Santa Monica Public Library

I SMP 00 0517315 T

S0-BZL-408

921 E   v.12

Emerson
Journals and miscellaneous notebooks
v.12: 1835-1862

Santa
Monica
Public
Library

4-WEEK LOAN

Date Due

NOV 11 1991

The Journals and Miscellaneous Notebooks

of

RALPH WALDO EMERSON

WILLIAM H. GILMAN   *Chief Editor*

ALFRED R. FERGUSON   *Senior Editor*

LINDA ALLARDT   HARRISON HAYFORD

RALPH H. ORTH   J. E. PARSONS

A. W. PLUMSTEAD

Editors

Emerson

The Journals and Miscellaneous Notebooks

of

RALPH WALDO EMERSON

VOLUME XII

1835–1862

EDITED BY

LINDA ALLARDT

THE BELKNAP PRESS
OF HARVARD UNIVERSITY PRESS

Cambridge, Massachusetts

1976

SANTA MONICA PUBLIC LIBRARY

NOV 19 1976

© *Copyright 1976 by the President and Fellows of Harvard College*
All rights reserved

CENTER FOR EDITIONS OF
AMERICAN AUTHORS
AN APPROVED TEXT
MODERN LANGUAGE
ASSOCIATION OF AMERICA

Library of Congress Catalog Card Number: 60–11554
ISBN 0–674–48475–4

Typography by Burton J Jones
Printed in the U.S.A.

SANTA MONICA PUBLIC LIBRARY

MAY 19 1976

921 E v.12

Preface

This volume could not have been completed without the contributions of many people. Ralph H. Orth edited Notebook L earlier for Volume VI where it was originally scheduled to appear. Suzy Q Groden collated L, Man, F No. 1, Δ, Φ, Ж, and Index Minor against the manuscript, and Linda Allardt collated them against photocopy and checked differences against the manuscript. Notebook BO Conduct was collated against the manuscript by William H. Gilman, A. W. Plumstead, and Niki Plumstead. Ruth H. Bennett did the research and additional manuscript collation and wrote the notes for BO Conduct. Linda Allardt added to Professor Orth's notes for Notebook L, did research and notes for all but Notebook BO Conduct, is responsible for the final form of both text and notes, and wrote the Foreword.

The editor wishes to thank a number of institutions and persons for help of various kinds. The Ralph Waldo Emerson Memorial Association, through the medium of David Emerson, has continued to provide regular grants-in-aid which have been indispensable to the progress of the edition. The Center for Editions of American Authors of the Modern Language Association of America provided generous financial support for the work of the editor and others from grants made by the National Endowment for the Humanities of the National Foundation on the Arts and the Humanities.

Special thanks are due to Rose Simon, for extraordinarily careful and dedicated work in checking and typing footnotes; and to Wallace E. Williams and James H. Justus, the present editors of the later lectures, who provided texts of the surviving lecture manuscripts from 1843 to 1862. Professor Williams has been especially generous of his time and his rich knowledge of both early and later lectures.

Joan Levine, Mary Leonard, and Frances T. Webb typed an

unusually difficult text. Other valuable help was given by Ordale Leermakers and Linda Kellner, who did preliminary research, William Miller, who compared collations, Katherine Mayberry Quill, who checked footnotes, and Russell Brubaker, Pamela Knight Hanke, Margaret B. Heminway, and Janet Parsons, all of whom assisted with typing and/or proofreading.

For other valuable assistance and courtesies the editor wishes to thank Miss Carolyn Jakeman, Professor William H. Bond, and the staff of Houghton Library; the staffs of Widener Library and Rush Rhees Library; Mr. William H. Loos, Curator of Rare Books of the Buffalo and Erie County Library; and Mrs. John Dempsey of the Emerson House in Concord.

All the editors named on the edition title page have responsibilities of various kinds for the edition as a whole. The Chief Editor has the primary responsibility for the edition, and for certification of individual volumes.

W. H. G.

William Henry Gilman

1911–1976

The death of William H. Gilman on February 17, 1976, brings to an end an era in the history of the Emerson journals edition, for he was one of the four founders of the project in 1954 and its chief editor for the last decade. His matchless energy, dedication, and spirit were a central factor in the success of the edition. It stands as his lasting monument.

Born in Boston, Professor Gilman received his undergraduate degree at Harvard in 1933, his M.A. from George Washington University in 1943, and his Ph.D. from Yale in 1948. After teaching at Robert College in Istanbul, Turkey, and Georgetown University's School for Foreign Service, he came to the University of Rochester in 1947 and began to establish his reputation as one of the foremost scholars in American literature. In 1953 he was awarded a fellowship from the Fund for the Advancement of Learning, and in 1960 and 1964 received fellowships from the Guggenheim Foundation. He was a visiting professor at Stanford University in 1959. At his death he was Roswell S. Burrows Professor of English at the University of Rochester. In his honor the University has established a prize fund for outstanding work in graduate study in literature.

Although the major scholarly labor of his life was this edition of the Emerson journals, he was also the author of what remains the definitive study of Melville's early years, *Melville's Early Life and Redburn* (1951), which grew out of his doctoral dissertation, and the coeditor, with his good friend Merrell R. Davis, of *The Letters of Herman Melville* (1960). He was in addition the coeditor, with Margaret Denny, of *The American Writer and the European Tradition* (1950); the editor of *Selected Writings of Ralph Waldo Emerson* (1965), a popular paperback anthology; and the author of numerous articles and reviews in scholarly journals.

But it was this edition of the Emerson journals which eventually absorbed all his energies. As the project grew in scope and complexity, Professor Gilman was chosen as chief editor by his colleagues, and thus assumed responsibility for the edition as a whole. He insisted, however, upon continuing to edit individual volumes with younger scholars, and was partially responsible for volumes VIII (1970) and XI (1975). Although he found the administrative and financial duties of the chief editorship oppressive at times—for with the beginning of federal support for definitive editions in 1966 both of these duties increased significantly—he worked unceasingly to provide his fellow editors with the freedom and support they needed to edit their volumes. His office at Rochester, which came to be known as the "Emerson factory," was a clearing house for information not only on Emerson but on the Transcendental circle as a whole. Even after he fell seriously ill in June of 1973, he continued to work to the limit of his capacity, both as chief editor and as coeditor of volume XI. Despite increasingly lengthy stays in the hospital, he had the gratification of holding the finished volume in his hands in December of 1975. At his death he was actively at work planning future volumes of the *JMN*.

When the edition began, his fellow editors were his contemporaries, but as the years passed he recruited younger scholars whom he carefully and wisely guided in the intricacies of textual study. Several had been students of his in graduate seminars at Rochester, where his passion for accuracy, keenness of mind, and unswerving devotion to ascertainable fact reflected his own unyieldingly high standards. He leaves a major bequest to the edition in the fact that, by recruiting new editors, he has ensured its continuity.

For those who knew and worked with Bill Gilman, his passing is a loss not to be repaired. He was a humanist in a largely antihumanist age, an ardent supporter of racial equality, a man opposed to the slightest evidence of cant, snobbery, or laziness of mind. His devotion to his large, vital family was an expression of his commitment to enduring personal values. His courage in his last years impressed all those who saw it. If it is true that a man's life can be judged by the effect he has had on those who knew him, there are many who can testify to the lasting respect and affection he inspired in them.

Contents

Illustrations

Foreword to Volume XII

THE LECTURE NOTEBOOKS FROM 1835 TO 1862

Nine of Emerson's notebooks are brought together in this volume, all primarily of the same kind, a complex mixture of index-like surveys of his journals and more narrowly focused collections of journal references, lists of topics and titles, salvaged journal passages and revisions, notes and translations from his reading, working notes, fragmentary drafts and near-outlines, all the various kinds of material Emerson collected for the composition of his lectures, articles, and essays. Taken by themselves, the lecture notebooks seem a "cold mechanical preparation," as Emerson fretted; but used as Emerson used them, as a working link between his journals on the one hand and his lectures, articles, and essays on the other, they reveal Emerson at work. There are gaps and false starts; the notes are often sketchy, largely undated, a many-layered tangle at times — one needs Emerson's "eye to see a navy in an acorn" — but they add to our understanding of Emerson's method of composition, and suggest the influence this method had on his journal keeping, the directions his thought took, his prose style, and the form of his lectures and published writings.

Emerson began the earliest of these, Notebook L, in the summer of 1835, when he was gathering material for the "Historical Discourse at Concord," and at the same time, judging from library records, was doing research for his lecture series on "English Literature." Notebook L is a double-ender, unusual in that Emerson seems to have used both sequences during the same time, writing notes on Concord history in one direction and, perhaps to keep them separate, turning the book back to front and upside down to enter notes on literature. The "English Literature" series was given before the Society for the Diffusion of Useful Knowledge, on a subject probably suggested by them; Emerson's notes for the lecture course and for the "Historical Discourse" are largely quotations from and paraphrases of his reading.

Emerson began the notebook now called F No. 1 in September, 1836, during early planning for the "Philosophy of History" series, the first under his own management, on a subject of his own choosing. This change in his lectures led to a marked change in his working methods and in the form of the lecture notebooks. He had trouble bringing the series into focus. In a letter dated October 4, 1836, he considered "some very broad name, say perhaps 'Intellectual Culture' to admit of stating my views of the tendencies of things around us, Religion, Literature, Science, Art, in this country, & to treat of the principles of them all, or indicate the foundations of them all in the nature of things." In F No. 1 he noted down three possible series titles, "Philosophy of History," "Intellectual Culture," and "Omnipresence of Spirit"; and listed possible subjects and lecture titles in several stages, beginning with "Man," under the heading "Intellectual Culture." It was a busy time; *Nature* had been published the second week of September; correspondence occupied him, including a long letter to Carlyle on September 17, and two days later he attended the preliminary meeting of "Hedge's Club" with its consideration of topics for discussion; and on October 30, Emerson's first son, Waldo, was born, delighting and further distracting him. On October 23, he wrote to his brother William, "I am still scheming my lectures which I advertise 'On the Philosophy of Modern History,' to be delivered on twelve Thursday evenings, from first Thursday of December. But how little masters we are of our wits! Mine run away with me; I don't know how to drive. I see them from far — then they whisk by me — I supplicate — I grieve — I point to the assembly that shall be, but the inexorable Thoughts will neither run in pairs nor in strings nor in any manageable system. But Necessity is Lord of all."

Emerson began Notebook Man on the following day, using it to salvage passages from his journals for the series or for the opening lecture; he scanned his journals for the preceding seven years, entering passages from Blotting Books Psi, Y, and III, and Journals Q, A, and B, most with only minor revisions of wording and punctuation, but some combined with passages from other journals, some revised or expanded. Many passages in Man and others from these early journals were used in the "Philosophy of History" series. Perhaps copying out passages proved cumbersome. Emerson set aside Man and, in gatherings for individual lectures of this series in Notebook F No. 1, began to evolve the more economical, indexlike listing of journal passages which became his working method for bringing together materials from the rich diversity of his journals for both lectures and essays over the next ten years. He began a new notebook for each of his next three lecture series, Δ in the fall of 1837 for the "Human Culture" series, Φ in October, 1838, for lectures on "Human Life," and Ж in the fall of 1839 for the "Present Age" series, working in much the same way, an increasingly meticulous routine. For the next four years he reused the notebooks he had; he began Index Minor in October, 1843, to gather material for *Essays, Second Series*, and in October, 1851, fell into his old pattern, beginning BO Conduct for the "Conduct of Life" series.

Emerson's working method. In 1840, Emerson wrote in his journal, "I ought to seek to lay myself out utterly, — large, enormous, prodigal, upon the subject of the week. But a hateful experience has taught me that I can only expend, say, twenty one hours on each lecture, if I would also be ready & able for the next." But the lecture notebooks make it plain that Emerson had done much preliminary work by the time he began the actual writing — wide-ranging surveys for the series as a whole, selection of topics and titles, and probably some preliminary collections for individual lectures.

Both the salvage of journal passages in Man and the indexlike collections are a natural outgrowth of Emerson's earlier journal keeping, of course. He was already in the habit of collecting quotations and sometimes his own sayings in Collectanea, Encyclopedia, and a series of Blotting Books, and in the effort to organize his thought had grown increasingly methodical in indexing his journals.

Before he announced each lecture series, generally eight weeks or more before the first lecture, Emerson scanned his journals for subject matter. The miscellaneous pages of F No. 1, the collection of Man from his journals, and the jotted page in Δ headed "Ethics, or Philosophy of Life, or Culture. What topics have we" probably represent early forms of this preliminary attempt to organize his available material. But by 1838, with planning for the "Human Life" series in Notebook Φ, this preliminary survey had become a systematic and extensive notation. Such surveys are easily recognizable by their order and scope. For example, a ten-page survey at the beginning of Notebook Ж for the "Present Age" series in 1839, headed "Miscellaneous Topics," scans Journal D page by page, entry by entry, sometimes even sentence by sentence, from page 244 to the end of D (probably October 7, 1839), then starts at the beginning of D and completes it. (See Plate III.) Only a handful of entries from Journal E (begun October 11) are added, along with scattered citations in C, B, and A. In 1841 Emerson extended this survey for six more pages with a survey for the "Times" series, going entry by entry through Journal G, followed by selected passages in F No. 2 and E.

It was probably from the preliminary surveys that he jotted down the lists of possible subjects or titles found on the back pages of all but L, Man, and BO Conduct and wrote the series announcements, choosing titles broad enough to encompass the as yet unblocked lectures; he probably transferred entries from the surveys to collections, some of which matured into individual lectures, some of which proved only trials; and he may have continued to refer to the surveys as he penciled final working notes. The surveys are heavily use-marked, and Emerson undoubtedly used and reused them long after they had served their original purpose; they will still serve the reader as they served Emerson for a convenient guide to the contents of the journals.

In October, 1837, Emerson wrote, "The very naming of a subject by a man of genius is the beginning of insight." His first list of possible subjects for the "Philosophy of History" series (see Plate I) includes several not in the series as it was finally given — "The Antique," "Reason & Understanding," "Literary History," "Poetry," "Rhetoric," "Life," "Goethe," "Literary Ethics" — and Emerson's index to F No. 1 shows that he set up pages under these heads and others, often in blocks of five to ten pages, and began collecting what belonged to each; he wrote, "I put like things together." So varied are the passages in some collections that the likeness must have been apparent only to Emerson — a measure of the elusiveness of his thought. In some cases he changed the title or worked the subject matter into a "Philosophy of History" lecture with other material; "Life" in the 1836 list evidently became the lecture "Ethics"; "The Antique" was worked into "Manners"; "Rhetoric" and "Literary Ethics" became part of the lecture "The Present Age"; the translations from Goethe contributed to "Humanity of Science."

Other topics were apparently discarded for lack of enough material for this series, but that was not the end of them. Simply scanning the indexes of the journals after this period shows that he continued to write on these subjects, and on the subjects he did use in the series as well. Some titles were used later. "Literary Ethics," first proposed as a lecture topic in Journal B on August 6, 1835, became the title of an oration at Dartmouth in 1838. "Goethe" eventually titled a lecture in the "Representative Men" series in 1846, after Emerson had considered it for both "Human Life" and "Present Age" series in the interval. Nor was he finished with the titles he used in the series — "Art," "Politics," and "Manners" became the titles of essays based only in part on these early lectures; "Literature," "Religion," "Trades," and "Ethics" all were reused at least once as lecture titles. "The Present Age" was considered again for the "Human Life" series in 1838 and became the title of the 1839 lecture series, while the subject itself was used in several related lectures, including the introductory lecture in the series on "The Times" in 1841 and as late as 1850 in "The Spirit of the Times."

The significance of this yearly stocktaking becomes increasingly evident as Emerson becomes more experienced as a lecturer. In 1842, he wrote in his journal, "This matter of the lectures, for instance. The engagement drives your thoughts & studies to a head, & enables you to do somewhat not otherwise practicable; that is the action. Then there is the reaction; for when you bring your discourse to your auditory, it shows differently. You have more power than you had thought of, or less. The thing fits, or does not fit; is good or detestable." Thus in planning for the "Human Life" series in 1838, he not only looked back to such topics as "Man" (there is scarcely a collection in this volume without mention of Man), "Labor," "Politics," and "Art," but listed "Friends," "Books," "Beauty," and "Riches," which were to become lectures or essays from six to twelve years later. The "Loci" for the "Present Age" lectures in 1839 repeated many of these, and suggested "Lectures" themselves as a topic, one treated later as part of an 1843 lecture. Biography had been, of course, the subject of his 1835 lecture series, but Emerson continued to list "Great Men," "Poet," "Skeptic," and "Representative," and work them into other lectures from 1838 until they culminated in the 1845–1846 "Representative Men" series.

Unlike his usual practice in regular journals, Emerson did not write consecutively through the lecture notebooks. In Notebook Δ, for example, he evidently began on page 5 with his search for a topic, turned to the back of the notebook to enter possible titles on page 170, and forward again to page 3 to copy his advertisement for the series; he turned again to back pages to jot down notes during actual writing of the lectures, beginning on page 151 with notes for the introductory lecture, and working back toward the front of the notebook with notes for succeeding lectures. The pattern holds roughly for the first use of the other lecture notebooks printed in this volume, but Emerson used them repeatedly over many years, filling in blank pages, writing over and sometimes adding to earlier notes, so that this order is often obscured.

Emerson used "*Collections*" as a heading for notes for "Literary Ethics" in L Concord, and the editor has adopted Emerson's term for similar gatherings of journal references on a single topic or for a specific lecture or essay. Resembling the preliminary surveys in appearance but narrower in scope, collections range through all stages from the earliest gatherings, in which passages are cited in more or less consecutive journal order and relatively few of the cited passages are used in a lecture or essay (trial topics among these), to near-final collections, almost outlines, in which a large number are used in the order listed. Trial topics and trial collections (those not apparently used for the lectures or essays being planned) can sometimes be linked with Emerson's lists of possible topics or titles, and might have been entered at any time between the preliminary survey and the delivery of the lectures.

In making his collections Emerson filled whole pages with entries, probably continuing to add to the page over a period of time, sometimes continuing down the page, but often inserting additional references at the ends of lines or within entries already inscribed. He often left a line or two blank between heading and collection, and these he sometimes filled in with added citations, some apparently taken from his journal indexes or earlier collections. Entries in such a collection generally consist of a key phrase, often a few words verbatim from the journal passage cited, but sometimes a summary phrase, along with one or more journal citations by abbreviated journal title and page number. Occasionally Emerson condensed so admirably that he used the summary phrase instead of, or in addition to, the passage listed; in "Spiritual Laws," for instance, such phrases from collections in Notebook F No. 1 are added as topic sentences to the paragraphs cited. Writing down terse phrases repeatedly in this way must certainly have contributed to Emerson's aphoristic style, but the full effect of this periodic extracting on his prose style remains to be explored.

Passages cited in a collection may be not only paragraphs but parts of paragraphs, sometimes only a few words, as well as sentences, quotations, and other units found in the journals. Perhaps as an outgrowth of this collection method, Emerson at times lettered entries in a journal or notebook to facilitate citation; salvaged journal passages and brief quotations in Notebook Φ, pages 4_2 and 160–161, are good examples. But the journal passages did not have to be actually lettered for Emerson to refer to them in this way; thus "4bc" in F No. 1, page 129, evidently refers to the second and third passages in Journal B, page 4. Furthermore, the page number given after an index word or phrase is not always the location of that passage but may be an additional citation, as in F No. 1, page 125_1, where the first paragraph is a draft for the lecture "Society," and "299" following it cites a paragraph in Journal B used following the draft in the lecture manuscript; single words and phrases may similarly indicate additional references, as in Notebook Φ, page 147_1, where "36 Day after day. Apercue" cites two passages in Journal D.

For collections, as for surveys, Emerson often started by scanning his most recent journals, but he included many references to earlier journals, occasionally, it seems, from a thorough rereading. He cites Journal A, for instance, not only in the 1836–1837 collections in F No. 1 but frequently in collections for the "Human Culture" and

xvii

"Human Life" series in Δ and Φ; he apparently went back to A as late as 1839 for scattered citations in Ж. Emerson undoubtedly drew on the surveys for single collections, of course, but they were only the starting point.

Entries in some collections, those on "Woman" in Notebook Φ, page 150$_1$, for example, seem to have been copied, complete with errors, from the indexes of earlier journals; and in Φ, pages 33 and 150$_1$, "Love; A" and "See Life in C" apparently cite the indexes directly. He sometimes used earlier collections as he used indexes; entries on "*Genius* & Talent" in Index Minor, page 67, for instance, may have been drawn from a collection headed "Intellect" in Φ, pages 43–45, and one headed "Genius" in Ж, page 97. His miscellaneous notebooks, especially Encyclopedia, were a frequent resource. He added some entries from memory, certainly, especially phrases repeated many times, such as the quincunx simile, and "Character cumulative," "Genius situated alike," or the often cited "Private Chapel B 61"; some, like "When you are sincerely pleased without any misgiving, you are nourished," he cited repeatedly but did not apparently use until many years later.

But his journals were not his only resource for collections. He wrote in his journal, "I do not feel myself a poet but a scribe. I write when I have thoughts & when my friends have thoughts." He not only draws on the conversation of family and friends such as his brother Charles and Elizabeth Hoar but cites the journals of others, "CS" (Caroline Sturgis), for instance. In several collections Emerson also cites his own earlier lecture and essay manuscripts as sources. Notes for "Self-Reliance" in F No. 1, pages 107–111, cite two 1837 lectures, "*Lect. Ethics,*" and "Phil Hist. Lect XII," as well as "H C Lect I p 32" from the 1837–1838 "Human Culture" series (in this case the journal source is given as well) and "*Home*" and "*Duty*" from the "Human Life" series in 1838–1839. And notes in Notebook Ж for several lectures of the "Present Age" series in 1839–1840 cite the manuscripts of four essays, apparently drafted but not yet published in *Essays [First Series]*.

Emerson often began a collection on a recto page, later filling in the blank verso page facing it with penciled working notes, so that the later stage seems to come before the earlier one; see Plates IV and V for one example. Emerson worked from the lecture collections into varying forms of working notes, outlines, and fragmentary drafts. They are treated here and in footnotes as distinct stages, but for Emerson they probably were not — collections grew into working notes, working notes into near-outlines, as the work in hand requized. Working notes were probably inscribed during actual writing of a lecture, presumably in the week before its delivery, or in the case of essays, in the rough draft stage. But exactly when Emerson did the collections for the lectures within a series, whether in the six to eight weeks between the announcement and the commencement of the course, or in the week of writing preceding a lecture, is uncertain. Trial collections such as those for the "Human Life" series were almost certainly done before final topics were settled on and composition begun. Furthermore, Emerson often used in an introductory lecture passages cited in collections for succeeding lectures, and in each series through at least 1839 concluded the introductory lecture with a summary of lectures to come, indicating the extent to which the lectures were already blocked. Certainly his letters mention some sort of work on lectures in the weeks before each series. On October 12, 1837, he wrote of the "Human Culture" lectures taking form, and on November 6 the following year he wrote of preparing the "Human Life" lectures; he mentioned looking over his notes in October, 1842, for the "New England" series, and setting down notes for it late in November.

He may have begun not only collecting but drafting some lectures before the start of a series. Less than a week before he left for Philadelphia to begin the "New England" series, he wrote, "I have in my portfolio the value of three pretty good lectures on New England, which may become five before they get spoken;" but more often they were still to be written. On the other hand, some of the collections may not have been made until the week of writing. There do not seem to be any preliminary collections, for instance, for the two lectures Emerson had hoped to include in the "Human Life" series, cut short by ill-health. There is no reason to suppose that he always worked in the same way, or at the same rate.

Working notes, usually in the form of rough pencil notes, often on the back pages of the notebooks, were obviously regarded by

Emerson as temporary and are frequently overwritten by later material. Working notes in Φ for a missing section of the lecture "Home" are overwritten in ink with notes and drafts for the lecture "Eloquence" and were recovered with difficulty; only a few words of what are probably working notes for "New England Reformers," "Nominalist and Realist," and "Experience" have been recovered from overwritten pages of Index Minor. In Ж, pencil notes for the lecture "Private Life" are overwritten by a collection for "Education," given in the same series only a month later.

Working notes are a mixture of repeated and added journal references, abbreviated phrases, partial drafts, incomplete sentences, abortive efforts at organization, and sometimes notes close enough to the final order to be called outlines. The nearest thing to a formal outline is one of "New England Reformers" in Index Minor that looks suspiciously as though it were done after the lecture was written, perhaps in revising it for print. But notes in an order that indicates the final stages of composition occur quite often. A collection in outline order for the lecture "The Protest" in Φ was clearly done in the final stages of composition; it cites a journal passage dated January 12, 1839, only four days before the lecture was given. Or see the sketchy outline for part of the lecture "Chaucer" in L Literature, page 82, the outline in F No. 1, page 5, for a section of "The Individual," and another sectional outline for the lecture "Manners" in F No. 1, page 39; such notes rarely cover more than a small section.

A similar function may have been served by what appear to be paragraphs in L Literature, pages 66 and 72; in reality they are summaries of the introductory lecture in the "English Literature" series. A similar brief paragraph in Δ, page 86, apparently outlines a section of "Heroism." Notes in paragraph form in F No. 1, page 164, summarize the introductory lecture in the "Philosophy of History" series, while sentences on page 135, closely related to a numbered outline on the preceding page, outline the entire series, and may have been the basis for a summary paragraph in the concluding lecture. Such paragraphs may be related to Emerson's habit of summarizing each lecture series in paragraphs in the introductory and final lectures.

The notes show Emerson considering the relationship of passages, trying them against one another in various combinations, adding and discarding, sometimes numbering entries, as in notes for the lecture "Tragedy" in Φ, page 78, or connecting passages by marginal lines as in notes for "Self-Reliance" in F No. 1, page 109, though not always in the order he finally used. Emerson repeats earlier working notes, often several times, as he approaches the final order, and often the journal locations are dropped; compare, for instance, near-final notes for "Doctrine of the Hands" in Δ, page 144, with the earlier collection for this lecture on the following page.

These late working notes are sometimes combined with fragmentary drafts, apparently original in the lecture notebooks, such as the short paragraphs in Δ used in "The Eye and Ear." There are many of these short drafts, though the largest proportion of the discursive prose in these notebooks is taken from the regular journals. A few longer drafts exist; an outline and a nine-page draft in F No. 1 are apparently all that survive of an 1837 lecture on slavery; also in F No. 1 is a partial draft, bearing some similarities to a letter to Carlyle, but probably for a review of Carlyle's *French Revolution* (drastically cut by the editor of the *Christian Examiner*) which Emerson salvaged later for an 1843 lecture. Notebook Δ contains drafts for Emerson's peace lecture, "War," for his preface to Carlyle's *Critical and Miscellaneous Essays,* and his introductory article, "The Editors to the Reader," in the first issue of *The Dial,* as well as a memorandum of events leading to an 1857 lawsuit, which gives a rare glimpse of the relationship of Emerson and Thoreau with their neighbors.

It is possible sometimes to see the subtle progress of Emerson's thought from collection to lecture; in a collection in Δ, page 130, for the lecture "The Head," for example, he lists a passage in Journal C, page 83; one sentence in the journal passage, "I put like things together," becomes in the lecture, "to string things by their true natures, not by their apparent." There are other instances where little is used verbatim from notes or collections, but the thought, reworded, remains recognizable; this is true of notes for the Divinity School Address in L Concord, or salvaged passages, such as the paragraph in Man, page 2, developed in the opening paragraphs of

"Humanity of Science." It is remarkable that these and other passages, extensively rewritten for early lectures, turn up in their original journal form in essays and later lectures.

In some cases, the regular journals show a concentration of passages used in a particular lecture or series, some of the entries apparently written later than collections in the notebooks, some clearly based on the notes, suggesting that Emerson wrote in his journal to fill out the partly drafted lecture. Journal E has such a concentration for the two lectures on "Literature" given in the "Present Age" series in December, 1839, and passages from Journal J, pages 43–45, in the lecture "Prospects" were apparently written later than collections for the lecture.

Quite often phrases from earlier journal passages listed in collections will survive in later journal passages actually used in a lecture or essay. A paragraph in D, page 162, beginning "It is observable . . . that even the science of the day is introversive," is used in "Doctrine of the Soul," where it is filled out with a phrase from B, page 284, an earlier source. One phrase in A, page 98, about an election, "everything to get the hurrah on our side," shows progressive revision as it appears in turn in B, page 59, Notebook F No. 1, page 72, and the 1837 lecture "Politics."

Many later journal passages are copies or revisions of earlier ones. Emerson used and revised everything, including his own letters to friends and the conversation of friends and relatives, and sometimes only the earliest mention identifies a significant source. For instance, Emerson used a passage from Journal TU, page 230, in "Behavior": "An old man who added an elevating culture to a large experience of life, said to me, 'When you come into the room, I think I will study how to make humanity beautiful to you.'" The "old man" was Jonathan Phillips, as the source in C, page 58, shows. Emerson used "The talent is the call" many times, but only in the earliest journal entry, in Blotting Book Psi, page 36, does Emerson identify it as a quotation from Abraham Tucker; similarly the source of a paragraph in B, page 284, used in "Being and Seeming," is found in A, page 6, to be "Bell on the Hand."

Far more early journal material was probably used than has been realized. A small amount has been noted; at least thirty-nine references to the early Blotting Books are to be found, for instance, not only throughout the early notebooks L Literature, F No. 1, and Δ, but in Φ, and two citations as late as 1841 in Ж. This volume, like others in this edition, supplies numerous cross-references to earlier journals and notebooks which serve to fill out and draw together the widely separated raw materials of Emerson's writings; but in so extensive a storehouse as Emerson's, much more undoubtedly remains to be discovered, and it is never safe to assume that the earliest draft of a passage has been located.

It should be emphasized that these notebooks do not hold complete collections, outlines, or working notes for any lecture or essay. Emerson occasionally used his regular journals for collections, working notes, and drafts, some probably in unrecovered erased or overwritten pencil writing; a few pages of collection and note material still exist, interleaved with lecture manuscripts, and are or will be printed in textual notes with the lectures; probably some loose material was discarded. Offset ink-lines in F No. 1, pages 104–105, evidently from cancellations or use marks on a loose sheet, may have been from such notes. But it is more likely that the extent of the notes varied with the difficulty of composition and that they were never more than sketchy. On the other hand, they contain much that was not finally used, and though there are notes probably for lectures for which no manuscript has been found, such as "General Views," "Character," "Manners," "Relation of Man to Nature," and the lectures in the "Representative Men" series, or for missing pages in lectures, "Duty" and "Private Life," for example, no passage cited was necessarily used in the completed lectures.

Dating. There are few dates in the lecture notebooks. Emerson dated the initial pages of Notebooks Man, F No. 1, Φ, Index Minor, and BO Conduct, probably when he began them, and dated some survey pages written later in Φ. The dates of the first entries can be given with reasonable certainty. But some other dates may have been added later and some are clearly in error. He gives the delivery dates of the lectures, not the dates of the working notes in L Concord and L Literature. And Emerson dated Notebook Δ 1841 both on its title page and in Index Summary (described on pages 518–519 below), but it was begun shortly before October 11, 1837, the date of an advertisement drafted on page 3. Moreover, Emerson used these notebooks repeatedly over many years, filling in blank pages, writing over and adding to earlier notes. It has not been possible, therefore, to date each page.

The editor has tried to provide a framework in time in footnotes and headnotes, but dating is largely conjectural. Dated journal passages are probably the surest basis for dating this material; that is, notes cannot be earlier than the latest dated journal passage cited in a continuous inscription on a page or block of pages, but they may be considerably later. It is assumed that the reader will refer to the journals as they are cited. But not all journal passages can be reliably dated, nor can later additions to the notebooks always be ascertained, and the editor has exercised great caution in dating pages which are apparently accretions over a period of time. Dates can also be inferred from Emerson's probable use of collections and notes, based on the number and order of the passages used in a lecture or essay, headings, on what is known from letters and journals about Emerson's habits of composition and the dates of composition of various works, and in some cases through comparisons of ink, pencil, and handwriting. The reader will find few certainties, many reasonable probabilities, and some thought-provoking possibilities provided with regard to both dates and probable uses.

Emerson's use of these notebooks can be roughly dated, however, and within that framework, his use and reuse of the lecture notebooks can be fitted together with his use of the regular journals and other miscellaneous notebooks, as he worked out the content, structure, and interrelationship of lectures within each series, drew together occasional lectures and addresses, built lecture series upon lecture series, and reworked lectures into essays, articles, and sometimes still later lectures, often from materials now partly or wholly vanished.

He began Notebook L during the summer of 1835, using the L Concord sequence until the "Historical Discourse" was delivered on September 12 and printed a short time later, and the L Literature sequence until January 14, 1836, when the "English Literature" series was completed.

He began the notebook now called F No. 1 in September, 1836, and used it through March 2, 1837, for the lectures in the "Philosophy of History" series. He also used his regular journals for lecture notes for this and later series; Journal B, which he was using during the early planning of this series, contains a partial outline for "Humanity of Science" and a concentration of October–November, 1836, entries used throughout the series; the early pages of Journal C, begun January 1, 1837, while he was giving the lectures, have passages used in the final lectures and probably written during composition.

Emerson turned to F No. 1 again, probably in October, 1837, to enter a list of titles which may be the first planning for *Essays* [*First Series*]. In the same month, he began Δ, preparing for the "Human Culture" series, but probably in November, 1837, he used F No. 1 again for drafts and an unusually complete outline for the now missing 1837 lecture on slavery, and for his review of Carlyle's *French Revolution.* He also used Journal C during planning for the "Human Culture" series for a partial outline, a list of the final titles, and probably some draft paragraphs, including one written only a day or two before the final lecture in which it was used. Emerson used Δ again in March, 1837, entering working notes and drafts for the lecture "War" on pages following the collections for "Heroism" which he probably reused for a section in "War," and for postal accounts running from December 11, 1837, to May 10, 1842. In late June he used blank pages in Δ (rather than Journal D, which he had begun June 7) to draft his preface to Carlyle's *Critical and Miscellaneous Essays.* In July, 1838, he took up Notebook L Concord for notes and collections for the Divinity School Address and "Literary Ethics," the address at Dartmouth, and probably used them while revising the addresses to print. But he returned to Δ to enter the names of the recipients of the printed addresses.

In October, 1838, he began Notebook Φ, using it through February 20, 1839, for the preparation of lectures in the "Human Life" series. He used Journal D during the same period for numerous brief drafts for the lectures, lists of subjects for consideration or expansion that may tie in with the topics listed under *"Human Life"* in Φ, page 166, and a sketchy outline for a section of "Tragedy."

At some time after October, 1838, probably in April, 1839, when he wrote in a letter, "I have been writing a little and arranging old papers more, and by and by, I hope to get a shapely book of Genesis," Emerson turned to Notebook F No. 1 again for collections and working notes for four essays, "History," "Self-Reliance," "Compensation," and "Spiritual Laws." Emerson's later use of the lecture notebooks is not quite as random as it sometimes seems. Working notes for these essays are probably in F No. 1 because they draw on the "Philosophy of History" lectures gathered there. "Spiritual Laws," for example, draws on five of them, "Literature," "Religion," "Manners," "Ethics," and "The Present Age"; "Compensation" uses "Politics," "Society," "Trades and Professions," and "Ethics"; "Self-Reliance" also draws on "Manners," "Ethics," "The Present Age," and "The Individual"; "History," notes for which appear to have been the last added, makes use of "Introductory," "Humanity of Science," "Art," "Society," "Manners," and "The Individual." Though Emerson undoubtedly returned to the journals for many passages, he did cite the lectures directly; notes for "Self-Reliance" in F No. 1, pages 107–111, cite "Ethics" and "Phil Hist. Lect XII," for example. Lectures in the "Human Culture," "Human Life," and the 1835 "English Literature" series are cited and used in these essays, too; "Compensation" and "Spiritual Laws" in particular seem to carry out Emerson's description of the two additional lectures he had envisioned for the "Human Life" series.

Although it is difficult to date the completion of these four essays precisely, Emerson wrote Carlyle on July 4, 1839, that he had three essays nearly done; by autumn he had four — "History," "Compensation," "Self-Reliance," and "Spiritual Laws" ("Simplicity") are cited, apparently as sources, in collections in Notebook Ж for lectures in the "Present Age" series (see Plate IV). The relationship between the essays and the "Present Age" series is complex; Emerson scattered passages from both "Spiritual Laws" and "Self-Reliance" through at least five of the lectures, but virtually nothing from "History" or "Compensation" has been found in the surviving lectures. (The eighth lecture, "Ethics," is missing.) Emerson undoubtedly added to "History" and "Self-Reliance" later; both contain journal passages dated late in 1840. A brief outline in Ж, page 74, of a paragraph in "Self-Reliance" may date from this later revision.

At the end of summer in 1839, Emerson put aside the essays and reluctantly prepared to lecture again. Several sentences in Φ, page 84, headed "Oct 1839" and indexed "New Subjects" may be part of the earliest stage. He began Notebook Ж to gather material for the "Present Age" series, probably shortly after he began Journal E on October 11, 1839; on October 18, he wrote in E, "In these golden days it behoves me once more to make my annual inventory of the world. For the five last years I have read each winter a new course of lectures in Boston, and each was my creed & confession of faith. Each told all I thought of the past, the present, & the future. Once more I must renew my work and I think only once in the same form though I see that he who thinks he does something for the last time ought not to do it at all." By October 28 he had found his subject, "the character, resources, & tendencies of the Present Age," and had begun expanding on lecture topics in his journal.

Emerson used Notebook Δ for unusually extensive drafts for The Present Age: "Introductory," and Journal E as well; an unusually large part of the lecture seems to have been written later than the brief early collection in Ж, pages 47–48. Emerson reworked this material for a number of later lectures, including "The Spirit of the Times" in the 1850s, and may also have reused the notes in writing the "Lecture on the Times."

Shortly after the completion of the "Present Age" series on February 12, 1840, Emerson began Journal F No. 2, which he used concurrently with Journal E until March, 1841, about the time Essays [First Series] was published. As usual, he continued to repeat his lectures throughout the spring, at Salem, New York, Providence, and Concord; in April, while lecturing in Concord, he used Notebook Δ again as well as Journal E to draft part of "The Editors to the Reader," his introductory article in the first issue of The Dial, perhaps because it bears some relation to the drafts in Δ for The Present Age: "Introductory."

Emerson evidently turned to the completion of the essays as soon as he was free of lecturing in late spring. Journal E contains a concentration of entries throughout May and June, 1840, for "Circles," and on June 11 he was revising the lecture "Love." With four essays all but completed, he filled out the volume with several based largely on single lectures — "Love" and "Prudence," and probably "Art" and "Heroism," though the lecture manuscripts are fragmentary or missing; other essays combine passages from several lectures. Emerson used the lecture notebooks, but the essay notes are scattered, usually added to notes for the lectures on which they were based. He used and added to notes for the lecture "Love" in Φ. Notes for "Friendship" were added to collections in Ж and Δ for "Private Life" and "The Heart," two lectures on which it was based, though a good deal of "Friendship" was newly written in E and F No. 2 during the summer. He probably used notes in Δ for the revision of "Prudence" and "Heroism," adding scattered passages from later lectures and journals; the opening paragraph in "Prudence" is dated February 10, 1841, so late that it must have been added to printer's proof.

While notes in F No. 1, page 102, apparently outline a section in "Doctrine of the Soul," Emerson may have outlined it in order to revise it for "The Over-Soul"; this complex essay draws on notes in F No. 1, Δ, Φ, and Ж for both 1837 and 1840 lectures on "Religion," "Doctrine of the Soul," "The School," "Holiness," and "Tendencies." Working notes apparently for "Circles" in Δ, page 167, may be tied in with the large amount of new writing done for "Circles" in the journals in June. Emerson probably used notes in Δ and Φ for "The Head" and "Genius" in drafting the essay "Intellect"; "Intellect" and "Art" also contain late journal passages that must have been added to proof. "Art" draws on notes in Δ and Φ originally for "The Eye and Ear" and "Genius"; Emerson may also have used notes in F No. 1 for the 1837 lecture "Art," including four pages now missing from the notebook, and notes surviving with the remnant of the lecture manuscript. Notes added in Φ, page 70, and Ж, pages 31–33, may be for an essay on "Nature" Emerson had hoped to finish for the essay volume, and notes in Δ, page 128, may be for a proposed "Essay entitled a Survey of the Time," though both may be for lectures in the "Times" series.

With his essays sent to press, Emerson used Notebook Ж for working notes for the lecture "Man the Reformer," January 25, 1841, adding to notes for the 1840 lecture "Reforms" and using a concentration of entries written at this time in Journals E and F

No. 2. This lecture may also draw on notes for "Doctrine of the Hands" in Δ; for example, the first entry in Δ, page 149, "Each art is a whole . . . flowers cold," is expanded in "Doctrine of the Hands" and again in F No. 1, page 48, summarized in "Compensation," rewritten and expanded again in Ж, page 65, and used in "Man the Reformer."

Emerson used Δ in August, 1841, for the names of recipients of "The Method of Nature." He used Ж again from the fall of 1841 to January, 1842, for collections and working notes for the lecture series on "The Times," but used Δ also in preparing the introductory lecture, perhaps reviewing drafts for The Present Age: "Introductory" in Δ as he added to a collection for it in Ж, page 48. Only two lectures in the "Times" series, "The Poet" and "Prospects," survive in manuscript and are printed in *The Early Lectures*, III. Three were printed in *The Dial* and partly reprinted in *W*, I, as "Lecture on the Times," "The Conservative," and "The Transcendentalist." A substantial part of the three missing lectures, "Manners," "Character," and "Relation of Man to Nature," may survive in the essays "Manners," "Character," and "Nature"; uses in these essays are noted, although no essay passage was necessarily in a lecture. Beyond recognizing journal passages too late to have been in the lectures, it has been difficult without the missing manuscripts to distinguish between lecture and essay notes.

Emerson used Journals G and H concurrently from September to November, 1841, writing a considerable part of the material that went into the "Times" series. But he did not decide finally to lecture that year until the first week of October, when the City Bank failed to pay a dividend, and planning for the series went slowly. It was the end of October before he decided on a series title; probably about that time he added a survey of G and E to the earlier "Present Age" survey in Notebook Ж. Other preliminary notes are unusually scattered; he apparently continued the survey of E on back pages headed "Miscellaneous," added to earlier pages headed "The True Life," "The Age," "Reform," and "Genius," reused other collections for the "Present Age" series, and gathered under the headings, "Our Boston Age" and "Optimates," passages used throughout the series. There are notes in Ж probably for all eight lectures on "The Times," but notes for "Prospects" are also in Journal H; notes for "The Conservative" and "The Transcendentalist," perhaps later than the intermixed notes for these paired lectures in Ж, are in Journal G (they include a page of erased but not overwritten pencil writing, and a loose sheet inserted between pages) and J, which was begun only shortly before the commencement of the series. Other notes possibly for this series are in Notebook Dialling.

In October, 1842, Emerson took up Φ again for an extensive survey and the rather sparse and wide-ranging notes that exist for the five lectures on "New England." He also added to notes for the lecture "Religion" in Ж, and entered several more pages of unsystematic notes for the series in Journal N, which he used from September to November, 1842. A number of drafts probably for these lectures are in the early pages of Journal Z[A], which he began in November. The fifth lecture remains uncertain; in Index Minor, Emerson identifies an outline, clearly for "New England Reformers," as "V Lecture on N. England," but it may have differed considerably on first delivery. Notes for the "New England" series may be incomplete, not only because the lectures were incomplete when he left Concord but because a new audience in Philadelphia enabled him to reuse parts of older lectures. In Φ he cites as sources "Character" from the "Times" series, several lectures in the "Present Age" series — "Tendencies," "Politics," "Education," and probably "Prospects" and "Private Life" — and even earlier, "Trades and Professions" and "Doctrine of the Hands." He also reused the paragraphs on Carlyle in F No. 1, and a considerable part of the 1835 lecture "Permanent Traits of the English National Genius."

In October, 1843, Emerson started Index Minor, probably first titled simply "Index" as it is on its title page, with a survey for his second book of essays. Although he determined not to write a new lecture course for that winter, he lectured steadily, repeating older lectures and writing at least two new ones, "The Young American" in February and the "Address at the Second Church" in March. He was interrupted by work on *The Dial* as well. But by February 16, 1844, he wrote to his brother, "You asked about my book. 'The Poet' is only one of its chapters though much the longest. The others that are ended or nearly so are 'Life' & 'Character.'" Six weeks later he wrote again, "Three good chapters which will almost fill a volume, are ready or nearly so for the printer. But I wish to have a book this time if the Muses will, which shall not displease me in a month after its publication." Lists of titles and the number of pages in each essay in Index Minor, pages 132–133, may date from this period.

The collection of materials for the "New England" series seems to have had a formative influence on the new essays; Emerson re-used the survey for the series and other 1842 pages in Notebook Φ, and used Φ for collections or working notes for "The Poet," "Experience," "Character," and "Nominalist and Realist." To round out the volume of essays he turned to the unpublished lectures in the "Times" series, reusing notes for them in ЖК for the essays "Manners," "Character," "Nature," and "The Poet." But extensive collections, notes, and drafts in Index Minor for all the essays except "Gifts," a brief article prepared for *The Dial* for which no working notes have been identified, indicate that he thoroughly rewrote even those built on lectures.

Notes and drafts for "Nominalist and Realist" and "Experience" are scattered through Φ and Index Minor, some in unrecovered erased or overwritten pencil writing; more are in the regular journals and probably on loose sheets as well. Emerson used Journal U for a concentration of passages for "Nominalist and Realist"; an outline for "Experience" is in Journal R, page 126, and a concentration of passages in Journal V argues for a late expansion of this essay in June and July, 1844; more material for essays may have been in unrecovered erased pencil inscriptions in U and V. Notes for "Experience" jotted on the back of a letter enclosure were found between the leaves of Φ; Notebook JK is made up of once loose leaves, several headed "For 2d vol Essay" or "For Vol II of Essay," inscribed with notes and salvaged journal passages probably gathered during the winter of 1843–1844 and later bound alphabetically. Some headings in Index Minor are repeated in JK. At some time during this period he used both Index Minor and Φ for outlines of "New England Reformers" for delivery as a lecture March 3, 1844, and for inclusion in *Essays, Second Series*, probably a late addition, since it is not in his nearly complete title list in Index Minor.

While working on the essays, he used Index Minor and much

of the same material and thought for the lecture "The Young American" in February, 1844, the "Address at the Second Church" in March, 1844, and the "Discourse at Middlebury College" in July, 1845. Emerson used Index Minor again for the 1845–1846 "Representative Men" lectures; the lecture manuscripts are missing, though a leaf probably from "Plato" is laid into Notebook BO Conduct, and there appear to be a few scattered lecture leaves in the printer's copy for *Representative Men*. Uses are given in *Representative Men*, published in 1850, subtitled "Seven Lectures," but the printed version contains some journal passages later than the lectures, and the printer's copy also shows revisions. Unlike earlier series, Emerson began to plan this one in early summer. He had delivered a single lecture on Napoleon in Lowell and Concord earlier in the year; this he revised for the series, and in late June planned lectures on Plato, Montaigne, and Swedenborg. He added the introductory "Uses of Great Men" and "Shakspeare" through the summer, and by September had decided to add "Goethe." A considerable number of earlier collections in Index Minor appear to have been added to in 1845. Reading notes for "Napoleon" make up a considerable part of Journal V, and working notes for other lectures in the series are scattered through V, W, and Y, as well as Index Minor.

In 1847, Emerson used both Index Minor and Φ for notes for the lecture on "Eloquence," a recurrent theme in his thought and his journals since his college years. In Φ, page 146 (see Plate II), working notes for "Eloquence" are written around earlier notes for "The School," while in Ж, page 90, notes possibly for "Eloquence" are added to those for the lecture "Education"; other notes for "Eloquence" are to be found in Journal O and Notebook JK. The lecture manuscript is incomplete (though much of it may survive in "Eloquence," *W*, VII, the printed text contains enough later journal material to indicate revision), but enough remains to invite deeper study of this wide-ranging lecture.

Emerson probably continued to refer to these notebooks in later years. Δ contains the titles of six lectures given in various combinations throughout 1848, 1849, and 1850, under the head "Mind & Manners in XIX Century"; the last lecture may have been "The Spirit of the Times," given under various titles, which uses parts of

The Present Age: "Introductory," notes for which are in Δ, and perhaps other related lectures on the Age or the Times. In 1851, when he began Notebook BO Conduct for the lectures (some new, some revised) in the "Conduct of Life" series, he entered notes indexed "1851 Salvage" in Ж; only fragments remain of these lectures, but the text printed in *W*, VI, incorporates a good deal of earlier journal material, and Emerson probably scanned Φ, Ж, and Index Minor for the series. In 1857, he took up Δ again for his memorandum of a lawsuit, and in 1862 used it again for notes for the lecture "Perpetual Forces," which makes considerable use of earlier thought.

These notebooks, then, span twenty-seven of Emerson's richest years, and contain notes for more than a hundred of his major lectures and essays.

Emerson's indexes. Because of the light Emerson's indexes shed on dates and probable uses of the material in the notebooks in this volume, they are printed and carefully described, as well as being included in the general index below as in previous volumes. The indexes, on the front cover verso of each notebook, vary in completeness and usefulness. As in the regular journals, Emerson usually began with a preliminary index, sometimes in page order, sometimes in apparently random order, though numerous additions over a period of time often obscure what pattern there is. In Φ, Ж, and Index Minor he derived from this initial index an alphabetical index to which he continued to add. Additions can be distinguished and sometimes dated by differences in ink and pencil and in Emerson's handwriting, and by comparison with the pages indexed, but the indexes alone are not conclusive. Only one of the notebooks seems to have been indexed close to the time it was begun. Others may have been compiled later when Emerson reused and added to earlier notes, demonstrating the increasingly systematic fashion in which he utilized his notebooks and journals.

The indexes to L Concord and L Literature are both in ink, written at various times, in apparently random order. Emerson added a penciled reference to his 1838 letter to Van Buren to the L Concord index, but did not index lecture notes inscribed later in 1838. The addition of a journal citation to the L Literature index suggests that it was compiled during composition of the "English Literature" lectures.

The brief index to Notebook Man begins with a section in ink in consecutive page order, using some page headings and summing up other pages in terms that suggest this part was done about the time of the "Philosophy of History" series. Penciled additions probably indicate reuse of the notebook for later lectures or essays; the pages indexed do not seem to have been inscribed later.

The F No. 1 index is more complex, reflecting the repeated use of this notebook. Most of the pages indexed in the first column were collected for the "Philosophy of History" series; several groups, probably the earliest pages, are in numerical order and still show the original structure of the notebook. But the first column includes "Love 106", which refers to a passage dated June 6, 1839; so Emerson probably did not begin to index F No. 1 until after that date, perhaps before beginning work on essays written that summer. Seven entries in the second column, probably added at three different times, index notes probably made in the summer of 1839, most of them for "Spiritual Laws," "Compensation," and "Self-Reliance." The last entry indexes the drafts on Carlyle probably written in November, 1837, but salvaged in 1843 for use in the lecture "Recent Literary and Spiritual Influences"; the entry closely resembles 1843 notes and may have been added then.

Emerson seems to have indexed Δ as he set it up, with blocks of pages, usually ten to a topic, for the "Human Culture" series, and this section, in ink and in consecutive page order, helps to identify the earliest notes and topics even though they were not all used in the series. He extended the index in pencil in the same small hand, and added more entries above it in pencil in a larger hand, all probably before completion of the "Human Culture" series, since he used only a few of the final titles; this helps in dating pages reused later. "The Soul p 25" and "Society p 30" appear to have been added at one time to the right; both pages are dated 1839 by internal evidence, but this suggests some connection; "Circles 167" was added after these, suggesting that this essay was composed somewhat later. An entry at the top of the page supplies the date "1841" for otherwise puzzling notes on "The Age," and three entries in a late hand are a clue to the reuse of some early notes in the 1862 lecture "Perpetual Forces."

The earliest surviving index in Φ is the alphabetical column at the left margin of the inside front cover, but faint traces of an earlier index in erased pencil are visible to the right of it. The pages indexed seem from content to be notes written in the fall of 1838 for the "Human Life" series. Three entries in pencil at the bottom of the center column, "New Subjects 84," "Progress 83," and "Protest 142, 134," are probably additions to the first column. A center column of added entries is headed "October 1842"; the date applies with certainty only to the first four entries following it, in the same dark pencil, but the next seven entries appear to have been written about the same time. This helps to place some puzzling pages in the period when Emerson was preparing for the "New England" series and perhaps revising earlier lectures for *Essays, Second Series*. Although the first seven entries indented below these may not all have been entered at the same time, they index pages dated 1842 by their contents, all probably notes for essays. "Poet 85," added at the top of the center column, indexes notes for the essay "The Poet," probably in 1843. The final alphabetical column includes "Poet 85" as well as entries in the center column through "LIFE 50" and ten entries selected from the left-hand column, perhaps pages Emerson used repeatedly. "Eloquence 146" appears to be in the same ink and hand as the three entries above it and the final alphabetical index; since the notes to which it refers are almost certainly dated 1846, all may have been inscribed in 1846 or later.

The index to Ж is less instructive. A preliminary index in partially erased pencil includes both 1839 and 1841 pages, and the alphabetized index adds only three entries to it; "Condition 138," "Fashion 126," and "Riches 132" may indicate later pages or only an oversight in doing the preliminary index. "Progressors" is omitted from the alphabetical index, perhaps an oversight, and page 67, headed "The Over-Soul," is included under "True Life," an otherwise unsuspected connection. The addition of "Lectures 128" to the top of the page and to the alphabetical index may indicate that this is a later page.

The partially erased preliminary index in Index Minor, mostly in numerical order, includes pages begun in 1843 for essays, a page of notes for "The Young American," given February 7, 1844, and one collection for the "Representative Men" series, headed "Skeptic" and probably begun no earlier than August, 1845. "Love 31" is an error corrected in the alphabetical index that was probably done a short time later and includes some but not all of the collections for the "Representative Men" series (1845–1846); the preliminary index was probably begun as Emerson began planning the series, and the alphabetical index· after only a small amount of work had been done for it. Entries added over the erased preliminary index and also inserted in the alphabetical column index collections for four of the lectures, "Uses of Great Men," "Plato, or the Philosopher," "Swedenborg, or the Mystic," and "Goethe, or the Writer." But the puzzling omission from the preliminary index of "Napoleon 20", almost certainly notes for the lecture "Bonaparte," given April 2, 1845, suggests caution in inferring the order of composition of the lectures from the index.

The brief index in BO Conduct, probably inscribed before the verses fitted in to the right of it, was begun in page order; the addition of the last three entries may indicate that these pages were inscribed or used later.

Using the lecture notebooks. The editor's aim has been to present an accurate text of the lecture notebooks, with some guidance as to their content, probable use, and date, not to undertake a complete critical study. But as the notebooks brought together journals, lectures, and works, detail by detail, they shed new light on both journals and writings, and suggested some promising areas for further study.

The titles of Emerson's journals and notebooks began to fall into place, for instance. References to Γ, probably Emerson's original title for F No. 1, survive in a cross-reference on page 24 of the notebook and on the cover. It is evident from references in F No. 1 that Journals A, B, and C were not given these designations until some time after the close of the "Philosophy of History" series early in March, 1837; these three journals are referred to as "J 1833," "J 1835," and "J 1837" until after that time. "J" alone usually means Emerson's current journal during this period, though in later notebooks it refers to Journal J. The letter titles may have arisen from difficulties in citation as his lecture method matured. Notebook Γ may have been titled at the same time as A, B, and C; it has not been determined when Emerson retitled it F No. 1, but he referred to the journal now titled F No. 2, probably begun in February, 1840, merely as "F" until September, 1845, or later. Emerson continued Greek letter titles for his lecture notebooks with Δ, Φ, and Ж (designated Notebook Psi by the editors; Emerson may have doubled the Greek letter Ψ — see Plate VI — to differentiate it from the Blotting Book he had earlier titled Ψ and continued to cite by Greek letter alone as late as 1847 in Index Major), while he titled the regular journals A, B, C, D, E, etc. Page references to "Θ" in the 1838–1839 or early 1840 pages of Notebooks Φ and Ж (see Φ, page 14) point to the possible existence of another notebook or manuscript in the Greek letter series (though in Ж, page 39, Emerson used Θ as a symbol for theology or God, not a notebook). Various references to "Spirit Mss" in early surveys for the "Human Culture" series and in notes for "Holiness" suggest the existence of yet another unlocated manuscript or notebook (see Δ, page 14). Later journal designations may also fall into a significant pattern, helpful in placing puzzling materials.

That Emerson continued to cite the early journals throughout, even in Notebook BO Conduct, underscores the need for familiarity with them in the study of supposedly later lectures and essays and the development of Emerson's prose style. More lecture notes may be recognized in the published journals; the as yet unpublished journals and notebooks, particularly those after 1847, may also include additional lecture materials.

These notebooks also provide clues to the contents of some leaves missing from journals (especially the 1843–1844 journals such as K, U, V, and Y), and in some cases to the lectures and essays where missing entries probably survive. Lecture notes help to place some lecture fragments, and list journal material Emerson considered for lectures or parts of lectures now missing. Research on the lecture notes is limited, of course, by the fact that not all of the lectures survive in manuscript, and many that do are incomplete despite impressive efforts by the editors of *The Early Lectures* to reconstruct them. Lectures for the 1843 "New England" series and later were still being edited as this volume was completed; the manuscripts are fragmentary and difficult to assemble since Emerson used and revised them for later readings, adding to and sometimes combining them, and taking out leaves for later lectures and essays. For lectures not yet published, the editor has relied on texts supplied by Wallace E. Williams and James H. Justus, the editors of the later lectures, and on background information generously supplied by Professor Williams out of his own surpassing knowledge of them. They also supplied texts of two fragments discovered too late for inclusion in *Lectures*, one belonging in "Duty," the other in "Private Life." But four more brief journal passages can be assigned to "Duty" from Emerson's references to them in essay collections in Φ and Index Minor, indicating that the manuscript was intact in October, 1843. One fragment printed conjecturally with "Private Life" seems to fit notes for the 1838 lecture "General Views," and a long paragraph from Journal E, pages 41–42, printed in "Reforms," is cited by Emerson in Ж as "In last years Lecture on Tendencies." Notes for a missing lecture sometimes lead to an essay where parts of the lecture may survive (though no passage cited in Emerson's notes was necessarily in a lecture); a torn leaf of "Politics" can be partly recovered from "The Fortune of the Republic," for instance; notes for the lecture "Home" lead to a section of "Domestic Life," and notes for the lecture "Character" not only lead to the essay "Character" but to fragments printed with notes in *Lectures* and at the end of Journal D in *JMN*, VII.

Materials now exist for a thorough study of Emerson's reuse and revision of lectures for articles and essays. The lecture notebooks also provide evidence that may help to establish the order in which essays were composed, and their completion dates. Working titles in notes for lectures and essays — "Laws of life" for "General Views," "Duties" for "Prospects," "Life" for "Experience," "Representative" for "Nominalist and Realist," for example — may unlock new sources for these writings through Emerson's index headings and topics (some of which he may have added to the journals during composition). While the intermixture of notes suggests that some lectures in each series are paired (such as "The Individual" and

"The Present Age" in 1837, and "Love" and "Tragedy" two years later), the repetition of journal references in widely separated collections also draws together related lectures and essays many years apart on recurrent topics — work and trade, the individual and society, the present age and history, the Soul, great men, literature.

New evidence will undoubtedly fill in gaps and clear up many of the mysteries in these notebooks. Scattered lecture leaves may be found to fit the notes; the letters of Emerson's family and friends may correct dates and supply clues to missing lectures; what has been suggested here of Emerson's way of working will certainly be enlarged and corrected by the vigorous investigation this material plainly invites. Together with the journals and lectures already in print, the publication of these notebooks rounds out the necessary resources for a searching reappraisal of the origins, composition, and interrelationship of Emerson's lectures and essays.

Editorial technique. The editorial process follows that described in volume I and the slight modifications introduced for prose in subsequent volumes of the edition. But these notebooks present new editorial problems necessitating new techniques. Although they contain some drafts for lectures and quite a number of passages copied from other journals, there is relatively little finished prose. Most of the material, ranging from the indexlike collections and surveys to rough working notes and outlines made during actual writing, can be termed notes. The editor has tried to distinguish between Emerson's notes and his discursive prose and to leave the notes as nearly as possible the way Emerson wrote them. Mixtures of notes and prose are normally edited as notes.

Emerson erased or partially erased many pages and frequently made entries in ink or pencil over earlier pencil inscriptions; since little of the material was copied elsewhere, and much of it seems to be notes jotted down during actual composition, a special effort has been made to recover as much as possible. Where a printed or copied version exists of a passage in erased or overwritten pencil writing, the editor has first recovered as much as possible without aid, and has then consulted another version, but has printed only what she has been able to see.

Except in a few special instances, punctuation which Emerson added is reported only to account for an otherwise illogical situation. Pages bearing four or more additions of accidentals, which are taken as signs of unusually careful revision, are listed in the headnotes to the individual notebooks. These notebooks, which Emerson looked over in 1877, show numerous small mendings in a fine hand, probably added much later by Emerson or another editor, and not reported. They also have notes in pencil, evidently instructions by another editor to a copyist, not reported, and some cancellations in pencil enclosed in penciled parentheses, possibly by an editor other than Emerson, which are reported in textual notes.

Whenever one of Emerson's hyphens coincides with the compositor's end-of-line hyphenation, two hyphens have been set, one at the end of the line and one at the beginning of the following line. When the text is quoted in the notes, no silent emendations are made; hence there are occasional variations between notes and text.

Emerson began to use several new types of use marks with his indexlike collections. The most frequent are horizontal use marks, either straight or wavy, and single use marks struck either horizontally, vertically, or diagonally through each page number on a line; since neither type can be physically distinguished from cancellations, they are indicated by the same diamond brackets used to indicate cancellations, set to include the nearest whole word, journal title, or page number. But unmistakable cancellations are noted. Brackets used to indicate use marks are omitted when the text is quoted in the notes. Marginal markings, usually single or double vertical or slightly diagonal short lines, which are probably a form of use mark, are described. As in previous volumes, diagonal or vertical use marks through a line or passage are carefully described, with special attention to the unusually large number of discontinuous or extended use marks found in these notebooks.

In accordance with the policies of the Center for Editions of American Authors, a list of silent emendations has been prepared; copies are to be deposited in the Rush Rhees Library of the University of Rochester, the Library of Congress, Houghton Library, Huntington Library, and Newberry Library. The following statement describes the silent or mostly silent emendations. These range from numerous — as with apostrophes, punctuation of items in a series, supplying periods at the ends of sentences if the next sentence begins with a capital, or expansion of contractions — to occasional, as with supplying quotation marks, dashes, or parentheses missing from intended pairs.

Emendation of prose. A period is silently added to any declarative sentence lacking terminal punctuation but followed in the same paragraph by a sentence beginning with a capital letter. If a declarative sentence lacking a period is followed by a sentence beginning with a small letter, either a bracketed semicolon is supplied, or a bracketed period is supplied and the small letter is silently capitalized. In the second instance the reader will automatically know that the capital was originally a small letter. If a direct question lacking terminal punctuation is followed by a sentence in the same paragraph beginning with a capital the question mark is silently added. Punctuation of items in a series, since Emerson habitually set them off, is silently inserted. Small letters at the beginning of unquestionable paragraphs or of sentences which follow a sentence ending with a silent period are silently capitalized. Where indispensable for clarity a silent period is added to an abbreviation. Quotation marks, dashes, and parentheses missing from intended pairs have been silently supplied; so have quotation marks at the beginning of each of a series of quotations. Apostrophes have been silently inserted or normalized in possessives and contractions. Superscripts have been lowered. Double underscorings (and overscorings used by Emerson in the lecture notebooks to emphasize titles of journals, lectures, and essay manuscripts) have been interpreted by italics. Common Emersonian contractions like y^t for *that*, y^e for *the*, y^s for *this*, y^r for *their*, y^m for *them*, y^n for *than*, *wh* for *which*, *wd*, *cd*, and *shd* for *would*, *could*, and *should*, *mt* for *might*, *thro* for *through*, and *bo't*, *thot*, and *brot* for *bought*, *thought*, and *brought* are silently expanded. His dates have been regularly normalized by the silent insertion of commas and periods where necessary.

Emendation of note material. Generally, Emerson's working notes, collections, and outlines have been left as they stand in the manuscript; apostrophes have been supplied, in accordance with the rules for emending prose, but only where Emerson's intention was unmistakable, and contractions are normally expanded. Abbreviations have been expanded in brackets only where necessary for understanding. Because of the nature of the material, the editor has tried to preserve Emerson's spacing whenever it might be significant, as far as possible in type. When inserted entries or those added after an appreciable time could be distinguished, the editor has indicated them by insertion arrows or in footnotes, but many pages without insertion arrows were not written at one time but are accretions.

Emendation of poetry. On the whole, Emerson's poetry has been left as it stands in the manuscript; apostrophes have been supplied in accordance with the rules for emending prose, but only where Emerson's intention was unmistakable.

The line numbers of poems as printed in *Poems, W,* IX, are supplied in brackets, by fives, except when the manuscript lines are not in the printed order, or where the line number cannot be deduced with certainty from other line numbers. A bracketed "x" means the line does not appear in the poem. No line of poetry in the manuscript is necessarily unchanged in *Poems.*

Certain materials are omitted, either silently or with descriptive annotation; these will not be reported in the list of emendations. Omitted silently are slips of the pen, false starts at words or numbers, careless repetitions of a single word, and Emerson's occasional caret under insertions (assimilated into the editor's insertion marks). Marginal marks in red crayon or pencil, probably not Emerson's, are silently omitted. Underscoring to indicate intended revisions, and lines separating page numbers from matter on the page or separating crowded entries and turnover lines are not normally reproduced. Omitted, but usually with descriptive annotation, are practice penmanship, isolated words or letters, and miscellaneous markings.

Annotation. The editor has tried first of all to bring out patterns of use shown in collections and working notes that point to the series, lecture, or essay Emerson may have been working toward. Care has been taken to show the exact order in which cited passages are used. Since Emerson repeats many references from collections to final working notes, this necessarily entails a certain amount of repetition in footnotes. Earlier and later uses of cited passages are given when in the editor's judgment their number indicates that Emerson may have based a lecture or essay on earlier manuscripts, or used substantial parts of a lecture or essay in a later work. With the added help of these notebooks, many new uses for journal passages, some of them previously unlocated, have been found and the new locations are noted at least on their first occurrence. Uses are given for most use-marked entries. But not all uses noted in earlier volumes of *JMN* are repeated each time they occur; locations in the journals are supplied in footnotes or text wherever possible and the reader is referred to those journals. Similarly, when quotations are identified and the sources given in another volume of *JMN*, this easily available information is not usually repeated though such quotations are indexed under the author in this volume. A bracketed location in the text does not necessarily imply that a passage or quotation is copied or used verbatim, but does indicate that it is unmistakably taken from the journal entry with only Emerson's usual small changes in wording and punctuation.

Since the largest part of these notebooks consists of Emerson's references to passages in his journals, journal references supplied by the editor in the text or cited in notes follow Emerson in citing journal title and manuscript page number. Those supplied in the text omit the manuscript page brackets used in notes and use abbreviated titles, following Emerson's own practice as closely as possible but expanding where necessary for understanding. Emerson sometimes listed only the page numbers; the editor has supplied the journal title only when necessary for understanding, such as when Emerson changes journals. Cross-references are designed to draw together the often widely scattered materials for a work found in other lecture notebooks, journals, and manuscripts, and to facilitate further research.

The first known delivery dates of lectures discussed in this volume are listed in the Chronology below. Emerson's journals and notebooks are listed in the Editorial Title List, *JMN*, I, 403–415; journals and notebooks published in this edition to date are listed, with their location in previous volumes and their probable dates, in Appendix I, p. 617 below.

CHRONOLOGY

The reference list below gives only the first known delivery dates of lectures cited in this volume and the publication dates of essays and articles.

See also William Charvat, *Emerson's American Lecture Engagements* (New York: The New York Public Library, 1961), and Chronologies in *JMN*, V–XI.

Title	Date
Biography: "Introductory"	Jan. 29, 1835
"Michel Angelo Buonaroti"	Feb. 5, 1835
"Martin Luther"	Feb. 12, 1835
"John Milton"	Feb. 19? 1835
"George Fox"	Feb. 26, 1835
"Edmund Burke"	March 5, 1835
"On the Best Mode of Inspiring a Correct Taste in English Literature"	Aug. 20? 1835
"Historical Discourse at Concord"	Sept. 12, 1835
English Literature: "Introductory"	Nov. 5, 1835
"Permanent Traits of the English National Genius"	Nov. 12, 1835
"The Age of Fable"	Nov. 19, 1835
"Chaucer"	Nov. 26, 1835
"Shakspear" [first lecture]	Dec. 10, 1835
"Shakspear" [second lecture]	Dec. 17, 1835
"Lord Bacon"	Dec. 24, 1835
"Ben Jonson, Herrick, Herbert, Wotton"	Dec. 31, 1835
"Ethical Writers"	Jan. 7, 1836
"Modern Aspects of Letters"	Jan. 14, 1836
The Philosophy of History: "Introductory"	Dec. 8, 1836
"Humanity of Science"	Dec. 22, 1836
"Art"	Dec. 29, 1836
"Literature"	Jan. 5, 1837
"Politics"	Jan. 12, 1837
"Religion"	Jan. 19, 1837
"Society"	Jan. 26, 1837
"Trades and Professions"	Feb. 2, 1837
"Manners"	Feb. 9, 1837
"Ethics"	Feb. 16, 1837
"The Present Age"	Feb. 23, 1837
"The Individual"	March 2, 1837
"Address on Education"	June 10, 1837
"The American Scholar"	Aug. 31, 1837
"Slavery"	Nov. 14? 1837
Human Culture: "Introductory"	Dec. 6, 1837
"Doctrine of the Hands"	Dec. 13, 1837
"The Head"	Dec. 20, 1837
"The Eye and Ear"	Dec. 27, 1837

"Character"	Jan. 6, 1842
"Relation of Man to Nature"	Jan. 13, 1842
"Prospects"	Jan. 20, 1842
"The Senses and the Soul," *The Dial*, II	Jan. 1842
"Lecture on the Times," *The Dial*, III	July 1842
"The Conservative," *The Dial*, III	Oct. 1842
"The Transcendentalist," *The Dial*, III	Jan. 1843
"New England" series:	
"Genius of the Anglo-Saxon Race"	Jan. 10, 1843
"Trade"	Jan. 17, 1843
"Manners and Customs of New England"	Jan. 28, 1843
"Recent Literary and Spiritual Influences"	Jan. 30, 1843
"Results and Tendencies"	Feb. 1, 1843
"Europe and European Books," *The Dial*, III	April 1843
"Address to the Temperance Society at Harvard Mass."	July 4, 1843
"Gifts," *The Dial*, IV	July 1843
"The Comic," *The Dial*, IV	Oct. 1843
"The Young American"	Feb. 7, 1844
"New England Reformers" (Lecture read to the Society in Amory Hall)	March 3, 1844
"Want of Distinctive National Character"	March 6, 1844
"Address at the Second Church"	March 10, 1844
"The Young American," *The Dial*, IV	April 1844
"The Tragic," *The Dial*, IV	April 1844
"Emancipation in the British West Indies"	Aug. 1, 1844
Essays, Second Series	October, 1844
"Bonaparte"	Jan. 8? 1845
"Discourse at Middlebury College"	July 22, 1845
"Representative Men" series:	
"Uses of Great Men"	Dec. 11, 1845
"Plato, or the Philosopher"	Dec. 18, 1845
"Swedenborg, or the Mystic"	Dec. 25, 1845
"Montaigne, or the Skeptic"	Jan. 1, 1846
"Napoleon, or the Man of the World"	Jan. 8, 1846
"Shakspeare, or the Poet"	Jan. 15, 1846
"Goethe, or the Writer"	Jan. 22, 1846
"Eloquence"	Dec. 16, 1846? Feb. 10, 1847
"Discourse at Nantucket"	May 8, 1847
"England"	Dec., 1848
"The Spirit of the Times"	Jan. 10, 1850
"Conduct of Life" series:	
"Fate"	Dec. 22, 1851
"Power"	Jan. 30, 1851, Dec. 29, 1851

"Wealth"	March 25, 1851, Jan. 5, 1852
"Economy"	March 27, 1851, Jan. 12, 1852
"Culture"	March 29, 1851, Jan. 19, 1852
"Worship"	April 1, 1851, Jan. 26, 1852
"Address to the Adelphic Union of Williamstown College"	Aug. 15, 1854
"Perpetual Forces"	Nov. 18, 1862

SYMBOLS AND ABBREVIATIONS

⟨ ⟩ Cancellation

↑ ↓ Insertion or addition

/ / Variant

‖ ... ‖ Unrecovered matter, normally unannotated. Three dots, one to five words; four dots, six to fifteen words; five dots, sixteen to thirty words. Matter lost by accidental mutilation but recovered conjecturally is inserted between the parallels.

⟨‖ ... ‖⟩ Unrecovered canceled matter

‖msm‖ Manuscript mutilated

[ ] Editorial insertion

[...] Editorial omission

[ ] Emerson's square brackets

⌐ ¬ Marginal matter inserted in text

[ ] Page numbers of original manuscript

n See Textual Notes

-- Two hyphens are set when the compositor's end-of-line hyphen coincides with Emerson's.

∧ Emerson's symbol for intended insertion

[R.W.E.] Editorial substitution for Emerson's symbol of original authorship. See volume I, plate VII.

* Emerson's note

epw Erased pencil writing

☞
☜ Hands pointing
☝

ABBREVIATIONS AND SHORT TITLES IN FOOTNOTES

CEC   *The Correspondence of Emerson and Carlyle.* Edited by Joseph
Slater. New York: Columbia University Press, 1964.

E t E   Kenneth W. Cameron. *Emerson the Essayist.* Raleigh, N.C.: The
Thistle Press, 1945. 2 vols.

J   *Journals of Ralph Waldo Emerson.* Edited by Edward Waldo
Emerson and Waldo Emerson Forbes. Boston and New York:
Houghton Mifflin Co., 1909–1914. 10 vols.

JMN   *The Journals and Miscellaneous Notebooks of Ralph Waldo
Emerson.* William H. Gilman, Chief Editor; Alfred R. Ferguson,
Senior Editor; Harrison Hayford, Ralph H. Orth, J. E. Parsons,
A. W. Plumstead, Editors (Volume I edited by William H. Gil-
man, Alfred R. Ferguson, George P. Clark, and Merrell R. Davis;
volumes II–VI, William H. Gilman, Alfred R. Ferguson, Merrell
R. Davis, Merton M. Sealts, Jr., Harrison Hayford; volumes VII–
XI, William H. Gilman, Alfred R. Ferguson, Harrison Hayford,
Ralph H. Orth, J. E. Parsons, A. W. Plumstead). Cambridge:
Harvard University Press, 1960–

L   *The Letters of Ralph Waldo Emerson.* Edited by Ralph L. Rusk.
New York: Columbia University Press, 1939. 6 vols.

Lectures   *The Early Lectures of Ralph Waldo Emerson.* Volume I, 1833–
1836, edited by Stephen E. Whicher and Robert E. Spiller; volume II, 1836–1838, edited by Stephen E. Whicher, Robert E.
Spiller, and Wallace E. Williams; volume III, 1838–1842, edited
by Robert E. Spiller and Wallace E. Williams. Cambridge: Harvard
University Press, 1959–1972.

Life   Ralph L. Rusk. *The Life of Ralph Waldo Emerson.* New York:
Charles Scribner's Sons, 1949.

W   *The Complete Works of Ralph Waldo Emerson.* With a Bio-
graphical Introduction and Notes, by Edward Waldo Emerson.
Centenary Edition. Boston and New York: Houghton Mifflin Co.,
1903–1904. 12 vols. I — *Nature Addresses and Lectures;* II —
Essays, First Series; III — *Essays, Second Series;* IV — *Repre-
sentative Men;* V — *English Traits;* VI — *Conduct of Life;*
VII — *Society and Solitude;* VIII — *Letters and Social Aims;*
IX — *Poems;* X — *Lectures and Biographical Sketches;* XI —
Miscellanies; XII — *Natural History of Intellect.*

Miscellaneous Notebooks

$\mathcal{L}$ *Concord*

1835, 1838

The major portion of this notebook consists of working notes for Emerson's "Historical Discourse at Concord," delivered on September 12, 1835. Three years later he used it again to draft his letter to President Van Buren on the removal of the Cherokees, sent April 25, 1838, and in preparing for the Divinity School Address, July 15, 1838, and his oration at Dartmouth on "Literary Ethics" on July 24, 1838.

Notebooks L Concord and L Literature comprise one double-ended notebook. The covers, which measure 17 x 20.3 cm, are brown and blue marbled boards, with a leather spine strip labeled "L". There are 162 pages, lightly ruled, measuring 16.1 x 19.6 cm. The section occupied by L Concord runs through page 92, although material from L Literature, which, with reference to L Concord, reads upside down and back to front, appears on pages 81–84, 89, 91, and 92. Emerson numbered pages in ink front to back to the end of the notebook, leaving 71 pages, usually the verso, unnumbered; he repeated 45, so pages 45$_1$–45$_2$ have been given subscript numbers to differentiate them. Of the first 92 pages, 15, 18–24, 32–40, 42–45$_1$, 47–54, 57–60, 66, and 80, a total of 35 pages, are blank. Pages 5 and 7 have four or more revisions of accidentals.

[front cover]

CONCORD

L

[front cover verso] ↑Battle of 19th April, ⟨19th,⟩ 1775, p. 45↓

Charter, Rights↑,↓ ⟨&c⟩p. 1
Courts   13
Church   5
Schools   55

3

Finance   17
Battle   p 45
Indian   6⟨0⟩1
Puritan   25
Town   67
Country   79
Concord   85
Revolution   41
↑Letter to Pressant↓ [1]

[1]   *Concord.* [2]

In 1643 the Massachusetts Colony was divided into four Counties
or Shires; Essex, Middlesex, Suffolk, & Norfolk. /Middlesex contained Charlestown, Camb[ridge]., Watert[own]., Sudbury, Concord,
Woburn, Medford, Lynn/ [3]

⟨1692   New Charter of Mass⟩
↑March↓ 1629 The Charter of Mass[achuse]↑tts↓. Bay Compy.

---

[1] "Letter to Pressant" is added in pencil.

[2] In a letter to Lemuel Shattuck, September 27, 1835, Emerson gave some details
of his extensive research into the early history of both his town and his state for the
"Historical Discourse at Concord" (*W*, XI, 27–86) which he delivered at the town's
Second Centennial celebration on September 12, 1835. Besides the proof sheets of
Shattuck's *A History of the Town of Concord*, Emerson says that "I have now on my
table the seven first volumes of the Town Records, and the Volume of Church Records;
all which books I have examined with great attention; I have Johnson's Wonder
Working Providence in the Historical Collections. I have here also Hubbard's Indian
Wars, Mathers Magnalia, Winthrops Journal Hutchinsons History & his Collection;
Minot; & Bradford; Bancroft's U. S. Peter Bulkeleys Gospel Covenant. Allens Biog.
Dictionary. Dr Ripley's Half Century Sermon & History of y⁰ Fight; Phinney; &
the Lexington Sermons; Brigham's Discourse at Grafton; &c — These books are &
have been before me. At Cambridge in August I made written extracts from Neal's
New Engd.; Shepards Clear Sunshine &c; Mourt; Higginson; Josselyn; Underhill;
Shepards Lamentation, &c." (*L*, I, 455.) Many of these works are quoted in this
notebook; full titles and probable editions are given on first mention. No attempt has
been made to determine the exact source of each of Emerson's hundreds of working
notes; the ones that Emerson does not identify seem to be largely from the Town
and Church Records.

[3] "In 1643 . . . Concord," is used in the "Historical Discourse," *W*, XI, 55.
The date "1643", in darker ink, was probably filled in later.

4

granted by Charles I established a Corporation of Governor & Compy of Mass. Bay in New England. There should be a Governor, Deputy, & eighteen Assistants to be annually elected by the stockholders or members of the Corporation. Four times a year or oftener a general assembly of the free men should be held. It was in the power of the corporation to establish the terms on which new members [n] [2] could be admitted to its freedom [4]

The Govt established was a Gov & 13 counsellors 8 to be appointed by the Corpn; 3 by the 8; 2 by Colony.

1630   By the Charter fundamental laws were to be enacted in the assembly of all the freemen of the Colony   Oct 19. A general court was convened at Boston to settle the Govt. More than 100 persons many of them old planters were admitted freemen [5]

1631 General Ct. reserved the right of annually making changes in the board of assistants.

"And to the end the body of the Commons may be preserved of honest & good men it was ordered & agreed that for the time to come no man shall be admitted to the freedom of this body politic but such as are members of some of the Ch[urc]h[es]. within the limits of the same."

1632 May 8   ⟨G⟩Agreed at the Genl. Court, that the Gov & assistants [3] [n] shall be annually chosen. Each town was ordered to choose two men to appear at the next court of assists. & concert the estab. of pub. Treasury.

1634 The Genl Ct. ordered that the rep[resentative]s. alone should raise money & dispose of lands. See Winthrop   Vol 1 p. 128 [6]

↑1633 This year the plantation Dorchester began the practice of choosing men↓

1635 Framed a body of grounds of laws in resemblance to a Magna Charta

[4] "The Charter . . . freedom" is used in the "Historical Discourse," W, XI, 42–43.

[5] "By the Charter . . . freemen" is used in the "Historical Discourse," W, XI, 43. It is from George Bancroft, *A History of the United States, From the Discovery of the American Continent to the Present Time*, 10 vols. (Boston, 1834–1875), I, 389; vol. I is in Emerson's library.

[6] John Winthrop, *The History of New England from 1630 to 1649*, ed. James Savage, 2 vols. (Boston, 1825–1826). The reference is circled.

↑1636 Gov. & council legislate, judge, &c.↓

1644 The Magistrates & the Deputies separated into two ⟨bo⟩houses, each with a negative on other.

1641 Every man freeman or not, inhabitant or not, might introduce any ⟨public⟩ business into a public meeting. Bancroft (Laws, ed. 166[0] p. 50.) [7]

↑1647 "By an estimate taken by the Townsmen this year" &c.↓

1662 Repealed the law concerning freemen & allowed Eng. subjects freeholders of a certain rate ↑10 s.↓ certified by the minister of the place to be orthodox & not vicious in their lives to be made freemen though not members of Ch[urch]. Hutchinson   p 212 [8]

1647   For a more equal & ready way of raising mon⟨ey⟩ies for defraying public charges in time to come & for preventing such inconveniences as have fallen out upon former [4] assessments it is ordered & enacted by the Authority of the Court that the treasurer for the time being shall from year to year in the 5th month send ⟨out⟩ ↑forth↓ his warrant to the Constables & selectmen of every town within this jurisdiction requiring of the Constables to call the inhabitants together, who, being assembled, shall choose some one of their freemen to be a Commissioner who, together with the Selectmen for the Prudential affairs, shall some time &c make rates.

	W[illiam]. E[merson]
[Edward] Wigglesworth	Mother
N L F[rothingham]	M[ary] M[oody] E[merson]
T[homas]. C[arlyle].	C[harles] C E[merson]
Dr [John] Farmer	R. B[ulkeley]. E[merson].
E[dward]. Eve[rett]	2 Plymouth
S[amuel]. Ripley	[Frederic Henry] Hedge

[7] Bancroft, *A History of the United States* . . . , 1834, I, 452. The citation in parentheses is Bancroft's footnote. The sentence is used in the "Historical Discourse," *W*, XI, 47.

[8] Thomas Hutchinson, *The History of Massachusetts, from the First Settlement Thereof in 1628, Until the Year 1750*, 3rd ed., 2 vols. (Boston, 1795), vol. I. A third volume, entitled *The History of the Province of Massachusetts Bay from 1749 to 1774, Comprising a Detailed Narrative of the Origin and Early Stages of the American Revolution*, was edited by John Hutchinson, and published in London in 1828.

D↑r↓ G Park   O[rville] Dewey
Abel Adams
2 Mrs L[incoln]. Ripley
E[zra]. Weston [Jr.]
Mrs [Paulina Tucker] Nash
Dr [John Gorham] Palfrey
H[enry] Ware Jr
⟨President Quincy⟩ or College
[Robert Charles] Winthrop
Miss [Harriet] Martineau
P[eter]. C[hardon]. Brooks
[Samuel] Greele [9]

[5]   *Ecclesiastical.*

1637   The 6 April, 1637, those of Concord set a day apart for the
ordination of their two ministers, Mr Jones to be their pastor, & Mr
Bulkley, to be their teacher. But neither the Governor, Mr Vane,
nor Mr Cotton, nor the two ruling elders, nor any other of Boston
Church would be present; because the two forementioned ministers
were looked upon in that hour of temptation as too legal preachers,
& therefore they would not ⟨p⟩be present to give approbation to their
ordination. Hubbard's Hist[ory]. of N[ew]. England. p. 274   Hist.
Coll.[10]

[9] The list of names, in pencil, may be a record of those who received Emerson's
"Historical Discourse at Concord," which was printed shortly after its delivery. In
addition to his family and others easily identified, it includes Edward Wigglesworth
(1804–1876), an 1822 graduate of Harvard and a Boston lawyer, editor, and businessman; Samuel Ripley, Emerson's half uncle; Abel Adams, his lifelong friend and
business adviser; Mrs. Lincoln Ripley, Emerson's aunt; Ezra Weston, Jr., a Boston
attorney and friend of Charles Emerson; Dr. Palfrey, editor of the *North American
Review*, who printed a joint review of Shattuck's *History* and Emerson's "Historical
Discourse" in the April, 1836, issue (XLII, 448–467); Henry Ware, Jr., Emerson's
predecessor as minister of the Second Church in Boston, and a professor in the Harvard
Divinity School; Lieutenant Colonel R. C. Winthrop, a descendant of the first governor of Massachusetts, who had attended the celebration; Peter Chardon Brooks
(1767–1849), a retired Boston merchant and philanthropist, and father-in-law of
N. L. Frothingham and Edward Everett; Samuel Greele of Boston, evidently a
deacon in the Federal Street Church (*L*, II, 122); and Orville Dewey, Emerson's
cousin, then pastor of the Second Unitarian Church in New York.

[10] William Hubbard, *A General History of New England, from the Discovery to
MDCLXXX* (Boston, 1815), in the *Collections of the Massachusetts Historical Society,
Second Series*, probably withdrawn from the Harvard College Library July 20, 1835.

Musketaquid.

1635. Sept. 2, The General Court at its session at New-Town, (Cambridge) granted to Mr Buckly (Bulkeley) and Major Simon Willard, merchant, & about twelve more families, to begin a town. See Shattuck's History p. 5 [11]

[6]   Discourse to Cambridge Theological School, 15 July, 1838. [12]

Topics.

              Present state of Christianity
The moral nature of man is to be preached

        Nothing is more real than the office of the moral teacher
        It cannot bear to suffer the deduction of a lie.
        Man is to be preached
        Ethical poetry   C.288 [13] 301   283, 304

        [7] Preaching is very bad. I
    It is of no use to point at times when it ⟨is⟩was worse, if faith was there; faith was character, Action, & the intellectual analysis could afford to sleep; but now the faith in texts is clean gone. A sermon of texts is dead & buried; the age is a scholar, an intellectual man, & if it have no thought, it is a degradation and a Dark Age.
Preaching is verbal; timid; useless; its success is a bad sign: It is beginning to indicate character & religion to withdraw from churches [14]
        Preaching gives no sign of life. It has not been lived.
        Everything accuses the bad preacher   D 22
        Foolishest preaching   D 24
        Speak the truth   D 29   Dispute not   C.289   D.[29]
Yield to the Spirit   D 30
        Have you had doubts & shames   D 32

[11] Lemuel Shattuck, *A History of the Town of Concord* (Boston, 1835); cf. the "Historical Discourse," *W*, XI, 32.

[12] Emerson used pp. [6]–[16] to collect materials for the Divinity School Address (*W*, I, 117–151). Emerson used the thought but little of the exact wording of this draft in the final version; he followed the outlines on pp. [14] and [16] closely.

[13] Cf. the Divinity School Address, *W*, I, 151.

[14] This sentence is used in the Divinity School Address, *W*, I, 143.

Poetry concealed in commonplaces of prayer   [D 43]
Distinction of the new Age   D 46
Test of the true faith   D 46
Veneration beautiful   D 46
Falsehood of preaching   D 53   C 67   C 148   284 [15]
The preacher's classes   C 120
        [8] Preacher a poet   C 295
The man that can speak well. *C* 346
It is wicked to go to church Sundays.[16] [C 249]   C 274

[9] From its infancy the history of Xy [Christianity] interests us as showing the invincible power of the moral element.ⁿ But from its infancy it has fallen on low places. It is the history of the personal, the positive, even of the ritual.[17] ⟨I⟩You standing in this Creative Hour, desire & aim to understand your relation to it. Redeem it. Be Christians. There have never been any. Jesus taught sentiments & stood on instincts. Do you so.
I have not taken it in hand to vindicate the moral sentiment. It will answer for itself as gravity, & heat, & light, & hydrogen do. But I have thought that a prophet might well arise who should say, Why stoops the human race like Nebuchadnezzar to the ground & eats grass. Why is it so jealous of its ill fame? Why does it resent being told that it is divine. Why so hug its despair & burn the blasphemer that declares that not only God was with it but God *is* with it.[18]
    Preach Christianity today. Say, as Christ did, God is in me, I am God; Have I been so long with you & hast thou not known me? Who hath seen me hath seen the Father.[19]

[15] Passages in Journal D, pp. [22], [29], [43], and [46], are used in the Divinity School Address, *W*, I, 140, 123, 139, and 136–137. Passages in C, pp. [67], [148], and [284], are used in the Divinity School Address, *W*, I, 138, 139, and 137–138, 138–139, and 141–142. Emerson evidently scanned D in order, then added references from C.
[16] This remark of Lidian Emerson's is used together with the passage from Journal C, p. [274], in the Divinity School Address, *W*, I, 143.
[17] This sentence is used in the Divinity School Address, *W*, I, 130.
[18] With this sentence, cf. Journal B, p. [4], used in the Divinity School Address, *W*, I, 144.
[19] With "God . . . God;", cf. John 14:10, 11; "Have I . . . Father." is from John 14:9.

9

Say this today. Be Christ; & you shall find you are the only Christian there & men [10] will still reject & crucify the true witness anew. Jesus belonged to the true race of the prophets. One man was true to that which is in you & me. Thus deep was his impression engraven on the history.

I see then, That, Moral Sentiment is Divine & deifying

> That the same sentiment seems to injure Jesus whilst really it does him honor, but with his honor we have no concern. Not with persons but with truth.
>
> That, the office of the preacher is perpetual
>
> That the office is poorly discharged now.

That the doctrine of Man's divine nature is almost forgotten: that the doctrine of Inspiration is almost lost; that the doctrine of the Crowd of the Majority has usurped the place of the Doctrine of the Soul — a very ⟨b⟩low doctrine indeed. ⟨We bid you⟩

⟨We bid you⟩

[11] There is no faith in the Soul.[20]
The greatness of the Soul is the first, second, & third faith of the man. Now that has disappeared & in consequence every thing is low; church, state, art, letters, life.

⟨The remedy⟩ These evils. False Christianity:

Great want of a Cultus.

Vicious preaching   All is going to pieces.

Remedy is in belief, in culture, in protest first, & then affirmation; in yea & nay; in loving virtue; & Jesus when the parrot world denies him.

Then in being the love & virtue & sane Self of the world & so preaching God.

A good preacher belongs to old or new [C 346]

[12] It is very foolish to manufacture a faith. Faith makes us, not we it. All attempts to supply a system are as cold & foolish as the new worship introduced by Robespierre to the Goddess of Reason ⟨ginger bread⟩ all pasteboard & fillagree, & end like that in madness

---

[20] "Soul." is followed by what may be the start of another letter, canceled.

& murder.[21] It must grow. The hope of mankind must rest in the sometime appearance of a true Messiah who shall complete the Epos of moral nature & write out those laws for the charmed world to read & to obey.

Meantime what grief that we & our successors should be deprived of that worship without, which we need & should have no discipline in the moral & religious world; that what makes the crown & blessing, the fragrant virtue that salts & sweetens life, & makes it sublime should be taken away & leave us mere utilitarians below. Angels might weep; the bond that joins us to them is cut[.]

[13]   Courts, Shire.
     Courts of Middlesex were held alternately at Cambridge
     & Charlestown till 1692
1692   Concord was added
1775   Charlestown left out [22]

A song of the Soul
Permanent good
Color of the moral sentiment
Kingdom of ideas
Speakers of ideas in all ages
Uplifting influence
Instant degradation & lie when the word is spoken without the spirit.

Illustrated by the history of religion alway
Jesus was a man & taught alone in history the greatness of man.
Instantly it was vitiated & Xy ever since has been false. It is only here & there has been a Xn. [Christian]
     Inspiration

[21] "Faith makes . . . murder." is used in the Divinity School Address, *W*, I, 150.
[22] "Courts of . . . out", notes for the "Historical Discourse" in 1835, is struck through in ink with a wavy diagonal line, probably to indicate cancellation in 1838 of the earlier material.

Miracles
Church

Injury done now by Xy to mankind.

[14] I wish to expose the ⟨e⟩fatal error to which the communication of religion is open.[23]
The soul is a law[24]
⟨The⟩ Religion is a joy that ⟨accompan⟩[n] attends the perception of the soul.
And the inexperience & indolence of the mind disposes man ever to take this thought at second hand.
⟨All⟩ Jesus was a teacher of the Soul: men have not received the Soul but Jesus.
And the effect is 1. second men not first men
And ⟨not⟩ 2. The moral law is not taught.

Preaching a real office.
Bad preaching

[15] [blank]
[16]   Beautiful Summer
        World of senses
        World of intellect
        World of Virtue
        Moral sentiment

        Moral sentiment a delight in the insight of the Soul[25]
↑I Foundation
of Religion↓   This sentiment is Religion; & permanent.
        All Expressions of it permanent
        Loss of it a Dark Age.

[23] Cf. the Divinity School Address, *W*, I, 130.
[24] This entry, struck through in ink with a diagonal use mark, and the rest of p. [14] are an outline of the Divinity School Address, *W*, I, 122–138.
[25] P. [16] to this point is an outline of the first five paragraphs of the Divinity School Address, *W*, I, 119–122.

History of Xy
Jesus a poet
Travestied & made noxious by the instant depar-
ture of the soul

II Cultus or Worship
⟨Our⟩ The office of priest real & perpetual
Our worship dead or dying
Our preaching lifeless
Misery of preacher   misery of people

III Remedy in return to the Soul.
Man infinite   We want soul soul
Let him protest   let him believe   let him affirm
Let him befriend their sublime thoughts

Let him have latent virtue & be an influence [26]

[17]   Financial   ↑Hutchinson   p 110↓ [27]
In 1642 a tax of £800 was apportioned
Boston, ↑£↓120. Concord £25
1640   A Rate of £1200   Boston 179   Concord £50
Winthrop   2 Vol p 2

	1834	1835
Schools	1400	1800
Poor	900	800
Town Charges	800	1200
Town Debts	400	400
Ministry	640	640
Music	75	75

[26] "I . . . Religion" is set off from "Moral sentiment a . . . This" by a curved line in ink. Emerson followed sections I–III of the outline on p. [16] in sections of the Divinity School Address, W, I, 126–129, 134–140, and 144–151, changing much of the wording.
[27] Thomas Hutchinson, *The History of Massachusetts* . . . , 1795, vol. I. Hutchinson cites a resolution of the House of Commons in 1642 exempting the colonies from taxation on transported goods. "In 1642 . . . Concord £25" is taken from a footnote on this page. "Hutchinson   p 110" is in pencil.

Paroch[ial] Expense   50   100
Sab[bath]. School   25   25
                           ‾‾‾‾‾   ‾‾‾‾‾‾‾‾
                            4290   ⟨64⟩5040 [28]

[18]–[24] [blank]
[25]   Puritan, Pilgrim, &c
Bring papers & Linseed oil for your windows
Our Indian Corn even the coarsest maketh as pleasant meal as rice;
therefore spare that unless to spend by the way
          E. W. Plymouth 11 Dec 1621
                    Mourt [29]

[26]   Literary Societies of Dartmouth College. [30]

Collections
⟨A great man escapes out of the Kingdom of t⟨h⟩ime⟩
                    sublimely patient — C 324   D 19
⟨Nature & the sublime get into everything⟩   C 325 —
⟨Gradually we bend our living to our idea   C⟩319
     ⟨Napoleon's Day Mine⟩   ⟨C 316⟩
⟨First men no glory   Be great where you are   C 317⟩
⟨Means & Ends   Napoleon   C 315⟩
⟨Napoleon, a great vascular man. A great man univ.⟩   C 312   ↑296↓
⟨Make your own estimate⟩   ⟨311⟩
⟨Natural History of the Reason (BF & RWE   308⟩
⟨Superiority of the poultry yard ⟨C⟩⟩   298
⟨No cultivated men in America   D⟩   C 2⟨2⟩93

----

[28] Emerson used the notes on p. [17] in the "Historical Discourse," *W*, XI, 54 and 82.

[29] G. Mourt, *A Relation Or Iournall of the beginning and proceedings of the English Plantation setled at Plimoth in New England*, first published at London in 1622. Emerson's edition is uncertain.

[30] The heading is framed in a heavy, irregular rectangle. Emerson used pp. [26]–[31] to collect material for "Literary Ethics," the address he gave at Dartmouth College July 24, 1838 (*W*, I, 153–187).

In this and subsequent lecture collections, some entries are struck through with horizontal lines, probably intended as horizontal use marks; since the editors cannot always distinguish between cancellations and use marks, both are indicated by cancellation symbols: ⟨ ⟩.

⟨All remains to be written⟩ C 29⟨3⟩1   D 18, 50, 55.

⟨Eclecticism⟩   C 276

⟨All things are mine   The 3 Kings of Cologne D 3⟩ ⟨D⟩

⟨Let us be silent & do chares for Culture's sake   D 4⟩

⟨Love of Beauty⟩   D 6

⟨Love of a Man   Ney.   D 10⟩

⟨Power of a Milton, a Homer, &c to brace me   D 12⟩ [31]

⟨On protesting⟩   ⟨D 15, 25⟩

⟨Unconsciousness of the Conscious   D 17⟩

      [27] ⟨Shakspear & Genius⟩   D 18

⟨Napoleon   Great laws & little   D 20⟩

⟨Owe thought to Antagonism   D 39 C 343⟩

⟨Tragedy of more & less   D 48⟩

⟨The distinction of the Coming Age⟩   D 46

⟨Scholar's commissions on all study⟩ [D 50]

⟨Moon   51 D⟩

⟨Scholar's reason for Solitude   C 331⟩

⟨Extempore speech⟩ ↑as↓ ⟨easy as silence   334 One mind⟩

⟨Valuable hint of Napoleon on the Bellerophon. C 343⟩

⟨Never allow⟩ ⟨Ignore difference of sentiment⟩ 343 ⟨D⟩C

⟨Injurious position of the Scholar⟩, ↑advising.↓ [n] C 345

⟨A man is piqued by any limitation of his genius⟩ ↑C↓ ⟨346⟩

⟨Who can speak well belongs to *new &*⟩ old. 346 [32]

All things are mine   3 Kings of Cologne D 3

Napoleon's day mine   C 316

[31] Passages cited in Journal C, pp. [316], [315], [312], [308], [291], and [276], are used in "Literary Ethics," *W*, I, 162–163, 179, 164–165, 165–166 and 167, 167–169, and 171–172. Passages in D, pp. [18], [50], [55], [3], [4], and [12], are used, *ibid.*, pp. 167 and 168, 170, 166–167 and 170–171, 159–160, 176 and 177–178, and 161–162. Passages in C, p. [324], and D, p. [6], were used in "Tragedy," *Lectures*, III, 116 and 117; C, p. [296], in "Tendencies," *Lectures*, III, 312; C, p. [311], in "Duty," *Lectures*, III, 139, and "Spiritual Laws," *W*, II, 143; C, p. [298], in "The Protest," *Lectures*, III, 98; and D, p. [10], in "Doctrine of the Soul," *Lectures*, III, 13 and 12.

[32] Material on the top half of the page, down to "*new & old.* 346", appears to have been written at the same time as p. [26]. Passages from Journal D, pp. [18], [20], [39], [48], and [50], are used in "Literary Ethics," *W*, I, 167, 180, 184, 164, and 184–185. Those from C, pp. [331], [334], [343], [345], and the first reference on p. [346] are used, *ibid.*, pp. 173–174, 166, 178–179, 183, and 164.

A man is piqued by any limitation   C 346 ↑Tragedy of more & less
                                                                            D 48↓

Power of a man   Milton   Homer   D 12 [33]
Value of a man. Ney.   D 10
Make your own estimate   C 311
First men no glory. Be great where you are   C 317
A great man escapes out of Time   C 324   D 19
Flexibility of a man. Speak well; old *and* new   C 346
The distinction of the coming age   D 46
[28] the rain dear hermitage of nature   D 21
Man can't sit down to see stars for consumption in his side   D 21
Agiocochook   D 44   Bivouac.[34]

      Literature yet unwritten   C.291   D 18   50   55
      Eclecticism   C 276 [35]
      Unconsciousness of the Conscious   D 17
      Nature & the sublime in everything   C 325
      Love of Beauty   D 6

      Let us protest   D 15   25
      Let us be private   C 331
      Let us owe thought to Antagonism   C 343   D 39
      Let us do Chares for Culture   D 4
      Scholar's commissions on all study   D ⟨46⟩ 50
      Gradually we bend our living to our idea   C 319
      Ignore difference of sentiment   C 343
      Let us be humble.   C 345
         Napoleon on Bellerophon [36]   [C 343]

---

[33] Matter from "All things" to the bottom of the page is in a smaller hand and may have been added later. Passages from Journal D, p. [3], C, p. [316], and D, pp. [48] and [12], are used in "Literary Ethics," W, I, 159–160, 162–163, 164, and 160–162. D, p. [48], is also used in "Tragedy," *Lectures*, III, 107.

[34] The first three entries on p. [28] are struck through in ink with three diagonal use marks, though only the first passage cited in Journal D, p. [21], and the paragraph in D, p. [44], have been located in "Literary Ethics," W, I, 175 and 169–170. With "Bivouac.", cf. "Self-Reliance," W, II, 87.

[35] Passages from Journal D, pp. [18], [50], and [55], and C, p. [276], are used in this order in "Literary Ethics," W, I, 167, 170, 166–167 and 170–171, and 171–172.

[36] Lines drawn in ink in the left margin connect "Let us owe . . . " with "Ignore

Means & Ends . . . . .   C 315

Great laws & little . . . . .   D 20

Let us be true. Great man escapes out of time [C 324]

Make your own estimate.[37]

Napoleon's merit. Universal   C 312, 296.

Extempore Speech easy as silence   C 334

Natural History of Reason   C 308 [38]

Shakspear & Genius   D 18

[29]   Love of Beauty   D 6

Moon   51 D

⟨S⟩No cultivated men in America   C 293   D

Superiority of Poultry Yard.   C 298

⟨Shakspear & Genius   D 18⟩

⟨Natural Hist. of Reason   C 308⟩

⟨The distinction of the coming age   D 46⟩[39]

Literary Ethics.

Who can speak well belongs to old & new   C 346

---

1. Resources of the Scholar not yet known
2. His subject new
3. ⟨His aims be n⟩Noble be his aims!
     He solitary
     humble

---

difference . . . " and "Let us do Chares . . . " with "Napoleon . . . "; passages in Journal C, p. [331], D, pp. [39], [4], and [50], and C, p. [345], and "Napoleon on Bellerophon" are used in "Literary Ethics," *W*, I, 173–174, 184, 176, 184–185, 183, 178–179.

[37] These two lines, "Let us . . . estimate.", in a smaller hand, may have been crowded in later. Passages from Journal C, p. [315], and D, p. [20], are used in "Literary Ethics," *W*, I, 179 and 180.

[38] "Napoleons . . . Natural" is struck through in ink with a diagonal use mark. Passages from Journal C, pp. [312], [334], and [308], are used in "Literary Ethics," *W*, I, 164–165, 166, and 165–166.

[39] The passage cited in Journal C, p. [308], is used in "Literary Ethics," *W*, I, 165–166, and that in D, p. [46], in "The Protest," *Lectures*, III, 89.

loving

true   D 42 [40]

[30] A solitary laborious charitable soul

III Aims [41]

> Let the scholar be alone
> Let him live, drudge, suffer,
>> Means to ends & the grand soul too

> Let him be true   Let him be true

There are laws that can only be learned by living. They are concealed under the details of daily action. ⟨They⟩ All action is an experiment upon them. The scholar equally with all men & more than all men is interested to know them. So let him be a great soldier & conqueror[.]
The greater man the more skilful.
That is a lesson which Napoleon taught.

[31] "To the persevering mortal" &c [T· 185]

True scholar has no rival.
↑D 50↓ Scholar always gets his commissions.[42]

If they say 'tis good, it's good; if bad, bad. 'Tis even so.[n] In all that we hear & read there ever is so much of nature, that a trifle hath some majesty, & the mediocre production may be cracked up by the affectionate into a sort of Olympian merit, & find allowance from us,

---

[40] Emerson followed this brief outline closely in "Literary Ethics," *W*, I, 158–186.

[41] The entire page [30] contains materials for section III of "Literary Ethics." Emerson followed the four-line outline below closely; see *W*, I, 173, 176, 179, and 183. "They are . . . upon them." and "That is . . . taught." are used in *W*, I, 177 and 178.

[42] The first two lines on p. [31] are marked with vertical bars in pencil in the left margin. With "True scholar . . . rival.", cf. Journal D, p. [57]. The paragraph in D, p. [50], is used in "Literary Ethics," *W*, I, 184–185.

though not its spontaneous praisers. Bowles's sonnets, Southey's Roderic, Wordsworth's Wagoner, may come to be esteemed very fine, such latitude of aboriginal worth nature yields to everything not contrarious. [C 325]

[32]–[40] [blank]
[41] [43]   Revolution
1776 25 June General Assembly of Mass resolved to raise 5000 militia for 6 ↑months↓ to reinforce the Continental Army

> "The numbers they say are large but this Court has the fullest assurance that their brethren on this occasion will not confer with flesh & blood but will without hesitation & with utmost alacrity & despatch fill up the numbers proportioned to the several towns"

£500000 were appropriated   Bradford 2. 113
On that occasion Concord furnished 48 men at an expense of 432£

1775 Of the Boston poor 82 were maintained here

1779 Tax in silver ⟨£⟩$6,281.
1782 d[itt]o   do ⟨£⟩$9544.   population 1300
1783 do   do   5208.

[42]–[45₁] [blank]
[44₂] [44]
[45₂]   Battle   19 April 1775
Captain Charles Miles ⟨to⟩said to Dr Ripley that he went to the services of the day with the same seriousness & acknowledgment of God which he carried to Church.

Luther Blanchard whilst his wound was dressed on hearing Mrs   remark that a little more & it would have killed you ⟨&⟩replied   And a little more and it would not have touched me

---

[43] The page, struck through in pencil with a diagonal use mark, is used in "Historical Discourse at Concord," *W*, XI, 79 and 78.
[44] P. [44₂] is blank except for "April . . . Boston", printed as an insertion on p. [45₂].

From W. Emerson's Journal

↑April 2. This Month ushered in with the alarming news of 15 Regiments more of British Troops on their passage to Boston↓ [45]
"Apr. 16   Preached all day from Genesis 6.9
       19   Battle at Concord & Lexington
       20   falsely alarmed with the report of the Troops returning to
              Concord by way of Lincoln
21   Attend prayers at the Meeting House   present 700 soldiers from the
frontier towns   Mr Webster gave an exhortation. Went to Cambridge &
Malden. Great Commotions the whole country universally alarmed
30   Preached from Ps. 56.3.   P.M. The Lord is my Rock
This month remarkable for the greatest events taking place in the
present age."

[46] "They (the people) were sulky." Gen Gage [46]

[47]–[54] [blank]
    [55] Schools, Education, &c

1653   Concord subscribed £5 for 7 years for Harvard College
                                              S[hattuck]. p. 45.

1642   None of the brethren shall suffer so much barbarism in their
            families as not to teach their children & apprentices so much learning
            as may enable them to read perfectly the English tongue

1647   To the end that learning may not be buried in the graves of ⟨their⟩
            ↑our↓ forefathers ordered that every township after the Lord hath
            increased them to ⟨50⟩ the number of 50 householders shall appoint
            one to teach all children to write & read & where any town shall in-
            crease to the number of 100 ⟨ho⟩families they shall set up a grammar
            school the masters thereof being able to instruct youth so far as they
            may be fitted for the university   Col. Laws 74. 186. apud Ban-
            croft   Vol 1 p 498.[47]

---

[45] "April 2 . . . Boston" was added on p. [44₂], circled, and its intended place
on the facing page, [45₂], was indicated by a hand sign between "From" and
" 'Apr. 16' ".
    [46] Thomas Gage (1721–1787), last royal governor of Massachusetts.
    [47] P. [55] is struck through in pencil with a diagonal use mark. "1653 . . .
College" and "1647 . . . university" are used in the "Historical Discourse," *W*, XI,
57 and 56–57.

[56] "We want good Schoolmasters, none being here allowed of but of ill principle, & till there be provision made to rectify the youth of this Country, there is no hopes that this people will prove loyal." E. Randolph to the Abp. Canterbury

Hutchinson   Coll. p 553 [48]

"Their Commencement kept yearly the 2 Aug[us]t in the meeting-house where the Governor & magistrates are present attended with throngs of illiterate elders & Church members who are entertained with English speeches & verses"   E. Randolph   Hutch. Coll. p. 501

[57]–[60] [blank]
[61]   *Indian*
        "Alas for them their day is o'er
        Their fires are out from hill & shore
        No more for them the wild deer bounds
        The plough is on their hunting grounds
        The pale man's ax rings thro their woods
        The pale man's sails skim↑s↓ o'er their floods
              Their pleasant springs are dry
        Their children — look by power oppressed
        Beyond the mountains of the West
              Their children go to die."
                                    Sprague [49]

_____

    When Canonchet knew that his sentence was death, he said, he liked it well that he was to die before his heart was soft, or he had spoken anything unworthy of himself. He would not deliver up a Wampanoag or the paring of a Wampanoag's nail!

_____

    John Monoco who burned Groton, ↑March,↓ 1676, boasted that he had burned Medfield & Lancaster, & would now burn Groton, Chelmsford, Concord, Watertown, Cambridge, Charlestown, Roxbury, Boston, adding "What me will, me do." He had 480 men but was hanged in Boston Sept. 26 16⟨2⟩76 [50]

[48] Thomas Hutchinson, *A Collection of Original Papers Relative to the History of the Colony of Massachusetts-bay* (Boston, 1769), which Emerson withdrew from the Boston Athenaeum Sept. 3-Oct. 7, 1835.
[49] Charles Sprague, "Centennial Ode," xix; Emerson used the first seven lines in the "Historical Discourse," *W*, XI, 62.
[50] This and the preceding entry, from Hubbard's *A Narrative of the Indian Wars*

[62]   ↑Indians.↓

It was in marching to the Indian towns around Wachusett that Gershom Bulkely was shot in the thigh & one of the party killed by Indns. Hubbard's Ind[ian]. W[ars]. p 205

The nameless hero of the Wampanoags butchered by the Mohegans [n] (Hubbard 244) leads the chronicler to say that Justice vindictive hath iron hands though leaden feet. They put him in a great circle that all their eyes might be fed & broke off successively & at intervals each one of his fingers and toes yet did he not relent or show a sign of anguish but being asked by his tormentors how he liked the War? he replied "he liked it well & found it as sweet as English men do their sugar." [51]

"This heart," said Uncas, sachem of the Mohicans, in 1638 "is not mine but yours." [Ibid., p. 56]

1676 A remarkable thaw in January ↑melted snow & opened the earth↓
enabled [n] Philip's Indians to come at the ground nuts otherwise they had starved
Philip fled from one swamp to another [52]

[63]   ↑Indians.↓
At beginning of Philip's War the Narragansets had 2000 ↑warriors↓

Their bowstrings were made of moose sinews the arrow of a young stick of the pithy elder.
Roger Williams says he has known them run between 80 & 100 miles in a summer's day & ba⟨g⟩ck again within 2 days.
they sit ⟨up⟩ around holes in the ice catching pickerel   breams   perch &c
Pounded parched corn or No cake
Hooker calls them the ruins of mankind
The Eng. alcohol has been more fatal than the sword [53]

---

in New England (Worcester, Mass., 1801), pp. 185 and 201–202, are used in the "Historical Discourse," W, XI, 58 and 59.

[51] The paragraph is used in the "Historical Discourse," W, XI, 59.

[52] "1676 . . . another" is used in the "Historical Discourse," W, XI, 60.

[53] "Their bowstrings . . . sword", struck through in pencil with a diagonal and a vertical use mark, is used in the "Historical Discourse," W, XI, 36–37 and 51.

R. Will[ia]ms says   They had a tradition that a crow brought the first grain of Ind. corn. not one Ind. in a hundred would kill them

John Smith pestered by instructions from the Company to convert the savages sent them one to England that they might convert him.

⟨N⟩Thos Morton N E Canaan says the savages have the sense of seeing far beyond any of our nation as sometimes when they have told ⟨o⟩us of a ship at sea sooner by one hour yea two hours sail sooner than any Englishman that stood by o⟨f⟩n purpose to look out their sight is so excellent.[54]

[64] 1634   The Pequods offered the G[eneral]. C[our]t. at Boston a great present of beavers, otter, ⟨wa⟩peag, &c with the expression that we might with part thereof procure their peace with the Narragansetts themselves disdaining to offer it of themselves. Winthrop   Vol I p. 386

"Blood for Blood," was their international code
Indians are bad neighbors.

[65] [55]   *Praying Indians.*

An object expressed in the charter ⟨o⟩was "to win the Indians to the knowledge & obedience of ⟨the⟩God."

1644   Squaw Sachem at Concord   two sachems at Wachusett & others submitted to the Eng. Govt. & said they would as opp[ortunit]y serves & the Eng. live among them learn to read God's word, know God aright, &c S[hattuck]. 20

Gen[eral]. C[our]t. ordered the county cts. to have them civilized & take order for their instruction in knowl. of God

1646   Oct 28   John Eliot preached his first sermon at Noonantum to Waban & others

Thither came *Tahattawan* & his sannaps & 29 orders agreed on among his men

---

[54] See Thomas Morton, *New English Canaan or New Canaan* (Amsterdam, 1637), pp. 47–48. This entry, struck through in pencil with two diagonal use marks, is used in the "Historical Discourse," *W*, XI, 36.

[55] Most of the information on p. [65] comes from Shattuck, *A History of the Town of Concord*, 1835, pp. 20–31, and is used in the "Historical Discourse," *W*, XI, 50, 51, 52, and 54.

↑1651 Wilson says the Indians sung the Psalm made Indian by ⟨|| ... ||⟩
↑Eliot in one of our ordinary Eng. tunes melodiously↓↓

1654 Nashobah lying near Nagog Pond ↑now↓ partly in Littleton
partly in Acton became an Indian town by grant of the Ct. & here
a part of the praying Ind[ia]ns of Concord gathered & had a
Ruler
They had orchards but got drunk
Waban son in law of Tahattawan was Ruler ↑at Natick↓

1660 ⟨at Natick⟩ Ten towns of P[raying]. I[ndians]. (Goffe) ap
Hu⟨c⟩tthinson [I] p. 156

1676 Total 567   117 men   The Nashobah or Conc[or]d. P[raying].
I[ndians]. were then 10 men   50 women & children.

1689   24 Ind. Preachers   6 Ch[urc]h[es]. 18 assemblies

[66] [blank]
[67]   Town
Town the miniature of th[e] State. A vein & what blood circulated
through the system the very same flowed in the vein.

Wiser teachers than office clerks[,] higher sentiments than ambition /devised/contrived/ th⟨ese⟩is simple & beautiful system. The wolf
was to be killed, the Indian was to be watched & resisted, wells were
to be dug, the forest felled, pastures cleared, town & farm lines run,
corn to be raised, roads to be cut,
The Nature of Man & his Condition in the world for the first time
within the period of certain history controlled the formation of the
State. ⟨There were all these things to be done⟩ Govern who might
these must be done & cold, famine, & sickness & the Indian arrow[,]
no respecters ⟨p⟩of persons[,] the governors being as liable as the governed[,] all govt as show[,] as gratification to personal vanity became
ridiculous, it was responsibility and for once ⟨God was permitted to
make⟩ God made the leaders since the qualified were chosen ⟨& Nature⟩
& the Convenience & necessity of the parties ⟨prescribed the⟩ ran the
town ↑& county↓ lines. Standish, Winslow, Church, & Willard were
the captains because they were born such & not because they were any
man's [68] sons or cousins. Their Wants, their poverty, their manifest
convenience made them bold to ask of the Governor & of the General
Court immunities or the defining of rights. Their words were heard

& weighed for the Governor & Council knew that it was /things/peti-
tioners/ that could not be slighted[;] it was the river or the winter or
the Pequods that spoke through them to the Governor & Council of
Massachusetts Bay.[56]

Nobody can doubt the advantage ⟨of the⟩ derived to our forms
of Govt. from the Indian. The fear of the Indian compelled them to
knit a strong social frame. ⟨Robt Blood w⟩ They would have otherwise
formed a very ⟨t|| . . . ||⟩lax bond, the least govt that need be. Many
symptoms appear of the spirit of the Persian noble who desired neither
to command nor to obey. Robert Blood 1685 (p. 65 Shattuck) agrees
with the town of Concord that his lands shall be annexed to the town
on condition that ⟨no service or office shall be⟩ he shall be exemp[t]ed
from all service or office on the one hand & all burdens on the other
excepting the minister's rates & the tax of a road [69] to his land. But
for the Indians I doubt not they would have relapsed into a state of
rural anarchy[.]

The perpetual mistake of men is that the spirit can be preserved
by preserving the form of an institution. The vote of 1641 was wise
because the nominal ⟨w⟩church was the real Church.

⟨The hist[ory] serves to show or⟩ We wish to know how a little
society of farmers left to administer their own affairs on a little plot
of field & meadow six miles square will behave[.]

See on the subject of *Towns* Mackintosh Hist of England
Vol I p 22 [57]
    Hutchinson History of Mass Vol I. p. 162
    Winthrop's Journal   Vol. I. p. 129

[70] Sir,[58]
   The seat you fill places you in a relation ⟨to every citizen that⟩ of

---

[56] "The wolf . . . Massachusetts Bay." is struck through in pencil with single
vertical use marks on pp. [67] and [68]. "The wolf . . . must be done", "necessity of . . . lines", and "Their Wants . . . Bay." are used in the "Historical Discourse," *W*, XI, 43–44.
 [57] Sir James Mackintosh, *The History of England* . . . , 3 vols. (London,
1830–1832), in Lardner's *The Cabinet History of England, Scotland, and Ireland*,
in Emerson's library.
 [58] Emerson filled pp. [70]–[78] with a draft of the letter he sent to President

⟨dearness⟩ credit & dearness ↑to every citizen↓. Every citizen is by right & natural position your friend. Before any acts can alienate the affections of any, each may look with hope & loving anticipations to your career. Each has the highest right to call your attention to such wants & actions as are of a public nature & as properly belong to the chief magistrate & the good magistrate will feel a joy in reciprocating such confidence. In this belief I ⟨shal⟩ hesitate not to ask your attention to a matter of public moment & the circumstance that my name will be utterly unknown to you will only give the fairer chance to what I say.

Sir, My communication respects the rumors that fill the country respecting the Cherokee people. The newspapers

[71] April 20, 1838

The newspapers inform the citizens of this part of the Country that a treaty was pretended to be made with the Cherokee nation in— —
that the fact afterwards appeared that these deputies did not represent the will of the nation, & that the vast majority of the nation ⟨refused⟩ protested.

It now appears that the Govt of the U S. consider this sham treaty as binding, & are proceeding to execute the same. Almost the entire Cherokee nation stand up & say, this is not our act. Behold us! Here are we: do not take that handful for us: And the American ⟨Sena⟩ ⟨Congress⟩ President, the Senate, & the House neither hear nor see. The⟨y⟩ir eyes are nailed to the question of finance[,] their ears hear only of the currency & they are proceeding to put this nation into carts & rafts & drag them over mountains & rivers

[72] In the name of God, Sir, the citizens of the town & neighborhood of Concord in Massachusetts ask you if this is so. Do the newspapers rightly inform us? Men & Women with pale & perplexed faces meet one another in streets & churches here & ask if this be so? We have inquired if this be ⟨one⟩[n] a gross misrepresentation of the party op-

Van Buren April 25, 1838, protesting the removal of the Cherokees from Georgia. The full text, printed in *W*, XI, 87–96, shows significant differences in wording and emphasis from this draft. For Emerson's reluctant participation in the protest, see *JMN*, V, 475, 477, and 479, n. 580, and *Life*, pp. 266–267.

posed to the Government & anxious to blacken it with the people. We have looked in newspapers of different parties & find a horrid confirmation of the tale. We cannot yet believe it. We are sure the Indians are misinformed & their remonstrance is premature & will turn out to be a needless act of ⟨fea⟩ terror. The piety, the principle that is left in these United States, the very coarsest form of a regard to the speech of men forbid us to entertain it as a fact. Such a dereliction of all faith & virtue[,] such a denial of justice & deafness to [73] screams for mercy ⟨th⟩was never heard of in times of peace & in the dealing of a nation with its own citizens since the ⟨wo⟩earth was made. Are the United States of America mad? Are they savage? Do they forget in the zeal of business the majesty of principles? [n] They shall not[,] they must not. We appeal to themselves[;] the justice[,] the mercy in every heart that is the heart's heart in all men from Maine to Georgia is to that extent the enemy until death of th⟨e⟩is measures. Sir we have no patience to argue this matter. ⟨We cry murder⟩ ⟨As men cry Murder! or [n] Fire! ⟨in⟩and do not prove⟩ when houses burn or assassins strike men cry ⟨M⟩Fire & Murder without attempting logic. ⟨W⟩So we only state the fact that a crime that confounds our wits by its magnitude[,] a crime that really deprives us as well as the Cherokees of a Country for we would not [74] call a ⟨pirate the diabolical⟩ conspiracy that shall crush these poor Indians our country any more. You sir would no longer be the president of men[;] we should be brute beasts of hell.

These Indians have our sympathies. We have seen some of them in our schools & colleges in New England where they were sent for education. We have seen with joy their improvement in civil arts. We have read their newspapers. We have seen the laudable literary efforts of some of them. Even to our distant state some good rumor of their living & labor has arrived. If there be any bowels of compassion in the American people[,] if they dwell in towns & families & love their own blood[,] their own dwelling-place & freedom[,] let them not perpetrate this great crime. I see the ⟨me⟩American [n] people sitting in a majestic extent & world defying pride over this vast region through different climates & soils listening to the wash of the sea on one side & the murmur of the Missisippi through their ⟨Under their national protection this handful⟩ [75] ⟨of Indians lie⟩ Their vast extent, their freedom, their fast swarming population ⟨give⟩ ↑make↓ them no unfit

27

representation of the human race. Under their protection this handful of Indians lies and it is not to be doubted the pleasure of all the families, the children, the matrons, & the men of this land that they shall be duly cared for[;] that they shall taste justice & love. I

Do not mistake us as connecting this remonstrance with any local or party feeling. It is in our hearts the simplest command of feeling. We expressly remonstrate upon this great & solemn claim upon national & human justice being huddled aside under the flimsy plea of its being a party act. We will not bear it. Sir the questions upon which the Govt & the people have been agitated the whole of the last year, the prostration of currency, the good & evil of banks, [76] the vicissitu⟨e⟩des of exchange, the questions of territory, are dust & ashes in the comparison[.]

They are grave questions for the common sense to agitate & decide but it is the chirping of insects to the immortal question whether justice shall be done by the race of ⟨ma⟩ civilized to the race of savage man. Whether all the attributes of reason, of civility, of justice, & even of mercy shall be put off by the civilized Americans & they shall assume the attitude & do the deed of devils by the Cherokee Nation.

⟨The grave⟩ It is fit that the government be admonished of a new historical fact of great meaning, namely, that the pursuit of great interests public & private in Congress for some years has had the effect to diminish if not to destroy the confidence of a great part of the northern people in the moral character of its Government. A general expression of despondency, of disbelief that any good will arise [7⟨5⟩7] from remonstrance on a↑n↓ act of fraud & robbery. Will the American Government steal? Will ⟨they⟩ it lie? My wiser neighbors shake their heads dubiously. Our counsellors & old statesmen here say that ten years ago they would have staked their life on the affirmation that the proposed measures ⟨agai⟩ⁿ regarding the Indians could not be put in force[,] that the unanimous nation would put them down. And now the⟨y are⟩ steps of the crime fast follow each other & the millions of virtuous men & women & whose agents the Government are ⟨the⟩ are pursuing their business in

⟨I have tried to sit still⟩ but I have not been able.

⟨Sir, it is scarcely becoming to suggest to your mind⟩ And any letter going to the address of this & suggesting to the mind of the Executive the plain obligations of man has a burlesque character in the apprehension of my friends. I sir will not beforehand treat you [78] with the contumely of this distrust. I will at least state to you the fact how plain & humane people whose love would be honor, regard the policy of the Government, & what injurious inferences they draw as to the mind of the Governors.

I would suggest to your mind the futility of opposition ⟨of⟩ to a moral sentiment. God is in it & it cannot be opposed. Your chair is rottenness, & this nation but a name against it & both will be annihilated. With it & in it they are immeasureably strong.

[7⟨7⟩9]   Country
1640 After a few years by hard labor & hard fare the land produced more than was consumed by the inhabitants. Hutchinson   p. 90 [59]
1679 Neal says   The people began to grow intolerably licentious in their morals.[60]

1689 Time of Andros's usurpation "The country people came armed into the town in the P.M. in such rage & heat that it made us all tremble to think what would follow." Letter to Plymouth
                              ap. Hutch[inson]   p. 336 [61]

"The farmers are numerous & wealthy   live in good houses, are given to hospitality & make good advantage by their corn   cattle   poultry   butter & cheese."
                    Edw. Randolph's Narrative 1676
                    Hutchinson's Col[lection]. p 48⟨5⟩4 [62]
1643 "Wine, sugar, cotton, very plentiful in the Country"
                              W[inthrop]. II 95 [63]

[59] *The History of Massachusetts . . .* , 1795, vol. I. Cf. the "Historical Discourse," *W*, XI, 54–55.
[60] See Daniel Neal, *The History of New-England*, 2 vols. (London, 1747), II, 32.
[61] "1689 . . . follow.' " is used in the "Historical Discourse," *W*, XI, 63; Emerson evidently went back to Hutchinson to expand the quotation, since he used more in the "Discourse" than is copied here.
[62] This entry is used in the "Historical Discourse," *W*, XI, 62–63.
[63] "presant", written in faint pencil three lines below "plentiful", may be an abbreviation for "president"; Emerson added "Letter to Pressant" in pencil to the index material on the front cover verso.

[80] [blank]

[81]–[84] [...] [64]

[85]   Concord Territory

1635   Musketaquid   6 miles square

1638   Go⟨u⟩v Winthrop   1200 ⎫ acres below Concord [65]
        Thos Dudley   1000 ⎭

      June, J. W   200

1639   Increase Nowell   500   acres
        Rev T. Allen   500

1640   Rev T. Weld   533
        A Hough   400 [66]   Blood's Farms ↑1685 annexed↓

  ↑Rev↓ P. Bulkeley   300
        W. Spencer   300

1643   "We think some quantity may be granted them N.W. of the
        town"

1652   Additional grants made

1655   5000 acres granted to the town

1665   5000 acres ↑/Total 15000 acres↓ [67]

                Bedford incorporated   Sept 23, 1729
                Acton   July 3, 1735
                Lincoln   Apr 14, 1754
                Carlisle   Feb 18, 1809

[86] [68]   Concord

1645   The petition to the Gen[eral]. C[our]t. states that 1/7 or
        1/8 part of the town had gone southward with Mr Jones.
        Johnson says (this year probably) the number of families is at
        present 50. The church of Xt consists of 70 souls.

1636   The foot company organized

[64] From this point on, material from Notebook L Literature, omitted here and
printed below, is indicated by [...].

[65] Cf. the "Historical Discourse," W, XI, 41.

[66] A short line to the right of "400" joined to a diagonal line almost up to
"below" separates "Bloods Farms . . . " from the column of numbers.

[67] "/Total . . . acres" is added in pencil.

[68] Emerson used most of the notes on p. [86] in the "Historical Discourse," W,
XI, 54–55.

1637   Robt. Fletcher chosen constable. ↑Died the Pequots.↓

1638   Lt. Willard allowed to sell wine & strong water.

Same Court, Freemen of Conc[or]d. & those not free that had a hand in the undue election of Mr Flint fined 6s. 8d. apiece

1639   Mr Flint, ⟨T⟩Lt. Willard, & Richd Griffin were appointed to have the ending of small matters this year.

1638   Capt Underhill's notice

Josselyn's Notice, same year.[69]

1640   Rate of ↑£↓1200 for the Colony Concord pd £50. ↑Winthrop↓ ↑All immigration ceased

Fish bad manure   H[utchinson]. p. 94

    1643 Colony divided into 4 Counties↓

1643 Corn was very scarce because of cold & wet summer & of pigeons in such flocks as beat down & eat up all sorts of Eng Grain. Mice also. Winthrop   2. 94

[87] 1646 Rev P. Bulkeley [70] saith to his people "We are brought out of a fat land into a wilderness & here we meet with necessities: God hath now set us besides our hopes & expectations   our props which we leaned upon are broken   our money is spent   our states are wasted   & our necessities begin to increase upon us & now we know not how to be supplied   the waters of the river are cut off   & now we begin to be full of cares & fears what we shall do" (p. 209)

"Sometimes the places we live in are hard & barren & this unsettles us we know not how to subsist. I deny not that one place may be better than another more desireable more fruitful in itself yet the Lord promiseth if we abide &c &c thither he will come & bless his people & what is wanting from the place shall be made up from the lord himself &c &c.

[69] John Underhill (c. 1597–1672), military leader and magistrate, published *Newes from America* in 1638. John Josselyn (fl. 1630–1675), traveler and writer, first visited New England in 1638; his *An Account of Two Voyages to New-England*, first printed in 1674, was also reprinted in the Massachusetts Historical Society Collection, vol. 23, 1833. See p. 4, n. 2 above.

[70] Peter Bulkeley, *The Gospel-Covenant; or The Covenant of Grace Opened* (London, 1651), withdrawn from the Boston Athenaeum Sept. 3–Oct. 7, 1835. The quotations, in order, actually occur on pp. 209, 210, 211, 300, 301, and 301.

For comfort unto godly & faithful parents that having come over hither have here spent their estates by which they [88] might have provided comfortably for their children" &c   p. 211

"We pretended to come hither for ordinances but now ordinances are light matters with us we are turn[e]d after the prey." &c
"We have among us excess & pride [n] of life pride in apparel daintiness in diet & that in those who in times past would have been glad to have been satisfied with bread. This the sin of the lowest of our people." [71]
      "A straight heartedness & close handedness towards the Lord"
                                                                  p. 301

[89] [72] [...]
[90] [73] 1654   Sept. ⟨Gen Ct⟩ Four Colonies agreed to raise 270 foot
      & 40 horse & appointed Maj Simon Willard to march to Ninigrate

1670   the Wampanoags began to grind their hatchets & mend their
      guns & insult the English. Philip came armed to confer with
      commissioners in Taunton meetinghouse [74]

[91] [75] [...]
      [92] I have read the Records with care & I find the history of the town marked with a uniform good sense. I find no ridiculous laws, no eavesdropping legislators, no hanging of witches, ↑no ghosts,↓ no whipping of Quakers, no unnatural crimes. The ↑old↓ town clerks d⟨o⟩id not spell very correctly but they contrive to make pretty intelligible the will of a free & just community. Somewhat saving they are though for the most part they deal generously by their minister & provide well for their poor. But economy is at once the virtue & the vice of our republic. It is in Concord very very rigid[.] [76]
[...]

---

      [71] This and the preceding entry, struck through in pencil with a diagonal use mark, are used in the "Historical Discourse," *W*, XI, 56.
      [72] Two sketches appear on the top half of the page: a man's face, and the standing figure of a woman in a long gown.
      [73] A sketch of a man's face in right profile appears between the two entries.
      [74] Both passages on p. [90] are used in the "Historical Discourse," *W*, XI, 57 and 57–58.
      [75] Four sketches of men's faces, three in left profile, appear at the top of the page.
      [76] Most of this paragraph appears in the "Historical Discourse," *W*, XI, 83–84.

L Literature

1835

Emerson devoted this notebook to quotations and working notes for his lecture series on English Literature, November 5, 1835–January 14, 1836. Emerson probably used L Concord and L Literature concurrently through the summer of 1835 and may have begun L Literature first.

Notebook L Literature comprises the other half of the double-ender of which L Concord is the larger section; see the bibliographical description on page 3 above. Beginning after the unnumbered inside back cover, Emerson numbered all but pages 2, 48, 50, 52, 54, 58, 60, and 62 of the L Literature sequence to page 70 in ink. The section occupied by L Literature runs through page 82, although material from L Concord appears on pages 71, 73, and 75–78. Page numbers on pages 1, 3, 14–19, 21–23, 26, 27, 31–33, 35, 36, 38–47, 49, 51, 55–57, and 68 are struck through diagonally in ink. Of the first 82 pages, 37 are blank: 10–12, 17, 20–22, 24–26, 28–30, 32–35, 38, 45–46, 48–50, 52–56, 58–63, 65, and 69–70. Pages 5 and 6 each bear a large circle drawn with a compass, but nothing else. Laid in between pages 6 and 7 is a small piece of paper with the penciled notation "to an assembly". Pages 18, 19, 20, 39, 40, 43, and 66 have four or more revisions of accidentals.

[front cover]   L

[front cover verso] [1]
    Hist[ory] of Eng[lish] literature   p. 1⟨6⟩4
    ⟨M⟩Characteristics of the Old Ages & the New

---

[1] "Hist of . . . song   43" appears to have been written at one time. "Fable" is in a larger hand and may have been added on a line left blank earlier; "p. 51" is added in pencil. "Symbolical Language" is in print-writing. "⟨Fable⟩" and "⟨51⟩" were finger-wiped while wet. "Anc. British . . . 1833" appears to have been added at one time. "page 71", in pencil, is inscribed upside down at the bottom of the front cover verso.

[1]   ⟨Low⟩————
             Salem 1 Tuesday March.³

             ————

Lecture   I   Theory of Literature
         II   British & Saxon Literature
        III   Normans. Romance. Fable. Crusades.
         IV   Chaucer
          V. ⟨Spenser⟩ Shakspear
         VI   Shakspear
        VII   ⟨Herbert Jonson⟩ Bacon
       VIII. ⟨Bacon⟩ Herbert, Herrick, Jonson, ⟨Chapman.⟩ Wotton.
         IX   Milton, ⟨Dryden⟩, Clarendon Locke Addison Johnson
          X   ⟨Johnson,⟩ Gibbon,⁴

---

² The passage on "God's mnemonics" is used in "Ben Jonson, Herrick, Herbert, Wotton," *Lectures*, I, 353–354, much revised.

³ Apparently Emerson's memorandum of his engagement to lecture in Salem on Tuesday, March 1, 1836, probably on Milton. See William Charvat, *Emerson's American Lecture Engagements: A Chronological List* (New York, 1961), p. 16.

⁴ These are preliminary titles for the ten lectures in the English Literature series; for the final titles, considerably different, see *Lectures*, I, ix–x.

[2][5] See Journal | *1835*, p. 86, ⟨81⟩
    1833   81[6]
p 101 Scholar p 119, 137. 77
        76
        65 good once good always[7]
        61 Hist of Lit.
        55 Books better than talk
        52 Imperfection of language
        51 Cudworth. Obj. of lit. Hist.[8]
    130   40 Composition.[9]
         7 Use of Aristotle to A & B, & C.

     Episodes. Women
          Gentleman p.[10]

[3]   Materials for Lectures, Nov. 1835.[11]
  ⟨Lit⟨sup⟩erature supposed ⟨of⟩ to interest few.[12] Show it to be the
concern of a man.⟩

[5] Like the materials on p. [3], this page is probably an early collection of materials for the English Literature series; passages listed on p. [2] are used in five different lectures. All the page numbers to the right of the line are in Journal B. Presumably the page numbers to the left of the line are all in A, but none have been located in the lectures.

[6] Passages from Journal B, p. [81], are used in "Lord Bacon," *Lectures*, I, 327, and "General Views," *Lectures*, II, 361.

[7] The passage cited in Journal B, p. [65], is used in "Chaucer," *Lectures*, I, 271.

[8] See "Ethical Writers," *Lectures*, I, 365, n. 16, and 529(notes), where the passage from Journal B, p. [51], is printed as a probable insertion.

[9] The passage cited in Journal B, p. [40], is used in "Shakspear" [second lecture], *Lectures*, I, 317–318.

[10] See Encyclopedia, pp. [117] and [221], headed "*Women.*" and p. [177], headed "GENTLEMAN.", passages from which were used in sections on the gentleman and women in "Chaucer," *Lectures*, I, 276–280 and 280–282.

[11] The "Introductory" lecture in the "English Literature" series was first given November 5, 1835. As with the "Historical Discourse at Concord," no attempt has been made to determine the exact source of each of Emerson's working notes beyond his own identifications, which are fairly complete. Full titles and probable editions of works cited are given on first mention.

[12] "⟨Lit⟨sup⟩erature . . . few.", repeated below, is used in English Literature: "Introductory," *Lectures*, I, 226. Except for a phrase from Journal B, p. [81], nothing else on p. [3] appears to have been used in the "English Literature" series.

The character of the scholar. Working with invisible tools to invisible ends; supposed an idler, or worse, ⟨a⟩ brainsick: defenceless to idle masons & clerks, that having done nothing all the day, pounce on him fresh for wasting him at night.   J. p. 60, 45,[13]

Claims of England; very great; yet how they sink before those of this country; and all countries & localities sink before the ⟨spiritual⟩ entire humanity.

Literature supposed to interest few. Show it to be the concern of man   p. 81 J. 1835   p. 76 also.   p. 62

Set Men upon thinking & you have been to them a god. The whole of History is poetry; the globe of facts whereon they tread, is bullion to the scientific eye: the meanest life is a thread of empyrean light. You have to convert for them the dishonored facts ⟨on⟩ which they know, into trees of life, their life into a garden of God by suggesting the Principle which classifies them. [B 128]

[4] The large topic of the Imagination; analysis of it; distinction betwixt it & Fancy. (p 83 J 1835) [B 82–83]

Natural language. [B 85]   Oegger. [B 71]   All ⟨great men⟩ memorable words of the world are figurative. J. p. 67 —[14] [B 66–67]

Reason & Understanding
Ideas
Imagination & Fancy
Wit & Humor
Genius & Talent [15]

Composition [16]

[13] "The character . . . 45," and "Set Men . . . classifies them." below, both struck through in ink with single diagonal use marks, also appear, with minor changes, in Journal B, p. [128], part of a collection of material on the Scholar. One paragraph in B, p. [45], is used in "Lord Bacon," *Lectures*, I, 332.

[14] The passages listed on page [4] to this point are used in English Literature: "Introductory," *Lectures*, I, 224, 220, and 222.

[15] Emerson used these nine terms throughout the English Literature series and combined all but "Wit & Humor" in a single sentence on Coleridge in "Modern Aspects of Letters," *Lectures*, I, 378–379.

[16] For discussions of Composition, see "Shakspear" [second lecture], *Lectures*,

[5]–[6] [17]

[7] If you would know what nobody knows, read what every body reads, *just one year afterwards*, & you shall be a fund of new & unheard of speculations; or, listen to the discourse of a wise man to ⟨a crowd in⟩ an assembly, in a perfect conviction that nobody hears it but you. [B 55]

The hist of lit is one of few facts & few ideas [B 61]

"No book was ever written down by any but itself." [18]

[8]   Literature of display.
           Apicius [B 53]
           Age of seeming   J.[B] p. 48

[9] One use of reading is that ⟨whils⟩ ofttimes whilst dealing with small persons we think all things have been said & the well of truth is dry; then comes by SHAKS↑peare↓ or Taylor & we believe again in its inexhaust↑ibleness.↓ⁿ Then how oft we receive intel. activity from an acting mind. I read some verses of Elliott's, & believed I could write verses. [19]
"To think is to act." [BB III, 60]

[10]–[12] [blank]
      [13] Who in this country will venture to speak of English literature? It needs a more liberal (extensive) & a more concentrated discipline than any of us have had. [20]

I, 317–318 (from Journal B, p. [40]; see p. [2] above), and "Modern Aspects of Letters," *Lectures*, I, 382.

[17] On each of these pages, a large circle has been drawn with a compass. Laid in between pp. [6] and [7] is a small piece of paper with the penciled notation "to an assembly".

[18] See the statement attributed to Richard Bentley in Encyclopedia, p. [186].

[19] "One use . . . acting mind." is used in English Literature: "Introductory," *Lectures*, I, 230. "I read . . . verses.", from Journal B, p. [47], is not used.

[20] The paragraph, near the bottom of the page, is struck through in ink with a diagonal use mark. Cf. English Literature: "Introductory," *Lectures*, I, 217.

[1⟨6⟩4]   Hist. English Literature

↑"The infusion of British into the English language appears to be scanty" Mackintosh   Hist. Eng Vol. 1, p. 22,↓ 21

Edw. III abolished the use of the Norman tongue in the pub[lic]. acts & ↑judicial proceed[in]gs.↓ But Chaucer manifestly first taught his countrymen to write English, & formed a style by naturalizing words from the Provençal, at that time the most polished dialect of any in Europe, & the best adapted to the purposes of poetical expression. *Warton* vol. 2. 179 22

"About the commencement of the 14 Century the Eng. language had undergone the whole change to which it was doomed, by the irruption of Norman words. Many French & Latin words have been introduced since, but by learning or pedantry rather than by the convenience of familiar intercourse between two branches of the same people. Many books perfectly intelligible to us, were written before Edw. III. Very shortly after the close of the reign of Edw. I, the Eng. language produced one of the earliest accounts of very remote regions in Mandeville." — Wickliffe, Chaucer 23

Edw. I. 1272 — 1307   Mackintosh England, Vol. I, p. 275

[1⟨7⟩5] On the dissolution of the Monasteries in England in & after Henry VIII, — "A visible revolution & decline in the ↑national↓ state of learning succeeded. Most of the youth of the Kingdom betook themselves to mechanical & other illiberal employments, the profession of letters being now supposed to be without support and reward. By the abolition of the relig. houses many towns & their adjacent villages were utterly deprived of their only means of instruction. At

---

21 Sir James Mackintosh, *The History of England* . . . , 1830–1832. The entry, struck through in ink with a diagonal use mark, is used in "Permanent Traits of the English National Genius," *Lectures*, I, 238.

22 Thomas Warton, *The History of English Poetry, from the Close of the Eleventh to the Commencement of the Eighteenth Century*, ed. Richard Price, 4 vols. (London, 1824), withdrawn from the Boston Athenaeum July 22–Dec. 10, 1835. The first sentence of this entry, struck through in ink with two diagonal use marks, is used in "The Age of Fable," *Lectures*, I, 254. With the rest of the paragraph, cf. "Chaucer," *Lectures*, I, 270.

23 The first sentence is struck through in ink with a diagonal use mark; the rest of the paragraph is struck through in ink with a diagonal use mark at right angles to the first. The first and last sentences are used in "The Age of Fable," *Lectures*, I, 254.

the beginning of the reign of Q. Eliz., Williams, speaker of the H. of Commons, complained to her majesty, that more than a hundred flourishing schools were destroyed in the demolition of the monasteries, & that ignorance had prevailed[n] ever since." Warton, Hist. Eng. Po. Vol 3 p. 268

"Some ages are so barbarous & ignorant that men may as easily be governed as sheep. But this princess (Elizabeth) lived in a learned & polite age; when it was impossible to be eminent without great parts & a singular habit of virtue." Bacon. Portrait of Q. Elizabeth [24]

"This is not a logical age. A friend lately gave me some political pamphlets of the time of Charles I & the Cromwellate. In them the ⟨deductions⟩ premises are frequently wrong, but the deductions almost always legitimate; whereas in the writings [16] of the present day the premises are commonly sound but the conclusions false." ⟨I think a⟩
Coleridge   Table Talk [I] p 40 [25]
"In the 16 & 17 centuries, almost all our ambassadors were distinguished men". Coleridge T[able]. T[alk]. [II, 131] "The third rate men of those day possessed an infinity of knowledge, & were intimately versed not only in the history but even in the heraldry of the countries in which they were resident. Men were almost always chosen for dexterity & experience"
Coleridge [*ibid.*, II, 132]

"How many books are still written & published about Charles I & his times! Such is the fresh & enduring interest of that grand crisis of morals, religion & govt.!"
Table Talk, [II] p. 141.

[1⟨9⟩7] [blank]
[⟨20⟩ 18] The present age Coleridge calls "a devil in a strait waistcoat."

Yet see the encouragement of the time[,] the appreciation of what is good. The good word spoken is heard[,] the good word written is

[24] "In Felicem Memoriam Elizabethae Angliae Reginae," *The Works of Francis Bacon*, 10 vols. (London, 1824), X, 280; in Emerson's library.
[25] Samuel Taylor Coleridge, *Specimens of the Table Talk of the Late Samuel Taylor Coleridge*, 2 vols. in 1 (New York, 1835), in Emerson's library, and cited throughout Notebook L Literature.

read, the nation is on tiptoe when Webster & Calhoun go by, Lafayette did not miss of his praise.

Language stereotyped. Even Edw. Everett only coins one word for a speech. The whole sermon or oration is now only a string of formulas: and literature but a ⟨game of⟩ sum in the arithmetical rule of permutation & combination [26]

————

Consider that all but vital works perish quickly. Therefore of any past age, we have no remains but colossal. But of our own age, though the ⟨thr⟩proportion of great works exists, yet the vast majority of books are ephemeral & worthless, & these obtrude so much that we contemn our times unjustly. ↑Hooker characterises *his* age as full of tongue and weak of brain.↓ ↑Agis.↓ [27]

————

'Tis the age of Parenthesis, you might put all we say into brackets & it would not be missed[.] [B 101]

————

Most of our life is mimetic. Society is the imitation of friendship. Churches are the imitation of religion[.] Agis   J 1835 p. 97,

[⟨21⟩19] Pray don't read American. ⟨Thot⟩ ↑Thought↓ is of no country. And it may well deserve the analysis of the most penetrating inquirers. What hinders the action of the Contemplative Spirit here? [n] The little book called "Observations on the Growth of the Mind" [28] is the only book this country has produced since Edwards on the Will, that is a work of the Reason saving sermons & the periodical literature. ——

What ages must pass to make Burton's Anat[omy]. [of] Melancholy possible

[26] "Language stereotyped . . . speech." and "literature but . . . combination" are from Journal B, p. [101].
[27] For Agis, see Journal B, p. [97].
[28] Sampson Reed, *Observations on the Growth of the Mind*. Originally printed at Boston, in 1826 (London, 1827); in Emerson's library. For Emerson's first impression, see *JMN*, III, 44–45.

In America The Edin[burgh]. Review query Who reads an American book? is unanswerable.[29] Why? ↑1.↓ Property is the p[r]edominant interest & nobody needs to be learned in order to speak & write creditably. 2. We have English literature.

[20]–[22] [blank]
[2⟨5⟩3] *What ideas predominated in the old English?*

In the period of 9, 10, 11, century the whole force of the pious & poetic principle was spent on the lives of the saints — in canonisation.

⟨Down to⟩ ↑In↓ the 14 century, Froissart says, In Scotland ye shall find no man lightly of honor or gentleness; they be like wild & savage people

Harold's oath to Wm Conqueror o⟨n⟩ver ⟨a⟩ concealed relics.

⟨Tall⟩ Their poet is not a Pope but a Talliafer who whilst he sings tosses his sword into the air, & catches it as it falls

The doctrine of *Gentle behaviour*. Chaucer   vol 1. p. 194
Coleridge, Table Talk, p. 132 vol 1 & p. 91
Mackintosh, Hist vol. 1. p 269. Elia, passim. Landor.
Wordsworth's definition of Honor.   Hospitality.[30]

Home is another Saxon idea.   sports

Humor

Objective religion, Luther a representative

[29] Sydney Smith's famous query occurred in "America," the *Edinburgh Review*, XXXIII (Jan. 1820), 79.
[30] "The doctrine . . . Honor." is used, except for "Elia, passim.", in "Chaucer," *Lectures*, I, 276–280. Though Charles Lamb's *Elia* is not listed in Emerson's library, he made a note to pay "G. P. Bradford for Elia, &c." in accounts dated Nov. 17, 1835 (*JMN*, VI, 244).

Love of truth.
English Melancholy; marked time by nights & winters.

Economical talent & not genius for art.   Utility.

Patriotism. Island less by Scotland & Wales.
Respe⟨t⟩ct for women; and for birth.[31]

[24]–[26] [blank]
[2⟨9⟩7] What is Literature?
It is the recorded thinking of Mankind.[32]

It is singular that every natural object how wearisome soever in daily observation is always agreeable in description & doubly so in illustration. ↑See also J 1833, p. 73 and p. 87↓ [33]

See 1833 J p. 107, 137 [34]

For the explanation of Fable, every man must recur to his own childhood.[35]
     Literature is essentially moral. Mme. de Stael's remark.[36] The poets   satirists   & reformers. The Northmen poets branded Piracy & it fell [37]

---

[31] Most of the traits listed in "Home . . . birth." are used in "Permanent Traits of the English National Genius," *Lectures*, I, 249. Several are repeated in "Chaucer," *Lectures*, I, 275–276 and 280. Emerson later used this and other sections of "Permanent Traits of the English National Genius" in the lecture "Genius of the Anglo-Saxon Race" (January 10, 1843).

[32] "What . . . Mankind.", struck through in ink with a diagonal use mark, is used in English Literature: "Introductory," *Lectures*, I, 218.

[33] "It is singular . . . illustration." is struck through in ink with a vertical use mark. Passages from Journal A, pp. [73] and [87], are used in English Literature: "Introductory," *Lectures*, I, 221 and 226–227.

[34] The passage in Journal A, p. [107], is used in English Literature: "Introductory," *Lectures*, I, 219. With the passage in A, p. [137], cf. *ibid.*, p. 229.

[35] With this sentence, struck through in ink with a diagonal use mark, cf. "The Age of Fable," *Lectures*, I, 259.

[36] This is probably the statement quoted in Journal B, p. [102], and "Ben Jonson, Herrick, Herbert, Wotton," *Lectures*, I, 341.

[37] Cf. "Permanent Traits of the English National Genius," *Lectures*, I, 243.

[28]–[30] [blank]

[31]   British, Saxon Northman, poets,

↑AD 617↓ The Queen of Redwald pleaded for the youthful exile (Edwin), "A king should not sell a distressed friend, nor violate his faith for gold; no ornament is so ennobling as good faith." S. T. p 139 [38]

But for the most part the British poetry is so barren & bloody, ↑—↓ a tasteless & senseless heap of eagles, wolves, lions, & slaughter — that none can regret its loss.

Cyndyllan.[39] and Child Dyring

[32]–[35] [blank]

[36]   ——

The old poets observers of nature [40]

——

The goddes have her holpen for pite
And in the sign of Taurus men may see
The stones of her crowne shine clear (Ariadne)
          Chaucer   Vol 2 p. 166 [41]

[37]   Brut —

Gesta Romanorum first printed in folio 1473
152 gests

[38] [blank]

[39]   Sir David the Bruse
          Was at distance
          When Edward the Baliot↑l↓fe
          Rade with his lance
          The north end of England

[38] Sharon Turner, *The History of the Anglo-Saxons* . . . , 2nd ed., 2 vols. (London, 1807), vol. I, withdrawn from the Boston Athenaeum Oct. [20]-Nov. 19, 1835.

[39] "The Queen . . . Cyndyllan." is struck through in ink with a diagonal use mark. "But for . . . Cyndyllan." is used in "Permanent Traits of the English National Genius," *Lectures*, I, 241 and 240.

[40] Cf. "The Age of Fable," *Lectures*, I, 262–266.

[41] "The Legend of Good Women," ll. 2222–2224, Emerson's edition unidentified.

Teached him to dance
When he was met on the moor
With mickle mischance
Sir Philip the Valayse
May him nought advance
The flowers that faire war
Are fallen in France
The flowers are now fallen
That fierce w⟨a⟩ere & fell
A boar with his battle
Has done them to dwell.
Sir David the Bruce
Said he should fonde   (attempt
To ride through all England
Would he nought wonde.   (wander
At the Westminster hall
Should his steeds stand
Whiles our King Edward
Was out of the land. Laurence Minot   1360 [42]

[40]   ↑*Edward's Victory over the Spaniards in a seafight.*↓

I would nought spare to speak
Wist I to speed
Of wight men with weapon
And worthly in wede
That now are driven to dale   (sorrow
And dead all their deed
They sail in the sea ground
Fishes to feed:
Foul fishes ⟨to⟩ ↑they↓ feed
For all their great fare
It was in the waniand   (waning of the moon
That they came there;
They sailed forth in the Swin,
In a summers tide
With trompets & taburns
And mi⟨k⟩ckle o⟨f⟩ther pride.
                    Laurence Minot
                    Warton   vol. 3. p. 434,

The "Nut Brown Maid" first appeared 1521

[42] Warton, *The History of English Poetry*, 1824, III, 433–434, 430.

"The imagery of Nature or KINDE sending forth his diseases from the planets at the command of Conscience & of his attendants Age & Death is conceived with sublimity"

Kinde Conscience then heard & came out of the planets
And sent forth his furious Feveris & Fluxes
[41]   Coughs & Cardiacles cramps & tooth aches
Reums & Redgounds & roynous skales
Boils & botches & burning Agues
Frensies & foul evils foragers of Kynde
There was "Harrow! & Helpe! here cometh Kynde!
With Death that is dreadful to undon us all"
The Lord that lyved after lust then loud cried
(Age the hoar he was in the vaward
And bare the banner before Death: by right he it claimed.)
Kynde came after with many keen sores
As Pockes & Pestilences & much people shent.
So Kynde thro corruptions killed full many
Death came driving after & all to dust pashed
Kings & knights Kaisors & popis
Many a lovely lady & lemans of knights
Swowed & sweltid for sorrow of Deaths dents
Conscience of his Courtesy to Kynde he besought
To cease & suffer & see whether they would
Leave Pride privily & be parfyt Christian
And Kynde ceased then to see the people ↑a↓mend
Robert Langland
⟨1362⟩ ↑1350↓ Visions of Piers Plowman.[43]
Warton   Vol 2 p. 121 [119–120]

[42] The armies approached. "This was not a time for interchange of civilities, for friendly greetings; no man asked his fellow for a violet, or a rose — &c. They chewed steel in death in the pain of wounds from spear or javelin."

Von Traum
Warton, Vol. ↑2↓, p 168

[43][44] Here is poetry written 555 years ago for Warton fixes it

[43] " 'The imagery . . . amend" is struck through in ink with single diagonal use marks on pp. [40] and [41]. " 'The imagery . . . Plowman." is used in "The Age of Fable," *Lectures*, I, 266.

[44] The page is struck through in ink with two diagonal use marks, one from "Here is poetry" to "Summer is", the second from "Summer is" to the bottom of the page. Pp. [43]–[44] are used in "The Age of Fable," *Lectures*, I, 265 and 263.

about 1280 by Robert of Glocester. It is from a poetical history of England from Brute to Edward the first.   At Arthur's Coronation

> The King was to his palace then the service was y do
> Ylad with his menye and the queen to hire also
> For they held the old usages that men with men were
> By themselve & women by themselve also there
> Then they were each one ysett as yt to her state ↑becom↓
> ⟨became⟩ Kay king of Anjou a thousand knights nome
> Of noblemen yclothed in ermine each one
> Of one suit & served at this noble feast anon
> Bedwer the butler king of Normandy
> Nom also in his half a fair com↑p↓any &c
>
> [Warton, I, 53]

But this love-song is by Warton's reckoning 635 years old

> Summer is icoming in
> Loud sing cuckow
> Groweth seed & bloweth mead
>   And springeth the wood now
>   Sing cuckow cuckow
> Ewe bleteth after lamb,
> Loweth after calf cow,
> Bullock start⟨s⟩eth, buck verteth,
>   Merrie sing cuckow
>   Well sings th↑o↓u, cuckow!
>   Nor cease thou never now
>   Sing cuckow now
>   Sing cuckow. [Warton, I, 32]

[44]

$$\begin{array}{r} 1835 \\ 635 \\ \hline 1200 \end{array}$$

[45]–[46] [blank]
[47]
                              ———
                    Symbolical Language.
                              ———

Who can see the river in a meditative hour, & not be reminded of the flux of all things? Heat & Light answer to Love & Knowledge. The circles in ⟨the w⟩ disturbed water, are the beautiful type of all influence.

46

The world shines on him with enigmatical light [45]

[48]–[50] [blank]
[51]   ⟨Li⟩Fable
___

Most valuable Essay on the Popular Mythology, Quarterly Rev. Jan. 1820 [46]
___

Certain fables agreeable to the human mind as the Wandering Jew, the Seven sleepers, the understanding the song of birds.

Certain others are of permanent convenience as expressions for human truths as Tantalus' cup which life is. Antaeus, for the beast force we acquire by low natural habits, &c. [47]

"The happy conception of extraordinary events is much more the production of tradition than of the poets" *De Stael   Infl[uence]. of Lit[erature].* [48]

"Nothing novel in the marvellous can be discovered when the Credulity of the multitude withdraws its aid." De Stael

For the explanation of Fable every man must recur to his own childhood

In *Brut* Arthur overcomes the mighty giant Ritho on the Mt. Arabius who had made himself a robe of the beards of the Kings whom he had killed. ↑Warton   XVII Vol I↓

The giants conveyed the stones which compose Stonehenge from the farthest coasts of Africa. They all have medicinal virtue

A terrible dragon flies from the west breathing fire & illuminating the whole country with the brightness of his eyes.

The Arabian romance of Alexander the Great says that Alex.

___

[45] "Who can see . . . light" is struck through in ink with a diagonal use mark. The paragraph is used in English Literature: "Introductory," *Lectures*, I, 220–221, in a section on symbolic language. It also appears in "Shakspear" [second lecture], *Lectures*, I, 289, probably an insertion for a later reading, according to the editors (*Lectures*, I, 287).

[46] Francis Cohen, "Popular Mythology of the Middle Ages," the *Quarterly Review*, XXII (Jan. 1820), 348–380.

[47] "Certain fables . . . habits, &c." is used in "The Age of Fable," *Lectures*, I, 256, and expanded in "History," *W*, II, 31, 32, and 34.

[48] Mme de Staël, *The Influence of Literature upon Society*, 2 vols. (Boston, 1813), I, 105 and 106. The first quotation is used in "Shakspear" [second lecture], *Lectures*, I, 317, the second in "The Age of Fable," *Lectures*, I, 262.

gave the signal to his army by a wonderful horn of immense magnitude which might be heard 60 miles & that it was blown or sounded by 60 men at once [49]

[52]–[56] [blank]
[57]   Language

"No fact is more certain within our knowledge of the past & our experience of the present than that words neither have been nor are now *invented*; but that they always have been compounded from existing roots in the dialect — or borrowed from some collateral source"

Editor [50] of Warton   Vol 1 p. 33

"In the Northern languages *elf* means a stream of running water & hence the name of the river Elbe. The ⟨g⟩Grecian νυμφη has the same import with the latin lympha" — nympholepsy"

Editor, Warton   Vol. 1, p. 52

Of 69 words which make up the Lord's prayer there are only 5 not Saxon; [51] the best example of the natural bent of the language & of the words apt to be chosen by those who speak & write it without design. Of 81 words in the soliloquy of Hamlet 13 only are of Latin origin. Even in a passage of 90 words in Milton ⟨whose diction is more learned than that of any other poet⟩ there are only 16 Latin words. In 4 verses of Genesis containing 130 words, 5 latin.

Mackintosh   Hist. Eng. vol 1. p. 81

―――――

"The Eng. court for more than 200 years after the Conquest was totally French," Warton [52]

[58]–[63] [blank]
[64]   On the duty of reflection.

Whoever shall purge himself to see things without superstition &

[49] "The giants . . . once" is from Warton, *The History of English Poetry*, 1824, I, xvii–xix and 136. "In *Brut* . . . once" is used in "The Age of Fable," *Lectures*, I, 256.

[50] See *JMN*, VI, 117–118.

[51] "Of 69 words . . . not Saxon;", struck through in ink with a diagonal use mark, is used in "Permanent Traits of the English National Genius," *Lectures*, I, 249.

[52] This entry, struck through in ink with a diagonal use mark, is used in "The Age of Fable," *Lectures*, I, 253.

without passion & shall with erect moral sense look at the world, the institutions, the opinions, & the faces of men shall see the world that God made & the beauty that inspired the song of angels.

But it is the Shame of our ⟨day⟩age that these are not times of thought[,] that the appeal is to empty ⟨r⟩names that tinkle well in people's ear or to some bugbear with which they have been used to be put to bed. The Noodle's Oration is the usual one. Has Masonry or Antimasonry or the Indian or the African or the Bank been argued up or down or has mere noise, most of it, interested noise, decided the fate of these things? [n]
The Newspaper ⟨is⟩ goes up & down & there is much speaking but men get for their money that which is not bread. Let the⟨m⟩ir reason be addressed, let them learn its grandeur so as to demand that it shall be. That is the reason why they go to Faneuil Hall when Otis or Webster speak, that they may rend the thin rinds of the visible & finite & come out into the world of sentiment & truth.

[65] [blank]
[66] [53] On the Nature of literature. founded in the intellect, in the super sensuous: i⟨t⟩n the belief of occult but universal relations between man & nature: in the belief that man exists to noble ends: in the belief of God. Every man's interest. It is the Second Religion; the public Depository of the Thoughts of the human race. Do what we can, we cannot make a leaf or a sunbeam or moment of time less wonderful, less poetical. We cannot stop the stream of thoughts that is ever entering (from who knows whence?) into the brains of men & who is he who would not ha⟨che⟩ve them watched & recorded? It is only sciolists that have made scholars suspected. The blacksmith & the truckman have an interest in keeping the poet free from common caresȋ, and would tooↄ. It is only ignorant or interested men who tax learning. Every man has his Parnassus somewhere, if it be in a band of music, or the theatre, or the walls of a barber's shop, or the psalm tune, or song⟨,⟩ he hums, or the caucus, or the vestry meeting. But these humble tanks receive their water from aquaducts, which brought

---

[53] P. [66], struck through in ink with a diagonal use mark, is a summary of English Literature: "Introductory," *Lectures*, I, 217–230. "the stream . . . brains of men" is also used in "The Head," *Lectures*, II, 250.

them from rivers, which came from the mountain⟨,⟩s, whose summits drew the water from the heavens. And so are Chaucer, Spenser, Bacon, Plato, ↑Luther↓ or some divine thinker always the authors, through a remote paternity, of the truths & sentiments in common circulation among us[.]

[67] [54] ⟨mor⟩
to learn the entertainments of the spirit; what & who.
more careful to record than judge of truth in confidence that history is poetry [B] p. 45
in the belief of the symbolical character of the world.

not numbers nor colleges but some divine savage shall say what we all believe must   p. 62   A principle is eye to see facts with. They are slipping by unknown that are gold & topaz. p 76
     Aristotle benefits m

for every blacksmith & truckman is also a man, &, as such, cares very little for his trade in comparison with some other things.

Aristotle benefits many more than who reads his Ethics ↑J↓ p 7.

[68] [55] The Character of the Man of letters: ⟨a⟩founded on natural gifts as specific & rare as military genius: the power to hold off his thoughts at arm's length; to form *il piu nell' uno*; studies the art of solitude; p. 60 ↑1835↓   He shows thought to be infinite which you

---

[54] The entries on this page are apparently designed for inclusion or substitution on p. [66], but Emerson does not indicate where. "to learn . . . poetry p. 45" (Journal B, p. [45], rewritten) is opposite "universal . . . belief that"; "in the belief . . . world." is opposite "belief of God." (cf. English Literature: "Introductory," *Lectures*, I, 224). "not numbers . . . p 76" (B, pp. [62] and [76], rewritten) and "Aristotle benefits m" are opposite "We cannot stop . . . brains of men &", and "for every blacksmith . . . things." is opposite "The blacksmith . . . in keeping". "Aristotle benefits . . . Ethics J p 7", unfinished above, is opposite "divine thinker . . . paternity of the". "Aristotle benefits many . . . Ethics" and additional material from B, p. [7], rewritten, is used in English Literature: "Introductory," *Lectures*, I, 229.

[55] Matter on this page is struck through in ink with a diagonal use mark; much of it is in Journal B, p. [128].

had thought exhausted ↑p 60↓   One who is gravelled in every discourse with common people   p 119 ↑1833↓   There is a real object
in nature to which the grocer turns, the intellectual man. p 137 ↑1833↓
    Theory of the Bard — an omniscient teacher.
        recognized by Chaucer, Spenser, Shakspear, & Milton; &
Ben Jonson eminently;
The Thinker, like Glauber, keeps what others throw away. He is
aware of God's way of hiding ⟨s⟩things[,] that is, as he does the stars,
in a deluge of light. [B 83] So principles are not seen, they are so
near us.
    Also he knows all by one   see J. 1835 — p 117

[69]-[70] [blank]
[71] 1 What is Literature
       2 'Tis founded in nature & condition of man
       3 'Tis stamped divine
       4 'Tis a virtual history of man
          Interest of all men. Man a poet
          Classes of men receivers; perceivers; & shapers;
          Interest the vile have in Homer
          Interest the vile have to Homerize
[...]⁵⁶

[72]⁵⁷ What is Literature
    It is founded in nature & condition of man. He thinks — is pris-
oner of his thoughts & his whole effort is to express those thoughts.
They make him what he is. They clothe themselves with institutions,
cities, languages, events. The most perfect utterance is language. But
see how this is formed. Here he is surrounded always by the same
company, i.e. by what he calls nature, the sun & moon, &c. These serve
as keys[,] the symbols of thought.
Nature is the mirror of the mind, & literature is the marriage of the

---

    ⁵⁶ From this point on, material from Notebook L Concord, printed above, is in-
dicated by [...].
    ⁵⁷ The page is a summary of English Literature: "Introductory," *Lectures*, I,
218–226. "It is founded . . . poets" is struck through in ink with a diagonal use
mark.

two. But besides that Nature is mirror of thought the Reason still looks for a higher harmony, viz of events with nature[.]

Then the human mind shall write out its thoughts as the march of society proceeds; its hopes & fears[,] its joy & pain[.]

So shall ⟨lit. the⟩ aim & effort of lit. be to represent in just images of nature the whole life of the world.

Thus is Lit the hist. of Man

This is the theory of lit. Let us now consider it in fact.

All men think; but rarely. All men can. To think is to ascend to the absolute & view things as objective. This the poet aims to do by pure intellectual excitement. But his very effort proves his belief that all men are poets[.]

[73] […]
[74] [58] England at the present day.

↑College, church, families, nobles, politeness, art, India, Polar expedition,↓

Royal Society; D. of Wellington's fète; Greenwich Observatory

the sun sets never upon her flag Scott, Coleridge, Wordsworth, Moore, Turner, Herschel,

Origin. out of the fiercest savages whom history trembles under

Britons, Saxons, Northmen. Alfieri's remark

Botany bay experience. Antaeus.

[75]—[78] […]
[79]   *Albion*

Britons, Cimmerians, & Celts.

Oriental extraction. The Welsh Cymry came, they say, from Constantinople. Oriental Castes, Druids, Transmigration of the Soul. taught by them. Stonehenge all their monument. *Be* a cimbric word.

A. C. 680 They were in Europe. Before their arrival, ⟨it⟩ ↑England↓ was occupied by bears, wolves, beavers, & oxen with large pro-

---

[58] The notes on p. [74], struck through in ink with a diagonal use mark, are used in "Permanent Traits of the English National Genius," *Lectures*, I, 235, 236, 237, 242, and 243, and the lecture "Genius of the Anglo-Saxon Race."

tuberances. Cimmerians dwelt underground. horsemilkers   Women prophesied among them.

They give name to the great masses of land & water   Prydain Helvellyn   &c.

mistletoe

   Ossian ↑A D.↓ 300
   Arthur b. 501
      Lessons of the Druids were conveyed in a great number of verses.

Taliessin A.D. 540   Aneurin & LLywarch [59] Hen. VI Century

[80] All Romance will be in the gross *Moral*
         Magic is an instinctive presentiment of Science
         Romantic powers & success a presentiment of heaven

The fairies did not like to be named
Who seeks a treasure should not speak
The money lasts so long as it is not counted
Fairy gifts not to be trusted [60]

[81]   Saxons
He
⟨AD. 449 Hengist's arrival⟩ [61]

———

———

[59] "Britons . . . LLywarch" is struck through in ink with a diagonal use mark; "Lessons of . . . verses." is struck through in ink with a second diagonal use mark. Much of this page is used in "Permanent Traits of the English National Genius," *Lectures*, I, 238–239, and part of it in the lecture "Genius of the Anglo-Saxon Race."

[60] The entire page [80] is used in "The Age of Fable," *Lectures*, I, 259–260. "All Romance . . . heaven" is struck through in ink with a diagonal use mark. "Magic is . . . Science", "The fairies . . . speak", and "Fairy . . . trusted" are used in "History," *W*, II, 34 and 35.

[61] "Saxons . . . arrival⟩", struck through in ink with what may be a curved diagonal use mark, may be a continuation of the notes on p. [79] above and is used in "Permanent Traits of the English National Genius," *Lectures*, I, 237–238, and the lecture "Genius of the Anglo-Saxon Race." The rest of the page and the first paragraph on p. [82] are an outline of "The Age of Fable," *Lectures*, I, 253–265, almost in its final order.

Lecture III

Eng. lit. begins   ↑AD 1128 Geoffrey of Monmouth
    Begins in fable   translated Brut and Turpin 870↓
        Fables of middle age prodigious.   diff
        Difference from Greek fable
        Yet had these & all a moral

Historical importance. Happy effect of the Rómance lit. that it restored the poet to the multitude.

Effect of Xy, trade, & politics. enlarging the resources of poetry.

⟨Homely earthy smell of Eng. poetry.⟩

Gradual fall of romance as ⟨the⟩ credulity withdrew its aid

these stories only entertaining that were once believed. Munchausen

It fell by its own excess   the more wild the wonders grew the sharper reprehension from the caustic sense and the moral indignation of conscientious persons. But it had disclosed wealth enough to drop this tinsel without loss.

Homely earthy smell of Eng. poetry

Cuccu. ⟨Lindsay.⟩ the effect of this popular origin popular institutions & undertook to *amuse*[n] the people instead of to instruct them. Abundance of ballads   It held fast to the market, the ⟨tavern⟩ inn, the street,

[82] It is the books of a people that require meat & not pap, to whom elegance is less native than truth & who must even have their ⟨native⟩ ↑⟨inn⟩constitutional↓ Utility remembered in ⟨the⟩ songs & ballads.

Chaucer [62]

We feel among our forbears

---

[62] What follows is an outline of the lecture "Chaucer." With the first entry, cf. *Lectures*, I, 271; "He borrows . . . Copernicus" is expanded on p. 284; "Real merits . . . religion" outlines pp. 272–280; with the last line, cf. pp. 272 and 274.

He borrows of Dante of Boccacio of Colonna
What of that? So do all men
Christ, Dumont, Jefferson ⟨Ga⟩ Copernicus

    Real merits of C.
        hilarity   strong sense humor pathos
wide knowledge, man of the world
observer of nature
A reformer & lashes the Romish Clergy
    A man, wise,
    English ideas, nobility, gentillesse.
            Woman
            Objective religion

A stronger sympathy with nature betrayed

Man

1836

Emerson began Notebook Man in October, 1836, evidently to gather material from his journals for use in his lecture series on "The Philosophy of History." The only dates are "October, 1836" on p. [i], and "24 Oct. 1836" on p. [1], but all but one of the located passages are drawn from journals dated December 10, 1836, or before; most of this notebook was probably completed within six weeks or less. Emerson drew on it most heavily for passages in the lecture "Ethics" and to a lesser extent for "The Present Age"; he used scattered passages throughout the series. He drew on Notebook Man again for a few passages in the "Human Culture" series the following year, and later for essays, perhaps by way of the lectures.

Notebook Man, the earlier half of a double-ender, the other half of which, Notebook Art, runs upside down and backward with relation to Man, is a copybook with light brown mottled boards measuring 17.4 x 20.7 cm and a brown leather spine. The front cover of the Man sequence is marked "M‖ . . . ‖" and "MAN." in faded or erased ink. Turned upside down, this cover is inscribed in ink "Art" and "Try the other door." set off by rules above and below; both the spine and the front cover in the Art sequence are marked "ART" in ink. The leaves, lightly ruled, measure 17.1 x 20.1 cm. Including 2 front and 2 back flyleaves, there are 174 pages; the leaf bearing pages 119–120 has been cut out. Material in the Man sequence occurs on the inside front cover and pages i, 1–11, 41, 47–53, 69–74, 91–92, 104–106, 116–118, and 121. Pages iii, iv, 12–40, 42–46, 54–68, 75–78, 80–87, 90, 94–96, 98–100, 103, 107, 108, and 111–112 are blank. In the 125 pages used for Man, material in the Art sequence occurs upside down on the inside front cover and page 121, together with matter for Man, and on pages ii, 13, 79, 88–89, 93, 97, 101, 102, 109–110, and 113–115. Numbered in ink in the Man sequence are pages 1–11, 13, 15, 17, 19, 21, 23, 25, 27, 29, 31, 33, 35, 40–41, 46–53, 55, 57, 59, 61, 63, 65, 67, 69, 71–74, 78, 82, 84, 88, 90–93, 95, 97, 99, 101, 103–108, 110, 112, 114, 116–118, and 121; numbers 1–5 are crossed through in ink. Tipped onto flyleaf iv is a sheet of white notepaper, lightly ruled, torn from a larger sheet to measure 16.4 x 20 cm; on one side are notes in ink which may belong with either sequence, printed as iv_b below; on the other side are ink blot designs. A dried crocus is pressed between pages 104–105. Pages 3, 48, 72, 117, and 118 have four or more revisions of accidentals.

[front cover] M‖ ... ‖
MAN.

[i]   R. W. Emerson.
October, 1836

Man.
"Os oculosque Jovi par." [2]

[ii] [...] [3]
[iii]–[iv_a] [blank]
[iv_b] [4] p. 240   Ceremonies & respects
232   top of page
230   economy
233   I find
228   ——————————

[1] 24 Oct., 1836 —
⟨Let me invent s⟩*Some descriptions of* ⟨m⟩*Man.*

——————

[1] "Intellect . . . Travel 9" is in pencil.
[2] "A mouth and eyes equal to Jove." (Ed.)
[3] From this point on, material from the back-to-front sequence, Notebook Art, which occurs frequently and is regularly omitted here, is indicated by [...].
[4] These notes are on a torn piece of notepaper tipped onto p. [iv] and described in the headnote above. The book or journal to which they refer has not been identified.

"Do but examine with impartiality the admirable form of Man, not as terminated by lines, & of such or such a size, but in its nature, which is that of an intelligent being in correspondence with all others, & as placed out of time & space, it will appear not so unworthy of divinity as some have thought it; it contains a kind of infinite, of which all other possible forms of life are only degradations." *Oegger*.[5]

Wherever goes a man, there goes a great soul. I never more fully possess myself than in slovenly or disagreeable circumstances. When I stamp through the mud in dirty boots, I hug myself with the feeling of my immortality. I then reflect complacently on whatever of delicacy is in my taste, of amplitude in my memory. In a university, I draw in my horns. On nothing does a wise man plume himself so much as on independence of circumstances, that in a kitchen, or dirty street, or sweltering stage coach, he can separate [2] himself from impure contact & embosom himself ·in the sublime society of his ⟨hopes & his⟩ recollections of his hopes & of his affections. ⟨The Ambassador⟩ It is a principle of international law, that the Ambassador carries his country with him. So does the mind. [BB Psi, 113]

A man is a method; a progressive arrangement, a selecting principle gathering his like to him wherever he goes. Half is more than the whole. Yes let the man of taste be the selector, and half is a good deal better than the whole; or, an infinitesimal part becomes a just representative of the All. A man of taste sent into Italy shall bring me a few objects that shall give me more lively ⟨pleasure⟩ and permanent pleasure than ↑would the possession of↓ galleries, cities, & mountain chains.[6] [B 125]

[3] Every man stands on the top of the world. When I look at the rainbow, I find myself the centre of its arch. But so is every one.[7]

[5] Copied from Journal B, p. [74], with only minor changes in punctuation. Emerson developed the thought in The Philosophy of History: "Introductory"; see especially *Lectures*, II, 9.

[6] "A man . . . goes." is used in "The School," *Lectures*, III, 36–37, and "Spiritual Laws," *W*, II, 144; the thought is developed in the opening paragraphs of "Humanity of Science," *Lectures*, II, 22–25.

[7] This paragraph, expanded from Blotting Book Y, p. [9], is used in "The Individual," *Lectures*, II, 185.

What is the grief we feel when a man dies[?] Is it not an uneasiness that nothing can be said?ⁿ He has done nothing, he has been merely passive to the common influences of Nature.ⁿ And now that the great endowments proper to a man have passed away from this flesh, we feel that the emptiness of life & character is deep dispraise, and the affectionate expressions of friendship are apologetic. Certainly the feeling would be very different if the departed man had been an earnest self-cultivator, scattering streams of useful influence on every side of him. Then every tear that flowed would be a tribute of eulogy. Friends would not need to say any thing; his acts would speak for him. They would keep a proud silence. A rich consolation would shine in all eyes. But now let our tears flow for the vanity of man! for the poor issues of a God's charity. [Q 81–82]

[4] Nothing is more ⟨melancholy⟩ ↑severely punished↓ than to treat men as pawns & ninepins. If I leave out their heart, they take out mine. But speak to the soul, & always the soul will reply. To treat of the nature of things, is to show his life in new glory to every man. When he sees he is not the sport of circumstances, but that all nature is his friend, & that he is related to natures so dread that if his private selfish good suffer shipwreck, he yet must rejoice, for therein is his universal nature vindicated, he shall reward his teacher with joyful assent.[8]

[5] ⟨What⟩ ↑What is a grown man but a knower↓ of laws? What is a good judgment but a knowledge of laws in that particular province in which the praise is attributed got by experience in that province?ⁿ Thereby slides the person ably & cheerfully in & out amidst all the terrors of nature, their master[,] not their slave; like the skilful engineer among his furnaces & boilers which daunt⟨s⟩ the beholder[.] v[ide]. J 1835 p. 221[9]

[8] "Nothing . . . rejoice," is copied, with some revision, from Journal B, p. [235]. "To treat . . . assent." also appears in Notebook F No. 1, p. [132] below. "Nothing . . . reply." is used in "Society," *Lectures*, II, 107; "Nothing . . . mine." is used in "Compensation," *W*, II, 110–111.

[9] "What is a grown . . . that province.", struck through in pencil with a diagonal use mark, is used in "Ethics," *Lectures*, II, 146. The added reference, "v. J 1835 p. 221", may refer to the passage from Journal B, p. [221], copied on p.

A wise man is a perfect index or table of Contents of the Universe in which he walks.

[6] Is not a man a little knot of roots whereof the world is the flower & fruit? Art, science, poetry, religion, law, — each is but the unfolding & perfection of some one seminal point in him.[10]

[7] Malthus revolts us by treating man as an animal. When the wrong handle is grasped, the tresses of beauty remind us of a mane. It ⟨a⟩disgusts when genius is treated as a medical fact, an inflammation of the brain, & thought & poetry as evacuations. I heard once a loathsome lecture on precocity & the dissection of the brain & the distortion of the body & genius, &c. a grim compost of blood & mud, that for a week I could scarce reflect without remembering ⟨the⟩ ↑my cerebral↓ vessels↑.↓ ⟨of the brain;⟩ Blessed, thought I, were those who, lost in their pursuits, never knew that they had a body or a mind.[11]

[8] I suppose the materials may now exist for a portraiture of man, which should be at once history & prophecy. Does it not seem as if a perfect parallelism existed between every great & fully developed man & every other? [n] [12] Take a man of strong nature, upon whom events have powerfully acted, Luther, or Socrates, or Sam Johnson, & you shall find no trait in him, no fear, no love, no talent, no dream, in one, that does not translate a similar love, fear, talent, dream, in the other. Luther's Pope & Turk & Devil & Grace & Justification & Catherine de Bore shall reappear under far other names in George Fox, in John Milton, in George Washington, in Goethe, or long ago in Zeno & Socrates. Their circles coincide. [A 101, 102]

---

[73] below and used in "Ethics," *Lectures*, II, 150, or to the last paragraph in B, p. [221], partly used in "The Present Age," *Lectures*, II, 158.

[10] This paragraph, struck through in ink with a vertical use mark, is used, rewritten, in The Philosophy of History: "Introductory," *Lectures*, II, 17 and 12. The lecture was given on December 8, 1836, and repeated December 15; the form of the first sentence in Journal B, p. [333] (dated December 10, 1836), reflects the lecture passage.

[11] "Malthus . . . I heard" is struck through in pencil with a diagonal use mark. "Malthus . . . animal." is in Journal B, p. [277]; "It ⟨a⟩disgusts . . . evacuations." and "I heard . . . a mind." are from A, pp. [88] and [129].

[12] With this sentence, cf. "The Individual," *Lectures*, II, 175.

[9] "It was to him gradually plain that only truth & faith make a man estimable, that the good must live genuinely in order to shame all laws, whilst another can neither evade them nor turn them to his advantage." Goethe   vol. 15, p 187 [13]

The moment we enter into the higher thoughts fame is no more affecting to the ear than the ⟨faint⟩ tinkle of ⟨a⟩ passing sleigh bells.

[B 149]

"Men are a sort of moving plants and like trees receive a great part of their nourishment from the air. You were observing the other day how sickly that row of trees in the Thuilleries looked, from being pent up between the terrace & the wall. It is just the same with men who keep too much at home: & it is for the same reason that women in general, who keep more within doors than men, are more unhealthy." *M. Le Grand* apud
Spence's Anecdotes. p 248 [14]

"Mr Pope was with Sir Godfrey Kneller one day when his nephew a Guinea [10] trader came in. "Nephew," said Sir Godfrey, "you have the honour of seeing the two greatest men in the world." —— "I don't know how great you may be (said the Guinea-man) but I don't like your looks. I have often bought a man much better than both of you together, all muscles & bones, for ten guineas." *Dr Warburton* in Spence's Anecdotes
p. 368 [15]

[11] 'Tis the fulness of man that runs over into objects, & makes his bibles & Shakspeares & Homers so great.[16]

↑printed in "Success"↓ See *NO* 42

[12]–[40] [blank]
[41] ——
No man is a master of controversy whom controversy masters.

[BB Y, 10]

[13] *Werke,* 55 vols. (Stuttgart and Tübingen, 1828–1833), in Emerson's library.
[14] Joseph Spence, *Anecdotes, Observations, and Characters of Books and Men* . . . (London, 1820).
[15] The anecdote, struck through in ink with three vertical use marks on p. [9] and one on p. [10], is used in "Montaigne," *W,* IV, 152–153.
[16] This entry, struck through in ink with two vertical use marks, is in a larger hand and was probably added later; it is used in "Success," *W,* VII, 295–296.

He who rides his hobby gently must always give way to him who rides his hobby hard. [Q 17]

I like the sayers of No better than the sayers of Yes. [Q 109]

Un tal⟨o⟩e le cui mani giugnevano spesso dove non arrivava la vista degli altri.
I Promessi Sposi   Vol 2 p. 121.[17]

"No man in God's wide world is either able or willing to help any other man." Pestalozzi [18]

[42]–[46] [blank]

[47]   LAWS.

J 1831 Sept 13

If a teacher have any opinion which he wishes to conceal, his pupils will become as fully indoctrinated into that as into any that he publishes. If you pour water into a vessel ever so twisted into coils & angles   it is in⟨v⟩ vain for you to say I will pour it only into this or that[;] it will find its level in all. Men feel & act the consequences of your doctrine without being able to show how they follow. Show us an arc of the curve & a good mathematician will find out the whole figure. We are always reasoning from the seen to the unseen.

A man cannot bury his meanings so deep in his book but time & likeminded men will find them. Plato had a secret doctrine, had he? What secret can he conceal from the eyes of Montaigne, of Bacon, of Kant? [19]

---

[17] See *JMN*, IV, 73, n. 162.

[18] " 'No man . . . man.' " is struck through in ink with three diagonal use marks. The sentence, quoted from Edward Biber, *Henry Pestalozzi and his Plan of Education* . . . (London, 1831), p. 203, which Emerson withdrew from the Boston Athenaeum Aug. 22–Oct. 3, 1836, is repeated in Journal B, p. [226], and used in "The American Scholar," *W*, I, 113. See also Q, p. [13], where the quotation is incomplete.

[19] This and the preceding paragraph are struck through in light pencil with a single vertical use mark; each paragraph is struck through in ink with a vertical use mark as well. The first, copied from Blotting Book III, p. [34], is used in "Ethics," *Lectures*, II, 148–149, and "Spiritual Laws," *W*, II, 146. In the second paragraph,

[48] Whoever is genuine his ambition is exactly proportioned to his powers. ⟨The height of the pinnacle determines the⟩The breadth of the base⟨.⟩ ⁿ determines the possible height of the pinnacle.[20]

Demosthenes said "Whoso hath an evil cause, the same hath no good fortune." [A 116]

I think the most devout persons to be the freest of their tongues in speaking of the Deity, as Luther, Fuller, Herbert, Milton, whose words are an offence to the pursed mouths which make formal prayers; &, beyond the word, they are free thinkers also.   See passage from Luther, *J* 1833, p. 114 [21]

The hearing man is good. Unhappy is the speaking man.[22]
[B 108]

The moment our higher faculties are called into activity we are domesticated, & our aukwardness or torpor or discomfort give place to natural & agreeable movements. [B 138] [23]

We do what we can, & then make a theory to prove our performance the best. [A 77] [24]

[49] All is economized. When you do any thing, you lose no time from your book, because you still study & still learn. Do what you will, you ⟨s⟩learn ⟨s⟩, — so that you have a right mind & a right heart. If not, I think you still learn, though all is mislearned. [B 207]

---

used following the first in both "Ethics" and "Spiritual Laws," "A man . . . find them." is from Journal B, p. [217], and "Plato . . . Kant?" from B, p. [32].

[20] The paragraph, rewritten from Journal Q, p. [52], and struck through in light pencil with a vertical use mark, is used in "Ethics," *Lectures*, II, 147–148, and "Spiritual Laws," *W*, II, 141.

[21] See Journal A, p. [114], for the entire paragraph.

[22] The entry, struck through in ink with a vertical use mark, is used in "The Head," *Lectures*, II, 257, and "Intellect," *W*, II, 342.

[23] Cf. "Manners," *Lectures*, II, 142.

[24] Cf. "Doctrine of the Soul," *Lectures*, III, 13, and "Considerations by the Way," *W*, VI, 246.

Why fret at particular events? For every thing you have missed, you have gained something else; & for every thing you gain, you lose something. [B 201]

Pains & Prayer will achieve anything. [B 207]
Can a man forget anything which he truly knows? No, for that which he knows, that is he. The more knower, the more man. [B 203] Quantum scimus, sumus. [BB Y, front cover, 13, 32]

The ship beating at sea against the wind gains yet a small commission of miles for her true course on every tack. So in life, our profession, our dilettantism gives us with much parade a little solid wisdom.[25] [B 236]

[50] I think profanity to be as real a violation of nature as any other crime. I have as sensible intimations from within of any profanation as I should have, if I stole. [B 125] [26]

The present is always too strong for the future.[27] ⟨F⟩Where knowledge does not make the future a part of the present the moment is served at the cost of the day. Thus the Esquimaux in the morn will sell his bed. Thus at sea we always ⟨th⟩ judge from the weather of the present hour of the length of the voyage. A single individual or a newspaper expressing malignant sentiments d⟨e⟩ispirits us for the republic. A declaimer of opposite sentiments renews our confidence in Man. A ragged coat looks sinister & revolutionary.[28]

[25] All four paragraphs on p. [49], struck through in pencil with a discontinuous diagonal use mark, are used in "Ethics," *Lectures*, II, 145–146. The first two paragraphs are struck through in pencil with another diagonal use mark, while the second is also struck through in ink with a vertical use mark; "For every . . . something." is used in "Compensation," *W*, II, 98. "Can a man . . . more man." is struck through in pencil with a diagonal use mark, and "more man . . . wisdom." is struck through in pencil with another. "The ship . . . tack.", rewritten in Journal D, p. [324], is used in "Tendencies," *Lectures*, III, 311, and "Self-Reliance," *W*, II, 59.
[26] The paragraph is used in "Holiness," *Lectures*, II, 344.
[27] See Notebook F No. 1, p. [12] below; the sentence may have been intended for insertion in the lecture "The Present Age."
[28] "Thus at sea . . . voyage." comes first from Journal Sea 1833, p. [23]; it is put together with "Thus the Esquimaux . . . bed." in Q, p. [143]; the last

[51] In Action is the power of Man, and, therefore, not in his goals, but in his transition from state to state is he great. Instantly he is dwarfed by self-indulgence.[29]

To a speculative inquiry whether the soul is immortal, God maketh no answer. No convincing argument can be found, but do your duty & you are already immortal: the fear of death has already vanished. [A 110]
There is a surprising tendency ⟨in⟩of man in action to believe in his continuance.[30] [A 97]

Not in his goals, but in his transition man is great. [A 91] The truest state of mind rested in, becomes false. Thought is the manna which cannot be stored. It will be sour if kept, & tomorrow must be gathered anew. Perpetually must we east ourselves, or we get into irrecoverable error, starting from the plainest truth & keeping, as we think, the straightest road of logic.[31] It is by magnifying God that men become Pantheists; it is by personifying him that they become idolaters. [B 39]

[52]   ↑Moral Sentiment.↓

———

As the flower precedes the fruit, & the bud the flower, so, long before the knowledge, comes the opinion, long before the opinion comes the instinct, that a particular act is unfriendly, unsuitable, wrong. We are wonderfully protected. [A 24₂][32]

———

———

sentence is from A, p. [93]. "Thus the Esquimaux . . . revolutionary." is expanded in "The Senses and the Soul," *The Dial*, II (Jan. 1842), 378, and *Lectures*, II, 362. ("The Senses and the Soul" is reprinted as the lecture "General Views" in *Lectures*, II, 357–364.)

[29] Journal A, p. [91], rewritten. The paragraph, partly repeated below, is used in "The Present Age," *Lectures*, II, 158.

[30] A vertical line in ink is in the left margin beside this paragraph.

[31] "The truest . . . of logic." is struck through in pencil with a vertical use mark; "Not in . . . false." is used in "The Present Age," and "The truest . . . logic." in "Religion," *Lectures*, II, 158 and 93.

[32] A revision of this paragraph in Journal B, p. [219], is used in "The Head," *Lectures*, II, 251, and the essay "The Intellect," W, II, 330.

Never a magnanimity fell to the ground. Always the heart of man greets it & accepts it unexpectedly. [B 334] It always discovers that the pusillanimous are magnanimous within.[33]

The order of things consents to virtue. ⟨↑&c J 1835 p 36↓⟩Such scenes as luxurious poets & novelists ⟨often⟩ paint where ↑the↓ temptation is out of all proportion to the power of resistance never ⟨or very rarely⟩ occur in real life.[34]

[53] What you love not, you cannot do[.] [35]
What pleases me will please many. [C 38]

[54]–[68] [blank]
[69] Because sentence is not executed speedily therefore the heart of men is fully set in them to do evil. How has the soldier acquired his formidable courage? By a rare occasional ⟨effo⟩ action? No[,] by eating his daily bread in danger of his life, by having seen a thousand times what resolution & combination can accomplish. H⟨is⟩ow is a firm cheerful conversation to be got? not by one effort but by spending days & years well & so having a divine support for such a frail nature to lean upon,[n] a divine support of all the virtue of his life. The volatile vanishing froth of the present which any shadow will alter, any breath blow away, any act annihilate[,] is every moment converted into the adamantine record of the past[,] the fragility of man into the eternity of God. The Present is always becoming the Past. We walk on molten lava on which the claw of a fly or the fall of a hair makes its impression which being received the mass hardens into flint & retains every impression forevermore. —— —— What makes [70] the majesty of Brougham, Webster, & Mackintosh? Brass will never be gold. The consciousness of an innocent life & the cumulative glory of so many witnesses behind. There they all stand & shed an united light on the

[33] The paragraph is struck through with a diagonal use mark in ink and a vertical use mark in pencil. "Never . . . unexpectedly." is used in "Religion," *Lectures*, II, 95, and "Spiritual Laws," *W*, II, 158–159. Cf. also "The Heart," *Lectures*, II, 294.
[34] "⟨&c . . . p 36⟩" was added in pencil after "to virtue." It is overwritten in ink by "Such . . . novelists ⟨often⟩", a revision of the rest of the paragraph in Journal B, p. [36]. See Notebook Φ, p. [17] below, for still another revision.
[35] "Doctrine of the Hands," *Lectures*, II, 236.

advancing actor. He is attended as by a visible escort of angels to every man's eye. ⟨It ne⟩

'It nerves his arm, it steels his sword,'

That is it that throws music into Channing's voice, & dignity into Washington's port, & America into Adams's eye.[36]

Who thinks kindly of the world? [n] Always those who do well themselves. Who receive hospitality? the hospitable. Who receive money⟨;⟩? the rich. Who receive wisdom? the wise. To whom do opportunities fall? To the prompt. Unto him that hath shall be given. For whom are the doors of the great flung wide open but for the diligent & the magnanimous? Who see the sweetest smiles of beauty? the insignificant dangler whom every one would shake off⟨,⟩↑?↓ or the brave & just man who cuts a straight path to whatever is most precious in the world? And [71] does the world bow to the cook & the ⟨taster⟩ & the Iachimo, & the self despised, or to the generous and abstemious self commander? [37]

If you would not be known to do any thing never do it. A man may play the fool in a pantry & say who can possibly tell it↑?↓ but he will betray his own secret unawares; pimples ⟨will⟩shall tell, a swinish look shall tell; incapacity of generous a⟨ims⟩cts; the want of knowledge he ought to have acquired in that hour of selfindulgence; — all these shall blab. Can a cook, a Chiffinch be mistaken for a Seneca? [Q 26] Confucius said, "How can a man be concealed? How can a man ⟨can⟩be concealed!" [T 190] ↑Solon said, "Such as the speech such is the life of the man."↓ [A 129] [38]

Do not believe that possibly you can escape the reward of your

[36] This and the preceding paragraph on pp. [69]–[70] are expanded from Journal Q, p. [25]. "The consciousness . . . Adams's eye." is struck through in ink with two parallel, discontinuous, diagonal use marks. "What makes . . . Adams's eye." is used in "Tendencies," *Lectures*, III, 311, and "Self-Reliance," *W*, II, 59–60.

[37] Emerson combined passages from Journal Q, pp. [24] and [27], in this paragraph. See Notebook F No. 1, p. [105] below.

[38] The paragraph is struck through with two diagonal use marks, one in ink and another in light pencil. "If you . . . concealed!' " is used, rewritten, in "Ethics," *Lectures*, II, 150, and "Spiritual Laws," *W*, II, 159. "Solon . . . man.' " was added in a smaller hand.

action. You serve an ungrateful master. Serve him the more. Be wholly his. Embrace any service, do what you will, & the Master of your Master, the Law of Laws will secure your Compensation. Every man is valued as he makes himself valuable. [Q 17][39]

[72] It seems as if a ⟨simple⟩ manly character should never make an apology, but always regard his past action with the ⟨same marble⟩ calmness ⟨as⟩ ↑of↓ Phocion when he admitted that the event was happy, yet regretted not his dissuasion from the action. [A 115][40]

When I am true to myself nations & ages do guide my pen & I perceive my commission to be coeval with the eldest causes.

> The privates of man's heart
> They speken and sound in his ear
> As tho' they loud winds were [B 50]

The true man has the ⟨universe⟩ ↑world↓ [41] at his back in every action.[42] Genius is the enemy of genius by excess of influence. All true greatness must rest on the foundation of God. Some people in Rhode Island saying to George Fox, that if they had money enough, they would hire him to be their minister he said, "Then it was time for him to be gone, for if their eye was to him or to any of them, they would never come to their own teacher." [43]

[73] Shall I not treat all men as gods? [44] [B 191]

[39] The thought of this paragraph is developed and the last sentence used in "Trades and Professions," *Lectures*, II, 125. The paragraph is copied into Notebook F No. 1, p. [105] below, and "You serve . . . more." used in "Compensation," *W*, II, 119. With the first sentence, cf. also "The Transcendentalist," *W*, I, 337.

[40] The cancellations are revisions of the passage in Journal A, p. [115]; the paragraph, further revised, is used in "Heroism," *Lectures*, II, 337.

[41] "universe" is canceled and "world" added in light pencil.

[42] "When I . . . every action." is from Journal B, p. [50]. With the first sentence, cf. also Q, p. [34], and A, p. [31]. The lines from Gower are used in "Ethics," *Lectures*, II, 150.

[43] "Genius . . . influence.", struck through in ink with a vertical use mark, is in Journal B, pp. [232] and [252], and C, p. [101]; it is used in "The American Scholar," *W*, I, 91. "Some people . . . teacher.'" is in B, p. [53].

[44] The sentence is used in "The Present Age," *Lectures*, II, 167, and "Politics," *Lectures*, III, 245; cf. also "Lecture on the Times," *W*, I, 280.

The wise man ⟨has no⟩ ↑has no↓ secrets. Secrets belong to the individual, local. He strives evermore to sink the individual in the universal. The friend who can bring him into a certain mood has a right to all the privacies that belong to that mood. Moreover he believes that no secrets can be: that the nature of the man does forever publish itself & that all laborious concealments lose their labor.

"I know not what you think of me," said my friend. Are you sure? You know all I think of you by those things I say to you. You know all which can be of any use to you. If I, if all your friends should draw your portrait to you, faults & graces, it would mislead you, embarrass you; you must not ask, how you please me? for curiosity. You must not look in the glass to see how handsome you are but to see if your face is clean. ⟨Certainly⟩ I know what impression I made on any man by remembering what communications he made to me.[45]

[B 220–221]

[74] Insist on yourself. Never imitate. For your own talent, you can present every moment, with all the force of a lifetime's cultivation, but of the adopted stolen talent of another, you have only a poor brief half-possession.[46] [A 88]

I would not have a man dainty in his conduct. Let him not be afraid of being besmirched by being advertised in the newspapers or by going into Atheneums, town meetings, & bar rooms or by making speeches in public. Let his chapel of private thoughts be so holy that it shall perfume & separate him unto the Lord though he lay in a kennel. Let not a man guard his dignity but let his dignity guard him.

[B 140]

[75]–[78] [blank]
[79] [...] .

[45] "The friend . . . that mood." and "I know what impression . . . to me." are used in "Ethics," *Lectures*, II, 150. With "The wise . . . that mood.", cf. "The Head," *Lectures*, II, 257. "The friend . . . that mood." is used in "Spiritual Laws," *W*, II, 145. "a right . . . your portrait" is struck through diagonally in faint pencil with what may be a use mark.

[46] The paragraph, struck through with two vertical use marks, one in ink and one in pencil, is used in "Ethics," *Lectures*, II, 151, and "Self-Reliance," *W*, II, 83.

[80]–[87] [blank]
[88]–[89] […]
[90] [blank]

[91] We have thoughts but we don't know what to do with them, materials that we can't manage or dispose. We cannot get high enough above them to see their order in Reason. We cannot get warm enough to have them exert their natural affinities, & throw themselves into crystal. We see a new sect devoted to certain ideas, & we go to individuals of it to have them explained. Vain expectation! They are possessed with the ideas, but do not possess them.[47] [Q 70]

The cotemporaneous diminution of Hope & of Memory is the tragedy of Man. [B 28] [48]

Speechmaking ⟨seems to⟩ turn↑s↓ the man out of doors, ⟨to⟩ change↑s↓ his timber into flowers, & make↑s↓ him like to Apicius who sold his house but kept the balcony to see & be seen in. [B 53] ⟨Un⟩-happy is the hearing man [49] [B 108]

———

Who can be sincere? The child is sincere & the man when he is alone, if he be not an author, but on the entrance of the second person, hypocrisy begins. [A 77] The abomination of desolation is not a burned town, nor a country wasted by war, but the discovery that the man who has moved you, is an enthusiast upon calculation.[50] [A 67]

[92] We improve easily up to the point at which our contem-

---

[47] Single pencil lines are drawn vertically in the left margin from "We have" to "new sect" and from "new sect" to "the ideas,".

[48] This sentence is used in "Tragedy," *Lectures*, III, 104, and "The Tragic," *W*, XII, 405.

[49] "Speechmaking . . . seen in." is used in "The Present Age," *Lectures*, II, 163. "⟨Un⟩happy . . . man", added in light pencil, is used in "The Head," *Lectures*, II, 257, and "Intellect," *W*, II, 342.

[50] "The child . . . begins." is used in "Being and Seeming," *Lectures*, II, 296. Other versions of the sentence in Journal A, p. [67], are in Encyclopedia, p. [193], Notebook Δ, p. [16] below, and R, p. [129₂]. See F No. 1, p. [13] below, where "Calculated Enthusiasm" is in a collection for the lecture "The Present Age."

poraries & countrymen have arrived.ⁿ There we stop for months[,] for years & very slowly gain anything beyond it.[51] [B 166]

I find it the worst thing in life that I can put it to no better use. One would say that he can have little value for time who sits down to so slow labor & of such doubtful return as studying Greek or German tongues. Yet I know not how better to employ a good many hours in the year.[52] [C 26]

[93]–[102] [...]
[103] [blank]
[104]   Particular Men.
Great men ⟨are our⟩ ↑serve us as↓ high water marks [Enc. 132]

I am bound by all my tastes to a reverence for Luther yet can I by no means find any but a subjective that is essential correspondence in me to his mind. I cannot reanimate & appropriate his difficulties & speculations. How then Jesus & his apostles? Sometimes it seems as if nations[,] ages were the body of shades of thought[.] [A 94]

Dampier's Irregular Men
Yankee's abundant canvas [53]

"Mr Canning was always great when he was jocular & always small when he was serious." Sidney Smith [B 115]

Some men seem formed for what is low & squalid, as it was said of one of the English painters, that he was "an angel at an ass and an ass at an angel." [54]

[51] The paragraph, struck through in ink with a vertical use mark, is used in "The Present Age," *Lectures*, II, 165. It is also copied into Notebook F No. 1, p. [151] below.
[52] The first sentence, marked in the left margin with two vertical lines in pencil, is used in "Being and Seeming," *Lectures*, II, 296.
[53] "Dampiers . . . canvas" is in pencil. See Journal Sea 1833, pp. [17]–[18], and "On the Relation of Man to the Globe," *Lectures*, I, 37–38 and 39, for some anecdotes about seamen from Dampier. "Yankees abundant canvas", from B, p. [294], is used in "Trades and Professions," *Lectures*, II, 128.
[54] See Journal Q, p. [29]. This and the preceding entry are marked in the left margin with vertical lines in pencil.

71

I count no man much because he cows or silences me. Any fool can do that. But if his conversation enriches or rejoices me, I must reckon him wise.[55] [A 21]

[105] Some people exist to ask each other conundrums; some to attend their fire or their front door; [56]

A system-grinder hates the truth. [B 81]

Perhaps a reason why one man apprehends physical science better than another is that his livelier fancy enables him to comply with the prescribed conditions of the problem long enough for the full apprehension of the law. Thus in learning the precession of the Equinoxes he can keep the picture of the sun where he ought in his mind & figure to himself the nutation of the axis of the Earth; &c. But I alas write my diagrams in water.[57] [B 93]

[106] I listened to Dr Ripley's prayer in the mourning house with excited attention because the probability that some touch of nature shall melt us is tenfold greater than we should feel in the rising of one of the city preachers of propriety — the fair house of Seem. These old semisavages do from the solitude in which they live & their remoteness from artificial society & their inevitable daily comparing man with beast, their inevitable a⟨n⟩cquaintance with the outward nature of man & with his strict dependence on sun, rain, wind, & frost; wood, worm, cow, & bird, get an education to the Homeric simplicity which all the libraries of the Reviews & the commentators in Boston do not countervail.[58]

[107]–[108] [blank]

[55] See Notebook Δ, pp. [7], [95], [97], and [136] below, where this passage is listed in collections for "The Heart" and probably "General Views." It is used in lecture pages printed conjecturally with "Private Life," *Lectures*, III, 249.

[56] "Some people . . . conundrums;" is taken in part from Blotting Book Y, p. [6].

[57] "he can keep . . . water." is marked in the left margin with a discontinuous vertical pencil line.

[58] The paragraph, rewritten from Journal B, p. [106], is struck through in pencil with a vertical use mark and used in "Manners," *Lectures*, II, 136–137.

[109]–[110] [...]
[111] [blank]
[112]–[115] [...]
[116]

The Scholar
The Philosopher

To know the laws of our being man must be an observer. But how we live on the outside of the world! Open the skin, the flesh; enter the skeleton, touch the heart, liver, or brain, ⟨of the man⟩, & you have come no nearer to the man than when you were still outside. All this is as strange & foreign to him as to you. You have almost as much property in his body as he has. The babe is formed in the womb of the mother quite outside of her system. It is carefully ⟨guarded⟩ ↑secured↓ from any interference with her constitution. So if you go into a family where you supposed a perfect understanding & intimate bonds subsisted, you find with surprise that all are in a degree strangers to each other, that the father has one interest, the son another, that husband & wife observe each other's acts with much of a stranger's curiosity.[59]

[B 228]

People think that husbands & wives have no *present time*, that they have long already established their mutual connexion, have nothing to learn of each other. [117] The wise man will discern the fact; viz. that they are chance-joined, little acquainted, & do observe each the other's carriage to the stranger as curiously as he doth.[60] [B 119]

And very difficult is the task of the observer, — Very subtile & ev⟨o⟩anescent the phenomena. It often seems that we do not record the true thoughts. We do not apprehend them. Those that we feel & live we cannot yet record. How far often is the thought that rises in the Soul from being lived, — or how remote yet from the hands! The friend, the spouse perceives unfitness in the friend, in the spouse: Yet periods of discipline, revolutions in State, must transpire before

------

[59] "But how . . . he has." and "So if . . . acts" are used in "Home," *Lectures*, III, 32.
[60] A short vertical pencil line is drawn in the right margin beside "each other." A version of this paragraph was canceled in the manuscript of "Home"; see *Lectures*, III, 399(notes).

that chasm which the far lightning of thought ⟨bridged⟩revealed, can be bridged over. [B 217]

We have many states of mind of a sad or practical influence which refuse to be recorded. I could as easily recal a fled dream as recal & describe the feeling I had yesterday of limited power & the small worth of a day to me. The impression is left; the self evidence is flown.[61]

[118] His virtue is to work for the love of the work; drawn by the love of truth — he explores, & thoughts he thinks. The auctioneers of imagination & philosophy who set truth to sale on the instant of her Epiphany, let him shun. This is the difference between Genius & Talent, that the one works for the delight of the work, & the other prostitutes the sublime faculties to sordid ends. I have seen a hawk wheeling up to heaven in a spiral flight, & every circle becoming a more brilliant point in the sunlight, until he vanished into the atmosphere. What could be more in unison with all pure & splendid images! Yet is the creature an unclean greedy eater, and all his geography from that grand observatory was a watching of barnyards or an inspection of moles & field mice. He is an apt emblem of the man of intellect who converts poetry & eloquence into an instrument for by-ends.[62]

[119]–[120] [leaf cut out]
[121] company. It is nothing   if he is nothing. The company is perfectly safe & he is not⟨c⟩ one of them though he is there. Let him come out & brag of his company. A well bred person will discover presently what place he occupied.[63]
[. . .]

[61] The paragraph, marked by a vertical pencil line in the left margin, is rewritten from Journal A, p. [128]. With this and the previous paragraph, cf. "Holiness," *Lectures*, II, 345.
[62] With "His virtue . . . sordid ends.", cf. Notebook Δ, p. [143] below, Journal B, p. [22], and *Lectures*, II, 404–405(notes), a passage canceled in the manuscript of the lecture "Society." "I have seen . . . field mice." is from A, p. [38]. "The auctioneers . . . field mice." is expanded from B, p. [225], and condensed in "The Present Age," *Lectures*, II, 161.
[63] The passage on p. [121], struck through in pencil with a diagonal use mark, is the end of a passage in Blotting Book III, pp. [106]–[107], used in "Ethics," *Lectures*, II, 149, and "Spiritual Laws," *W*, II, 149.

ℱ No. 1

1836–1840

Emerson began this notebook, probably first titled "Γ," in September, 1836, while preparing to announce his lectures on "The Philosophy of History," and used it for notes and outlines in writing the lectures, given December 8, 1836, to March 2, 1837. He entered a list of titles, probably in October, 1837, which may be the earliest planning for his first book of essays, and a short time later used it to draft a now missing lecture on slavery given in Concord in November, 1837. He used blank pages to draft paragraphs on Carlyle, probably for a review written in November, 1837, but used in the 1843 lecture "Recent Literary and Spiritual Influences." Although he began Notebook Δ for the "Human Culture" series given in the winter of 1837–1838, he used and added to his 1836–1837 notes for at least one of the new lectures. The only other date given is 1839, when he entered some notes on literature, but at some time between October, 1838, and the summer of 1839, he used this notebook extensively for collections and working notes apparently for the essays "History," "Self-Reliance," "Compensation," and "Spiritual Laws," some parts of which were probably used in lectures in the "Present Age" series in the winter of 1839–1840. At some time after this Emerson retitled it "F" and "F No. 1".

Notebook F No. 1 is a copybook with stiff cover boards measuring 16.1 x 19.9 cm and covered with orange paper marbled black and yellow, and a spine of cracked brown leather marked "F" in ink. The front cover is inscribed "1836-7." retraced over an earlier "1836", with a small "Γ" to the right, and "F" retraced over "Γ"; near the bottom, in pencil, is a diamond with a cross within and a circle at each point. The leaves, ledger ruled, measure 15.8 x 19.3 cm. Including 2 front (Emerson numbered the second flyleaf 1) and 2 back flyleaves, there are 172 pages. Numbered in ink are pages 1–28, 30–36, 38–40, 42–48, 50–60, 62–68, 70, 72–108, 110, 112–113, 116, 120, 12⟨0⟩2–123, 128–130, 13⟨0⟩2–134, 13⟨6⟩8–146, 148, 150–154, 156, 158, 160, and 162–168; pages numbered in pencil are 69, 126, and 135. The rest are unnumbered. Two pages are numbered 63; the editor has renumbered them 63₁ and 63₂; Emerson omitted number 65, going from 64 to 66. Pages misnumbered 78 and 79 were corrected to 80 and 81. The page misnumbered 82 was corrected to 84. Following this page, one or more leaves are probably missing, though no stub remains. The following page was numbered 85, then corrected to 89, and pages marked 88, 89, and 90 were corrected to 90, 91, and 92. Following 99, verso pages were num-

bered 98 and 100, then corrected to 100 and 102. Two verso pages were numbered
110, and the second corrected to 112. Two verso pages were numbered 120 and the
second corrected to 122. Two verso pages were numbered 130 and the second corrected
to 132. Following pages 136–137, which are blank and unnumbered, Emerson numbered verso pages 136–148, followed by 149, 150, 151, and 152, then corrected them
to 138–154. Two verso pages were numbered 154 and the page following the second
was unnumbered; the editor designates them 154₁, 155₁, 154₂, and 155₂. Pages 19,
41, 60–61, 117, 127, 136–137, 139, 142–143, 146–147, 150, 152, 160–161, 163,
and 165 are blank. The following pages have four or more revisions of accidentals:
18, 30, 40, 46–53, 58, 62, 63₁, 66, 67, 74, 77–80, 82–84, 90, 94, 95, 98, 100–103,
105, 121, 124₂, 125₂, 129, 140, 144, 145, 148, 149, 154₁–155₂, 158, 159, 162,
and 164.

[front cover]   ⟨1836⟩1836–7.   Γ
                                        ⟨Γ⟩F

[front cover verso] [1] ⟨*Examined this book*⟩ *March 1877*
    Contents

Realism	p 1	Slavery 113
Religion	p 50	
Art	p. ⟨‖ . . . ‖⟩ 80	Ethics p. 21
Criticism	p. 58	
Science	p. 62	Ethics miscellany 43
Poetry	p. 106	One mind 96
Miscellanies	138	Science 104
Chivalry	146	Realism 70 82 98
The Present p. 10		Literature 18
Politics	72↑, 82,↓	Compensation 103
Rhetoric	p. 100	Self-Trust 107
Love	106	Carlyle, p. *154 to 162*
Literary Ethics 1⟨40⟩51		
Outline	⟨166⟩ 166	

[1] "⟨*Examined* . . . *1877*" and "*Contents*" were added in pencil at different
times. In the first column "The Present p. 10" was probably added at the same time
corrections in the preceding two lines are in heavier ink. "Eloquence   126" is in
as "Ethics miscellany 43" in the second column. "Life   128", in print-writing, and
pencil; the last three entries in the column appear to have been added at the same
time. "Slavery 113" and "Ethics p. 21" were added later in a large hand. "One
mind . . . Literature 18" was apparently added at one time, and the two lines below it at another. "Carlyle . . . 162" was added later in blacker ink.

↑Life 128↓
Value of Knowledge 154
Philosopher 112
The Antique 20
Literary History 30
Trade 92
Society 122
Eloquence 126
The Individual 26
Manners 35
Character 42

[i]

R. W. Emerson.
September, 1836.
F NO I.[2]

[ii] Mr R W Emerson proposes to deliver a course of Lectures on the Philosophy of ⟨History⟩ Modern History. The subjects to be treated are the foundations of Religion, Politics, Science, Literature, & Art in the nature of things; the action of general causes upon them at the present day, the condition & tendencies of these elements of civilization, the popular sciences, & the men of gen⟨us⟩ius as these illustrate the general subject and the intellectual duties of the existing generation[.]

The course will consist of at least twelve lectures to commence on the first Thursday of December & to be given every ⟨E⟩Thursday Evening at the Masonic Temple. Tickets, ⟨T⟩two dollars each.[3]

[1]   Realism.
Only the perception of principles can give stability to the character. Men of great phlegm & apparent strength have a merely superficial tranquillity. — Under a marble brow their thoughts are a tossing sea. The inconveniences of fear are however so great that we ought to

[2] "superficial", in pencil, is overwritten in ink by "F NO I.", which is enclosed in an octagon.

[3] See pp. [171]–[inside back cover] below for Emerson's accounting of the series, which he began on December 8, 1836.

thank God that he has taken it away from honesty.[4] Any pain which a mob can inflict is trifling compared with the humiliation of obeying them. In times of anarchy to die is an elegancy. Love is the greatest of elegances & of that please God anarchy shall never bereave me. The conservative principle is Love. The separating principle is Truth.

[2] Periods of Belief—↑are always attractive V[ide]. Milton's Areopagitica; the notice of intel. activity in time of the Commonwealth.↓
⟨Pe⟩Men of faith always noble.[5]
Every principle is a war-note.[6]

All history is in the mind as thought long long before it is enacted.
[B 322]

———

Every man explicable by his history   J 1835 p 31 [7]

———

"A single house will show all that is done & suffered in the world." [8]
[Enc. 191]

———

A Revolution illustrates at large the difference of two tendencies in man

———

[3]   Between the acting of a dreadful thing
           And the first motion, all the interim is
           Like a phantasma or a hideous dream
           The genius & the mortal instruments
           Are then in Council; & the state of man
           Like to a little Kingdom, suffers then
           The nature of an insurrection.
                           Jul[ius]. Caes[ar]. — [II, i, 63–69]

    [4] This sentence is used in "The Individual," *Lectures*, II, 182.
    [5] "Periods . . . noble." is used in "Religion," *Lectures*, II, 96. "V. Miltons . . . Commonwealth." is added after "noble." and partly circled to show its intended position.
    [6] See Notebook Δ, pp. [82] and [83] below. The sentence is used in "Perpetual Forces," *W*, X, 87.
    [7] "All history . . . history" is used in The Philosophy of History: "Introductory," *Lectures*, II, 13, and "History," *W*, II, 3. With "All history . . . enacted.", cf. also "Religion," *Lectures*, III, 272.
    [8] The quotation is used in "Ethics," *Lectures*, II, 144.

It is easy to solve the problem of individual existence. Why Milton, Shakspear, or Canova should be there is reason enough. But why the million should exist drunk with the opium of Time & Custom, does not appear.[9] [B 138]

[4]   L⟨ec⟩ast Lecture [10]
Story of Luther's Wife   [B] 280
⟨Study all men in one   117⟩ [11]
⟨Nature never quite reached⟩ [12]
⟨Civilization loses what it gains. watch & sun⟩
          ⟨Christ[ianit]y emasculated⟩ [13]
Reflection makes gods of men⟨; Olympian huts⟩ [14]
Progress is of the Individual ⟨138⟩ 218   223   ↑1833↓ ⟨44⟩
     Dulness of the Age   [B] 228   207 [15]
Value of knowledge ↑(This book   154)↓ [16]
Plutarch's Athenian youth [17]
     He that saves souls ↑transports them not in bundles↓ [Enc. 99]
     Sublime ambition of the Individual (1837) p 2 [18]
Genius always situated alike [C 3]

[9] The paragraph is in pencil; "the million . . . Custom," is used in "Being and Seeming," *Lectures*, II, 296.

[10] The last lecture in the "Philosophy of History" series was "The Individual," *Lectures*, II, 173–188. Emerson collected material for this lecture here and on pp. [5] and [135] below. P. [4] is in pencil.

[11] This and the preceding entry are used in "The Individual," *Lectures*, II, 178–179.

[12] Cf. Journal B, p. [303], "Nature was still inaccessible," used in "The Individual," *Lectures*, II, 185.

[13] These notes are expanded in "The Individual," *Lectures*, II, 174–175, and "Self-Reliance," *W*, II, 85; cf. Journal B, p. [51].

[14] "Olympian huts" is also circled in pencil. Cf. "The Individual," *Lectures*, II, 184.

[15] Passages from Journal B, pp. [218], [223], and [228], and A, p. [44], are used in "The Individual," *Lectures*, II, 175–176. See also p. [26] below. The paragraph from B, p. [228], is partly transcribed in Notebook Δ, p. [133] below; "The only . . . individual." (B, p. [228]) is expanded in B, p. [322], which is used in The Philosophy of History: "Introductory," *Lectures*, II, 13–14.

[16] "The value of knowledge" is in "The Individual," *Lectures*, II, 182, but the passage on p. [154] below is not used.

[17] Emerson may be referring to the quotation from Plutarch he had inscribed in Notebook Composition, p. [42].

[18] This passage is used in "The Individual," *Lectures*, II, 186.

Thought of Jesus or Plato [B] 303 [19]

[5] Use of knowledge to free
Use of reflection to counteract the dwarfing of circumstances
        Magnitude nothing to science [B 208]
        drop & sea [20] [B 199, 208]

        Use of Hist to magnify the present
        Use of society to magnify the Individual
        Society never advances, Individual does
        Society a Wave [A 44]
        Individual passes through all states
        Study all men in one [B 117]
        Travelling [B 117]
        Position of the Individual [21]
        Use of knowledge to emancipate
        Use of reflection to counteract dwarfing Circ.ⁿ
                Magnitude nothing to science
                Drop & sea
                Drops & sands
        Su⸓render of individuality   Which Schiller [22]

[6] E. P. Peabody's Synopsis of the Lectures; September 1837 [23]

_____

                God with us
                illustrated

[19] This passage is used in "The Individual," *Lectures*, II, 187, and "History," *W*, II, 26–27.

[20] P. [5] is in pencil, written over seven ampersands in light pencil. "Use of knowledge . . . sea", repeated below, is an outline of "The Individual," *Lectures*, II, 182–185.

[21] "Use of Hist . . . of the Individual", the first four lines of which are struck through in pencil with single diagonal use marks, is an outline for "The Individual," *Lectures*, II, 174–180.

[22] "Tongue" is written in an ornate hand to the left of this line and may have been inscribed on the page earlier. "Which Schiller", from Journal Q, p. [77], is used in "The Individual," *Lectures*, II, 185.

[23] Elizabeth Palmer Peabody's "Synopsis", possibly her suggestions for publication, is derived from the "Philosophy of History" series, though "the Ideal" is the central theme of the "Introductory" lecture in the "Human Culture" series, which

by ⎫ or:
The Philosophic Idea ⎬ Hints of the
of History ⎭ Ideal
of Science
of Art
of Literature
of Politics
of Society
of Trades & Professions
of Manners
of The Present Age

A Second Volume to be made
of Ethics
of Religion
of the Individual

[7] One Mind
⟦The Soul⟧
Science
Art
Genius
Virtue
Heroism
Holiness
Love
Prudence
Realism
Offsets [24]

Emerson may have been considering at this time. For evidence that he was also con-
sidering a new book in early October, see a letter from Lidian quoted in Eleanor
Tilton, "Emerson's Lecture Schedule — 1837–1838 — Revised," *Harvard Library
Bulletin*, XXI (Oct. 1973), 385–386.

[24] The topics on p. [7], in heavy print-writing, may be suggested titles for the
"Human Culture" series; see Notebook Δ, pp. [170]–[171] below, where "Heroism"
is in similar print-writing, and "Art" becomes "The Eye & Ear." However, "Art,"
"Heroism," and "Prudence" are also titles in *Essays [First Series]*; "Offsets." appears
on p. [27] below in a collection used for "Compensation"; and pp. [69], [70], [82],
and [98] below, indexed or headed "Realism" by Emerson, are collections for
"Spiritual Laws."

[8]   Popular theology is low
         Contradicted by silence
              by ascetic thought
              by literature & proverbs
These all indicate the Compensation perfect   they are in the
nature of things, & so Eternal & present
    Compensation in Nature
              in Condition
              in Action
              in labor

         We seek to sever
         This is the Omnipresence [25]

[9]   All things are sold
         You cannot cheat Nature
         You cannot lose
         Goodness is God & therefore Virtue is Heaven
         Compensations of calamity [26] [D 298]

[10]   The Present.
    The value of history is the estimate it gives to the present hour.
To give value to the Eternal Now is the tendency of Science [27]
    The Geologist shows us that the amazing ⟨con⟩ revolutions of
the surface of the planet are attributable to Causes now active.
    What is doing now?

[25] P. [8], in pencil, outlines sections of "Compensation"; with "Popular
theology . . . present", cf. *W*, II, 95, 96, 104, 106–109, and 110; "Compensation
in . . . labor" is developed in *W*, II, 96–98, 110, and 114; the last two entries are
used in *W*, II, 103 and 101. For "Compensation in . . . Condition", see also "Duty,"
Lectures, III, 145 and 146. Since roughly the first third of the manuscript of "Duty"
is missing, part or all of "Popular theology . . . present" may have been in the lecture.

[26] P. [9] outlines "Compensation," *W*, II, 107, 119, 122, and 126–127. "Parties
Parties", in pencil, is overwritten by "things are sold" and "cheat Nature" in the
first two lines.

[27] "The Present . . . Science" is struck through in pencil with a vertical use
mark. Both sentences are used in "The Present Age," *Lectures*, II, 157 and 158.
The first sentence is also used in The Philosophy of History: "Introductory," and
"The Individual," *Lectures*, II, 16 and 174.

Mountains of salt are being formed at the bottom of the Mediterranean like those of Poland. Niagara Falls are receding at the rate of ↑50 yards in 40 years↓ to Lake Erie.   Who thinks at what a cost of ⟨p⟩organs & processes a tree is formed? Yet what regions of forests Vesuvius burns.

J 1835 p. 53   Display.[28]

[11] The present is reflective.[29] The present age deciphers ↑nat.↓ history from organic remains & civil from a few facts[.]

good of jacobinism, *J.* 1835 p. 259

What is said now, will be heard.[30]

The age of voluntary association

Carlyle assured me that Colburn & Bentley the London publishers expended in one year £10,000, in puffing.

French journals announce *Pantheon Litteraire*; "Collection Universelle des Chefs d'oeuvre de l'esprit humain," to consist of 100 thick volumes so printed as to contain the quantity of 1000 ordinary ones at 10 francs each   M. Buchon editor. F[oreign]. Q[uarterly]. Rev[iew]   July 1836 [31]

In this last year appeared in France 6700 works in French German Eng Span Ital Portug. Greek & Latin
In Germany the Leipzig Fair Catalogue has 4003 new works or new editions [32]

---

[28] "this speechmaking . . . seen in.", in Journal B, p. [53], is used in a paragraph on "The love of display" in "The Present Age," *Lectures*, II, 163.

[29] There are sections on the reflective age in both "The Present Age," and "The Individual," *Lectures*, II, 168–171 and 180–188.

[30] With this sentence, also in Notebook L Literature, p. [18] above, cf. Journal B, p. [239], used in "Literature," *Lectures*, II, 68.

[31] Cf. Journal C, p. [227], used in "The Head," *Lectures*, II, 254, and "Intellect," *W*, II, 334.

[32] "In this last . . . editions", struck through in pencil with a vertical use mark, is used in "The Present Age," *Lectures*, II, 166.

[12]   Single facts
Humboldt
The negro slave
Pompeii
Liberia
The Peace Society —   Congress of Nations
The Temperance Society
Universal Association. Mediation of Nations.
National Education.
     Sunday School
     Prison Discipline
     Charlestown Bridge
     Mobs [33]
          Insert in Lecture XI, Pius VII — [B] p 280
          Present too strong for the future [34]

[13] Age of /decorum/Seem/ Webster's scream [B] 21, 60,[35]
The Reflective   26, 90, 216, 302, 304 [36]
Idea of Jacksonism &c   28, 319,[37]
Causes of Principle as Abolition &c   33. 78 [38]

[33] "Liberia", "Congress of Nations", and "Mediation of Nations." are used in
"Politics," *Lectures*, II, 82. "Mobs" are discussed, *ibid.*, pp. 74 and 81, and "Compensation," *W*, II, 119. "The Temperance Society" and "Prison Discipline" are
mentioned in "Society," *Lectures*, II, 106, and "Humboldt" and "Pompeii" in "The
Present Age," *Lectures*, II, 172 and 159.

[34] "Insert . . . future" is in pencil. "The Present Age" was the eleventh lecture in the "Philosophy of History" series; the passage from Journal B, p. [280],
does not appear in the lecture as printed in *Lectures*, II, 157–172, but see p. [13]
below, where "Pius VII   280" is included in a collection for "The Present Age."
For "Present . . . future", see Notebook Man, p. [50] above.

[35] P. [13] is in pencil. "Age of" is struck through in pencil with a short diagonal
use mark. Passages from Journal B, pp. [21] and [60], are used in "The Present
Age," *Lectures*, II, 162–163. Pp. [13]–[17] list passages used in both "The Present
Age" and "The Individual"; Emerson may have conceived them as one lecture in
this early stage.

[36] All five passages cited here are used in "The Present Age," *Lectures*, II, 168–
171, in a section on the reflective character of the age. The passage in Journal B, p.
[216], is also used in "Tendencies," *Lectures*, III, 311, and "Self-Reliance," *W*, II,
58.

[37] Cf. "The Present Age," *Lectures*, II, 171.

[38] Emerson later used the passage in Journal B, p. [33], in The Present Age:
"Introductory," *Lectures*, III, 197.

Chapel of secret thought   61
Calculated Enthusiasm [39]
The Vanity stricken   101
> Age of Parenthesis &c   101 [40]
> Compare our proprieties with Bacon's nonsense   105
> Individuals & the million   138, 218, 223,[41]
> We improve easily to the point of contemp   166, 226,[42]
> Young men   226 [43]
> Jacobinism   259
> Ethics of Intellect   259
> Pius VII   280
> Age of Trade   294 [44]
> Our Politics   307
> After thirty [B 83]
> Archidamus [45] [B 97]

[14] The reflective makes gods of men & heaven of time makes free & cheerful
makes cottages Olympian & so makes amends for loss of old metropolitan feeling

Civilization loses what it gains; watch loses the sun, Xy emasculated [46]

---

[39] See Notebook Man, p. [91] above.

[40] "Age" is struck through in pencil with a short diagonal use mark. The passage in Journal B, p. [101], is used in "The Present Age," *Lectures*, II, 163.

[41] These three passages are also listed in collections for the lecture "The Individual" on pp. [3] and [4] above; passages from Journal B, pp. [218] and [223], are used in "The Individual," *Lectures*, II, 175 and 174.

[42] "We" is struck through in pencil with a short diagonal use mark; passages from Journal B, pp. [166] and [226], are used in "The Present Age," *Lectures*, II, 165 and 170. The first passage is also transcribed in Notebook Man, p. [92] above.

[43] "Young" is struck through in pencil with a short diagonal use mark; the passage is used in "The Present Age," *Lectures*, II, 170.

[44] The passage in Journal B, p. [294], is used in "The Present Age," *Lectures*, II, 160–161.

[45] "After thirty" and "Archidamus", each struck through in pencil with a short diagonal use mark, are used in "The Present Age," *Lectures*, II, 169 and 170.

[46] P. [14] is in pencil. "Civilization . . . emasculated", repeated below, is used in "The Individual," *Lectures*, II, 174–175. With "The reflective . . . feeling", cf. sections in both "The Present Age," and "The Individual," *Lectures*, II, 168–171 and 180–188.

Before every new party & gazette Reflection stands inquisitive to learn the Idea. *They*[n] know it never.

It is alleged that the cultivated intellect of the time is reflective not instinctive. Age of second thought, [B] 26
Wordsworth [B 90][47]　　Hereby we lose what civ[ilization] gains, watch & sun
Xy emasculated.

Hence after 30 [48]
　　Young men　166, 226
　　Archidamus [B 97]

[15] The Present is the conflux of two Eternities. To value the Present is the best doctrine of History. The antagonist principles are the Universal & the Individual.[49]
The Universal hath nothing new: gives a family & country name

The Individual hath its own name, property, wife, son, thought;

"There is a wise presumption in favor of the old." And every reformer aims anxiously to make a historical argument

Nature never quite reached [50]

[16]　　　　　　　Age of precocity not learning

[47] "It is alleged . . . Wordsworth" is used in "The Present Age," *Lectures*, II, 168.
[48] This and the two entries following, each struck through in pencil with a diagonal use mark, are used in "The Present Age," *Lectures*, II, 169, 165, and 170.
[49] "The Present . . . Individual." is written in ink over the same in pencil, except for the second sentence, which begins "The Present to value is . . .". With the first sentence, cf. "The Present Age," *Lectures*, II, 159; the second is used in The Philosophy of History: "Introductory," "The Present Age," and "The Individual," *Lectures*, II, 16, 157, and 174, and the third in "Religion," *Lectures*, II, 84.
[50] "The Universal . . . reached" is in pencil. " 'There is . . . argument", struck through in pencil with a diagonal use mark, is used in "The Present Age," *Lectures*, II, 157. "Nature . . . reached" is used in "The Individual," *Lectures*, II, 185; cf. Journal B, p. [303].

Age of decorum   not ⟨n⟩passion
↑love of hist arg.   Webster scream↓
Age of exactness   not boldness
Age of facts   not principles
    Principle slips away (D of I)

Age of reflection not instinct

Good of the Age of Reflection

Under the great & permanent influence of nature all others seem insignificant [B 303] [51]

[17]   Best use of History   teach value of Present
    Men disesteem the present
    wise presumption in favor of old
    The good instinct ⟨clusters⟩ twines round the old
        unwilling to think   unwilling to be bad [52]
↑Ours the Age of Reflection   of second thought↓ [53]
    Age of Unconsciousness
    Character of Moderns
            Evils
            Goods

The appeal is always open from these vague acc[oun]ts of masses to the Individual. What man has felt any bars
    Suicide
The conventions of society press very sorely upon large numbers. There is not a balance in the active & passive power [54]

[51] P. [16] is in pencil. "Age of precocity . . . instinct" is an outline of "The Present Age," *Lectures*, II, 164, 162, 166–167, and 168. The last two entries are used in both "The Present Age," and "The Individual," *Lectures*, II, 171, 159, 180, and 187.
[52] "Best use . . . be bad", in pencil, is an outline of "The Present Age," *Lectures*, II, 157–158.
[53] "Ours . . . thought", in ink, is used in "The Present Age," *Lectures*, II, 168; "the Age of Reflection" is repeated in "The Individual," *Lectures*, II, 180.
[54] "Age of Unconsciousness . . . passive power" is in pencil. "Age of . . . Goods" outlines sections of "The Present Age," *Lectures*, II, 168–170; cf. also "The

Sacrifice not the man to the writer, as Milton, Chaucer, Wordsworth, do not. C 221
Humanity of the great poets   C 179   B 225
Knowledge alters every thing for use   C 178 [55]
Every man write literature for himself   B 98

[19] [blank]
[20]   The Antique.
"Beauty with the ancients was the tongue on the balance of expression," said Win[c]kelmann [56] [B 17]

Abernethy says that the eye sockets are so formed in the gods & heroes of Greek Sculpture, that it would be impossible for such eyes to squint & take furtive glances on this side & that. They must turn the whole head. [A 86] [57]

———

Eternal beauty is in the fable of ⟨the⟩ Endymion, of Pandora, of Orpheus, of Cassandra, & the Sybil, of Pygmalion, of Icarus, of Proteus,

'Bacchus the vinum mundi: Apollo conscious intellect.'
There is but one mind. Of course, the Antique is merely a distinction of circumstances and always they reappear for some & so Greeks are sprinkled [58]

———

Individual," *Lectures*, II, 180. With "The appeal . . . Individual.", cf. "The Individual," *Lectures*, II, 176. "Suicide" is struck through in pencil with a diagonal use mark; cf. "The Present Age," *Lectures*, II, 161 and 170.

[55] With the first three passages ("Sacrifice . . . poets"), cf. "Doctrine of the Soul," and "Literature" [first lecture], *Lectures*, III, 17 and 218, and "The Over-Soul," *W*, II, 288–289. The passage cited in Journal C, p. [178], is used in "The Poet," *W*, III, 17.

[56] The quotation is used in "Genius," *Lectures*, III, 72, and "History," *W*, II, 15.

[57] The paragraph, struck through in pencil with a diagonal use mark, is used in "Manners," *Lectures*, II, 133, and "History," *W*, II, 24.

[58] With "Of course . . . sprinkled", struck through in pencil with a vertical use mark, cf. "Manners," *Lectures*, II, 135, and "History," *W*, II, 26.

The admiration of the Antique is not admiration of the old but of the natural.[59] [B 234]

[21]   Ethics
Realism   ↑You must Be.↓[60]   ↑p. 69↓[61]
⟨The talent is the call⟩[62]
Affinity makes society[63]
⟨Solus docet qui dat⟩[64] [Enc. 31, C 192]
Pertinence is deep thought
⟨Faces never lie⟩ [B 201]
⟨What is appears⟩[65]
⟨What you believe you must say⟩
⟨Your unbelief discredits⟩
⟨Truth tyrannizes over us⟩[66]
Punishment is in the crime. Glaucus.
Reward of a↑n↓ ⟨th⟩act is to have done it
      House praises carpenter [B 257]

---

[59] The sentence, struck through in pencil with a vertical use mark, is used in "Manners," *Lectures*, II, 134, and "History," *W*, II, 25.

[60] Cf. "Being and Seeming," *Lectures*, II, 298–299, and "Spiritual Laws," *W*, II, 160.

[61] "p. 69" is in pencil. P. [69] below, headed "Realism.   *Being*.", contains working notes probably for "Spiritual Laws," as do pp. [21], [23], [68], [70], [71], and [98]. It is possible, however, that this and other 1839 pages headed "Ethics" in Notebook F No. 1 may be working notes for the lecture "Ethics" (January 29, 1840), the manuscript of which is missing. Emerson evidently wrote at least four essays, including "Compensation" and "Spiritual Laws" (then titled "Simplicity"), before the 1839–1840 series on "The Present Age" (see Notebook Ж, pp. [56], [84], [88], and [95] below), then drew on the not yet published essays for several different lectures. He may have reworked parts of "Compensation" and "Spiritual Laws" for use in "Ethics."

[62] See Blotting Book Psi, p. [36], for the source of this phrase, a quotation from Abraham Tucker. It is used in "Ethics," *Lectures*, II, 147, and "Spiritual Laws," *W*, II, 140.

[63] Cf. "Ethics," *Lectures*, II, 147, 150, and "Spiritual Laws," *W*, II, 150–151.

[64] Emerson used a translation of the Latin in "Education," *Lectures*, III, 502 (notes), and "Spiritual Laws," *W*, II, 152.

[65] "Pertinence . . . appears" is used in "Spiritual Laws," *W*, II, 153, 156, and 158. The first entry is also used in "Ethics," *Lectures*, II, 147 and 148. With the second and third entries, cf. also "Religion," *Lectures*, II, 94–95.

[66] This and the preceding entry are used in "Spiritual Laws," *W*, II, 156 and 157.

A man passes for his worth [67]
⟨A writing'⟨e⟩s effect is proportioned to its depth *
⟨An action's effect, — to the depth of the sentiment⟩ [68]
⟨⟨W⟩He may have what place he will take⟩   [⟨Protest⟩] [69]
⟨He may trust only the good that grows from his nature⟩
⟨We can see only what we are⟩   [⟨Demonology⟩]
⟨We can read only what we know⟩ [70]
We can associate only with what is ours
⟨You have a right to your own everywhere⟩
        ⟨Secrets. Narbonne.⟩ [71] [C 314–315]
Economy of time is selfreliance [72]
Magnanimity greatens

[22]   Ethics
Wisdom is justified
Drive out nature with a fork she runs back again [D 61]
World is a multiplication table   quincunx [73]

                                    * See p. 69 of this book &

[67] "Punishment . . . worth" is struck through in ink with a vertical use mark. The story of Glaucus, found in Herodotus, *History*, VI, 86, and "Reward of . . . carpenter" are used in "Duty," *Lectures*, III, 147–148 and 149. See Notebook Φ, p. [19] below. See also p. [70] below. With "Punishment . . . done it", cf. "Compensation," *W*, II, 102–103. "A man . . . worth" is used in "Religion," *Lectures*, II, 95, and "Spiritual Laws," *W*, II, 157 and 159.

[68] With "A writing'⟨e⟩s . . . depth", cf. Journal D, p. [141], and "Spiritual Laws," *W*, II, 153. With "An action's . . . sentiment", cf. "Spiritual Laws," *W*, II, 155. Variants of both sentences occur on p. [69] below.

[69] See Journal D, p. [87], "it is an universal maxim . . . acquiesce.", used in "The Protest," *Lectures*, III, 101, and "Spiritual Laws," *W*, II, 151.

[70] With this and the preceding entry, cf. "Ethics," *Lectures*, II, 149, and "Demonology," *Lectures*, III, 155–156, used in "Spiritual Laws," *W*, II, 148.

[71] With "We can associate . . . Narbonne.", cf. "Spiritual Laws," *W*, II, 149–151 and 145.

[72] Cf. Journal B, pp. [4] and [275], and "Ethics," *Lectures*, II, 146. For still another version, see C, p. [211], used in "The Head," *Lectures*, II, p. 257.

[73] All three entries on p. [22] are used in "Compensation," *W*, II, 120, 105, and 102. The last entry is also used in "Demonology," *Lectures*, III, 156, in a fragment printed with "Private Life," *Lectures*, III, 252, "Self-Reliance," *W*, II, 58, and "Spiritual Laws," *W*, II, 148; cf. Blotting Book III, p. [93], and Journal B, p. [216].

[23]   Ethics
    Concealment impossible
In will out
Sin blabs, daubs. [B 241]
Virtue shines
⟨Pretension versus Performance⟩
Every secret is told
⟨Truth tyrannizes⟩
⟨Eyes never lie⟩   Faces   D 145
⟨Your unbelief discredits you⟩
Result of society an estimate ⟨D⟩C 223 [74]
Every thing hangs out its flag [D 292]
All men live in glass houses

[24]   Ethics
    Tit for tat   in Nature
Chain slave chain lord
⟨long neck short tail⟩
⟨grain of wit grain of folly   finest wits have their sediment⟩
Harm watch   Harm catch
Bad counsel is the bane of the counsellor
Opinion reacts
The gun recoils: the curses come home
pride humbles
defects enrich   oyster
⟨Magnanimity greatens⟩
Wisdom is justified
⟨Furies watch the Sun⟩.
⟨Darkness, light; ebb, flood; heat, cold.⟩
⟨⟨L⟩Every loss a gain, every gain a loss.⟩
↑⟨Gather too much & it comes out of gatherer. Manna⟩↓
⟨Every secret is told.⟩
⟨Every crime is punished every virtue rewarded⟩
⟨World is a multiplication table.   a quincunx.⟩

[74] Notes on p. [23] to this point are developed or used in "Spiritual Laws," *W*,
II, 145 and 156–159; Emerson may have been working from the earlier lectures,
"Ethics" and "Religion."

oyster mends her shell with pearl [75]
Society   ⟨th⟩ Γ 43 [76]

[25]   Ethics
⟨These laws execute themselves⟩ [77]
Tit for Tat   in Man in Will
        You must pay [D 214]
        Eye for eye   blood for blood
        Revenge is wild justice
        You shall have what is thine
        Nothing venture nothing have
        Nothing is given everything is sold
        You cannot do wrong without suffering wrong [78]
        The curse causeless shall not come
        Harm watch   Harm catch
        Bad counsel bane of counsellor
        Opinion reacts   Gun recoils   Curse comes home
        Chain slave   chain lord [79]

[75] "Tit for tat . . . quincunx." is struck through in ink with a vertical use mark. "oyster", in line 11, and "oyster mends . . . pearl" are added in pencil. Though phrases in ll. 3–6 and 14–16 are used in "Ethics," *Lectures*, II, 153, 154, and 145–146, the page is probably a collection for "Compensation," where most of it is used. Phrases on ll. 2–9, except "finest wits . . . sediment" (Journal B, p. [53]), are used in "Compensation," *W*, II, 109, 97, 98, 109, 110, 107, and 109. With "pride humbles . . . enrich" (ll. 10–11), cf. "Compensation," *W*, II, 110 and 117, and "Ethics," *Lectures*, II, 147 and 153. "oyster" (ll. 11 and 21) is used in "Compensation," *W*, II, 117. For ll. 13–20, see "Compensation," *W*, II, 120, 107, 96, 98, and 102. For "quincunx.", see p. [22] above.

[76] See p. [43] below. Emerson apparently first titled this notebook "Γ" and changed it to "F" at some time later than this inscription, probably made in the summer or fall of 1839.

[77] Cf. "Ethics," *Lectures*, II, 147 and 148, the Divinity School Address, *W*, I, 122, "Tendencies," *Lectures*, III, 312–313, "Compensation," and "Spiritual Laws," *W*, II, 110 and 135. P. [25] is apparently a collection for "Compensation."

[78] Ll. 5 ("Eye for . . . blood"), 7, 8, and 10 are struck through in ink with single vertical use marks. The phrases in ll. 3–6 and 8–10 are used in "Compensation," *W*, II, 109–110, 113, 109, 100, 109, 107, and 110. Proverbs in ll. 5 and 8 were also used in "Ethics," *Lectures*, II, 152. "You shall . . . thine" is developed in "Spiritual Laws," *W*, II, 145–146; cf. also "Ethics," *Lectures*, II, 149.

[79] "Harm watch . . . lord" is struck through in ink with a vertical use mark. Entries on all four lines are used in "Compensation," *W*, II, 109, 110, and 107. The first and last proverbs are also in "Ethics," *Lectures*, II, 153 and 154.

Every crime punishes: virtue rewards.
Love for love
Pride humbles   Defects enrich. Oyster [80]
Treat men as pawn & ninepins & you suffer [B 235]
Men resist being made things
Safe is Blame   D 136
All love mathematically just [B 246]   [Society]
Exclusive & exclusionist
Beware of too much good [81]

[26]   ⟨The Individual
The able man is as rich as the world &c   see p. 74 this book
A man knows no more to any purpose than he practices
Dulness of the age &c⟩   [B] p 228 ↑207↓ [82]
                    ↑Ethics

Self Trust↓
Know one know all
The barometer's mile alike everywhere [BB III, 80]
Sit at home with might & main
⟨For every loss a gain   for every gain a loss⟩
Don't interfere
World a quincunx; acrostic; [83]

[80] "Every crime . . . Oyster" is used in "Compensation," *W*, II, 102, 116, and 117. "Love for love" is also in "Ethics," *Lectures*, II, 152.

[81] "Treat men . . . things" is struck through in ink and "Safe is . . . good" in pencil with single vertical use marks; "Exclusive & exclusionist" is in pencil. All six entries are used in "Compensation," *W*, II, 110–111, 118, 116, 110, and 113. The passages in Journal B, pp. [235] and [246], are both used in "Society," *Lectures*, II, 107 and 103; the sentences in the essay are apparently taken from the lecture, not the journal, and shortened.

[82] "The able man . . . world &c", copied from Journal B, p. [251], on p. [74] below, is used in "Trades and Professions," *Lectures*, II, 124. "A man . . . practices", from Blotting Book Y, p. [32], and B, p. [279], is used in "Ethics," *Lectures*, II, 146; cf. also B, p. [203], and Notebook Man, p. [49] above. The passage on B, p. [228], is copied into Notebook Δ, p. [133] below; cf. "The Individual," *Lectures*, II, 175 and 176. "207" is added in pencil. Passages in B, p. [207], are used in both "Ethics," and "Trades and Professions," *Lectures*, II, 146 and 125.

[83] "Know one . . . acrostic;" is probably notes for the "Philosophy of History" series, but may have been used also in writing several essays. With "Know one know all", cf. "Ethics," and "The Individual," *Lectures*, II, 143 and 178. "The barometer's . . . everywhere" is used in "Ethics," *Lectures*, II, 151. With "Sit at . . . main",

[27] [84] ⟦Borrow R H's horse & you pay the highest price for it
1 Everything is sold
2 What is, appears or, You must *Be*
All is bipolar

All is one	Unity
All is bipolar	Polarity
All appears	Being
All is sold	⟨Equivalents⟩ Offsets.[85]

———

The world reappears in each drop & atom

———

God with all his parts in a lichen

———

That is Omnipresence

———

We falsify by severing; disjoining; [86]

Ethics
These laws Execute themselves
Nature not to be cheated

———

cf. "The Individual," *Lectures*, II, 179, "Politics," *Lectures*, III, 242, "History,"
and "Self-Reliance," *W*, II, 8 and 71. "For every . . . a loss" is used in "Ethics,"
Lectures, II, 145–146, and "Compensation," *W*, II, 98. With "Don't interfere", cf.
"Ethics," *Lectures*, II, 147, and "Spiritual Laws," *W*, II, 135. "World a . . .
acrostic;" is used in "Self-Reliance," "Compensation," and "Spiritual Laws," *W*,
II, 58, 102, and 148.
  [84] "⟦Borrow R H's . . . bipolar" (l. 4), in pencil, is probably the earliest inscription on p. [27]; it is overwritten in ink by "Ethics . . . spiritual laws",
printed below, probably the last to be added. "All is one . . . Offsets.", also in pencil,
which follows "We are begirt . . . laws" on the page, is probably a continuation
of the first inscription. "The world . . . disjoining;", in ink following "All is
. . . Offsets.", may belong with either layer.
  [85] "⟦Borrow R H's . . . bipolar" (ll. 1–4) is struck through in pencil with a
diagonal use mark. With "Borrow R H's . . . Offsets.", cf. "Compensation," *W*,
II, 112–113, 107, 102 and 121, 96–97, and 101. "Offsets" appears on p. [7] above
in a list of titles. With "All is bipolar . . . Polarity", cf. also "Ethics," *Lectures*,
II, 154 and 153. "All appears   Being" is developed more fully in "Spiritual
Laws," *W*, II, 158–160.
  [86] "The world . . . disjoining;" is developed in "Compensation," *W*, II, 101
and 103–104. Cf. Journal D, p. [274].

Ask & you shall have
Ask not & you are not indebted
Do not interfere
⟨The world is a⟩
Life is a good deal easier than we think it
We miscreate our evils   Let well alone
The world should be a happier place
We are begirt with spiritual laws[87] [C 97]

[28][88]   Ethics
  Men wish to outwit nature
            to be great without tax
  Sow poison dust[89]
When a stone falls to the earth the earth falls to the stone. When you move the air with your hand the whole atmosphere is moved[;] a pebble in the water disturbs the level of all the waters of Ocean.
All care for him who cares for all; none care for him who cares for none.[90]
  Serve self you serve society
  Serve society serve yourself
  Liar is never believed
↑The↓ House praises the Carpenter [B 257]
The reward of a good action is to have done it [C 9]
  Ali's peck measure[91]

[29]   All is bipolar   in Condition
        Darkness-light, ebb-flow, heat-cold, inhale exhale, systole-
-diastole.   action reaction.

---

[87] "These laws . . . themselves" and "Do not . . . laws" are used in "Spiritual Laws," *W*, II, 135 and 148. "These laws . . . cheated" and "Life is . . . laws" are used in "Tendencies," *Lectures*, III, 307 and 312–313.
    [88] Overwritten by the matter on p. [28] are pencil sketches of two men in left profile, and the word "Individual" enclosed in a heart.
    [89] "Men wish . . . tax" is developed in "Duty," *Lectures*, III, 146–147, and "Compensation," *W*, II, 103–105, from Journal D, p. [180]. "Sow poison dust" is used in a fragment printed with "Private Life," *Lectures*, III, 252.
    [90] All or part of "When a stone . . . for none." may have been added later; the last three words are crowded in.
    [91] "Ali's peck measure" is in Journal D, p. [292]; part of the paragraph in which it appears, but not the anecdote, is used in "Compensation," *W*, II, 116.

Every excess makes a defect: Every defect an excess
Long neck   short tail
Every sweet its sour: Every bad its good
For every gain a loss   for every loss a gain
Grain of wit   grain of folly. Finest wits sediment
Gather too much; 'tis out of the gatherer
Furies watch the Sun.
Polarity   C 35
Greatness its tax   Riches its tax
All things double [92]

[30]   Literature
The history of editions of books is a valuable part of ⟨h⟩Civil history.
Thus if I knew the fortunes of the Bible in each age & country since
its first books w⟨r⟩ere written, I could ⟨do without⟩ ↑spare↓ Muller.

Sir J Mackintosh said that nothing which was popular could be
uninteresting to a philosopher. Therefore novels were & they addressed a part of man which sermons did not reach.

Six months in a Convent made the fortune of Russell & Shattuck.
Orders came from Natchez.

So a story of a miraculous Medal is announced in German in Munster,
of which 75000 copies were sold in France in 183⟨5⟩4 & 5

Bunyan's ↑born 1628↓ Pilgrim's Progress published from Bedford
jail. He died 1688. Before 1786 the book passed through more than
50 editions

Thomas A Kempis [93]

[92] "All is bipolar" is partly circled. "Darkness-light . . . Greatness its tax" is
struck through in ink with a vertical use mark. "All things double" is in pencil. Except
for "Finest wits sediment" (Journal B, p. [53]), the entire page is used in "Compensation," W, II, 96–99, 107, and 109. Emerson had used six of these entries in "Ethics,"
Lectures, II, 153.
[93] "The history . . . fortunes of" and "Sir J Mackintosh . . . philosopher" are
struck through in ink with diagonal use marks. Both passages, plus references to
Bunyan and "Thomas A Kempis," are incorporated in a paragraph in "Literature,"
Lectures, II, 59. See Encyclopedia, p. [115], for a similar quotation from Mackintosh.

[31] The history of ⟨sto⟩ nursery literature, even of Mother Goose & Grimm's Tales exacts attention & could it be understood would unfold more than Brown, Reid, or Stewart. ⟨Baron Grimm⟩ The fables that have been agreeable to the sense of mankind

Literature the record of thought — all passions have their books. Necessity of literature. Man paints himself out with secular patience. ↑How can a great genius endure to make paste jewels↓ The words of Orestes & Electra are like actions. So live the thoughts of Shakspear. They have a necessary being. They live like men. To such productions it is obviously necessary that they should take that form which is then alive before the poet. The playhouse must have been the daily resort of Shakspear & that profession on which his circumstances had concentrated his attention. That is essential to the production of his plays. Quite otherwise with Taylor Van Arteveldt. His playhouse & muse is the reading of Shakspear. Sermons were thus a living form to Ta⟨l⟩ylor & Barrow[.] Novels & parliam. speeches since Fielding & Burke Instauratio was a natural effect of the Revival of Ancient Learning. But thus it [32] always must be that the true work of genius should proceed out of the wants & deeds of the age as well as the writer & so be the first form with which his genius combines as sculpture was perfect in Phidias's age because the marble was the first form with which the creative genius combined. Homer the only true Epic. Milton is to him what Michel Angelo is to Phidias. But Shakspear is like Homer & Phidias himself. Do that which lies next you, O Man! 1835 J. p 166 [94]

Of Composition &c illust. by Kings College, &c	J. p 233
Of the delight of a thought written	p 243
Of the extent desireable in writer	p. 310
Of the delight a written thought may give	315
That the word never covers the thing	303
The man of genius apprises not of *his* but *our* wealth	285

[94] These three paragraphs, struck through in ink on p. [31] with a wavy diagonal use mark from "Literature the record" to the bottom of the page, and on p. [32] with diagonal use marks through "always must . . . O Man!" and "perfect . . . 166", are used in "Literature," *Lectures*, II, 56, 60, and 61. "How can . . . O Man!" is copied from Journal B, pp. [165]–[166].

The fit word comes as the voice pitches itself to the area   271
Passages sublime in their place   231
Dignity of office felt by Bards; & humanity   225
Estimate a book by the number of things in it. [B 156] see p 58
this bk.[95]

[33] Bacon's perfect law of inquiry after truth was that nothing should be in the globe of matter which was not also in the globe of crystal[,] that is nothing should ⟨exist⟩ ↑take place↓ as event in life, which did not also exist as truth in the mind.[96] [Enc. 147]

[34]   Country ⎫
          Wealth's ⎪
          Army   ⎬ Manners[97]
          Jacobin ⎪
          fashionable ⎪
          heroic ⎭

The Men who at public meetings of whatever kind[,] the writers who in books or papers of whatever kind put manner for matter should learn that they have lost their time. The writer who takes his subject from his ear & not from his heart should know th⟨e⟩at he has lost as much as he seems to have gained & when the empty book has gathered all its praise, & half the people say what Poetry[!] what genius[!] it still takes an ounce to balance an ounce. Nature cannot be cheated.

[95] Of these ten lines, ll. 1, 2, 3, 7, 9, and 10 are struck through in ink with short diagonal use marks; the passages from Journal B, pp. [233], [243], [310], [271], [225], and [156], are used in "Literature," Lectures, II, 63–64, 58–59, 61–63, and 66. Emerson later used passages from B, pp. [243], [310], [303], and [225], in "Intellect," W, II, 327, "Literary Ethics," W, I, 182, "The Individual," Lectures, II, 185, and "Literature" [first lecture], Lectures, III, 218.

    A loose leaf found in A between pages [40] and [41] and numbered "40a" in pencil, omitted in printing A, also contains a collection for "Literature" and is printed in Appendix II below.

[96] The quotation, also listed in Journal B, p. [128], is used in "Lord Bacon," Lectures, I, 327, and "The Head," Lectures, II, 252. "R" is written twice in pencil under "which did . . . the mind."

[97] In pencil, and overwritten in ink by "people say . . . impart life", printed below, this is an outline for a section of "Manners," Lectures, II, 136–140. See p. [39] below for a similar outline.

That only profits which is profitable. Life alone can impart life. And though we burst we can only be valued as we make ourselves valuable.

See also, Lecture before the Institute
"   on Literature
"   on ⟨Virtue⟩ Duty [98]

[35]   Manners [99]

Sheridan	J 1835	327 [100]
Honor		319 [101]
Oaths	109	261
Gruff Jacobin manners		259
		254

⟨Goethe's Householder of the North⟩ [102]
     Country & town   Dr R.   106 [103]
       J 1833, 41, 57   84 [104]

---

[98] The paragraph is copied from the lecture "Modern Aspects of Letters" (*Lectures*, I, 381–382), rewritten from Journal B, p. [48]; "Nature cannot . . . valuable." is used in "Literature" [first lecture], *Lectures*, III, 206; "The writer . . . genius" and "That only . . . valuable." are used in "Spiritual Laws," *W*, II, 153–154, where they are followed by a passage from "Literature," *Lectures*, II, 65–66, which in turn was rewritten from "On the Best Mode of Inspiring a Correct Taste in English Literature," *Lectures*, I, 212, delivered before the American Institute of Instruction. Emerson drew on "Duty" for a passage in "Spiritual Laws," *W*, II, 152–153.

[99] "Manners", "Honor 319", "254", and "Goethes . . . North" are in ink; the rest of p. [35] and all of p. [36] are in pencil. Emerson was apparently scanning his journals for material for the lecture "Manners," first reading backward from Journal B, p. [327] (November 30, 1836), later front to back in both B and A; only about half of the material on pp. [35]–[36] was actually used in the lecture.

[100] This passage, and those in Journal B, pp. [109] and [261] below, were used in "Being and Seeming," *Lectures*, II, 301, 297–298.

[101] The passage cited is used in "Manners," *Lectures*, II, 140, and "Self-Reliance," *W*, II, 60.

[102] This line is deleted with three horizontal pencil lines. Emerson mentions the effect of climate on manners in "Manners," *Lectures*, II, 130, but the quotation is used in "Trades and Professions," *Lectures*, II, 122.

[103] "Country" is struck through in pencil with a short diagonal use mark. The paragraph on Dr. Ezra Ripley, also copied into Notebook Man, p. [106] above, is used in "Manners," *Lectures*, II, 136–137.

[104] All three passages from Journal A are used in "Manners," *Lectures*, II, 141–142.

flowing courtesy   [T 70]
Puckler Muskau   [B] 130
Mme de Stael
Natural Chivalry   (1835)   p 12 [105]
Wrath is not worth carrying home &c [B 21]
Genius nonchalant
Saturn & children   [B 26] [106]
wealth   47 [107]
core of ⟨ma⟩ young man   61
Manners of Wordsworth & Co   65
Mr Hoar   (1833) 133   & (1835)   83 [108]
New Acquaintance   93
Miss Martineau   124
Awkwardness gives place to ideas   138 (1833) 57 [109]
faces never lie &c   [B] 201 [110]
Scholars opium manners   205 [111]
ecclesiastical manners   234
Claverhouse manners   302 [112]
[36]   Experience   1833   p 7
Strong will   & Pepperel   8   87 [113]

[105] "flowing" is struck through in pencil with a diagonal use mark, "flowing
. . . Puckler" with another, and "flowing . . . Natural" with still another. "flowing
courtesy" is the story of the Duke of Buckingham in "Manners," *Lectures*, II, 138.
Emerson used a quotation from Mme de Staël (Notebook T, p. [181]) in "Manners,"
Lectures, II, 141. The passage from Journal B, p. [12], is used in "History," *W*,
II, 18.
[106] This anecdote is used in "The Present Age," *Lectures*, II, 168.
[107] "wealth" is struck through in pencil with a short diagonal use mark; the
passage is used in "Manners," *Lectures*, II, 138–139.
[108] Cf. "Manners," *Lectures*, II, 140–141, Emerson's description of the "Man
of honor."
[109] "Awkwardness" is struck through in pencil with a short diagonal use mark;
both passages cited are used in "Manners," *Lectures*, II, 142.
[110] "faces" is struck through in pencil with a short diagonal use mark; "faces
never lie" is in "Spiritual Laws," *W*, II, 156, but the last sentence of the paragraph
in Journal B, p. [201], is used in "Manners," *Lectures*, II, 129.
[111] This paragraph is used in *Nature*, *W*, I, 46.
[112] "Claverhouse" is struck through in pencil with a short diagonal use mark.
The passage is used in "Manners," *Lectures*, II, 138.
[113] Passages in Journal A, pp. [8] and [87], were rewritten in B, p. [47],
which was in turn used in "Manners," *Lectures*, II, 139; see p. [35] above.

Bard or hero cannot look down upon the word or gesture of a child.

It is as great as they   p 72 [114]

Iarnos   1833   80

Ambitious young man   84 [115]

    Fra Cristoforo   [A 85]

    Greek heads   86 [116]

Variety of manners   88 [117]

    Duke of Ormond

Lord Falkland [118]

Duke of Buckingham [119]

Mr Canning's rank

Not to be doubted that every man's character writes itself out on his person

Cato's Commendation [B 256] [120]

Fashion [121]

Greatest simplicity   greatest elegance

[37]   Oaths

          Games

          Theatre

          Court customs [122]

[114] "Bard . . . they", struck through in pencil with a diagonal use mark, is used in "Manners," *Lectures*, II, 135.

[115] The sentence cited in Journal A, p. [84], is used in "Manners," *Lectures*, II, 142.

[116] "Greek" is struck through in pencil with a short diagonal use mark. The passage is used in "Manners," *Lectures*, II, 133, and "History," *W*, II, 24. See p. [20] above.

[117] Cf. "the diversity of manners", "Manners," *Lectures*, II, 132, and p. [40] below.

[118] "Lord Falkland", struck through in pencil with a short diagonal use mark, is included in a list of men of heroic manners, "Manners," *Lectures*, II, 140.

[119] This and the two entries following it, struck through in pencil with a discontinuous diagonal use mark, are used in "Manners," *Lectures*, II, 138 and 132. For Canning, see Journal A, p. [66], and B, p. [301].

[120] "Manners," *Lectures*, II, 140.

[121] "Fashion" is struck through in pencil with a vertical use mark. See "Manners," *Lectures*, II, 139.

[122] These four topics are in pencil; for "Oaths", see Journal B, pp. [261] and [109], used in "Being and Seeming," *Lectures*, II, 297–298.

Manners betray instantly the amount of individual energy because the force of condition is inert & the individual force overcomes it in proportion to its intensity. It is a trial of strength to lift weights. Where the private force is very little a perfect conformity will be seen to the place & time. Where it is very great the place & time will be hardly discernible in the manners.

All manners impress us with pleasure & veneration in proportion to the dignity of the spirit which they betray.

They are robes of ornament & badges of power.[123]

[38] Manners may be defined the ⟨expression of c⟩ silent expression of character. History is the record of what men are, is the record of the character of the human race. Human character does evermore publish itself. It will not be concealed. It hates darkness. It will ↑in↓to the light. The most fugitive deed & word[,] the mere air of doing a thing[,] the intimated purpose expresses character & the remote results of character are civil history & events that shake or settle the world. If you act you show character; if you sit still you show it; if you sleep you show it.[124]

[39]   Manners a sign
                a sure sign
                a near sign
          Washington is but a man
⟨Make history⟩
Infuse animal heat into history
          Heroic Age of the Greeks
          Greeks & Romans

---

[123] "Manners betray . . . power." is struck through in pencil with a vertical use mark. The first two paragraphs are used in "Manners," *Lectures*, II, 130 and 132.

[124] The paragraph, expanded from Journal B, pp. [201] and [326], is used in "Manners," *Lectures*, II, 129–130. Emerson also used the passages from B in "Spiritual Laws," *W*, II, 156, but in their original journal form. See C, p. [80], for the response of some of Emerson's audience to this passage. The paragraph is struck through in pencil with two vertical use marks, and "Manners may . . . publish itself" with a third; "& the remote . . . world." is struck through in ink with two diagonal lines which may indicate cancellation rather than use.

⟨but⟩these grow straight out of their state; want of mechanic
arts, a sparse population, war
honor of courage over all things

Manners of the Country   [B] 106

of wealth   [A] 8, 87,
of army   [B] 302
of fashion   130   12
of jacobin
of heroism
     plainness [125] [A 66]

[40] A fact of much importance is this, every individual nature
has its own beauty. One who goes with eyes open about the world, is
struck in every company, at every table, with the riches of nature,
when he hears so many new tones, sees original manners, & new expression of face.
He feels that nature has given here the foundations of a divine building, if the soul will build thereon. There is no face or feature, no form
or voice, that one cannot easily imagine to belong to prodigious power
of intellect or greatness of soul.[126]

[41] [blank]
[42] [127]   Actions   ↑Character
                    J 1835   p 326, 256
                    This book p 145↓

The house praises the carpenter
Courthouse, Commencement;
     ↑Moxon, &c.   J.1835   p 201↓
     compensation   185

[125] P. [39], in pencil, is an outline for the lecture "Manners." For "Manners a
sign . . . all things", see *Lectures*, II, 129–134; the rest of the page repeats material on pp. [34]–[36] above.
[126] This paragraph, in pencil and struck through in pencil with a vertical use
mark, is used in "Manners," *Lectures*, II, 132. With the first sentence, cf. Blotting
Book Y, p. [58].
[127] "Character . . . p 145" and "Moxon, &c . . . 201" are in ink; "Actions"
and the rest of p. [42] are in pencil.

What is once well done lasts forever
    Not fear being besmirched   p 140
    How can a man remain concealed [Q 26, B 132]
        Earnestness   p 61
    Retention of simple & high sentiments (1833) p 13

        Not in nature, but in man is all the good he sees [C 1]
        If men be worlds there is in every one — [C 89]
        People are not the better for the sun & moon [C 211] [128]

[43]   ⟨Society⟩ *Ethics*
                          Miscellany [129]

    The longer the speech the less society   D 69

    Eloquence   D 71 [D 7⟨1⟩2]

    Fourth of July Orations   D 247

    ⟨Institutions are optical illusions: Great man knew not what he did   D 263⟩

    ⟨Safe to be blamed   D 136⟩

    ⟨resist being made things of   D 59⟩

    Faces   D 145

    Destructionism vain   D 143

[128] Passages in Journal B, pp. [326], [256], and [201], are used in "Manners," and passages on p. [145] below, and in B, p. [185], and Q, p. [26], in "Ethics," *Lectures*, II, 129–130, 140, 129, 151, 152, and 150. Emerson may have conceived the two lectures as one at this early point. "Not in nature . . . moon", struck through in pencil with a curved vertical use mark, was probably added later; passages in C, pp. [1] and [211], and the passages in B, pp. [326] and [201], F No. 1, p. [145], and Q, p. [26], listed in the earlier collection above, are used in "Spiritual Laws," *W*, II, 147, 156, 158, and 159.

[129] Both "⟨Society⟩" and "Miscellany" are set off by short rules above and below.

⟨Not in nature but in man is all the good he sees   C 1⟩

Fear God & where you are men walk in cathedrals   C 2

Best use of money   C 8

⟨Polarity   C 35⟩

⟨"If men be worlds there is in every one"   C 89⟩

We are begirt with spiritual laws [C 97]

⟨There are graces in a polished man lost on the churl   C 101⟩
The motto on palace doors is Hush [C 141]

⟨People are not the better for sun & moon   C⟩ 211

The result of all social intercourse an estimate   C 223

⟨The thing uttered in words is not therefore affirmed.⟩ [B 44]
                                                    [⟨Present Age⟩]
Men are the poetry of God in whom our nature is manifest [Society]

⟨All love is mathematically just.⟩ [B 246] [Society] [130]

⟨Treat men as pawns & ninepins & you shall suffer as well as they.⟩
                                                    [B 235] [131]

---

[130] For this and the two preceding entries, see *Lectures*, II, 163, 100, and 103.

[131] The passages cited in Journal D, pp. [247] and [263], C, pp. [1], [97], [101], [211], and [223], and B, p. [44], are used in "Spiritual Laws," *W*, II, 152, 155, 147, 135, 157, and 152–153; with D, p. [145], cf. *ibid.*, p. 156. "Safe to be blamed" and the paragraph in D, p. [136], are used in "Self-Reliance," *W*, II, 118. The passages cited in C, p. [35], and B, pp. [246] and [235], are used in "Compensation," *W*, II, 96–97, 116, and 110–111; with "resist being . . . of", cf. *ibid.*, p. 111. The passages cited in D, pp. [69] and [143], and C, p. [97], are used in "Tendencies," *Lectures*, III, 314, 305, and 313.

105

[44] ——

Winds ⟨r⟩blow & waters roll
Strength to the brave & power & deity
Yet in themselves are nothing [132]

The armies sent against the Poles

The exclusive & exclusioni↑s↓t [133]

There is no luck

Οι κυβοι Διος αει ευπιπτουσι [Enc. 185]

The Devil is an ass [Enc. 209]

"Nothing can work me mischief except myself. The harm that I sustain I carry about with me & never am a real sufferer but by my own fault"
St. Bernard.[134] [BB II, 34]

Everything hangs out its own flag. [D 292]

Be sure your sin will find you out

A man is valued as he makes himself valuable. [B 48] [135]
Every thing hath its own price & that price must be paid or not that thing but some other thing will be bought.
The highest price of a thing is to ask for it [136] [Enc. 186]

[132] "Sonnets Dedicated to Liberty," Part I, Sonnet XI, ll. 10–12; the lines are marked with a marginal line in Emerson's copy of *The Poetical Works of William Wordsworth*, 4 vols. (Boston, 1824), II, 324.
[133] The first four lines on p. [44], struck through in ink with one vertical use mark, and the fifth line, struck through with another, are used in "Compensation," *W*, II, 116 and 110.
[134] Emerson first struck "Οι . . . ευπιπτουσι" and " 'Nothing . . . fault' " through in ink with single vertical use marks, then connected them with a curved use mark through "The Devil is an ass". All three quotations are used in "Compensation," *W*, II, 102, 109, and 123.
[135] See p. [34] above.
[136] "Every thing . . . for it" is struck through in ink with a vertical use mark. Both sentences are used in "Compensation," *W*, II, 115 and 113.

[45]   Compensation in Labor
                    in Politics
                    in Love
                    in intellectuals
                    in Condition
                    in Action [137]

Cheapest is the dearest labor
You cannot cheat nature
Swindler swindles
real price of labor is knowledge   swindler & quack get no knowledge

Yet is there somewhat that pays no tax: right & truth

———

I do not wish to find a dollar   D 264 [138]

———

What is Justice? *p. 90*

———

Property is timid

———

Prosperity haunted by a looking for of Eumenides.[139]
Every thing is an apologue to the same text. ⟨An⟩ The adventures of
an apple or a planet or a poet ↑or a lover↓ or a law case or a ⟨heathen
god⟩ mythology[,] every fact & every fiction or fact in masquerade
will ⟨r⟩make the same thing plain.

[46] If a man steals, it is known; if he borrows, it is known; if
he receive gifts, it is known. If I accept important benefits from another in secret, or in public, there arises of course from the deed a
secret acknowledgment of benefit on his part, & of debt on mine; or,
in other words, of superiority & of inferiority.[140]

---

[137] These six topics are developed in "Compensation," *W*, II, 114–115, 99 and
100, 116, 99–100, 98, and 102–104 and 110.
    [138] "Cheapest . . . D 264" is struck through in ink with a curved, mended,
diagonal use mark. "Cheapest . . . knowledge" is used in "Compensation," *W*, II,
114. With "Yet is there . . . D 264", cf. *ibid.*, pp. 122 and 123.
    [139] With "What is Justice . . . Eumenides.", cf. "Compensation," *W*, II, 102
and 103, 111, and 112.
    [140] Cf. "Compensation," *W*, II, 112.

Nature dual
Condition dual
Action dual

This

It seems that every act rewards itself or in other words executes itself utterly in a twofold manner; first; in the thing: & secondly; in the circumstance. Men call retribution only the circumstance. The causal retribution is in the thing, & is seen by the Soul. The circumstance ⟨is inseparable⟩ is seen by the understanding; it is inseparable from the ⟨Cause⟩ thing; but is often not seen until some time after.[141]

[47]   Polarity or Reaction everywhere
    or Nature dual.
        So is each particle dual
        Condition dual   or all things sold
        President; Prophet; Genius; snows & silence
        This ⟨is⟩ baulks all artifice
        This fact indicates Omnipresence
        It is the Soul
        Whilst thus the World will be dual, we wish to sever.
        Life invests itself with conditions. The dodgers are blind.
        Literature true to these facts.
        Proverbs
        Action Dual
        Labor
        No gain by cheating
        No loss by virtue   Sandwich Island
        Virtue absolute Being [142]

Popular theology far behind [143]

[48] Everything is made of one hidden stuff as a horse is only a

---

[141] "Nature . . . Action dual" is developed in "Compensation," *W*, II, 96–97, 98, and 102–104. The paragraph is used, *ibid.*, pp. 102–103.

[142] "Polarity . . . Being" is an outline in final order of "Compensation," *W*, II, 96–122. "snows & silence" and "Sandwich Island" have not been located in the essay.

[143] Cf. "Compensation," *W*, II, 95–96.

⟨metamorphosed⟩ ↑running↓ man, and a fish a swimming man, a bird a flying man, a tree a rooted man, and each repeats not only the main history, but, part for part, all the details, all the aims, furtherances, hindrances, energies, & system of every other. Every occupation, trade, art, transaction, is a compend of the world, & a correlative of every other. And whatever you find remarkable in any one, there is somewhat tantamount to it in every other. The clothier fears moth, the gardener frost, the brewer heat, the painter rain, the iron↑-↓monger rust, the sailor tempest, the miller the fall of the wind, the carpenter the rot & the warping of lumber.[144]
The gardener must weed, the iron monger wipe, the brewer strain, the cloth↑i↓er ventilate & fumigate, the butcher refrigerate. ↑&c↓

A ship is a man's sailing apparatus, a [49] house his dwelling apparatus, a garden his growing, a kitchen his cooking, an army his fighting, a government his political,[n] a hatter's shop his hatting, and each of these must somehow accommodate the whole creature & recite his destiny. Well we put our life into every act. The world globes itself in a drop of dew. You cannot find with telescope an animalcule who is less perfect for being ⟨small⟩ ↑little↓. Eye, ear, taste, smell, sensation; resistance; past; future; & eternity made visible in his organs of reproduction; all find room to consist in the small creature. This is the omnipresence, & in this manner does the ⟨virtue⟩ value of the Universe contrive ⟨or⟩to throw itself into every act. If the good is there, so is the evil; if the gain, so the loss; if the ⟨virtue⟩ ↑force↓,[n] so the limitation.[145]

[50]   Religion[146]
   J. 1835   p. 161

[144] "Everything is . . . correlative of every other." is used in "Compensation," W, II, 101. Cf. "Humanity of Science," Lectures, II, 28, and pp. [64]–[68] below for its probable source in Goethe. With "Every occupation . . . lumber.", cf. Journal C, p. [200], Notebook Δ, pp. [148]–[149] below, "Doctrine of the Hands," Lectures, II, 234 and 243, and "Prudence," W, II, 234. See also Notebook 冰, p. [65] below, for the draft of a similar paragraph used in "Man the Reformer," W, I, 238.

[145] "and each . . . limitation." is used in "Compensation," W, II, 101–102. With "omnipresence," cf. "Humanity of Science," Lectures, II, 29.

[146] Emerson used pp. [50]–[57] to collect materials for "Religion," Lectures, II, 83–97.

I remark the increasing earnestness of the cry which swells from every quarter that a systematic moral education is needed. Channing Coleridge Wordsworth Owen Degerando Spurzheim Bentham Pestalozzi [A 90]

In this age we are learning to look as on chivalry at the sweetness of the ancient piety which makes the genius of A Kempis, Scougal, Herbert, Taylor. It is a beautiful mean equidistant from the hard sour Puritan on one side, & the empty negation of the Unitarian on the other. It is the spirit of David & of Paul. Who shall restore to us the odoriferous Sabbaths which that sweet spirit bestowed on human life, & which made the earth & the humble roof a sanctity? This spirit of course involved that of Stoicism as in its turn stoicism did this. Yet how much more attractive & true that this piety should be the central trait, & the stern virtues follow, than that stoicism should [51] face the Gods & put Jove on his defence. That sentiment is a refutation of every skeptical doubt. David is a beauty, & read 3d Chapter of Ephesians. And yet I see not very well how the rose of Sharon could bloom so freshly in our affection, but for these ancient men, who, like great gardens with banks of flowers, do send out their perfumed breath across the great tracts of time. How needful is Paul, David, Leighton, A Kempis, Fenelon, to our idea! ⟨o⟩Of these writers, of this spirit which deified them, I will say with Confucius, "If in the morning, I hear about the right way, &, in the evening, die, I can be happy."
[B 161–162] [147]

"The sinner is the savage who hews down the whole tree in order to come at the fruit." *Puckler Muskau* [B 130]

Why should the poet bereave himself of the sweetest as well as grandest thoughts by yielding d⟨i⟩eference to the miserly indigent unbelief of this age, & leaving God & moral nature out of his catalogue of beings. [B 130] C. threatened to read Phaedo to E.E.   J 1835 P 34 [148]

---

[147] This and the preceding paragraph, struck through in pencil with single vertical use marks on pp. [50] and [51], are used in "Religion," *Lectures*, II, 97 and 93–94.

[148] "Why should . . . to E.E." is struck through in pencil with a vertical use mark. "Why should . . . beings." is used in "Religion," *Lectures*, II, 97.

Good has been a term of ⟨reproach⟩ contempt. [BB Y, 7, B 279]

Sects fatten on each others' faults. How many people get a living in New England by ⟨showin⟩ ↑calling↓ the Unitarians prayerless, or by showing the Calvinists to be bigots. Hallet feeds on the Masons; M'Gavin on the Catholics; M'Dowell on the libertines. The [52] poor man that only sees faults in himself will die in his sins. [B 24]

The high, the generous, the self-devoted sect will always instruct & command mankind. [B 24]

All the devils respect virtue. [T 182]

The whole of Virtue consists in substituting Being for Seeming, & therefore God properly saith, *I AM*.[149] [B 47, C 6]

Character is not ephemeral but cumulative.[150]

Sects J 1835	p 256, 290,[151]
God & man the Universal & individual	p 281
Evil merely privative	331 [B 332]
⟨Religion nears the Nature of things⟩	23⟨8⟩9[–240] [152]
Ecclesiastical manners	234
Relation to Deity	200
Personality	184
Desire of truth desire of repose	123
Objective devil of Middle Age	108
Religious theory	105
Goodness always smiles	259 [153]

[149] "The high . . . *I AM*.", struck through in pencil with a vertical use mark, is all in Journal C, p. [6], and is used in "Religion," *Lectures*, II, 94–95, and "Spiritual Laws," *W*, II, 158 and 160.

[150] Cf. Journal Q, p. [25], "Tendencies," *Lectures*, III, 311, and "Self-Reliance," *W*, II, 59.

[151] "Sects" is struck through in ink with a diagonal use mark. The passage in Journal B, p. [290], is used in "Society," *Lectures*, II, 108–109.

[152] Emerson struck "God & man . . . privative" through in ink with a diagonal use mark, then extended it through "Religion . . . things". The passages cited in Journal B, pp. [281] and [239]–[240], are used in "Religion," and B, p. [332], in "Ethics," *Lectures*, II, 84 and 85, 95 and 94, and 155.

[153] The passages cited in Journal B, pp. [234], [200], and [105], are used in

[53] "God does not need a house, but man does need that God should have a house." ↑*Donne.*↓ [BB Y, 27]

Dangers or evils of reformation; licen⟨c⟩tiousness; remember Luther's wife.[154] As in chemical decompositions & recompositions there is usually explosion, effervescence, & some foul smell, so there will be with a Reform bill some folly; broken glass, broken heads, & foolish wrath.

Religious literature, Thomas A Kempis.[155]
A superstition is a hamper or basket to carry useful lessons in. [B 313]

In proportion to a man's alienation from wisdom & goodness, do they seem to him another & not himself; that is to say; the Deity becomes more objective.

A man must ⟨do⟩speak the truth not because it is profitable to all, but because it is the truth.[156]

[54]   ⟨Art⟩
⟨J 1835 p 185, 186, 115,⟩[157]

⟨Reality⟩ Nature of the ethical or religious principle
Its elastic, subtle, celestial force.
It resides in all men identical
        Makes men always young. ↑Its opposite, irreligion. absolute
                                                        badness. p. 331↓

"Ethics," *Lectures*, II, 147, 148 and 146, and 149. The passages cited in B, pp. [184] and [259], were used later in "Holiness," and B, p. [123], in "The Head," *Lectures*, II, 353–354, 344–345, and 256.

[154] Cf. Journal B, pp. [225] and [280], used in "The Individual," *Lectures*, II, 178, and "History," *W*, II, 29.

[155] Cf. p. [50] above, and Journal B, p. [161], used in "Religion," *Lectures*, II, 93.

[156] "In proportion . . . objective." and "A man . . . truth.", each struck through in pencil with a vertical use mark, are used in "Religion," *Lectures*, II, 96 and 87.

[157] The three passages cited are used in "Thoughts on Art," *The Dial*, I (Jan. 1841), 369 and 372, and *Lectures* II, 44–45 and 47–48, where "Thoughts on Art" is reprinted as the lecture "Art"; they are also used in "Art," *W*, VII, 41–42 and 46–47.

↑Jesus, Menu, Confucius↓

The Church

Unhappy fact that this Beauty admits no handselling

Touched, it soils, & is no longer the same thing

Endures never two moments, but must spring new all the time, no vows, no formulas, no c⟨on⟩reeds, can keep it more than light or electricity.

Its

Its appearance in history: prodigious efficacy

Necessity ⟨co⟩of influence

    no counterfeit possible

    ⟨no⟩

    Belief in God

Obstinate tendency of men to persons

Impossibility of personality in ↑the↓ common sense ↑of that word↓

Every man strives to become impersonal   p 281 [158]

Solution may be

But certainty not yet for us

[55]   Rust, mould, cobwebs, & barnacles, that collect on forms

    Our ch⟨r⟩urches smell old

    Traditions fall

        Nothing but truth lasts

    General unbelief. Age of Prudence, Religion never degraded

        ↑to serve a turn without loss.↓

        Belief unlovely

        Remedy in opening the eye to the True

        Unanimous demand ⟨tha⟩for Moral Education

        Leibnitz's saying

        Pestalozzi

        Religion nears the nature of things [159]

The most original writer feels in every sentence the influence of the

---

[158] "Art . . . 115," and "Reality" are heavily canceled; the rest of the page is probably notes for the lecture "Religion"; cf. *Lectures*, II, 83–85, 92–93, and 96. The passage cited in Journal B, p. [281], is used, *ibid.*, pp. 84 and 85.

[159] Notes to this point on p. [55] are probably a continuation of the notes above for "Religion"; cf. *Lectures*, II, 96–97.

great writers who have established the conventions of composition ↑&↓ the religious revolution ⟨a⟩effected by Jesus Christ insensibly or avowedly models each of these succeeding reforms. The boldest ⟨re⟩vision of the prophet communing with [160] God only, is confined & colored & expressed according to the resistless example of the Jewish. [B 3]

[56]   The Un↑i↓versal Mind
                Its dictates are Virtue
                Whenever it speaks the individual is rebuked

                The Universal Mind
                    Its dictate is Virtue
                    Antagonism of persons
                    ⟨Its perception⟩ Universal Mind is God
↑signs of sentiment of Duty↓
1   The Universal not founded in numbers, but by one
2   The Profitable, a sign; but its decree ultimate
3   The Elevating a sign
                Always attended by Enthusiasm
The prophet   Jesus   Stoic Socrates Plotinus Fox Behme Swedenborg
The Revelation
The Church
                Injury to Church from Sense & ⟨Tr⟩Understanding
                Now see the Necessity that it underlies [161]

[57]   "High instincts before which our mortal nature
                Did tremble like a guilty thing surprized

                    Which, be they what they may,
                Are yet the fountain light of all our day
                Are yet a master light of ⟨o⟩all our seeing
                Uphold us, cherish, & have power to make
                Our noisy years seem moments in the being
                Of the eternal silence: truths that wake
                    To perish never
                Which neither listlessness nor mad endeavor

[160] "Its appearance in history" is written in pencil under "prophet communing with"; see p. [54] above.
[161] P. [56] contains an outline for "Religion," Lectures, II, 83–94.

Nor Man nor Boy
Nor all that is at enmity with joy
Can utterly abolish or destroy." [162]
↑*Wordsworth*.↓ ["Ode: Intimations of Immortality Recollected
From Early Childhood," ll. 150–151, 154–164]

[58]   Criticism
    J. 1835 p ⟨164⟩ 156 ↑p. ⟨5⟩101,↓ [163]
He only is a good writer who keeps but one eye on his page & with
the other sweeps over things. So that every sentence brings us a new
contribution of observation.   p. 164
    "A good book never written down by any but itself"

"The light of the public square will best test its merit." I cultivate
ever my humanity. This I would always propitiate & judge of a book
as a peasant does[,] not as a book by pedantic & individual measures,
but by number & weight, counting the things, the ⟨things⟩ ↑realities↓
that are in it. My debt to Plato is a certain number of sentences: the
like to Aristotle. A larger number yet still a ⟨certain⟩ ↑finite↓ number
make the worth of Milton, of Shakspeare, to me. ⟨I would therefore
run over what⟩ [164] [B 156]

    That statement only is fit to be made public which you have got
at in attempting to satisfy your own curiosity. For ⟨a ma⟩ himself a
man only wants to know how the thing is; it is for other people that
he wants to know what may be said about it. [165] [Q 74]

[162] All thirteen lines of poetry are struck through in pencil with a diagonal use
mark; all but the last four are used in "Religion," *Lectures*, II, 85.
[163] Passages from Journal B, pp. [164] and [156], are copied below; that from
B, p. [101], is copied on pp. [100]–[101] below. Pp. [58] and [59] were probably collected for the "Philosophy of History" series, but four of the entries are used
in "Spiritual Laws."
[164] The two quotations, struck through in pencil with a diagonal use mark,
are used in "Literature," *Lectures*, II, 65 and 66, and "Spiritual Laws," *W*, II, 154
and 155; the first is also used in "Literature" [first lecture], *Lectures*, III, 206. "I
cultivate . . . would therefore" is struck through in pencil with a straight diagonal
use mark, and "propitiate . . . therefore" with a wavy diagonal use mark; the
passage is used in "Literature," *Lectures*, II, 66.
[165] This paragraph, struck through in pencil with a diagonal use mark, and
marked with a pencil line in the left margin from "a man" to "know what", is used
in "Ethics," *Lectures*, II, 151, and "Spiritual Laws," *W*, II, 153.

[59] The argument which has not power to reach my own practice, I may well fear has not power to reach yours.[166] [BB Y, 55]

Before you urge a duty, be sure it is one; Patriotism for example.
[B 96]

[60]–[61] [blank]
[62]   Science [167]
It will perhaps be the effect of the popularisation of Science at the present day to keep in the eye of Scientific men that *human side* of ⟨thing⟩ nature wherein lie grandest truths. The poet, the priest must not only live with God, but feel a necessity to bring his oracles low down to men in the market. And why not Newton. Tendency of Science is from analysis back to synthesis. Ideology mixes therewith. The Education of the people forces the savant to show the people something of his lore which they can comprehend.
⟦It is observable that even the science of the day is introversive: and Geology looks no longer for histories, but examines the earth that it may be its own chronicle.⟧ [D 162]
& that he is taught by their taste to look for what humanity ⟨there⟩ ↑yet↓ remains in his Science, & now calls to mind (seeing how it is valued) much that he had forgotten. Geoffroy de St Hilaire   Cuvier Hunter, Everard Home, Davy.
        Why 5 or 10 petals? Why colors? [168]

[166] This sentence is used in "Spiritual Laws," *W*, II, 153.
[167] Matter on pp. [62]–[68] was probably collected for the lecture "Humanity of Science," where nearly half of it is used. For more notes for this lecture, see Journal B, pp. [163] and [198].
[168] "It will . . . Tendency" is struck through in pencil with two diagonal use marks. Both use marks are then extended in pencil through "Tendency . . . they can comprehend.", which is from Journal B, p. [261], and may have been added; the remainder of the paragraph in B, p. [261], is continued below after "⟦It is observable . . . chronicle.⟧" and is struck through in pencil with two diagonal use marks. "It will . . . comprehend." is used in "Humanity of Science," *Lectures*, II, 38. Emerson extended his brackets to partly circle "It is observable . . . chronicle." The entry is expanded in D, p. [162], and is used in "Doctrine of the Soul," *Lectures*, III, 9.

[63₁]¹⁶⁹ "In the economy of the world," said Hutton, "I can find no traces of a beginning, no prospect of an end." ¹⁷⁰

———

Science had much charlatanism once of magic, & gowns, & methods; now it is reduced to strict observation. Its very experiments are simple & cheap; & it perceives the truth that the Universal fact is what happens once. [B 236] Nature lets out every secret somewhere. [A 20] It works too with a certain praise of the mind towards simplicity, Unity in process & cause. Davy, Black, Decandolle, ⟨Black⟩, Cuvier, LaPlace, Arago, are its names.¹⁷¹ [B 236]

How is Science possible? How to such an animal six feet long, walking, & in the earth, is the solar system measurable & the nature of matter universally. Because a straw shows how the stream runs & the wind blows, — because, as falls the apple, so falls the moon; because, as grows one inch of one vegetable, in a flowerpot, so grow all the forests; & as one animal ⟨is f⟩of one species is formed, so are formed all animals of all species; because, in short, the wide Universe is made up of a few elements & a few laws, perhaps of one element & one law.   See also J. 1835, p. 258 ↑Learn the history of a cranberry.↓ ¹⁷²

[63₂] The progress of Science is ever to the simple, to the one. God hides facts by placing them next us, as he hides the stars by day in a deluge of light.¹⁷³

¹⁶⁹ The page number is repeated.
¹⁷⁰ See "Humanity of Science," *Lectures*, II, 32, n. 14. The sentence is struck-through in pencil with a vertical use mark.
¹⁷¹ With "Nature . . . names.", cf. "Humanity of Science," *Lectures*, II, 26, 37, and 39. "Nature . . . somewhere.", paraphrased from Goethe, is also used in The Philosophy of History: "Introductory," *Lectures*, II, 16.
¹⁷² The paragraph, struck through in pencil with a vertical use mark, is used in "Humanity of Science," *Lectures*, II, 25–26; the passage in Journal B, p. [258], is used in the following paragraph, *ibid.*, p. 26. For "Learn . . . cranberry.", see B, p. [25]; one phrase from the passage is used in "Humanity of Science," *Lectures*, II, 30.
¹⁷³ A favorite simile of Emerson's, the paragraph, struck through in pencil with two diagonal use marks, is rewritten from Journal B, p. [83], and used in "Humanity of Science," *Lectures*, II, 31.

There is no object so foul, said I, that intense light will not make beautiful. [A 146] In like manner, is there nothing in nature disagreeable which Science does not b⟨re⟩ereave of its offence↑s↓ as anatomy may witness.[174]

When Phrenology came, men listened with alarm to the adept who seemed to insinuate with knowing look that they had let out their secret that ↑spite of themselves↓ he was reading them to the bone & marrow. They were presently comforted by learning that their human incognito would be indulged to them a short time longer until the artists had settled what allowance was to be made for temperament & what for counteracting organs, which trifling circumstances hindered the most ⟨tr⟩ exact observation from being of any value.[175] [C 145]

[64] passenger pigeon	J [B]	p. 257
study one object	"	p. 258
antecedence of spirit	"	260
Unifying tendency	"	264
Nature works unique through many forms	J. p. 273	
Unity of Nature never invites to indolence	" 275	
Character of natural phenomena	285	

Every law will some time or other become fact. [B 250]
Science is ⟨the reconstruction of nature in the mind.⟩ [176]

Buffon said, There is an original & Universal type (vorzeichnung) which may be followed very far. G. N. W. ⟨p⟩ Vol 10 p. 2⟨4⟩18

To separate & to knit up are two inseparable acts of life; it is forbidden to go out of the All into the particular, or out of the particular into the All & the more strictly these functions of the Spirit like inspiring & expiring breath, unite, the better for science & its lovers:

The Analogon of a form as the fore arm is not to mistake how far soever it goes as in fowl's wing though the extremities diminish in

---

[174] The paragraph is struck through in pencil with two diagonal use marks; "is there nothing . . . witness." is used in "Humanity of Science," *Lectures*, II, 33.

[175] This paragraph is struck through in ink with a diagonal use mark.

[176] The last part of this sentence is canceled in pencil. Except for the passage in Journal B, p. [250], parts of all these passages are used in "Humanity of Science," *Lectures*, II, 28, 26, 29–30 and 33, 22, 26, 33, 31–32, and 27.

number & show their identity sometimes by a monstrous formation as when the fingers ⟨are⟩ locked up in a horse's hoof sometimes show themselves.[177]

[66][178]   ⟨Poetry⟩
⟨The true poem sings itself⟩
Hence the two principles
1. a particular bone may always be found in its proper neighborhood however disguised

2. Economical nature spends justly, &c.[179]

Buffon confesses to a primitive & general design which can be followed far according to which all seems to have been conceived [180]

All parts of the Creature in particulars as in wholes will be found in all beasts

All variety of form springs from an overweight of this or that member in the Creature over the rest.
Giraffe   head & neck
Mole   body & rump
snake indefinitely long for no helforgans. Lizard
To no part is aught given without some thing being taken from some other part.[181]

---

[177] "Buffon said . . . themselves." is in pencil. Emerson is translating from Goethe, *Werke*, 1828–1833, L, 218, 223, 241, and 237; the fifteen volumes of *Nachgelassene Werke* are volumes 41–55 of *Werke* (see *JMN*, V, 127, n. 390). With "The Analogon . . . themselves.", cf. "Humanity of Science," *Lectures*, II, 28.

[178] Emerson omitted 65 in numbering to correct his pagination.

[179] "Poetry . . . itself" is canceled heavily; it is repeated on p. [106] below. Emerson wrote "Hence the . . . justly," in ink over almost the same in pencil, changing "latent" to "disguised" and adding the numbers and "&c." It is Emerson's translation from Goethe, *Werke*, 1828–1833, L, 240 and 241.

[180] "Buffon confesses . . . conceived", in pencil, is Emerson's translation from Buffon's French, quoted by Goethe in *Werke*, 1828–1833, L, 245.

[181] "All variety . . . rump" and "To no part . . . other part." are translations of and notes on Goethe, *Werke*, 1828–1833, LV, 205–206. With "snake indefinitely . . . Lizard", cf. *ibid.*, p. 208.

The abstract animal is to be deemed a small world, which ↑exists↓
for itself & through itself↑.↓ ⟨exists⟩ So is every animal its own aim &
because [67] all its parts stand in immediate reciprocity, have a relation
to each other, & thereby still renew the circle of life; so is every animal
to be esteemed physiologically perfect. No part of it is, inly seen,
useless or as they sometimes ⟨dep⟩represent it quite wilfully produced
through the plastic power, although parts outwardly may appear useless since the inner dependence of the beast nature so formed them,
without troubling itself about the external proportions. Of such members we should ask e.g. the —— tooth of Sus Barbirussa, not whereto
they serve, but whence spring they? It will not be said, A steer has
horns that he may push, but it will be inquired *how* he could have
horns in order to push.[182]

Camper followed the harmony of form, out even into the race
of fishes.

This also had we gained to be able to maintain unshamed that all more
perfect organic natures   under which we include fishes, Amphibiae,
fowls, Mammalia, & at top of the last man, are all formed after one [183]

[68] ↑NachG.W.   Vol 10 p 224↓ "Here were now the place to
say that the naturalist in this way first & easiest learns to know the
worth of a law, of a rule. If we see always the normal, we think it
must be so; forever is it so prescribed & therefore stable. But if we see
deviations, degradations, monsters, we learn, that the Law certainly
is firm & eternal, but also is alive; that the Creature can convert itself
⟨certainly⟩ not indeed out of itself, but within the same into defor-
mity, — but always as with bit & bridle holden back, must obey the
inexorable mastery of the law." [184]

Talent is call
Ambition proportioned [Q 52]

[182] Emerson translated the paragraph from Goethe, *Werke*, 1828–1833, LV,
206–207.

[183] "Camper . . . after one" is Emerson's translation from Goethe, *Werke*, 1828–
1833, LV, 261.

[184] Goethe, *Nachgelassene Werke*; volume 10 is volume L of the 55-volume edition of *Werke*, 1828–1833, in Emerson's library. The paragraph is struck through
in pencil with two curved, vertical use marks. Emerson used it, after revising his
translation, in "Humanity of Science," *Lectures*, II, 30.

⟨He⟩ ↑Each↓ has this ⟨thi⟩and none has other
All nature calls him to this
No competition but universal furtherance
He may have what good is intrinsic
He may see what he maketh
He may read what he writeth
↑He may solve secrets↓
He may associate as he is
He may have what place he will
He may teach [185]

[69]   Realism.   *Being.*[186]

What is appears. Every secret is told
Faces never lie
Truth tyrannizes over us
What you believe you must say [187]
↑It is said over your head↓
Your unbelief discredits you [188]
In will out   Sin blabs & daubs   Virtue shines
Concealment impossible

A man passes for his worth [189]
Do what you can do. Talent is Call
↑Ambition proportioned↓ [190]
He may have what place he will take

---

[185] "Talent . . . teach", in pencil, is an outline for "Spiritual Laws," *W*, II, 140–152. See p. [21] above. Emerson had used the first two entries in "Ethics," *Lectures*, II, 147–148.

[186] Cf. "Religion," *Lectures*, II, 95, and "Spiritual Laws," *W*, II, 160. P. [69], in pencil, continues the collection for "Spiritual Laws" begun on p. [68].

[187] These four entries are developed in "Spiritual Laws," *W*, II, 156–157. With the last two, cf. also "Being and Seeming," *Lectures*, II, 300–301.

[188] This entry refers to a paragraph in Journal C, p. [176], used in "Being and Seeming," *Lectures*, II, 300, and "Spiritual Laws," *W*, II, 156–157.

[189] With this and the two preceding entries, cf. "Religion," and "Ethics," *Lectures*, II, 95 and 150–151, and "Spiritual Laws," *W*, II, 157 and 159.

[190] This and the preceding entry are used in "Ethics," *Lectures*, II, 147–148, and "Spiritual Laws," *W*, II, 140–141.

He may have what society he is related to [191]
He may have what good is intrinsic
He may see what he maketh
He may read what he writeth
He may solve his secrets everywhere
He may teach by doing & not otherwise
    The effect of the writing is its truth. Bentley
    The effect of the action   its depth [192]
    The Man must be in the Manners or they are naught
    The preacher's classes [C 120] [193]

[70]   Being is all [194]
House praises the carpenter
Virtue its reward
The Crime is the punishment. Glaucus [195]
⟨Ec⟩Selfreliance is Economy
⟨Pertin⟩Depth of thought is pertinence

You may take your own everywhere [196]
Men lock up facts in secrets ·
          pictures in cabinets
          truth in mysteries
          Sympathy

[71]   Life m[igh]t. be simpler

[191] With this and the preceding entry (which refers to a passage from Journal D, p. [87], also used in "The Protest," *Lectures*, III, 101), cf. "Spiritual Laws," *W*, II, 150 and 151.

[192] These seven lines are an outline of "Spiritual Laws," *W*, II, 143–155. With the last two, cf. Journal D, p. [141]. A quotation ascribed to Bentley is used in "Literature," *Lectures*, II, 65, and "Spiritual Laws," *W*, II, 154; cf. Encyclopedia, p. [186].

[193] The passage in Journal C, p. [120], listed also in Notebook L Concord, p. [7] above, and on pp. [96] and [99] below, is used in "Eloquence," *W*, VII, 94.

[194] P. [70], in pencil, is probably a continuation of the collection for "Spiritual Laws" on pp. [68] and [69]. See p. [21] above. With "Being is all", cf. "Spiritual Laws," *W*, II, 160.

[195] See p. [21] above.

[196] With this and the preceding entry, cf. "Spiritual Laws," *W*, II, 144–145 and 153.

No need of convulsions   struggles   despairs
no need of knowing so much
We make ourselves unhappy
⟨Life⟩ ↑world↓ should be ↑a↓ happier place
Do not interfere
We miscreate our evils. Let well alone
We are begirt with spiritual laws [C 97]
Which execute themselves.[197]

We are full of mechanical actions. Our benevolence is unhappy. Our Sunday Schools and churches & Pauper societies are yokes to the neck. We pain ourselves to pleasure nobody. But be a good man & you help by looking, by speaking, by acting, Virtue goes out of you: you make humanity lovely. Why should all give dollars? [n] It is very inconvenient ↑to us,↓ and we do not think any good will come of it. We have not dollars. Merchants have. Let them give them. Farmers will give corn. Laborers labor.

Time enough to answer a question when it is asked. Don't drag your class to ask questions [198]

[72]   Politics [199]

The object of the modern politician is "to get the hurra on our side." [A 98, B 59]

Knowledge transfers the censorship from the statehouse to the reason of every citizen & compels every man to mount guard over himself & puts shame & remorse for Sargeants & maces. [A 146]

Every great man does in all his nature point at & imply the existence & well being of all the institutions & orders of a state. He is full of reverence. He is by inclination though far remote in position the defender of the Grammar School, the Almshouse, the Sabbath, the priest, the judge, the legislator, & the executive arm. Throughout his

---

[197] These nine entries, struck through in ink with a diagonal use mark, are developed in "Spiritual Laws," W, II, 135. Cf. also "Tendencies," Lectures, III, 312–313.

[198] "We are . . . nobody." is struck through in ink with five diagonal and three vertical use marks. "Why should . . . questions" is struck through in ink with four diagonal and two vertical use marks. The marked passages are used in "Spiritual Laws," W, II, 135–136.

[199] Pp. [72]–[79] contain material collected for the lecture "Politics," Lectures, II, 69–82.

being is he loyal. Such was Luther, Milton, Burke; each was an aristocrat though by position the champion of the people. [A 146]

————

The sea is the ring by which the nations are married [B 50]

————

Every one has a trust of power, — every man, every boy a jurisdiction, if it be only over a cow, or a rood of a potato ⟨p⟩field, or a fleet of ships, or the laws of a state. [B 214]
Wise was the word, "Stablish a democracy in your house." [BP I, 25]

In London, last year, they wrote on the walls "Of what use are the Lords?"[200] [B 115]

[73]   ↑PARTY↓
The aliases of the father of William the Conqueror who was called Robert the Magnificent or Robert the Devil, are a good specimen of every man's Janus reputation. [B 105]

————

A sect or party is an elegant incognito devised to save a man from the vexation of thinking. [BB Psi, 110]

————

⟨There would be no sect if there were no sect.⟩ Something has been overstated by the antecedent sect, & the human mind feels itself wronged, & overstates on the other side. Each sect is an extreme statement, See J. 1835 p. 290

"Call that which is just, equal; not that which is equal, just," said the Spartan.
                    V[ide]. Plut[arch's]. Mor[als] Vol 3 p. 432

In our age every party has written history for itself, as ⟨Li⟩Gibbon, Lingard, Brodie, Hume, Mitford, Hallam,[201]

[200] "The object . . . side.' " is struck through in pencil with a vertical use mark which is extended first through "Knowledge transfers . . . of the people." and then through "The Sea . . . married". The first three paragraphs are used in "Politics," *Lectures*, II, 81 and 78, while "The Sea . . . married" is used in "Trades and Professions," *Lectures*, II, 116 (see p. [92] below). "Every one . . . state.", though not use marked, and "In London. . . Lords?' ", struck through in pencil with a vertical use mark, are used in "Politics," *Lectures*, II, 77 and 80–81.
[201] "The aliases . . . Spartan." is struck through in pencil with two vertical

[74] Every cent in a dollar covers its worth; perhaps also covers its wo. If you covet the wealth of London, undoubtedly it would be a great power & convenience, but each pound & penny is a representative of so much commodity — so much corn & labor, — & of necessity also of so much evil. Could your wish transfer out of London a million pounds sterling into your chest, so would also against your wish just so massive an ill will & fear concentrate its black rays on you, — darkness that m[igh]t. be felt. It follows that whatever property you have must pay its full tax: if it come not out of the head it comes out of the tail. Pay the state its full dividend, & if your means increase pay society its full dividend by new exertion of your faculty for its service or you must pay the debt to fate, — to the Eumenides, in such dooms of loss, degradation, or death, as they shall choose[.] [B 250–251]

An able man is as rich as the world. How much water is there? You ask when the rain begins to fall; why all in the planet if wanted. And an able merchant takes up into his operations first & last all the property of the world. He bases his projects upon it. [B 251] [202]

[75] Vulgar princes think that the art of governing is the art of dissembling. Alfred did not. Charles V. [B 121]

Politics are now studied & practised ⟨in c⟩on the principles of Commerce.

"The English lawmakers took away our lands when they had given us rum." said the poor Indian of Maine.

The root & seed of democracy is the doctrine, Reverence thyself. How is he greater than I if he be not more just? It is the inevitable effect of that doctrine, where it has any effect, (which is rare) to insulate the partisan, to make each man a state.

---

use marks. Although "Party" is discussed in "Politics," *Lectures*, II, 81, the first three paragraphs are used in "Society," *Lectures*, II, 108. The quotation from Plutarch (from the London, 1718, edition in Emerson's library), struck through in ink with two additional diagonal use marks, and "In our age . . . Hallam," struck through in pencil with one vertical use mark, are used in "Politics," *Lectures*, II, 72 and 81.

[202] The first paragraph on p. [74] is struck through in pencil with two vertical use marks, each extended to the bottom of the page. "Every cent . . . tail." is used in "Politics," *Lectures*, II, 79. With this paragraph, cf. also "Compensation," *W*, II, 112–113. The last paragraph is used in "Trades and Professions," *Lectures*, II, 124.

"The speculative opinions of men in general between the ages of twenty &
thirty   the one great source of political prophecy." [203]

It is in vain that we affect indifference to the omens of public
change & depravation. Like ostriches we but hide our head in the sand.
We are like cabin passengers ⟨in⟩ who amuse themselves with cards
or music during a storm [204]
[76] It is the great man that makes the great place[.]
A very hard nut to crack. Gen Washington appears half-divine to the
people in his state followed by a nation's eyes. Some ambitious but
stupid person sees him & thinks it is the place alone that makes him
so great & that if he sat in the same chair he would be as much admired. All means are used[,] all sorts of degradation added to his
original mud & at last he sits in the high seat to be the pity & scorn of
all good men. Not beautiful to the eye.

"Democracy is a poor regulator but a powerful spring." Mitford. [BB I, 23]

———

The democrat abroad is a despot at home [BB I, 17]

Our age seems to be dis↑t↓inguished by the separation of real
power from its forms & the continual interference of the popular
opinion between the executive & its will. An unknown levity arises.
Thus the word Revolution is stripped of its terrors, & they may have
many in a year, [77] and they say in Paris, "there will be no revolution today, for it rains."
        ↑Read of Political Economy J. 1835 p 250, 326↓ [205]
If America should be sold today it would fetch more than yesterday.

[203] "Politics are . . . Commerce." is struck through in pencil with a vertical
use mark, and "The root . . . state." and " 'The speculative . . . prophecy.' "
with single diagonal ones. With "Vulgar princes . . . Charles V.", cf. "Ethics,"
and "Politics," *Lectures*, II, 154 and 79. With "Politics are . . . Commerce.", cf.
"The Present Age," *Lectures*, II, 161. "How is . . . just?" (Journal Q, p. [72])
and " 'The speculative . . . prophecy.' " are used in "Politics," *Lectures*, II, 70–71
and 78.
        [204] With "cabin passengers", cf. Notebook Δ, p. [74₁] below, and "Prudence,"
Lectures, II, 322.
        [205] "It is . . . eye." and "Our age . . . year," are struck through in pencil
with single vertical use marks on p. [76]; "Read of . . . 326" is added in pencil.
Both paragraphs and the passage cited in Journal B, p. [250], are used in "Politics,"
Lectures, II, 79–81. Cf. also *JMN*, IV, 169.

The low can best win the low, & all men like to be made much of. [B 308]

When fear enters the heart of a man at hearing the names of candidates, & the reading of laws that are proposed, then is the state safe; but when these things are heard without regard, as above or below us, then is the commonwealth sick or dead. [B 308]

When the philosopher comforts himself with general views over particular disasters to the state, let him not feel that he has any right to his solace so long as it is only derived ⟨from⟩ from the diversion of his mind, the mere hiding of his head in the sand ostrich-like, — not until he[n] sees that his consolation arises out of the evil itself, — that the relief which he contemplates is already working, — let him dare to give sleep to his eyelids, or joy to his soul.[206] [B 308]
Geology, Botany, ⟨b⟩Astronomy become ignominious, if cowardly sought. This is the demerit of Germany. [B 308]

[78] Civil History   J 1835   p. 280, 300

Quam parva sapientia. All society & govt seems to be making believe when we see such hollow boys with a grave countenance taking their places as legislators, presidents, & so forth. This could not be but that at intervals throughout society there are real men intermixed whose natural basis is broad enough to sustain these paper men in common times, as the carpenter puts one iron bar in his banister to five or six wooden ones.[207] [A 72]

Now will men burn down their neighbor's house to bake their own loaf[.]

Politics are also founded on the nature of things. It is very charming to have the reins not of corn, wine, or wool but of man. Few men can get the reins of the soul but they can of the body. They can hold the bread basket, & Govt. is nothing more; it is the boardinghouse. Agreeable as the most conspicuous interest, — that which puts[n] the individual into relation with all nations. Easier way to monopolize men than through the intellect, & admitting Counterfeit, easier.

[206] "The low . . . low," is used in "Politics," *Lectures*, III, 244–245. "When the philosopher . . . soul." is used in "Prudence," *Lectures*, II, 321–322.
[207] "All society . . . ones.", struck through in pencil with a vertical use mark, is used in "Politics," *Lectures*, II, 80.

[79] Res nolunt diu male administrari [BB II, 6, C 3, 8]

Govt. now admiñistered↓ on commercial principles
Dissimulation its art, — House of Seem.
Democracy in the nature of things. Every one has a trust of power
[B 214, F No. 1, 72]
⟨Use of⟩ ⟨abuse⟩ of power as in Alexander the Great [C 4]
Optimism is the faith of all minds
Antagonism of War & Trade
Congress of nations now possible
Forms no dam to nature.
Cent has its power, & person his power, let the law say what it
will. [B 250–251]

Strange, said the Dean of Peterboro, that Harrington should be the first to find out so evident & demonstrable a truth as that of property being the true basis & measure of power. [BB Y, 18]

Every pennyworth of corn preserves its radical nature through all its influence.[208]

Jan. 14. Insert in the Lecture the saying of Napoleon in J. 1835 p. 276

[⟨78⟩80]   ART
⟨J 1835 p. 185, 186, 115,⟩ [209]
"who speaks not clearly to the sense speaks also not clearly to the soul." Goethe.
"Every work of art sets us in that temper in which the author was when he made it. Was that cheerful & free, so shall we feel. Was that constrained, anxious, & careful; so draws it us likewise into a corner." [210]
Goethe

---

[208] Entries in ll. 1, 3–6, and 8–11 on p. [79] are used or developed in "Politics," *Lectures*, II, 75–82, though not in this order. With "Every pennyworth . . . influence.", cf. *ibid.*, p. 77.

[209] See p. [54] above, where the same references appear. The line is canceled in pencil.

[210] Cf. Journal C, p. [176], "The Eye and Ear," *Lectures*, II, 270, and "Spiritual Laws," *W*, II, 157.

The Arts languish now because their scope is exhibition; when they originated, it was to serve the gods. The Catholic Religion has turned them to continual account in its service. Now, they are mere flourishes.[211] Is it strange they perish? Poetry to be sterling must be more than a show, must have or be an earnest meaning. Chaucer, Wordswor↑t↓h vs Moore, Byron.

———

"You have practised your eye & hand; now practise your understanding."

———

"Our signboards show there has been a Titian in the world."

[BB II, 1, BB III, 57, B 7]

Art is a mixture of the human mind with nature.

[⟨79⟩81] Of useful art, I think the ↑decimal↓ cipher ⟨(zero⟩ to be the most elegant invention[212]

Art

[82]   ↑*ART*.↓

Our ⟨b⟩society is encumbered by ponderous machinery which ⟨will appear ludicrous⟩ resembles the infinite aquaducts which the Romans built over hill & dale & which are all superseded by the Discovery of the law that water ⟨finds its own⟩ rises to the level of its source; or the Chinese Wall which any nimble Tartar can jump over; or a standing army, which ⟨a peace⟩ ↑international law↓ supersedes; or a graduated ti⟨t⟩tled pampered royalty or Empire, which is quite unnecessary,— town meetings answering just as well.

———

Nature always works by short ways. *D* 247
        A Dis-inclination to society better than a bolt.
        House praises carpenter[213] [B 257]

---

[211] Cf. "Art," *Lectures*, II, 54.

[212] The sentence is struck through in pencil with a diagonal use mark. Cf. "Art," *Lectures*, II, 43.

[213] Both the paragraph above and the passage in Journal D, p. [247], are used in "Spiritual Laws," *W*, II, 136–137. "international law" and "Nature always . . . carpenter" are added in a smaller hand; "House . . . carpenter" is used in "Duty," *Lectures*, III, 149.

[83]   ↑ART.↓

⟨t⟩There's a divinity that shapes our ends
Roughhew them how we will [B 186]

Nothing bizarre, nothing whimsical will endure. Nature is ever inter-
fering with Art. ⟨y⟩You cannot build your house or pagoda as you will,
but as you must. There is a quick bound set to our caprice. The leaning
tower can only lean so far. The verandah or the pagoda roof can curve
upward only to a certain point. The s⟨t⟩lope of the roof is determined
by the weight of the snow. Gravity, wind, sun, rain, the size of men
& animals & such other aliens have more to say than the architect.
Beneath the almighty necessity ⟨r⟩therefore, I regard what is artificial
in man's life & works as petty & insignificant by the side of what is
natural. Every violation, every suicide, every miracle, every wilfulness, however large it may show near us, melts quickly into the All,
& at a distance is not seen. The outline is as smooth as the curve of
the moon.

And as nature controls us thus to our good, so does she yield
us, — ⟨m⟩the kind mother — all her strength when docile we yield to
her. All powerful action is performed [84] by bringing the forces of
nature to bear upon our objects. We do not grind corn or lift the loom
by our own strength, but we build a mill, & set the north wind to play
upon our instrument, or the expansive force of steam, or the ebb &
flow of the sea. So in our manipulations we do few things by muscular
force but we place ourselves in such attitudes as to bring the force of
gravity, the weight of the planet, that is, to bear upon the spade or the
axe we wield. — What is it that gives force to the blow of the axe, or
crow-bar? Is it the muscles of the laborer's arm, or is it the attraction
of the whole globe below it on the axe or bar? In short, in all our
operations, we seek not to use our own, but to bring a quite infinite
force to bear.

In a quite analogous manner are our intellectual works done. We
are to hinder our individuality from acting; we are to bring the whole
omniscience of Reason upon the sub- [214]

[214] P. [83] is struck through in pencil with a vertical use mark from "Nothing
bizarre," to the bottom of the page; "*ART*" is also added in ink at the top of p.
[84], and the page struck through in pencil with two vertical use marks. "⟨t⟩There's
a divinity . . . point." and "Gravity . . . moon." are copied from Journal B, p.

[85]–[88] [215] [2 leaves missing]
[8⟨7⟩9] principles of Art. J. 1835   p 242
    analogies of art   p 258 [216]

        Polarity through all things
        Everything a Half

        In animals compensation
        In faculties, fortunes, opportunities,
        in greatness
        in riches
        in bravoes
These facts teach the Omnipresence in atoms
We seek to be partial, to sever,
God to Integrate
Our detaching counteracted
Nor could be but for Ophthalmia
Inward Soul, Outward Law,
Inevitable conditions
Proverbs   Anecdotes   Trivial instances
Must pay
In Labor, no cheating
Goodness always gains; out of defects & disasters
Execution of the Law interior & essential [217]

[⟨88⟩90] What is justice but the universal necessity by which the whole ⟨is⟩appears wherever a part appears. If you see smoke there must be fire. If you see ↑a hand or↓ ⟨a⟩ limb, the trunk will be there also. ⟨If y⟩ [n] Often the specific stripes follow late after the offence, but

---

[186]. "All powerful action" to the end of p. [84] is copied from B, p. [188], but the order is changed. All three paragraphs are used in "Art," *Lectures*, II, 44, 45, and 49.

[215] Two leaves, at the center of a gathering, are missing between pp. [84] and [89], leaving no stub.

[216] These passages in Journal B, pp. [242] and [258], are used in "Thoughts on Art," *The Dial*, I (Jan. 1841), 375 and 376 (*Lectures*, II, 51 and 52); the first is also used in "Art," *W*, VII, 52–53, and the second in "History," *W*, II, 20–21.

[217] "Polarity . . . essential" is an outline in final order of "Compensation," *W*, II, 96–121.

they follow, because they attend. In the moment of offence they entered, though their celebration in some act to the tardy senses, may not be until long after.[218]

A scientific statement ↑of this law↓ is at once beautiful & salutary.

Every person who comes to me has two offices, — ⟨A⟩a present & a prophetical. He is at once ⟨the⟩ ↑a↓ fulfilment & a prediction. He is the long expected son returned, & he is a herald of a coming Friend.

[⟨8⟩91] [219]

[9⟨0⟩2]   Trade↑s & Professions↓ [220]
The sea is the ring by which the Nations are married. [B 50]
Savage on NW America holds up a shell & cries A Dollar [B 293]
        Sublime is in a ledger. [B] ↑p. 297↓
Antagonist of War inasmuch as it acquaints people. I will fight a Turk, for I do not know him; I will not fight an Englishman, for I have been in London.

Modern & American   Trade J. [B] p 294, 293 p. 272
        Am. vessel
Able man as rich as the world   J p 251
Trade   J. p.111 [221]

---

[218] This paragraph, struck through in ink with a vertical use mark, is used in "Compensation," W, II, 102 and 103.

[219] What may be a word in Greek, the only decipherable letters being "$\kappa\nu$", is written diagonally in the center of the page.

[220] "s & Professions" is added in pencil. Pp. [92]–[95] contain outlines and material collected for "Trades and Professions," Lectures, II, 113–128. Most of this material is used in the lecture, but not in this order. Emerson probably used and may have added to these notes in preparing the 1837 lecture "Doctrine of the Hands."

[221] "The sea . . . married." and "Savage on . . . people." are struck through in pencil with single diagonal use marks. "Sublime is . . . know him;" is struck through in pencil with a vertical use mark, while "know him . . . American" is struck through in pencil with a diagonal use mark which Emerson extended first through "Am. vessel" and then through "J. p.111". "p. 297", "Modern & . . . 272", and "Able man . . . 251" are in pencil. "The sea . . . married.", copied on p. [72] above, and "Savage on . . . A Dollar" are used in "Trades and Professions," Lectures, II, 116 and 128, and the lecture "Trade" (January 17, 1843). "Sublime

Potato, silk, tobacco, teaplant, Caoutchouc,
Solon's iron & gold [B 280]
Blessing of the Bay [B 280]
    Hold the plough or drive
    Buy by acre   sell by foot
Baseless   [B] p 23
    Climate; Naples & the North
To produce a pound of bread or of cloth what acquaintance with nature is needed
    Love of labor   World is full of allusion [222]

[93] Hand of artist is in his art is pure

    Moralities of trade
      Usefulness
        Morale of mining & crafts
        Dampier: advantage of steady pursuit. hammer & saw

      paying money in cities in lieu of kind
      native differences are the basis of each calling

    Anton Fugger

---

is . . . ledger." is used in "Trades and Professions," *Lectures*, II, 127, but cf. also "Sublime ubique" in Notebook Δ, pp. [144] and [145] below, and "Doctrine of the Hands," *Lectures*, II, 244. With "Antagonist of War", cf. "Politics," *Lectures*, II, 81, the lecture "Trade," and "War," *W*, XI, 156–157. Passages in Journal B, pp. [294], [293], [272], and [251], are used in "Trades and Professions," *Lectures*, II, 128 and 124; with "Am. vessel", cf. "Trade" also.

[222] "Solons iron . . . allusion" is in pencil. "Solons iron . . . Bay", struck through in pencil with a diagonal use mark, is used in "Trades and Professions," *Lectures*, II, 118 and 128; "Blessing of the Bay" is used in the lecture "Trade." "Hold the . . . foot" also appears in Notebook Δ, pp. [29], [144], and [145] below, in collections for "Doctrine of the Hands"; "Buy by . . . foot" is used in "Prudence," *Lectures*, II, 317. With "Baseless", cf. Journal C, p. [200], "Doctrine of the Hands," *Lectures*, II, 243, and "Prudence," *W*, II, 234–235. "Climate; Naples . . . labor" is struck through in pencil with one diagonal use mark and "To produce . . . needed" with another; cf. "Trades and Professions," *Lectures*, II, 122 and 119, 117, and 124; with "Climate; Naples . . . North", cf. also "Prudence," *Lectures*, II, 313–314, and *W*, II, 226. With "World is . . . allusion", cf. "Doctrine of the Hands," *Lectures*, II, 231–233.

Usefulness the true measure of respectability

    talk with carpenter   earth made of wood
    Mr ⟨Brunel⟩ Brindley

    Goethe's return of benefit
    Italy
    Sailor [223]
    ⟨The dearest labor is cheapest⟩ [B 208]
    The world owes us a living [224]

[94] How strongly guarded is the common sense [B] p 260

Power is never far from necessity
Labor is the soul in action upon the apparent world

Want is a growing giant, & *Have* could never cut a coat large
enow to cover him. [B 254]

    The heroic in work is to love the work better than the price. "For
the narrow mind whatever he attempts is still a trade[,] for the higher
an art & the highest in doing one thing does all or to speak less para-
doxically in the one thing he does rightly he sees the likeness of all
which is done rightly"

"All that frees talent without increasing self command is noxious"
                                       [B 164]
Nature gives us no sudden advantages. By the time we have acquired

[223] "Hand of . . . Sailor" is in pencil. The first line, struck through in pencil
with a vertical use mark, and "Moralities of . . . & saw" with a diagonal one, are
used in "Trades and Professions," *Lectures*, II, 124–126. See also Notebook Δ, p.
[144] below, "Doctrine of the Hands," *Lectures*, II, 245, and the lecture "Trade."
"paying money . . . calling" is also listed in Notebook Δ, pp. [29] and [145]
below; "native differences . . . calling" is developed in "Doctrine of the Hands,"
Lectures, II, 235–236. "Usefulness the . . . respectability", struck through in pencil
with a vertical use mark, is used in "Trades and Professions," *Lectures*, II, 124.
"talk with . . . Goethes", "Goethes return . . . Sailor", and "Sailor", each struck
through in pencil with a single diagonal use mark, are used in "Trades and Professions," *Lectures*, II, 125–126, 119–123, and 116–117.

[224] "The dearest . . . living" is struck through in pencil with a diagonal use
mark. The paragraph in Journal B, p. [208], is used in "Trades and Professions,"
Lectures, II, 127. See also Notebook Δ, pp. [29] and [145] below.

great power, we have acquired therewith enough wisdom to use it well.[225] Animal magnetism inspires the prudent & moral with a certain terror. Men are not good enough to be intrusted with such power[.]
[B 164]

[95] Cheapest say the Prudent is the dearest labor. In my garden I find it best to pay a man's price or to buy good sense applied to gardening; in the house, good sense applied to painting; good sense applied to building; &c. So do I multiply myself. [B 208]

An able man is as rich as the world [B 251]
He alone seems to me rich who is informed.
A man knows no more to any purpose than he practises. [B 279]
Values [B] p. 326
Saul son of Kish [226]

[96] [227]   One Mind
Preacher's classes [C 120]
Engineer's charity [C 63]
What pleases me pleases many [C 38]
Community   Identity of Nature   the ground of trust   C 128
⟨Conversation embarrassed by identity of conscio⟨s⟩usness⟩ D 79

[225] "How strongly . . . rightly' " is in pencil. "*Want* is . . . is to love the work" and "Nature gives . . . use it well.", struck through in pencil with single diagonal use marks, are used in "Trades and Professions," *Lectures*, II, 114 and 124–125.

[226] "An able . . . world" and "Values   p. 326" are in pencil. "Cheapest . . . myself." is struck through in pencil with a diagonal use mark, which Emerson extended through "An able . . . world". Both entries are used in "Trades and Professions," *Lectures*, II, 127 and 124; the first paragraph is also used in "Compensation," *W*, II, 114. With "He alone . . . informed.", cf. Journal B, p. [272], and "Trades and Professions," *Lectures*, II, 124; "A man . . . practises." is used in "Ethics," *Lectures*, II, 146. "Saul son of Kish", struck through in pencil with a diagonal use mark, is used in "Trades and Professions," *Lectures*, II, 115.

[227] Pp. [96] and [97], written not earlier than March 26, 1839, may be early notes for *Essays* [*First Series*]; with "One Mind", cf. p. [7] above. The notes on p. [96] are written over three small sketches in ink, one the figure of a man seen from the back, the other two heads in left profile, and a large pencil sketch of a man in left profile. Notes on p. [97] are written over a pencil sketch of a man's head and shoulders in left profile filling most of the page.

Intelligence of the Artwork makes it mine   D 83
Repentance of sin,   of the One mind   D 94
⟨Tacit reference in all conversation to a third party⟩ D 94
Science & Antiquities—effort to find myself ↑impersonal↓ in these
                                        things   D 160, 268

Anciently friends exchanged names   D 162
⟨A⟩Each man is one radius of my orb. D 168
In Shakspear's King Dick finds himself   D 211
        ⟨"And each ⁿ brave foe was in his heart a friend"   D 241⟩
                            ⟨Hector⟩
Why peep about to read Brant's story   Read ⟨your⟩ own   D 259
Epaminondas is Thou   D 267 ²²⁸
Literature is a looking glass   D 268
Books! Thou art the book's book. Protest.

[97] ↑That there is↓ One mind in all men
                    in conversation
                    in eloquence
                    in love
                    in virtue   Engineer's charity [C 63]
                    in biography
                    in Works of men; Antiquities
                    in literature

↑That↓ ⟨the soul is greater than its works⟩
        The same mind that man is of, made the world.
        Man lies in it, the ⟨less⟩ part in the whole
        Science is At-one-ment   D 160, 268 ²²⁹
        Art is connate with nature
        Genius & Virtue are eruptions of the Soul

²²⁸ The passages cited in Journal D, pp. [94], [259], and [267], are used in
"Spiritual Laws," D, p. [94], in "The Over-Soul," D, p. [160], in "History," and
D, p. [162], in "Friendship," *W*, II, 133–134, 164–165, and 162–163, 277, 11,
and 212.
    ²²⁹ With the entries in ll. 1, 3, and 6–9 on p. [97], cf. "History," *W*, II, 3, 38,
21, 23, 29 and 7. Part of the passage cited in Journal D, p. [160], is used, *ibid.*, p.
11. One sentence in D, p. [268], is used in "Intellect," *W*, II, 340.

[98]   Simplicity. Be & Seem [230]

We see all persons not natural with pity. D 307, ↑247↓ [231]

The Sabbath & the Prayer accuse the week & the day   D 308

Laws, letters, creeds, a travestie   D 304

We have surrendered to children the romance   D 305

Modern Heroism the wise life   D 304   299

A man amenable for the choice of his profession   D 303 [232]

Garden discovery   D 300

The moral of all Realism is truth of Character

Do not believe in *size* but in integrity   D 286, 289, 298 [233]

Strike sail to none ⟨F⟩D 287   You shall have your own friends. [234]

Always scorn appearances & you always may. D 269

Be greatly content. D 266   261 [235]

Conformist's two not two. D 265 [236]

Peeping   D 264, 259   Isolation 260, 280,

We care not for Fourth July orators   D 247

Nature always works by short ^{n} ways;   ⎡ Falling ^{n} D 247
                                          ⎣ ↑Heat   C 333↓ [237]

---

[230] See Journal F No. 2, p. [25], where "Simplicity" appears in a list of suggested essay titles; it may have been an early title for "Spiritual Laws"; the first 17 lines on p. [98] are probably an early collection for that essay. See also a paragraph on the "simplicity of the universe" in "Spiritual Laws," *W*, II, 137–138. With "Be & Seem", cf. "Ethics," *Lectures*, II, 150, "Being and Seeming," *Lectures*, II, 295–309 (parts of which are used in "Spiritual Laws"), and "Spiritual Laws," *W*, II, 160.

[231] The paragraph in Journal D, p. [247], is used in "Spiritual Laws," *W*, II, 152.

[232] This paragraph in Journal D, p. [303], is used in "Spiritual Laws," *W*, II, 140.

[233] This line is struck through in ink with two short diagonal use marks. All three passages are used in "Spiritual Laws," *W*, II, 160–161, 161–162, and 163. Those in Journal D, pp. [289] and [298], are also used in "Reforms," *Lectures*, III, 266–267 and 267–268.

[234] Cf. "Spiritual Laws," *W*, II, 150–151, where the paragraph in Journal D, p. [287], is used.

[235] This line is struck through in ink with a diagonal use mark. The passage in Journal D, p. [266], is used in "Reforms," and that in D, p. [261], in "Literature" [second lecture], *Lectures*, III, 267 and 230–231; both are used in "Spiritual Laws," *W*, II, 162–163 and 164.

[236] This passage and that in Journal D, p. [269], above, are used in "Tendencies," *Lectures*, III, 309 and 311, and "Self-Reliance," *W*, II, 54–55 and 59.

[237] "Peeping" is struck through in ink with a diagonal use mark which is ex-

History Subjective   Every man may live it all.

We are always coming up with the poetry & the history that have delighted us. Only there seems an unnecessary variety of persons.

↑D ⟨219⟩, ⟨274⟩, ⟨300⟩, ⟨314⟩, ⟨322⟩, ⟨8,⟩ ⟨8⟨2⟩9,⟩ ⟨205b, 206a, 217,⟩ C ⟨52⟩, ⟨128   146   155   175⟩ ⟨184, 179, 250,⟩ ⟨286,⟩↓ ²³⁸

    Travelling ⟨D 303   C 143⟩ ²³⁹

    Great man among small objects   D 310, 55,

    Two absolutions ⟨D 312   C 328⟩ ²⁴⁰

    Self trust ⟨D 320⟩, ⟨10, 30, 68,⟩ ⟨143,⟩ ⟨97, 98⟩,²⁴¹ C ⟨96, 102⟩, ⟨149⟩ ⟨B 202⟩ ⟨D 50⟩, ⟨Q 71,⟩ ²⁴²

[99] Plain greatness ⟨D 37⟩ ²⁴³

The sick & insane have a good deal to teach the plain dealer   166 D ²⁴⁴

---

tended through "We care" and then through "Nature". Another diagonal use mark strikes through "Isolation" and "Fourth" and is extended through "works by". Passages in Journal D, pp. [264] and [259], are used in "Literature" [second lecture], *Lectures*, III, 230 and 231, and "Spiritual Laws," *W*, II, 164–165. The two passages on "Isolation" are used in "Self-Reliance," *W*, II, 71–72. The first passage listed in D, p. [247], is used in "Politics," and the second in The Present Age: "Introductory," *Lectures*, III, 244 and 189; both are used in "Spiritual Laws," *W*, II, 152 and 137. The passage in C, p. [333], is used in "Nature," *W*, III, 179.

  ²³⁸ "History Subjective . . . 286," is apparently a collection for the essay "History." "History Subjective . . . persons." is used in "History," *W*, II, 9–10. Passages from all the pages listed in Journal D are used in "History," *W*, II, 27–28, 9 and 23, 10 and 28, 10, 18, 7 and 18, 9 and 5–6, 16, and 27. Passages from C, pp. [52], [146], [155], [184], and [286], are used in "History," *W*, II, 33, 4, 10, 11–12 and 10–11, and 28. See p. [101] below.

  ²³⁹ Passages from Journal D, p. [303], and C, p. [143], are used in "Self-Reliance," *W*, II, 81–82 and 45.

  ²⁴⁰ Passages from Journal D, p. [312], and C, p. [328], are used in "Self-Reliance," *W*, II, 74.

  ²⁴¹ All seven passages cited in Journal D are used in "Self-Reliance," *W*, II, 72 and 73, 47, 57, 49, 61, and 56. That from D, p. [10], is also used in "Duty," *Lectures*, III, 139, and those from D, pp. [97] and [98], in "Tendencies," *Lectures*, III, 310. Passages in D, p. [143], are used in both "Tendencies," and "Politics," *Lectures*, III, 305 and 243.

  ²⁴² Passages from Journal C, pp. [96] and [102]–[103], B, p. [202], and Q, p. [71], are used in "Self-Reliance," *W*, II, 46, 48, 53, and 45 and 83. C, p. [102], is also used in "The American Scholar," *W*, I, 105; B, p. [202], in "Ethics," *Lectures*, II, 152; and D, p. [50], in "Literary Ethics," *W*, I, 170 and 184–185.

  ²⁴³ The paragraph in Journal D, p. [37], is used in "Religion," *Lectures*, III, 284–285, and "The Over-Soul," *W*, II, 290.

  ²⁴⁴ The passage in Journal D, p. [166], is used in "The School," *Lectures*, III, 42.

Identity — indifferency of things   D 265   55   C 164 [245]
[Crump; [246] See Montaigne sentence   C p. 9
      Wherever we are we stand for Man, & for the world.[247]
              ↑Jonathan Phillips↓ [C 58]
    Every thing is my cousin   C 120
    One mind   C ⟨128⟩
Foolish face of praise   C 138
True man belongs to his age   C 143 [248]
Learn the whole for yourself. ⟨C 155⟩

[Tree gets $\dfrac{19}{20}$ from air   C 157

    [Thinker & Doer   C 309 [249]

    Civilization fast becomes Barbarism as baggage impedimenta. Sol-
diers carrying all   C ⟨31⟨7⟩5⟩
Bivouac ⟨C 329⟩ [250]
Every man should write literature for himself   D 190   B 98
Jesus to be lived   D ⟨219⟩
    The Foreworld is the Inworld ⟨D 274⟩
    Self reliance. ⟨Ze⟩New Zeno. D 300
    No history but biography   D ⟨300⟩, 322
    Alcott the Stylite   D ⟨314⟩   Sardanapalus ⟨C 175⟩

[245] With "indifferency of things", cf. "all circumstances indifferent." in "Self-Reliance," W, II, 61. The passage Emerson probably meant in Journal D, p. [265], is used in "Art," W, II, 355–356, but the second paragraph on the page is used in "Tendencies," Lectures, III, 309, and "Self-Reliance," W, II, 54–55. The passage in C, p. [164], is used in "The Head," Lectures, II, 253–254, and "Intellect," W, II, 332–333.

[246] Cf. Journal D, p. [94], used in "Spiritual Laws," W, II, 134.

[247] Cf. "I will stand here for humanity," in "Self-Reliance," W, II, 60.

[248] The passage cited in Journal C, p. [138], is used in "Tendencies," and that in C, p. [143], in "Politics," Lectures, III, 309–310 and 242. Both passages are used in "Self-Reliance," W, II, 55 and 60–61.

[249] With "Thinker & Doer", cf. "Doctrine of the Soul," The Present Age: "Introductory," and "Politics," Lectures, III, 7, 188, and 242, and "Self-Reliance," W, II, 60.

[250] With this and the preceding entry, cf. "Self-Reliance," W, II, 86–87, where Emerson uses a quotation from Las Cases copied in Journal C, p. [315].

I see the creation of sun & moon ⟨D 8⟩ (Socrates [C] ⟨286⟩
E. H.'s Fairies D ⟨89⟩
Life stuck round with Egypt ↑D↓ ⟨205⟩
Manners like Parthenon friezes   D 206
Tripod   D ⟨217⟩
New Faust ⟨C 52⟩ [251]

[⟨98⟩100]   Rhetoric
Once I was present at Academical exercises & heard what was
called the best performance but it was founded on nothing & led to
nothing. Then arose a speaker & made as if he was in earnest with
pathetic tones & gesture & most admired expressions and all about
nothing & he was answered by others with equal apparent earnestness
& still it was all nothing. The building seemed to grudge its rent if
the assembly did not their time. Stetson who jokes seems the only wise
man. Pity that 300 men should make believe Debate. [B 60]

Who is the most decorous man? not ⟨w⟩Who speaks most truth? In
the orations of Demosthenes & Burke ⟨c⟩how many irrelevant things,
⟨of w⟩sentences, words, letters are there? Not one. ⟨Go into⟩ ↑Enter↓
one of our cool Churches & begin to count the words that might be
spared, & in most places the entire sermon will go. One sentence kept
another in countenance, but not one by its own weight could have
justified the saying of it. It is the Age of Parenthesis: You might put
all we say in bracketts, it would not be missed. I hope the time will
come when phrases will [101] be gazetted as no longer current. Now
literature is nothing but a sum in the Arithmetical rule of Permutation
& Combination. [B 101] [252]
          Who sees necessity of Fr. Rev. C ⟨128⟩
     History Subjective. Every man may live all. C ⟨146⟩, ⟨184⟩ 179 [253]

---

[251] "Jesus . . . ⟨C 52⟩" is crowded in in a smaller hand at the bottom of the
page. All the passages listed except "Self reliance . . . D 300" and "⟨C 175⟩" are
used in "History," W, II, 27–28, 9 and 23, 10 and 28, 18, 28, 18, 9 and 5–6, 16,
27, and 33. For "Self reliance. . . . D 300", see Journal D, pp. [299]–[300], used
in "Self-Reliance," W, II, 75–76, and "Reforms," Lectures, III, 264–265.

[252] P. [100] is struck through in pencil with a wavy vertical use mark; "be
gazetted . . . Combination.", on p. [101], is struck through in ink with five diagonal
use marks. Both paragraphs are used in "The Present Age," Lectures, II, 163.

[253] "History Subjective . . . all." and passages from Journal C, pp. [146] and

Every soul the whole lesson   C 155, 175
Be the man that made the minster   C 184 [254]
Why defer to Pym & Vane. C 178, 173 [255]
Modern Antiquity   C ⟨250⟩ [256]
Not by running after Napoleon   D 261 [257]
    Self action best. D 141

    Every body will judge you by your own rule   Q 122 [258]
There is one mind
That wrote history & must read it
The hero, the sage, the saint, was there for man & for me.
I learn to read proudly: to transfer the point of view: Egypt ⟨and⟩
Greece   what are you to me. I sit at home.
    I must learn all by myself
I learn that a few facts outvalue many.
      that effects are many, but causes few, & I learn these.
      form mutable
      Greek history
      origin of the arts
      All study in thought
      same principle a wide variety of surface action as Itera-
                    tion
So in all Fable it is the same, I bring it home [259]

[10⟨0⟩2]   The Soul a Light not a faculty

---

[184], are used in "History," W, II, 10, 8, 4, and 11–12 and 10–11. The passage
from C, p. [179], is used in "Private Life," Lectures, III, 250.
   [254] The passages cited in Journal C, pp. [155] and [184], are used in "History,"
W, II, 10 and 12. The second is also used in "The Eye and Ear," Lectures, II, 268.
   [255] Passages from Journal C, pp. [178] and [173], are used in "Self-Reliance,"
W, II, 62–63. The sentence cited in C, p. [173], is also used in "Heroism," W, II,
258 (Lectures, II, 335).
   [256] All of Journal C, p. [250], is used in Human Culture: "Introductory,"
Lectures, II, 225–226.
   [257] This passage in Journal D, p. [261], is used in "Literature" [second lecture],
Lectures, III, 230–231, and "Spiritual Laws," W, II, 164, but cf. also "History,"
W, II, 8.
   [258] A computation inscribed earlier in pencil underlies this and the preceding six
lines.
   [259] "There is one mind . . . home" is an outline of "History," W, II, 3–30.

when it ⟨breathes⟩ ↑pours↓ [260] through the intellect it is
genius.
When it breathes through the Will it is virtue,
And the sickness of the intellect ⟨is⟩& of the Will   is
          Interference.

The soul broods over every society
A common sense

          Humanity of Shakspeare
                    of Wordsworth
                    Homer
                    Milton [B 225]

          The soul a discerner of spirits [261] [D 225]

[103] The borrower runs in his own debt. Has a man gained
anything who has received a hundred favors & rendered none? [n] Has
he gained anything by borrowing his neighbor's wares or horses? The
transaction remains in the memory of himself & his neighbor and
every transaction alters their relation to each other. He ⟨will⟩ ↑may↓
soon come to see that he had better have broken his own bones than
to have ridden in his neighbor's coach, and that the highest price ⟨of⟩
↑he can pay for↓ a thing is to ask for it. [262]

I have a present. It makes it clearer to me that I am paid for
every thing I do, & I need not be too solicitous ⟨of⟩ about the mode.
The difference betwixt the present & the receiv.[in]g. payment of a
bill is a lively pleasure which rewards the trustfulness of him who
did not stipulate for his price. Still more the ⟨joy of a⟩ burst of admiration at your magnanimity & long suffering in some ⟨th⟩ unthanked

[260] The cancellation and "pours" are in pencil.
[261] P. [102] contains notes for "Doctrine of the Soul," *Lectures*, III, 15–18,
used in this order in the lecture. The same passages are used in "The Over-Soul," *W*,
II, 270, 271, 278, 276, 288, and 285. In the left margin is a diagonal mark in ink
from "genius." to "And the sickness".
[262] Emerson indexed p. [103] "Compensation". This paragraph, struck through
in pencil with a diagonal use mark, is used in "Compensation," *W*, II, 112–113.
With "the highest . . . ask for it.", cf. a quotation from Landor in Encyclopedia,
p. [186].

ben↑e↓ficence, awakens a far livelier joy in your heart which returns to you the rare good of kindness done without hope of kindness, & without spectator. Then [263]

[104] [264]   Science
Nature revealed as the production of the Soul
    Science is At-one-ment   D 160, 268
    Not sufficient to know one thing   D 284
Doctrine of the Metamorphosis   D 58
    Apercues. D 101
    See D 319 [265]

[105] serve. If you serve an ungrateful master serve him the more assiduously. Be wholly his. And like the Indian Rajah the Universe becomes indebted to you. The Hours & the Centuries must pay.[266] I like well the sublime indifference of the Buddhist to favors. "Never flatter your benefactors," he saith.[267] They are paid for every kernel of rice. Why should I doubt the justice of Nature by profuse thanks.
I pass for what I am↑;↓ ⟨worth⟩ & I am content to pass for what I am.

Do not believe that possibly you can escape the reward of your action. You serve an ungrateful master: Serve him the more. Be wholly his. Embrace any service, do what you will, & the master of

---

[263] Continued on p. [105] below. "It makes . . . the mode." is written over two capital D's in pencil.

[264] Emerson apparently laid a loose sheet, with five lines crossed through horizontally and with one diagonal line, first on p. [104] and then on p. [105]; both pages show traces of ink offset at different angles.

[265] This collection is probably for a later reading of "Humanity of Science," made some time after June 18, 1839. The passage in Journal D, p. [284], is printed as part of "Humanity of Science," *Lectures*, II, 26. The passage in D, p. [160], is used in "Home," *Lectures*, III, 30, and "History," *W*, II, 11, and the passage in D, p. [268], in "Intellect," *W*, II, 340. Two paragraphs in D, p. [101], are used in "The School," *Lectures*, III, 49 and 46–47. A passage in D, p. [319], is used in "History," *W*, II, 16–17.

[266] "If you serve . . . more", from the paragraph in Journal Q, p. [17], transcribed below, is used, and "the Universe . . . must pay." is paraphrased, in "Compensation," *W*, II, 119.

[267] Cf. Journal E, p. [155]; the quotation is used in "The Transcendentalist," *W*, I, 337, and "Gifts," *W*, III, 163–164.

your master, the law of laws, will secure your compensation. Every man is valued as he makes himself valuable.[268] [Q 17]

Who receive hospitality? the hospitable. Q 24   27[269]

[106]   Poetry.
    The true poem sings itself[270]

Love is a thauma⟨r⟩turgist. See how he converts a chair, a table, a scrap of paper, a lock of hair, a faded weed into amulets worth the world. Who can see o⟨f⟩ut of what straws he builds his Elysium, without understanding somewhat of miracles?[n] [D 309][271]

> Be not hindered by name of goodness
> Nothing sacred but your integrity
> If I am the devil's child   B 50
> ⟨Be not hindered by the name of goodness⟩
> Coat & boots   C 293[272]

Out with it, man. Let their ears tingle. Let them say   We never saw it in this manner.

> I am owner of the sphere
> Of the seven stars & the solar year
> Of Caesar's hand and Plato's brain
> Of Jesus' heart & Shakspeare's strain[273]

---

[268] The first sentence in this paragraph is used in "The Transcendentalist," *W*, I, 337, with the quotation above; the second is used in "Compensation," *W*, II, 119, and the last in "Trades and Professions," *Lectures*, II, 125. The entire paragraph is transcribed in Notebook Man, p. [71] above.

[269] Emerson developed this sentence in two different paragraphs in Journal Q, pp. [24] and [27]; he combined them in Notebook Man, pp. [70]–[71] above.

[270] Cf. Journal D, p. [213]. The sentence is canceled on p. [66] above and transcribed in Encyclopedia, p. [92].

[271] This paragraph is used in "Religion," *Lectures*, III, 279. "Endives" is written below it in ink in an ornate hand, probably practice penmanship.

[272] "Be not . . . C 293", in a smaller hand like that of p. [107] following, is struck through in ink with two vertical use marks. All four passages (one is repeated) are used in "Self-Reliance," *W*, II, 50 and 51. The first two passages are used in "Tendencies," *Lectures*, III, 308–309.

[273] These lines, from "The Informing Spirit," ll. 5–8, *W*, IX, 282, are used as the motto to "History," *W*, II, 2.

[107]   Self trust
               Truth of Character
⟨We must abandon ourselves to the Eternal in the heart   D 10⟩
⟨Cumber yourself never with the Past or consistency   D 30, 334   112
                                                                    B 216⟩
⟨True scholar's word would put men in fear   D 68⟩
⟨Tom & Dick are possibilities as great as Caesar   D 143⟩
⟨Value of sour faces⟩ D 98
⟨Keep a sweet face   D 97   even when the mud boils   D 97⟩
⟨Abide by y[ou]rself chiefly when all say the contrary   C 96⟩
⟨Infancy   youth   puberty have their own charm   C 103⟩ [274]
Good intention the back bone of the world   C 149
⟨If I am the devil's child I will be the devil's⟩ child   B 50
⟨You will always find those who think they know your duty better
than you⟩ B 202
⟨Foolish face of praise   C⟩ 138
⟨Admonition of an original thought C 143,⟩ True man measures you
                                                    C 143, [275] Bruce
⟨I believe in the being God   C 56⟩
⟨If you admire the world admire yourself   C 155⟩
⟨Schelling   Kant   & Spinoza only return myself. C 165⟩ [276]
⟨When private men shall act with vast views the man king comes,
                                                    C 173   178⟩ [277]
⟨Don't accept the fame of Aeschylus   C 181⟩ [278]

[274] The eleven passages listed above are all used in "Self-Reliance," W, II, 47,
57, 58, 49, 61, 56, 46, and 48. Journal D, p. [10], was used earlier in "Duty,"
Lectures, III, 139; D, pp. [334], [98], and [97], were also used in "Tendencies,"
and D, p. [143], in "Politics," Lectures, III, 310 and 242–243; B, p. [216], was
used earlier in "Ethics," Lectures, II, 149.

[275] Passages in Journal B, pp. [50] and [202], C, p. [138] and both passages
in C, p. [143], are used in "Self-Reliance," W, II, 50, 53, 55, 45, and 60–61. That
in B, p. [202], was used earlier in "Ethics," Lectures, II, 152; C, p. [138], was also
used in "Tendencies," Lectures, III, 309–310; and C, p. [143], in "The Head,"
Lectures, II, 260, and "Politics," Lectures, III, 242.

[276] The passage in Journal C, p. [165], is used in "The Head," Lectures, II, 260–
261, and "Intellect," W, II, 344–345.

[277] Passages in Journal C, pp. [173] and [178], are used in "Self-Reliance," W,
II, 62–63.

[278] The passage in Journal C, p. [181], is used in "The Head," Lectures, II, 260,
and "Intellect," W, II, 344.

⟨The soul no charity boy or bastard, C 186   H. C. Lect. I p 32⟩ [279]
When you are sincerely pleased without misgiving you are nourished
[C 188]

Wild men & tame men   C 188   Man in love
⟨Shakspeare will never be made by the study of Shakspear   C.113.⟩
⟨Treat things books sovereign genius as a sovereign   C 113⟩ [280]
Pride is selftrust [281] [C 121]
Nail box   C 129 [282]
⟨Over-influence of a coat & boots & hypocrites   C 293⟩
⟨What I do is all that concerns me not what they think   C 306⟩
⟨Genius deserts me when I desert myself, C 306⟩
⟨We are a mob   D 259⟩
⟨Kings make their own scale   D 263⟩
⟨Ask nothing of men & thou oh firm column &c   D 284⟩
⟨Keep thy state do not all descend   D 280⟩ [283]
[108]   ⟨Believe your own thought [B 185] Lect.⟩ Ethics
          ⟨Never imitate [A 88] Ethics⟩
          ⟨Nothing sacred but your integrity   Ethics⟩ [284]
          ⟨Cumulative power of character⟩
     ⟨Do not regret calamities even but do your work   C 82⟩ [285]
          ⟨Secondariness   D 41⟩
          Man-Magazine   C 57, 70, 260. D 1, 10   C 293   A 126
          ⟨Self reliance of Genius   B 102⟩ [286]

[279] The passage in Journal C, p. [186], used earlier in Human Culture: "Introductory," Lectures, II, 223, is used in "Self-Reliance," W, II, 61–62.
[280] Emerson used the first of these two sentences in Journal C, p. [113], in "Self-Reliance," W, II, 83; the second he had used earlier in "The Head," Lectures, II, 260.
[281] Cf. "Private Life," Lectures, III, 248–249.
[282] The passage in Journal C, p. [129], is used in "Prudence," Lectures, II, 314, and "Prudence," W, II, 227.
[283] Passages in Journal C, pp. [293] and [306], and D, pp. [259], [263], [284], and [280], are used in "Self-Reliance," W, II, 51, 47, 71, 63, 89, and 72.
[284] These three passages, taken from "Ethics," Lectures, II, 152 and 151, are used in "Self-Reliance," W, II, 45, 83, and 50.
[285] "Cumulative . . . character" and the paragraph in Journal C, p. [82], are used in "Self-Reliance," W, II, 59 and 78; the first is also used in "Tendencies," Lectures, III, 311, and cf. "Duty," Lectures, III, 144.
[286] Passages from Journal D, p. [10], C, p. [293], A, p. [126], and B, p. [102], are used in "Self-Reliance," W, II, 47, 51, 61, and 45–46. B, p. [102], is also used in "Genius," Lectures, III, 77.

⟨The Reason of Self Trust is indeed very deep.⟩ [287]
⟨Bivouac [C] 329, 315,⟩ [288]　　　　↑Phil Hist. Lect XII↓ [289]
⟨Travelling　C 143　D 303⟩
⟨Be Sacred　D 320⟩
⟨Two absolutions　C 328　D 312⟩
New Zeno　D 300 [290]
⟨He only can teach himself　Q 71⟩ [291]
⟨Always scorn appearances & you may　D 269⟩
↑⟨Cumulative power of character⟩↓
⟨Conformist's two not two. D 265⟩ [292]
⟨Plain greatness　D 37⟩ [293]
⟨Be not deceived by this buzz about progress there is none
but to the individual⟩
⟨Phil. Hist. Lect XII⟩
　　Reason of trust is very deep
"Selfreliance is reliance on God" Bettina
　　If you admire the world admire yourself　C 155
　　We must abandon us to the Eternal within　D 10 [294]
　　⟨I believe in the Being God　C 56⟩
　　⟨Trouble yourself not with Consistency　B 216⟩ D 30
　　　　　　　　112　334　324　337 [295]

[287] This sentence is used in "Genius," *Lectures*, III, 78, and cf. "Self-Reliance,"
W, II, 63.

[288] Cf. "Self-Reliance," *W*, II, 87.

[289] See "The Individual," *Lectures*, II, 174–175, for a long passage used in
"Self-Reliance," *W*, II, 84–87. See also "Be not deceived . . . XII" below.

[290] Passages in Journal C, p. [143], D, pp. [303], [320], [312], and
[300], are all used in "Self-Reliance," *W*, II, 60–61, 81–82, 72 and 73, 74, and
75–76. With "Two absolutions" and C, p. [328], cf. "Self-Reliance," *W*, II, 74.

[291] Two passages in Journal Q, p. [71], are used in "Self-Reliance," *W*, II, 45
and 83.

[292] The passage in Journal D, p. [269], "Cumulative . . . character", and a
passage in D, pp. [265]–[266], are used in "Self-Reliance," *W*, II, 59 and 54–55,
and "Tendencies," *Lectures*, III, 311 and 309. A curved line in the left margin connects "Cumulative" with "Trouble" below.

[293] See p. [99] above.

[294] "Reason of . . . D 10" is struck through in ink with a vertical use mark.
With the first two entries, cf. "Self-Reliance," *W*, II, 63–64. The passage in Journal
D, p. [10], is used in "Duty," *Lectures*, III, 139, and "Self-Reliance," *W*, II, 47.

[295] "B 216 . . . 337" is written in a slanting column in the right margin and
struck through in ink with a diagonal use mark. All the passages cited are used in

⟨True man measures the world   C 143⟩
        ⟨puts men in fear   D 68⟩
        ⟨draws all men unto him   D 284⟩
⟨Infancy youth &c their own charm   C 103⟩ [296]
When you are pleased you grow [297]
[109] ⟨Admonition of original thought⟩ ⟨C 143⟩   ⟨Ethics⟩
⟨Believe your own thought⟩   ⟨Ethics⟩
⟨Never imitate [A 88] *Ethics* Genius deserts me when I desert⟩
                                                         ⟨C 3ʋ6⟩

⟨Shakspear not made by study of Shakspear⟩   ⟨C 113⟩
⟨He only can teach himself⟩ ⟨Q 71⟩
⟨Self reliance of genius⟩ ⟨B 102⟩ [298]
⟨Treat things books sov genius as thyself sovereign⟩ C 113
⟨Schelling   Kant   Spinosa   C 165   Aeschylus   C 181⟩ [299]
⟨There is for me now the large utterance of the early gods
                                          D 274⟩ [300]

⟨Abide by yourself then most when contradicted   C 96⟩
⟨What I do is all that concerns me, not what they think   C 306⟩
⟨Conformist's two not two   D 265⟩
⟨You will always find those who know your duty   B 202⟩
⟨Foolish face of praise   C 138⟩

"Self-Reliance," *W*, II, 58, 57, 59, and 54. The first had been used in "Ethics,"
Lectures, II, 149, and the last three are also used in "Tendencies," *Lectures*, III, 310,
311, and 309.

[296] Passages from Journal C, p. [143], D, pp. [68] and [284], and C, p. [103],
are used in "Self-Reliance," *W*, II, 60–61, 49, 89, and 48. The first is also used in
"Politics," *Lectures*, III, 242.

[297] Cf. Journal C, p. [188], p. [107] above, and Notebook Δ, p. [20] below.

[298] "Admonition . . . B 102" is struck through in ink with a vertical use mark.
A curved ink line in the left margin connects "Never" with "There is" in l. 9
below. All seven passages are used in "Self-Reliance," *W*, II, 45, 83, 47, 83, and
45–46. The first three are from "Ethics," *Lectures*, II, 151–152.

[299] This and the preceding entry are connected by a brace in ink in the left
margin; a curved ink line in the left margin extends from the brace to between
"Soul" and "Tom" in ll. 18 and 19 below. All three passages from Journal C, pp.
[113], [165], and [181], are used in "The Head," *Lectures*, II, 260–261, and
"Intellect," *W*, II, 344–345.

[300] This line is struck through in ink with a vertical use mark. The passage in
Journal D, p. [274], is used in "Self-Reliance," *W*, II, 83–84.

⟨Sweet faces⟩⌉
⟨Sour faces⟩ ⌋ D 97, 98 [301]

We are a mob   D 259
⟨Soul no charity boy or bastard   H C Lect I p 32   C 186⟩
Tom & Dick possibilities of Caesar   D 143
Kings make their own scale   D 263 ⟨Man king   C 173, 178.⟩
⟨Keep thy state   D 280,⟩ 2
Be Sacred   ⟨D 320⟩
            ↑⟨Isolation must precede⟩↓ [D 260]
But Be
Two Absolutions   C 328   D 312 [302]
Plain Greatness   D 37 [303]

[110]   Do not wail but do your work   C 82
                Don't fret & pout   All men are great as ↑you↓
                ⟨well as you⟩ C 57
                Be you somebody (to offer) C 70
                Excuse not thyself with words   D 308 [304]

The divine economy of selftrust

The Church does not respect Man   D 259

Explain yourself by doing your work   D 337 [305]

[301] All seven passages cited in "Abide by . . . 98" are used in "Self-Reliance," W, II, 46, 53, 54–55, 53, 55, and 56. The passage in Journal B, p. [202], was also used in "Ethics," Lectures, II, 152; those in C, p. [138], and D, pp. [265], [97], and [98], are used in "Tendencies," Lectures, III, 309–310. The passage on "Sweet faces" in D, p. [97], is also used in "Culture," W, VI, 159.

[302] All eleven passages cited from "We are a mob . . . D 312" are used in "Self-Reliance," W, II, 61–74, though not in the order listed. Emerson used the passage in Journal C, p. [186], in Human Culture: "Introductory," Lectures, II, 223, and the passage in D, p. [143], in "Politics," Lectures, III, 242–243.

[303] See p. [99] above.

[304] Only the passage in Journal C, p. [82], is used in "Self-Reliance," W, II, 78, but cf. "Self-Reliance," W, II, 47 and 77, for the ideas in C, p. [57], and D, p. [308].

[305] Passages in Journal D, pp. [259] and [337], are used in "Self-Reliance," W, II, 71 and 54; the second is also in "Tendencies," Lectures, III, 309.

Be

We are fed when pleased [C 188]
Be somebody to offer [C 70]

Reason of selfreliance is in the great fact of Spontaneity

Roses   D 331   338

After p. 35 [306]

[111] Secondariness   D 41
    Travelling   C 143   D 303
    Imitation   *Home*
    Society or progress of species ⟨Phil Hist⟩ ↑Φιλ-Ιστ↓ Lect 12 [307]
    The Bivouac better   C 315, 329, [308]

Audate's meaning lies in our endeavors
Our valours are our best gods.
Prayer of the sower & sailor [309]

	Praying	
	Wailing	
	Travelling	look abroad
	Imitation	
⟨and⟩	Discipleship	
↑and	Property↓ [310]	

---

[306] "Reason . . . Spontaneity" is developed in "Self-Reliance," *W*, II, 63–64. The passages in Journal D, pp. [331] and [338], are used in "Religion," *Lectures*, III, 283, and "Self-Reliance," *W*, II, 67. "After p. 35" may refer to D, p. [35], used in "Self-Reliance," *W*, II, 79–80.

[307] With the paragraph in Journal D, p. [41], cf. "Self-Reliance," *W*, II, 79. The passage in D, p. [303], is used, *ibid.*, pp. 81–82, where it is followed by a section on imitation; see also "Home," *Lectures*, III, 31, n. 11. With "Society or . . . Lect 12", cf. "The Individual," *Lectures*, II, 174–175, used in "Self-Reliance," *W*, II, 84–87.

[308] Cf. "Self-Reliance," *W*, II, 87.

[309] "Audate's . . . sailor", combined in Journal D, p. [314], is used in "Self-Reliance," *W*, II, 77–78.

[310] "Praying . . . Property" is an outline of "Self-Reliance," *W*, II, 77–89. Emerson first drew the brace from "Praying" to "Discipleship", then extended it around "Property".

Kings teach us.
>   Royal blood never pays
>   Make their own scale   D 263, *Duty* p.
>   Represent a cause [311]

[11⟨o⟩2]   The Philosopher
>   The Scholar
>   Value of Principles.

The eye to see a navy in an acorn. [A 43]

See J. 1835 p. 117,[312]

———

>   Selden

———

>   Duty to us
>   Duty to Negro
>   Practicability
>   Slavery ⟨self destructive⟩
>   wholly iniquitous
>   self destructive
>   a dreadful reagent.

The [313] abolitionist; his plan
>   to awaken the conscience &c
>   Its aspect to us
>   A question for discussion
>   A question for action
>   for New England
>   Importance of discussion
>   The vote   & the assertion of his right

[311] "Kings . . . cause" is an outline of a paragraph in "Self-Reliance," *W*, II, 63.

[312] The page to this point may be a collection for "The Individual"; with the first three entries, cf. *Lectures*, II, 179 and 181–182. The paragraph in Journal B, p. [117], is used in "The Individual," *Lectures*, II, 178–179.

[313] A pen stroke above "The" may be either the start of a letter or the number "1".

Beyond this I do not feel a call to act
Nearer duties [314]

[113]   The present aspects of the Slavery Question.

I   The one important revolution is the new value of the private
man
      Let him know the truth
      〈s〉Shall fear hinder, or decorum, or interest.
Who shall muzzle the lion
      〈The〉 ↑Our↓ great duty on this matter is to open our halls to the
discussion of this question steadily day after day[,] year after year
until no man dare wag his finger at us. That first, for the great duty
of freedom [n] 〈thought〉 or duty to ourselves.

II   The duty to our fellow man the Slave
We are to assert his right in all companies
      An amiable joyous race who for ages have not been permitted to
unfold their natural powers we are to befriend
      I think it cannot be maintained by any candid person that the
African race have ever occupied or do promise ever to occupy any very
high place in the human family. Their present condition [114] is the
strongest proof that they cannot. The Irish cannot; the American
Indian cannot; the Chinese cannot. Before the energy of the Caucasian
race all the other races have quailed and 〈ser〉 done obeisance
      Yet the colony at Liberia is somewhat. The black merchants are
so fond of their lucrative occupations that it is with difficulty any of
them can be prevailed upon to take office in the Colony. They dislike
the trouble of it. Civilized arts are found to be as attractive to the wild
negro as they are disagreeable to the wild Indian.[315] [B 328]

      [314] "Selden" and "Duty to us" are struck through in pencil with a vertical use
mark. "Duty to us . . . duties" is probably an outline for the address on "Slavery"
first delivered in the Second Church in Concord in November, 1837; the manuscript
is missing. The material on pp. [113], [114], [116], [118]-[121], and [124₂]-
[125₁] follows this outline in part and was probably used in the lecture. See James
Elliot Cabot, *A Memoir of Ralph Waldo Emerson*, 2 vols. (Boston, 1887), II, 424-
433, and *Lectures*, II, xvii.
      [315] "is the strongest . . . Indian." is struck through in ink with a vertical use
mark.

[115] P   Selfreliance

A greater respect for Man indicated by the movements
of   Antigovernment
    Anti Association   ↑their pursuits
    Anti Monopoly   politics
    Anti Church   education
    ⟨Anti A⟩   religion↓
    Democracy
    ↑Anti money↓

[116] [316] The professed aim of the abolition↑i↓st is to awaken the conscience of the Northern States in the hope thereby to awaken the conscience of the Southern states: a hope just & sublime.   A high compliment they pass upon the integrity & moral force of New England which I hope we shall not disappoint. Old England, as all the history of Europe for centuries shows, has been the public of Europe[;] the things which were suppressed, extinguished, expunged in the sleepy empires of Austria, France & Italy, Russia ⟨th⟩ emerged to the light & air in England & there got the benefit of a verdict and the moral force of a jury's verdict. Despotism is like that vampire bat which ⟨lulls the⟩ whilst it sucks the blood of the sleeping ⟨m⟩traveller, lulls the pain & soothes him to sleep by the ⟨flitting⟩ fanning of his wings.

[117] [blank]
    [118] [317] Is it thought that there is a race of beings in this earth[,] an exception to all which we have yet found in nature, one, namely, whose existence cannot be maintained except by another's usurping its independence: except by crime? [n]

There is a little plain prose which has got I know to be somewhat tedious by often repetition which yet needs to be said again & again, until it has perforated the thick ↑deaf↓ ear, that no man can hold

---

[316] P. [116] is struck through in ink with a vertical use mark.
[317] Each of the paragraphs on p. [118] is struck through in ink with a vertical use mark.

property in Man; that Reason is not a chattel; cannot be bought &
sold; and that every pretended traffic in such stock is invalid & criminal.

[119] [318] Our duty in the matter is to Settle the right & wrong
so that whenever we are called to vote in the matter, we may not
dodge the question; we may not trifle with it. We may not be ignorant
but do an act of reason & justice in the vote we cast. A vote of a free-
holder is a rising power. Now nothing is of less worth. It is scarce
more than a whim. And of course it has little honor. No grave & good
man ⟨sees⟩ ↑admires↓ the absurd acts of our state & national governments because of the multitudes & majorities by which they are ap-
plauded but to a section however small which is known to be well
informed & well principled & much more to the vote of one man
known to be independent & virtuous, all men look. That is a great
fact. That shows not what the majority think, far otherwise, but it
tells what the majority, yea what all mankind and all future ages
will think when the provocations of persons & interest & local politics
have passed out of memory.

[120] [319] The vote is to mend its reputation with the advancing
intelligence & worth of society. We have one security for its right, that
honesty is the best policy.
By & by↑, the fact↓ that a vote went so & so, will be tantamount to the
⟨ju⟩ decision of our Supreme Court.

But when we have settled the right & wrong of this question I think
we have done all we can. A man can only extend his active attention
to a certain finite amount of claims. We have much nearer duties than
to the poor black slaves of Carolina and the effect of the present
excitement is to exaggerate that.

Far be it from me to reproach the planter. ↑I think↓ His misfor-
tune is greater than his sin.

[121] Slavery is important as a test of the times. There is a great
deal of unbelief, of distrust of man's nature, of open apology for the

---

[318] P. [119] is struck through in ink with crossed diagonal use marks.
[319] P. [120] is struck through in ink with a diagonal use mark.

wrong on the plea that it is expedient. The familiar reply of the Southerner to the charge of the iniquity of Slavery, is, "but we shall not buy at your market." Well, let him not buy to the end of the world. What then? Why then ⟨we shall⟩ sugar will be dearer, & cotton shirts & gowns will be dearer, & worse⟨,⟩ yet, we shall not be able to sell so many shoes & clocks and books & ↑fur↓ caps as we do now; the Southerner will cut his own lumber out of his own woods. Very like, Very like, and what then? We can buy Egyptian & East Indian Cotton, we can make maple or beet sugar, or can go without. ⟨?⟩ What go without? And is that all? Why let every true man choose to have sugar, coffee, and tobacco & to feel mean; or no sugar & coffee & be a man; Which shall it be? Why rather potato, a loghouse, & a peat fire, dressed in broadcloth, made of the wool of our own mountain sheep woven by the [320]

[1⟨20⟩22]   Society [321]

One Soul   [B] ↑112   149   285   282   (1833) 75↓ [322]
    Sympathy
    Otherism   saying of Novalis   H & N. [323]
    Others acquaint us with our solitude [B] ↑273↓ [324]
    Solitude in relation to Reason
    Fresh interest given to stale thought by a pupil; Letter   185,
                                                      35, [325]

    Eloquence —   ↑112   158↓
       Diff. manner of speaking to one & to many ↑55↓ [326]
       Cannonade   ↑302↓

[320] Continued on p. [124₂] below. P. [121] is struck through in ink with a diagonal use mark.
[321] Pp. [122]–[125₁] contain outlines for "Society," *Lectures*, II, 98–112, in close to the final order.
[322] "112 . . . 75" is in pencil. Passages from Journal B, pp. [285] and [282], and A, p. [75], are used, rewritten, in "Society," *Lectures*, II, 99.
[323] "Sympathy" is discussed in "Society," *Lectures*, II, 99. Passages indexed "Otherism" in Journal B, pp. [184] and [316], and the "saying of Novalis", B, p. [30], are used in "Society," pp. 100–101.
[324] "273" is in pencil.
[325] Both passages cited are used in "Society," *Lectures*, II, 101.
[326] The passages cited in Journal B, pp. [158] and [55], are used in "Society," *Lectures*, II, 110. "112   158" and "55" are in pencil.

Sect or Party. Dyspathy   ↑290↓ [327]

Duty to Society   J 1833 p 35

[123] [328] There is one mind —
Inspiration larger reception
Genius more like, not less like all men [B] 285 plagiarism
What hits one deeply, hits all.
W

Gener⟨al⟩ic Nature
Individuality.
             Newly bound by that for every one can do what no
                                                              other can
             Morally necessary to make good the law
             But not only helpful but joy making is it
In Lit. we showed the pleasure of objectivity
More blessed is objectivity in a person
Other⟨s⟩ism   saying of Novalis   H. & N. p 219
      Freshness to the stale   185   35

      Marriage   ↑246↓ [329]
         La Place
         Its moral laws

Sect & Party
      Age of association [330]
Powers of Society limited by the Eternal Necessity
      Strong for right   weak for wrong

[327] See p. [73] above. "302" and "290" are in pencil.
[328] P. [123] is struck through in pencil with a curved diagonal use mark. In the upper right quarter of the page are pencil sketches of a beribboned hat and a man in left profile, and below them some arithmetic in pencil, partly overwritten at the bottom of the page by "by the Eternal . . . antislavery".
[329] "246" is in pencil.
[330] The sections on "Sect & Party" and "association" were reversed in "Society," *Lectures*, II, 108 and 106; see a similar outline on p. [124₁] below and a final outline printed from the lecture manuscript in *Lectures*, II, 405 (notes).

Societies of principle.   antislavery
[1241] Society of nature; Marriage
Society of friendship; friends
   of power; States
   of opinion; sect & party
   of philanthropy
   of eloquence

Him whom disaster
& vice have undone [331]

[1251] [332] No never let man be addressed by any motive that is unworthy a man. The ⟨lowest⟩ wretch that has reason shall be no wretch when his Reason is addressed. How pitiful then is the patronizing tone   [B] 299

The law of all society is spiritual
of friends [n] that a man should live where can act himself
of marriage;
of association; that only the hearty individual that is in you avails;
  numbers & means nothing
of states; only their spiritual union [333]

[1242] waterfall of our New Hampshire hills and in honest poverty say what we think & do what the heart of Nature prompts

Again slavery is the most striking example in the history of the world of the evil of taking one wrong step. The introduction of slaves unfor-

---

[331] "Society of nature . . . undone", the earliest inscription on the page, is in pencil; the first two lines are overwritten by "in honest . . . heart" and the last two by "unmixed evil . . . freedom", both printed on p. [1242] below. "Society of nature . . . of eloquence" and "Him whom . . . undone" are struck through in pencil with single diagonal use marks.

[332] "No never . . . union", in pencil, is overwritten by "it is amputation . . . governments, they", printed on p. [1252] below.

[333] "No never . . . addressed." (not from Journal B, p. [299]) is used in "Society," *Lectures*, II, 107, followed by the last passage on p. [1241] above; the passage in B, p. [299], follows in the manuscript of the lecture but is canceled; see *Lectures*, II, 407–408 (notes). "The law . . . union" is used in "Society," *Lectures*, II, 102–107.

tunately distinguishable by color has entailed all these crimes on the states.

I

It is an almost unmixed evil to the Southerner. The hope of freedom is there: all things ⟨contend⟩ work against wrong. The trials of the master are innumerable & inappreciable by the ⟨whites⟩ ↑northerner↓. The gain is apparent, — the loss is real. The slave earns a dollar, but the master loses the estate; or, the planters gain on estates, but the whole state loses³³⁴ [125₂] in the possibility of cultivation. It is barbarism; it is amputation of so much of the moral & intellectual attributes of man. Se⟨tt⟩lling so much manhood to buy so much luxury.

It has long been maintained by the English economists, that Great Britain was a loser, ⟨in⟩on the whole, by the possession of the West Indian Colonies; the West Indians finding that without bounties & monopolies & protecting duties & protecting garrisons, & expensive governments, they could not realize adequate profits from the ↑forced &↓ dilatory ⟨& compelled⟩ labor of the slave.³³⁵

[126]   Eloquence
"Lord Coventry" says Clarendon "had in the plain way of speaking & delivery without much ornament of elocution a strange way of making himself believed, the only justifiable design of eloquence."³³⁶

[127] [blank]
[128]   Life

Behind us as we go all things assume pleasing forms as clouds do far off &c   ⟨J 1835 p. 111⟩
                                                       ⟨p 201⟩

³³⁴ "waterfall . . . prompts" (continued from p. [121] above) and "Again slavery . . . states." are struck through in ink with single vertical use marks, and "It is an . . . loses" with a diagonal one.
³³⁵ "in the possibility . . . governments," is struck through in pencil with a diagonal use mark; Emerson extended the use mark in ink through "they could not . . . slave.", which may have been added.
³³⁶ See Encyclopedia, p. [22]. The quotation is struck through in ink with a diagonal use mark. Emerson used part of the quotation earlier in "Ethical Writers," *Lectures*, I, 365.

Why fret at particular events? For every thing you have missed you have gained something else: And for every thing you gain you lose something — [B 201]

The ship beating at sea gains a small commission of miles for her true course on every tack. So in life our profession[,] our dilettantism gives us with much parade a little solid wisdom. The days & hours of Reason shine with steady light as the life of life & all the other days & weeks appear as hyphens to join these [B 236]

The order of things consents to virtue. Such scenes as luxurious poets & novelists paint, where temptation has a quite overcoming force never or very rarely occur in real life[.] [B 36]

A single house will show all that is done or suffered in the world [337] [Enc. 191]

[129] ⟨No man need be perplexed in speculation⟩	[B] 316
Nature with doors ajar is silent.	315
Room for all gifts: happy the hearing ear	309
Politics ↑too↓ easy to a philosopher	308
Pestalozzi's sentence	
⟨Particular experience supplies no other particular exp.⟩	⟨3⟩221 [n]
Fear not to be besmirched	140
Private chapel	61
Either hold the plough or drive	[B 35]
⟨Never unhappy⟩	19
Routine	
⟨Measures of the value of time⟩	4 bc
⟨Genius & Talents⟩ (Man. p 118)	
Genius always s⟨u⟩ituated alike J 1837	3
Magic of learning languages J 1833	64
Individual force	88
Phocion	115 [338]

[337] The first three entries are struck through in ink with a diagonal use mark and used in "Ethics," *Lectures*, II, 144 and 145–146. The first sentence is also used in "Spiritual Laws," *W*, II, 131, and the passage from B, p. [201], in "Compensation," *W*, II, 98. "A single . . . world", struck through in pencil with a diagonal use mark, is used in "Ethics," *Lectures*, II, 144.

[338] P. [129] may be an early collection of materials for the lecture "Ethics";

Con

[130]   ↑Man p 5, 71, 72   74↓ 339
Live with God, with living nature as the Roses do
Wilfulness vitiates & enslaves, but the leaf partakes of the sublime
of All.
Live with Roses   which do not point backwards & do not peep
forward 340

> One mind
> Inviolability of its laws
> ⟨One mind⟩
> You tell what you conceal
> You ⟨are⟩ can see only what you have *
> You are not in the comp[an]y uncongenial
> You cannot read my book
> Spirit publishes
> The relation between persons 'tis vain to define
> it makes itself

> Manner never did the work of matter 341

[131]   Ethics

          T. You will always find those who think they know what is

          * ambition proportioned to its powers

---

see Notebook Δ, pp. [16] and [130] below. The horizontal use marks are in pencil;
"No", "Particular", "experience", "Never", "Measures", and "Genius" are also
struck through in pencil with short diagonal use marks. Passages from Journal B,
pp. [316], [19], and [4], and A, p. [88], are used in "Ethics," *Lectures*, II, 145,
144, 146, and 151.
          339 "Man . . . 74" is added in pencil; the passages from Notebook Man are used
in "Ethics," *Lectures*, II, 146, 150, and 151.
          340 With "Live with God . . . forward", cf. Journal D, pp. [331] and [338],
used in "Religion," *Lectures*, III, 283–284, and "Self-Reliance," *W*, II, 67.
          341 "One mind . . . matter", in pencil, is used in "Ethics," *Lectures*, II, 147–
151, in the order outlined on p. [130], but most of it is also used in "Spiritual
Laws"; see *W*, II, 139, 135, 146 and 159, 149 and 150, 149, 156–159, and 149–
151. With "You tell . . . uncongenial", cf. Blotting Book III, pp. [34], [106],
and [107], and Journal Q, p. [26]. Emerson's footnote, "ambition . . . powers",

your duty far better than you know it yourself [B 202]

To believe your own thought that is genius [B] 185

Truth   Capt. ⟨Back⟩ ↑Ross↓ 124 [342]

[13⟨0⟩2] The private life yields more affecting illustrations of the irresistible nature of the laws of the human spirit than masses of men or long periods can.

> We are embosomed in beauty
> ↑We need not be unhappy↓
> We need not be perplexed with other questions [B 316]
> We gain as much as we lose [B 201]
> Different measures of time
> Deliv Talent the call [B] p. 199 [343]

To treat of the nature of things is to show his life in new glory to every man. When he sees he is no sport of circumstances but that all nature is his friend & he is related to natures so great that if his private selfish good suffer shipwreck he yet must rejoice for therein is his Universal nature vindicated[,] he shall reward his teacher with assent [344]

> ˣ⟨The conclusion from these views is Self trust⟩ˣ

And as ⟨s⟩Self Trust is the rule so compensation is the ⟨a⟩↑re↓ward pervading nature

---

in pencil, is copied into Notebook Man, p. [48] above, from Q, p. [52], and used in "Ethics," *Lectures*, II, 148, and "Spiritual Laws," *W*, II, 141.

[342] P. [131] is in pencil. "T." is circled. The first two entries are used in both "Ethics," *Lectures*, II, 152, and "Self-Reliance," *W*, II, 53 and 45. The story of Captain Ross is used in "Prudence," *Lectures*, II, 318–319.

[343] P. [132] is in pencil. Three diagonal use marks in pencil are struck through "The private . . . time", "We are . . . measures", and "We are . . . the call". Except for "We need . . . unhappy", all the entries to this point are used in "Ethics," *Lectures*, II, 144–147. "We are . . . questions" and "Deliv Talent the call" (see " 'The delivery of the talent is the call' ", a quotation from Abraham Tucker in Blotting Book Psi, p. [36]), and the passage in Journal B, p. [199], are used in "Spiritual Laws," *W*, II, 131, 135, 132, and 140–141. The passage in B, p. [201], is also used in "Compensation," *W*, II, 98.

[344] This paragraph is also in Notebook Man, p. [4] above; "To treat . . . rejoice" is from Journal B, p. [235].

Stand not on a shovel [345]

[133] The laws of the mind transcend all positive rules & ⟨establish⟩ ↑execute↓ themselves. The mind wants no other laws than its own. Its checks are complete. ⟨Its⟩ Wake the mind & it will be vocation, ear, judge, apology, guard, physician, prophet, heaven unto itself.

———

Every faculty which is a receiver of pleasure has an equal penalty put on its abuse: it is to answer for its moderation with its life. [B 306]

———

It is easy in the world to live after the world's opinion. It is easy in solitude to live after our own. But the great man is he who in the midst of the crowd keeps with perfect sweetness the independence of solitude[.] [A 133] [346]

[134] [347]

1 {	One soul	
{	Relation of soul to the world	
2	Science	Mind seeks a row
		Nature is in a row
		perfect Unity
3	Art	The conscious utterance of the soul
		& consists in subordinating individual to Universal
4	Literature	Delight of having the subjective made objective
		Every age place man hath its fixed word

[345] "⟨ˣThe conclusion . . . trustˣ⟩" is written after "suffer" in the paragraph above, which was probably written later around it. The sentence is struck through and partly circled in pencil, with an arrow drawn to the blank line above "And as ⟨s⟩Self Trust". "And as . . . nature" and "Stand not on a shovel" are struck through in pencil with single diagonal use marks. These three sentences are used in "Ethics," *Lectures*, II, 151–152.

[346] P. [133] is in pencil. Each paragraph is struck through in pencil with a diagonal use mark; all three are used in "Ethics," *Lectures*, II, 147, 153, and 152. With the first paragraph, cf. "The Head," *Lectures*, II, 250, and "Intellect," *W*, II, 327–328, where the thought is rephrased. The second is also used in "Compensation," *W*, II, 98, and the third in "Self-Reliance," *W*, II, 53–54.

[347] P. [134], in pencil, is an outline of the entire "Philosophy of History" series, possibly derived from the summary on p. [135]. Cf. earlier forms in Journal B, pp. [262] and [268]–[269]; comparison with Emerson's index on the front cover verso above suggests that he set aside blocks of pages under these and related headings.

5   Politics — Persons & Property
              Inalienable power of each
6   Society possible by one soul

7   Religion

8   Trades

9   Manners impress us all the dignity of the spirit betrayed

10 Ethics

11 Age

[135] [348] There is one soul
      It is related to the world
      Art is its action thereon
      Science finds its method
      Literature ↑is↓ its record
      Religion is the emotion of reverence it inspires [n]
      Ethics is the Soul illustrated in human life
      Society is the finding of this soul by individuals in each other
      ⟨Politics⟩ Trades are the learning the soul in nature by labor
      Politics is the activity of the soul illustrated in power
      Manners are silent & mediate expressions of Soul

[136]–[137] [blank]
[13⟨6⟩8]   Objection↑s↓
But this real knowledge is the most formal & tedious. It destroys
illusions. It would build in squares & build barns; garden in diagrams,
a quaker world. It destroys hope
      Answer. "As from fire, heat cannot be separated, no more can
beauty from the eternal." [349] [Enc. 144]

---

[348] P. [135] is in pencil. While each of these thoughts may be traced in individual
lectures of the "Philosophy of History" series, this is an outline of one paragraph in
"The Individual," *Lectures*, II, 181.
      [349] Emerson uses a similar translation in "The Eye and Ear," *Lectures*, II, 264.

163

[139] [blank]
[⟨138⟩140] [350]   *Miscellanies.*

Animal Magnetism; facts beforehand of science. Unnatural separation. Precocious.

Telescopes &c hurt the bad. J. 1835, p. 164

The mind masters ⟨the⟩ ↑a↓ fact by an Idea; no otherwise: the moment the Unity is perceived in it, it is hallowed & not profane.

How the world looks to the Scholar! It is his experimenting room. The people come up; [n] he reads their names & history written on their forms in letters invisible to themselves but in a Universal language which those of every nation can read. God puts a glass in their bosoms & every gesture & act is Confession. Without ⟨a fee⟩ ↑suspicion↓ [351] & without form, he sits in the Confessor's chair & they without design & against their will ↑un↓ravel ⟨out⟩ to him their weaved up follies. "How can a man be concealed? how can a man be concealed?" said Chee. [352] The little flower, a stranger in the soil, whose leaf has puzzled the inquirer, when now at last urged by an irresistible nature, it forms the bud, then opens it to the day, does not more ⟨fully⟩ surely ⟨tel⟩ publish to the botanist the whole secret of [141] its order, class, & species, than does the man by every involuntary act of his life.

Men know what you conceal as well as what you show
"faces never lie." Moxon [353]
Man makes the whole interest of the world & in Man wisdom & virtue: Scipio, ⟨w⟩Milton well calls the "height of Rome." ⟨The interest of Spain was concentrated on the *wild man*, on Columbus's return.⟩

[350] "Extern" is written diagonally in the upper left corner of the page, partly under the page number.
[351] "suspicion" is added in pencil.
[352] Emerson copied the quotation into Journal B, p. [132], and Notebook T, p. [190], and used it in "Ethics," *Lectures*, II, 150, and "Spiritual Laws," *W*, II, 159. See also Notebook Man, p. [71] above.
[353] "Men know . . . Moxon" is struck through in pencil with a diagonal use mark. Cf. Journal B, p. [201], "Manners," *Lectures*, II, 129–130, and "Spiritual Laws," *W*, II, 156 and 159.

The ⟨one⟩ main object of curiosity to Spain, on the return of Columbus, was the wild man.[354]

[142]–[143] [blank]
[144] The education of the mind consists in a continual substitution of thoughts for words as in petrifaction a particle of stone replaces a particle of wood. But what are called facts are commonly words, as my friend who called himself the practical man. [A 92] See J 1832 14 Nov [Q 84]
the iron rail in the banister. 1833 p 73 [A 72] [355]

[145] The light of the public square will best test its merit
His works do follow him saith the blessed revelation & the world echoes Amen. What hath he done? is the divine question which searches souls & transpierces the paper shield of every false reputation. A fop may sit in any chair of the world nor be distinguis⟨e⟩hed for his hour from Homer & Washington but there can never be any doubt concerning the respective ability of human beings when we seek the truth. — Pretension may sit still but cannot act. Pretension never feigned an act of real greatness. Pretension never wrote an Iliad, nor drove back Xerxes, nor Christianized the world, nor abolished slavery. Coleridge has thrown ↑many↓ new truths into circulation; Southey, never one.

Let us call a spade a spade
Go into a court & you are guaged. or to Commencement.[356]

---

[354] This sentence, a revision of the canceled sentence above, is struck through in pencil with a diagonal use mark. Cf. Journal C, p. [1], used in "Literature," *Lectures*, II, 56; cf. also "Being and Seeming," *Lectures*, II, 306.
[355] "The education . . . man." is used in "Ethics," *Lectures*, II, 150. "the iron rail in the banister.", struck through in ink with a diagonal use mark, is used in "Politics," *Lectures*, II, 80. The lower part of the page is filled with pencil sketches of a raised arm, a left-hand sign, and an unfinished figure.
[356] P. [145] may be a collection for "Spiritual Laws," but see p. [42] above. The first sentence, struck through in ink with a diagonal use mark, is used in "Literature," *Lectures*, II, 66, and "Spiritual Laws," *W*, II, 155. "His works . . . slavery." is struck through in pencil with a vertical use mark; "What hath . . . slavery." is used in "Ethics," *Lectures*, II, 151, and "Spiritual Laws," *W*, II, 158.

[14⟨4⟩6]–[147] [blank]

[14⟨6⟩8] All pomps & ceremonies of courts do only flourish & idealize the simple facts in which that state began as the orders of Architecture do in every ornament refer to some essential part of the building. The Pope performeth all ecclesiastic jurisdiction as in Consistory among his cardinals which were originally but the parish priests of Rome. Milton Vol. I, p. 16, so to the wise eye an etiquette is a history. [A 145] The whole of heraldry is in Courtesy. A man of fine manners ⟨y⟩ can pronounce your name in his conversation with all the charm that ever 'My Lord' or 'Your Highness' or 'your grace' could have had to ⟨his⟩your ear.[B 12]
↑v[ide]. also.↓ J 1835 p 158

"Ceremonies are the translation of virtue into our own language"
                                    Bacon. [BB I, 21] [357]

[149] and when greater than Napoleon, Trade with his teams & locomotive cars had crossed the military lines, bridged the fosse, broken the bastion, & by dint of trampling with hoofs & wheels worn a road through every fortification.

  With a birthplace & an era thus favorable to extended observation his own literary culture has conspired.[358]

[1⟨48⟩50] [blank]
[⟨149⟩ 151]   Literary Ethics
  Evils considered
⟨P⟩The Present is a period of despair, of unbelief.
There is no religion.
We improve easily up to the point at which our contemporaries &

With the last entry, cf. Journal B, pp. [33] and [227], C, pp. [176] and [223], "The Heart," *Lectures*, II, 285, "Being and Seeming," *Lectures*, II, 300 and 301–302, and "Spiritual Laws," *W*, II, 157.

[357] The entire page, which is indexed "Chivalry", is summarized in "Thoughts on Art," *The Dial*, I (Jan. 1841), 377 (*Lectures*, II, 53). "The whole . . . ear.", struck through in pencil with a vertical use mark, is used in "History," *W*, II, 18. See also Journal B, p. [244].

[358] Both paragraphs, on Carlyle, probably written in November, 1837, for a review of Carlyle's *French Revolution* (see Journal C, p. [232]), are used in the lecture "Recent Literary and Spiritual Influences" (January 30, 1843). See pp. [154₁]–[162] below for more material on Carlyle used in the same lecture.

countrymen have arrived. There we stop for months[,] for years & very ⟨c⟩slowly gain anything beyond it.

At the age ludicrously called the age of discretion every hopeful young man is shipwrecked. The burdensome possession of himself he cannot dispose of. Up to that hour others have directed him & he has gone triumphantly. Then he ⟨learns⟩begins to direct himself & all hope, wisdom, & power sink flat down. Sleep creeps over him & he lies down in the snow. [B 226]
    See words of Sir C Wren   J. 1835 p 255 [359]

[15⟨0⟩2] [blank]
    [15⟨1⟩3] The Arts & Sciences are the only Cosmopolites.[360]
                                                    [B 152]

    Every intellectual acquisition is mainly prospective & hence the scholar's assurance of eternity quite aloof from his moral convictions
                                                    [B 111]

    "He should be ↑born↓ robust who ⟨undertakes to⟩ ↑would↓ explore his interior self without becoming morbid."
Truth first.

    [15₄1] Good is promoted by the worst. Don't despise even the Kneelands & Andrew Jacksons. In the great cycle they find their place, & like the insect that fertilizes the soil with worm casts or the scavenger bustard that removes carrion they perform a beneficence they know not of & cannot hinder if they would. [A 38]
[This belongs to the head *Value of Knowledge.*] [361]

    "Two gifts has the poet to thank God for   Cheerfulness & Knowledge; Knowledge that he may not fear what is dreadful, Cheerfulness that he may know how to describe all things sportively." [T 183]

---

[359] "We improve . . . beyond it." and "At the . . . snow.", struck through in pencil with single vertical use marks, are used in "The Present Age," *Lectures*, II, 165 and 170. The entire page is probably a collection for that lecture. "See words . . . p 255" is in pencil.
    [360] This sentence is struck through in ink with a diagonal use mark.
    [361] See p. [4] above.

Harvey's account of insensibility of the Heart [362]

CARLYLE

Strong he is[,] upright, noble, & sweet & makes good how much of our human nature[.] [363] [C 2]

Mirabeau. This piece will establish his kingdom, I forebode, in the mind of his countrymen. How he gropes with giant fingers into the dark of man,[n] into the obscure recesses of power in human will, & we are encouraged by his word [155₁] to feel the might that is in a man. "Come the raggedest hour that spite & fate ⟨&⟩ dare bring to frown upon the enraged Northumberland" — Gigantic portrait-painting. [C 17] Yet he adds mirth. Much like those terrible Africants↓ at the sources of the Nile, who ran with explosions of laughter to the battle.[364]

The Diamond Necklace, I doubt not, is the sifted story, — the veritable fact as it fell out, yet so strangely told by a series of pictures, cloud upon cloud, that the eye of the exact men is speedily confused & annoyed. It seems to me his genius is the redolence of London, — the great Metropolis. So vast, — enormous, with endless details, & so related to all the world is he. It would seem as if no baker's shop, no mutton stall, no academy, church, placard, Coronation, but he saw & sympathized with all, & took up all into his omnivorous memory: & hence his panoramic style, & this encyclopediacal allusion [154₂] [365] to all knowables.[366] [C 17–18]
Then he is a worshipper of strength, heedless whether its present

---

[362] See "The Individual," *Lectures*, II, 183.

[363] This sentence is expanded in the lecture "Recent Literary and Spiritual Influences."

[364] "How he gropes . . . in a man." and "those terrible . . . battle.", struck through in ink on pp. [154₁] and [155₁] with single vertical use marks, and "Gigantic portrait-painting." are used in the lecture "Recent Literary and Spiritual Influences."

[365] Emerson repeated the page number.

[366] Emerson extended the use mark above ("those terrible . . . battle.") first through "his genius", then to the bottom of page [155₁]. "It seems . . . knowables." is used in the lecture "Recent Literary and Spiritual Influences"; with "It seems . . . is he.", cf. p. [162] below.

phase be divine or diabolic; [367] Burns, Fox, Luther, & those unclean beasts, Diderot, Danton, Mirabeau, whose sinews are their own, & who trample on the tutoring & Conventions of society, he loves. For he believes that every noble nature was made by God, & contains,— if savage passions, also fit checks, & grand impulses within it,—hath its own resources, &, however erring, will return from far. Then he writes English & crowds meaning into all the nooks & corners of his sentences. [C 18]

He is never encumbered by the particles & circumlocutions of speech, but inflates them all with his soul, so that his work, like a bird, is distended with air to the extremity of every bone & plumule of the body.

So that, once read, he is but half read. [C 18]

I think he has seen as no other in our time how inexhaustible a mine is the language of conversation. [155₂] He does not use the written dialect of the time in which scholars, pamphleteers, & the clergy write, nor the parliamentary, in which the lawyer & the statesman↑,↓ ⟨write⟩ & the better newspapers write; but he draws strength & motherwit out of a poetic use of the spoken vocabulary, so that his paragraphs are all a sort of splendid conversation.[368] [C 18]

It needs a well-read, variously-informed man, to read ⟨c⟩Carlyle, from his infinite allusion. He knows every joke that ever was cracked.
[C 220]

His power of critical analysis is novel in English literature. His utter independence of all canons, his ready appeal to the unalterable laws of Nature & the scope of his mind which is like nothing but the cap of an observatory commanding an entire horizon—the earth below, the heaven above—[369]

---

[367] The page to this point is struck through in ink with two vertical use marks. "Then he is . . . diabolic;" is used in the lecture "Recent Literary and Spiritual Influences."

[368] "noble nature . . . splendid conversation.", struck through in ink with single vertical use marks on pp. [154₂] and [155₂], is used in the lecture "Recent Literary and Spiritual Influences."

[369] "He knows . . . above —", struck through in ink with a vertical use mark, is used in the lecture "Recent Literary and Spiritual Influences."

[156]³⁷⁰   Carlyle a critic
                                        biographer
                                        translator
                                        philosopher
                    His accomplishments
                                        learning
                                        wit
                                        humor
                                        moral sentiment
                                        earnestness
                                        love of strength
                                        hatred of Cant

[157]   Carlyle a fruit of 19th Century
                                        in London
                                        cultured by Germany

                              Antagonism to conventions

                              His private genius
                                        Moral sentiment
                                        Earnest
                                        Sportive
                                        Delighting in strength
                                        Hating Cant.
                                        Humor
                                        Poetic Skill

[158] We suppose all readers come to one opinion in regard to his style. It is stamped all over with a sort of defiance of the existing conventions as if he would say: I drew my wit from other lands. [It is full of allusion to all regions of geography, all manual arts, all the annals of time] The vice is that the parts are not duly subordinated to aid the effect of the whole. — One is forever stopping in mid career to pick up & examine these golden apples. Yet is there no

---

³⁷⁰ Pp. [156]–[157] are apparently outlines of the section on Carlyle used in the lecture "Recent Literary and Spiritual Influences."

gratuitous ornament[,] no varnishing or veneering, the ornament is in the grain, & evinces the ⟨matchless⟩ⁿ richness & qualities of the root. We travel on an errand of weight through a South American Grove, where the palm & the mahogany trees rise side by side, & vines like enormous serpents interweave acres into solid mats of vegetation[.] [371]

⟨Of course⟩ there are ⟨many⟩ places where the reader is cloyed with richness, & where ⟨the⟩ⁿ ⟨a sharp⟩ the plainest statement would be worth more than all the commentary [159] (The Diamond Necklace for example) [372]

& many a timeⁿ in the French Revolution we think the reader would prefer that ↑t↓his horseman of the sun should trot or walk a little way, & not execute so many celestial caracoles.

But whoever reads will find that no living writer has shown equal acquaintance with all the resources of the English tongue. He crowds meaning into all the nooks & corners of his sentences &c [373]

[160]–[161] [blank]
[162] ⟨Carlyle's genius is the redolence of London, the centre of Christendom, the Heart where all the ⟨currents⟩ ↑cataracts↓ of national life rush to mingle, & the pulse of the world beats in audible tumult; ⟨th⟩ where all arts & all actions ↑coexist,↓ where every interest finds its representative & official apparatus, & where a nation is gathered within the circle of a wall.⟩

His genius is the redolence of London; of London the centre of Christendom, the congre⟨gation⟩ss of mankind, where all arts & all actions ↑conditions.↓ coexist; where every interest finds its organ, & where a nation is gathered as within four walls; where from a thousand thoroughfares of land & water the couriers of the earth pass & repass

---

[371] "a sort of . . . conventions" and "It is full . . . vegetation" are used in "Recent Literary and Spiritual Influences."

[372] A short diagonal ink line links "(The Diamond . . .)" with a short vertical ink line between "stamped all" on p. [158], and "& many" on p. [159], probably for insertion. The parentheses are in pencil.

[373] "no living . . . sentences &c" is used in the lecture "Recent Literary and Spiritual Influences."

with tidings ⟨of all parts⟩ ↑in every tongue↓. Such another London is this style,ⁿ so vast, ⟨so⟩ enormous, & related to all ⟨nature⟩ the world.³⁷⁴

[163] [blank]

[164] Man.³⁷⁵ his ⟨Allness⟩ ↑Universality↓: his relation to Geography, to Astronomy, to all the sciences; to ⟨U⟩History, as the Rom. Empire, to Fr. Revolution (which makes the Fr. Rev. solvable by him by insight into his own structure as well as by external causation). Man of whom the Godlike is no less a property than pleasure & sweetmeats; man, mirrored in all nature prophesied by crystal, plant, animal; husband of nature; who reacts on nature the ganglion Talbot; a knot of roots which flower into the Universe. All things have their foundation in his nature.
Axioms A, B, C, D, E, & F.

To all men One Mind: Eloquence: Duty of the scholar to address this mind & to present principles. ↑Secondary importance of system.↓ Nobleness of Faith. Hope reinstated as soon as a principle is beheld. These are the light of all our day —

[165] [blank]
[166] Intellectual Culture ³⁷⁶
    Reason & Understanding
    Mystics.
    Goethe
    Intellectual duties. What crusades were, commerce is
    Position of Religion. — Education from the church

---

³⁷⁴ This paragraph, the first draft of which is canceled above, is used in the lecture "Recent Literary and Spiritual Influences."

³⁷⁵ Notes on p. [164], probably written in October, 1836, are developed in The Philosophy of History: "Introductory." For "Talbot" and "a knot . . . Universe.", see *Lectures*, II, 17–18, and "History," *W*, II, 36 and 37; with the last paragraph, cf. *Lectures*, II, 20. For the "Axioms", see Journal B, pp. [268]–[269].

³⁷⁶ "Intellectual Culture" was apparently an early title for the "Philosophy of History" lectures; see pp. [168] and [170] below. The notes on pp. [166] and [167] may have been written in October, 1836, about the same time as Emerson's advertisement for the series on p. [ii] above, but before the lectures were written or titles decided.

No progress of Society. Progress ↑is↓ of Individualsⁿ J 1835
p 223, 218, J.1833, p. 44.[377]
Every Society needs its own culture, books, philosophy, govt.
We Bunker hill mon[umen]t mechanical improvements. Stock com-
panies,[378] What is said now, will be heard.[379]
⟨On the philosophy⟩
On the philosophy that rests on the nature of things: phrenology, ani-
mal magnetism, infidelity, Utilitarianism, grow out of it physiog-
nomy
Criticism founds itself on principles
Art is founded on things *Goethe*
Religion must be founded on things
Poetry
Rhetoric
Science

[167] Realism of the day attested by the character of the great
men. Malthus, Bentham, Goethe, Wordsworth
Goethe's theories of customs & structures
Wordsworth's Preface —
On the power of principles in men.
On the overlaying the spiritual by the material J 1833 p. 31
Plutarch's Athenians who took oath to consider the vine,
olives, & barley as the boundaries of Attica [BB I, 21]

[168]   Intellectual Culture
1   ⟨Introductory Lecture⟩
2   The Antique
3   Reason & Understanding
4   Literary History
5   Art
6   Poetry

---

[377] "J 1835 . . . p. 44." is written on p. [167] and connected by an ink line
with p. [166]. The entry on p. [166] and passages from Journal B, pp. [223] and
[218], and A, p. [44], are used in "The Individual," *Lectures*, II, 174–176, and
"Self-Reliance," *W*, II, 84, 86, and 87.
[378] Cf. Journal B, pp. [168] and [230].
[379] Cf. Notebook L Literature, p. [18], above, and "Literature," *Lectures*, II, 68.

7 Rhetoric
8 Religion
9 Science
10 Life ⟨[J 1835 p 236] 264, 201⟩,
11 Goethe
12 Literary Ethics
    Trades & Professions
    Manners & Customs
    The Individual [380]

	Man	1	Man
	Science	2	Science
	Art	3	Art
	Literature	4	Literature
	Religion	5	Politics
	Politics	6	Religion
	History	7	Society
	Poetry	8	Trades & Professions
X	General aspect of the Age	9	Manners
	Goethe	10	Ethics
	Lit. Ethics	11.	The Age
	Literary Ethics [381]	12	The Individual [382]

[380] P. [168] shows three stages in the development of titles for the "Philosophy of History" series, titled "Intellectual Culture" at an early stage (see *L*, II, 39, and p. [170] below). "1 Introductory . . . Individual", the column nearest the left margin (see Plate I), is probably the earliest. "Introductory Lecture", "Art", "Religion", and "Science", all final lecture titles, are struck through in ink with single diagonal use marks. P. [20] above, headed "The Antique", is a collection for "Manners"; pp. [100]–[101] and [151] above, headed "Rhetoric" and "Literary Ethics", are collections for "The Present Age"; p. [128] above, headed "Life.", is a collection for "Ethics." Passages in Journal B, pp. [236] and [201], are used in "Ethics," *Lectures*, II, 146 and 145–146; both are transcribed in Notebook Man, p. [49] above. "Reason & Understanding" is discussed in "Religion" and Goethe is quoted in "Trades and Professions."

[381] "Man . . . Literary Ethics", in pencil, is written to the right of the first column on p. [168] and partially overwritten by "1 Man . . . 12 The Individual", the column printed to the right. Though "Man" was evidently the title of the first lecture at this stage, Emerson wrote "Introductory Lecture . . ." on the first page of the manuscript (see *Lectures*, II, 7).

[382] This column is written in ink so far to the right that "Professions" runs over

[169]³⁸³ Society   Manners
        〈Puckler Muskau's Dandy〉 [B 130]
        〈Society〉 Miss Martineau   124
             chance pleasures   307
                                     273
        ⎰Manners   256   130
        ⎱Ormond   [Enc. 269]
        〈Ld Falkland〉 [BB III, 97]
             talents   ⟍
             genius   ⟍
             〈eloquence〉

             〈marriage〉
             〈Be & Seem〉
             experience
             〈Strong will〉
             present too strong for the future
             The Antique

[170]   Philosophy of History
                         Intellectual Culture
                         Omnipresence of Spirit³⁸⁴

[171] The Course of Lectures on the Philosophy of History w〈ere〉as delivered at the Masonic Temple on Thursday Evenings commencing 8 December, 1836, & closing 2 March, 1837. The audience attending them 〈av〉might average 350 persons. The amount received from sale of tickets about $600.00. The Expense of the hall &c 169.00. Expense of advertising — ↑60.80 (see next pages)↓³⁸⁵

[172]³⁸⁶ Gave tickets   3 to T. H[askins]   W.C.M[artin].
   〈2 Mrs Ripley〉   2 to T W H[askins]   26 tickets sold
1 A A _____   4   A[bel] A[dams] total sum recd 149.55

onto p. [169] which faces it. "Science" became "Humanity of Science" and "The Age" became "The Present Age," but this is the final order.

³⁸³ P. [169] is in pencil. Notes below are developed in both "Society" and "Manners"; see p. [35] above.

³⁸⁴ These three titles are enclosed on three sides by an ornate pattern in pencil.

³⁸⁵ "60.80 . . . pages)" is in pencil.

³⁸⁶ P. [172] is in pencil except for "W.C.M. . . . 149.55", the last two names

1 [R. C.] Waterston

4	E[lizabeth] P P[eabody]	
2	M[argaret] F[uller]	
2	A B A[lcott]	
1	S B	195
2	C.T.J[ackson].	26
2	G B E[merson]	16
2	O[restes] A B[rownson]	237
2	N.L.F[rothingham].	
⟨2⟩3	E[zra].B.R[ipley].	
1	Courier	
1	Advertiser	
1	Post	}papers
1	Transcript	
1	Mrs M.B.	
3	E[lizabeth].H[oar].	
1	Dr B[artlett].	
1	Dr J[ackson].	
3	Mrs Greele	
↑1↓	Mr Blagden	
↑1↓	Mr [Barzillai] Frost	
↑1↓	Dr [Artemis] Stebbins	
↑2	E[zra] Ripley	
⟨M⟩1	Mrs Millel↓ [387]	

---

and the last five numbers on the page, which were added in ink. Later "Watertown", "Concord" (twice), "Boston", "Cam", and other practice penmanship were scrawled over the page in ink.

[387] In addition to those previously or easily identified, this list includes Emerson's uncle Thomas Haskins, and his cousin Thomas Waldo Haskins; Robert Cassie Waterston (1812–1893), then a student at the Harvard Divinity College and later one of the committee who corresponded with Emerson about the Divinity School Address; W. C. Martin, then superintendent of the Masonic Temple in Boston; George Barrell Emerson, another cousin; Ezra B. Ripley, son of Samuel Ripley and grandson of Dr. Ezra Ripley, Emerson's stepgrandfather; Elizabeth Hoar, who had been engaged to Emerson's brother Charles at the time of his death in May, 1836; Dr. Josiah Bartlett, the Emerson family physician; George Washington Blagden, minister of the Salem Street Church in Boston; Barzillai Frost, an assistant and later successor to Ezra Ripley at Concord's First Church; and Dr. Artemis Stebbins (1787–1871), both a doctor of medicine and a sporadic Swedenborgian preacher in New Bedford.

Intellectual Culture

1	Introductory Lecture	1. Man
2	The Antique	2 Science
3	Reason & Understanding	3 Art
4	Literary History	4 Literature
5	Art	5 Politics
6	Poetry	6 Religion
7	Rhetoric	7. Society
8	Religion	8 Trades & Profs
9	Science	9 Manners
10	Life ~~Frankfort 10s, 20s,~~	10 Ethics
11	Goethe	11. The Age
12	Literary Ethics	12 The Individual
	Trades & Professions	
	Manners & Customs	
	The Individual	

Plate I   Notebook F No. 1, page 168   Text, pages 173–174
Titles for the "Philosophy of History" series

146   Eloquence
Brasidas   The School

Health   Posthumous effect K 2
          Ashburton dinner E 331
          Boy playing ball is Jove E 159
          Pericles. Cousin VI. 108
                Plato
      activity   Test objects O 306 294 J 39
Classification D 35 120 207 Webster eloquence force U 161

Eloquent man must not speak too much
St Cecilia V. J O 112
   Gratitude O 80

Realism of Swedenborg Creed O 349

Plate II   Notebook Φ, page 146   Text, pages 392–393, 397
Notes for "Eloquence" added to notes for "The School"

4

If I love you ~~what is that~~ to ~~you~~ D 295
Allstons Genius & defect D 296, 314, 332,
If the Absolute theory of life is wrong use votes D 297
The ~~poor~~ mean must have ~~what~~ D 298
The Compensations of Calamity D 298
Self-help must be preached. Yankee boy D 299
The garden discovery D 300
No History, only biography. D 300, 322,
We disbelieve in the puissance of Today D 301-2
Nature says, So hot Sir! D 302
A man amenable for his vocation D 303
A mans self travels ghost like with him D 303
Manual labor. Heroism of 1839 D 304
Why give & Children all ye romance of life 305
Lotus eaters: Damper of reform D 306
We fear for the Not-Natural D 307
Compression of style ellipsis. D 307, 350, 356
Language, spolia prima D 307
Our Scholars not learned or unnoble D 308
The Consecration of Sabbath owns ye desecration of D 308
List of reforms D 309
Foreigners write as well as natives D 309
My life a may game D 309
Love thaumaturgic D 309
Great man among small matters shows the divine in them 310
The riches of Nature in Dartmouth sheriff D 310
Doctrine of the Soul D 311

313, 304, 323

Plate III   Notebook Ж, page 4   Text, pages 426–428
Survey for the "Present Age" series, marginal markings
and horizontal and vertical use marks

Manual labor *Self* 630
Temperance
Antimoney
Non resistance
        Objection to modes E 14, 25,
        Temperance hateful
        I hate yr personalities
        Caution to martyrs
        One idea bad C 255
        dont vaunt principles
        Value of Inaction Sup 78

        Nobleness of reform
        Honor yr station
        Obligation to reform D 237
        Dont quarrel with a man to persu. E 98
        Great men liker to be conciliated D 204
        Reality ten of world D 354
        Nonconformity Self r 49 ~3

Plate IV   *Notebook Ж, page 56*   *Text, pages 463–464*
Working notes for "Reforms"

Reform
~~Reforms~~

Obligation to the Reformers D 337
Reform in housekeeping D 342
The problem how to spend a day nobly D 350 & E 21
Manual labor D 304, 313, 328, 131,
  The garden discovery D 300
  Dangers of reform D 306
  List of reforms D 309
  Reform must not be partial D 328
  Consecration of Sunday desecration of monday D 308
  Objection to conforming D 337
  The Doctrine of Silence S 353, 152, Epaminondas D 244,
  Temperance conscious is not temperance S 131, E 22,
  Doctrine of Hatred S 336, E 22
  Licenses D 96
  Potatoes D 184
  ~~How many men will measure with a ton of oats D 311~~
  Advantage of the orators of a principle B 33
  Anti money D 154
  Health E 34
Nothing gained by admitting omnipotence of limitation E 11
  ~~I cannot vote for your measure &c good E 14~~
  ~~Extent of new world &c D 111~~
  ~~Trust thyself E 51~~

  Honor the Philanthropies of yr day D 287,
  Progresses Janus faced D 258
  Fear goes before rottenness D 293

Plate V   Notebook Ж, page 57   Text, pages 464–465
                 Collection for "Reforms"

90

the Carpenters cord if you hold your
ear close enough is musical in
the breezes.

It is well said by Taylor in note to Pro
clus that the infirmities ascribed
to the gods, as lameness to Vulcan
blindness to Love &c express transcendences (See Proclus in Tim. vol. 1, p. 120

Nature in 𝕏 p 33

Poetry is "wanton heed & giddy Cunning."

Real words good as real actions 2 226
all poems unfinished H 112
music first before thought 1. 55
Every word a trope 6 43, 57, 60.
Power to affect me in natural objects
impersonal & unrepenting. H 45
Every promise many fulfilments F 112

Perpetual Miracle wonder &
rapture See Lecture

Plate VI   Notebook Φ, page 90   Text, page 347
Notes for the essay "The Poet"

[inside back cover] [388]
↑Art 80, 82, 84.↓   A partial *Index* inside *front* cover

_____

          James Munroe sold ⟨3⟩tickets   3
          H Gray & Co   198
          W.C. Martin   72
          S Colman   27
↑Carlyle 154, 158, 162,↓   300

                                $600.00
          Expense of Hall &c   169
                                    431
     600   16   50
                                    381
Expense of Advertising
          Dutton & Wentworth's bill   13 50
          Daily Advertiser   15.71
          Courier   14.97
          Morning Post   16 62
                                       60 80
                     Hall   169.
          Expense of Tickets   9.25   600 00
                               239 05   239 05
                                            360.95

[388] "Carlyle . . . 162," is written in ink over "S Colman"; "Art . . . 84.",
in the same ink and hand, was probably added at the same time. See also the front
cover verso above, where the pages on Carlyle are indexed in the same ink and hand.
The rest of the page is in pencil.

Δ

1837–1841, 1850, 1857, 1862

Emerson first used Notebook Δ in 1837 for collections and notes for the ten lectures in the "Human Culture" series, probably beginning it shortly before October 11, when he advertised the series, and continuing till the final lecture on February 7, 1838. From December 11, 1837, to May 10, 1842, he used part of it for postal accounts. He also used it in drafting "War," a lecture delivered March 12, 1838. In June, 1838, he used two blank pages for a draft of his preface to Carlyle's *Critical and Miscellaneous Essays*. In August and September, 1838, he entered the names of people to whom he sent copies of the Divinity School Address and the Dartmouth Oration. A year later, in November or early December, 1839, he took it up for notes and drafts of the "Introductory" lecture and others in the "Present Age" series. In April, 1840, he used it for a draft of his introductory article, "The Editors to the Reader," in the first issue of *The Dial*. Later in 1840 or early in 1841 he added notes for "Friendship" (some may have been used in the lecture "Private Life") to earlier notes for "The Heart," and an outline of the essay "Circles." He used it for another list of names, probably recipients of "The Method of Nature" in August, 1841, and for a draft for the introductory "Lecture on the Times," probably in December, 1841. He jotted down the titles of lectures probably given in 1850. In 1857 he entered his recollections of a lawsuit, using some blank pages and writing over some earlier material, and in 1862 he wrote notes for the lecture "Perpetual Forces" over earlier notes.

Notebook Δ is a copybook with stiff cover boards measuring 16.7 x 21.4 cm and covered with blue, red, and brown marbled paper, and a worn brown leather spine marked "Δ 1837" in ink. The cover is labeled "Δ". The leaves, faintly ruled, measure 16.4 x 20.6 cm. Including 2 front and 2 back flyleaves, there are 174 pages. The leaf bearing pages 79–80 has been torn out. Emerson numbered the first flyleaf 1. Pages numbered in ink are 1, 3, 5–7, 9–19, 22–23, 29, 34–35, 41, 47, 53–54, 62–63, 66, 68–69, 72–73, 82–87, 89–93, and 167; pages numbered in pencil are 20–21, 24, 27–28, 36–38, 40, 42–46, 49–52, 56–59, 64–65, 67, 70–71, 74–78, 81, 88, 94–97, 100–113, 116–117, 120–140, 142–166, 172–173, and 175–176; page 118 was numbered in pencil in the earlier sequence, then renumbered 108 in ink and the following page numbered 109 in ink in 1862. Pages 30–31, 39, and 98–99 are numbered in ink over the same in pencil. Turning the notebook upside down Emerson began numbering the first ruled page 1 (172 in the front to back sequence) continuing to 11; all but the first number are erased, and only one entry on page 11 (162) was made in this sequence. The rest of the pages are unnumbered. Pages 26, 33–34, 37–39, 45, 60–62, 101, 114–115, 142, 159, 161, 163, 165, and 168–169 are blank. Pasted to the bottom of page 3 is a newspaper clipping of the announcement drafted above it for the "Human Culture" series. Between pages 4 and 5 (but photographed between pages 26 and 27 in 1955) is an engraved portrait of James Ferguson with a piece of blue paper pasted to its back. Pages 17, 29, 64, 72, 106–109, 131, 133, 134, 136, 137, 144, 148, 152, and 164 have four or more revisions of accidentals.

[front cover]   Δ

[front cover verso] [1] ⟨128⟩   The Age 128   [1841]

Earnestness	21	The Soul	p 25
Comic	24	Society	p 30
Heart	95	Circles	167
The Prudent	75		
Laws of life	1⟨0⟩36		
Miscellanies	13		
Instincts	23		
Nature	19		
B⟨y⟩uy & sell	29	Pym	63
The Unconscious	35	Hist. of Liberty,	94
Being vs Seeming	41		
The Age	47		
Ethics	53	Perpetual Forces	106
Politics	63		
Means	73		
Heroic	83		
End	93		
Culture	103		
Convenient	113		
Lecture	156		

[1] Emerson began Notebook Δ methodically. The earliest entries in the index, "Miscellanies 13 . . . Convenient 113", in ink, are probably trial topics for the "Human Culture" series, with six pages set aside for each of five topics, ten pages for each of the rest. "Lecture 156 . . . The Holy 123" is in pencil. "Earnestness 21 . . . life 1⟨0⟩36" is in pencil in a larger hand. "The Soul . . . 167" is in ink, the first two entries probably written at the same time. "⟨128⟩ . . . [1841]" was added later in pencil. "Pym 63 . . . 106", in pencil in a late hand, was probably added in 1862.

[1]   R. W. Emerson.

                                        1841

                                   Δ

[1857 Notes of the case in court of Bartlett
          vs. Emerson. p. 6⟨6⟩5]

[2] Divinity College Address sent to[2]

	Dr J. Dalton	"	E. Hoar.	"
o	Dr C. Francis	"	S. Hoar Esq	"
o	Dr Frothingham	"	E. R. Hoar	"
	Dr Ware	"	H.D. Thoreau	"
o	Dr Ware Jr	"	J. Bartlett	"
o	Dr Palfrey	"	A.H. Nelson, Esq.	"
2	Mr S Ripley	"	J. Keyes, Esq.	"
	Dr Ripley	"	T. Carlyle	"
	Mr Frost	"	C.S. Wheeler.	
o	Mr Stetson	"	Hayward	
	Mr Furness	"	Miss Searle	

[2] The Divinity College Address (see Notebook L Concord, pp. [6]–[16] above) was published by August 21, 1838. Recipients not previously or easily identified include Convers Francis, a Watertown pastor, and the Reverend Caleb Stetson, a Harvard classmate, both members of the Transcendental Club; the Reverend Leonard Withington (1789–1885), a Congregational minister at Newbury, Mass.; George Partridge Bradford, a lifelong friend; probably the Reverend George Moore, a friend of William Emerson; Edmund Hosmer, a Concord neighbor; John Milton Cheney, a Harvard classmate and cashier of the Concord bank; Albert Hobart Nelson, a Concord lawyer and socialite; John Keyes, a Concord lawyer, county treasurer, and director of several Concord corporations; Charles Stearns Wheeler (1816–1843), an instructor in history at Harvard who had aided Emerson in preparing Carlyle's *Miscellanies*; the Reverend George Bush (1796–1859), a Presbyterian minister; and probably William Mackay Prichard, an 1833 Harvard graduate and a friend and later partner of William Emerson. Both Bush and Withington spoke at Dartmouth the same day Emerson delivered his Oration.

	James F. Clark	"	Dr C.T. Jackson	
	Rev. L. Withington	"	Rev O Dewey	
o	Mr Alcott	"	Rev G. Bush	
	Miss Fuller	"	Mr Prichard	
	Miss Peabody	"	M.M.E.	
	W. Emerson	"		
	G. P. Bradford	"		⟨7⟩150
F	H. Hedge	"		5
	Mrs Brown	"		750
o	Dr John Ware	"		75
o	P. C. Brooks	"		25
o	E. Everett	"		
	G. Moore	"		
	E. Hosmer	"		
	J. M. Cheney.	"		

[3]   [Advertisement of 11 October, 1837.]

Mr R. W. Emerson proposes to deliver a Course of Lectures on the Principles, the Means, & the End of Human Culture. The subject will be illustrated by historical & biographical notices, and will be treated in reference to the condition & interests of Society at the present day. The Course will comprise ten or more lectures to be delivered at the Masonic Temple once a week; beginning, probably, on the first Wednesday of December.[3]

[4]   Dartmouth Oration sent to [4]

"	Rev Dr Frothingham	"	Dr J. Bartlett.
"	C A Bartol	"	S. Hoar.
"	C Robbins	"	J.M. Cheney

[3] Emerson delivered the first of the ten lectures in this course on Wednesday, December 6, 1837. A clipping of this advertisement is pasted at the bottom of the page; it ends, "beginning on the first Wednesday of December, at 7 o'clock, PM.

"Tickets to the course, at Two Dollars each, may be had of C. C. Little & James Brown, 112, Washington street, or of James Munroe & Co. 134, Washington st."

[4] Emerson delivered the address "Literary Ethics" (W, I, 153–187) at Dartmouth on July 24, 1838; it was published by September 8, 1838. Recipients not previously or easily identified include Cyrus Augustus Bartol, a Boston pastor, and Chandler Robbins, Emerson's successor at the Second Church, both members of the

" Dr Francis	" N. Brooks
" Dr Palfrey	" C.W. Upham
" H Ware Jr	" T. Carlyle 9 copies
" J. Ware M D	" H Martineau
" E. Everett	" J Sterling
" P.C. Brooks	" J. Wilder
" Rev C Stetson	" J.R Lowell
" Mr A B Alcott	" Geo Briggs
H S McKean	" W.M. Jackson
" Dr G. Bradford	" S. Searle
Mrs Brown	" B[oston].D[aily]. Advertiser
" G.P Bradford	" A Adams
" Rev. S. Ripley	" Isaac Hedge
" Rev B Frost	" G.W. Haven
" Rev E Ripley	B Rodman
" M M E.	Rev E.B. Hall
" Miss Peabody	D.A. White
" J F Clarke	Miss Burley
" ⟨M⟩S. M. Fuller	E. Palmer
" Rev L Withington	J L Russell
" J. Keyes Esq	T.W. Haskins
Dr Adams	2 E Palmer
Dr [A. D.] Hobbs	J. Very

Transcendental Club; Henry S. McKean, a young enginee⸱ in Cambridge who had volunteered to correct the proofs of Carlyle's *Miscellanies*; Dr. Gamaliel Bradford, a mentor since Emerson's Latin School days, a physician, lecturer, and writer; Drs. Adams and Hobbs, apparently residents of Waltham, who had sent Emerson a gift of 31 trees in May, 1837; Mary Howland Russell, a Plymouth friend of Lidian Emerson; Nathan Brooks, a prominent Concord lawyer, bank director, and secretary of an insurance company; Charles Wentworth Upham, a Harvard classmate; the Reverend John Wilder, a Concord pastor from 1833 to 1839; George Ware Briggs, associate pastor of the First Congregational Church in Plymouth and a member of the Transcendental Club; William M. Jackson, a family friend of Lidian in Plymouth; George Wallis Haven, a Portsmouth lawyer and brother-in-law of William Emerson; Benjamin Rodman, a New Bedford friend and correspondent; the Reverend Edward B. Hall, a fellow student at Harvard and a Unitarian minister; Daniel A. White, Judge of Probate of Salem; Susan Burley, who had recently lent Emerson some books (see *L*, II, 154 and 174); Edward Palmer, a reformer and itinerant preacher, the "No-Money" man who visited Emerson in October, 1838; and John Lewis Russell, a Harvard classmate of Charles Emerson.

C.S. Wheeler
   " F.H. Hedge
    C T Jackson
   " Mary Russell

[5] Ethics, or Philosophy of Life, or Culture.
What topics have we [5]

> Society. Have it on your own terms
>
> ⟨V⟩Trade or Calling. Your own; but where circumstances oppose, have this consolation — that — he who uses life symbolically makes little account whether cups or platters they be he works.[6]
>
> Universality of the Individual
>
>> Capacity of Poetry — as a harp by ⟨being⟩ⁿ tightening the strings, is made sonorous to the wind so every man may put himself into the state of unison with nature.
>>
>> N.Y. broker.
>>
>> Write verses without larks & nightingales drawing your alphabet from *your*ⁿ eyes.
>>
>> The Glance.
>>
>> Importance of one individual. An opinion how rare. an action.
>>
>> We feel as the last company we saw affect us. A ragged coat looks revolutionary [7]
>>
>> Every body knows as much as the Savant. Waken the soul & you will find quick how much you know. The dark walls

---

[5] The notes that follow are probably the earliest planning for Emerson's 1837–1838 lecture series. The title, undecided here, became "Human Culture" by October 11, 1837, when he advertised the course. Passages cited on the page are used in several different lectures.

[6] "Have it . . . works." is struck through in ink with a vertical use mark. With "cups or platters", cf. Journal C, p. [50], used in "Prudence," *Lectures*, II, 326.

[7] "The Glance . . . revolutionary" is struck through in ink with a vertical use mark. With "The Glance.", cf. "The Heart," *Lectures*, II, 283–284. With "An opinion how rare.", cf. Journal C, p. [33], used in "Being and Seeming," *Lectures*, II, 304, and cf. p. [130] below. "A ragged . . . revolutionary", in A, p. [93], and Notebook Man, p. [50] above, is used in "The Senses and the Soul," *The Dial*, II (Jan. 1842), 378 (*Lectures*, II, 362).

of your mind are scrawled all over with facts & thoughts.
Bring a light & read the inscriptions [8]

[6] ⟨It seems as if⟩ no man entertains just views of the human
capacity. All things are in the human constitution. And life is wast⟨y⟩ed
if various & bold trials are not made. To bring heaven into the family
& the day labor is my aim.
I doubt not that ⟨par⟩ men are now educated that party, dependence,
sense & sin do also teach but as I believe self trust will be a more rapid
assumption of the manly robe I am constrained to speak[.]
    Why shines this Ideal evermore in the mind? Is it not accom-
panied with an oath of God that it is true & practicable? But men it is
gravely said are not perfect. However gravely & ⟨de⟩ pardonably this
may be said for mankind, never can it with pardon be assumed for the
individual himself. It damns him to mediocrity & to deterioration.
Supreme value of facts
Science
Judge of their value by the use you make of those laws you have.
Could you spare any?

[7] Demonology   Dreams
    Superstition
    Animal Magnetism
    Society   Conversation   A 21   ⌐
    Self-life of young men   B 61
    Capt Franklin's floating ice   B 25
    Solitude of the Heartless   A 114
    Compound origin of man; & debt   A 116
    Advantage of a Cause like Abolition   B 33 [9]

    [8] "Every body . . . inscriptions", struck through in ink with a vertical use
mark and in pencil with a diagonal use mark, is used in "The Head," Lectures, II,
251. Cf. Journal C, p. [164], used in "Intellect," W, II, 332–333. See p. [131]
below.
    [9] The first three lines on p. [7] are in ink, the rest in pencil. The page may be
a collection for "General Views," the last lecture in the "Human Culture" series;
see pp. [106] and [136]–[140] below, probably collections for the same lecture.
"Demonology   Dreams" and the passage from Journal B, p. [25], are used in
"The Senses and the Soul," The Dial, II (Jan. 1842), 375 and 379 (Lectures, II,
359 and 363). Passages in A, pp. [21] (also copied in Notebook Man, p. [104]

[8] The Editor offers to the public these volumes ⟨at st⟩ in obedience to their call. ↑⟨To most⟩ To all but a few the contents of these vols. will be new.↓ Many readers will here find pages which spoke to their youthful mind in the scattered anonymous ⟨p⟩sheets of magazines with emphasis that ⟨did not suff⟩ hindered them from sleep. They will be glad to see in this collection the spiritual history of the author[,] the record of his studies & know the course of his reading & what outward materials went to the edification of the man. In undertaking this publication it was thought that a larger portion of the miscellanies would be absorbed in two volumes. Two more volumes will presently be printed which will contain all the scattered articles of the Author up to the present time.

Add to these the translation of Wilhelm Meister (in three volumes ↑12 mo↓, London 1824), the German Romance (4 vols 12 mo London 1827), & the life of Schiller,   Sartor Resartus, Boston 1835 & the French Revolution[.]

[9] To the voluntary labors of two friends of the Editor residing in Cambridge the public are indebted for the correction of numerous ↑typographical↓ errors in the original volumes.

Mr Carlyle has expressed in letters to the editor & other individuals a great satisfaction in the success of his literary labors in this country.   himself prepared the list of his complete works ⟨after which by⟩ which has been exactly followed in the present volumes[.]
⟨Th⟩ Many young men will remember with pleasure the rich & wise genius who ⟨spoke⟩ ↑wrote↓ with so much wit & so much hope when ⟨the⟩^{n} amidst the mediocrity of modern teaching they complained that none of them spoke to their Condition.[10]

---

above) and [116], are used in a manuscript fragment printed as part of "Private Life," *Lectures*, III, 249 and 251–252, but possibly part of the missing manuscript of "General Views" (see p. [136] below and notes in *Lectures*, II, 480); the pasage in B, p. [33], is used in The Present Age: "Introductory," *Lectures*, III, 197 and 198.

[10] Emerson used both paragraphs on p. [8] and the second and third paragraphs on p. [9] in "Advertisement," his preface to volume I of Thomas Carlyle's *Critical and Miscellaneous Essays*, 4 vols. (Boston, 1838–1839), dating it "*Concord, June 24, 1838.*"

[10]¹¹   Unbelief grows out of analysis

Analysis destroys the Infinite that overhangs all things by confining the attention on the economical

Prerogative is gone

Astrology, Magic, Palmistry,

Authority falls in ⟨C⟩Bench Church College Medicine

E⟨p⟩xperiment alone is credible

There is somewhat ghastly about this empiricism.

At first delighted with the exercise of the intellect, & the surprise of the results, & the sense of power that accrues we are like hunters on the scent & soldiers who rush to battle; but when the game is caught[,] when the enemy ⁿ ⟨no⟩lies cold in his blood at our feet we are alarmed at our solitude[;] we would vainly recal the life that so offended us & the face seems no longer that of an enemy, we are willing to turn the sword on our own breast.

Want of faith in Church   C 65   E 67   D 330

Aurora   D 350

In Medicine   C 191

No art   D 338

No learning   D 99   96   308   190¹²

---

¹¹ Emerson used pages [10]–[12], left blank earlier, for notes and drafts for The Present Age: "Introductory," *Lectures*, III, 185–201; more notes for this lecture are on pp. [17] and [27]–[32] below, and Notebook Ж, pp. [47]–[48] below. Some of the use marked passages not located in the lecture may have been used in five leaves missing from the lecture manuscript. Some are found in "The Spirit of the Times," a lecture manuscript of the 1850's partly recast from The Present Age: "Introductory," and in "Historic Notes of Life and Letters in New England," *W*, X, 323–370, and "Boston," *W*, XII, 181–211, both lectures put together in the 1860's from earlier material.

¹² "Unbelief grows . . . delighted" is struck through in ink with a diagonal use mark, which Emerson extended first through "our own breast.", then through "308   190". "Unbelief grows . . . economical" is developed, and "Prerogative . . . Palmistry," and passages in Journal C, p. [65], E, p. [67], D, pp. [351]–[352] (the "Aurora" passage), [338], [99], and [308], are used in The Present Age: "Introductory," *Lectures*, III, 190–191, 193–194, 192, 194, 195, and 194. For "Prerogative is gone", "Authority . . . College Medicine", and the passages in C, p. [191], and D, p. [96], see cancellations printed in The Present Age: "Introductory," *Lectures*, III, 456–457 (notes); see also "Historic Notes of Life and Letters in New England," *W*, X, 327 and 329, where "Authority . . . credible" is used.

[11] "If you count 10 stars you will fall down dead" Let us
see   1 2 3 4 5 6 7 8 9 10 & laughs aloud. If you spill the Salt, if you
cross your knife & fork. If you make hay on Sunday. if you tell a lie
The King is anointed of God & God will avenge him. They insulted,
⟨a⟩restrained, imprisoned & beheaded the King & the whole land
eat & slept as well as usual. The Church ⟨is⟩ hath the keys of
heaven. Episcopal ordination is sacred & the weal of the world
stands in that. Well[,] Men ordained themselves, the laity appointed things themselves, the laity preached, exhorted, prayed,
gave the Lord's supper & found as good order in their church as
in that out of which they came. ⟨The Judicial cannot⟩ See how
petulantly the attorney squints at the Bench & questions its authority, see how the client questions the office of the attorney, &
proposes to argue his own case.[13]

[12] Side by side with this analysis is the surviving tradition[,]
a vast ⟨a⟩numerical amount of Minds inactive, weak, vicious, who find
themselves heirs of the old forms & fancy that these may last their
day. They defend their altars & hearths but not in the faith of the altar
or the love of the hearth but for the good of property only. The
assailants meantime ⟨a⟩degenerate also. They ⟨apply the s⟩ ↑⟨lo⟩↓ [n] lose
the sentiment & learn to apply their weapons of logic & philosophy
only to destroy. Every sentiment builds. ⟨The Understanding without⟩
Analysis without sentiment razes. They destroy for wages as their
opponents build for wages,[n] hirelings on both sides. Hence the immense talkativness of the time. E
     Life is feeble. Men are sick   ocular   meddlesome

The Defence of forms has the worst effect upon the intellect. Deprived
of real objects it withers to a dwarf[;] it has no food[;] it becomes a
mere talker. The life of the senses grows[;] men are sick   ocular
meddlesome.[14]

---

[13] P. [11] is struck through in ink with a curved, vertical use mark; " 'If you
count . . . usual." is used in The Present Age: "Introductory," Lectures, III, 191,
followed in the manuscript by two missing leaves. Cf. also "Tragedy," Lectures, III,
106. With "⟨The Judicial . . . case.", cf. a canceled passage in The Present Age:
"Introductory," Lectures, III, 457(notes).
     [14] "Side by . . . both sides." and "The Defence . . . it becomes" are struck

[13]   Miscellanies

Most men have a conventional and ostentatious, and a business side. Be introduced to them, visit them at their houses and you see the first. Deal with them in trade or affairs of tender interest to them, and you know the other. One is sour & pompous; the other hearty & suppliant. They resemble the two entrances of all our Concord houses. The front door is very fair to see, painted green, with a brass knocker, but is always bolted, and you might as well beat the stone wall, as tap there; but the farmer slides round the house into a quiet back-door that admits him at once to his warm fire & loaded table.[15]
We aim to forward reform dynamically, or by votes, public opinion, laws, ↑associations,↓ & not spiritually by the omnipotence of private thought.[16]

[14] Happy is the hearing man unhappy the speaking man B 309
                                                      C 167 [17]

Nothing is useless. A superstition is a hamper or basket to carry useful lessons in. [B 313]

Do they not make a bridge somewhere of such construction that the strength of the whole is made to bear the strain on any one plank? Do they not charter banks sometimes on the provision that the entire property of all the stockholders is accountable for every dollar of their issue? Such a bridge, such a bank is a man. [B 284]
    Life & death. We are like children brought up in towns who

---

through in ink with single vertical use marks. "Side by . . . tradition" is used in The Present Age: "Introductory," *Lectures,* III, 197. With "They defend . . . sides." and "The Defence . . . talker", cf. a canceled passage, *ibid.,* p. 460(notes). "Men . . . ocular" is used in the lecture "The Spirit of the Times."
    [15] "Most men . . . resemble" and "resemble . . . table." are struck through in ink with single vertical use marks, and the paragraph is circumscribed in ink. See p. [21] below. "They resemble . . . table." is expanded from Journal B, p. [313].
    [16] This sentence is struck through in ink with a vertical use mark.
    [17] "Happy is . . . man" (cf. Journal B, p. [108], and Notebook Man, p. [48]· above) and the passages cited in B, p. [309], and C, p. [167], are used in "The Head," *Lectures,* II, 257–258, and "Intellect," *W,* II, 342 and 343.

think the sun & moon a part of the municipal illumination like the gas lanthorns & wonder how the poor country folks can see. — [18]
Sp[irit]. Mss 80 [19]

[15] Chapter on Time   B 275 [20]
   Oaths   B 109, 261, [21]

As history's best use is to enhance our estimate of the present hour so the value of such an observer as Goethe who draws out of our consciousness some familiar fact & makes it glorious by showing it in the light of thought is this[:] that he makes us prize all our being by suggesting its inexhaustible wealth; for we feel that all our experience is thus convertible into jewels. He moves our wonder at the mystery of ↑our↓ life.

Leave father mother for my sake   B 210

Reception. Keep the organs open as for life: Hate egotism & pride for they shut & seal. Hate ambition for it delirates. See Fontanes on perfection in B [300]. See a page on greeting disgrace   C. p. 158 & 166 [22]

[18] "Do they not make . . . man." is struck through in pencil with a diagonal use mark, in ink with a diagonal use mark extended through the second paragraph, and "Do they not make . . . on the provision" with a third vertical use mark in ink, possibly a false start with a dry pen. The paragraph from Journal B, p. [284], is used in "Being and Seeming," *Lectures*, II, 295–296; cf. A, p. [6].

[19] For other probable references to "Sp[irit]. Mss" see pp. [16], [121₁], [122₁], and [123] below; no such manuscript has been located. It had at least 81 pages, and may have been made up, like Notebook Man, of passages copied from other journals; the latest such passage identified, from Journal B, p. [184], is dated May 22, 1836. Several entries listed were used in the lecture "Holiness."

[20] The "Chapter on Time" is three sentences taken from Journal B, pp. [259], [236], and [133], and a fourth added later, a variation of sentences in B, pp. [4] and [49], used in "On the Best Mode of Inspiring a Correct Taste in English Literature," *Lectures*, I, 213, and "Ethics," and "The Head," *Lectures*, II, 146 and 257.

[21] Both passages are used in "Being and Seeming," *Lectures*, II, 297–298.

[22] Passages in Journal B, p. [210], and C, pp. [158] and [166], are used in "The Head," *Lectures*, II, 258–259. B, p. [210], is also used in "Intellect," *W*, II, 343–344, and C, p. [158], in "Compensation," *W*, II, 117–118.

[16] We do what we can & then make a theory to prove our practice the best. [A 77] [23]

Cant. The abomination of desolation is an affected enthusiasm[.] [24]
Not know where to find him, &c. *Mss ⟨spirit⟩S* 41

We should cleave to the usage until we are clear it is wrong
Never apologize & you never need. Phocion ↑S 50↓ [25]
Nothing but humility is a match for pride [26] Spirit Mss p. 81
The peace principle   C 144 [27]
Persons   *Mss ⟨spirit⟩S* 67 [B 184] [28]
Desire of truth & desire of repose   B [123]
Room for all gifts; happy the Ear   B 309 [29]
Private Chapel   B 61 [30]
Fear not to be besmirched   B 140
Genius always situated alike   C 3 [31]
Politics too easy to a philosopher   B 308 [32]

---

[23] See Notebook Man, p. [48] above. Cf. "Doctrine of the Soul," *Lectures*, III, 13.

[24] See Notebook Man, p. [91] above.

[25] This entry is struck through in ink with a vertical use mark. "*S*" may mean "Spirit Mss"; see n. 19 above. The passage, from Journal A, p. [115], is transcribed in Notebook Man, p. [72] above, and used in "Heroism," *W*, II, 260 (*Lectures*, II, 337). It is also listed on p. [82] below and in F No. 1, p. [129] above, as are seven other entries on p. [16]. This line and the rest of the page, in a smaller hand, may be part of a survey of the journals during early planning for the "Human Culture" series.

[26] This sentence is used in "Holiness," *Lectures*, II, 347.

[27] Emerson developed this passage throughout "War," his address before the American Peace Society in Boston on March 12, 1838. See *W*, XI, 149–176.

[28] See p. [123] below. The passage cited is used in "Holiness," *Lectures*, II, 353–354.

[29] This and the preceding entry are struck through in ink with a vertical use mark. Both passages cited are used in "The Head," *Lectures*, II, 256 and 257, and "Intellect," *W*, II, 341–342. The second passage is also listed in collections on pp. [14] above and [130] below, and in Notebook F No. 1, p. [129] above.

[30] Emerson listed this paragraph several times; see p. [7] above and Notebook F No. 1, pp. [13], [35], [42], and [129] above. Cf. also Man, p. [74] above, a related passage transcribed from Journal B, p. [140], listed below.

[31] See also p. [130] below and Notebook F No. 1, pp. [4] and [129] above.

[32] This entry is struck through in ink with a vertical use mark. Emerson copied

Magic of learning languages	*A* 64
Individual force	*A* 88
Words of C. Wren	B 255
The guage of Courthouse & Commencement	B [33]
Truth, Story of Capt. Ross	B [124] [34]
Character not ephemeral but cumulative [35]	
Retention of simple & high sentiments	*A* 13 [36]

[17] Sheridan   B 327 [37]
          Demonology   B 240 [38]

The gayest petal serves the flower; the finest form in woman is only perfectest health.[39] [B 231]

The moment the intellect outstrips the active power, there is a recoil of shame & emptiness. If we speak a greater holiness than our will consents unto, we are devils to ourselves presently. Nature & the Spirit will be obeyed. You shall speak only when ⟨they⟩ ↑it↓ commands & stop on the instant it withdraws[.]

We will the act of suicide when we have talked too well at Sunday Schools or preached too well at Church.

It seems a War betwixt the Intellect & the Affection. It seems a crack in Nature which split Christendom into Old & New, Calvinism into old & new School. Quakerism into old & new. Methodism into old & new, England into Reform & Conservation, America into Whig

---

the paragraph in Notebook F No. 1, p. [77] above, and used it in "Prudence," *Lectures*, II, 321–322.

[33] See p. [21] below.

[34] This line is struck through in ink with a vertical use mark; the anecdote was used in "Prudence," *Lectures*, II, 318–319.

[35] See Notebook F No. 1, p. [52] above.

[36] This line is struck through in ink with a vertical use mark; the passage is used in "Heroism," *W*, II, 262 (*Lectures*, II, 338).

[37] "Sheridan" is struck through in ink with a vertical use mark. The passage is used in "Being and Seeming," *Lectures*, II, 301.

[38] "B 240" is in pencil; cf. "Demonology," *Lectures*, III, 163–164.

[39] "The gayest . . . health." is in pencil.

& Democrat, Philosophy into Impulse & Rule,   The very Turk
has put on a Frankish uniform & Frank learns to sit in a chair.[40]
  History accurate now which was wild then
  Burton's Anat. p ⟨6⟩5

[18]   Topics
    The Heroic
    Vocation   The Hands
    Art   Beauty
    Intellect   Books   Composition
    The Holy
    Social   Conversation   Peace & War
    The Mystic
    The Convenient
    Proportion [41]
Childhood is holy. The Intellect advances at first holily but instantly
detects falsehood in its objects of worship;[n] then it outruns the Affection & we have the ⟨cold⟩ heartless dissector only warmed by the
activity of mind[,] not by the fire of the heart. Again & again he recalls
the sentiment but finds it hopeless to attach himself again to the God
of his infancy. He must arise & journey into new regions of thought —
& there & not in the land of his fathers will God manifest himself
unto him. .

[19]   Nature
Botany or buying wood   B 304
Wealth of Nature   B 315 [42]
Sleep   B 298 [43]

[40] "It seems . . . chair." is used in The Present Age: "Introductory," *Lectures*,
III, 187–188.
  [41] "Topics . . . Proportion", in pencil, is evidently an early list of topics for
the "Human Culture" series; see pp. [170]–[171] below.
  [42] "Botany" and "Wealth" are struck through with two diagonal use marks, one
ink and one erased pencil. The first passage is used in "The Eye and Ear," *Lectures*,
II, 274–275; the second passage is used in "Doctrine of the Hands," *Lectures*, II,
235, and "Powers and Laws of Thought," *W*, XII, 28.
  [43] "Sleep" is struck through in ink with a vertical use mark. The passage cited
is used in "Prudence," *Lectures*, II, 322–323.

American aspects of the forest	B 293 C 137 [44]
Approach of Winter	B 292
Appetite for natural influences	C 136 [45]
Passenger pigeon	B 257
Sun & Moon	C 211 [46]

But whence comes this Sickness & Hollowness & Despondency?
It comes when the Will is inactive; when we know better than we do;
when we shrink to accept this new law;

It comes never to those who have taken their part, who follow the
Genius with peril of all convenience. But the Intellect loves safely to
picture out the new Republic before it denies its allegiance to the old
government, & get at once the ⟨c⟩praise of wit & the credit of loyalty.

[20] A man should stand among his fellow men as one coal lies
in the fire it has kindled radiating heat but lost in the general flame [47]

[B 149]

When you are sincerely pleased without any misgiving you are
nourished [C 188]
The virtue of society is really the basis of its stability. C 154

Put the heart in	Integrity
Palermo	Society corrupts
Natural relations or none	Trust instinct
[C 98]	
Creation is genius [C 60]	Something is
Simplicity	Fall back on Bei↑n↓g
Wild man attracts [C 188]	Silence Sleep
Self confiding boy [C 103]	Might of natural action
Foolish face [C 138]	Dr. J. Mr. H. Swedenborg [48]

[44] Both passages cited are used in "Literary Ethics," *W*, I, 169.

[45] This paragraph in Journal C, p. [136], is used in "The Eye and Ear,"
Lectures, II, 275, and "Nature," *W*, III, 171.

[46] This line is in pencil. The sentence in Journal C, p. [211], is used in
"Spiritual Laws," *W*, II, 147.

[47] P. [20] is in pencil. This sentence is used in "Holiness," *Lectures*, II, 356.

[48] "Put the heart in" and the passages from Journal C, pp. [154], [60], and

[21] [49]   Be & seem   The Heart continued
Cant   C 82   92 [50]
Simplicity
Put the heart in a Palermitan [51]
Guage of Court house &c   B 227, 33, [52]
Capt Ross. [B 124]   Truth [53]
Bifaced men p 13 ⟨B⟩ above [54]
Foolish face of praise   [C] 138   238
Natural relations or none   C 98
Conversation & life   C 60
Law of visits   B 124, 16
Dependence of the proud
The family culture   C 242
Why should we lie so   C 207
Appeal to the Future [C 185]
Dr J's speaking   B 157 [55]
Very hard to live well one day
Geo Chapman's verses   B 264 [56]
Bridge & Bank   B 284

-----

[188], are used in "Being and Seeming," *Lectures*, II, 305–309. In the first column, the paragraph in C, p. [98], is used in "Prudence," *Lectures*, II, 321, and *W*, II, 240, and the last two entries in "Self-Reliance," *W*, II, 48 and 55; "Foolish face" is also used in "Tendencies," *Lectures*, III, 309–310. The second column is an outline of "Being and Seeming," *Lectures*, II, 295–300.

[49] P. [21], in pencil, and indexed "Earnestness", is probably a collection for the lecture "Being and Seeming," though only half the entries are used there; the first paragraph (*Lectures*, II, 295) makes it clear that "Being and Seeming" was a continuation of the lecture "The Heart."

[50] The passage in Journal C, p. [92], is used in "Being and Seeming," *Lectures*, II, 300–301, and "Spiritual Laws," *W*, II, 153.

[51] This and the preceding entry are struck through in pencil with single vertical use marks. "Put the heart in" (a quotation from Scott) and "a Palermitan" (Journal C, p. [60]) are used in "Being and Seeming," *Lectures*, II, 308–309.

[52] The passage in Journal B, p. [33], is rewritten in C, p. [223], and used with a sentence from B, p. [227], in "Being and Seeming," *Lectures*, II, 301, and "Spiritual Laws," *W*, II, 157.

[53] Cf. "Prudence," *Lectures*, II, 318–319.

[54] Cf. Journal B, p. [313].

[55] "Why shd . . . Future", struck through in pencil with a vertical use mark, is used in "Being and Seeming," *Lectures*, II, 302–303 and 303; Emerson extended the use mark through "Dr J's . . . B 157", used, *ibid.*, p. 300.

[56] This and the preceding line are struck through in pencil with four lines, which may be either use marks or cancellations.

Sheridan   B 327
Well meaning is the backbone   C 149
Say what you believe   C 176   & write it   C 92 [57]
Wild man attracts   C 188 [58]
Self confident boy   C 103   Self truth   B.39
Creation is genius   C 60
You show character   C 80   expression   C 174 [59]
Young women   C 147, 163,
Boys know   C 175
Shadow follows body   C 211 [60]

[22]   Foot board of the pulpit   [A 51]

A man esteems himself as a mere circumstance & not as the solid adamant mundane ground plan of a universal man.
He thinks his internals are evanescent opal shades & won't bear scrutiny & description. Let him turn the telescope of Reflection on them. Let him compare them with durable things. He will find they outshine the sun & will grind to powder the iron & the stone of outward permanence. [Sicily 32]

When I see how near alike men all are & that always they seem to be on the edge of all that is great & yet invisibly retained in inactivity & unacquaintance with our powers it seems as if men were like the neuters of the hive[,] every one of which is capable of transformation into the queenbee[.] [A 73]

[57] "Bridge", "Sheridan", and "Say" are each struck through in pencil with single vertical use marks; "Sheridan . . . Say" is struck through in pencil with a diagonal use mark. All five passages are used in "Being and Seeming," *Lectures*, II, 295, 301, 299, and 300–301. Passages in Journal C, pp. [176] and [92], are also used in "Spiritual Laws," *W*, II, 156–157 and 153.

[58] "Wild man attracts" is struck through in pencil with two vertical use marks. The passage is used in "Being and Seeming," *Lectures*, II, 306.

[59] The paragraph in Journal C, p. [60]("Creation . . ."), is used in "Being and Seeming," *Lectures*, II, 304 and 308–309. With C, p. [80], used in "Spiritual Laws," *W*, II, 156, cf. "Being and Seeming," *Lectures*, II, 298. With "expression   C 174", cf. "The Eye and Ear," *Lectures*, II, 264–265, and C, p. [63].

[60] This and the two preceding lines are struck through in pencil with a vertical use mark. Passages in Journal C, pp. [147], [175], and [211], are used in "Being and Seeming," *Lectures*, II, 302 and 301. The last two passages are also used in "Spiritual Laws," *W*, II, 157–158.

The child is sincere & the man when he is alone but on the entrance of the second person hypocrisy begins.[61] [A 77]

[23]   Instincts

Respect yourself. You have first an instinct[,] then an opinion, then a knowledge, as the plant has root, bud, & fruit. Trust the instinct to the end though you cannot tell why or see why. It is vain to hurry it. By trusting it it shall ripen into thought & truth & you shall know why you believe.[62] [B 219]

We want faith in human nature ↑Chapman p 13↓

Society full of pretension   all the professions

Noble savages are disgusted at the general tameness

The game is not worth the candle. It is not that I[,] it's nobody uses it well

What remedy? Sincerity. Abstain.

Immense strength of natural action

  Trust Being: shadow, body:

  Truth first

  Don't profess. Why need you lie?

  Appeal to the future. Be a spectator   coal

↑Yet↓ There is salient energy to this common life & whatever trust we lay on it is well bestowed

Only so much as Being comes in does life rise

  1   The Seemers are all sustained by the Real

  2   Opinion action   The Heart performs miracles

   Put the heart in; Palermo;[63]

[24]   Comic

⟨C p 9⟩[64]

---

[61] P. [22] is in pencil. The first and third paragraphs, struck through in pencil with single vertical use marks, are used in "Being and Seeming," *Lectures*, II, 297 and 296.

[62] This paragraph, struck through in pencil with a diagonal use mark, is used in "The Head," *Lectures*, II, 251, and "Intellect," *W*, II, 330; cf. also "The Heart," *Lectures*, II, 293.

[63] "We want faith . . . Palermo;", in pencil, is a collection for "Being and Seeming," *Lectures*, II, 296–309.

[64] "Comic" and "⟨C p 9⟩" are in pencil; the passage is used in "Comedy," *Lectures*, III, 127.

Routine
Acceptance
No thoughts
No actions
Only so much as reality so much power
And this is the value of the R.H. & J.S.'s
But seeming does not get its own end
We are interested only by reality
Love
Genius
Genius is Being & Doing
Only Being can make
But all men have Genius if they will [65]
Self-Reliance
S [(Salvage)] p 40, 44, 45
Events that shake the state show what feeble folk we are
it is base to owe my house to the government or my living to ⟨the⟩ chance,

[25]   The Soul
We cannot forgive any body his limitations   D 246
Teaching ab extra & ab intra   D 233, 235,
Books & men are ⟨thy⟩ luxuries   the instincts thy bread

We cannot afford to scan our friends much   D 321

⟨Effect⟩ Relation of the Soul to Facts. *School* p.

The doctrine of immortality is not preached from the Soul but always from the Understanding   D 345 [66]

---

[65] "Routine . . . they will", in pencil, is an outline of "Being and Seeming," *Lectures*, II, 304–308.
[66] "The Soul" is partly circled. The passage cited in Journal D, p. [246], is canceled in the manuscript of "Education," *Lectures*, III, 497(notes), and used in "Circles," *W*, II, 308. The passage cited in D, p. [233], is used in "The Over-Soul," and D, p. [321], in "Friendship," *W*, II, 287 and 214–216. With "Relation of . . . Facts.", cf. "The School," *Lectures*, III, 47–49. With "The doctrine . . . Understanding", cf. "Religion," *Lectures*, III, 277.

[26] [blank]

[27] [67] Beside Analysis is Tradition. Strong yet

    Its defenders   ↑Burke Coleridge Scott↓

    the affectionate

    the feeble

    Retrospective Review &c

Age of Severance   Dissociation   Analysis   Dissection   Detachment.

    Genius is always not of its Age

    Mechanical

    Detaching "I speak for myself" Freedom, Free trade, No Church

No turnpike   no toll-bridge   no tax   no Bank

    Dissociation   (Shelley's Divorce; Aristotle's chastity).

Yet Nature has room for us all[;] the stately pinetree stands alone[;] so do a thousand in the wood. The sentiment of patriotism has become weak. And all Veneration. It is the age of the first person singular. Dissection. The natural sentiments feebler. People grow more philosophical[.] Rebel against Mediation or saints or any Nobility in the Unseen. It is All souls day. Anciently Sacred Band   Theban Phalanx; None now. College Classes[,] Military Corps ⟨W⟩fancy themselves indissoluble for an instant over their cups. 'Tis a painted hoop, has no girth.

But two Parties endure[,] the Old & the New[,] the preachers of Con⟨s⟩- & of Dis-sociation. It is true the party which represents this Dis. represents it so basely that most of those who sympathize in the movement have no connexion with it abhor it —

The Party of the Past & the Party of the Future [68]

---

[67] Emerson used pages [27], [28], the lower parts of [29] and [30], and [31]–[32], left blank earlier, for notes and drafts for The Present Age: "Introductory," probably shortly before its delivery December 4, 1839. "⟨Barbecue⟩" is written diagonally to the right of ll. 3–5.

[68] "Beside Analysis . . . Review &c" is developed in The Present Age: "Introductory," *Lectures*, III, 197–198; for "Its defenders . . . Scott", canceled in the lecture manuscript, see *Lectures*, III, 459(notes). "Age of Severance . . . Detachment." and "Detaching . . . Dissociation" are developed, and "The sentiment . . . Dis-sociation" and "The Party . . . Future" used, though not in this order, in The Present Age: "Introductory," *Lectures*, III, 188–189, the lecture "The Spirit of the Times," and "Historic Notes of Life and Letters in New England," *W*, X, 325–327. For "Genius is . . . Mechanical" and "It is true . . . abhor it", see *Lectures*, III, 462, 454, 459, and 460(notes).

[28] Commerce realizes this autocracy to the senses. Analysis like the Devil promised the world to the man if he would sell his soul and Commerce is the fulfilment of the bargain.[69] The honored of today is the man of impulse. We are all calculators and ⁿ New England the very metropolis of the Multiplication Table[.]
A Man of Impulse who is attached to the Future is adored. The most remarkable ↑literary↓ work of the age describes this Analysis, I mean *Faust.*

The foregoing ages seem to have had some Integrity or Wholeness. The institutions preserved an inactive wholeness after ↑the Vital Unity ceased↓
Greece & Rome w⟨h⟩ere whole. The Crusader whole. The Elizabethan had a normal wholeness. Analysis has no religion. It is ⟨a stepping forward⟩ the Understanding taking a step forward of the Soul and so it has the freedom of an evil spirit.[70] Once Magic, Animal Magnetism had been forbidden science. The Religion of the middle Age forbid them after the man could seek them. But we have [71]

[29]   Buy and Sell

The world owes us a living
Native differences are the basis of each calling
On paying money in cities in lieu of kind
Hold the plough or drive
Buy by the acre sell by the foot
A rich man is, a habit of care.
The Ship & letter B.
In a money transaction the main thing is not money.
When ⟨tin⟩ ↑corn↓ is dear, the tinman must cut his tin econom-
                                                              ically.
C 200, 43, 36,[72]

---

[69] "Commerce . . . bargain.", struck through in ink with a vertical use mark, is canceled in the manuscript of The Present Age: "Introductory"; see *Lectures*, III, 454(notes).
[70] "The foregoing . . . spirit." is struck through in ink with a vertical use mark; "It is . . . spirit." is used in The Present Age: "Introductory," *Lectures*, III, 190.
[71] Continued on the lower part of page [29] below.
[72] See page [145] below, where eight of these entries are listed in a collection

⟨Type⟩

F. Parkman	A. B. Alcott	W. L. Garrison
N. L. Frothingham	J. S. Dwight	Leggett
J. Quincy	E. Palmer	
L. Woods		

G. P. B.	G. Bancroft
E. G. L.	O. Brownson
	Leggett

no religion. We are up to everything divine & devilish. But the Universe must still be propitiated,[n] let the members gain what they may. Being divided the man's aims are steadily baulked. Commerce has subdued the world[,] holds all nature in fee & yet the merchant is not more a man than the farmer or soldier he has supplanted.[73] And yet as far as I can read the signs of my heaven [74]

[30] "The establishment of a ⟨a⟩ba⟨k⟩nk in any place immediately advances the pecuniary value of a ↑good↓ moral character. — — — There is many a man who would be deterred from dishonesty by the frown of a banker who might care little for the admonitions of a bishop"

London Paper.

Society

Office of Conversation   D 262

Men do not converse they chat

---

the evil time is passing, ⟨the C⟩I seem to descry the approaches of a celestial visitant[;] this cold eclipse will end[;] the light already breaks

---

for the lecture "Doctrine of the Hands." "Buy by . . . foot", and "In a money . . . money.", which is written in ink over the same in pencil, are used in "Prudence," *Lectures*, II, 317 and 326. Passages in Journal C, pp. [200] and [43], are used in "Doctrine of the Hands," *Lectures*, II, 243 and 238–239; C, p. [200], is also used in "Prudence," *W*, II, 234–235. One sentence from C, p. [36], is used in "Tendencies," *Lectures*, III, 306.

[73] "no religion . . . supplanted.", struck through in ink with a vertical use mark, is canceled in The Present Age: "Introductory"; see *Lectures*, III, 455 (notes).

[74] Continued on the lower half of p. [30] below.

from the outer limb of the sun[,] the earth will be reconciled to the heaven and Nature be One.

We cut ourselves with our own tools. We must needs conjure a spirit we cannot lay. We boast of this magical invention of *credit* & suddenly the nations are impoverished & governments shaken by its cruel convulsions. Bankruptcy, Cholera, Party, War, [31] Mob [75]
I think it very evident that the books of our day are much clearer of credulity & nonsense than those of the foregoing ages. Read Burton's Melancholy. And you shall see the madness of Scholars. see p. 58 & 63 [76]

[⟨Analysis⟩ denotes at last the movement of the Soul which is ⟨the⟩ affirmation, the claiming a stake. *I ↑also↓ am.* I
Men think, which they did not before as a separate act
They destroy, but,[n] underneath, a bud pushes off the old leaf.
Analysis hastens synthesis, Skepticism enforces faith   r
Analysis revises reputations, reforms institutions.] [77]

But I look at the age with another feeling. It is to me an Oracle that I cannot bring myself to ⟨d⟩ undervalue. I cannot look down on it. I must think & write up to it ever. It is to me Heaven and the temple of the Highest. Meantime it is dear. I look not at its hand but into its eye. I see it in the persons it forms, — a fair & sacred choir[n] in ⟨those⟩ my friends; in those to whom I speak & in those who speak to me. It knows its own

[32] And in my love is my only claim to ⟨r⟩be heard by you. E 55 [78]

[33]–[34] [blank]
[35]   The Unconscious   ↑see p. 23↓
My son cannot replace me. I could not replace myself. I am the child of [B 104]

---

[75] With this paragraph, cf. "Tendencies," *Lectures,* III, 305–306.
[76] With this paragraph, cf. "Literature" [first lecture], *Lectures,* III, 211–213.
[77] With "⟨Analysis⟩ . . . leaf.", cf. The Present Age: "Introductory," *Lectures,* III, 189. "Analysis hastens . . . institutions." is developed, *ibid.,* pp. 195–196.
[78] The last paragraph on p. [31], and the passage cited in Journal E, p. [55], are combined in The Present Age: "Introductory," *Lectures,* III, 201.

"Power is never far from necessity." [BB I, 15]

The drawing of Circles   C 135
C 192 [79]

[36]   *Prudence*
Prudence is false when detached, it is only legitimately taught when it is merely the natural history of the soul incarnate, when it shows the beauty of the soul's laws even in the confinement of the senses[.]
If taught for itself it is base [80]
    The wisdom of Gleaning

[37]–[39] [blank]
[40] [...] [81]
[41]   Be, not seem
What illustrates realism more than this law from Goethe? "Every work of art sets us in that temper in which the author was when he made it. Was that cheerful & free? so shall we feel. Was that constrained[,] anxious & careful? So draws it us likewise into a (cramp)".
"Who speaks not clearly to the sense speaks not clearly to the soul"
                              Goethe.

See further   C p. 176
The house praises the carpenter
Sheridan   B.327 [82]
Value of life is always Cumulative,[83] if life be right; the whole past

---

[79] "see p. 23" is added in pencil. With Journal B, p. [104], and C, p. [192], cf. "The School," *Lectures*, III, 37 and 42. The passage cited in C, p. [135], is used in "Circles," *W*, II, 304 and 305.

[80] Cf. "Prudence," *Lectures*, II, 311 and 312.

[81] Postal accounts, running from December 11, 1837, to May 10, 1842, are omitted on pp. [40], [42]–[44], [46], [47]–[52], and [54]–[59] and are indicated by [...].

[82] "What illustrates . . . made it." is struck through in pencil with a diagonal use mark; the quotation is used in "The Eye and Ear," *Lectures*, II, 270; it is paraphrased in Journal C, p. [176], which is used in "Being and Seeming," *Lectures*, II, 300, and "Spiritual Laws," *W*, II, 157. The passage cited in B, p. [327], is used in "Being and Seeming," *Lectures*, II, 301.

[83] Cf. Journal Q, p. [25], "Being and Seeming," *Lectures*, II, 300, "Tendencies," *Lectures*, III, 311, and "Self-Reliance," *W*, II, 59.

is our purchase wherefrom to work on the future. If not, then peni-
tence, shame, undoing, & doing over again.

[...]
[42]–[44] [...]
[45] [blank]
[46] [...]
[47]   ⟨The Age⟩
⟨It is observable that even the Science of the day is introversive
and geology looks no longer for histories but examines the earth that
it may be its own chronicle.⟩ [D 162]
    Compare our proprieties with Bacon's nonsense   B 105
    Pius VII   B 280 [84]
[...]
[48]–[52] [...]
[53]   Ethics
    Before you urge a duty, be sure it is one; Patriotism for example
                                                            [B 96]
The argument which has not power to reach my own practice, I may
well ⟨doubt⟩ fear has not power to reach yours. [BB Y, 55]

    That every man's art should make him happy
That every man should yield himself to the Universal soul [85]
    It sounds to me very reasonable what Charles I said when his
Chaplain Mainwaring was accused by the Commons, "He that will
preach other than he can prove, let him suffer."

[54]–[59] [...]
[60]–[62] [blank]
[63] [86]   Politics
↑John↓ Pym referred to all the multitude of grants that had in his-

[84] "The Age . . . chronicle.", which is heavily canceled, is used in "Doctrine
of the Soul," *Lectures*, III, 9. "Compare our . . . B 280" may have been added
later; the passage cited in Journal B, p. [105], is used in "Literature" [first lecture],
Lectures, III, 211–212.
    [85] "That every man's . . . soul" is in pencil. "The argument . . . yours." is
used in "Spiritual Laws," *W*, II, 153. "That every man's . . . happy" is used in
"Doctrine of the Soul," *Lectures*, II, 238.
    [86] Although material on p. [63] was probably written earlier, Emerson added
"Pym 63" to the index at the same time he indexed material used in the lecture
"Perpetual Forces" in 1862. See *JMN*, VI, 335.

tory been made to the King, and then exclaimed "But of ↑what↓ avail have all these grants & prerogatives been? They were now so alienated[,] anticipated or overcharged with annuities & assignments that no means were ⟨a⟩left for the pressing & important occasions but one, and that one the voluntary & free gift of the subjects in Parliament. It is that one which is now assailed; but trust me, my lords, the hearts of the people & their bounty in Parliament are the only ⟨true⟩ constant treasure & revenue of the crown which cannot be exhausted, alienated, anticipated, ⟨a⟩or otherwise charged & encumbered."

Accusation of Dr Mainwaring ————————

⟨Take from⟩
"Take from us our property[,] our subsistence, we are no more a people. It will be time enough to settle rules to live by when we are sure to live."

Extract from speech (supposed) of Pym.

v[ide]. Lardner Cab. Cyc. Vol. 91; p. 142

"As if," said Pym, "their kingdoms were for them, and not they for their kingdoms." [87]

[64] When the great man comes, he will have that social strength that Dr Kirkland or Franklin or Burns had, and will so engage us to the moment that we shall not suspect his greatness until late afterward in some dull hour we shall say behold I am enlarged[;] how dull I was! how grand of late ha⟨ve⟩s my horizon grown! This man[,] this man must be divine.

One thing more: As the solar system moves forward in the system certain stars close up behind us & certain others open before us so is man's life. The reputations that were great & inaccessible they change & tarnish. How great were once Lord Bacon's dimensions[;] he is grown but a middle sized man and many another star has turned out to be a planet or an asteroid. Only a few are the fixed stars which have no parallax or none for us[:] Plato, Jesus, & Shakspeare. These are the gracious marks of our own growth. Slowly ⟨& th⟩[n] like light of morning it steals on us[,] the new fact that we who were pupils & aspirants are now society[,] do now compose a portion of that head & heart we are wont to think worthy [65₁] of all reverence & heed,

[87] This quotation is set off by double vertical lines in heavy ink in both margins.

we are the representative of religion & intellect & stand in the light of Ideas wh⟨ich⟩ose light streams through us to those younger & more in the dark [88]

[...]

[66]–[72] [...]

[73₁]   Means.

Always give a boy a room alone when he asks for it, though you sell your horse.

Keep a journal [89]

[...]

[74₁] [90] Put a house under the wind   out of the dirt; [BB I, 42] ↑cap
                                                & shoes   C 179↓

 Let a Scholar study solitude   B 60

 Humility a timesaver   B 76   Time 27

 Truth always prudent   B 124 [91]

 Half more than the whole   B 125

↑The↓ Sinner is the savage who hews down the whole tree in order to come at the fruit [B 130]

My pill is the sun; & Sleep; Love   B ⟨131⟩, 298, ↑C 244↓ [92]

---

[88] Pp. [64] and [65] to this point are in pencil. Both paragraphs are in Journal H, pp. [100]–[101]; the second is used in "Lecture on the Times," *W*, I, 266–267. "of all . . . the dark", the first inscription at the top of p. [65], is partially overwritten in ink by the date and first line of Emerson's account of a lawsuit in 1857; the entire account, which Emerson continued on pp. [66]–[72] and inscribed around or over earlier notes on pp. [73], [74], and [77]–[78], is omitted here, indicated by [...] and printed following p. [78₁] below as pp. [65₂], [66]–[72], [73₂]–[74₂], and [77₂]–[78₂].

[89] "Always . . . journal", struck through in ink with a diagonal use mark and set off from the 1857 material below it by a long rule, is used in "The Head," *Lectures*, II, 261.

[90] Emerson first inscribed p. [74] in pencil with what is probably a collection for the lecture "Prudence." For other collections for the same lecture, see pp. [36] above and [75]–[78] below. "Put a house . . . always be" is overwritten in ink by the 1857 notes printed as p. [74₂] below.

[91] The passages cited in Journal B, pp. [76] and [124], are used in "Prudence," *Lectures*, II, 320, and 318–319 and 322. With "Put a house . . . dirt;", cf. "Montaigne," *W*, IV, 160.

[92] "*My pill is the sun*;", struck through in pencil with a vertical use mark, is in Journal B, p. [131], and is used in "Prudence," *Lectures*, II, 323. A passage on

Women less accurate measure of time [B 130]
Chee's mountain of earth   B 133
        This Hour is an edifice
        Which the omnipotent cannot rebuild
        Anywhere but here [93]
    ⟨Stick to your work   B 187⟩
    ⟨I pay no rent for the woods⟩ B 202 [94]
    Every one a trust of power   B 214 [95]
Dentist's fine prints [B 250]
    Event modified by the man it befals   B 257

_____

    ⟨He that despises little things⟩ [B 279]

_____

    ⟨Every minute its monetary value⟩
    ⟨always be sticking a tree Jock⟩ [96] [BB III, 89]
    Best use of money to pay debts
    ⟨Love an eyewater   C 24⟩   Economy 60
    Aid of fine manners   C 42, 203,
    Goethe's cups & platters   C 50
    Courage is prudent. Every little measure a great error. The gale
threatens the cabin passenger [97]
[. . .]

[75]   The Prudent

⟨B 254⟩ ↑smoky room↓ ⟨204⟩ ↑⟨opium eaters⟩↓

_____

sleep on the same page is used in "Demonology," _Lectures_, III, 152, but not in
"Prudence." Passages on sleep in B, p. [298], and C, p. [244], are used in
"Prudence," _Lectures_, II, 322–323.
   [93] Cf. Journal B, p. [140], _JMN_, V, 145, n. 435, and "Fragments on Nature
and Life," V, _W_, IX, 350.
   [94] Cf. "Prudence," _Lectures_, II, 324.
   [95] See Notebook F No. 1, p. [72] above.
   [96] This and the two preceding entries are used in "Prudence," _Lectures_, II, 315
and 317, and _W_, II, 232 and 234.
   [97] The last five lines are struck through in pencil with a vertical use mark. Passages in Journal C, pp. [24], [42], [203], and [50], and "Courage . . . passenger" are used in "Prudence," _Lectures_, II, 320–321, 325, 326, and 319 and 322. C,
p. [24], was used later in "Prudence," _W_, II, 238, and C, p. [42], in "Manners,"
_W_, III, 126–127.

⟨Climate   B 185⟩ [98]

⟨B 204   C 205   Goethe's Tasso⟩

⟨C 7   Every change its sign⟩

⟨B 110 Door painted⟩

⟨The domestic man   A 132⟩ [99]

C 159   comfortmaking women [100]

⟨C.32   The perpendicular in painting⟩

⟨C 37   The pillars of society⟩ R Heard [101]

   140   ⟨Afternoon man⟩ [102]

   166   The Coat

       Dampier [Q 143]

⟨To find in life the greatest number of happy moments⟩ B 146

Love those who are near   C 64

Have friends in natural relations   C 98 [103]

⟨Nail box   C 129⟩

Mountains   Z [104]

Sleep   C 244   B 131   298

Scholar a cannon   C 231

---

[98] P. [75], in pencil, is a collection for the lecture "Prudence." The first two entries are struck through in pencil with a vertical use mark. Passages in Journal B, pp. [204] and [185], are used in "Prudence," *Lectures*, II, 316 and 313, and *W*, II, 233 and 226.

[99] Emerson struck vertical use marks through "B 204 . . . painted" in heavy pencil, and "B 110 . . . A 132" in light pencil. Passages in Journal C, pp. [205] and [7], B, p. [110], and A, p. [132], are used in "Prudence," *Lectures*, II, 315–316, 322, 313, and 314; all but "C 7" are also used in "Prudence," *W*, II, 232–233, 225, and 227.

[100] See "Love," *Lectures*, III, 63.

[101] "C.32 . . . C 37" is struck through in pencil with a vertical use mark. The first passage is used in "Prudence," *Lectures*, II, 315, and *W*, II, 229–230; the second passage is used in "Being and Seeming," *Lectures*, II, 305.

[102] Traces of an earlier layer of erased pencil writing, none of which is recovered, are discernible from this line to the bottom of the page. For this phrase, see Human Culture: "Introductory," and "Prudence," *Lectures*, II, 229 and 315, and *W*, II, 229.

[103] "To find . . . Have friends" is struck through in pencil with a vertical use mark. All three passages cited are used in "Prudence," *Lectures*, II, 317 and 321; those passages in Journal C, pp. [64] and [98], are also in "Prudence," *W*, II, 240.

[104] This and the preceding entry are struck through in pencil with a vertical use mark. The passage in Journal C, p. [129], is used in "Prudence," *Lectures*, II, 314, and *W*, II, 227.

Sardanapalize   C 122   175 [105]
England *Alfieri*   C 202
English Manners   203
⟨Commerce & pine ship   B 42⟩ [106]
Allston's house   B 49
⟨Do what we can summer has flies   B 50⟩
Prudence about opinions [107]
[76] [108] Regret calamities if you can help   C 82 [109]
　　E Hosmer & SHS   C 83
　　A walk near the sea & a sail near the shore [C 132]
　　Unbuttoned slovenliness [110]
　　Esquimaux   Dampier
　　⟨Fear of Mr Bacon   C 181⟩ [111]
　　Italy & England   C 202
It is strife with nature makes the Northerner wise
　　Buy by acre sell by foot [Enc. 183]
　　Make night night & day day [Enc. 58]
　　　self control

　　All the satire of the forms & conventions of society goes on the supposition that they are exclusively regarded. If a man sees clearly their source & uses them merely for a convenience [112]

　　[105] "Sleep . . . Sardanapalize" is struck through in pencil with a vertical use mark. Passages in Journal C, p. [244], and B, p. [298], are used in "Prudence," *Lectures*, II, 322 and 323; with "Sardanapalize", cf. *ibid.*, p. 324. Passages in B, p. [131], and C, p. [231], are used in "Demonology," *Lectures*, III, 152, and "Prospects," *Lectures*, III, 370–371.
　　[106] This line is struck through in pencil with a vertical use mark; the paragraphs cited in Journal C, p. [203], and B, p. [42], are used in "Prudence," *Lectures*, II, 325 and 317; only B, p. [42], is used in the essay, *W*, II, 235–236.
　　[107] "Do what . . . B 50" is struck through in pencil with a vertical use mark; the passage cited is used in "Prudence," *Lectures*, II, 313, and *W*, II, 225–226. With "Prudence about opinions", cf. "Prudence," *Lectures*, II, 310.
　　[108] P. [76], in pencil, is a continuation of the collection for "Prudence" on pp. [74] and [75].
　　[109] This passage is used in "Self-Reliance," *W*, II, 78.
　　[110] Cf. Journal C, p. [205].
　　[111] This entry is struck through in pencil with a vertical use mark; the passage cited is used in "Prudence," *Lectures*, II, 320, and *W*, II, 238. With "Esquimaux" in the preceding entry, cf. Journal B, p. [124], used in "Prudence," *Lectures*, II, 318–319.
　　[112] "It is strife . . . self control", struck through in pencil with a vertical use

[77₁] [113] There are two prudences[,] one a small, one a great. Small is comical

Live according to the law of the outward

The great prudence relies on instincts
   Humility saves time [114]
   True economy
   Half more than the whole
   Truth is prudent
   Sinner savage
   Sleep sun
   Love
   Courage
   Manners
    Sleep   Sun

        Trust your instincts in the care of your health. Use the great medicines of Sleep Exercise fasting & diversion. The woods & the mountains you pay no rent for & no tax The sun is your pill & Sardanapalize [115]
[. . .]

[78₁] That there are two prudences
_____

that the one is very low indeed
_____

that the true prudence is a regard to externals
_____

that the condition of it is simple recognition that internals are
_____

mark, is developed in "Prudence," *Lectures*, II, 313 and 317, and *W*, II, 226, 234, and 235. With "All the satire . . . convenience", cf. "Prudence," *Lectures*, II, 324–325.

[113] Pp. [77₁] and [78₁], both in pencil, continue Emerson's collection for "Prudence." Both pages are overwritten in ink by 1857 notes, printed below as pp. [77₂] and [78₂].

[114] "There are . . . time" is developed in "Prudence," *Lectures*, II, 312–313, 322, and 320, and partly used in "Prudence," *W*, II, 223–224.

[115] "Truth is prudent" is used in "Prudence," *Lectures*, II, 322; cf. also "Prudence," *W*, II, 240. Except for "Sinner savage", the rest of the page is developed in "Prudence," *Lectures*, II, 319–325, part of which is used in "Prudence," *W*, II, 237–238.

then it will reward every degree of attention
     Do actions have clear perceptions
     We have somewhat to do with climate house field tree
Northern man wise; Esquimaux
Our education is in these schools
     Nail box, ⟨smoky room⟩, ⟨flies⟩, mountains
     Door to be painted
     Nature sternly punishes any neglect [116]

[65₂] 1857. June 17.

Yesterday, The Jury who heard the evidence on the Walden ⟨lot⟩-Woodlot case reported that they could not agree on a verdict, & were discharged. I bought the lot in Nov. 1845, of Abel Moore & John Hosmer, 41 acres, 52 roods, at $30. per acre, for $1239.56. — I was carefully shown all the bounds by Moore & Hosmer. I saw the pinnacle, the blazed trees below it, & fragments of the stone wall to & past the stake & stones, and, as I believe, one or two blazed trees before coming to the pinetree-with-the-stone-against-it, which was a principal mark, and, below that, [66] the remains of the old stone wall, down to the foot of the valley & the run of water. Thence, we drew a line across to the rail road, where a stone boundary was placed. I ⟨the⟩was told by them that Dr Abiel Heywood had shown or marked these boundaries (at the time they bought the land) on the part of, or, as the friend of, or at the request of, the widow, Mrs   Heywood, (whom Bartlett now represents). There was then no dispute of bounds. At Mr Hoar's office, ⟨I met Bartlett⟩ where the deed was given me Moore said We will sell this as 40 acres more or less for 1200. or we will have it measured & sell it at 30 per acre. I said, You [67] shall measure it. It was measured, and I have always supposed that my *plan* given me at the time [n] was Cyrus Hubbard's plan, *then made*. I gave this plan with my deed to Goodnow, last year, but I learn now, that it was ruled out of court, as being a copy made by Reuben Moore

[116] Notes on p. [78₁] are developed in "Prudence," *Lectures*, II, 312–314, and partly used in "Prudence," *W*, II, 223–228.

from Cyrus Hubbard. Now, this plan of mine does not appear. Mrs Goodnow & J. Moore cannot find it.

Not long after I bought the land I met Bartlett by chance on lot or near it & we went together along the boundary line between us and I found with satisfaction that he knew & accepted the same marks as I. I should think we begun somewhere along the ridge not far from the Lincoln line & went ⟨d⟩to the pinnacle & down thence past the stake & stones to the pinetree with the stone & to the end of the stone wall & the run but did not cross to the railroad but returned through [68] my path along the edge of the meadow and so up to the wood path which runs parallel to the bank of Walden, until we came to the stone wall whereat, or wherethrough my lot is entered by anyone coming from the ⟨N⟩Lincoln road. I remember this well enough in connexion with one circumstance, Bartlett's wood was then large & well grown. Mine had been mainly cut off, when M & H had ⟨b⟩first bought. I said to B., in the first part of our walk, that "his were the woods, & mine the bushes." When we came to the ⟨run⟩bottom of my valley & afterwards to large wood on both sides & at the end of our walk ⟨on⟩large wood on the right hand, Bartlett said, "No, you have good woods also" or to that effect.

In 1846 or 7 Bartlett cut down some large trees of mine not far from the place where once they crossed the meadow by means of [69] laying trees or boughs to what is called the "island" over which the railroad runs. I was informed that he had cut them, (I should think ↑I was informed↓ by Edmund Hosmer,) and either to me or to Hosmer, Bartlett said, that it was a mistake, he did not mean to have it done, ⟨& that he would have the sticks hauled to the mill ⟨&⟩for me or I believe⟩ that he had already hauled them to Britton's steam mill, & would have them marked with my name, & I should find them there. I was satisfied, and went to the mill, & found two or more sticks of pine (I believe) marked E, and, when they were sawed, I had them brought home to my house.

[70] The tops were hauled home to my wood pile from the woods, I do not remember when Bartlett first told me about his old deed, but it was ⟨m⟩several years ago, say, seven or eight. I remember that he told me whether before he found this old deed or not I do not know

that he did not think he had all the land that belonged to him for the deed or a deed ⟨s⟩called it twenty or twenty two or three (I know not how many) acres, and he did not think that his bounds included so much. At some time, in the woodlot, he told me that he had found or had an ancient deed which made him think that Moore & Hosmer [71] had sold me what ought to belong to him & he had showed it to some persons & they thought so too. I went to J. Hosmer & to John Moore, & told them this but they made light of it as did Geo Heywood & Edmund Hosmer. So I gave it no further attention.   Now as I remember these rare conversations with Bartlett [for I seldom talked with him & always unwillingly on account of his misbehaviour about the grass which he cut from my meadow & refused to pay for & on account of his cutting into my wood lot along the ridge & burning into me &c &c] [72] I believe he did not newly find the deed but had it at our first conversation but did not yet esteem it so highly, and I think that he now pretends to have found it later, because if he had it then it would be fatal to him to have admitted my claims by restoring the sticks of timber he cut in 1846 or 7[.]

On my return from Eng[lan]d in   1848 he had bought some grass in my meadow of Henry D. Thoreau & had got it away contrary to agreement without paying. Henry T. was vexed at this and I went to Mr Hoar [73₂] senior & asked him to collect the money which I think was $20. Geo Heywo⟨d⟩od was then in Mr H's office, & did soon after collect it & pay me.

One day, I met Bartlett & told him we would, if he liked, go over the bounds, & mark them anew at our common expense. He agreed to it. I was going one day with Thoreau to the lot, for the purpose of marking the Lincoln line through my lot. We stopped at Bartlett's house, & proposed to him to go now with us, & let Mr Thoreau [74₂] as surveyor, ⟨draw⟩find or refind & mark anew the old bounds between us. He consented. Then Thoreau said, he would not go (if it were a joint expense) until Bartlett should pay his part, since Bartlett had cheated him in the matter of the grass. Bartlett then said, he would never pay for any work until it was done. So we left him at home, & Thoreau went with me & surveyed the ⟨line between⟩ Lincoln line through my lot.

[77₂] 1857 June. Thoreau went with me to the woodlot & read there the copy of Bartlett's old deed. He said ____ means to sell meadow: he must cross the brook & meadow ↑from the valley↓ to a point "on his woodland" & keep "along his woodland" ↑to the dam↓. These conditions will be fulfilled either by the line which Bartlett would draw from O T′ or by the line which Emerson would draw Q T′[.]
But he proposes to sell only meadow & pasture, not woodland. But if he draws the line as claimed by Bartlett, he is selling woodland too.

The deed speaks all along of "the stone wall" and it would be natural ↑interpretation of it↓ to follow the stone wall down to its termination at the ⟨valle⟩ natural valley.
[78₂] But chiefly the question arises which valley? Emerson draws the line from Q. at the bottom of the natural valley where the water runs. And if the premises be approached from what we call "Bartlett's road" it will be seen, that this is the only valley of importance. Bartlett claims to draw from a stake & stones at ⟨C⟩O, where also is a depression, or lesser valley.

[79]–[80] [leaf torn out]
[81] Our religion is indigent
    The canons of our criticism are slavish
    The Glory is lost sight of

Of course if our Journal is a leaf from this plant, it cannot now know how far it shall extend or in what form. Its criticism should be poetic[,] unpredictable[,] superseding as every new thought does, all foregone thought & casting a new light on the whole world[.]

Then in letters the antidote to all narrowness is the comparison of the record with nature which at once shames the record & stimulates to new attempts. Whilst we look at this we wonder how anything has been thought worthy to be preserved[.] [117]

[117] This and the preceding paragraph are used in "The Editors to the Reader," *The Dial*, I (July 1840), 3. See also Journal D, p. [358], and E, pp. [127]–[128].

[82] [118] Life has dangers also
    Every principle a warnote [B 227]
    Every man must have a frigate
       Hospitality Charity Temperance   scorn of commodity & of
making an ill figure;
Self trust   Hardening   Truth [119]

Heroism is a boundless selftrust
Very attractive   Hence war's attraction & pride's
    preference of the high impulse with disregard of prudent con-
siderations out of confidence in the powers of the soul to repair [120]

       Your nature also is noble   C 103
          Bide your time   C 185
          Trust the Ideal   ↑C↓ 220   ↑Cleave to the Soul   C 204↓
          Never make apology   A 115
          Never tell charity   B 46   A 33
          Obstinately retain   A 13
↑coal coals;↓ Be lowly firm;   Let them rave; [121]

[83]   The Heroic

A man must always take both reputation & life in his hand & with
perfect urbanity dare the gibbet & the mob in every company by the
absolute truth of his speech.

[118] P. [82], in pencil, and pp. [83]–[86] below, are probably collections for
the lecture "Heroism." The lecture manuscript is missing; the first edition text of the
essay "Heroism" is printed in *Lectures*, II, 327–339, in place of the lecture, but this
contains at least four passages from journals written later than the lecture and is about
one-third shorter than other lectures in the series; use marked and repeated passages
not located in the essay were probably in the lecture.

[119] "Life . . . also" and "Hospitality . . . Truth" are developed in "Heroism,"
W, II, 249–262 (*Lectures*, II, 327–339). With "Every man . . . frigate", cf.
"War," *W*, XI, 163, 164, and 165. "Every principle a warnote" is used in "Perpetual Forces," *W*, X, 87; notes for this 1862 lecture are on pp. [116₂]–[122₂]
below.

[120] With "Heroism . . . repair", cf. "Heroism," *W*, II, 250–251 (*Lectures*, II,
330–331), and "War," *W*, XI, 171–173.

[121] "Cleave . . . rave;" is used in "Heroism," *W*, II, 260–263 (*Lectures*, II,
336–338), except for "coal coals;" (Journal B, p. [149]), used in "Holiness,"
Lectures, II, 356.

C. 204, 103, ↑proud boy↓ 195, women [122]
Retention of high sentiments   A ⟨5⟩13
Prince Hal's considerations   Cleopatra
Milton & Shakspeare are the books of heroism [123]
Sidney
Cervantes
"Honor bright"
The Romances
Every principle is a war note   B 227
Barkeepers   B 151 [124]
Chee of Yaou   B 134
See what is said of Wordsworth   B 110
Charities   B 46
B ⟨227⟩, 166   A[s]cetic of Scholar
Eliot's Temperance
Lord Evandale
⟨Ver⟩ Socrates in Montaigne [125]
Marriage
Miss Edgeworth

[122] "103 . . . women" is in pencil. "A man . . . 103," is struck through in pencil with a diagonal use mark. The first sentence is used in "Heroism," *W*, II, 249–250 (*Lectures*, II, 330); cf. also "War," *W*, XI, 173–174. The passage in Journal C, p. [204], and one paragraph of the passage on women in C, pp. [195]–[196], are used in "Heroism," *W*, II, 260 and 259 (*Lectures*, II, 336–337 and 336). "proud boy" (C, p. [103]) is used in "Self-Reliance," *W*, II, 48.

[123] Use marks above and below "103 . . . A ⟨5⟩13" are connected through it with a faint vertical use mark in pencil; the sentence in Journal A, p. [13], is used in "Heroism," *W*, II, 262 (*Lectures*, II, 338). "Prince Hal's considerations", struck through in ink with a vertical use mark, refers to a quotation used in "Heroism," *W*, II, 252–253 (*Lectures*, II, 332). "Cleopatra" is in pencil. "Milton & Shakspeare" is struck through in pencil with a vertical use mark; Milton and Shakespeare are not mentioned in the essay, but Emerson discusses "the books of heroism" in "Heroism," *W*, II, 245–248 (*Lectures*, II, 327–330).

[124] "Every principle . . . pride   C 121" is in pencil. "The Romances . . . Barkeepers B 151" is struck through in pencil with a discontinuous vertical use mark. One sentence in Journal B, p. [151], is used in "Heroism," *W*, II, 252 (*Lectures*, II, 332).

[125] "Charities   B 46", struck through in pencil with a vertical use mark, is used in "Heroism," *W*, II, 261 (*Lectures*, II, 337). With passages in Journal B, pp. [227] and [166], cf. "Heroism," *W*, II, 261–262 (*Lectures*, II, 337). "Eliots . . . Socrates", struck through in pencil with a vertical use mark, is developed in "Heroism," *W*, II, 254–255, 247, and 256 (*Lectures*, II, 333, 329, and 334).

Hospitality   C 104   B 124

Falkland   C 105

Our sympathy is with pride   C 121 [126]

[84] Greatness where you are   C 144, 173, 178   A 134. [127]

       Heroic young man   C 185, 220, 61, 140 B   166 B [128]

       Heroic women   C 254, 195,

Say of your Sottise   Well 'tis a part of my office   A 7

Don't higgle for commodity   A 31

M M E   A 33   Never tell charities   B 46

Never make an apology   A 115 [129]

Coal among coals [B 149]

Ecclesiastical manners   B 234

Chapman   B 264

   Selftruth   B 39   A 88 Hoppin

Young American   Alcott Sewall Lovejoy

   Be lowly firm   The great sleep sweet in their grave [130]

[85] In thinking on these things I at least have felt that there is something in great actions which does not allow us to go behind them

Now the Soul as it appears to each Individual seems in relation to all this evil ⟨that⟩ ⟨exists⟩ [n] to take a hostile attitude & affirms ⟨to him⟩ [n] its own ⟨ample⟩ [n] ability to cope with & vanquish this dismal army of

----

[126] Emerson used the passage in Journal C, p. [105], later in the lecture "Doctrine of the Soul," and the passage in C, p. [121], in a fragment printed with "Private Life," *Lectures*, III, 8 and 248–249.

[127] P. [84] is in pencil. Passages in Journal C, pp. [144] and [173], are used, and A, p. [134], revised, in "Heroism," *W*, II, 257–258 (*Lectures*, II, 335). Cf. also "Self-Reliance," *W*, II, 62–63.

[128] "61, 140 B" is circumscribed in pencil; Emerson may mean Journal B, pp. [61], [140], and [166]. With "Heroic young man", cf. "Heroism," *W*, II, 258–262 (*Lectures*, II, 335–338).

[129] "Heroic women . . . A 7" is struck through in pencil with a vertical use mark which Emerson extended through "Never . . . A 115"; the passages cited are used in "Heroism," *W*, II, 259–261 and 255 (*Lectures*, II, 336–337 and 333–334).

[130] "Chapman B 264" is struck through in pencil with a vertical use mark. "Young American" may refer to the passage in Journal C, p. [23], used in "Heroism," *W*, II, 258–259 (*Lectures*, II, 335–336). "Lovejoy" (C, p. [241]) and "The great . . . grave" (A, p. [90]) are used in "Heroism," *W*, II, 262 and 263 (*Lectures*, II, 338).

enemies. It represents to the private man his all sufficiency against a world in arms. This divine instinct breaks out in savage & warlike nations in the contempt for life & ease & the attractiveness of war undoubtedly is that it presents the imagination this always grateful image of the conquest of the flesh by the immaterial principle. The hero is a mind of such equilibrium that no disturbances can shake his will but pleasantly & as it were merrily he moves at his own music in the frightful alarms or the extremes of dissoluteness [131]

[86] Where are all the ideals   Young men   young women Come let them live up to their mark; be new; strike sail to none.[132]

Peace [133] ↑(Pr. in War)↓

War necessary once; vastly useful.
The progress of man has opened the new idea
It is now seen to be needless. Peace seen to be practicable
The warlike principle incontestibly a part of nature, of vast energy
All History is the record of its perversion.
Its office is to resist wrong, to conquer matter, to conquer flesh, to brave labor   danger, fine people,[134]
A degree of rebellion seems necessary to fine character.
The attractiveness of War must stand for somewhat: it is spiritual energy always that defies Material injury.[135]

In the new meetinghouse we see what built the meetinghouse, pride,

[131] P. [85], in pencil, is used, with some revisions, in "Heroism," *W*, II, 250 (*Lectures*, II, 330–331). But with "the attractiveness of war", cf. "War," *W*, XI, 171–173, and p. [86] below.

[132] "Where . . . none.", in pencil, is probably an outline of a section of "Heroism"; cf. *W*, II, 258–259 (*Lectures*, II, 335–336). "mark" is overwritten by the rule above "Peace" below.

[133] On March 12, 1838, Emerson read "a lecture on Peace" (Journal C, p. [282]) in Boston before the American Peace Society. "(Pr. in War)" is added in pencil; see *W*, XI, 149–176. Most of the material on pp. [86]–[92], and on the lower portions of pp. [93] and [94] below, is used in the lecture, in revised form and order.

[134] With "War necessary . . . people," cf. "War," *W*, XI, 151, 160, 155, 154, and 155.

[135] With this sentence, cf. "War," *W*, XI, 171–172 and 173.

spite & religion & decorum. In the fort & navy yard we may as well feel the building of that in our heart also. That quivering lip that cold hating eye built frigates [136]

[87] We surround us with images of ourselves, be it feasts, or poems, or cannons, or churches.

If we made the frigate, we can burn it.[137]

Idle people want excitement[,] boys kill cats[.]

The southerner talks of *whipping*. He has yet no other image of manly activity & virtue, charity none; endurance, perseverance, none; attainment of truth none.[138]

But it is laughable[,] not Saxon robur but French or Neapolitan giddiness to expect to accomplish anything by votes & societies. In some of our cities they choose noted duellists presidents & officers of Antiduelling societies. The men bitten by this big dog called Public Opinion are rabid for public meetings as if they could do anything; [n] they vote & vote & go home, no man responsible, no man caring a pin. At the next season an Indian War[,] a French or Turkish aggression on our commerce; or the party this man votes with have an appropriation to carry through the Congress. Instantly he wags his head the other way & cries War, War. No it is to be accomplished by men,[n] by the formation of great true brave men, who [88] shall in their mind feel the connexion of opinions & shall give up wrong-doing. It is very easy to see what must & shall be, & that bayonet will first be hid as halters & gibbets are now: inviting only relations & friends: & then will be transferred to the museums of the curious as poisoning & torturing tools are now,[139]

It cannot be done by papering or painting[;] it cannot be done by signing or by peacemaking; it is a state of mind only, it is only trust, love, ⟨wis⟩ knowledge, that loves the unbolted door & the unguarded coach, & wagon; pride & selfishness & avarice & ignorance do as nat-

---

[136] With this paragraph, cf. "War," *W*, XI, 163–164 and 165.

[137] With this and the preceding sentence, cf. "War," *W*, XI, 164.

[138] "Idle . . . none." is used in "War," *W*, XI, 155–156.

[139] "In some . . . War, War." is used in "War," *W*, XI, 170. With "No it is . . . wrong-doing", cf. *ibid.*, pp. 168–169 and 171. The last sentence is used, *ibid.*, p. 166.

urally ↑levy troops↓ build forts & forge cannon as seed corn germinates into green blades.[140]

Peace & War thus resolve themselves into a mercury of the state of Cultivation. At a certain stage of his progress, the man fights if he be of a sound body & mind; at a certain higher stage, he makes no offensive demonstration but is alert to repel, & of an unconquerable heart; [89] at a still higher stage he has come into the region of holiness. Passion has passed away from him; his warlike nature is all converted into an active medicinal principle, he sacrifices himself & accepts wearisome tasks but being attacked he bears it & turns the other cheek [141]

The attractiveness of War shows one thing through all the throats of artillery, the thunde[r]s of so many sieges, the jousts of so much chivalry —— this namely, the conviction of man universally that a man should be himself responsible with goods, health, & life for his behavior — that he should hold himself ready to peril all for the preservation of his name & of his rights. And he should and if Peace is sought to be defended or preserved for the safety of the luxurious & the timid it is a sham & the peace will be broken. If peace is to be maintained it must be by brave men[,] men who have come up to the same height as the hero to hold their life in their hand & imperil it at any instant for their principle but who have gone one step beyond [90] & will not seek another man's life,ⁿ ⟨n⟩ who do not think their property or their own life a sufficient good to be bought by such dereliction of principle as the treating a man like mutton.[142]

There are cases frequently put by the curious, moral problems like those problems in arithmetic which in long winter evenings the rustics try the hardness of their heads in ciphering out. And it is said What will you do when wife & children are assaulted[,] are murdered in your sight? Will your non resistance go this extent? If you say yes

[140] With this paragraph, cf. "War," *W*, XI, 170, 163–164, 162, and 165.
[141] This uncompleted paragraph is used in "War," *W*, XI, 166–167.
[142] This paragraph is used in "War," *W*, XI, 171, 173, and 174.

then you only invite the robber & the assassin and a few b⟨r⟩loody minded desperadoes would soon butcher the good.[143]

We answer I. the positive as well as negative force of virtue

II We are not careful to answer in this matter. A wise man will never impawn his future being & action & decide beforehand what he shall do in a given extreme crisis. Nature & God [91] will instruct him in that hour.[144]

[92] [145] Trade   Learning   Christianity   Intercourse
all put down war
    The Italian towns
    The Pope
    The prison
    The Art
        What a progress! Only in Elizabeth's time Cavendish. Assacombuit   "No peace beyond"

[93]   End.
To entertain oneself —
To be manly happy
To be content with your art. `
To reconcile cities with thoughts
To find in life the greatest number of wise & happy moments.
To inspire Hope.
To make no end.
Proportion.[146]

        War was necessary
        And very useful. Alexander

[143] This paragraph is used in "War," *W*, XI, 167 and 168.
[144] With "We answer . . . virtue", cf. "War," *W*, XI, 168. The last paragraph is used, *ibid.*, p. 169.
[145] The notes on p. [92], in pencil, are used in "War," *W*, XI, 156, 157, and 158–159.
[146] P. [93] to this point may have been early notes for the "Human Culture" series as a whole, or for the Introductory lecture. "End.", "Hope.", and "Proportion." are developed in "Introductory," *Lectures*, II, 215, 224, and 226–227. Other entries are developed throughout the series; "To find . . . moments." is used in "Prudence," *Lectures*, II, 317, and with "To reconcile . . . thoughts", cf. "The Eye and Ear," *Lectures*, II, 273.

It covered a divine principle
But it was extreme youth & idleness
Very barren: spoils conversation
Now has arisen the Peace idea
The Idea is the Epoch
Its growth
It looks ludicrous: the tough Actual:
See you not what an Idea can do
How is the Peace to be established
    Not by votes
    Not by cowards
    Not by nations [147]

[94]   Identical nature [C] ⟨27   124⟩   C 128 [148]
    Real insulation of a Soul   ⟨C 75, 74, ⟨124⟩⟩
    Otherism ⟨136⟩   238   ⟨241⟩ [149]
    Fear   181   236   138   71   96   119
    Real kindness ⟨154⟩   A 57[-58]   C 198, 131,   B 132 [150]

To Each his own   C 61, 80,

Fear   sense of violating
Fear removed

[147] "War was . . . nations", in light pencil, is an outline of "War," *W*, XI, 151-176.

[148] "Identical nature . . . temperately C 71", in pencil, is probably a collection for the lecture "The Heart." See also pp. [95]-[98] and [103] below. Passages in Journal C, pp. [27] and [124], are used in "The Heart," *Lectures*, II, 283. With C, p. [128], cf. *ibid.*, p. 284. Emerson also used the first passage in "Love," *Lectures*, III, 64-66, and *W*, II, 184-187, and the third passage in "The American Scholar," *W*, I, 112-113.

[149] Passages in Journal C, pp. [74], [124], [136], and [241], are used in "The Heart," *Lectures*, II, 279-280, 283, and 287.

[150] Passages in Journal C, pp. [236], [96], [119], [154], and [198], A, p. [57], and B, p. [132], are used in "The Heart," *Lectures*, II, 280, 285-286, 282, 293-294, 282-283, and 282; the passage in C, p. [154], is also in "Friendship," *W*, II, 191. Emerson used the paragraph in C, p. [181], in "Prudence," *Lectures*, II, 320, and *W*, II, 238. He used the paragraph in C, p. [138], later in "Tendencies," *Lectures*, III, 309-310, and "Self-Reliance," *W*, II, 55, and the lines in C, p. [131], in "Private Life," *Lectures*, III, 253, and "Domestic Life," *W*, VII, 128.

Conversation

Talk heartily   C ⟨225⟩   ⟨122⟩   ⟨73⟩   ⟨157⟩

Talk temperately   C 71 [151]

"The wounds inflicted by iron are to be healed by iron & not by words,"
said the elder Cancellieri & ordered the hand of Lore to be struck off.

Muller Vol 3 p 14 [B 120]

"No peace beyond the Line" "No prey no pay."

In the 12(?) century the principal cities in the north of Italy
having grown strong & populous reduced the castles of the rural
nobility & compelled them to reside in ↑the↓ towns [152]

[95]   Heart

Chee   B.134, ⟨132⟩

True & false relations to people   C 223

The Glance   C 124   27   ⟨of Epaminondas also⟩ [153]

Conversation A 21, C 225, 60 ↑tides↓ 71 157 ↑principles↓ ⟨122⟩ 73 [154]

See Above p. 13

Heart in a cultivated nature   C 198   Monti [C 201]

Welcome each to his part in you   C 61

No contact   C 73

[151] Passages in Journal C, pp. [61] and [80], are used in "The Heart," *Lectures*, II, 291–292. "Fear   sense . . . Conversation" is developed, *ibid.*, pp. 284–286 and 292. Passages in C, pp. [225], [122], [73], [157], and [71], are all used, *ibid.*, pp. 292–293.

[152] " 'No peace . . . towns" is used in "War," W, XI, 158 and 157. Although " 'The wounds . . . towns" was probably written in 1838, Emerson added "Hist. of Liberty, 94" to the index at the same time he indexed material used in the lecture "Perpetual Forces" in 1862. Emerson discusses "the history of political liberty" in "The Emancipation Proclamation," given in September, 1862 (W, XI, 315–316), but neither of these entries on p. [94] is used in that address.

[153] P. [95], in pencil, is a collection for the lecture "The Heart." "Chee . . . The Glance" is struck through in pencil with a vertical use mark; "True" is also struck through in pencil with a diagonal use mark, and "The Glance" with a vertical use mark. Passages in Journal C, pp. [223], [124], and one sentence from C, pp. [27]–[28] (the paragraph used in "Love," *Lectures*, III, 64–66, and W, II, 184–187), are used in "The Heart," *Lectures*, II, 285 and 283. The sentence in C, p. [223], is also used in "Being and Seeming," *Lectures*, II, 301, and "Spiritual Laws," W, II, 157. For "Epaminondas", see "The Heart," *Lectures*, II, 284.

[154] For "A 21" see Notebook Man, p. [104] above, and p. [136] below. Passages in Journal C, pp. [225], [71], [157], [122], and [73], are used in "The Heart," *Lectures*, II, 292–293 and 279.

Conversation superficial — central   C 73
Acquaintance separates   C 74
Unfit guest   C 80
Deference to a companion   C 136 [155]
False conversation — foolish face ⟨1⟩C 138 ↑71↓ Animal Magn ibid.
                                           ↑220↓ [156]

Real kindness everywhere   ⟨1⟩C 154
Fear —   Mr Bacon — C 181
Caducous relations   C 124 [157]
Friendship C 131   204   144 [158]
Love those who are near   C 64
On your own terms C 98   or natural relations [159]
Selfsubsistency of Bulrushes   C 236 [160]
Law of visits   B 124, 16,
The family   C 242
Effect on me of other men's virtues   C 241 [161]
   "   "   "   " opinions   C 238
Scholar works not well near 231   Dr B
Individuals represent classes   ↑C↓ 231

[155] "Heart . . . Welcome", "No contact . . . Conversation", "Conversation . . . Acquaintance", and "Unfit" are struck through in pencil with single vertical use marks, and "Deference" with three. All eight passages are used in "The Heart," *Lectures*, II, 293–294, 293, 291, 279, 292, 279–280, 291–292, and 287.

[156] "71" and "220" are added below the short line; both passages are on "False conversation". With Emerson's footnote in Journal C, p. [71], cf. "The Heart," *Lectures*, II, 292. The "foolish face" paragraph in C, p. [138], is used in "Tendencies," *Lectures*, III, 309–310, and "Self-Reliance," *W*, II, 55.

[157] "Real" is struck through in pencil with a diagonal use mark; "kindness . . . Caducous" is struck through in pencil with a curved vertical use mark, and "Caducous" with another short vertical use mark. The passage in Journal C, p. [154], is used in "The Heart," *Lectures*, II, 282, and "Friendship," *W*, II, 191. The passage in C, p. [181], is used in "Prudence," *Lectures*, II, 320, and *W*, II, 238. With C, p. [124], cf. "The Heart," *Lectures*, II, 279.

[158] With Journal C, p. [144], cf. "The Heart," *Lectures*, II, 283. For "C 131", see p. [94] above.

[159] This and the preceding entry, struck through in pencil with a vertical use mark, are used in "Prudence," *Lectures*, II, 321, and *W*, II, 240.

[160] This entry, struck through in pencil with a vertical use mark, is used in "The Heart," *Lectures*, II, 280.

[161] This entry, struck through in pencil with a vertical use mark, is used in "The Heart," *Lectures*, II, 287. With the preceding entry, used in "Domestic Life," *W*, VII, 119–121, cf. "Home," *Lectures*, III, 399–400(notes).

Faneuil Hall   C 227 [162]
Tea parties   C 220
[96] The merged or average soul   C 139 [163]
Identical nature   C 128,
Dependence of the proud   C 111
Mush of concession odious   A 144
Kindness better than Corinna   A 57
Persons for a thousand years   A 126
Don't mix waters
It takes two men to make friends
Monti's mother   C 201
Seraphim & Cherubim
Sneer
⟨O⟩Never look behind. First thoughts.[164]

It takes men
Mush of concession
Natural relations
Don't mix
Persons for 1000 years
Montaigne [165]

[97] [166] I count no man much because he cows or silences me[;] any

---

[162] The first paragraph in Journal C, p. [231], is used in "Prospects," the second in a fragment printed with "Private Life," *Lectures*, III, 370–371 and 251; but with the second, cf. "The Heart," *Lectures*, II, 279. Emerson used the paragraph on Faneuil Hall in "Genius," *Lectures*, III, 83.

[163] P. [96], in pencil, continues a collection for "The Heart." This entry, struck through in pencil with a vertical use mark, is used in "The Heart," *Lectures*, II, 289, and "Friendship," *W*, II, 207.

[164] "Mush of concession . . . Monti's mother" is struck through in pencil with a diagonal use mark, which Emerson then extended to beyond "Sneer". The passage in Journal A, p. [144], is used in "The Heart," *Lectures*, II, 289, and "Friendship," *W*, II, 208. A paragraph on kindness and lines from Felicia Hemans' "To Corinna at the Capitol" in A, p. [58], are used in "The Heart," *Lectures*, II, 282–283. The next seven entries are used, *ibid.*, pp. 290, 288, 288–289, 293, 281, and 284. For "Don't mix . . . friends", see "Friendship," *W*, II, 207–209.

[165] These six entries, all but the last repeated from pp. [95]–[96] above, are found in "The Heart," *Lectures*, II, 288–291.

[166] P. [97] is in pencil.

fool can do that. But if his conversation enriches or rejoices me I must reckon him wise[.] [A 21] [167]

It is ⟨a⟩felt as a defect in any man the want of heart even by those who have no heart.

There are men who suffer cruelly from a suspicion of suspicion
Fear is the violation of society [168]
Affliction leve⟨s⟩ls all

I think it must be felt that over all & through all is a superior nature not to be analysed[,] not to be used but to be obeyed. It is a little prejudiced by acumen. Women who do not reason yield themselves to it more than men. It is always unconscious. & Culture only teaches to yield to it. Culture teaches us to trust our instincts & gives us back to them[.]

This common soul saves the drowning man, rushes to the rearing horse, leaps into the ⟨fire⟩ burning house to rescue the cradle. This takes counsel only of itself & sneers never, imputes never a low motive. Its eye is clear as the heaven[.] [169]

[98]   Friendship.

Real insulation of Man
Actual association

The pervading Soul or the Heart
Kindness
Owned by the Glance
Heart enjoins true relations
False relations punished by fear
Courage
Friendship   the individualisation of Heart

Of course the end of friendship is *One life*[,] a cooperation more entire

---

[167] See Notebook Man, p. [104] above, and p. [136] below.

[168] "It is . . . heart." and "Fear . . . society" are used in "The Heart," *Lectures*, II, 282, and 284 and 285.

[169] "I think . . . heaven", struck through in pencil with a diagonal use mark, is used in "The Heart," *Lectures*, II, 281 and 293.

than any in our experience but we cannot go too slowly towards that re⟨no⟩mote end.

The simplest goods are the best. Can we not be so great as to offer tenderness to our friend? n 170

[99]   Friendship
Do you know your friend at once or in a long time? "Both."
"If you do not like my friend at first you will never like him." Indeed!
I had not thought so. I did not, I remember, like you at first, yet we man↑a↓ge to converse without disgust. [D 360]

Better have friends full grown before they are made acquainted.171
They have the surprise of the result. A man & a man. As character is more to us, our fellow men cease to exist to us in space & time, & we hold them by real ties.

Blessed be the friend! & Blessed also be the eternal power for those whom my law⟨t⟩less fancy even cannot strip of beauty & who never for a moment seem to me profane.

I see well ⟨fo⟩that for all his purple cloaks I shall not like him unless he is at last a poor Greek like me[.] [E 114]
How did you know he was a God? 172 Because n [100] I was content the moment my eye fell on him. [E 117]

The soul puts out friends as the tree puts out leaves. [E 169] 173

---

170 "Real insulation . . . of Heart" is in pencil and may be a continuation of Emerson's collection for "The Heart"; cf. *Lectures*, II, 279, 281, 283, 284, 285, and 288. "Friendship." and the rest of the page are in ink and, like pp. [99]–[100] below, may be notes for the essay "Friendship," added in 1840; "goods" is struck through in pencil with what may be a diagonal use mark; with "Can we not . . . friend.", cf. Journal E, p. [165], and "Friendship," *W*, II, 204.
171 Cf. "The Heart," *Lectures*, II, 290.
172 From "Blessed be the friend!" to the bottom, the page is struck through in ink with a vertical use mark. "I see . . . like me" is used in "Friendship," *W*, II, 197.
173 "Friendship" is added at the top of p. [100]. The paragraph in Journal E, p. [117], is used in "Character," *W*, III, 90, and see notes to "Private Life," *Lec-*

Is it not possible that I should go into a man's house without losing sight of the landscape? If not, better never go under a roof again. Better with the Douglas hear the lark sing than the mouse cheep. Yet now a morose or a little man tyrannizes over it, & hinders me of its influences,

Why this unseemly haste to work & live together? [n]

[101] [blank]
   [102] [174] Milton
⟨C. C E's love a new fact⟩
The age has already lost the Controversialist
C.C.E. a new fact
   The inspiring character
   Milton's claim
   Physique
   Education
     language

[103]   Culture: Progress
C 201 [175]

[104]   Eye & Ear [176]
Retzch
Retzch Gothic   C 29
Tischbein's end of painting   C 29   Tischbein & Granduke 31
Plotinus on art   C 53

---

tures, III, 483. The paragraph in E, p. [169], is used in "Friendship," *W*, II, 197, but with this sentence, cf. C, p. [124], and "The Heart," *Lectures*, II, 279.

[174] P. [102] is in pencil. The bottom half of the page contains three columns of arithmetic and "Jonathan" in ink, probably practice penmanship. This and the following page are covered with sketches in pencil, upside down on the page, and possibly those of a child, of seven urns, two with flowers, several partial figures, one of a woman in left profile, another of a crowned man labeled "EDWARD THE SECOND", a castle, a sword, a crown, and a kite.

[175] Both paragraphs in Journal C, p. [201], are used in "The Heart," *Lectures*, II, 293.

[176] Pp. [104]–[111], in pencil, contain collections and drafts for "The Eye and Ear," *Lectures*, II, 262–277.

Laocoon ⁿ ↑C↓ 170

American artist   C 137

Fluctuation of form ↑C↓ 181

   Imitation not the end of art   C 208 [177]

   Carpets & paper hangings & Thom's statues   C 16   ↑Egypt 179↓

Goethe   C 50   B 145

   Design — (invention   C 13) ↑C↓ 63   220 ↑Graeter↓   251 ↑Human form↓ [178]

Walk with a painter   C 176

Tomb ornaments   C 177

Primi in proeliis oculi   C 244

Life tends to be picturesque   C 11

Paule de Viguier   C 30 [179]   Beauty welcome   203

Beauty 34, 102, 152,

Inward Beauty 147 [180]

Nature's Beauty   188, 40, 83, ⟨183⟩, ⟨103⟩   107 ↑Walden↓   136

    ↑water↓ ⟨218⟩ ↑miracles↓ 101 ↑chesnut↓ 224 ↑darkness↓ [181]

Proportion   194

[177] This entry is struck through in pencil with a vertical use mark; the sentence cited is used in "The Eye and Ear," *Lectures*, II, 266. Passages in Journal C, p. [31], are used in "Prudence," *Lectures*, II, 315, and *W*, II, 229–230, and "Literature" [first lecture], *Lectures*, III, 221, and "Thoughts on Modern Literature," *The Dial*, I (Oct. 1840), 153 (*W*, XII, 325–326). With C, p. [137], cf. "Literary Ethics," *W*, I, 169. The paragraph in C, p. [181], is used in "History," *W*, II, 14.

[178] The passage in Journal C, p. [179], is used in a fragment printed with "Private Life," *Lectures*, III, 250. Emerson quotes or paraphrases Goethe throughout "The Eye and Ear"; with the last paragraph in C, p. [50], cf. *Lectures*, II, 269 and 271; the quotation in B, p. [145], is used, *ibid.*, p. 265. Of the notes on design, only the paragraph in C, p. [63], is used, *ibid.*, pp. 264–265. The passage in C, p. [13], is used in "Being and Seeming," *Lectures*, II, 308, and C, p. [251], in "Genius," *Lectures*, III, 74, and "Intellect," *W*, II, 337.

[179] Three lines, "Primi . . . C 30", are struck through in pencil with a vertical use mark. The first passage is used in "Prudence," *Lectures*, II, 319–320, and *W*, II, 237; the second and third are in "The Eye and Ear," *Lectures*, II, 273 and 276.

[180] One phrase in Journal C, p. [34], is used in "The Eye and Ear," *Lectures*, II, 264 and 275. The passages in C, pp. [203], [34], and [102], are used in "Love," *Lectures*, III, 59 and 56. The paragraph in C, p. [147], is used in "Being and Seeming," *Lectures*, II, 302.

[181] The passages cited in Journal C, pp. [183], [103], and [218], are used in "The Eye and Ear," *Lectures*, II, 273–274. The paragraph in C, p. [136], is used, *ibid.*, p. 275, and in "Nature," *W*, III, 171.

People no better for sun & moon ↑C↓ 211 [182]
Music   C 233   96 ↑Culture↓   99 ↑Richter↓
The man that made the minster   C 184 [183]
American aspects of the forest   B 293   C 137
Approach of Winter   B 292
Botany or Buying Wood   B 304 [184]
Sun's Music, Chee, B 134
[105] Design C 63   251
 Form 181   Goethe   B 145
 Proportion [C 194]
  Life tends to the picturesque [C 11]
  Beauty of nature
  Buying wood [B 304]
  Approach of winter [B 292]
  American aspects
  Beauty of Man   Paule [C 30]

  Plotinus on Art [C 53]
  Imitation not the end [C 208]
  Tischbein [C 29]
  Taste.   Art [Enc. 143]
  The man that made the Minster [C 184] [185]

Every body that can speak can sing
Music

[182] The paragraph in Journal C, p. [194], is used in "The Eye and Ear," *Lectures*, II, 265. The sentence in C, p. [211], is used in "Spiritual Laws," *W*, II, 147.

[183] This line is struck through in pencil with a vertical use mark. The paragraph cited is used in "The Eye and Ear," *Lectures*, II, 268, and "History," *W*, II, 11–12. The passage on Richter in Journal C, p. [99] (see also Encyclopedia, p. [215], and D, p. [203]), is used in "Love," *Lectures*, III, 60, and *W*, II, 179.

[184] Both passages cited on "American aspects of the forest" are used in "Literary Ethics," *W*, I, 169. The paragraph in Journal B, p. [304], is used in "The Eye and Ear," *Lectures*, II, 274–275.

[185] "Life" and "Buying" are struck through in pencil with single diagonal use marks. See p. [104] for all entries except "Taste.   Art". Three entries in the first three lines on p. [105] are used in "The Eye and Ear," *Lectures*, II, 264–265, five in "Life tends . . . Paule", *ibid.*, pp. 273–276, and three in "Plotinus . . . Minster", *ibid.*, pp. 266–268.

Eloquence
A man should know the language of God
Beauty is everywhere   The eye the eye
When we are shown a beauty we feel compunction
Lincoln bell [186] [A 63]

[106]   Laws of life
⟨C 180⟩ ⟨In the fine day we despise the house.⟩ ⟨Esquimaux bed.⟩
C.80, 7, 109, at top, ⟨159⟩, 184, ⟨191⟩, ⟨22⟩, ⟨35⟩
B 216, 164 [187]

    Spenser   B 65
    Beauty depends on the interior truth
    Beauty is the pilot
    Science is a Venus & Graces
    All cultivation of the man decks the object
    The laws of beauty very deep   Pity he should not know them,
pity he should be a connoisseur & a devil too
    [I suppose if he were selfunited he would not contemplate the
beauty apart as now]
    Now his knowledge of art is for display
Cultivation is local   rub one place [on] a log of wood & you can excite
electricity
    Explanation of deformity   A shadow not handsome but helps

---

[186] "Beauty . . . eye" and "Lincoln bell" are used in "The Eye and Ear,"
Lectures, II, 269 and 272.

[187] The page to this point may be a collection for the last lecture in the "Human
Culture" series; see pp. [170]–[171] below, where "The Laws of Life" is listed
among titles for that series, and pp. [136]–[137] below, probably a collection for
the last lecture, "General Views," where all but three of these entries are repeated.
"C 180 . . . bed." is used in "The Senses and the Soul," *The Dial*, II (Jan. 1842),
378, and *Lectures*, II, 362, where "The Senses and the Soul" is reprinted as "General
Views." With Journal C, p. [22], and B, p. [216], cf. a fragment printed with
"Private Life," *Lectures*, III, 252, but possibly part of "General Views." The paragraph in C, p. [35], is used in "Compensation," *W*, II, 96–97; the passage in C,
p. [159], is used in "Love," *Lectures*, III, 63, and the passages in C, p. [184], are
used in "The Eye and Ear," *Lectures*, II, 268, and "History," *W*, II, 10–11 and
11–12; for the last entry see "Demonology," *Lectures*, III, 450–451 (notes), and
W, X, 20–21.

the lights.   a hybrid not deformed to the scientific as it proves the rule [188]

[107] ⟨A man⟩ Live in the Country
Beauty will be found an hourly neighbor of a true life
The factory is loathsome to us as the jail of young unwilling boys & girls. But the forge in Schiller is pleasing.
Bacon's best part of beauty
Il piu nell uno [B 128]
The beautiful a manifestation of secret laws [189]

Curious the divorce now between the eye & the soul so that people think it foolish to suppose a connexion. Great authors have wished to lead a genteel life without & to write poems from the imagination. Great preachers think it a pretty fancy your talking of the spiritual meaning of horse & plough & like to get on the solid ground of historical evidence — that a book was writ by somebody [190]

[108] Very superficial notions of Beauty exist
It is thought superficial
Form is not supposed to have anything to do with Soul
Walter Scott & ministers
Doctrine of Beauty is deep
And always so taught by Seers
As it depends on the heart of things, Science decks
Power of Form
Life un-beautiful which should be beautiful
Because untrue —

[188] "Spenser . . . the rule" is struck through in pencil with a diagonal use mark. The first entry is used in "The Eye and Ear," *Lectures*, II, 264, "The Poet," *W*, III, 14, and one line in *English Traits*, *W*, V, 242. The rest is developed in "The Eye and Ear," *Lectures*, II, 263, 264, 269, and 272–273.
[189] "Live in the Country", which may have been added, is developed in "The Eye and Ear," *Lectures*, II, 273–275. "Beauty . . . girls." is struck through in pencil with a vertical use mark; the first sentence is used, *ibid.*, p. 273. An English version of "Il piu nell uno", struck through in pencil with a diagonal use mark, is used, *ibid.*, p. 264. See Encyclopedia, pp. [143]–[144].
[190] This paragraph, struck through in pencil with a diagonal use mark, is used in "The Eye and Ear," *Lectures*, II, 263, and "The Poet," *W*, III, 3–4.

Distant from nature
The Great Miracle [C 218–219]
Botany   Coal

Beauty of Man deep [191]

[109]   Beauty everywhere   the eye the eye
Beauty has never been locked up in Vaticans. It is there but it is not less here. A graceful thought will instantly create it. In the plainest apartment in this city where an imaginative & pure mind acts with others beauty will each moment be born[,] beauty for the outward eye & ear as well as for the soul.

I say we hide ourselves from the influences of nature but how can we, — the fire in the chimney is here, the steam of the kettle, the beam of light, the air we breathe, the vibrations of sound, the faces & forms we behold[.]

We read with eager inclination of sounds heard & sights seen by others & imagine our being would be enriched had we them also but remember for every thing we miss we have gained something else; for every thing we gain we lose something. The world is a plenum. I cannot doubt but that fidelity to oneself, to one's place, is rewarded by a circle of Fair as well as Good in which something is found for every thing wanting. Remember that the Artist created his work without model save Life, Household life & personal relations, the beating heart, the meeting eyes.[192]

[110] Consenting with these views are the ⟨rules⟩ theory & the rules of Art.
The organism of the man should coincide with World
The soul seeks to produce what it is compelled to do.

---

[191] "Very superficial . . . Seers" and "Power of Form" are an outline of "The Eye and Ear," *Lectures*, II, 262–264; with "As it depends . . . decks", cf. *ibid.*, p. 269; the rest of the page is an outline of pp. 272–275.

[192] "Beauty everywhere . . . the eye" is used in "The Eye and Ear," *Lectures*, II, 269. "Beauty has never . . . meeting eyes." is struck through in pencil with a curved diagonal use mark. "Beauty has never . . . behold" is used, *ibid.*, pp. 271–272; with "We read . . . enriched", cf. *ibid.*, p. 272; the last sentence is used on p. 270.

Art not an imitation of nature but of ideal
⟨tr⟩The work of art brings you into that state of mind in which the man was that made it [193]
True art again is not imitation of Greeks   be Greek yourself. Moller

[111]   Beauty deep
         Beauty of art from the Universal & therefore all ours
         Theory of art

         Beauty o⟨b⟩verflows life
         Only it wants Eye

         True Culture therefore General, Moral,
         All this in *us*. Man that made the minster

    ⟨That⟩ Music seeks also ⟨this⟩ to express this universal beauty

    In a moment of great peace we are susceptible to the beauty which overflows all nature [194]

[112] Mind & Manners in XIX Century [195]
1   Intellect
2   Identity of Thought & Nature; & Byelaws
3   Instinct & Inspiration; & Tendencies & duties of Men of Thought
4   Eloquence —

---

[193] "Consenting . . . made it" is struck through in pencil with a diagonal use mark. With "Art not . . . ideal", cf. Journal C, p. [208]; with "⟨tr⟩The work . . . made it", cf. C, p. [176]; both are used in "The Eye and Ear," *Lectures*, II, 266 and 270.

[194] With "Beauty deep . . . minster", struck through in pencil with a discontinuous diagonal use mark, cf. "The Eye and Ear," *Lectures*, II, 263, 267, 273, 269, 275, 268, 266, and 273. "In a moment . . . nature", struck through in pencil with a diagonal use mark, is used, *ibid.*, p. 273.

[195] Emerson gave a series of six lectures under this heading in London in June, 1848; some of the titles were similar. He gave the lecture "England" for the first time in December, 1848, after his return. He repeated the series, with variations, several times in 1849 and 1850; this list is probably for one of these American readings. A collection for "Intellect" is in Journal GH, pp. [8]–[11]. See also O, pp. [164] and [310].

5 England —
6 Spirit of the Age —

[113]   The Convenient.
⟨Fire club⟩
Opposite of the Heroic
Evenus [C 132]
   Bad roads C.17   Mountains Z [196]

[114]–[115] [blank]
   [116₁] [197] I the imperfect adore my own perfect
I am somehow receptive of the Great God & therefore I do over-look
the sun & stars & feel them to be within or below my sphere[.]
   Heroism is proud[;] the soul advancing recognises the identical
nature of all men & sees how vain is all opposition to it[,] that it is the
invincible mistress of its own honor & can very well afford to contemn
all hostility & to distinguish between the actual & ideal nature of the
opponent so far as to impledge itself to his benefit[.]
When a man in this age wrote On the aversion of men of taste to
Evang[elical]. Relig[ion]. he had good reason for his
   It then renounces pride. It burns with love. It
Holiness is ⟨the mathematical⟩ a life mathematically true to the law of
nature with no rebellious individual thought. It soars above tradition
& sect. In the contemplation of principles Unitarianism[,] Romanism
are boyish. When I rest in perfect humility   When I burn with
pure love [198]
[...]

[117₁] Moral sentiment the essence of man

[196] See pp. [170]–[171] below, where "The Convenient" is evidently an early
title for the lecture "Prudence." A quotation from Evenus is used in "Prudence,"
Lectures, II, 324. The last line is in pencil.
   [197] Pp. [116₁] and [117₁] are in pencil. The lower half of p. [116] and the
following six pages are overwritten in ink by lecture notes written in 1862, indicated
by [...] and printed following p. [122₁] below.
   [198] Entries on p. [116₁] are used in "Holiness," *Lectures*, II, 355, 346–347,
341, and 346. "In the contemplation . . . boyish." is from Journal C, p. [207],
and "When I rest . . . pure love" from A, p. [155]. See pp. [117₁] and [120₁]–
[125] below, for more notes for "Holiness."

Vitiated instantly by being secondary not primary

Now it is historical

It seems sad that the world should be defrauded & that in God's name ever of the highest

Its habit should be adoration. It will come to see the perennial miracle & then the turning water into wine will not astonish [199]

[...]

[118]-[119] [...]

[120₁] [200]   Heroism exalts individual

Moral sentiment or Holiness

Heroism esteems the soul its private property

Saint esteems it God's or St Paul's

   Holiness unattractive

   Soul owns the instinct to venerate; but also

    owns the instinct of self trust

  And Tradition says Venerate this Saint & Law

Impossible: this imported faith may varnish whom it will — it may serve for seeming — for Being never.

But neither is unbelief good

See how we live from God

  1 We & events from else

  2 Our thoughts from above

  3 the command of Conscience

  4 Profanity

  5 beauty of worship

⟨Let us e⟩Explore the sentiment of Morals

———

[B] ↑p 259.↓

———

[199] "Moral sentiment . . . historical" is developed in "Holiness," *Lectures*, II, 345, 355, and 341–342. "Its habit . . . astonish" is used, *ibid.*, pp. 346 and 356.

[200] P. [120₁], in pencil, is an outline of "Holiness," *Lectures*, II, 340–351. The first two lines are overwritten by matter in the 1862 sequence.

Uniform, ultimate, impersonal, ravishing, superior to division
Humility a match for pride
Humility a self trust
Illustrated in Manzoni & Silvio
Humility prospective
[. . .]

[121₁] Explore further Moral sentiment
A man its mouthpiece
Impersonal ever
Occulted God
Plutarch's Egyptians & Jews.
S.67 [B 184]
Culture reaches

No positive all moral obligation   C 150 [201]
[. . .]

[122₁] [202] Unconscious
        ↑Events↓
        Thoughts
        ↑Conscience↓
        profanity
        prayer

The religious moment
Unites
        Humility   O virgin [A 9] / S.81 / A 78 / Forgive virtue↑s↓

Let the soul come without superstition to this contemplation that
the highest is made known to it through the sentiment of Duty ——

[201] P. [121₁], in pencil, is an outline of "Holiness," *Lectures*, II, 352–356. See
p. [123] below for "S.67". The last line is erased and overwritten by matter in the
1862 sequence.

[202] P. [122₁], in pencil, is an outline of "Holiness," *Lectures*, II, 343–346,
351, and 355–356. All but the last three lines are overwritten by matter in the 1862
sequence. A pencil sketch of a man's head in left profile is in the upper right
quarter of the page, overwritten by both pencil and ink layers.

that the highest dwells with man; with you & me
that in our own religious hours we understand all sacred lore
that the soul is defrauded if the sentiment be not primary
    commandment & commander
that the world is a perennial miracle
   no profane all sacred history
It is the soul not the Indiv. ever
If Jesus came into the world——
[...]

[116_2] [203] What each brings is power of classifying VA 180

 Locomotive

 Temperament ↑V↓ snapping turtle

 Persuade gunpowder to explode gently

 Sensibility VA 169 194
Shallow complainers [n] of poverty of nature [VA 169]
Color is a million fathoms deep [VA 169] [204]
[117_2] Anvil VA 233
 Navy *WAR*
 Every man at the mercy of his son ' VA 225
 Every one has his tyrant *VA 221*
 Resources of poet & chemist VA 113
 drubbed by Fate

[203] Emerson added "Perpetual Forces 106" to his index in a late hand; since pp. [118] and [119] were renumbered "108" and "109", he undoubtedly meant p. [116]. See pp. [63] and [94] above, indexed at the same time. Notes on pp. [116_2]– [122_2] were probably for the lecture "Perpetual Forces," November 18, 1862; many of these passages are in the lecture manuscript, which is incomplete, and others survive in "Perpetual Forces," W, X, 67–88, which drew on this lecture. See also Journal VA, p. [197], for similar notes.
[204] "What each . . . classifying", from Journal VA, p. [183], is struck through in ink with a vertical use mark and used with a passage from VA, p. [180], in "Perpetual Forces," W, X, 76–77, and in the lecture. "Temperament . . . turtle" and "Sensibility" are in the lecture. "Sensibility . . . deep" is struck through in ink with two vertical use marks. One sentence in VA, p. [194], is used in "Perpetual Forces," W, X, 82.

Expense of war "to slay a soldier." *WAR* 15

—

Proclamation defined every man's position   VA [209]

—

Recoils   V*A* 186
Riches of Memory   VA 182
My resources   VA 180

—

French civilization exceptional
admits all men to society [205]

—

[⟨118⟩108] Nov 1862
Inventory of our powers a consolation
⟦Man in nature
a suction pipe through which the world flows. No force but is his force.⟧
World machine
powers of a day, of a year,
the gross elements
Water   Air   Fire
Rock of Ages
Gravity   Electricity   Heat
Affinity
Circulation
Vegetation
*Anima*tion [206]

[109 [119]] Man in Nature

Fate
Temperament
Intellect

[205] "Resources of . . . chemist" and "My resources . . . society" are struck through in ink with single vertical use marks. "Riches of Memory . . . society" is used in the lecture "Perpetual Forces." The paragraph in Journal VA, pp. [180]–[181], is used in "Perpetual Forces," *W*, X, 76–77.
[206] "Inventory . . . force.⟧" is struck through in ink with a vertical use mark. "Inventory . . . powers of a day," "Water   Air   Fire", and "Gravity . . . *Anima*tion" are used in the lecture "Perpetual Forces"; with "Inventory . . . Heat" and "Vegetation", cf. "Perpetual Forces," *W*, X, 69–76.

⟨Will⟩
Memory
Talents, Music, Geometry,
    WILL   opinions of men
The acts of nations are not casualties, but must be as the men are, &
may be predicted if you know the men.

———

Freedom is as the virtue [VA 236]

———

Absurd pudency of Virtue [VA 32]

———

We arrive at virtue only by taking its direction instead of im-
posing ours[207]
That too is the difference between [120₂] Talent & Genius

Keep Shop

[121₂] The forces of nature seen from outside are Fate,[208]— seen
from within, are ours. We are chosen into the club. Our club. How
we swim! What a dust we kick up, said the fly.

[122₂] Forces of all kinds
not only of health but of recovery
    (

Manꜛ's↓ⁿ ⟨has⟩ whole frame is responsive to the world, part for part,
every sense, every pore, to a new element.[209]

[123]   The Holy
⟨See B.⟨259⟩ ⟨234⟩ ⟨2⟩⟩

[207] Below "Man in Nature", a hand sign points to "[Man in Nature . . .
force.]" on p. [118₂] opposite it. "Man in Nature . . . of men" is in the lecture
"Perpetual Forces"; cf. also "Perpetual Forces," *W*, X, 72, 73, 78, 80, and 82.
"Freedom is . . . virtue", "Absurd . . . Virtue", and "We arrive . . . ours",
each struck through in ink with a vertical use mark, are used in both lecture and
essay, *W*, X, 86, 87–88, and 83 and 84.
    [208] "The forces . . . Fate," is used in "Perpetual Forces," in both lecture and
essay, *W*, X, 73.
    [209] This sentence is used in "Perpetual Forces," in both lecture and essay, *W*, X,
74.

⟨Of profanity B 125⟩ [210]
Preaching B 112 C 148 B 334
⟨Idea of God B 93⟩
⟨Love of Virtue B 79⟩
     ⟨C 121⟩
Ecclesiastical Manners B 234.
⟨Marlboro Hotel prayer⟩
⟨Fra Cristoforo⟩   & Silvio
⟨What can Calvin or Swedenborg say S 12⟩ [211]
Cant
⟨Persons S 67,⟩ B 184
Best persons freest speakers A 114, B.41
⟨O virgin mother daughter of thy Son   S⟩ 81 [A 9] [212]
Commandment & Commander A 52
Connecticutt Sunday A 76
Attention to the obscure A 78
Satan of the past age   A 94
"⟨Forgive his virtues too⟩" [213] [A 106]
Idea of God in lonely place A 106   B 93
If I could persuade men to believe their interior conviction A 110
(⟨Saints of seemed blasphemers B 41⟩)
God occult B ⟨83⟩, 93
Goethe's mental prayer B 147
Religious soul speaks to Soul B 161
Duty a god in disguise. B.167 —
⟨Persons B 184⟩ [214] Curious concerning others faith B 256

[210] Pp. [123]–[125], in pencil, are collections for the lecture "Holiness." The passage cited in Journal B, p. [259], is used in "Holiness," *Lectures*, II, 344–345. "Of profanity B 125" is apparently canceled with a wavy line, but the passage is used, *ibid.*, p. 344.

[211] "Idea . . . C 121", "Marlboro . . . Cristoforo", and "What . . . S 12" are all apparently canceled with single wavy lines, but "Marlboro . . . say" is used in "Holiness," *Lectures*, II, 344, 347–351, and 346. "S" is probably "Spirit Mss". See p. [14] above.

[212] Passages in Journal B, pp. [184] and [41], and A, p. [9], are used in "Holiness," *Lectures*, II, 353–354 and 351. "S" is probably "Spirit Mss". The sentence in A, p. [114], is used in "Genius," *Lectures*, III, 81. (See Notebook Man, p. [48] above.)

[213] This and other lines from Young are used in "Holiness," *Lectures*, II, 352.

[214] Passages in Journal B, pp. [83] and [184], are used in "Holiness," *Lec-

[124] [215] Mor. sent.   Essence of the soul   B.259
Providence not to be read like a newspaper ↑C 22↓
Doctrine of Immortality   C 40, 206, ↑S↓
Our position absolute   C 41
Puritanic education   C.65
    Moral sentiment works miracles   C 121
    ⟨Preaching   C 148⟩
    ⟨No positive all moral obligation   C 150⟩
Lidian gives money for text's sake   C 223
    ↑Crocodile, lotus,↓

[125] Pure in heart shall be God   C 29
If Jesus came now into the world he would say You; he said I;
[C 121]
The habitual attitude of the wise mind must be adoration
⟨When the Conversation soars to principles Unitarianism is boyish⟩ [216]
[C 207]

    Were it the will of Heaven an osier bough
    Were vessel safe enough the seas to plough [217] [A 167]

It is hard to be simple enough to be good.
The Coal. [B 149] [218]

[126]–[127] [219]
[128] [220] Phrenology   does justice to surface

---

tures, II, 352–353 and 353–354. Though other passages cited on p. [123] have not been located, Emerson used the thought of many of them throughout the lecture. The sentence cited in A, p. [106], was used later in "The Over-Soul," *W*, II, 292.

[215] Only the first and last entries on p. [124] have been located in "Holiness," *Lectures*, II, 344–345 and 353. Journal C, p. [40], was used later in "Religion," *Lectures*, III, 277, and "The Over-Soul," *W*, II, 283–284; C, p. [121], in "Self-Reliance," *W*, II, 89; and C, p. [148], in the Divinity School Address, *W*, I, 139.

[216] "When . . . boyish", apparently canceled with a wavy line, is used in "Holiness," *Lectures*, II, 346.

[217] The lines of Pindar are used in "The School," *Lectures*, III, 41.

[218] The sentence cited in Journal B, p. [149], is used in "Holiness," *Lectures*, II, 356.

[219] Pp. [126]–[127] are covered with a child's pencil sketches of sailing ships and two small sketches by an adult of a ship and a sprig of evergreen.

[220] P. [128], in pencil, is indexed "The Age 128 [1841]". It may be early

Animal Magnetism to subsurface   •
Photography
Mechan. Arts. Railroad show healthy hands or perhaps that is merely
    a fact of population, results from a great census
Transcendentalism is spiritualism
Caoutchouc
Religion: pious, meek, loving women.
I do not see then but the grasp of this age is as great as any
Representative Government
State Rights

[129] [221]
[130]   Culture of the Intellect [222]

Economy of time   C 211   Sincerity   C 92
Goethe's Tasso   C 205
Proportion of Writing   C 194
Appeal to the future   C 185
AEschylus must win me also   C 181[–182], 165, 143, 113 [223]
Great poets plain   C 179
Hearing better than speaking ↑C↓ 167   B 309
Observing   C 166, ⟨164⟩, 158
Truth & Repose   B 123   B 210 [224]

---

notes for the series on "The Times," but Emerson also considered "an Essay entitled
a Survey of the Time" for *Essays* [*First Series*]; see Journal F No. 2, p. [25].

[221] A child's pencil drawings of pitchers, cups, a fireplace, and two seated figures, most of them upside down, cover two-thirds of the page.

[222] Pp. [130]–[135], in pencil, contain notes for "The Head," *Lectures*, II,
246–261. See also pp. [15] and [73₁] above.

[223] This and the preceding line are struck through in pencil with single diagonal
use marks. Passages cited in Journal C, pp. [211], [181], [165], [143], and
[113], are used in "The Head," *Lectures*, II, 257 and 260–261. With "Sincerity",
cf. *ibid.*, pp. 256–257, but the passages in C, pp. [92] and [185], are used in
"Being and Seeming," *Lectures*, II, 300–301 and 303. Emerson later used C, pp.
[181], [165], and [113], in "Intellect," *W*, II, 344–345, and C, p. [143], in
"Politics," *Lectures*, III, 242, and "Self-Reliance," *W*, II, 60–61.

[224] "Hearing", "Observing", and "Truth" are struck through in pencil with
single diagonal use marks. With Journal B, p. [309], cf. "The Head," *Lectures*, II,
257. The other six passages are all used, *ibid.*, pp. 257–258, 259, 253–254, 258–259,
256, and 258. The passages cited in C, pp. [167] and [164], and B, pp. [123] and

Spontaneous action ↑C↓ 140
Draw circles   C 135   progress
Unity of Men   C 134
The past lies in the mind for the future   C 120 [225]
Always on the brink of great thought   C 105
⟨Sincerity   C 92⟩
The Minister's office ↑C↓ 6⟨6⟩7 [226]
Genius   C 60, 3,
An opinion rare   C 33, 80
We all are stocked with facts. bring a light [C 164] See above p 5
Instincts (See above p. 23) [227]
Scholar   C 23   42   83   127   115
Literature
What↑ever↓ the mind saith is after a law ⟨1⟩C 152
Scientific Analogy   C 152 [228]
Truth & originality go abreast always   [B 206]
Scholar like the opium eaters   B 204
Objectivity & Subjectivity
[131] Do not fear the multitude of books   B 202
Every intellectual acquisition is mainly prospective [C 164]
God the substratum of the mind   C 85
We do not like to have any man give us thoughts

---

[210], are also used in "Intellect," *W*, II, 342 and 343, 332–333, 341–342, and 343–344.

[225] This and the preceding line are struck through in pencil with single diagonal use marks. Passages in Journal C, pp. [140], [135], [134], and [120], are all used in "The Head," *Lectures*, II, 250, 254–255, 255, and 254; the passages in C, pp. [140] and [120], were used later in "Intellect," *W*, II, 328 and 333–334, and C, pp. [135] and [134], in "Circles," *W*, II, 304–305 and 308.

[226] This and the preceding line are struck through in pencil with a diagonal use mark. The paragraph in Journal C, pp. [105]–[106], is used in "The Head," *Lectures*, II, 251–252, and "Intellect," *W*, II, 331–332. See above for "Sincerity   C 92". With the paragraph in C, p. [67], cf. the Address on Education, *Lectures*, II, 202–203; part of the paragraph is used in the Divinity School Address, *W*, I, 138.

[227] This and the preceding line are struck through in pencil with a vertical use mark. Both passages are used in "The Head," *Lectures*, II, 254 and 251, and "Intellect," *W*, II, 330. Passages in Journal C, pp. [60] and [33], cited above, are used in "Being and Seeming," *Lectures*, II, 308–309 and 304, and the passage in C, p. [80], in "Spiritual Laws," *W*, II, 156.

[228] Both brief passages in Journal C, p. [152], are used in "The Head," *Lectures*, II, 250 and 253; with "Scholar" and "Literature", cf. *ibid.*, pp. 256–258.

Dry light.   Secrets [229]
        Truth & Repose
        Unity of men   God the substratum
        Every soul must learn all [C 155]
        ⟨Acquisition⟩ ⟨C.164, 120⟩   Above p 5.
        The soul sublimates   127–8,
        Poet too high for partisan
        Hearing better than speaking [C 167]
        Observing 240   166   158   167
        Appeal to the future [C 185] [230]
Spontaneous; Instinct: Aeschylus; Schleiermacher
  We all have facts. a light; [231]
        Treat genius as yourself a genius   113
        True man measures you & all   143
        Insist that the ontologist shall render y[ou]r consciousn[ess]
                              165

        AEschylus must delight *me* also   181

        Leave father & mother   B 210
        Hundred vols of Univ. Hist. in self   C 227
        Why should we lie so   C 207
        You shan't integrate too fast   141 [232]

[132]   Culture of the Head [233]
    What is the Intellect

---

[229] Passages in Journal C, pp. [164] and [85], and "Dry . . . Secrets" are used in "The Head," *Lectures*, II, 253, 252, 249, and 251.

[230] The passage cited in Journal C, p. [155], is used in "History," *W*, II, 10, and the passage in C, p. [185], in "Being and Seeming," *Lectures*, II, 303. The rest of these entries, from "Truth & Repose . . . 167", are used in "The Head," *Lectures*, II, 249–260, some surviving only in a phrase or two.

[231] See p. [5] above. This and the preceding line list passages used in "The Head," *Lectures*, II, 250, 260, and 251.

[232] "Treat genius . . . 141", in darker pencil, is used in "The Head," *Lectures*, II, 260–261, 258, 254, and 253, except for "Why shd . . . 207", which is used in "Being and Seeming," *Lectures*, II, 302–303. The passage in Journal C, p. [143], was used later in "Self-Reliance," *W*, II, 60–61, and those in B, p. [210], and C, pp. [227], [181], and [165], in "Intellect," *W*, II, 343–345 and 334.

[233] P. [132] is an outline of "The Head," *Lectures*, II, 246–258.

Somewhat infinite & reverable flowing into us evermore after a law of its own which we must honor & obey

Law of Progress
Every soul must learn all

Rules of Culture
Sincerity is Economy
Love defeat

[133] What is the Intellect
How doth it grow
What can we do for it

Sincerity Solitude Journal
Truth & repose

Provisions negative

Let it grow or choose truth.
Live alone
Speak what you think
Love defeat
Trust yourself
Leave father & mother
Worship the Truth [234]

["]Dulness of the age["] What age was not dull? When were not the majority wicked or what progress was ever made by society[?] ⟨S⟩The only progress ever known was of the Individual. A great wit is at any time great Solitude. A barnyard is full of chirping & cackle but no fowl clappeth wings on Chimborazo[.] [B 228]

[134] At last comes the period of conscious thought & we consider an abstract truth
⟨I think⟩ We then labor to know how the fact stands[,] inquire for

---

[234] The first three lines on p. [133] are used in one paragraph and developed throughout "The Head," *Lectures*, II, 247 and 249–261. The rest of the notes to this point are developed, *ibid.*, pp. 256, 261, 256, 255, 256, 261, 257, 258, 260, 258, and 256.

example what is the basis of Civil Government. Yet the oracles come still & are the best part. But they come because we had previously laid siege to the Shrine. It seems undulation through life our intellectual action. Now labor   now vision

Dry Light free from affection   considers every person or thing impersonally   as a fact existing for its own sake [235]

Jan 7 Add a passage to the lecture out of B p 86 & B 150 [236]

[135] Deus anima   brutorum
                     infantum
                     intellectus

The object of the intellect is principles
Lord Bacon's globe of crystal [237]

B 86—   We have little control of our thoughts[;] we are pensioners upon Ideas, they catch us up for moments into their heavens & so fully possess us that we take no thought for the morrow[,] gaze like children without an effort to make them our own. By & by we fall out of that rapture & then bethink us where we have been & what we have seen & go painfully gleaning up the grains that have fallen from the sheaf[.]

When I see the doors by which God entereth into the mind[,] that there is no sot ↑nor fop↓ or ruffian nor pedant into whom thoughts do not enter by passages which the individual never left open[,] I can expect any revolution[.] [238]

B 150 — Strange is it to me how man is holden by a curb rein & hin-

---

[235] P. [134] to this point is used, rewritten, in "The Head," *Lectures*, II, 251, 252, and 249.

[236] See p. [135] below, where the passages are copied.

[237] P. [135] to this point is developed in "The Head," *Lectures*, II, 247–248 and 252.

[238] The first paragraph copied from Journal B, p. [86], is used in "Intellect," *W*, II, 328–329, and was probably inserted in "The Head"; see *Lectures*, II, 453 (notes); the second paragraph, rewritten in "The Head," *Lectures*, II, 250, is used in "The School," *Lectures*, III, 35, and "Education," *W*, X, 133.

dered from knowing & drop by drop & shade by shade thoughts trickle or loiter upon him & no reason can he give or get glimpse of why he should not grow wiser faster . . . . moving about in worlds not realized.

[136]   Laws of life [239]

⟨C 180   In fine day we scorn the house; Esquimaux⟩;

↑C↓166   Coat ↑174↓; ⟨sea voyage⟩; [240]

C 22   Genius of Div. Providence

C 35   Polarity

C 159   Good housewife

C 191   Our sympathetic nature

C 80   You show character   B 201

S   Life & Death

C 110   ⟨I thank those who teach me not to be easily depressed⟩

C 143   ⟨Allston⟩

[A 21]   ⟨I count not him much that cows.⟩ [241]

C 121   All literature writes the character of Wise

C 122   Least effect of oration on orator

C 130   Bad counsel so the gods ordain is &c

C 138   foolish face of praise

C 144   Fangs of spirit —   Peace Soc.

C 150   ⟨Every day new⟩

C 160   ⟨If you don't like the world make it suit⟩ [242]

---

[239] See p. [106] above. Pp. [136]–[140], in pencil, are probably collections for the last lecture in the "Human Culture" series, the manuscript of which is missing. See *Lectures*, II, 357–364, where "The Senses and the Soul" (*The Dial*, II [Jan. 1842], 374–379) is reprinted as "General Views," and *Lectures*, III, 249–253, where a fragment, printed with "Private Life," uses at least ten of the passages cited in this collection and may be part of the missing manuscript of "General Views."

[240] Passages cited in this and the preceding line are used in "The Senses and the Soul," *The Dial*, II (Jan. 1842), 378 (*Lectures*, II, 362).

[241] The passages cited in Journal C, pp. [110] and [143], and A, p. [21], are used in a manuscript fragment printed in *Lectures*, III, 249; with "C 22 . . . Providence" above, cf. *Lectures*, III, 252, also. For "S   Life & Death", probably "Spirit Mss", see p. [14] above.

[242] Emerson was scanning Journal C, an indication that this was a preliminary collection; for the passage cited in C, p. [150], see *Lectures*, III, 249; "If you . . . suit" is used in "Doctrine of the Hands," *Lectures*, II, 230.

C 160   Animal magnetism
C 168   Destiny
⟨1⟩C 169   Pym
C 176   New eyes
C 178   ⟨Past in the present   A 116⟩   Time   C 180 243
C 99   Richter   Music
C 180   Custom
C 182   Greek gods
C 242   Family   B 170
[137] ↑B↓ 164   All that frees talent without increasing self command
is noxious
B 216   Character an acrostic or quincunx
        Earth goes on the Earth
B 33   Cause like Abolition
B 25   ⟨Franklin's floating ice⟩ 244

Esquimaux. In fine day
At sea the passengers augur from the moment's weather
a ragged coat looks revolutionary 245

Spiritual energy
        Before it time usually so strong is feeble. We think in idle
hours that the ancients are far off & dead & still. In excited hours we
shake hands with them across the ages.
                See what a man's being is[,] the whole past now, feeds
him. ↑A 116↓   He is the past in the present   C 179 246

243 The paragraph on "Past in the present" is in Journal C, p. [179], not p.
[178]; for this and the paragraph in A, pp. [116]–[117], see the section on Time,
Lectures, III, 250 and 251–252.
    244 This passage and "Earth . . . Earth" above are used in "The Senses and
the Soul," *The Dial*, II (Jan. 1842), 379 (*Lectures*, II, 363); see also p. [7]
above. "Character . . . quincunx" is used in the fragment in *Lectures*, III, 252,
"Demonology," *Lectures*, III, 156, and "Self-Reliance," and "Spiritual Laws," *W*,
II, 58 and 148. The paragraph in Journal B, p. [164], is used in "Demonology,"
W, X, 20–21; see also *Lectures*, III, 450–451 (notes), and the lecture "The Spirit
of the Times."
    245 See Notebook Man, p. [50] above; these three lines outline part of a para-
graph in "The Senses and the Soul," *The Dial*, II (Jan. 1842), 378 (*Lectures*, II,
362).
    246 The four passages cited in "Spiritual . . . C 179" are used in the fragment
in *Lectures*, III, 249, 250, 251–252, and 250.

[138] Greatness of the private man
    full of superstition
    yet amenable to principles all
    Immense surface

        Every day new [C 150]
        New eyes ——
        Past in the present [C 179]
        Time
        Custom
        ⟨Y⟩Make your own world: Asia & Europe with you [247]

[139] let his culture go on proportionately; knowledge noxious
without self command

        Strange position of man   Beautiful World
    Fate Love Dreams Omens Sleep Death
    Laughter Music

        full of superstition
        immense inaction
        living from the senses; Esquimaux
        floating ice   Earth goes on the earth

        Yet amenable to principles
        I thank those that teach me not to be depressed [248]

[140] preceding attempts owned inadequate
    So is all literature

[247] With "yet amenable . . . surface" and "Custom", cf. "The Senses and the Soul," *The Dial*, II (Jan. 1842), 377, 374, and 378–379 (*Lectures*, II, 362, 358, and 362–363). Passages in Journal C, pp. [150] and [179], are used in the fragment in *Lectures*, III, 249 and 250; "Time" and "⟨Y⟩Make . . . with you" are developed, *ibid.*, pp. 249–252. With "Greatness of the private man" and "Custom", cf. also Human Culture: "Introductory," *Lectures*, II, 214–215 and 218–219.

[248] "Strange position . . . Music", and "immense inaction . . . principles" are developed in "The Senses and the Soul," *The Dial*, II (Jan. 1842), 374–375, 377–379, and 377 (*Lectures*, II, 358–359, ·362–363, and 362). "I thank . . . depressed" is used in the fragment in *Lectures*, III, 249. With "immense inaction", cf. also Human Culture: "Introductory," *Lectures*, II, 215.

We sail on Earth
Come out on the crust & they bid us not think
We think but cannot learn
Hope, Sleep, Music, Laughter, Death

See how much Superstition
Go to Atheneum
    how little
So of literature   very little
The few: Genius:
Men love truth
But the senses barbarize
    We serve the moment
    All serve the moment
This Culture redresses
    end of Culture
It speaks to the Individual not society
    Every day new
    Present in past [249]

[141] [250]
[142] [blank]
[143] [251] The ideal demands that every man work
                 that he work after his genius
                 that he love his work
                 that there be no routine but
                 that it be progressive

Use of manual labor
         manual
         literary

[249] "preceding attempts . . . All serve the moment" is developed in "The Senses and the Soul," *The Dial*, II (Jan. 1842), 374–379 (*Lectures*, II, 358–363). "This Culture redresses . . . past" is developed in the fragment in *Lectures*, III, 249–250.
[250] P. [141] is filled with a child's pencil drawings of some ships sailing, an upside down house, and some details of rigging.
[251] Pp. [143]–[150], in pencil, are collections for "Doctrine of the Hands"; p. [143] outlines sections in *Lectures*, II, 233–237 and 231–232. See also Notebook Man, p. [118] above, and Notebook Ж, pp. [55]–[56] below.

[144] Wealth of nature [B 315]
World owes us a living
Native differences basis of each calling
New York Broker
Every man's art should make him happy
*Do yours. If not, yet use life symbolically.
Failing merchant [C 43]
　　*Manufacturing int of N.E. [C 33]
　　Heroism of labor　C 212

⟨Eternity⟩ [252]

Morals of Labor
Hold the plough or drive
If any man work not let him not eat
Death & rates are sure
Sublime ubique
In a money transaction, money not the main thing
Skate fast. [C 200] Haymaker's rule. [253] [C 102]

Labor honorable　　what can he do?
Moral use of a Bank [Δ 30]
　　Best use of money ˙
Beauty of Use see p. 164
Times of labor　times of rest. Eng. gentleman Hampden [254]

[145]　　　　　Vocation or the Hands
Wealth of Nature　B ⟨315⟩

[252] "Eternity" is canceled. Except for ll. 2 and 4, entries to this point are used in "Doctrine of the Hands," *Lectures*, II, 235, 238, 236, 238–239, 237, and 240. For "If not . . . symbolically.", see p. [5] above, and "Prudence," *Lectures*, II, 326.

[253] "Morals of Labor" and "Skate . . . rule." are used in "Doctrine of the Hands," *Lectures*, II, 243. See also "Prudence," *W*, II, 234–235. With "Sublime ubique", cf. "Doctrine of the Hands," *Lectures*, II, 243–244, and Journal C, p. [98], used in "Compensation," *W*, II, 115.

[254] "Labor honorable . . . do?" and "Beauty of Use" are used in "Doctrine of the Hands," *Lectures*, II, 244 and 245. With "Times of . . . rest.", cf. "The Head," *Lectures*, II, 252. "Eng. gentleman Hampden", Journal C, p. [180], is used in "Prudence," *Lectures*, II, 324.

The world owes us a living   C ⟨199⟩, 146,

Native differences the basis of each calling   C.⟨225⟩

Hold the plough or drive [B 35]

In a money transaction the main thing is not money [255]

On paying money in cities in lieu of kind

C   200   ⟨43⟩   36 [256]

Moral use of a bank [Δ] p. 30

The house praises the carpenter [B 257]

Every man's art should make him happy [257]

Buying Wood   B 304

New York Broker

Do your own work; if you cannot, yet use life symbolically. Goethe's saying.

The best use of money is to pay debts with it [258] [C 8]

procession of wagons   C.27

Manufacturing interest of N. England   C.33

Labor honorable in New England   C.56, 145,

How can he fight? vs. What can he do? C.161

Skate fast for your life! C.200

Failing Merchant   C.43

Rule for raking hay. [C 102]

Sublime ubique   C.98

If any man will not work neither shall he eat

Death & rates are sure

Instruction in Nature

---

[255] The first three lines on p. [145], "Wealth . . . C.⟨225⟩", are struck through in pencil with single diagonal use marks, the last of which Emerson extended through "Hold . . . money"; the passages cited in the first three lines are used in "Doctrine of the Hands," *Lectures*, II, 235, 240 and 242, 239–240, and 235–236. "In a money . . . money" is used in "Prudence," *Lectures*, II, 326.

[256] "On paying . . . kind" is developed in the lecture "The Spirit of the Times." Passages in Journal C, pp. [200] and [43], are used in "Doctrine of the Hands," *Lectures*, II, 243 and 238–239; C, p. [200], is also used in "Prudence," *W*, II, 234–235, and cf. Notebook F No. 1, p. [48] above, also.

[257] This line, struck through in pencil with a diagonal use mark, is used in "Doctrine of the Hands," *Lectures*, II, 238. The preceding line is used in "Duty," *Lectures*, III, 149.

[258] "New York Broker" is struck through in pencil with one diagonal use mark, and "Do your . . . with it" with another. For "Do your . . . saying." see p. [5] above, Journal C, p. [50], and "Prudence," *Lectures*, II, 326.

Ideal of a trade. The proud cook [259]

[146] ⟨P⟩shelling corn, picking peas, ploughing a field, I learn somewhat universal. I learn ethics[;] I learn language; Walter Scott, Goethe,

How should men learn the same but by a compulsory study in this *real* School

> New England Labor honorable
> All serve
> What can he do [260] [C 161]

> 3 kinds of people who live to symbol & substance [261]
> We translate every thing into a money value

It is a maxim out of the heart of nature   What you ⟨cann⟩ love not you cannot do [262] [C 38]

[147] Society is barbarous until every industrious man can get his living   without

The good coat   C 166

He is not yet man until he knows how to earn ⟨his⟩ a blameless livelihood   [C] p 146 [263]

---

[259] "Manufacturing" is struck through in pencil with a vertical use mark, "Labor . . . Sublime" with another, possibly discontinuous, and "Sublime . . . cook" with another. Passages cited in Journal C, pp. [33], [56], [145], [161], [200], [43], [102], and [98], are used in "Doctrine of the Hands," *Lectures*, II, 237, 244–245, 244, 243, 238–239, 243, and cf. 243–244. The last two lines are used, *ibid.*, pp. 231 and 239.
[260] "⟨P⟩shelling . . . School", struck through in pencil with a diagonal use mark, is developed in "Doctrine of the Hands," *Lectures*, II, 231–233. Emerson extended the use mark through "What can he do"; "New England . . . do" is used, *ibid.*, p. 244. With "I learn ethics", cf. "Trades and Professions," *Lectures*, II, 126.
[261] This line is developed in "Prudence," *Lectures*, II, 311.
[262] "It is . . . do", struck through in pencil with a diagonal use mark, is used in "Doctrine of the Hands," *Lectures*, II, 236. "Endless" is written in an ornate hand above "maxim out of" and on p. [147] below above "suppose that".
[263] "Society . . . without" and "He is not . . . p 146", struck through in pencil with single diagonal use marks, are used in "Doctrine of the Hands," *Lectures*, II, 240 and 242.

I suppose that the high laws which each man sees implicated ever in those processes with which he is conversant[,] the stern ethics which sparkle on his chisel edge[,] are measured by his plumb & footrule[,] do recommend to him his trade & exalt it to his imagination though never spoken of[.] [264]

[148] Do not all the arts resemble each other; Medicine seeks the health, Divinity the reason, Law the right[.]

The strictest analogy would be found to unite all them & they all have analogous dangers to ward & all teach the same rules[.]

The man engaged by the necessity of bread to the intimate study of some part of nature & because of that necessity cannot slur it[;] otherwise if there's any quackery & he plants rotten wheat, wheat will not spring & he shall have no bread in his basket

In the trades the degree in which Culture is an end makes the dignity & beauty of each
In the professions we loathe quackery because it defeats this end.

The trades introduce men favorably to each other for knowing really no ceremony but what can you do Sir [265]
Dr Stebbins   Alcott pedlar

[149] Each art is a whole in itself[;] it has its own precautions, its own helps, its rules, its symbols, its proverbs, ↑its heroes↓ & anciently its god, Ceres for the farmer, Vulcan for the smith, Neptune for the sailor & so on

Hardware rust   wool moth   provisions heat   flowers cold

The doctrine of the Hands is   If you do not like the world make it to suit you

---

[264] This paragraph, struck through in pencil with a vertical use mark, is used in "Doctrine of the Hands," *Lectures*, II, 243–244, and "Compensation," *W*, II, 115; cf. Journal C, p. [98].

[265] "The strictest . . . study", "The man engaged . . . this end.", and "The trades . . . knowing", each struck through in pencil with a single vertical use mark, are used in "Doctrine of the Hands," *Lectures*, II, 233–234 and 244.

There are many incidental advantages of Culture[;] the mutual helpfulness is rightly taught. None can get on a day without the other & the various craftsmen meet each other on the simplest footing of mutual need & skill[266]

[150] A man is a pair of Hands[,] pretty dangerous tools, able to subdue the world or to ⟨keep it in⟩ unbuild & destroy much faster than others can build

What is their law
> They must work
> Why
> For the possession of Nature
> All their works teach the Head
> They do not incline to do the same thing

There should be no routine. If a man will carry into his trade the faith that it is to be made a worthy occupation of all his time[,] yea of all his nature[,] so that it might be continued indefinite time & he continue advancing it becomes a fine art[.]

It shows how far wrong we are that our picture of Heaven excludes these employments[.] [267]

Add the account of S.J. May & Co   B 78

[151] My course proposes to consider in turn the main parts of human nature, the senses, the intellect, the active powers, the affections, the cultivation of the Prudent, the Heroic, & the Holy.

The Ideal is the presence of the Universal mind to the Particular. ⟨Every⟩ There is always sublimity about every the least ⟨c⟩inclining

[266] "Each art . . . suit you" and "There are . . . skill", struck through in pencil with single vertical use marks, are used in "Doctrine of the Hands," *Lectures*, II, 234, 230, and 233. "If you . . . suit you" is in Journal C, p. [160].

[267] "A man . . . law" and "There should . . . employments" are struck through in pencil with single vertical use marks. With the first sentence, cf. "Doctrine of the Hands," *Lectures*, II, 230–231; "What is . . . thing" is an outline of pp. 231–236, and "There should . . . employments" is used, *ibid.*, p. 237. With "For the possession of Nature", cf. "Trades and Professions," *Lectures*, II, 114–115.

to the suggestions. It breathes a fragrancy over the whole carr↑i↓age
& form.

The Ideal gave all ↑the↓ value that inheres in existing institutions.

The Ideal is at home forever. It belongs to the man of the senses
to ascribe honor only to the Ancient & to the Remote.[n] He who can
open his private mind to the incursions of truth, will see that Glory
⟨to⟩belongs to the present hour, to the [268]

[152] I think it proper to ask the question Why are there no
heroes? Why is not every man venerable to his brethren? Why should
men be vulgar & vile[?]

For culture it suffices not to despond but to hope highly of oneself. No faculty is marked with a broad arrow. Whoever is alive may
be good & wise. A man must have that end & lay himself generously
open to the influences of Heaven & earth[.]

The toughness of the Actual evil is only a measure of the despondency
of the good.

He should be porous to principles

A man is not in harmony with nature

Is a man↑'s body↓ to be regarded as a philosophic apparatus or designed
only for the taste of sugar, salt, & wine & for agreeable sensations? [n]

See our mendicant respect hang on the names of Milton, Washington, Howard, as if each man did not embrace all their virtues in
his own. We think so meanly of man that 'tis thought a profanity to
call Jesus one [269]

---

[268] Pp. [151]–[157], in pencil, contain Emerson's notes for Human Culture:
"Introductory," *Lectures*, II, 213–229; see also Journal C, p. [248]. P. [151],
struck through in pencil with a vertical use mark, is used in Human Culture: "Introductory," *Lectures*, II, 228–229 and 219–220.

[269] "I think . . . vile" and "No faculty . . . Heaven & earth", each struck
through in pencil with a vertical use mark, and "Is a . . . sensations.", struck
through in pencil with a diagonal use mark which Emerson extended through "Howard", are used in Human Culture: "Introductory," *Lectures*, II, 228–229.

[153] The Related Nature of Man
    Range of affinities
    Same thing taught everywhere
    Always the scene changes
    In the presence of various objects
            of the beloved
            of the great
            of pain & failure
            of need & crisis
            of the martial
  Sympathy
  Every science but the name of a sympathy

I will not deny that so far from limiting I wish to inspire fresh confidence in this Ideal Nature. Nor can I do otherwise for it haunts me by day & by night. I cannot refuse absolute belief to its suggestions[.] [270]

[154] [271]   The Ideal
God is the moral ideal, the ideal of Character

If there were only you & me the ideal would be executed; but we are encumbered by so many actuals against one Ideal
    Papa writes on the
Ideal is the Basis of C.
    Define Ideal opposed to Actual Not Real
            is Real; Justice; Circle;
      Its universal presence to man, Lover   Patriot
      Reformer Artist Naturalist
          Conscience
          Heaven
          God
          Its efficiency as a spring
          Its revelations in regard to the World

[270] Notes on p. [153] are developed in Human Culture: "Introductory," *Lectures*, II, 220–224, 216–217, 225, and 229.
[271] P. [154] is an outline of Human Culture: "Introductory," *Lectures*, II, 217–220; with the last sentence, cf. *ibid.*, p. 229.

The Actual
The inspirations of Hope
If any should ask   What is this Ideal whose effects we have described
he has touched all the springs of wonder and I leave him to float in
the deeps of the problem.

[155] Revolution historical in point of ⟨view⟩ aim
        Ancients looked at success glory brilliant multitudinous effect at
        the state at the King
        Moderns subordinate the state to every Individual
        A Man
                Data   Xy   Reformation.   Eng. Rev.   Calvin, Fox,
                Am. Independ.   Xn Missions, Charity   Politics   Votes
                Trades   Unions   Education
Philosophic view
        Culture proposes the unfolding of Man as his chief end.
        Its basis is the Ideal
        Its means rest on the related nature of man
                Related Nature
                Scope
                Unites the poles

Individuality —   Bacon's Idols [C 238]
                Riches of the individ   [C] ↑227↓
Univ. & Indiv. reconciled in Proportion   212
        Scale is Himself
                Faith in the Scale   p. 240 [272]

[156] Lecture I

        Truth or Repose? Which? [B 123]
        ⟨Related Nature of Man⟩
        He exists to the end of Culture

----

[272] Notes on p. [155] are developed or used in Human Culture: "Introductory,"
Lectures, II, 213–220, 222, and 226–228, in nearly the order listed. The passage cited
in Journal C, p. [227], is used in "The Head," *Lectures*, II, 254, and "Intellect,"
W, II, 334.

What is the Scale?   Proportion
Himself
End of Culture
Apparatus: his related nature
Advantages of different time & place
Culture in New England

Hope
Latent Heat
A man prospectively seen is another creature from actually seen.

[157] Description of Culture
It is founded on the related nature of man
Its scope
Unites the poles
Man has a necessary being
The Ideal
Riches of every individual   [C] 227

of proportionate univ. Cult. p. 212
Our being floats on the whole Culture of the past the whole Hope of the future
It is the Enterprize by lot of the Present Age [273]

[158] [274] Composition   Every act Composite & every thought; drawing on all our experience. One word of this sentence I learned in Boston, one in Cambridge, one in Europe. The weight that is put on a bridge is spread equally on every square inch. I have no fact, no sensation, no emotion to spare.
Value of a Journal. A sentence now; a sentence last year[;] a sentence yesterday. Tomorrow a question comes that for the first time brings together these three & shows them to be the three fractions of an Unit.

---

[273] Passages in Journal B, p. [123] (cf. "Man has . . . being"), and C, p. [227], are used in "The Head," *Lectures*, II, 256 and 254, and "Intellect," *W*, II, 341–342 and 334. The rest of the notes on pp. [156]–[157] are developed in Human Culture: "Introductory," *Lectures*, II, 215–228, though not in this order. "Scale" is discussed in both lectures.
[274] P. [158] is in pencil.

[159] [blank]

[160] [275] Art. That Art is something to me. Yea Every thing is something to me. Whatever appears is the growth of Me. I have unfolded so far that the new object has become part of my domain.

Westminster Abbey is an experiment on me. The weather cultivates us[,] the clouds & fields paint for me every day

[161] [blank]

[162]   Pindar

"Mind the color of the Marine beast & so converse cunningly in all cities." the Polypus being said to take the color of the stone whereon he lies.[276]

[163] [blank]

[164] Do that which you can do
        The world will feel its need of you

Leave the charge of your comeli⟨m⟩ness with God. Every creature has his own & every one a new beauty impaired always by any attempt to import another's beauty into it.

We do not look at the *features* of a man at work: we are then receivers of a higher charm

Then the beauty of Work   of Use

It is the vice of our infancy to see piecemeal[;] we look at noses & hair. The pervading bathing beauty that appears in each soul which is knit to the whole world by Truth & Duty & beameth tenderness & splendid auguries in spite of crooked features[,] baldness[,] we do not see today, we shall see in the long Morrow[.] [277]

What you are, you can only find (that secret of gods!) by working. Every day you work on the ground of others you lose so much knowledge of yourself. Not quite all for all work is yours but it ought all to be done from your need as a starting place.

[275] P. [160] is in pencil. Cf. "The Eye and Ear," *Lectures*, II, 267.
[276] "Pindar . . . lies." is upside down on the page.
[277] P. [164], in pencil, is probably a draft for "Doctrine of the Hands." "Do that . . . Morrow" is struck through in pencil with a wavy, vertical use mark; the first sentence and "We do . . . Morrow" are used in "Doctrine of the Hands," *Lectures*, II, 236 and 245.

[165] [blank]

[166] [278] On Books; English genius; Shelley; What is poetry
        Milton: Humanity of the great poets;
        Ben Jonson. What kind of Mediocre can be
        Pym's Eulogy
           C. p 181

S G Ward
N L F[rothingham]
G[eorge] P B[radford]
H[enry] D T[horeau]
M[ary] R[ussell]
Mrs R[uth] E[merson]
L[idian].
M M E
S[amuel]. R[ipley].
L[ucy] C B[rown]
E[lizabeth] H[oar]
C[aroline] S[turgis]
M[argaret] F[uller]
A[bel] A[dams]
O[restes]. A. B[rownson].
A B[ronson] A[lcott]
F[rederick] H H[edge]
Mebzar Gardner
W[illiam]. E. C[hanning]
1 C[harles] S W[heeler]
5 W[illiam] E[merson]
W.C.Bryant
H Greeley
C.P Cranch
5 Carlyle
1 Gambardella
Dr Palfrey
W H Furness [279]

---

[278] P. [166] is in pencil.

[279] A pencil line is drawn in the left margin from "S G Ward" down to "W.
E. C" and another from "W.C.Bryant" down to "W H Furness". This is probably

[167]   Circles
A man a nest of boxes
Progress hateful

Divine moments abolish contrition
A fact a fact is all [E 196]

Degrees in Idealism
Degrees in Justice
Degrees in intelligence of nature
Degrees in Prudence
Degrees in thought; danger of a thinker
⟨Character⟩ Degrees in friendship

Degrees in Conversation
Degrees in Permanence

Always the interior commanded by the exterior
      Christianity must be seen from an outer thought.
All skill in rhetoric is this

Our moods do not believe in each other
Character
Practical power — Conquests of fanatics [280]

---

a list of those to whom Emerson sent copies of "The Method of Nature" (*W*, I, 189–224), delivered August 11, 1841, before the Society of the Adelphi at Waterville College, Maine, and published in mid-October. Persons not previously or easily identified include Samuel Gray Ward (1817–1907), a Boston businessman, literary and artistic patron, contributor to *The Dial*, and one of Emerson's closest friends; Christopher Pearse Cranch (1813–1892), a Unitarian minister until 1842, when he became a painter, critic, and poet, and a *Dial* contributor; and Spiridione Gambardella, an Italian political refugee and artist, whom Emerson had recently met.

[280] Most of the notes on p. [167] are developed in "Circles," but not in this order. With "Progress hateful . . . all", cf. "Circles," *W*, II, 305, 317, and 306; "Degrees in Idealism . . . Permanence" is developed, *ibid.*, pp. 309, 315–316, 313–314, 314–315, 308, 307, 310–311, and 302–303; with "Always the . . . thought.", cf. *ibid.*, pp. 303–304 and 313; and with "Our moods . . . power", cf. *ibid.*, pp. 306, 321, and 320.

[168]–[169] [blank]

[170]

⟨I Culture

II Culture from the Convenient & Common; Prudence.

III " " " Vocation; or The Hands

IV " of the Intellect; or, The Head

V " of Art; or The Eye & Ear

VI " of Society or The Heart

VII " from the Laws of Life

VIII " from the Individual or The Name

IX " of the Heroic

X " of the Holy⟩

I Human Culture

  ⟨Instinct⟩

I Culture

II Vocation or The Hands

III Intellect or The Head

IV Art or The Eye & Ear or Beauty

V Society or The Heart

VI Being & Seeming, or, The Heart, continued

VII Prudence

VIII Heroism

IX Holiness

X Position of man in nature.

[171] ⟨Lectures on Culture

I Culture

II Vocation the hands

III. Intellect the head

IV. Art the eye & ear

V. Society the heart

VI. ⟨The Individual the name⟩ Being & Seeming

VII. ⟨The He[roic]⟩ [n] Prudence

VIII. The Holy Heroism

IX.   The Convenient
X   The Laws of Life.⟩ [281]

$\langle 2 \rangle 420$

8

$\quad\quad 80$

$\quad\quad 30$ L.C B

31

12

372

$\langle 3 \rangle 530$

372

902

[172]
    given   83
sold   151
      138
      30.

        319
$\langle 5 \rangle 91$
  54
$\langle 2 \rangle 228$
   373   37   on average   1 evg.
             439   persons in the audience

[173]   Tickets sent to [282]   single Tickets
4 to A Adams   1 Miles   3 Dr Hobbs

[281] Titles for the "Human Culture" series, December 6, 1837–February 7, 1838, the two lists at the top of pp. [170] and [171], are heavily crossed through in ink. The list on the lower half of p. [170], probably the last written, is correct except for lecture X, which Emerson announced as "General Views."

[282] This is probably a list of those to whom Emerson sent tickets for the "Human Culture" series, given December 6, 1837–February 7, 1838, at the Masonic Temple in Boston. All the names except "Dr Geo Parkman", "C.S Bartoll", and "Wilson . . . AA's g" are struck through in ink with vertical, discontinuous but linked lines. Recipients not previously or easily identified include Robert Haskins, probably Emerson's cousin; George Ripley (1802–1880), a friend of Emerson since college days, a founder of Brook Farm, and a member of the Transcendental Club; Dr. George Parkman (1791–1849), a physician, and the brother of the Reverend Francis Parkman; Benjamin Dodge, a correspondent of Emerson; George Stillman Hillard, a Harvard classmate of Charles Emerson, and a Boston lawyer; Cyrus Bartol, a graduate of the Harvard Divinity School and a member of the Transcendental Club; probably Charles Miles, a Concord neighbor; Artemas Bowers Muzzey (1802–c. 1884), an 1828 graduate of Harvard Divinity School and a Unitarian

2 to R. Haskins, Jr.
 2 G. Ripley
 2 N.L. Frothingham
 2 G.B. Emerson
 2 A B Alcott
⟨4⟩5 S. Ripley
 Dr Geo. Parkman
2 B. Dodge
 2 T.W. Haskins
 3 S. Greele
 2 Dr J. Ware
 2 H. Ware, Jr
 2 Rev. C Francis
⟨2⟩5 Dr C.T. Jackson
 3 Miss Peabody
 2 Miss Fuller
 2 E. Hoar
 2 C. Robbins
 1 J.S. Dwight
 1 Dr Bartlett
 2 G.S. Hillard
 2 J. Pierpont
 C.S Bartoll
 1 R C Waterston
 2 A Morell
 3 T. Haskins
 1 O A Brownson
 1 J G Palfrey

2 Dr Dalton
1 T. Hopkinson
1 C. Larkin
1 A B Muzzey
1 W. Burton
⟨2 P.C. Brooks⟩
1 C Stetson
2 C Sprague
2 Peabody
1 CW Warren
1 Sibley
1 Alger
⟨1 Burton⟩
1 Wilson
2 Searle
1 Larkin
2 AA's g

[174] *1838–9* [283]
 6 ⟨A. Adams⟩   1 J. Very

---

minister in Concord, New Hampshire; C. W. Warren, a Concord neighbor; and William Dexter Wilson, one of the Divinity School students who invited Emerson to address their class in 1838, and a contributor to the first issue of *The Dial*. The Larkins may have been relatives of Abel Adams' wife, and the Searles, one of whom had served as William Emerson's financial agent while he was in Europe, were Boston import dealers.

[283] The date is circumscribed in ink. This is probably a list of those to whom

2 ⟨J.F. Clarke⟩

2 ⟨N.L. Frothingham⟩

2 ⟨G B Emerson⟩

8 ⟨A.B. Alcott⟩

⟨2⟩3 ⟨T.W. Haskins⟩

2 ⟨Rev Dr Francis⟩

2 ⟨Mrs Sampson⟩

3 ⟨T. Haskins⟩

4 ⟨T W. Haskins⟩

⟨6⟩9 ⟨E. Palmer⟩

1 ⟨J.S. Dwight⟩

2 ⟨B Dodge⟩

1 ⟨W. Evarts⟩

1 ⟨P.C. Brooks⟩

3 ⟨S. Greele⟩

2 ⟨Dr J. Ware⟩

10 Rev S Ripley 5 single

2 ⟨H. Ware Jr⟩

2 ⟨G.S. Hillard⟩

2 ⟨Rev Geo Ripley⟩

1 ⟨E.R. Hoar⟩

2 ⟨C. Stetson⟩

2 ⟨C.A. Bartol⟩

2 E.S Gannett

2 A. Young

2 F. Parkman

2 A. Washburn

2 J. Pierpont

1 B. Frost

2 N. Hall

2 W.G. Ladd

1 R. Bartlett

1 H. Blake

1 C.F. Barnard

1 H Crooker

⟨1⟩2 Miss Searle

2 H. Thoreau

2 L.C. Brown

2 E. Hoar

L. Payson

J. Sibley

J. Devens

J Alger

O.A. Bro[w]nson.

Emerson gave tickets to the "Human Life" series, delivered at the Masonic Temple in Boston December 5, 1838–February 20, 1839. Recipients not previously or easily identified include Mrs. Sampson, probably the widow of George A. Sampson, a good friend of Emerson from 1829, when he was a parishioner at the Second Church, till his death in 1834; Elizabeth Prichard, sister of William MacKay Prichard; Ezra Stiles Gannett, an old college mate; the Reverend Alexander Young (1800–1854), a minister at the New South Unitarian Church in Boston; the Reverend Francis Parkman (1788–1852), a Unitarian minister at the New North Church in Boston, and a participant in Emerson's ordination in 1829; probably Abdiel Washburn, Jr., a relative of Ellen Tucker Emerson; Nathaniel Hall (1805–1875), an 1834 graduate of Harvard Divinity School and minister of a Unitarian parish in Dorchester, Mass.; William G. Ladd, husband of Emerson's aunt, Mary Haskins Ladd; Robert Bartlett, a Latin tutor at Harvard; Harrison Gray Otis Blake, a friend of Henry Thoreau, and one of the Divinity School students who had asked Emerson to address their class in 1838, and who had visited Emerson in mid-November, 1838; Charles F. Barnard, founder of the Warren St. Chapel; and J. Devens, probably a Concord neighbor.

```
 1 G.P. Bradford 3 single          310
 3 ⟨E P Peabody⟩                   246
 2 ⟨C Robbins⟩                      46
 2 ⟨M⟩ Fuller                      ───
⟨2⟩3 C.T. Jackson                   602
 2 H Thoreau
 1 E Prichard
```

[175] 1838

↑Dec↓ 6 Recd of C.C. Little & Co   10 tickets
12 Recd of   d[itt]o   10 tickets
 5 Recd of W.C Martin ⟨8 tickets tak⟩ 15 single tickets taken at door
11 Recd of W C M   ──   ──   13 single t. taken at door

```
                    1839
        Jan ⟨10⟩9  Recd of W C M       50 single
        Jan    30  Recd of W C M       21 single [284]
        Feb    20  Recd of W C M       20
                                      ───
                               119 average    ⟨1⟩  ⟨9⟩12
                passes 180 = ⟨260⟩ average           26
                                                    117

Sold by C C Little   Comp T.      117
                     single    ·  ⟨53⟩
Given by me                       130               130
⟨Munroe⟩                          ───               150
                                  626               ───
                                                    435


        Little & Co.  Course Tickets    117
        Martin        Course T           17
Martin's passes  292 average             29
        Given                           130
                                        ───
                                        293
Average of single tickets ⟨sold by⟩     12
                                        ───
                                        305
Munroe (supposed)                       150
                                        ───
                                        455  total average audience
```

[284] This word and the rest of the page are in pencil.

[176] 1839
Nov 13 At Concord Lyceum read Introd. Lecture on Philosophy of
Hist.

27 At   d[itt]o   Lecture on Trades & Professions

[inside back cover] Kendall a/c   p. 40 [285]

---

[285] This entry is in pencil.

Φ

1838–1844? 1847–1851?

Emerson dated the first flyleaf of Notebook Φ "Oct. 1838"; he began it with a survey of his journals, from which he apparently derived possible topics for the "Human Life" lecture series, made trial collections for them, entered a list of possible titles, and used back pages for working notes during composition of the lectures, given from December 5, 1838, to February 20, 1839. In October, 1842, he used the notebook for another survey of journals and working notes for lectures in the "New England" series, given from January 10 to February 1, 1843. Notes headed "Lect. V", probably 1842 notes for the fifth "New England" lecture, may have been added or added to in 1844 for "New England Reformers." He used the notebook, probably later in 1843, for notes, drafts, and outlines for the essay "The Poet," and probably for others in *Essays, Second Series*, including "Experience" and "Nominalist and Realist," and adding to 1838 collections. Emerson wrote notes for the lecture "Eloquence," given in 1847, over and around 1838 notes, and may have used the notebook for reference in preparing the "Conduct of Life" lectures from 1847 to 1851.

Notebook Φ is a copybook with hard coverboards measuring 17 x 21.2 cm and covered in dark purple cloth embossed with diagonal stripes, and a spine of worn black leather; seven of a probable eight horizontal gold lines remain on the spine. The cover is marked "Φ" in ink and has two ink blots. The leaves, faintly ruled, measure 16.8 x 20.5 cm. Including 2 front and 2 back flyleaves, there are 176 pages. The binding threads are loose, and the 2 front flyleaves are separated from the binding. Emerson numbered the verso of the first flyleaf 1 in ink; he repeated 1 on the first ruled page and corrected it to 4, then numbered the verso 2 in pencil and the following leaf 3 and 4 in ink; the editor has renumbered the pages 2_1, 3_1, $\langle 1 \rangle 4_1$, 2_2, 3_2, and 4_2. The leaf following page 26 was numbered 26 and 27 in pencil, and corrected to 27 and 28 in ink. Two verso pages are numbered 122, and the following recto pages are 123 and unnumbered; the editor has renumbered them 122_1, 123_1, 122_2, and 123_2. The verso of page 125 is numbered 128. Pages numbered in ink are 1_1–$\langle 1 \rangle 4_1$, 3_2–7, 19, 22, 29, 51, 56–57, 59–64, 66–67, 69–72, 74–75, 83–85, 90, 92–93, 95, 97, 100–101, 103–104, 107, 110, 112, 116, 118, 120, 122–123, 122_2, 124, 128, 130, 140, 148, 150, 152, 154, 156–164, 166, 169, and 171. Pages numbered in pencil are 2_2, 8–17, 20–21, 23, 30–31, 33, 36, 39, 42–43, 52, 54–55, 82, 84, 86, 88, 94,

96, 98–99, 102, 132, 134, 138, 141–144, and 153. Pages 18, 24–26, 32, 34–35, 37–38, 40–41, 44–50, 76–80, 108, and 146 are numbered in ink over the same in pencil. The rest are unnumbered. Pages 36, 42, 53, 62, 66, 68, 73, 106, and 136 are blank. Fastened to page 51 with sealing wax is a slip of white notepaper measuring 11.5 x 18.8 cm, once folded as an enclosure and addressed to Emerson on one side, with notes on the other. A piece of blue paper torn down the right side and measuring 6.1 x 12 cm, inscribed in pencil with "No 2   Profile Mountain," and a sketch of a mountainside, is pasted onto the bottom of page 61. Pages with four or more revisions of accidentals are 92, 93, and 138.

[front cover]   Φ

[front cover verso] [1]

			Age	15
	Poet 85		Art	51
Age	15		Beauty	23
Art	51	October 1842	Character	38
Brook Farm 76		Literature	102	Conservatism	22
Beauty	23	Miscellanies	110	Condition	63
Classes	37	Manners	163	Demonology	14
Comic	27	Reform	34	Domestic Life	57
Condition	63	Men	108	↑FATE…32↓
Culture	67	Scholar	128	Genius	140
Carlyle	102	Character	38	History	59

[1] Emerson's index to Notebook Φ was written in at least four different periods. Traces of a preliminary index of twenty-two entries, in pencil, each crossed through horizontally and erased, are visible between the first and second columns below; only a few initial letters are recovered. In the first column, probably inscribed in 1838, "Age 15" is in pencil, "Art 51" is in ink written over the same in pencil, and "Beauty . . . Culture 67" and "Demonology . . . Woman 31" are in pencil. In the center column, "October 1842" is circled in pencil; "October 1842 . . . Reform 34", in dark pencil, and "Men . . . The Spirit 64", in lighter pencil, appear to have been written at about the same time; the rest of the center column is in a smaller hand; "Realism . . . Skeptic 77", "New Subjects 84", and "Progress . . . Protest 142, 134" are in pencil. "W.E.C's Poems 72", in pencil in a larger hand, may have been added later. "Poet 85", at the top of the center column, in ink in a large hand, was probably added in 1843. The right-hand column, in ink in a small hand, was written later than "Poet 85", and combines entries from the earlier columns. "Brook Farm 76", "Carlyle 102", and "Clare 115" in the first column and "Swedenborg . . . Eloquence 146" and "Edward's sketching, 101" in the second column, are in ink in a small hand like that of the third column, and may have been added at the same time.

Clare 115

Demonology 14

Εν και παν 4

Ethics 17

Genius 140

History 59

Intellect 43

Laws of the world 40

Literature 12

Love 33

Man 47

Men 10

Miscellany 71, 160

NATURE 69

↑Politics 75↓

Realism 11

Society 55

↑Theology..... 21

Tragedy..... 79

Woman .... 31↓

Transcendentalism 61

Religion 164

Domestic Life 57

The Spirit 64

Realism ⟨11⟩, 154

Society 5⟨5⟩4

Marriage 100

Skeptic 77

Swedenborg 82

Conservatism 22

LIFE 50

Eloquence 146

New Subjects 84

Edward's sketching, 101

Progress 83   P

Protest 142, 134

W.E.C's Poems 72   11⟨0⟩7

Intellect 43

Literature 102

↑Life 50↓

Manners 163

Marriage 100

Men 108

Miscellanies 110

Nature 69

Poet 85

Politics 75

Religion 164

Realism 154

Reform 34

Scholar 128

Skeptic 77

Society 54

Spirit 64

Swedenborg 82

Scott 123   116

Transcendm 61

Woman 31

Divine persons 107

[i]

R.W. Emerson.

Oct. 1838 —

Φ

[1]² Religion & Trade

Genius   Manners   Hunger   Eloquence   Education

² P. [1] is in pencil. "Lect . . . Affirmative p 156" is an addition to Emerson's index; pp. [156] and [159] below both contain notes probably for the 1843 lecture series on New England. "Religion & Trade" is in a larger hand than the rest of the notes on the page, which are probably topics and early notes for the "New England" series. See similar notes in Journal N, pp. [114]–[120], and pp. [21]–[32] and [166]–[169] below.

Recent Spiritual Influences   Association
     Coleridge
     Wordsworth   Bulwer   J 142
     Carlyle
     Everett
     Webster
     Channing
     Alcott
     Swedenborg   Divinity behind prayer &
                pottage   N 83

                Community
Poet   Never will have men but halves
                       N 127

↑Lect V. p 159   Advantage in women   N 140
Affirmative p 156 —↓   Ideal Union, magic   N 136
               Cities are phalanxes   N 2
       K 60 | People cannot live together in any but
            | necessary ways & only the lame will go

        Institution in Institutor   K 85

        Must fix the price of bread   K 90

K 49   Compassion for one who must meet an
                       expectation
        He dwarfs himself by union   K 50[3]
        Astor House   E 238
        Individuals save better than Associations
                       Z 133
        Good neighborhood   J 84

[3] The passages cited in Journal N, pp. [127] and [136], and K, p. [50], are used in "New England Reformers" (identified as "V Lecture on N. England" in Index Minor, p. [93] below, and see p. [159] below), *W*, III, 264–267; with the paragraph in K, p. [60], cf. *ibid.*, p. 264. The paragraph on Bulwer in J, p. [142], is used in "Europe and European Books," *The Dial*, III (April 1843), 519. The paragraph cited in K, p. [90], is used in "The Young American," *W*, I, 382–383.

Shaker farms   N 69
Feudality   J 20
Love of hard work   J 116

[2₁]   New England   ——

                                        Parker's Erratum [4]

                    ————

Barrooms E 78
Rowdies & Paddies make the law   H.75   N 42
Rhine of the Divinity School   H 85
The Community   N 127, 140   K 60, 85, 90, ↑49↓ 50, 46, H 30, J 84
                    ↑⟨116⟩↓ E 238   Z 133 ↑G 116↓ [5]
Praise of Cities   N.44, 122   K 15
Harvard University   J 34   Lect on P[resent]. Age p 54
Calvinism   N 72   E 309, 310, *Lect P.A.* 32,
Everett   N 52
Shakers
⟨Country unpeopled of good brains   N 63⟩
Merchants   N 45   Lect. P.Age p. 50; Lect. on Trades   E 264
Farm   N 77   Farmers: Lect. on Trades &c
Carlyle   D 15, F 32   E 184, G 17,
Wordsworth
Channing ↑N 92   87↓
Boston ⟨12⟩N 122, 44, E 200   N 83
Good-Meaning. N 35
New England population, idealist. N 16
Village traits   Φ 37
Americans love intoxication   E 164, N 76
Column of Am. population   E 283 [6]

⁴ "Parker's Erratum" and the rules above and below it are written in a curve
in the upper right-hand corner of the page. See bibliographical note above.

⁵ "49" is added in pencil. See p. [1] above, where ten of these entries are expanded.

⁶ For "Lect on P. Age p 54", "*Lect P.A.* 32," and "Lect. P.Age p 50;", see
The Present Age: "Introductory," *Lectures*, III, 197, 193, and 196. "Country unpeopled . . . N 63" is struck through in pencil with one horizontal and three
diagonal use marks. "N 92   87" is added in pencil. For the two references to "Lect.
on Trades", see "Trades and Professions," *Lectures*, II, 115–117. The passages on
Calvinism in Journal E, pp. [309]–[310], and "*Lect P.A.* 32," and the paragraph

Unitarianism E 311 313 N 38
No musical composer
[3₁] Lectures E.18, 58, N ⟨38⟩ 21,
     America peddles   E 280,
     Value of a Scholar to America N 108 D 99, .
     Indian names N 76
     American hunger N 76   JQA H.48
     American manners N 76
     Phrenology C 145
     Northerner & Southerner E 352
     Education E 350 N 47, 83, [J] 120   Dr Bradford J 94
     Internal Improvements O
     Thanksgiving sermon O
Cornwallis [E 9–10]
Faneuil Hall C 227, 306
     School of Medicine & Divinity *Lect P.A.* 39
     Sacs & Foxes C 209
Labor S 147 Hands; Lect. on *Trades.*
     Man of strong will (Tendencies 38) C 313 D 214, E 90
     Books. Silvio P[ellico].; Bettina; Manzoni;
     Sailor. Lect. on Trades
Yankee Z 137 Pedlar⁷
     Yankee pedlar, schoolmaster, ↑N 22↓ book agent, preacher,

---

in N, p. [16], are used in the lecture "Genius of the Anglo-Saxon Race." The passages cited in E, p. [78], N, p. [44], J, p. [34], N, p. [63], the passages from "Lect. on Trades", N, pp. [77] and [83], and E, p. [283], are used in the lecture "Trade." The passages in N, p. [52], E, p. [164], and N, p. [76], are used in the lecture "Manners and Customs of New England." The passages in E, p. [184], and G, p. [17], are used in the lecture "Recent Literary and Spiritual Influences." The sentence cited in N, p. [35], is used in "New England Reformers," W, III, 278–279.

⁷ The passages cited in Journal E, pp. [9]–[10], C, p. [209], Notebook S (Salvage), p. [147] (used in "Doctrine of the Hands," *Lectures*, II, 230–231), "Lect. on Trades" ("Trades and Professions," *Lectures*, II, 115–117), and Z[A], p. [137], are used in the lecture "Trade." The passages cited in E, pp. [18] and [280], N, p. [76], H, p. [48], E, p. [352], and C, p. [227], are used in the lecture "Manners and Customs of New England." "Manzoni" is discussed in the lecture "Recent Literary and Spiritual Influences." The passages cited in H, p. [48], E, p. [350], and "*Lect P.A.* 39" (The Present Age: "Introductory," *Lectures*, III, 457 [notes] and 195), are used in "New England Reformers," W, III, 274 and 258–260.

New England flowers   K 94

Indian summer   N 108

[⟨1⟩4₁] Our trade is wild & incalculable, not scientific; our brick houses tumble; our steamboats explode; our people eat fast; our enterprizes rash; our legislation fluctuating; diff. between pounds & dollars;

Melancholy of the Saxon Mind   B 117   D 11, 103

Wagon   C 27

Mesmerism ↑J 118↓

Teamsters' mottos   D 355

I love Sunday   D 366

   Mob   C 314, 254

↑True↓ Germany in N. Eng. D 178

When the great Yankee shall come   N 73   Dickens

Relation of Old & New England

N England the manufacturer of America   C 33

Elbowroom in America & no noise   G 143

Woman inspires   J 9

That the Soul is God   J 126

Intellect needed to check moral tendencies   J 126 Shaks &
                                       Swed   N [K] 83 [8]

[2₂] Genius   Manners

We mistake ↑a↓ tulip for timber   G 139

We are too slight & easily pleased | Phrenology &
                                     | Mesmerism & Dickens

[The most difficult of tasks to keep   K 121

Persistency   N 88   They follow success not skill   N 45

Thirst for Eloquence

Everett. Lyceum. Value of a Scholar to America

[8] "J 118" and "Woman inspires . . . N 83" are in pencil. "Our trade . . . fluctuating;" and the passage cited in Journal J, pp. [118]–[119], are used in the lecture "Manners and Customs of New England." The passages cited in C, p. [27], and D, p. [355], are used in the lecture "Trade." The sentence cited in N, p. [73], "Relation of . . . England", and the passage in K, p. [83], are used in the lecture "Recent Literary and Spiritual Influences."

Their spirit of detail gets represented in W.
N & S
Strong will   N 40   *Tendencies*
                              Spirit of detail in N E
Wilhelm Meister   J 90
Institution in institutor   K 85, 49,
Wordsworth   N 73   Dom Life
Carlyle   Phrenology
Novels
St Simon
Alcott ⟨N⟩ Z 163
We travel but we find but what we carry   J 136 [9]

[32] Every man would be a Benefactor   N 12   G 58
Every man would be convicted   39   G 58
Defeated all the time yet to victory born   K 79
Equality of apprehender to poet   E 331   G 52
Every one would make the dare God & dare devil experiment   N 102
I wonder not at Bible or divine man but that all are not   K 23, 53,
                                                    54   E 330

Here or nowhere the whole fact [J 108]
See that you work paid or unpaid J 138   G 43
Wine glass system [E 354]
Intellect grows by obedience   J 95
The fact abides   N 34   if I cannot explain it & College Mates
Wonder [G 147] (Duties)   and Little Grey Man [N 26–27]
Americans too easily pleas⟨d⟩ed [H 91] [Duties]
Staring Theorist [J 19] [Duties]
Rankest tories convertible. Want of thought. Scarcity of opinion
                                                    ↑G 169↓

---

[9] P. [22] is in pencil. The last line is marked with a short vertical line in the left margin. "We mistake . . . in N E" is probably notes for the lecture "Manners and Customs of New England," where "We are . . . Mesmerism", the paragraph cited in Journal N, p. [45], "Thirst for . . . Lyceum.", "spirit of detail" and "N & S" are used or developed. With "Strong will", cf. "Tendencies," *Lectures*, III, 312. "Carlyle" and "Novels" are developed in the lecture "Recent Literary and Spiritual Influences." The passage cited in Z[A], p. [163], is used in "New England Reformers," *W*, III, 280. The passages cited in J, pp. [90] and [136], are used in "Europe and European Books," *The Dial*, III (April 1843), 520–521 and 512.

Our housekeeping. What a house stands for.　Osman　Dom Life
Value of a man & of a cent　　Politics
Force of men whose part is taken　Z 163
A & B will set the town right　J 135
You should never ask what I can do
 Fable of Galileo　　　　　　　　　｜　The fact abides
   A man not holden by profession　｜　⟨W⟩A & B will set the
    but belief　　　　　　　｜　town right
Man equal to the State to the Ch & to　｜　Work paid or unpaid
 Shaksp or every other man　　Defeated all the time & yet
  As I am so I see　G 128　　Intellect grows by obedience
       Owes to defeats & rages
   Every man would be convict; benefac; radical [10]

[42] Eν και παν [11] B 152, C, 86, 310, 348, D 31, 65, 101, 205
 ↑Expression↓
b Nature is too thin a screen: the glory of the One breaks through
everywhere. [C 86]
Trees　D 58
A few facts avail, one even; D 101　　　Decisive trifles. D 225 a & c,
 When we study architecture, all looks architectural; if painting,
 picturesque, &c. B 258　　So Camper　C 30,
All in Each　B 256, 158,
Every thing that can be said capable of infinite meaning　B 158

 [10] "Every man would be convicted　39" (see p. [39] below), "Here or . . .
fact", "Wine glass system", "The fact . . . Mates", "Americans too . . . Theorist
[Duties]", and "Our housekeeping. . . . radical" are in pencil. "Duties" is evidently the lecture "Prospects"; for the three passages cited, see *Lectures*, III, 378, 374,
and 376. "Politics" has a curved pencil line above it; the passage is in "Politics,"
Lectures, II, 79. The passages cited in Journal N, p. [12], "Every man would be
convicted", K, p. [79], E, p. [331], J, pp. [108] and [138], N, p. [34],
"Rankest tories convertible.", Z[A], p. [163], J, p. [135], and "Man equal . . .
man" are used in "New England Reformers," *W*, III, 277–278, 283, 281, 278,
283, 282, 272, 280, 284, and 279 and 280.
 [11] See Journal B, pp. [142] and [151], for Emerson's sources in Xenophanes,
Goethe, Cudworth, and Gérando. Emerson used the Greek phrase or variations of his
translation, "All in Each", below, as an index heading and may have considered
it as a possible subject for a lecture during early planning for the "Human Life"
series.

[5] [12] The moment we enter into the higher thoughts, fame is no more affecting to the ear than the faint tinkle of the passing sleigh-bell.[13] [B 149]

The moment our higher faculties are called into action we are domesticated & our aukwardness or torpor or discomfort give place to natural & agreeable movements. [B 138]

"Our country is where we can live as we ought." [B 157]

Waking moments   B 183, 289   D 112   B 200,[14]
Plato will have a man to be a heavenly tree growing with his root, which is his head, upward.

The doctrine we preach in life is taught in architecture
19/20 of its nourishment the tree draws from the air by aerial roots the leaves [C 157]
Interior life not melancholy   C 166 [15]

True greatness will preach its own contentment[;] it will not sneer[:] it will not scold[, —] it will smile [at] the pompencumbered king[,] it will pity those who harness themselves with cares &c   C 261

In the highest moments we are a vision &c   C 289 [16]
In spite of all we can do every moment is new [C 308]
Dualism   C ⟨2⟩310
Eternity a state of mind. We are spirits   C 333
We are now men   D 10, ⟨H⟩112,
A sense of want & ignorance is a fine inuendo by which the soul makes its enormous claim.[17]

---

[12] P. [5] may have been collected during early planning for the "Human Life" lecture series.
[13] This sentence, struck through in ink with a diagonal use mark, is inscribed in Notebook Man, p. [9] above, and used in "Tendencies," *Lectures*, III, 312.
[14] " 'Our . . . ought.' ", struck through in pencil with a diagonal use mark, and part of a paragraph in Journal B, p. [289], are used in "Home," *Lectures*, III, 26–27 and 32; the rest of the paragraph in B, p. [289], used in "Domestic Life," *W*, VII, 103, may also have been in "Home," the manuscript of which is incomplete. The last paragraph in D, p. [112], is used in "Love," *Lectures*, III, 67.
[15] This line is struck through in pencil with two diagonal use marks. Emerson used part of the paragraph cited in Journal C, p. [166], in "Tragedy," *Lectures*, III, 104 and 113.
[16] This line is struck through in pencil with three diagonal use marks. The paragraph cited is used in "Duty," *Lectures*, III, 143, and "Self-Reliance," *W*, II, 69.
[17] "We are spirits   C 333" is struck through in pencil with two diagonal use

[6] Task work is good for idlers and Man is an idler. Its greatest disadvan⟨d⟩tage is that when you accept mechanical measures instead of spiritual ones you are prone to fill up the chasms of your prophecy with prose

There is a limit to the effect of written eloquence &c   D 56

Infusion of the spirit into quibbles by Herbert   D 55

23

Beneath low hills in the broad interval   [26]
Through which our gentle Indian river flows
Still mindful of the sannup and the squaw
Whose pipe & arrow oft the plough reveals
Here in pine houses which were lately trees   [30]
Nature's next brood the husbandmen abide   [x]
Traveller, to thee perchance a tedious road   [32]
Or it may be a picture to these men
The landscape [18]   [34]

[7] It is remarkable that the greater the material apparatus the more the material disappears as in Alps & Niagara in St Peter's & Naples [B 137]

See Belzoni also. T [55–56]   See also what is said of Size of Man   B 121, D 192 [19]

As character is more to us, our fellowmen cease to ex⟨s⟩ist to us in space & time, & we hold them by real ties.

In the broad ⟨plain thro which⟩ the river   [26–27]

⟨Base of the⟩ ↑Beneath low↓ hills ↑i↓n the broad interval
Through which ⟨the well loved⟩ ↑our↓ Indian river flows

---

marks. "We are now men", struck through in pencil with a diagonal use mark, is used in "Duty," *Lectures*, III, 139, and "Self-Reliance," *W*, II, 47. "A sense . . . claim." is struck through in ink with a diagonal use mark.

[18] "Musketaquid," *W*, IX, 142. On page [7], facing this, are an earlier version and, below it, a later version of these lines. See also *JMN*, VIII, 458, 465, and 466.

[19] Parts of the paragraph in Journal D, p. [192], are used in "The Protest," *Lectures*, III, 95.

Still mindful of ⟨its Indian name⟩ ↑the sannup & the
     squaw↓
Whose pipe⟨s⟩ & arrow⟨s⟩ the plough daily shews
Here in pine houses which grew late in trees   [30]
Nature's next growth   [x]

Beneath low hills in the broad interval   [26]
Through which at ⟨leisure⟩ ↑will↓ our Indian rivulet
⟨Slides⟩ ↑Winds↓ mindful still of sannup & of squaw
Whose pipe & arrow oft the ploughboy marks,
Here in pine houses which the grove supplied   [30]
⟨Late on that spot, the husbandmen abide⟩   [x]
⟨Nature's next growth supplant the sagamore⟩   [x]
Supplanters of the tribe the farmers dwell [20]   [31]

[8] [21] ⟨Despotism of sleep   B 131⟩
⟨Law of hospitality ⟨D⟩B 124⟩
⟨Melancholy of the Saxon mind   B 117⟩
⟨The inspired man is now galvanized   B 113⟩
⟨Inspiration   B 113, 109,⟩
⟨Blind side of great men, Bacon's nonsense   B 105, ↑53,↓ See M M E
                                         ↑in B 53↓⟩

⟨Ill success of almost all orations &c⟩
⟨Abuse of the superlative.   B 98, 46, 328, D 116, 171,⟩
⟨Earnestness   B 61⟩
⟨"We cannot disimagine the existence of truth" &c   B 60⟩
⟨Of Books   B 55, 77, 25   36, 311, C 229, D 68, 114, 126, 141⟩
⟨Our politics   B 307, C 153. 297, 318,   D 142, 144⟩
⟨Persons   B 53, C 139, 288, 300, 349   D 10, 143,⟩
⟨Resistlessness of conventions in literature & religion   B 3⟩

---

[20] "Musketaquid," *W*, IX, 142.
[21] Notes on pp. [8]–[9] are probably a survey of the journals during early
planning for the "Human Life" lecture series. In addition to the vertical use marks
described in the following note, every line on both pages is struck through horizontally; since most of the entries are listed in other collections in Notebook Φ, this
may indicate transfer rather than use. Passages listed are used throughout the "Human
Life" series, at least eleven in "The School," one in "Love," five in "Genius," six
in "Tragedy," two in "Comedy," and one in "Demonology."

⟨Our sympathy with men of genius affects our view of Nature   B 16⟩
⟨B 16⟩

⟨Tragedy of common life   B 16, C 166, D 48, 79,⟩ 95, 152, 174
⟨Benefit of Society   B 48⟩
"⟨Wrath is not worth carrying home tho' a man should ride⟩."
⟨Degrees of merits   B 22⟩
⟨East & west conversers   B 23⟩
⟨Conversation   B 23, 24, C 60, 254, 280 ⟨T⟩D 13, 15,⟩
⟨Music. B. 27⟩
⟨Life a defensive War ⟨D⟩B 28⟩
⟨The quotation stronger than the ⁿ writer's own word   B 30⟩
⟨Advantage of the Abolitionist   B 33⟩
⟨Controversy blinds. B 37⟩
⟨Which are the Hard Times? B 38⟩
[9] ⟨Man a ⟨m⟩selector, a choice, B 125, 98   C 187   D 68⟩
⟨A thought comes single like a foreign traveller but if you can find out
its name you shall find it related to a powerful & numerous family⟩
B 90, 334

⟨Every one has a trust of power   B 214⟩
⟨The wit of man is more elastic than the air our bodies breath[e].
A whole nation will subsist for centuries on one thought & then every
individual man will be oppressed by the rush of his conceptions &
always a plenum with one grain or 60 atmospheres.⟩
⟨Knowledge is easy to carry.⟩
⟨Objectiveness of the ancients   B 297, 107,⟩
⟨The child & the snow   B 292⟩
⟨Some talents must be kept under naphtha⟩ B 288
⟨Genius surprises   B 286, C 129,⟩ D 18
⟨Time   B 275   C 180, 261, 324, D 19, 49,⟩
⟨Common Sense   B 260   C 309,⟩ 324, D 115
⟨Genius works ever in sport & goodness hath ever a smile⟩ [B 259]

⟨When we study Architecture everything looks architectural; if
painting, picturesque; &c   B 258   So Camper; C p 30⟩
⟨We are screened from premature ideas   B⟩ 150
⟨The true miracle or Nature's contraventions   B 257⟩
⟨Architecture   B 255⟩
⟨The dentist's pictures   250⟩

281

⟨By the permanence of nature minds are trained alike & made intelligible to each other⟩ [22] [B 183]

[10]   Men
Wordsworth B 110, 109, 92   C 82, D 59, ↑N 73↓

Montaigne B 94, 59, C 205   278 D 95,

Goethe B 274, 148   153   158   144   C 25, 38, 50, 208, D 7, 15,
18 D 128, C 31, *A* 59,

Tennyson D 117, 55   C 283
Landor B 21, 25, 45, 186,
Napoleon C 348, 349, 314, 315,

Shakspeare D 207, 212, 211, 217, 102,
Shelley

Swedenborg B 130, 127,   D 25, 35, 41, 48, 148,[23]

[22] On p. [8], Emerson struck through ll. 1–8 with a vertical use mark in ink, then extended it, first through l. 15, then through ll. 16 and 17, then from l. 17 to the bottom of the page. On p. [9], he struck through "Man a selector . . . B 292" with a vertical use mark in ink, extended it through "ever a smile", then through each of the entries down to "Architecture B 255", then to the bottom of the page; p. [9] is also struck through in ink with a wavy vertical use mark. Passages in Journal B, pp. [113] and [109], C, p. [229], D, pp. [114] and [141], C, p. [300], B, pp. [125] and [98], D, p. [68], and B, pp. [214] and [183], have been located in text or notes of "The School," *Lectures*, III, 36, 405(notes), 46, 402 (notes), 43, 36–37, 40, and 41. The passage in D, p. [95], is used in "Love," *Lectures*, III, 54–55. Passages in B, pp. [109] and [16], C, p. [129], D, p. [18], and B, p. [259], are used in "Genius," *Lectures*, III, 76, 82, 79, and 80. Passages in B, p. [117], C, p. [166], D, p. [174], B, p. [28], C, p. [324], and D, p. [49], are used in "Tragedy," *Lectures*, III, 104, 113, 108, 104, 116, and 114. The passages in D, p. [142], and C, p. [30], are used in "Comedy," *Lectures*, III, 135–136 and 130, and a sentence in B, p. [131], is used in "Demonology," *Lectures*, III, 152.

[23] "Men of letters" is listed on p. [167] below among subjects Emerson was considering for lectures in the "Human Life" series. Though he used much of this material in later lectures and essays, he used only a few passages in the 1838–1839 series. Parts of passages on Shakespeare in Journal D, pp. [207]–[209], [211], and [102], are used in "Doctrine of the Soul," *Lectures*, III, 19, 21, and 18; part of the first is used in "The School," *Lectures*, III, 46. The sentence on Landor in B, p.

[11] Realism   B.96, 50, C 182, 342,
Farewells of the realist   B 16
Every man a philosopher once   B 313
Realism of literature   C 182 ↑Mythology↓   D 129, 173, C 220,
Realism in society   C 223, D 186c,
Realism in teaching   C 268, 342, 120,
Spite of all we can do every moment is new [C 308]
The argument which has not power to reach my own practice I may
      well ↑doubt has not power to reach yours↓ [BB Y, 55]
Which are the Hard Times? B 38 Which is the Atheist D [162]
Insight   outsight   C 220,
The house praises the carpenter [B 257]

"The reward of a thing well done is to have done ⁿ it" ↑Seneca↓ 24 [C 9]
  " 'Tis you that say it, not I; you do the deeds
  And your ungodly deeds find me the words." [B 14]

 A & B will set the town right respecting themselves   J 135
 Work! paid or unpaid   J 138, G 43 25

[45], is used in "Love," *Lectures*, III, 60. Passages in D, pp. [35], [41], and [48], under "Swedenborg", are used in "Duty," *Lectures*, III, 140–141. Emerson copied the entries on Goethe, Shakespeare, and Swedenborg in Index Minor, pp. [38], [56], and [81] below.

24 Emerson listed "Realism" among possible topics for the "Human Life" series on pp. [166] and [167] below, but little of the material listed above was used in the series; it may have been intended for one of the lectures Emerson planned but dropped from the series (see *Lectures*, III, 3[notes] and 170). The paragraph in Journal B, p. [313], is used in "Genius," part of paragraph "c" in D, p. [186], in "The Protest," and "The house . . . Seneca", struck through in pencil with a diagonal use mark, in "Duty," *Lectures*, III, 82, 96, and 149; " 'The reward . . . done it' " is also used in "New England Reformers," *W*, III, 283. Emerson added to the page in 1842 (see next note) and used the passage in C, p. [182], in "Compensation," and one in C, p. [342], in "Spiritual Laws," *W*, II, 106 and 152. "Mytholology" is separated from "D 129," by a partial bracket; passages in D, pp. [129]–[130] and [173], are used in "Literature" [second lecture], *Lectures*, III, 227–228 and 230. "Realism in teaching" is connected with "The argument" by a line in the left margin; part of the paragraph in C, p. [268], is used in "Education," *Lectures*, III, 289, and "New England Reformers," *W*, III, 258; the paragraph in C, p. [342], and "The argument . . . yours" are used in "Spiritual Laws," *W*, II, 152 and 153.

25 This and the preceding line, struck through in ink with a vertical use mark, were added in 1842; both passages cited in Journal J are used in "New England

Beneath low hills in the broad interval   [26]
Through which at will our Indian rivulet
Winds mindful still of sannup & of squaw
Whose pipe & arrow oft the plough reveals
Here in pine houses which the grove supplied   [30]
Supplanters of the tribe the farmers dwell [26]   [31]

[12]   Literature [27]

Poetry: poetic form   B 53, 31, ↑C↓ 211,

Language   B 52, 305   C 108, 153, 289,
Man of genius cannot finish his work   B 12   E.49
Moment of *casting* important   B 12
⟨Effect of⟩ Books   B 36, 311, — D 68, 114, 126, 141 [28]   B 55, 77,
                                                                                25, 311, C 229
Advertise the reader that you will speak Realism   B 31, 41   D 77
                                                                                B 49, 53,

The highest class ethical   B 315, ⟨3⟩C 301
The artist appeals to Eternity   B 255, 228
Be not ashamed of your gospel   B 186
Every man has a Parnassus   B 183
⟨T⟩Observe without ceasing   B 164
Identity of work of Art & Nature   C 86 [29]
Dense Poetry   C 111
Clarendon's (style Italian) C 112, 105,
The preacher's classes   C 120

Reformers," *W*, III, 284 and 283. See also p. [154] below, headed *"Reality"*, and
p. [32] above, both written in 1842, where the entries are repeated.
    [26] "Musketaquid," *W*, IX, 142; see pp. [6] and [7] above for earlier versions.
    [27] "Literature" is one of the topics listed on p. [167] during early planning
for the "Human Life" series, but only a few of the ninety-seven passages on pp.
[12]–[13] are used in the series, nine in "Doctrine of the Soul," four in "The
School," three in "Genius," and one in "Duty." Emerson used six of them a year
later in two lectures on "Literature" in the "Present Age" series, and at least one in
the "Introductory" lecture of that series.
    [28] The passage cited in Journal D, p. [114], is used in section IV, headed
"Books.", in "The School," *Lectures*, III, 46. "D. 141" is added in pencil to the
lecture manuscript and may have been intended for insertion in section I; see *Lectures*, III, 402 (notes).
    [29] This passage is used in "Genius," *Lectures*, III, 76.

All Literature writes the character of the Wise man C 121, D 89,[30] 24,
The Educated class: least effect of oration on orator C 122, 254, 314,
                              338   D 148, 150   190[31]
A good style   C 126
Saxon, C 153, Z
⟨We⟩The great poets /plain/human/ C 179   221, B 225 [32]
The ⟨si⟩ detached fact & the placed fact [33] C 181
Mythology   C 181
Proportion in Composition   C 194
Fable, superstition, a good hamper or basket
Force of a sentence   C 223   D 225,
Self reliance of poets   C 269 [34]
[13] Resistlessness of conventions in literature & religion   B 3
The final place of writers   C 305
Against Cliques   C 309
⟨Fe⟩Indifferency of some compositions   C 325, & pictures   D 343.
⟨Caricatures are history   C 329⟩
Tediousness of Scholars, C 338
Two emphases of teachers, Human life & Thought   C 339
Everett puts things in amber   D 11
Write to the great   D 15   77
Art of writing   D 26

[30] The quotation from Clarendon in Journal C, p. [105], is expanded in "Doctrine of the Soul," *Lectures*, III, 8. Passages in C, p. [121], and D, p. [89], are used in "Doctrine of the Soul," *Lectures*, III, 21–22, and "History," *W*, II, 7.

[31] The paragraph cited in Journal D, p. [150], is used in "Duty," and a passage in D, p. [190], in "Doctrine of the Soul," *Lectures*, III, 144 and 16. The anecdote in C, p. [314], is used in The Present Age: "Introductory," *Lectures*, III, 195, immediately after a two-leaf gap in the manuscript; the passages in C, pp. [122], [254], and [314], are used together in "The Spirit of the Times," an 1850 lecture partly derived from "Introductory." Another paragraph in D, p. [190], is used in "Literature" [first lecture], *Lectures*, III, 221–222.

[32] Emerson drew on these three passages for a paragraph in "Doctrine of the Soul," *Lectures*, III, 17, and "The Over-Soul," *W*, II, 288–289; cf. also "Doctrine of the Soul," *Lectures*, III, 16, "Literature," *Lectures*, II, 62, and "Literature" [first lecture], *Lectures*, III, 218.

[33] "The detached . . . fact" is in Journal D, p. [114], and is used in "The School," *Lectures*, III, 49; Emerson may have connected it with the first sentence in C, p. [181].

[34] Cf. "Genius," *Lectures*, III, 77–78, where Emerson adds lines from Wordsworth.

285

The unsaid part of the discourse   D 46
Wordsworth & Milton   D 59
Until History is interesting, it is not yet written.[35] [D 61]
True Scholar formidable   D 68↑, 118↓
Proverbs   D 91, 115,
Irresponsibility of the Recorder   D 100
Entire literature unfair: we skip the obvious   D 101
Read great books to know how poor are all books   D 102
The Wings of beauty   D 123 [36]
Read famed books   D 126
Philosophy of history   D 129
Poet   D 154, 233,
Short history of literature   D 173 [37]
Abuse of the superlative   B 46, 98, 328, D 116, 171,
The quotation stronger than the writer's own word   B 30
Quotation of Scripture   D 155. [157]
Shakspeare's threnes   B 225

[14]   Demonology [38]
B 240, 123, C 160   Θ 35,[39] B 46, 45 [40]

[35] With the passages in Journal D, p. [46], cf. B, p. [52], and "Doctrine of the Soul," Lectures, III, 16. "Until History . . . written." is used in "Literature" [first lecture], Lectures, III, 210.

[36] "Irresponsibility . . . D 100" is struck through in ink with a diagonal use mark. Two paragraphs following it, on p. [101], are used in "The School," Lectures, III, 49, 405 and 406(notes), and 46–47; that on D, p. [102], is used in "Doctrine of the Soul," Lectures, III, 18, and "The Over-Soul," W, II, 289. The "agaric" passage in D, p. [123], is used in both "Genius," Lectures, III, 74–75, and "The Poet," W, III, 22–24.

[37] Most of the long paragraph in Journal D, pp. [129]–[130], and two of the collection of sayings about Literature in D, p. [173], are used in "Literature" [second lecture], Lectures, III, 227–228 and 230.

[38] Spacing indicates that either the heading or the line below it was added later. The collection below is for the lecture "Demonology," much of which was used in "Demonology," W, X, 1–28; see pp. [130]–[132] below for later notes. "Demonology" appears to have been a later addition to the list of topics on p. [167], and p. [14] may also have been written later than the surrounding pages.

[39] For references to "Θ", see pp. [23], [63], [79], [150₁], and [158] below and Notebook Ж, p. [95] below; no Notebook or Journal Θ has been located. It had at least 122 pages, and may have been a collection of quotations or salvaged journal passages; it is cited in these 1838–1839 or early 1840 collections.

[40] All five journal passages listed on this line are used or rewritten in "De-

Dreams B 27, C 134, 178   258, 300, ϴ 122, Encyc. 201, D 211,
↑A 54↓ 41

Young men's genius   B 46
Goethe Nachg. Werke: vol 8 p. 178
Animal magnetism   C 160   D 36, 241,
Animals   C 208, 181, ↑A 54↓ 42
Augury   D 143
Ambiguity of Past & present   A 132
Memory   B 6   C 272
Circumambient soul   C 192
Apples & men   D 127   224
Turns
Lucky hand   C 314
Growth of nocturnal napoleons   C 296
    You can't speak little enow of y[ou]r family   C 139 or of y[ou]r
sickness   C 221 43

"Manifest virtues procure reputation; occult ones fortune,"
Bacon. [Enc. 35]

One omen is good to die for one's country. [BB I, 39, Enc. 37]

    Howbeit, I will steer my rudder true.⁴⁴ [Enc. 167]

---

monology," *Lectures,* III, 163–164, 156, 168, 162, and 168 and 169; the passage in Journal B, p. [123], is not used in the essay "Demonology."

    ⁴¹ "A 54" is added in pencil. Of the nine passages on "Dreams", all but "ϴ 122 . . . D 211," are used in "Demonology," *Lectures,* III, 154 and 155, 155 and 156, 155, 153, 155, and 154; the passage in Journal C, p. [178], is omitted in the essay "Demonology." The sentence in C, p. [178], and one from C, p. [134], went into "Spiritual Laws," *W,* II, 148; the passage in D, p. [211], is used in "Genius," *Lectures,* III, 74, and "Intellect," *W,* II, 337.

    ⁴² The paragraph in Journal B, p. [46], Emerson's translation of the quotation from Goethe (see B, pp. [164] and [240]), part of the paragraph in C, p. [160], a sentence in D, p. [36], and one phrase in D, p. [241], are used in "Demonology," *Lectures,* III, 162, 163–164, 152 (cf. pp. 167 and 168 also), 167, and 167–168. "A 54" is added in pencil; the passage cited is used in "Demonology," *Lectures,* III, 154.

    ⁴³ "Ambiguity . . . 221" is in pencil. The paragraph in Journal A, p. [132], "the circumambient soul" from C, p. [192], and the quotation in C, p. [314], are used in "Demonology," *Lectures,* III, 153, 169, and 161.

    ⁴⁴ This and the two preceding quotations are used in "Demonology," *Lectures,* III, 159 and 166.

No there is a necessity in Fate Why still the brave bold man is fortunate
[Enc. 63]

Coincidences signs presentiments   D 182 [45]

"Drunkenness & phrensy have a near approach to the nature of Divination."
Plutarch "Why the Oracles cease"

Sortilege
Omens *as* valuable in trifles as in bigger things. E 330½

[15]   The Age [46]
Advantage of the orators of a principle   B.33
Opinion of President Fontanes   B 300
Studies organic remains   B 284, D 162,
Our age is ocular. [C 71] travelling.   sick,[47]
The Age is decorous & of course the thinkers decry cant
Bancroft's History   C:153,
Animal Magnetism [48]
Airing   C 205, D 49,
The great questions   C 245   D 11, 154,
Cant   C 293, 306, ⟨41⟩D 41, C 82, 92,[49]

---

[45] This passage is used, rewritten, in "Demonology," *Lectures*, III, 156.

[46] "The Present Age" is listed on p. [166] below among possible topics for the "Human Life" series, but only seven of the entries on p. [15] are used in lectures in that series. Emerson returned to the topic for a series on "The Present Age" in 1839–1840, and the "Lecture on the Times" in 1841, where more of these entries are used. See Notebook Ж, pp. [47]–[48] below, a collection probably for The Present Age: "Introductory," also headed "The Age", where some of these entries are repeated.

[47] Emerson used passages in Journal B, p. [300], and D, p. [162] (derived from B, p. [284]), in "Doctrine of the Soul," *Lectures*, III, 13 and 9. The paragraph cited in B, p. [33], is used in The Present Age: "Introductory," *Lectures*, III, 197, and in the lecture "Eloquence." "Our age . . . sick," is used in "The Spirit of the Times," an 1850 lecture derived from The Present Age: "Introductory," and the entry is listed in notes for "Introductory" in Notebook Ж, p. [47] below; see also a draft of the same lecture in Δ, p. [12] above. All or part of a section on travelling, now in "Self-Reliance," *W*, II, 80–82, may also have been in missing leaves of "Home," *Lectures*, III, 31.

[48] "Animal Magnetism" (mesmerism) is discussed in "Demonology," *Lectures*, III, 167, and in the lecture "The Spirit of the Times."

[49] The paragraph cited in Journal D, p. [49], is used in "Tragedy," *Lectures*,

Democrat   C 297, D.14⟨5⟩2,
Sincerity surprises   C 307
Bivouac   C 329
Protestants   D 25
Vulgar reformers   D 53, 154, 173,
Americans apolo⟨z⟩gize for learning. D 99
Despond⟨ent⟩ing   D 103, C 96,⁵⁰
Needs religious culture   D 145, [D 119]
Anti-money   D 154
Phrenology   C 145
Martyrs chiefly Pseudo   C 343, 347, D 97, 98,⁵¹ 99, 206, B 101
⟨C⟩Our politics   B 307   C 153, 297, 318, D 142, 144,

The New Age   D 46,⁵²

[16]⁵³ The sentiment one & the same in
                        Selftrust
                        Humility
                        ↑Veneration↓
                        Benevolence
                        Justice
Beautiful is the (even mistaken) veneration of men   D 46⁵⁴
Man never appears to such advantage as with melting voice   224

III, 114. Four paragraphs in C, pp. [245]–[246], are used in both "Reforms," *Lectures*, III, 256–257, and "Lecture on the Times," *W*, I, 269–270. Under "Cant", Emerson used a paragraph in D, p. [41], in "Duty," *Lectures*, III, 140, and part of C, p. [293], in "Self-Reliance," *W*, II, 51.

⁵⁰ Emerson used the sentence in Journal D, p. [99], in The Present Age: "Introductory," *Lectures*, III, 195, and a passage in D, p. [103], in "Tragedy," *Lectures*, III, 104, and the lecture "Manners and Customs of New England" (January 28, 1843).

⁵¹ The paragraph in Journal C, p. [347], is used (and cf. also the first paragraph in D, p. [97]) in "Reforms," *Lectures*, III, 268. The second paragraph in D, p. [97], and part of a paragraph in D, p. [98], are used in "Tendencies," *Lectures*, III, 310.

⁵² With the paragraph in Journal D, p. [46], cf. "The Protest," *Lectures*, III, 89, where Emerson has reversed the meaning.

⁵³ P. [16] is in pencil.

⁵⁴ Index Minor, p. [2] below, lists "Beautiful is reverence in men   Duty 17", but the first eighteen pages of the manuscript of the lecture "Duty" are missing. All of p. [16] may be notes for "Duty," as are pp. [17]–[20] following.

He should revere even folly & sin & exchange names with enemy

C 325

[17]   Ethics [55]
The order of things consents to Virtue. Such scenes as luxurious poets
& novelists ↑often↓ paint where temptation has a quite overmastering
⟨effect⟩ force, never or very rarely occur in real life. [B 36]

     See also B 21
Honor no ephemeris B 319
"All that frees talent without increasing self-command is noxious." &c

B.164.

     My whole being is my pledge   not a signature of ink   B 140
     Treat all men as gods   B 140
Benevolence   T 33, C 63, ⟨326⟩,[56]
Falkland cared only that his actions should be just not that they should
be acceptable. C 105
Punishment grows out of the same stem as crime [C 107]
Who perceives the Moral sentiment rights himself   C 121
Self-trust; charge of pride pleasant   C 121

         Bad Counsel so the gods ordain
         Is most of all the adviser's bane   Plut. [C 130]

Utter yourself. C 292   l'abandon]
Always pay   C 302, D 214,[57]

[55] The collection in ink on pp. [17]–[18] and notes in pencil on pp. [18]–[20]
below are almost certainly for the lecture "Duty," *Lectures*, III, 138–150, but Emerson used the same heading for the 1837 lecture "Ethics" in Notebook F No. 1, p.
[131] above, notes for "Compensation" and "Spiritual Laws" in F No. 1, pp. [21]–
[28] and [43] above, and what may be notes for the missing 1840 lecture, "Ethics,"
in ЖК, p. [75] below. Emerson may have used these notes again in writing the essays.
[56] "My whole . . . ink" is used in "Duty," *Lectures*, III, 140. "Treat all . . .
gods" is paraphrased in B, p. [140], but see the sentence in B, p. [191], and in
Notebook Man, p. [73] above. Index Minor, p. [2] below, lists "Virtue surprises in
an engineer   Duty 4" (C, p. [63]); p. [4] is missing from the lecture manuscript.
Most of the paragraph cited in C, pp. [326]–[327], is used in "Tragedy," *Lectures*,
III, 119–120.
[57] "Punishment grows . . . crime", struck through in pencil with a diagonal
use mark, is used in "Compensation," *W*, II, 103, where it is followed by a passage
from "Duty," *Lectures*, III, 145–146. "Who perceives . . . himself C 121" is struck
through in pencil with a diagonal use mark; part of the passage cited is used in

Compensation   C 302, 3⟨2⟩13, 323, D 62, 84, 96, 141, ↑Φ 161i,↓ [58]
The condition of influence by virtue is time   C 302
Do *your*ⁿ work   C ⟨3⟨60⟩06⟩, 306, 82
Endure   C 324, 348
Venerate   C ⟨2⟩326 [59]
Humble yourself   C 328   San Filippo Neri
The good Compensation. love. C 340
Never dispute   B 37, D 29, ↑55↓   C.289, 290, 343,[60]
[18] Cumber not yourself with your own past, D 30, 112,
Tranquillity   D 32, 78   90, 240,[61]
Benefits   C 318, D 84,   C 279
Truth, Goethe Vol 9 p. 63, ⟨128⟩ D 128, 139, C 311,[62]
Never rely on your memory even in acts of memory. D 112, 118,

---

"Self-Reliance," *W*, II, 89. Emerson struck through "Self-trust" with a diagonal use mark in pencil, then extended it successively through "Is most" and "Always pay"; "Utter yourself." is struck through in pencil with another diagonal use mark. The passage in Journal C, p. [121] ("Self-trust . . . pleasant"), is used, along with paragraphs in C, p. [313], cited below, in a manuscript fragment printed with "Private Life," *Lectures*, III, 248–249. "Bad Counsel . . . bane" is used in "Duty," *Lectures*, III, 146; cf. "Compensation," *W*, II, 109. The passage cited in C, p. [292], which includes "l'abandon⟧", is used in "Duty" (ms. Houghton Library) and "Spiritual Laws," *W*, II, 141–142. The paragraph in D, p. [214], probably expanded from C, p. [302], is used in "Duty," *Lectures*, III, 149 and 150, and parts of it in "Self-Reliance," and "Compensation," *W*, II, 89–90 and 113.

[58] Passages in Journal C, pp. [323]–[324], and D, pp. [84] and [141], are used in "Duty," *Lectures*, III, 148–149, 149–150, and 145. Passages in C, pp. [323]–[324], D, p. [84], and the quotation cited on p. [161] below, are used in "Compensation," *W*, II, 121 and 113.

[59] Passages in Journal C, pp. [306] and [82], are used in "Self-Reliance," *W*, II, 47, 53, and 78. Passages in C, pp. [324], [348], and [326], are used in "Tragedy," *Lectures*, III, 116, 115, and 119–120.

[60] Emerson used one sentence in Journal C, p. [340], and the last paragraph in C, p. [289], in "Duty," *Lectures*, III, 143. Passages in D, p. [29], C, pp. [289] (the first paragraph) and [343], are used in "Prudence," *W*, II, 238–239.

[61] "D 32" is listed for addition to "Tragedy," *Lectures*, III, 431(notes); passages in Journal D, pp. [78], [90], and [240], are used in "Tragedy," *Lectures*, III, 113, 112–113, and 113–114.

[62] The passage cited in Journal D, p. [84], is used in "Duty," *Lectures*, III, 149–150, and "Compensation," *W*, II, 113. Passages on "Truth" in D, p. [128], and C, p. [311], are used in "Duty," *Lectures*, III, 139–140 and 139, and "Spiritual Laws," *W*, II, 139 and 143; D, p. [128], is also partly used in "Religion," *Lectures*, III, 281.

Live entire   D 128, 140   Φ 158; D 163, C 319,[63]
Do not choose   D 128, 59,
Do not degrade yourself to society   D 153, C 319 [64]
Philosophize pleasantly   C 131 [65]
Self regard ridiculous: Newspaper & Wordsworth   C 340,
External standards of action   D 154,
Be free   D 200, C 319,
Piously follow. D 10, 224,
Mathematics of Benefit C 279 [66] Condition of influence of virtue time
 Honor no ephemeris
 Character cumulative [67]

[19] [68] Virtue sans cant   D 150   Compensation
⟨Spontaneous virtue   D⟩ 94   ↑D↓141 ⟨Revenge⟩
Ungoodied temperance   D 51   paragraph by depth of thought
Speak to virtue   D 149   145 faces
Why choose   D 128, 59,   Saddle
⟨Forget that you exist⟩ D 109   148 Every thing must come round
⟨Goodies⟩ D 41   180 Inevitable conditions
⟨Character   D 94⟩   Greatness pays tax
⟨Who perceives the mor. sent. rights himself⟩ C 121

[63] The sentence cited in Journal D, p. [118], is used in "The Protest," and listed for addition to "The School," *Lectures*, III, 95 and 404(notes). For "D 128", used in "Duty," see the preceding note. Lines from Jonson inscribed on p. [158] below, and the passage in C, p. [319], are used in "Duty," *Lectures*, III, 149 and 143–144.

[64] "D 128" and "C 319", both passages used in "Duty," are listed above. The sentence cited in Journal D, p. [59], is used in "Religion," *Lectures*, III, 281, and "The Over-Soul," *W*, II, 293.

[65] This line is struck through in pencil with a diagonal use mark. The paragraph in Journal C, p. [131], a quotation from Plutarch, is used in "Comedy," *Lectures*, III, 126.

[66] "C 319," a passage used in "Duty," is listed above. The paragraph in Journal D, p. [10], is used in "Duty," *Lectures*, III, 139, and "Self-Reliance," *W*, II, 47. Emerson discusses "Benefit" in "Duty," *Lectures*, III, 149–150, but nothing from C, p. [279], has been located in the lecture.

[67] "Condition of influence . . . cumulative" is in pencil and may belong with "Punishment out . . . counsel" on p. [19] facing, with which it is aligned horizontally. See p. [17] above. "Character cumulative" (cf. Journal Q, p. [25]) is used in "Duty," and "Tendencies," *Lectures*, III, 144 and 311, and "Self-Reliance," *W*, II, 59.

[68] Pp. [19] and [20] are in pencil.

⟨L'Abandon   C 292⟩
Piously follow ⟨D 10⟩ 224 [69]

62 Whortleberry girl
84 Benefits
96 Not several numerical retribution

136 Tender Ruffians
↑214 Always pay↓
C⟨8⟩323 See a Spiritual retrib
302 Be not too shrewd [70]

Compensation   D 141   145   148, 180, 62, 84, 96,   C 80, 323, 302,
313, 323 [71]

Punishment out of same stem [C 107]
House & carpenter [B 257]
Bad counsel [C 130]
Reward of a thing [C 9]
Highest price is to ask [Enc. 186]
No true valor in bad [Q 30]
Greatness of thought.   its danger   D 180
Ethics of opinion   C 80
Always pay   C 302   D 214 [72]

[69] In the column above, passages in Journal D, pp. [150], [149], [128], [41], and [10], are used in "Duty," *Lectures*, III, 144, 144–145, 139–140, 140, and 139. With the passage in D, p. [94], used later in "Spiritual Laws," *W*, II, 133–134, cf. "Duty," *Lectures*, III, 140 and 144, where Emerson summarizes a section on Virtue which was probably in missing pages of the lecture manuscript. The passages cited in D, p. [109], and C, p. [292], are also used in "Duty" (ms. Houghton Library).

[70] In the column above, each line of "Saddle . . . tax" is struck through in pencil with a vertical use mark; passages in Journal D, pp. [141] (both paragraphs), [148], [180] (both paragraphs), [84], [136], and [214], and C, p. [323], are used in "Duty," *Lectures*, III, 145 and 146, 145, 148 and 146–147, 149–150, 147, 149 and 150, and 148–149. The passages in D, pp. [180], [84], [136], and [214], and C, p. [323], are also used in "Compensation," *W*, II, 105, 104 and 99–100, 113, 99, 113, and 121–122. "paragraph by . . . thot" (D, p. [141]) is used in "Spiritual Laws," *W*, II, 153.

[71] Except for "C 80", a passage used in "Spiritual Laws," *W*, II, 156, each of these entries is repeated from pp. [17]–[19] above; five passages are used in "Duty."

[72] Except for "House & Carpenter" and "Reward of . . . bad", the entries in the column above are repeated from pp. [17] and [19] above. The passages cited in Journal B, p. [257], C, pp. [130] and [9], and D, pp. [180] and [214], are used in "Duty," *Lectures*, III, 149, 146, 149, 146–147, and 149 and 150. Passages in C, pp. [107] and [130], Encylopedia, p. [186], and D, pp. [180] and [214], are used in "Compensation," *W*, II, 103, 109, 113, 104, 99–100 and 104, and 113.

↑Everything must come round↓ [D 148]

Punishment [C 107]   D 214 Always pay

Revenge [D 141]   C 302 Be not too shrewd

House & carp [B 257]   D 84 Benefits

Reward [C 9]   C 3⟨22⟩23 See a spiritual

Bad counsel [C 130]   Highest price to ask [73]

D 145 ⟨Saddle⟩ ↑Opinion↓ ↑paragraph by↓

Greatness pays tax [D 180]

↑paragraph↓ [D 141]

D 180 Inevitable conditions [74]

[20] Essence of Virtue   spontaneity

One substance, give way to that

All else receptacle

Spontaneous virtue   pious following, l'abandon, forget &c

Hence our dislike to mechanical aids

Pledges [B 140]

Goodies [D 41]

Creeds or Classifs

⟨Hence our discernment in trifles⟩

It must be spontaneous

Hence the terror of tradition

Speak to virtue

But speak heathenly [D 149]

The world

was made by it [75] [John 1:10]

---

[73] All the entries in this column are repeated above. The passages cited in Journal D, pp. [214] and [84], and C, p. [323], are used in "Duty," *Lectures*, III, 149–150 and 148–149.

[74] All the entries in this column are repeated above, and all but "D 145 . . . Opinion" are used in "Duty," *Lectures*, III, 145, 148, 149 and 150, and 146–147.

[75] "pious following," and "Pledges . . . Classifs" are an outline of "Duty," *Lectures*, III, 139–141. "pious following . . . aids" outlines pp. [19]–[22] of the lecture manuscript (ms. Houghton Library), where the passage in Journal D, p. [10] ("pious following,"), is canceled. "Hence our . . . trifles" is canceled. With "It must be spontaneous", cf. *ibid.*, pp. 140 and 144. With "Hence the . . . tradition", cf. Journal D, pp. [219]–[222], partly used, *ibid.*, pp. 141–143. "Speak to . . . by it" continues the outline for "Duty," *ibid.*, pp. 144–145.

[21]   Theology [76]

In the peculiar use I make of the word Ethics I need another higher division for other facts.

The Genius of the Divine Providence ⟨2⟩C 22, 183, 192   D 50

Immortality of duration never taught   C 40 [77]

Our position in the Universe   C 41

Omnipresence   C 62, 112

Always suppose God   C 112

Circumambient Soul   C 192

Christianity   C 278   303, D 56,

Worship   C 287, 2⟨8⟩98, 347   D 10, 59, 149,

. C 288

Theism   C 289   D 10, 17, 47, 94, 139, 152, Σ 14, D 240 [78]

The standing miracle   C 303   D 59

Dualism   C 310

God in Nature   C 341

Commandment & commander   A 52,

They call it Christianity I call it consciousness. [D 35] See also D 56

  ↑A Church↓ ⎫
                  ⎬ D 35
  A creed   ⎭

Swedenborg   D 25, 35, 48, 41, 148,

[76] See p. [167] below, where Emerson listed "Church" as a possible topic for the "Human Life" series. The first sentence below on p. [21] suggests that Emerson planned to use notes on this page for a lecture following "Duty," not completed when the series was cut short. A few of the listed passages are used in other lectures in the series, in the 1840 lecture "Religion," and in "The Over-Soul."

[77] Part of the paragraph cited in Journal C, p. [40], is used in "Religion," *Lectures*, III, 277, and "The Over-Soul," *W*, II, 283–284.

[78] Passages in Journal C, p. [303], and D, pp. [59] and [152], are used in "Religion," *Lectures*, III, 278 and 279–280, 281, and 280 and 284; D, pp. [59] and [152], are also used in "The Over-Soul," *W*, II, 293 and 269. Passages in D, p. [149], C, p. [289], and D, p. [10], are used in "Duty," *Lectures*, III, 144–145, 143, and 139; C, p. [289], and D, p. [10], were used later in "Self-Reliance," *W*, II, 69 and 47. The paragraph in D, p. [17], is used in "Doctrine of the Soul," *Lectures*, III, 10, and partly in "Intellect," *W*, II, 328. The last paragraph in D, p. [94], is used in "The School," *Lectures*, III, 43, and "The Over-Soul," *W*, II, 277. The paragraph in D, p. [240], is used in "Tragedy," *Lectures*, III, 113–114.

Popular religion   D 22, 23, 24, 53, 100, 105, 201,[79]

[22]   Conservatism
England held up by all dollars   N 75
Merchants   N 45, 104
Praise of cities   N 44
Harvard University [J 34]
Gold represents labor; labor is higher   J 140
Masses   J 28,[80] 70, 72
Talent makes comfort ⟨c⟩J 88
Credit eternal   J 33
Purest needs a law ⟨o⟩founded on force   N 101
Conservatism   N 10, 97

[23]   Beauty [81]
Flowers   C 40
Music   C 99, 233, 322, B.27   D 7, 72, ↑Θ 103↓
Manners   C 101, D 343
Personal beauty   C 102, 152, 203, ↑D 9↓
The detached fact & the fact in place   C 181, 255, ↑D 114, 146,↓
Nature's termini & outlines   C 188
Shadows   C 145   Softness of darkness   C 22⟨5⟩4
Memories   B 6, C.272
Proportion (in writing C 194) ↑Σ 12,↓
Forms   C 226, 251   317, D 41, 79, 93, ↑C 181↓
Voice of nature   C 268, 307   D 10, 31.[82]

---

[79] Passages in Journal D, pp. [35] and [48], are used in "Duty," *Lectures*, III, 140–141. The sentence cited in D, p. [105], is used in "Religion," *Lectures*, III, 278.

[80] The sentence cited in Journal N, p. [75], is used in the lecture "Genius of the Anglo-Saxon Race." The passages cited in N, p. [44], and J, pp. [34] and [28], are used in the lecture "Trade." The paragraph in N, p. [45], is used in the lecture "Manners and Customs of New England."

[81] "Beauty" is listed among possible topics for the "Human Life" series on p. [167] below.

[82] Passages listed above in Journal C, pp. [99], [102], [203], and [272], and B, p. [6], are used in "Love," *Lectures*, III, 60, 56, 59, 54, and 56–57. The passage in D, p. [9], is used in "Comedy," *Lectures*, III, 121–122. The paragraph in D, p. [114], is used in "The School," *Lectures*, III, 49. The passage cited in C, p. [145], is used in "Domestic Life," *W*, VII, 104, and is listed in notes for the lecture "Home"

Hens handsomer than men   C 298 [83]
Night   C 329   D 42, 51, 87
A birdwhile   C 333
Joy of beauty; safety, eternity   D 6,[84] ↑117↓
Hand   D 45
Nature   D 51, 59, 87, 104, 117
Face subordinates the body   D 70 [85]
Fitness of Architecture to the beautiful soul   D 83,
The Antique balance   D 90
Beauty invites us from within outward   D 110
Beauty a power of pe⟨p⟩rpetuity   D 123 [86]
Indifference to beauty Librarian & Custode   C 211
⟨Pro⟩Astronomy sedative   C 287 [87]
Variety of uniformities   B 255
Straight lines   B 255
In the Will.   D 343,

[24] [88] ⟨The wagons   C 27   see also the times   C.84, 294, 305⟩

---

on p. [150₁] below; see *Lectures*, III, 23(notes). One phrase in D, p. [31], is used in "Home," *Lectures*, III, 31. The paragraph in C, p. [251], is used in "Genius," *Lectures*, III, 74. Passages in C, p. [317], and D, p. [10], are used in "Duty," *Lectures*, III, 138–139.

[83] This line is struck through in pencil with a diagonal use mark; the paragraph in Journal C, p. [298], is used in "The Protest," *Lectures*, III, 98.

[84] The beginning of the paragraph in Journal D, p. [6], is used in "Tragedy," and the end in "Love," *Lectures*, III, 117 and 58.

[85] This line is struck through in pencil with a diagonal use mark; the paragraph cited is used in "Comedy," *Lectures*, III, 133–134.

[86] "The Antique . . . D 90" is struck through in pencil with a diagonal use mark; the passages cited in Journal D, pp. [90] and [123], are used in "Genius," *Lectures*, III, 72 and 74–75. D, p. [123], is the "agaric" paragraph used later in "The Poet," *W*, III, 22–24.

[87] This line is struck through in pencil with a diagonal use mark; the paragraph cited is used in "Tragedy," *Lectures*, III, 117.

[88] Notes on pp. [24]–[26] are probably an early survey of the journals for the "Human Life" lecture series, possibly a continuation of the survey on pp. [8]–[9] above. Every line on pp. [24]–[26] except "Faces . . . 145," on p. [24] is struck through horizontally, in addition to the vertical use marks described in the next notes. Passages listed are used throughout the "Human Life" series, one in "Home," four in "The School," four in "Love," three in "Genius," six in "The Protest," eleven in "Tragedy," one in "Comedy," and five in "Duty."

⟨The Man magazine   C.57   D.1, C 70, 260, D 70⟩
⟨Charm of Property   C 63,⟩
⟨Identity of Nature   ⟨C⟩human   C.63, 145, 312,⟩
⟨Turns   C 68   231   D 101, 119, 132, 146,⟩
⟨A man should behave himself as a guest of nature not as a drone./⟩
           [C 109]

⟨I would taste my time   C 122⟩
⟨Phidias's friezes   C 124⟩
⟨Philosophize pleasantly. C.131⟩
⟨Clapping   C 137⟩
⟨The foolish face of praise   C 138⟩
Faces   C 138, D 9, 31, 98, 97, 104, 145,
⟨Eloquence   C 145   D 72, 171⟩
⟨Phrenology   C 145⟩
⟨Distribution or Tempering of pain   C 151⟩
⟨We do not love him who gives thoughts   C 156⟩
⟨The Coat. C 166, 174,⟩
⟨Destiny   C 168⟩
⟨How is a man wise? By perception of a principle.⟩ [C 164]
⟨Laocoon   C 170⟩
⟨Chinese & English   C 171⟩
⟨American Pomp negro fine   C 173⟩
⟨Expression   C 166, 174, 175, 176, B.6, C 249, 269, 311, D 104⟩
⟨Tombs   C 177, 190, 97,⟩
⟨When you are sincerely pleased without misgiving, you are fed.⟩
           [C 188]

⟨Sympathy   C 191   D 31⟩ [89]
[25] ⟨Physician ⟨2⟩C 25, 191, D 153⟩
⟨Mutual instruction, C.192⟩

[89] Lines 1–5 are struck through in ink with a vertical use mark, which Emerson successively extended through ll. 5–9, 10, 11, 12, 12–14, 14–24, 24–25, and 26–27. Passages in Journal C, pp. [294], [109], and [151], are used in "Tragedy," *Lectures*, III, 108, 113, and 112; passages in C, pp. [63] and [249], are used in "The School," *Lectures*, III, 40 and 37–38; sentences in C, pp. [145] and [269], are used in "Genius," *Lectures*, III, 83 and 77; a sentence in C, p. [124], is used in "The Protest," *Lectures*, III, 93; the quotation from Plutarch cited in C, p. [131], is used in "Comedy," *Lectures*, III, 126; passages in B, p. [6], and D, p. [31], are used in "Love," *Lectures*, III, 56–57 and 59; the paragraph in C, p. [311], is used in "Duty," *Lectures*, III, 139.

⟨Woman   C 195, 196,⟩
⟨Places   C 202⟩
⟨Airing   C 205   D 49⟩
⟨Death   C 206   B 110   C 247, 348⟩
⟨Animals   C 208⟩
⟨Sacs & Foxes   C 209⟩
⟨Indifference to beauty. Librarians & Custodes   C 211⟩
⟨Village traits   C 217, 265, 266, 279, D 92⟩
⟨A man out of place is a dangler.⟩ [C 219]
⟨Insight outsight   C 220⟩
⟨Faneuil Hall   C 227, 306⟩
⟨Scholar   C 231, 280, 305, D 68, 73, 86,⟩
⟨Progress of Man ↑C↓ 231, 296   D 8, 37⟩
⟨Otherism   C 238   D 92, 101,⟩
⟨Buds   C 240⟩
⟨Culture needs no costly apparatus   C 242. T 19⟩
⟨Slavery   C 245⟩
⟨Condition   C 248, 261, 281, 287, 294, 308, D 100, 138,⟩
⟨The active happy   Napoleon gaped.⟩
⟨Of alms   C 279⟩
⟨Riches   C 281   D 100, 155,⟩
⟨The Past   C 287, D 30,⟩
·⟨Never dispute   C 289, 290. 343, D 29, B.37,⟩
⟨A man rare   C 293⟩
⟨Courage of 2 o'clock A.M.   C 299⟩ [90]
[26] ⟨Limitation   C 308, 318, 320, D 6, 11, 13, 16⟩
⟨Uses of distinction   C 311⟩
⟨Advantage of insusceptible Napoleon Temperament   C 313, 348,⟩
⟨The first men had no glory   C 317⟩

[90] Emerson struck through ll. 1–2 with a vertical use mark in ink, then extended it successively through ll. 2–4, 4–6, 7, 7–10, 10–17, 17–19, and 19–27. The passages cited in C, p. [192], and D, p. [68], are used in "The School," *Lectures*, III, 42 and 36–37; one sentence in C, p. [196], is used in "Love," *Lectures*, III, 62; passages in D, p. [49], and C, pp. [206], [247], and [281], are used in "Tragedy," *Lectures*, III, 114, 109, and 107–108; with D, p. [100], cf. "Tragedy," *Lectures*, III, 108; parts of the paragraph in C, p. [227], are used in "Genius," *Lectures*, III, 83; passages in D, pp. [86]–[87], and C, pp. [287] and [258], are used in "The Protest," *Lectures*, III, 101 and 102, 97, and 89.

⟨Martyrs   C 347   343   D 97, 98, 99⟩
⟨Bifronted is every Master   C 346⟩
⟨Benefits, C 318 . D 84⟩
⟨Feeble influence of thought on life   C 319⟩
⟨Anniversaries ↑C↓ 320⟩
⟨Put in a little heat   C 333⟩
⟨Self regard ridiculous. ⟨C⟩Newspaper & Wordsworth   C⟩ 340
⟨Health   D 21⟩
⟨Garden   D 35, 55, 108⟩
⟨The new age   D 46⟩
⟨Our meeting house   D 78⟩
⟨When the mud boils   D 97⟩
⟨Housekeeping   D 108⟩
⟨Aunts   D 115, 2,⟩
⟨A man ought to know how to plant or fish   D 137⟩
⟨Poor should pray for the rich. D 138⟩
⟨Animal spirits   D 141⟩
⟨External standards of action   D 154,⟩
⟨Quotation of ⟨see⟩scripture   D 155⟩ [91] [157]

[⟨26⟩27]   Comic [92]
To run after one's hat is ludicrous [C 86]
Love of Spoons   D 48 [93]
Deacon Parkman   D 92

[91] Emerson struck through ll. 1–10 with a vertical use mark in ink, then extended it successively through ll. 10–12, 12–14, 15–16, 16–18, 19–20, and 21–23. The first part of the paragraph in D, p. [6], is used in "Tragedy" and the last part in "Love," *Lectures*, III, 117 and 58; passages in C, p. [348], and D, p. [21], are also used in "Tragedy," *Lectures*, III, 115 and 106–107; passages in D, pp. [16] and [46], are used in "The Protest," *Lectures*, III, 100 and 89; passages in C, pp. [317] and [319], and D, pp. [84] and [141], are used in "Duty," *Lectures*, III, 138–139, 143–144, 149–150, and 146; most of the paragraph in D, p. [108], is used in "Home," *Lectures*, III, 24–25.

[92] Notes on pp. [27]–[31] below are for the lecture "Comedy," *Lectures*, III, 121–137, most of which was used, though with substantial revision, in the essay "The Comic," *The Dial*, IV (Oct. 1843), 247–256, and *W*, VIII, 155–174.

[93] With "To run . . . ludicrous", struck through in pencil with a diagonal use mark, cf. "Comedy," *Lectures*, III, 132. "Love of . . . D 48" is struck through in ink with a diagonal use mark; most of the paragraph cited is used in "Comedy," *Lectures*, III, 133.

Stetson   D 93, C 9 [94]

Mushroom   D 113

Names   D 115

"The Understanding's man finds all laughable; the Reason's man nothing" *Goethe*

Ancient Comic not parody   Z 23,

The Dentist's pictures   C 250

Do not laugh   D 166 [95]

Word blunders. C 280. "old hang zoin"   "snew"

Self regard ridiculous   C 340

Aunts   D 115, 2, A 139

Animal Spirits   D 141, 98,

Village traits   C 217, 265–6, 279, D 92

Airing   C 205   D 49

Chinese & English   C 171

Clapping   C 137

Domestics

Head subordinates   D 70 [96]

G Minot   D 11

Modern Martyrs

Cliques

Carlini   Encyc.86

The most diligent enquirer into causes of sleep. Encyc.87

Astley's vest. Nil habet infelix paupertas durius &c   Enc. 89 [97] ↑D 7↓

No man likes any body's intemperance but his own ↑C 312↓ [98]

---

[94] This line is struck through in pencil with a diagonal use mark. The passage cited in Journal C, p. [9], is used in "Comedy," *Lectures*, III, 127. See Notebook Δ, p. [24] above, which Emerson apparently started to use for this lecture.

[95] This line is struck through in ink with a diagonal use mark; the sentence cited is canceled in the manuscript of "Comedy," *Lectures*, III, 438(notes). With the passages in Journal D, p. [113], and the Goethe quotation, listed above, cf. "Comedy," *Lectures*, III, 127 and 123–124.

[96] This line is struck through in ink with a diagonal use mark; the paragraph cited is used in "Comedy," *Lectures*, III, 133–134.

[97] "Carlini" and "Astleys vest." are struck through in ink with single diagonal use marks; both anecdotes and an English translation of the lines from Juvenal are used in "Comedy," *Lectures*, III, 137, 132, and 131.

[98] This line is struck through in pencil with a diagonal use mark; "C 312" is in pencil. The paragraph cited and one following it in Journal C, pp. [312]–[313], are used in a manuscript fragment printed with "Private Life," *Lectures*, III, 249.

[⟨27⟩28] Jokes of the Paris drawingrooms　C ⟨47⟩　45 [99]

M M E's watcher　C 104

Dr. Hurd's correct [n] apoplexy. ↑C, 340.↓ Camper [C 30]

We require the perception of the comic in a fine character [100]

The young mirthful, humorous, funny.

Men more than women

Nonsense of great men　　grain of wit　grain of folly

Man a pendulum betwixt a smile & tear

Story of Tamurlain

Boy & W [101] [A 42]

No joke in Nature [102]

None in Greek & Roman

Normans, French, English, joke
Paper bullets
Pretension ridiculous
↑Care of body↓　Tamerlane & the queue
↑Love of Spoons [D 48]
Mandibles.↓ [103]

[99] This line is struck through in ink with a vertical use mark; "47" is canceled; the passage in Journal C, p. [45], is used in "Comedy," *Lectures*, III, 134.

[100] This and the preceding line are struck through in ink with single diagonal use marks; "We require . . . character" and both journal passages cited are used in "Comedy," *Lectures*, III, 125 and 130.

[101] This and the preceding line are struck through in ink with single diagonal use marks; both anecdotes are told in "Comedy," *Lectures*, III, 134–135 and 131.

[102] Cf. "Comedy," *Lectures*, III, 122.

[103] With "Care of body . . . Mandibles.", struck through in ink with a diagonal

↑Ignorance↓
Colleges
↑Patriotism↓
Wit like ice   or skunk
The form of man a pledge of goodness & truth
Cheap joking at Sacred things [104]
Joke falls if the jokee keeps his countenance   if he look resolute &
solemn   it enhances the joke
Laughter in the morning
Tottipotimoy [105]

———

⟨o⟩Or there are no snakes
The Lord Mayor hunting
[29] ———
John Smith sending an Indian to be converted [106]

———

Tiber↑i↓us & the Trojans

———

I never was in the pillory but once

———

As fast as Mrs C. rows, Mr C backs water [B 172]

———

Mr C. seizes hold of every piece of iron that is sinking in the sea.
C. Slow was born so near the end of the year that he came near not
being born at all [B 67]
S Smith said it was so hot he wished he could take off his flesh & sit
in his bones

———

Lie there, Five dollars!

---

use mark, cf. "Comedy," *Lectures*, III, 131–136, a section on "Pretension ridiculous".
    [104] This and the two preceding lines are struck through in ink with single diagonal
use marks; "Patriotism", "Wit like ice", "The form . . . truth", and "Cheap joking
. . . things" are used in "Comedy," *Lectures*, III, 135, 126, 124, and 129.
    [105] "Tottipotimoy" is struck through in ink with a diagonal use mark. The lines
from Butler's *Hudibras* to which it refers are used in "Comedy," *Lectures*, III,
128–129.
    [106] This line, struck through in ink with a diagonal use mark, is expanded in
"Comedy," *Lectures*, III, 128.

Back & front doors

Brummel jokes
Leo Byzantinus

Dost thou think because thou art virtuous there shall be no more cakes & ale? [107] [Shakespeare, *Twelfth Night*, II, iii, 123–125]

The jokes of the Greeks rarely make one laugh
We are educated by laughter as by tears

Alphonso could have given some advice at the creation
Some people have been put to death by tickling.[108]

Caricatures are often the truest history of the time.

'Tis merry in hall when beards wag all

Old King Coal was a jolly old soul.

[30] [109] Poverty
    Coat [D 158]
    Vest [Enc. 89]   Bitterness
                      Comfort

pedantry	Form of Man pledge of a whole
Camper	All halfness ludicrous when not dangerous
Dr Hurd	Perception of halfness
Boy & W	Reason makes whole
Cliques	Understanding
Habit	Man the sole joker
Dea Parkman	Reason jokes not

[107] "Brummel jokes" and "Dost thou . . . ale?", struck through in ink with single diagonal use marks, are used in "Comedy," *Lectures*, III, 133 and 126.
[108] "We are . . . tears" and "Alphonso . . . creation", struck through in ink with single diagonal use marks, and "Some people . . . tickling.", struck through with two, are used in "Comedy," *Lectures*, III, 125 and 136, 130, and 137.
[109] P. [30] is in pencil.

But the best of all jokes is the contemplation of
the philosopher's point of view by the Understanding.

M
Paper bullet
Lord Mayor

Alcott & G P B   D Q & Sancho
Prince Hal

In religion the joke is a rite which pretends
to be religion & is none at all
Tottipottimoy
John Smith
science mistaking the form for the thing
patriotism entire selfishness
poverty   coat [110] [D 158]

[31]   Woman
Housekeeper   C 159, ⟨195, 196,⟩ D 19, 108,
Woman   C 195, 196, 298, 297, D 7, 66, 91, 109, 137, 236,[111]

Poverty: the surrender of the man to the appearance as
in Santa Lucia

Astley's vest [Enc. 89]	The Comic our lesson
mandibles	But not our home
love of spoons [D 48]	Do not laugh too much
Brummel jokes	How hollow: death by ticklin[g]
hat [C 103]	Carlini
head subordinates [D 70]	

The perception of the comic
Wit like ice
Stetson   C 9

[110] "Poverty . . . Boy & W", in the left column, and "Form of Man . . . Prince
Hal" and "In religion . . . coat", in the right column, are developed in "Comedy,"
Lectures, III, 130–132, 122–125, and 127–132, though not always in the order
Emerson lists. "Habit . . . Parkman", apparently not used, is set off from matter to
the right by three large pencil brackets.

[111] "Woman . . . 236," set off from the rest of the page by a partial pencil
bracket in the left margin, may have been a trial topic for the "Human Life" lecture
series. Passages in Journal C, pp. [159], [196], and [298], and D, pp. [137] and
[236], are used in "Love," *Lectures*, III, 62–63 and 55–56; part of the paragraph
in D, p. [108], is used in "Home," *Lectures*, III, 24–25. See also p. [150₁] below,
where "Woman" is listed in notes for "Home."

Carlini [Enc. 86]
Man a pendulum
Do not laugh   Death by tickling
The ↑(dentist's pictures↓ [B 250]

Ignorance
     Lord Mayor superfluous courage
          surrender ⟨app⟩of man to appearance
          Paris drawing rooms [C 45]
          Tamerlane
          the queue
          Leo Byzantinus [112]

[32]   FATE
Calvinism complexional   J 85
Differences of opinion organic   J 110
We read for Fate   J 121
Fate takes in the holidays & work minutes   J.131
The music box   J 131

[33]   Love

     "Unvanquished love! whatever else deceives
     Our trust, 'tis this our very selves outlives." [C 131]
     "Not on the store of sprightly wine" &c   C 131

C 189, 216, B 6, C 264. 265, 269, 326, 340, D 31, 49, 120
     D 155, 156   C.27, T 43,
My Casella   D 120, C 27, A 126, C 260
Eberhard of Wirtemb⟨i⟩erg, Σ 13,   Henry Foundling T.33
Hampden & Eliot   T 45,
Christianity is Love. See Milton's thought   A p 39
It does not hurt weak eyes to look into human eyes ever so long [D 31]

---

[112] "Poverty: the surrender . . . Byzantinus", notes for the lecture "Comedy,"
is in pencil. "Poverty . . . vest" is developed in "Comedy," *Lectures*, III, 131–133;
"mandibles . . . subordinates", *ibid.*, p. 133; "The Comic . . . ticklin[g] Carlini",
ibid., pp. 136–137; "The perception . . . comic", *ibid.*, p. 123; "Wit like . . .
C 9", *ibid.*, pp. 126–127; "Carlini" and "Do not . . . tickling", *ibid.*, p. 137; and
"surrender ⟨app⟩of . . . Tamerlane", *ibid.*, p. 134.

"Stern Jove has in some angry mood
Bereft us of his solitude" [C 131]

Love; *A*
True Love & Faint Love: B 92
In Life all finding is not that thing we sought but somewhat else &c:
&c.   C 27
Gulf betwixt man & woman   B 16, 21 [113]
Love thaumaturgic   D 309
Love in Age   D 305
⟨"If I love you what is that to you"⟩ D 295
Be true & be loved   D 287
Beaumont & Fletcher's Viola   D 276
You must love me as I am &c. C 264
⟨Beauty never alone⟩ D 249
Love impersonal   D [114] [187]

[34]   *Oct 18⟨3⟩42*   *Reformers* & *Reform.*

Property. The Rich & the Poor   N 42   ↑Theanor & Amph. Z 161↓
Pedantry to give such importance to property   G 114
Gold represents Labor but Labor admits to higher secrets   J 140
All are on the Property side   G 164
Men should live by their strength not by their weakness   K 122
Reform dangerous because partial   K 130
Sunset wanted men.   *E* 332,
Don't be so grand with your one objection   J 39, 118,

[113] Notes to this point on p. [33] are probably a collection for "Love," *Lectures,*
III, 51–67, most of which was used in the essay "Love," *W*, II, 167–188. See also
pp. [138]–[139] below. "It does . . . long" is struck through in ink with 13 vertical use or cancellation marks. Passages in Journal B, p. [6], D, pp. [31] and
[120], and C, p. [27], are used in "Love," *Lectures,* III, 56–57, 59, 63–66, and 64,
65, and 66. The passage in D, p. [31], is omitted in the essay. "Love; *A*" may refer
to the only passage indexed "Love" in A, verses from Euripides on p. [135], paraphrased in "Love," *Lectures,* III, 58. Emerson used passages in C, p. [326], and D,
p. [49], in "Tragedy," *Lectures,* III, 119–120 and 107.
[114] "Love thaumaturgic . . . impersonal D", in a smaller hand, may have been
added later during revision of the lecture "Love" for *Essays* [*First Series*]; most of
the passages listed were written later than the lecture, and those in D, pp. [295],
[249], and [187], are used in "Love," *W*, II, 180–181, 178, and 178–179.

Good men must not obey the laws   J 112, E 42
We have never seen a man   K 99
⟨Men should live by their strength not by their weakness⟩ K 122
Wise man leaves the few as well as the many [K 122] J 120
We owe behaviour, we offer money   E 331½
Believe in the rule not in the exception [G 58]
The life of love   E 162
Animals; &c   Porphyry, E 283, 277,
We marry no worse than we eat or dress or speak. [J 118]
Philanthropic Meetings   C 306
Osman & Schill   G 1, 48, 110   F 37
Indian rule & Graham rule   E 165   War at no set diet
Pirates do not live on nuts   E 283
Whites have no rights. [E 255]
Abolitionists   E 352
Egotism of spiritualists   E 125 [115]
[35] We have not quite served up to our thought   J [H] 120
Why Cupid did not assault Muses   *Rabelais* III p 25 [H 142]
Compound interest on Temperance   J 141
Spirit of landscape will not come out to Coffee   K 17

As life comes into union with nature his thoughts run parallel with creation's laws   K 55

⟨Tipsy with water⟩ Φ 93
Temperance the Rus Ruris. N 87
Reform begins with the good, when the Reform Association is dis-
solved   N 88
Obedience to the genius the only Liberation   N 86
Concert when there are individuals. E 29⟨4⟩3,

[115] "& *Reform*." may have been added. "Pedantry to . . . G 114" is struck through in ink with a vertical use mark. "Egotism of . . . 125" is in pencil. The passages cited in Journal G, pp. [114] and [164], K, p. [130], J, pp. [39], [118], and [112], are used in "New England Reformers," *W*, III, 261–263 and 280; with K, pp. [99]–[100], cf. *ibid*., p. 279. "Good men . . . laws" is used in "Politics," *W*, III, 208. "Believe in . . . exception" is used in "Experience," *W*, III, 74. The passage cited in E, p. [352], is partly used in the lecture "Manners and Customs of New England."

Education K 69 (Pericles)   E 350
Conversation with A.B.A.   Z 168
Unleavened bread   Z 110[116]

[36] [blank]
[37]   Classes
Physician   C 25   191   D 153
Scholar   C 231   280   305   D 68   73   86
Farmer   D 9, 11, 100,
Protestants   D 231, 25,
Child   D 219
Aunts   D 2, 115, ↑A 139↓
When the mud boils   D 97
The Coat   C 166, 174,
Village traits   C 217, 265, 266, 279. D 92, 236,
Preachers   B 185

Animals   C 208,[117]

[38]   Character

Abide by truth   K 1
Man should command by the eye   K 16
Osric great in present moment   K 19
Character must be trusted   J 96
The taking my cloak is beautiful if original   J 15, 18
Character is told over my head   G 1⟨2⟩3
        History of Christ document of Character   K 71 [76]

[116] The paragraph cited in Journal H, p. [120] (Emerson's error), is used in "Character," W, III, 102. The passages cited in K, p. [17], and p. [93] below (cf. R, p. [125₂]), are used in "The Poet," W, III, 29. The passages cited in N, p. [86], E, pp. [293] and [350], and Z[A], p. [110], are used in "New England Reformers," W, III, 284–285, 265–266, 258–260, and 252.

[117] "Classes" may have been a trial topic for the "Human Life" series; most of the entries above are also listed on pp. [24]–[26] above, a survey for that series. A paragraph in Journal D, pp. [68]–[69], is used in "The School," Lectures, III, 36–37. Part of a paragraph in D, pp. [86]–[87], and passages in D, pp. [231] and [25], are used in "The Protest," Lectures, III, 101 and 102, 91, 96 and 90. The passage in D, p. [9], is used in "Comedy," Lectures, III, 121–122. The paragraph in D, p. [236], is used in "Love," Lectures, III, 55–56. "A 139" is added in pencil.

Fate & Character　K 78
We owe behavior & we offer money [E 331½]
Never apologize to the person aggrieved　K 115
Wise man leaves the few as well as the many ↑K↓ 122
Given a bandit & opportunity to save wit by wit　N 40, D 214　343
I am not ashamed that I am ashamed　K 118
Institution in the Institutor　K 85
In reading Lord of the Isles, I felt &c　K 14
Pure of the many & ⟨o⟩pure of the few　J 120, K 122
↑A↓ Man not praiseable nor insultable　H 17, ↑nor victimizable
　　　　　　　　　　　　　　　　　　　　　　　　N 121↓

Munificence the only insight　H 33
Men of aim must always rule the aimless　N 136, 112, 141, Z
⎰ It is only low merits can be enumerated　E 51
⎱ Riemer ↑N 79　In lect. o⟨f⟩n "Character." Charitable men not
　　　　　　　　　　　　　　　　　　　　　　　　　givers↓

―――

Privacy of elevation of sentiment. C S Journal

―――

Although I never spoke nor heard the truth, it is mine　K 77 [118]

―――

A beauty of character that could make ugliness of no account
　The Man — it is his attitude　K 22
[39] Unwillingly the soul is deprived of truth [BB II, 36]
Every man would be convicted　　Few opinions　J 109
Every man would be a Benefactor [N 12]
Every man would give all for erect demeanor [119] [J 44]
F

―――

[118] P. [38] is probably a collection for the essay "Character," *W*, III, 87–115.
"N 79　In lect. . . . givers" is added in pencil. The passages cited in Journal J,
p. [96], K, pp. [76], [85], and [122], H, p. [17], N, pp. [121] and [112], E, p.
[51], and N, p. [79], are used, *ibid.*, pp. 109, 114, 101–102, 100, 106–107, 99–100,
and 103–104. K, p. [115], is torn out, but cf. *ibid.*, pp. 102–103. The manuscript
of the lecture "Character" does not survive, but cf. *ibid.*, p. 103. For "Privacy of . . .
sentiment.", see *Lectures*, III, 524(notes); "C S" may be Caroline Sturgis. The
passages cited in J, p. [15], N, p. [141], and K, p. [77], are used in "New England
Reformers," *W*, III, 254, 278–279, and 282.
　[119] P. [39] is in pencil. "Unwillingly . . . convicted" and "Every man would
give . . . demeanor" are used in "New England Reformers," *W*, III, 271, 273,

[40]   *Laws of the World.*[120]
    In nature all growth is contemporary ⟨C⟩D 6
    Put in a little heat   C 333
Alternation is limitation   D 6, 13,[121]
The far, the near. D 21, 42, 137,
Limitation   D 21, 40, 60,
Healt⟨th⟩h   D 21, 89, 126,[122]
May, D 26
Value of facts   D 36, 43, 44, 50; 145, 146, ↑114↓[123]
The Divine soul takes care for heroes   D 47
Time   B 275   C 180, 261, ⟨23⟩324, D 19, 49, 78, C 122, 26⟨0⟩1,
                                            Σ 17, T 39, ↑C 111,↓[124]

Look for a thing in its place   D 53
Price of the picture   D 56.

⟨Naturam expellas furca tamen usque recurret.⟩ [D 61]

⟨The sun & the moon are the great formalists⟩ [D 62]
Actual & Ideal   D 95
⟨⟨When the⟩Naturlangsamkeit in⟩ men & things   D 114

277–278, and 275. With "Few opinions", cf. "Experience," *W*, III, 47, and Journal J, p. [110].

[120] Emerson listed "Laws of the world," among possible topics for the "Human Life" lecture series on p. [166] below and as the subject of a lecture omitted when he shortened the series (see *Lectures*, III, 170, where he lists "Time, Space, Dualism, Alternation, Climate, and other boundaries that wall us in," under this head), but passages listed on pp. [40]–[41] are used in seven other lectures in the series, at least nine in "Tragedy," eight in "The School," three each in "Love" and "Genius," two in "Demonology," and one each in "The Protest" and "Duty."

[121] Emerson used part of the passage cited in Journal D, p. [6], in "Love," *Lectures*, III, 58, and a passage in D, p. [13], in "Literary Ethics," *W*, I, 175.

[122] Passages in Journal D, pp. [21], [89], and [126], are used in "Tragedy," *Lectures*, III, 106–107, 112, and 106.

[123] The lines on May in Journal D, p. [26], are used in "Love," *Lectures*, III, 53. Passages in D, pp. [36], [43], and [114], are used in "The School," *Lectures*, III, 47–48, 48, and 49; "114" is added in pencil. With D, p. [146], cf. "The School," *Lectures*, III, 49.

[124] "T 39," in darker ink, may have been added; "C 111," is added in pencil. Passages in Journal C, p. [324], and D, pp. [49] and [78], are used in "Tragedy," *Lectures*, III, 116, 114, and 113.

Things are united in nature   D 114, 152,
Hard to begin an action   D 116,
Nature ↑self↓insured   D 117, 123,[125]
Nature cants not   D 116
Apples & men   D 127, 224,
Nearness & distinctness convertible   D 137
Turns   C 68, 231, D 101   119, 132, 146[126]
Finiteness. Division, D 152,
Plenty: wagons. C 27   the times ⟨E⟩C 84, 294, 305, ↑Potatoes   D 154↓
Sleep. B.131,[127]
The true miracle or Nature's contraventions   B 257,
[41] Persons   B 53, C 139, 288, 300, 349, D 10, 143,[128]

Distribution or tempering of pain   C 151
Destiny   C 168, Σ 1,[129]
Expression   B 6, C 166   174   175   176, 249   269, 310, D 104,
225, 161, Φ 4, b[130]

Buds   C 240,

Death   C 206   B 110, C 247,[131] 348

[125] Part of the paragraph cited in Journal D, p. [56], is used in "The School," part of it in "Genius," *Lectures*, III, 45 and 78–79. "The sun . . . formalists" and the last paragraph in D, p. [114], are used in "The School," *Lectures*, III, 40 and 49. The passage on "Actual & Ideal" in D, p. [95], is used in "Love," *W*, II, 54–55. A sentence in D, p. [116], is used in "The Protest," and the paragraph in D, p. [123], in "Genius," *Lectures*, III, 87 and 74–75.

[123] Two paragraphs in Journal D, p. [101], are used in "The School," *Lectures*, III, 49 and 46–47. Emerson later used passages in C, p. [68], and D, pp. [119], [132], and [146], in "Nominalist and Realist," *W*, III, 238, 238–239, 246–247, and 239.

[127] Emerson used the paragraph in Journal C, p. [294], in "Tragedy," and the sentence in B, p. [131], in "Demonology," *Lectures*, III, 108 and 152.

[128] The paragraph in Journal C, p. [300], is used in "The School," and the last paragraph of the passage cited in D, p. [10], in "Duty," *Lectures*, III, 43 and 139.

[129] The paragraph in Journal C, p. [151], and the story of Solomon and the Angel of Death in Notebook Σ, p. [1], are used in "Tragedy," *Lectures*, III, 112 and 114–115, and 105–106.

[130] The paragraph in Journal C, p. [249], is used in "The School," the passage in C, p. [269], is expanded in "Genius," and the paragraph in D, p. [161], is used in "Demonology," *Lectures*, III, 37–38, 77, and 157. See p. [42] above; the sentence marked "b" is used in "Religion," *Lectures*, III, 276.

[131] With passages in Journal C, pp. [206] and [247], cf. "Tragedy," *Lectures*,

↑*Polarity*↓
Dualism[n] C 310, 35, D 112,
War   D 241

[42] [blank]
[43]   Intellect [132]
Truth   B 60

Ignorance   *C* 262
Dispute, *C* 289, 290,
Express yourself   *C* 292
Genius never smells of fagots   *C* 295   Φ 157, *A* 39 [133]
Persons & thoughts   *C* 300
Judgment of Art   *D* 2
Classification   *D* 35, 120
Observe evermore   *D* 42 [134]
⟨Advancing na⟩ ↑Nature becoming↓ thought   *D* 44, 51, 99, 101, 142,
                                                                                                146
Growth by doctrine   *D* 48,
Genius   *D* 56 [135]
Insanity   *D* 61, 73, 195, 166, 195   C 64

III, 109. "Death", "*Polarity*", and "*Dualism*" are listed in "The School," *Lectures*, III, 40; see also *Lectures*, III, 170, Emerson's plan for two omitted lectures.

[132] "Intellect" may have been a trial topic for the "Human Life" lecture series; of the passages listed on p. [43], the first four lines on p. [44], and p. [45] below, at least ten are used in "The School," six in "Genius," six in "Duty," and one each in "Doctrine of the Soul," "Home," and "The Protest."

[133] "Genius . . . fagots" is struck through in pencil with a diagonal use mark. The passage cited in Journal C, p. [295], and a quotation from Scaliger on p. [157] below, are used in "Genius," *Lectures*, III, 80–81. The passage cited in C, p. [292], is used in the lecture "Duty" (ms. Houghton Library).

[134] The paragraph in Journal C, p. [300], and part of the long paragraph in D, pp. [42]–[43], are used in "The School," *Lectures*, III, 43 and 48; other parts of two paragraphs in D, pp. [42]–[43], are used in "The Protest," and the passage cited in D, p. [35], is used in "Duty," *Lectures*, III, 98, 99 and 100, and 140 and 141.

[135] The sentence cited in Journal D, p. [99], is used in "Home," *Lectures*, III, 30. Passages in D, pp. [101], [142], and part of [56], are used in "The School," *Lectures*, III, 49, 41, and 45 (with D, p. [146], cf. p. 49); the end of the paragraph in D, p. [56], is used in "Genius," *Lectures*, III, 78–79. The sentence cited in D, p. [48], is used in "Duty," *Lectures*, III, 141.

Receptive of all of Nature   *T* 184, *C* 237 [136]

Outruns affection   *D* 91

Tune or temper   *D* 77, 92,

Fancy & imagination   *D* 93

Not the fact avails but the use you make of it, *D* 101

Needs a religious culture   *D* 119

Order of Cause & Effect   *D* 120, 126

Reproduction   *D* 123

Life becoming thought, *D* 140   Σ 15   *C* 237, *D* 95,

Self-action be⟨t⟩st   *D* 141

Effect ⟨of⟩proportioned to depth of thought   *D* 141, *C* 33, [137]

The Poet   *D* 14⟨3⟩6, 154, Φ 157,

Wisdom in the Common   *C* 237   *D* 95

[44] Inspirati⟨d⟩on   B 113, 109, Φ 161,e, 162a.

Advantage of the Abolitionist   B 33, D 170,b,

Feeble influence of thought on life   *C* 319

Onesidedness   *C* 255 [138]

Genius an emanation of the thing it tel⟨s⟩ls of [D 234] [*Duty* p 5

Goodwill makes insight   N [J] 129

Intellect grows by moral obedience ⟨N⟩J 95

A new relation as good as new object. N 3 [139]

---

[136] With the paragraph cited in Journal D, p. [61], cf. "The Protest," *Lectures*, III, 85. The paragraph in D, p. [166], and lines from Bunyan in C, p. [237], are used in "The School," *Lectures*, III, 42 and 49–50.

[137] The paragraph in Journal D, p. [123], is used in "Genius," *Lectures*, III, 74–75. "D. 141" is added to the manuscript of "The School"; see *Lectures*, III, 402 (notes); D, p. [141] ("Effect . . ."), and the last paragraph in C, p. [33], are used in "Duty," *Lectures*, III, 146.

[138] Notes to this point on p. [44] are probably a continuation of those on p. [43] above; the rest of the notes on p. [44] were probably added in 1842. Passages in Journal B, pp. [113] and [109], and two paragraphs marked "e" on pp. [160]–[161] below, are used in "The School," *Lectures*, III, 36 and 37. With the quotation from Guizot cited in D, p. [170], cf. p. [168] below and "Doctrine of the Soul," *Lectures*, III, 17. The passage cited in C, p. [319], is used in "Duty," *Lectures*, III, 143–144, and is also listed in the manuscript of "Doctrine of the Soul," *Lectures*, III, 391 (notes).

[139] "Genius an emanation . . . N 3" was added later. The first passage cited is used in "Discourse at Middlebury College," the second in the lecture "Recent Literary and Spiritual Influences," and the third in "Discourse at Nantucket."

[45] ——
A thought comes single like a foreign traveller, but find out its name
& it is related to a powerful & numerous family   B 90, 334,

——

The wit of man is more elastic than the air our bodies breathe. A
nation will subsist for centuries on one thought & then every indi-
viddual will be oppressed by the rush of his ideas. & always a plenum
with one grain or 6⟨at⟩o atmospheres.
Knowledge is easy to carry.
Genius surprises   B 286   C 129   D 18
Genius works ever in sport & goodness hath ever a smile [140] [B 259]
Common Sense   B 260, C 309, 324, D 115
Some talents must be kept under naphtha. B 288

[46]   Soul
                        Home
                        Love
                        Study
                        ↑Poetry↓
                        Duty
                       ˙Condition

                   Man related to the Universe [141]

[47]   Man [142]
His nature   D ⟨17⟩, 20   T 184   C 85   ⟨D 216,⟩

[140] The passages cited in Journal C, p. [129], and D, p. [18], are used in
"Genius," *Lectures*, III, 79 and 80; with "Genius works . . . sport", cf. *ibid.*, p. 80.
    [141] "Soul . . . Universe", written in pencil in the upper right quadrant of p.
[46], is a list of tentative titles for the "Human Life" series in 1838–1839, probably
later than the topics on pp. [166] and [167] but earlier than the final titles on
p. [169] below. "Condition" and "Man related to the Universe" may have been
titles for the two lectures that were to have followed "Duty" (see *Lectures*, III, 170).
    [142] Emerson listed "Man" among possible topics for the "Human Life" series on
p. [166] below. See also "Man related to the Universe" on p. [46], facing this.
Emerson drew on pp. [47]–[49] for most of the lectures in the series, using at least
seventeen of the passages listed in "Doctrine of the Soul," four in "Home," eleven
in "The School," six in "Love," two in "Genius," ten in "The Protest," nine in
"Tragedy," one in "Comedy," and nine in "Duty." A frequent topic, "Man" had
been the subject of the "Philosophy of History" series in 1836–1837, and Emerson
used passages listed on these pages in many later lectures and essays.

Unconsciousness ⟨D 17,⟩ 94,[143]

Each individual better than he has done   D 24, 102,   ↑& wiser than

he has known   D 174, 178, C 251   D 208   211   225

1⟨6⟩83   167   190↓[144]

Progress of man   C 231, 296, D 8, 37, 42, 51, 57, 58, 70, ⟨92⟩ 97,

112, 116, 139   B 22   C 27[145]

What hinders? D 38

Limitation   C 308   318   320   D 6, 11, 13, 16, 38, 48, 60, 61, 90,

95, 99, 116, 152, B 150[146]

Monotones   D 39, 35

Secondariness   D 41

When you are deeply pleased without misgiving, you are nourished.

[C 188]

His Veneration   D 46, 224

The Heroic   D 51, 61, C 299, D 154, 86, 97, 136, 137, C 61,

---

[143] Paragraphs in Journal D, pp. [17] and [216], and one phrase in C, p. [85], are used in "Doctrine of the Soul," *Lectures*, III, 10, 14, and 16. Emerson used parts of the passages in D, p. [17], and C, p. [85], later in "Intellect," *W*, II, 328 and 332, sentences in D, p. [20], and C, p. [85], in "The Over-Soul," *W*, II, 267 and 268, and part of D, p. [94], in "Spiritual Laws," *W*, II, 133–134. The paragraph in D, p. [94], may have been used in missing pages of "Duty," where spontaneity is discussed; see *Lectures*, III, 140 and 144, and p. [19] above.

[144] Passages in Journal D, pp. [102], [178], [208], [211], [225], [167], and [190], are used in "Doctrine of the Soul," *Lectures*, III, 18, 17, 19, 21, 18–19, 16–17, and 16, and all but D, p. [211], in "The Over-Soul," *W*, II, 289, 280, 278–279, 285–286, 279–280, and 278; one sentence from D, p. [208], is used in "The Protest," *Lectures*, III, 96. The passage in D, p. [211], was used later in "History," *W*, II, 6 and 7. The paragraph in C, p. [251], is used in "Genius," *Lectures*, III, 74, and "Intellect," *W*, II, 337.

[145] Emerson discusses the "Progress of man" in "Doctrine of the Soul," *Lectures*, III, 20, but none of these passages is used. A passage in Journal D, p. [42], was used in "The Protest," one in D, p. [57], in "Tragedy," and a paragraph in D, p. [112], in "Love," *Lectures*, III, 98, 107, and 67. Emerson used C, p. [296], later in "Tendencies," and D, p. [37], in "Religion," *Lectures*, III, 312 and 284–285; both are used in "The Over-Soul," *W*, II, 274–275 and 290.

[146] "What hinders? D 38" is used partly in "The Protest," *Lectures*, III, 95, and partly in "Literary Ethics," *W*, I, 185. Of the entries on "Limitation", Emerson used passages in Journal D, pp. [6] and [48]–[49], in "Tragedy," *Lectures*, III, 117 and 107; D, pp. [6], [11], and [95], in "Love," *Lectures*, III, 58, 54, and 54–55; and D, pp. [16], [38], [61], and [99], and [116], in "The Protest," *Lectures*, III, 95–96 and 100, 95, 96, 88, and 87. Passages in D, pp. [13] and [48], are also in "Literary Ethics," *W*, I, 175 and 164. The passage in D, p. [152], was later used in "Religion," *Lectures*, III, 280 and 284, and "The Over-Soul," *W*, II, 269.

Fancies   D 51, 191

No rival   D 57,

Odious mistakes   D 60

Our sympathy too strong   D 61, 89,

Reason & understanding   D 62

How is man wise? By perception of a principle. [C 164]   —D 240 [147]

That work agreeable which is not due now   D 68

⟨Society   D 69⟩

Greatest whose sympathy goes lowest   D 70,

Eyes   D 47, 112, 224

Man must be in temper & tune   D 77

Great men acknowledge an ideal standard   D 78

Greatness   D 47, 78, 89, 94   105, 120, 128, 136, 145, 154, C 261,

                                                  Encyc. p. 167,

Man wife & son   D 85, M 117,

The priest profanes the Man, Now. D 87, 95, 201,

Praise & Blame   D 89, 116, 136, 187, 92 [148]

[48] Composure   D 90   32   78   240 [149]

Intellect outruns affection   D 91

Individual private partial worthless   D 92,

Observer formidable   D 93, 86, 99, 112, 118, [150]

[147] One phrase in Journal D, p. [39], and the paragraph in D, p. [89], are used in "Doctrine of the Soul," *Lectures*, III, 15 and 21–22. Passages in D, pp. [35] and [41], are used in "Duty," *Lectures*, III, 140–141. Passages in D, pp. [61] and [87], are used in "The Protest," *Lectures*, III, 96, and 101 and 102. Paragraphs in D, pp. [57] and [240], are used in "Tragedy," *Lectures*, III, 107 and 113–114.

[148] The sentence in Journal D, p. [68], is used in "Works and Days," *W*, VII, 177. Paragraphs on "Greatness" in D, pp. [78] and [89], are used in "Doctrine of the Soul," *Lectures*, III, 20 and 21–22; D, p. [89], was later used in "History," *W*, II, 7; paragraphs in D, pp. [120] and [128], are used in "Love," and "Duty," and a quotation in Encyclopedia, p. [167], is used in "Demonology," *Lectures*, III, 63–66, 139–140, and 159; D, p. [128], was used later in "Spiritual Laws," *W*, II, 139. For "M 117", see Notebook Man, p. [117] above, and a passage canceled in "Home," *Lectures*, III, 399(notes). The passage in D, p. [87], is used in "The Protest," *Lectures*, III, 101 and 102, and partly used later in "Spiritual Laws," *W*, II, 151. The paragraph in D, p. [136], headed "Censure & Praise", is used in "Compensation," *W*, II, 118.

[149] Passages on "Composure" in Journal D, pp. [90], [78], and [240], are used in "Tragedy," *Lectures*, III, 112–113, 113, and 113–114. D, p. [32], may also have been used; see *Lectures*, III, 431(notes).

[150] Part of the paragraph in Journal D, pp. [86]–[87], and the sentence in D,

Impersonality   D 94, C 349, 111, B 200
Licence   D 96, 186d
The Vast an element   D 105, 143 [151]
Forget that *you* ^{n} exist ⟨D 109⟩ [152]
Nomads   D 111, 112, 127,
A man as ⟨st⟩much a stranger in his own body as in yours ⟨D 111, ↑M 116,↓⟩ [153]

Affections & objects subordinate   D 112   115
Bashfulness   D 114
Scale   D 116
Loves the infinite   D 119, 105, 116,
Health is sound relation to externals ⟨D 126⟩
Abstract truth practical. D 136,
A vice is only an exaggeration of a necessary & virtuous function [154]
Love of law   D 141
Effect of the paragraph proportioned to depth   D 141 [155]

---

p. [118], are used in "The Protest," *Lectures*, III, 101 and 102, and 95; the first was used later in "Spiritual Laws," *W*, II, 151, and the second may also have been used in "The School"; see *Lectures*, III, 404(notes). A paragraph in D, p. [112], was used in "Love," *Lectures*, III, 67. D, p. [93], was used later in "Self-Reliance," *W*, II, 48–49.

[151] A paragraph on "Impersonality" in Journal D, p. [94], is used in "The School," *Lectures*, III, 43, and "The Over-Soul," *W*, II, 277. "The Vast an element" is a repeated theme in lectures of 1838–1840; cf. "Doctrine of the Soul," The Present Age: "Introductory," "Politics," and "Education," *Lectures*, III, 8–9, 196, 242–243, and 287 and 291; the paragraph in D, p. [143], is also used in "Self-Reliance," *W*, II, 61.

[152] This line is struck through in pencil with a diagonal use mark. The passage cited is used in the lecture "Duty" (ms. Houghton Library).

[153] All three passages on "Nomads" are used in "History," *W*, II, 22–23. "A man . . . yours" is struck through in pencil with a diagonal use mark; both passages, a paragraph copied in Notebook Man, p. [116] above, from B, p. [228], and the paragraph in D, p. [111], are used in "Home," *Lectures*, III, 32.

[154] The paragraph in Journal D, p. [112], is used in "Love," *Lectures*, III, 67. There are two paragraphs on "Bashfulness" in D, p. [114]; the first is used in "Education," *Lectures*, III, 295, and "Self-Reliance," *W*, II, 48, the second in "Friendship," *W*, II, 200. A sentence in D, p. [126], is used in "Tragedy," *Lectures*, III, 106. "A vice . . . function" (D, p. [138]) is struck through in pencil with a diagonal use mark.

[155] This line is struck through in pencil with a diagonal use mark; both passages cited in Journal D, p. [141], are used in "Duty," *Lectures*, III, 145 and 146; the second is also in "Spiritual Laws," *W*, II, 153.

Augury D 143
Persons D 143, B 200
Aspect of facts D 144.   As a man thinketh so is he.
Succession, division, parts, D 152,
The Man Magazine C 57, 70, 260, D 1, 10, C 293, A 126,
Courage [of 2 o'clock A.M. C.299] C 15, 348, 145, Φ.158, D 240 [156]
Inspiration B 113, 109
Hope [D] 199 [157]
[49] Man a selector, a choice, B 125, 98, C 187, D 68, 234, [158]
Otherism or Reference C 238 D 92, 101, 187, 68, 11,
Man the least part of himself C 26. [159]
Animal spirits D 98, 141
ONE MIND D 162, 79, 83, 94, 160,   C 63, 145, 312 [160]
Blind side of great men (Bacon's nonsense B 105) 53 Φ 161f
Magic of learning languages A 64
Character not ephemeral but cumulative
Convertibleness of every man. B 86,
We are screened from premature ideas B 255, D 195,
Earnestness B 61, C 293

[156] The paragraph on "Persons" in Journal D, p. [143], is used in "Politics," *Lectures*, III, 242–243, and "Self-Reliance," *W*, II, 61. "As a man . . . is he." is used in "The School," *Lectures*, III, 36. Emerson used the paragraph in D, p. [152], later in "Religion," *Lectures*, III, 280 and 284, and "The Over-Soul," *W*, II, 269. With "The Man Magazine", cf. "Doctrine of the Soul," *Lectures*, III, 11–13, which includes passages in D, pp. [1] and [10]. Of the four quotations on p. [158] below, one is used in "Duty" and another in "The School," *Lectures*, III, 149 and 41. The paragraph in D, p. [240], is used in "Tragedy," *Lectures*, III, 113–114.

[157] "Inspiration" is set off by two vertical lines in pencil in the left margin; the paragraph in Journal B, p. [113], is used in "The School," *Lectures*, III, 36; with B, p. [109], cf. also "Genius," *Lectures*, III, 76. The sentence on "Hope" in D, p. [199], is used in both "Duty," *Lectures*, III, 143, and "Self-Reliance," *W*, II, 69.

[158] Passages in Journal B, pp. [125] and [98], and D, pp. [68] and [234], are used in "The School," *Lectures*, III, 36–38, and "Spiritual Laws," *W*, II, 133 and 144–145.

[159] One sentence on "Otherism" in Journal D, p. [11], is used in "Love," *Lectures*, III, 54. "Man the . . . himself", struck through in pencil with a diagonal use mark, is used in "Doctrine of the Soul," *Lectures*, III, 16.

[160] Paragraphs in Journal D, p. [94], and C, p. [63], are used in "The School," *Lectures*, III, 43 and 40; the first is also in "The Over-Soul," *W*, II, 277. The paragraph in D, p. [160], is used in "Home," *Lectures*, III, 30, and partly in "History," *W*, II, 11.

Faces   C 138   D 9, 31, 98, 97, 104, 145, 187,[161]
Melancholy   D 95, 11, 103
Tone (of mind) D 231
Power of recurring to the sublime   C 318
Manners   C 324
Consonancy of a man with himself   B 216[162]
Size of great men   B 121
Hatred. C 344

[50]   LIFE[163]
Nonsense of men also educates them   N 83
⟨Riemer ⟨th⟩counts Goethe's virtuous actions⟩ N 79, E 51, ↑Character
                                                                p 47↓[164]

War, said Archidamus, cannot be kept at a set diet. [G 97]
Our faculties warrant inceptions only   D 191
Double consciousness in our biography   G 15
Asiatic sentences resemble life   G 16
Great success to begin like a fool & slip up   G 48
Genius takes 3 steps or 4   G 109
Today always trivial   E 192, 258
Game of life   H 48, 49,
We can seldom strike a direct stroke   J 20
World does not drop like a ripe peach   G 43 ⟨J 62⟩

---

[161] With "Character . . . cumulative", cf. Journal Q, p. [25], "Duty," and "Tendencies," *Lectures*, III, 144 and 311, and "Self-Reliance," *W*, II, 59. The sentence in B, p. [86], is used in "The School," *Lectures*, III, 35. C, p. [293], is partly in "Self-Reliance," *W*, II, 51. Passages on "Faces" in C, p. [138], and D, pp. [98] and [97], are used in both "Tendencies," *Lectures*, III, 309–310, and "Self-Reliance," *W*, II, 55 and 56; the passage in D, p. [9], is used in "Comedy," *Lectures*, III, 121–122; the paragraph in D, p. [187], is in "Love," *W*, II, 178–179, but not in the lecture.

[162] Passages on "Melancholy" in Journal D, pp. [95] and [11], are used in "Love," *Lectures*, III, 54–55; the passage in D, p. [103], is used in "Tragedy," *Lectures*, III, 104. The paragraph on "Tone" in D, p. [231], is used in "Doctrine of the Soul," *Lectures*, III, 20, and "The Over-Soul," *W*, II, 286–287. The passage in B, p. [216], the "quincunx" simile, is used in "Demonology," *Lectures*, III, 156, as well as several later lectures and essays.

[163] "LIFE" was probably Emerson's working title for "Experience," *W*, III, 43–86; see Index Minor, pp. [45]–[48] and [132]–[133] below.

[164] "Character p 47" is added in pencil; see p. [38] above.

⟨Hard drivers J.Q A, Trelawney &c H.48⟩   Grief   J 62
You shall have power, *Or* joy.   N.112
The Music Box   N 11 [9]
You must either lay to ↑more↓ labor, or whet the knife   N 20
The world never speaks of crime so lightly as it thinks.
Life in the middle zone   K 4, 131, N 90, D 126,
Life headlong, but the moment is all. K 14, 19, G 106   J 102
Life advertisement of faculty   H 49,
We shed our contritions   F 97,
Friends are expedients like stoves   F 108
Every promise of the soul has 20 000 fulfilments   F 112
↑Believe↓ Rule not exception   G 58
Universe our bride   G 74 [165]

[50a] [166] As I am so I see   G 128
Use what language we will we can never say anything but what we are.
Roads of life   J 129
Greatest genius like a geologist in my farm   J 131
We can only dispose of our own facts   N 24
Crime ⟨R⟩N 41, 49   N 122
All nonsense educative   N 83
We cannot spare the coarsest guard of Virtue   N 101
The chief art to give stuff & marrow to the world is *fidelity*.
World does not drop like a peach
Culture ends in headache   R 101, 109

———

Experience therefore indispensable.[167]

[165] The passages cited in Journal N, p. [83], "The world . . . thinks.", K, pp. [4] and [131]–[132], N, p. [90], H, p. [49], "Believe . . . exception", and G, p. [74], are used in "Experience," *W*, III, 57–58, 78, 62, 63–64, 62–63, 73, 74, and 77; with E, pp. [192] and [258], cf. *ibid.*, p. 46. The passages cited in N, p. [79], E, p. [51], and K, p. [14], are used in "Character," *W*, III, 103–104 and 113. Part of H, p. [48], is used in "New England Reformers," *W*, III, 274.

[166] Emerson jotted these notes for "Experience" on the back of a letter enclosure, stuck to p. [51] by its own sealing wax; see p. 270 above.

[167] "As I am . . . we are.", "Greatest genius . . . J 131", "We can . . . N 24", "All nonsense . . . N 83", "The chief . . . peach", and "Culture ends . . . 109" are struck through in ink with single vertical use marks. "Crime N 41, 49 122" is in pencil, overwritten in ink by "R 41" and "N 122". "We cannot . . . N 101" is

But all is musty again without Idea.

[51]   ART
||Etru||scan vase of the sky   D 40
||Lao||cöon [168] C 170
Idealizing   D 63, 67, C 341, D 80
Pictures   D 2, 63, 88, C 29
Phidias's Friezes   C 124, D ⟨1⟨8⟩9⟩ 19,
Head subordinates   D 70
Architecture   D 80, 83, B 255, E 136,
Nach Falconet   Z 27
Plotinus   C 53,
Eloquence   C 145, D 72, 171,
Drawing   C 251, D 211,
Artist at expense of Man   D 213
The price of the picture shows how false is our state; far from ideal
                                                 power. D 56   238

l'Abandon   C 292
Proportion Σ^n 12,
Retzch   C 29
My European lessons   D 332
Raphael   E 79   (Heliodorus) D 64,
Durer's pencil   D 275
Allston's Sisters   D 257
G. S. Newton   D 246
Brant's head   D 257 [169]

---

in pencil. "As I am . . . we are." and the passages cited in Journal J, p. [131], N, pp. [41], [49], [122], and [83], are used in "Experience," W, III, 80, 79, and 57–58; with R, p. [101], and "Experience . . . indispensable.", cf. *ibid.*, pp. 54 and 67.

[168] This and the word above it are obscured by the sealing wax on the insert printed as p. [50a] above.

[169] "Art" is listed among possible topics for the "Human Life" lecture series on pp. [166] and [167] below. "C 145, . . . D 211," is struck through in pencil with a zigzag line that may be either use mark or cancellation. The passages cited in Journal D, pp. [88] and [19], B, p. [255], C, pp. [145] and [251], and D, pp. [211] and [56], are used in "Genius," *Lectures*, III, 73 and 413(notes), 80, 77, 83, 74, and 78–79; passages cited in D, pp. [88] and [332], are used in "Art," and C, p. [251], and D, p. [211], in "Intellect," W, II, 351–352 and 360–362, and 337.

No property in Art   E 72
Chance pictures   D 326
Dark pictures   D 327
Guido   E 79
Rogers' Italy   D 272
[52] Drums for pillars   G 8
Architect throws up his reason when he builds a meetinghouse G 4⟨8⟩9
Blue sky for background makes the fine building   G 49
Art & artist   Z 15⟨2⟩3, 4,[170]
American Artist should make a different woodgod from Italian C 137

[53] [blank]
[54]   Society
Community advantage of seeing friends   H 30   J 84
Rowdies & paddies make law   H 75   N 42
Two liberties   J 33
Use of bores   J 77
Wilhelm Meister   J 90
In cities, surface   K 15
Phalanx   K 46, 90, 50, N 127   E 353
G[eorge]. R[ipley].   K 49, 85, G 116, E 238
Meeting of gentlemen   K 96½   .
We are bound to gentilize society   K 126
Society a delicate result   N 111, 121, 127
Olympians meet to exchange snuff boxes. N 111   ↑Silence rather↓
Society should be shower of rockets   N 113
Hospitality, thing of fate   N 127.
No persons could live together on their merits   G 34
Monastery & convent did not quite fail   E 207
I have pleasure in coming near   G 28

Passages in D, pp. [56] and [238], are used in "The School," C, p. [124], and D, p. [213], in "The Protest," and D, pp. [70] and [64], in "Comedy," *Lectures*, III, 45, 92 and 93, and 133–134. Passages cited in D, pp. [67] and [257], and C, p. [341], are used in "History," and C, p. [292], in the lecture "Duty" (ms. Houghton Library) and "Spiritual Laws," *W*, II, 16 and 18–20, and 141–142.
[170] "Blue sky . . . building" is used in "Nature," and one sentence in Journal Z[A], pp. [154]–[153], in "Experience," *W*, III, 174 and 67.

Orphic problem of Communities   E 353 [171]

[55]   SOCIETY [172]
Speech indicates difference   D 69, 72, 79, 152,
Sympathy   D 69, 70, C 191   D 31, 98, 126, 149, 61, 225,
False Society   D 77, 89, 192 [173] C 271
False persons. false position   D 79
Man, wife, & son. D 85 — 102, 105, M 116,
Antagonisms   D 87, 153, 98, A 52, D 241,
Within society is solitude   D 94, 138 [174]
Conversation   B 23, 24, C 60, 254, 280, D 13, 15, 147,
Benefit of Society   B 48, D 149   190, 166, [175]
A cheerful face makes society   D 97 [176]
A disinclination to society will keep out more visiters than a good
bolt. [D 100]

[171] Notes on p. [54] and the lower part of p. [56] below are 1842 additions to the notes headed "Society" on pp. [55]–[56] below. "Hospitality, thing . . . N 127." and "Orphic problem . . . E 353" are marked in the left margin with short double vertical pencil lines. The paragraph in Journal K, p. [90], is used in "The Young American," W, I, 382–383. The passages cited in K, p. [50], and N, p. [127] ("Phalanx"), are used in "New England Reformers," W, III, 264–265 and 267.

[172] "Society" is listed among possible topics for the "Human Life" lecture series on p. [167] below. Passages listed in the collection on p. [55] and the first six lines of p. [56] are used in several lectures in the series, four each in "Duty," "The School," and "The Protest," three in "Doctrine of the Soul," two each in "Home" and "Genius," and one in "Tragedy."

[173] The paragraph in Journal D, p. [149], is used in "Duty," Lectures, III, 144–145. Passages in D, pp. [61] and [192], are used in "The Protest," Lectures, III, 96 and 95. The first paragraph in D, p. [225], is used in "Doctrine of the Soul," Lectures, III, 18–19.

[174] The passages cited in Journal D, p. [102], and Notebook Man, p. [116] above, are used in "Home," Lectures, III, 32–33. The passage in D, p. [87], is expanded, and the paragraph in D, p. [138], used in "The Protest," Lectures, III, 101 and 102, and 96. The last paragraph in D, p. [94], is used in "The School," Lectures, III, 43.

[175] The passages cited in Journal D, pp. [147] and [166], are used in "The School," Lectures, III, 43 (see also notes, p. 404) and 42. One sentence in D, p. [190], is used in "Doctrine of the Soul," Lectures, III, 16.

[176] This entry is marked in the left margin with two short vertical pencil lines; this and other markings on p. [55], similar to those on pp. [54] above and [56] below, may have been added in 1842. The passage cited in Journal D, p. [97], is used in "Culture," W, VI, 159.

Natural affection is Opportunity   D 102
⟨Stranger   D 104, 107, 110⟩
⟨Intelligence the strongest bond   D 126⟩, C 33,
Nature will have society   D 135
⟨Tender ruffians   D 136⟩
The best of society is the fruit of solitude   D 138, 141
Provoke virtue   D 149,[177]
Society a compromise   D 153,[178]
Do not degrade yourself to society   D 153, 208,
We do not love him who gives thoughts   C.156, 283,
Law of Hospitality   B 124
Faneuil Hall   C 227, 306,
Solitude of the heartless   A 114
Mutual Instruction   C 192 [179]
Our sympathy with men of genius affects our view of nature   B 16,[180]
⟨The foolish face of praise⟩ C 138
[56] Soirees   C 220, D 186, 192
Rotten ripe   D 224
True society Jove to Jove   D 206, 208, Σ^n 13,
        Chimborazo   B 228
Visits   B 16, 124 [181]
Superlatives   B 98

Mutual gravitation   G 61
Persians & Dorians   Li 166

[177] One sentence in Journal D, p. [107], is used in "Tragedy," *Lectures*, III, 106. The passages cited in C, p. [33], and D, pp. [136], [141], and [149], are used in "Duty," *Lectures*, III, 146, 147, 146, and 144–145.

[178] This entry is marked in the left margin with a short vertical pencil line; the passage cited is used in "Friendship," *W*, II, 199.

[179] Part of the passage in Journal D, p. [208], is used in "Doctrine of the Soul," and one phrase also in "The Protest," *Lectures*, III, 19 and 96. "Law of Hospitality B 124" is marked in the left margin with a question mark and a short vertical line in pencil. Parts of the passage cited in C, pp. [227]–[228], are used in "Genius," *Lectures*, III, 83. Part of the passage cited in C, p. [192], is used in "The School," *Lectures*, III, 42.

[180] This entry is marked in the left margin with a short diagonal line in ink; the paragraph cited is used in "Genius," *Lectures*, III, 82.

[181] This entry is in pencil. See p. [55] above for D, pp. [192] and [208], which are repeated.

Few as I have seen I could do with fewer   H 128
We ask all things of society   J 10
You shall not accept any man's person   J 82   K 6
Every man baulks expectation   J 82   G 166, 151
Sane & insane   J 124
Grand is a good understanding betwixt two   J 84
Come ever so near men so there be bounds   J 84
Whitewashing   G 88   K 46
Gods are to each other not unknown [J 95]
Objections to phalanxes   K 60, 85, 46, 90, 50,
Impossibility of intercourse   H.71
The Community   H.30   J 84   E 238 [182]
You should never ask what I can do   K 70
Perfect Eloquence   D 72
Th

[57]   Private Life
Gifts   J 9, 11, N 39, 79,
We have never seen a man K 99, 121   Divine persons K 52, 53, 23,
Institution must be in Institutor [K 85]   E 238
Community, advantage of seeing friends   H 30   J 84, K 46, 90,
Bores   J 77
⟨I⟩Sculpture good for calm manners   N 41, 48,
Boy; Mrs Wells verses   E.201
Work! paid or unpaid   J 138   G 43
Grand is the good understanding betwixt two   J 84   72
The good Aunt   D 115
Subjects of greek gems   D 356, E 299,
⟨My house is here for the culture of the county⟩ K 126
City & Country life: Temperance Rus ruris   N 87
Wilhelm Meister   J 90
Come ever so near men, so there be bounds   J 84
Gold represents labor but labor is higher   J 140

---

[182] "Gods are . . . unknown" and "The Community . . . E 238" are marked
in the left margin with double vertical pencil lines; "Objections to . . . 50," is
marked in the left margin with a question mark and a single vertical pencil line.
See p. [54] above for repeated entries.

Babe not disconcerted   K 96½
Sunset wanted men   E 332
Mr C & his Boston house   E 339
⟨We owe men behaviour & we offer money⟩ E 331½
Marriage   N 112
Books are false: Morality always rare & commanding at N. *Orleans*[n]
↑G 26↓ & at Calcutta: Can you not read a little more proudly?

Domesticated by virtue
My facts & yours. I a /party/*cause*/ to my misfortunes   N 24
Moment   K 14,[183] 19   G 106   J 102
[58][184] Anecdotes about trifles shows each should make his own   J 138
In cities, surface   K 15
Do not live for show nor expectation   K 49, 85,
As life ⟨ca⟩comes to nature, thought to truth   K 55
Our vocation. You should not ask what I can do   K 70
⟨Carpenter's cord   K⟩ 114
Magic real   N 31

[59]   History [185]
Ancient Egyptian cultivation   D 81
Negro   D 82, 118, 125, 133   C 245, C 24, M 9,
History   D 85, C 349
Until history is interesting it is not yet written. [D 61] See D 130
The Antique   C 19
Ancient objectiveness   B 297, 107,

---

[183] Lines 4, 5, 12, and 20 on p. [57] are marked in the left margin with short double vertical pencil lines; a penciled question mark has been added to the last. "Moment . . . J 102" is in pencil. The passages cited in Journal J, pp. [9] and [11], and N, p. [39], are used in "Gifts," *W*, III, 162–163 and 159–161. The passages cited in N, p. [79], K, pp. [99], [85], and [14], and "Divine persons" are used in "Character," *W*, III, 103–104, 113–114, 101, and 108. The paragraph in K, p. [90], is used in "The Young American," *W*, I, 382–383. The paragraph cited in J, p. [138], is used in "New England Reformers," *W*, III, 283. The passage cited in E, p. [332], is used in "Nature," *W*, III, 178.

[184] P. [58] is in pencil. The sentence cited in Journal K, p. [114], is used in "The Poet," *W*, III, 13.

[185] "History" is listed on p. [167] below among possible topics for the "Human Life" lecture series, but only six of the passages listed below were used in that series; five were used later in the essay "History," and two in the essay "Manners."

Philosophy of History   D 129
Commerce of the Desert   D 133, 135, Σ 18,
Ancient Oriental education   D 138
Gournou   D 147,
Chinese & English   C 171
Caricatures are history, C.329.
Slavery   C 245, 24, M 9,
American pomp negro fine   C 173
Sacs & Foxes   C 209
France   C 44
The Trilobite is the beginning of History
Savages   C 15
The Irishman's country is a wheelbarrow [A 116, B 280]
Mountaineers
Melancholy of the Saxon mind   B 117, D 11, 103,
Pius VII's repeal of edicts against the Copernican system   B 280
The Past   C 287, D 30,
Clarendon de Falkland   C 105
History should awaken such emotion as the landscape does   D 130
Nomads   D 67, 111, 112, 127,
Real history is the Miltonic sketch of London. *Prose Works Vol. 2*
p. 60 & 63[186]

[60] The Fall of Man   C 135[187]

[61]   Transcendentalism
Transcendentalism   J 25
Nature & literature subjective phenomena   E 337
Poet disposes of facts very fast   N 46, 75, 23,   E 331

---

[186] *A Selection from the English Prose Works of John Milton*, ed. Jenks, 2 vols. (Boston, 1826). Passages cited in Journal B, p. [117], and D, p. [103], are used in "Tragedy," *Lectures*, III, 104; D, p. [11], in "Love," *Lectures*, III, 54; C, p. [287], in "The Protest," *Lectures*, III, 97; and C, p. [105], and the quotation from Milton in "Doctrine of the Soul," *Lectures*, III, 8 and 7. Passages in C, p. [349], and D, pp. [67], [111], [112], and [127], were used later in "History," *W*, II, 9 and 21–23. Passages in D, pp. [125] and [147], were used in "Manners," *W*, III, 119–120. "History should . . . D 130" is in pencil; the passage cited was used in "Literature" [second lecture], *Lectures*, III, 227–228.

[187] This entry may be a continuation of the notes headed "History". With the passage cited, cf. "The Protest," *Lectures*, III, 86.

Good men must not obey the laws too well   J 112
Genius unsettles everything   G 56
Time inverse measure of spirit   G 140
Corporal Spohn true   N 90
Divinity behind prayer & pottage   saint & city   N 83
Try Olympian experiments   N 85   Criticism   E 334
Osman & Schill   G 1, 48, 110, 112,
Our force ubiquitous   J 79 [78] [188]
J. and Calvinism   R [85]
Transcendental criticism   E 334, N 38, 43
Buddhism   E 353
Egotism of spiritualists   E 125 [189]

[62] [blank]
[63]   CONDITION [190]
Condition   C 248, 261, 281, 287, 294, 308   D 100, 138, B 28

Riches   C 281   D 100, 155, ⟨D⟩138
The active happy. Napoleon gaped.
A man out of place is a dangler [C 219]
Places   C 202
Charm of property, C 63
Every one has a trust of power   B 214
Uses of distinction   C 311,[191]

---

[188] "Try Olympian . . . N 85" is marked in the left margin with a short vertical pencil line; "Criticism E 334" may have been added. The passages cited in Journal E, p. [337], N, p. [83], and J, p. [79], are used in "Experience," *W*, III, 50, 57–58, and 74–75. The passages cited in N, pp. [46] and [75], are used in "The Poet," and J, p. [112], in "New England Reformers," *W*, III, 18–19 and 280.

[189] "Buddhism E 353", added in a larger hand, is used in "Domestic Life," *W*, VII, 124. "Egotism of . . . E 125" is added in pencil.

[190] "Condition" is listed among possible titles for the "Human Life" lecture series on pp. [46] above and [167] below; the topic is treated briefly in "The School," *Lectures*, III, 34 and 40–41, but Emerson had planned to expand it in a lecture following "Duty"; see *Lectures*, III, 170. Passages listed on this page are used in seven lectures in the series, at least six in "Tragedy," three each in "The School" and "The Protest," two in "Duty," and one each in "Home," "Love," and "Demonology."

[191] Passages cited in Journal C, pp. [281] and [294], and B, p. [28], are used in "Tragedy," *Lectures*, III, 107–108 and 104; with the paragraph in D, p. [100], cf. "Tragedy," *Lectures*, III, 108. Passages in C, pp. [287] and [258]("Napoleon

Housekeeping   D 108, 19,[192]
Man should know how to plant or fish   D 137
Garden   D 35, 55, 108,
The first men had no glory   C 317, D 213,
The child & the snow   B 292
The Golden mean, Θ.73   C 237
Tragedy of common life   B 16   C 166   D 48, 79, 95, 152, ↑174,↓
                               Θ 101   D 225

Destiny. Σ 1,[193] C 168, D 196,
Mountaineers   Z
Tombs   C 97, 177, 190
Anniversaries   C 320
Genius always situated alike   C 3
G. Minot, the Wise Limitation   D 11,
Power of recurring to the sublime   C 318
A man responsible for his condition   N 22 [194]

[64]   Spiritualism
                    ↑[See Religion p 164]↓ [195]
Why answer catechism in Words when the fact ⟨is omnipresent⟩ to be
     translated is omnipresent? N 34
Shaker Faith   N 71
Mary Rotch   N 105
Mutual Gravitation   G 61
         When each the other shall avoid,

---

gaped."), are used in "The Protest," passages in C, p. [63], and B, p. [214], in "The School," and a passage in C, p. [311], in "Duty," *Lectures*, III, 97, 89, 40, and 139.

[192] This entry is set off by two short vertical pencil lines in the left margin; most of the paragraph in Journal D, p. [108], is used in "Home," *Lectures*, III, 24–25.

[193] The passage in Journal C, p. [317], is used in "Duty," and part of the paragraph in D, p. [213], in "The Protest," *Lectures*, III, 138–139, and 92 and 93. For "Θ", see p. [14] above. The last eight lines in C, p. [237], are used in "The School," *Lectures*, III, 49–50. Passages in C, p. [166], and D, pp. [48] and [174], are used in "Tragedy," *Lectures*, III, 104, 107, and 108. The passage cited in D, p. [95], is used in "Love," *Lectures*, III, 54–55. The story of Masollam the Jew in Notebook Σ, pp. [1]–[2], is used in "Demonology," *Lectures*, III, 159–160.

[194] This entry was probably added in 1842.

[195] See p. [164] below.

Shall each by each be most enjoyed.

["The Celestial Love," ll. 97–98; G 61]

Men not pious but lovers of the pious. N 72, E 330½

Lecture on George Fox [196]

Here or nowhere the whole fact   J 108

Mrs Black   K 97½

Jones Very   D 168, 185, 230, 177, 316, 322, N 123,

I am not ashamed that I am ashamed. [K 118]

After all our accumulation of facts we are just as poor in thought Z 3

Time an inverse measure of spirit   G 140

Moment is all in all noble relations   K 14, 19   G 106   J 102

We believe in ecstasy   K 53

You are not good enough to be a Reformer   J 139

Swedenborgianism Manicheeism   D 148

Literature of Spirit   D 188

Life in the spiritual trance   D 322

⟨Fox & Beh⟨e⟩men & Swed. do not complain⟩ of not being admitted to

Ch[urc]h. D 346 [197]

Ecstasy   E 253 ↑257↓   Blessed they who have no powers. [E 252]

Boldness, yes, but whence boldness? K 122

[65] Mysticism what. N 123

Nonsense of men educates them   N 83

What does not hold the world is forbidden or wrong   K 68

Virtue not to be taught: Pericles. K 69

Spiritual advertisements   H 139

Our force ubiquitous   J 79 [198]

---

[196] See *Lectures*, I, 164–182.

[197] "When each . . . enjoyed." is struck through in ink with a diagonal use mark. "Moment is . . . relations" is marked in the left margin with a short vertical line. The passages cited in Journal G, p. [61], and K, p. [14], are used in "Character," *W*, III, 112 and 113. The passage cited in N, p. [34], is used in "New England Reformers," *W*, III, 282; with D, p. [346], cf. *ibid.*, p. 279. The passages cited in N, pp. [71] and [105], are used in "Discourse at Nantucket," and N, pp. [105] and [123], in "Address at the Second Church"; the passages cited in N, p. [71], and K, pp. [19] and [53], were later used in "Worship," *W*, VI, 237, 234, and 213.

[198] The passage cited in Journal N, p. [123], is used in "The Poet," and N, p. [83], and J, p. [79], in "Experience," *W*, III, 34–35, 57–58, and 74–75.

[66] [blank]

[67]   CULTURE

Culture needs no costly apparatus, C 242   T 19
Which are the Hard Times?
Feeble influence of thought on life   C 319
Bifronted is every master   C 346,
Best persons freest speakers   A 114, B 41, A 39,
⟨C⟩A cheerful face   D 97   Repose, D 195, 90,
Unconscious Culture   C 34 [199]

[68] [blank]

[69]   NATURE [200]
What does the love of Nature show. D 185, 230, C 298
Love of nature rhetorical sometimes   D.196,

Advantage of insusceptible Napoleon temperament   C 313, 348,

A few things suffice   C 307
Animals   C 208
Buds   C 240
Put in a little heat   C 333
May   D 26
Trees   D 58, 142,
Fire   D 218

---

[199] "CULTURE" may have been a trial topic for the "Human Life" lecture
series; the passage cited in Journal C, p. [319], is used in "Duty," the sentence in A,
p. [114], in "Genius," the paragraph in D, p. [90], in "Tragedy," and the paragraph
in C, p. [34], in "Love," *Lectures*, III, 143–144, 81, 112–113, and 59–60.

[200] "Nature" is listed on p. [167] below among possible topics for the "Human
Life" lecture series, and Emerson may have begun p. [69] as a trial collection; the
following page, however, headed "Nature (continued)", was begun not earlier than
June, 1839, at which time Emerson had begun work on the essays published in *Essays
[First Series]*; for evidence that he began an essay on "Nature" for that volume, see
Journal E, p. [174], F No. 2, p. [25], and L, II, 387. He may have drawn on p. [69]
for notes in Notebook Ж, p. [31] below, probably a collection for "Relation of Man
to Nature" (January 13, 1842), the manuscript of which is missing. Emerson evidently
used pp. [69]–[70] again, and added to p. [70], while preparing the essay "Nature,"
W, III, 167–196; see note 203 below.

Heat   D 8, 60,
Night   D 8, C 268, 329,
All growth cotemporary. D 6,
Sun & Moon   C 211
Nature in Memory   D 218
Natural science an asylum   D 202   *A* [48]   D 117
Nature Knowing   D 117
Nature a deist   D 117
The Mushroom   D 113
Significance of Nature   D 142,
Return from Nature to the Actual   D 87
Astronomy sedative   C 287 [201]
The Woods   B 204, 203
Birds   D 218, C 87,

[70]   Nature (continued)
Perception of identity a measure of progress   D 268
Influence of nature   People no better for sun & moon   C 211
Miracles have not ceased in the woods   C 218
Ripening days of September   C 136
Hawks   C 136
⟨Gather apples in sunshine   C 120⟩
   Influence of the city on my personal feeling [202]
   There is a necessity to be beautiful in the landscape   J 125
      Plants are the young of the World   N 45
      Tremendous energies flow through the babe   K 64
      Sunset wanted men   E 332
      Nature interrogates   J 143

[201] "A few . . . C 307", "Sun & Moon C 211", and "Natural science . . . D 117" are in pencil. The passages cited above in Journal D, pp. [185] and [230], and C, p. [298], are used in "The Protest," *Lectures*, III, 98. Passages in C, pp. [348] and [287], and D, pp. [202] and [117], are used in "Tragedy," *Lectures*, III, 115 and 117–118. The couplet in D, p. [26], is used in "Love," and the paragraph in D, p. [142], in "The School," *Lectures*, III, 53 and 41. Passages in D, pp. [185] and [230], [117] and [58], and C, p. [333], are used in "Nature," *W*, III, 178, 186, 181, and 179.
[202] With "Ripening days . . . C 136", cf. "Nature," *W*, III, 169; with "Influence of the . . . feeling", cf. Journal C, p. [136], a sentence used in "Nature," *W*, III, 171.

Flowers jilt us   K 93
Dewey's Report on Botany   K 90
Indian summer   N 108
Nature never cares that the scholar can't express   G 151
Is Nature also Dilettante   G 1
Nature not enjoyable until man finds his completion   E 334
⟨Surprize & casualty are the apples of her eyes⟩. [JK 64]
Nature has no exaggeration   E 333 [203]

[71]   Miscellany
Our meeting house   D 78
Clapping   C 137,
Asylums   D 6, 117, 141, 202, C 318 [204]

[72]   W E C's Poems
H.17
Our poetry like cat bird's   J 86
Ellery   E 343, 342 [205]

[73] [blank]
[74] Horne Tooke [D 144]
Distressing class of reformers   J 115
Conservative   K 22
Pecunia alter sanguis. [N 87]
Good men must not obey the laws   E 42, J 112,
Population of the world conditional   K 57
The state a trick

[203] "Influence of the . . . E 333" was probably added to p. [70] in 1842 while Emerson was preparing the essay "Nature" for *Essays, Second Series*; see Index Minor, pp. [97]–[98] below. "Plants are . . . N 45" is marked in the left margin with three short horizontal ink lines and struck through in ink with a diagonal use mark; "Flowers . . . K 93" is struck through in ink with a diagonal use mark. The passages cited in Journal J, p. [125], N, p. [45], E, p. [332], and K, pp. [93] and [90], are used in "Nature," *W*, III, 176, 181–182, 178, 182, and 172.

[204] Passages in Journal D, pp. [6], [117], and [202], are used in "Tragedy," *Lectures*, III, 117–118.

[205] "Our poetry . . . 342" is in pencil. The sentence cited in Journal H, p. [17], is used in "Character," *W*, III, 105. Part of the paragraph in E, p. [343], is used in "The Poet," *W*, III, 8.

Democracy malignant, not creative   selffed   happy   grim
      Treat Poetically [E 101]
         Idea ↑of↓ state   persons & property [Z[A] 159]
                       Right got done by might
           I think very modestly of any state we have seen[,]
very highly [n] of a few men. Population is contingent, & state is as good
as we can have; but great faith in the necessity of [206]

[75]   Politics

"As if their kingdoms were for them & not they for their kingdoms,"
said Pym
     See also   Δ 63
True Politics   Σ[n] 13,
     The low can best win the low & all people like to be made much of
                                     [B 308]
If America were to be sold today it would fetch more than it did
yesterday
Base Politics   C 318   A 92   B 307, 294   D[n] 142, 144
This country governed in barrooms   E 78 [207]
Rowdies & paddies *rightly* make the law   H 75   N 42
Leaders of great causes cunning   H 89
Parties wish all to be partisans   H 97
Whig & Democrat, today   N.97
Bryant & Bancroft   N 4

---

[206] Notes on p. [74], probably an addition to notes on p. [75] below, may be
for a revision of the 1840 lecture "Politics" for a reading in New York, March 7,
1843; see *Lectures*, III, 238: "Democracy malignant . . . necessity of" is in pencil.
"Good men . . . laws" and "The state a trick" are used in "Politics," *W*, III, 208.
With "Democracy malignant . . . grim", cf. Journal Z[A], pp. [158] and [85],
and "Politics," *W*, III, 209 and 210. The paragraph in E, p. [101], is used in
"Politics," *Lectures*, III, 239–240. With "Idea of state", cf. *ibid.*, p. 246, and, more
fully, "Politics," *W*, III, 212–213. The passage cited in Z[A], p. [159], is used,
ibid., pp. 205, 206, 203, and 204. With "Right got . . . might" and "but great . . .
of", cf. *ibid.*, pp. 220 and 212. "Population is . . . have;" is from K, p. [57].

[207] The notes to this point on p. [75] may have been copied from Notebook Ж,
pp. [83]–[84] below. "The low . . . yesterday" is in pencil. "A 92", in ink, is
written over "A 9" in pencil. The quotation from Luther in Notebook Σ, pp. [13]–
[14], "The low . . . of", and "This country . . . barrooms" are used in "Politics,"
Lectures, III, 246 and 244–245.

"All these people mean to vote right" [N 35]
I expect more from Kendall than Webster   G 54
⟨A⟩Editors wish to call Webster to account   H 49
Sign of public virtue the split of Harrison party   H 49
The pocketing power↑, The Accident,↓ the Target-King, The Paren-
thesis

Rich & Poor   N 42   K 24   D 356
Clare's poor man   K 24   Robin hood   J 1,   Milnes
Whig paternal ⟨J⟩G 26
Hands   S [(Salvage)] 147²⁰⁸
⟨Expect more from a Kendall than from Webster   G 54⟩
Harvest best preserved by selfishness   Z 133
Malthusian   Z 133

[76]   Brook-Farm times.
S. Robbins & the egg. K 7
E Palmer. K 46
Mrs Black. K 97½
Objections to Phalanxes   K 50, 60,
The Institution must be in the Institutor. K 85
Dial. K 13
Socialism, K 49, 50, 60, 85, 90,²⁰⁹ J 84,   ⟨C⟩
Transcendentalism   J 25   Osric, K 19

[77]   The Skeptic   ↑See G 136↓
A good exception is as good as a rule   N 78
We suppose defects organic   D 345
We want More; the gods can't help us   N 38
Skeptical scholars speak the sheriff fair   E 237

---

²⁰⁸ " 'All these . . . right' ", struck through in ink with a diagonal use mark,
is used in "New England Reformers," *W*, III, 279. ", The Accident," is added in
pencil. For the passage on "Hands" in Notebook S (Salvage), p. [147], see "Doctrine
of the Hands," *Lectures*, II, 230–231.
²⁰⁹ The paragraph cited in Journal K, p. [50], is used in "New England Reformers," *W*, III, 264–265; with K, p. [60], cf. *ibid*., p. 264. The paragraph in
K, p. [85], is used in "Character," *W*, III, 101–102. The paragraph in K, p. [90],
is used in "The Young American," *W*, I, 382–383. The passages in K, pp. [60] and
[49], are used in "Life and Letters in New England," *W*, X, 368 and 354.

Kitty & her tail   N 30
Wineglass system   G 113   E 354
Divine persons chuckle   K 52
Preacher is cunning   K 87
Understanding lame & laughable   J 124
Understanding is a Malthusian   E 331½
To wish for war is atheism   K 118
Masses   N 37, J 70   D 281
Panurge, N 104   Wall street has nothing new   N 104
I curse my visitor at 9 o'clock, said F   N 105
Ed.H[osmer]. Skeptical   N 22
Faith says, I meddle not with others' facts. N 24
Equivocal generation or life from sour paste
⟨t⟩Trilobite is the beginning of history
To wish for war is atheism [K 118]
Men follow success & not skill as in P. J.   N 45 [210]
Vulgar man licentious when he travels   G 26
Skepticism is unbelief in man   H.131   G 135–6
Vast skepticism   G 136,
Undue power of a fact   D 144
Olympian Criticism   E 334
Opinion of President Fontanes   B 300
Skepticism believes ignorance organic   G 136   D 345

[78]   Skeptic (continued)
⟨Paper⟩ ↑inflated↓ currency instantly increases population
        Destiny [211]
                Death

[210] "Kitty & . . . N 30" is struck through in ink with a diagonal use mark; the page cited is used in "Experience," *W*, III, 80. With the passages cited in Journal G, pp. [135]–[136], and D, p. [345], cf. "New England Reformers," *W*, III, 268, 270, and 278. The passage cited in N, p. [22], is used in the lecture "Trade," and N, p. [45], in the lecture "Manners and Customs of New England." The paragraph cited in E, p. [331½], is used in "The Young American," *W*, I, 374. The passage cited in E, p. [237], is developed, and E, p. [354], used in "Discourse at Middlebury College."

[211] "Destiny", in pencil, as is the rest of the page, is overwritten by "⟨Paper⟩ currency", printed above. Emerson probably wrote these notes for the lecture "Tragedy," *Lectures*, III, 103–120, after the collection on p. [79]; more notes and outlines for "Tragedy" follow on pp. [80]–[81].

Disease   Insecurity   Sleep
Poverty; More & Less
Affection crossed
Details or Actual
Parts
↑Woman the victim because affection & Condition↓
     Ter[r]or is the Nemesis & Teacher   D 32   C 324
               protects Woman
               punishes avarice
3 Philosophy   punishes worldness
   Interior life
   See the uses   C 324
   Asylums   Reliefs 2 Nap. Temperam[ent]
   Astronomy [C 287]   3 Philosophy   Asylums
   Interior life   4 Character.   Love,
1 Chee Koong   2 [T 189]   1 Time
   recurrence to the sublime
   Composure [D 90]

   Destiny   Temperament [D 244] society full of sick
      Oedipus   Donne [C 90]
      Kehama   Taste for grief
      Death 212

[79]   Tragedy of Life
"Perfect through suffering"   Hebrews [2:10]
Highest gifts not secure   D 174
Donne's verses   "O how feeble is man's power" [C 90]
Temperament

212 With "Destiny . . . Insecurity" and "Poverty; More & Less", cf. "Tragedy,"
Lectures, III, 105–109. "Teachers D 32" is added to the lecture manuscript; see *Lectures*, III, 431 (notes to p. 116); the paragraph cited in Journal C, p. [324], is used
in "Tragedy," *Lectures*, III, 116; in the left column, "3 Philosophy . . . Astronomy"
lists passages on pp. 114, 118, 116, 117–118, and 117; the quotation from Notebook
T, p. [189], is used on pp. 118–119, "recurrence to yᵉ sublime" developed on p. 115,
and the paragraph in D, p. [90], used on pp. 112–113; in the right column, "Reliefs
. . . 1 Time" lists sections of "Tragedy" on pp. 114, 115, 117–118, 118, 119–120,
and 114; "Destiny . . . Death" and "Temperament . . . grief" outline sections on
pp. 105–106, 108–109, and 110.

Tragedy of genius   C 25
Dull hours instruct masters   C 324
Sleep   C 320
Interior life not melancholy   C 166 [213]
Tragedy of common life   B 16   C 166   D 48, 79, 95, 152, 174, 225
Θ 101 [214]

Melancholy of the Saxon mind   B 117   D 11, 103, 95,[215]
Solitude of the Heartless   A 114
That work agreeable which is not due now   D 68
Man must be in temper & tune   D 77, 92,
Feeble influence of thought on life   C 319 ↑D 226↓ [216]
Insanity   D 61, 73, 166   195
Distribution of pain   C 151 [217]
Woman   C 195   196 ⟨298, 297⟩, ⟨D 7⟩   66, ⟨91⟩, 109, ↑J W↓   ⟨137⟩
⟨236⟩ 79 ↑E P↓ [218]

Flowers   C 40
Asylums   D 6, 117, 141, 202,   Astron. C.287
Farewells of the realist   B 16
Wear the white seam of others' needs   C [327]
The Compensation of disease in "Bell on the Hand" [219] [BB IV[A], 20]

[213] "Highest gifts . . . Temperament" is struck through in pencil with a vertical use mark; the paragraphs cited in Journal D, p. [174], and "Donne's verses" are used in "Tragedy," *Lectures*, III, 108 and 110; the "Temperament" section of the lecture begins on p. 114. "Tragedy of genius . . . C 166" is in pencil. "Dull hours . . . C 324", struck through in pencil with a vertical use mark, and the passage cited in C, p. [166], are used, *ibid.*, pp. 116, 104, and 113.

[214] For "Θ", see p. [14] above. In addition to "C 166", listed above, the passages cited in Journal D, pp. [48] and [174], are used in "Tragedy," *Lectures*, III, 107 and 108.

[215] Passages cited in Journal B, p. [117], and D, p. [103], are used in "Tragedy," *Lectures*, III, 104. The passage cited in D, p. [95], is used in "Love," *Lectures*, III, 54-55.

[216] "D 226" is added in pencil.

[217] This entry is struck through in pencil with a vertical use mark; parts of the paragraph cited are used in "Tragedy," *Lectures*, III, 112 and 114-115.

[218] The use marks or cancellations in this line and "J W", "79", and "E P" are in pencil. Emerson used passages in Journal C, p. [298], and D, pp. [137] and [236], in "Love," *Lectures*, III, 63, 62, and 55-56.

[219] "Asylums" is struck through in pencil with a vertical use mark, and "Astron. C.287", also cited below, is in pencil. Passages in D, pp. [6], [117], and [202], and C, p. [287], are used in "Tragedy," *Lectures*, III, 117-118. "Wear the . . .

Should & Would   B 236
College jubilee 1836   8 Sept   B 227
Dark hours   B 28
Tragedy of details   D 95
Astronomy sedative   C 287
"He knows you not ye heavenly powers." [220] [A 62]

[80] 2 My Private satisfaction opposed by the Laws of the world

3   opposed by vice of others
        [Terror.] Solitude is fearsome because in it the man is dis-
        joined from men; & if he is appropriating & not imparting.
        Society is not because in it he is in some sort joined to the
        universe[.]
        Idleness is terrible for then there is no pledge
        Labor is happy
        Property is timid
        ⟨L⟩Charity is brave
        Too much sympathy with persons is anxious
        The love of beauty thought & virtue are already safe [221]

            And who the fool that does not know
            How bloom & beauty ⟨&⟩come & go
            And how disease & change & sorrow
            May chance today may chance tomorrow
            Unto the merriest of us all [Byron? W 96]

A pathetic thing that we allow men of talents to which we are allied to
go by without heed   D 225

Hand' " is struck through in pencil with a vertical use mark; both passages cited are
used in "Tragedy," *Lectures*, III, 119–120 and 115.

[220] The paragraph in Journal B, p. [28], is used in "Tragedy," *Lectures*, III,
104. "D 95" is in pencil; the passage cited is used in "Love," *Lectures*, III, 54–55.
"Astronomy sedative   C 287", in pencil (see above), and " 'He knows . . . powers.' "
are struck through in pencil with a vertical use mark.

[221] "2 My private . . . already safe" is in pencil; "2 My private . . . world"
is overwritten in ink by "And how . . . merriest" and "3" by "the fact.", printed
below. With "2 My private . . . [Terror.]", cf. sections of "Tragedy," *Lectures*,
III, beginning on pp. 106, 109, and 110; "Solitude is . . . brave" is expanded in
a paragraph, *ibid.*, p. 118.

Sadness is always the comparison of the idea with the fact.
Doubts & perturbations of college boys   D 32

Bitter farewells of the Realist   B 16
C.C.E.'s tragedy. C 15
Tragedy dissection parts particles; therefore the All seen cures. D 152

"I turned from all she bro't to all she could not bring." [222] [C 99]

[81] [223] All tragedy an illusion
It comes never near me
Others always
If a man says "lo! I suffer" he suffers not
An illusion   As it comes it has its supports   soldiers   sailors   ⟨poor,⟩
paupers; the glass bell will support a thousand pds water or iron if
filled with the same

Sickness   D 21

Poverty
Poverty   C 281 ↑Skin↓   D 100, ↑same way as now↓   ⟨138⟩,
⟨155⟩, 48, ↑more & less↓   C ⟨81⟩ ⟨280⟩ 294 ↑farmer↓
Terror, (of death)   of indef. evil; fearsome
Dislocation
Insecurity   D 174
Dis⟨s⟩union   D 225
Tedium

Want — More & less — [D 48]
Advantage of riches in the skin [C 281]
farmer fears not want [C 294]

---

[222] "And who . . . us all", used in "Tragedy," *Lectures*, III, 103–104, is written
partly over pencil notes for "Tragedy" (see the preceding note), but "A pathetic . . .
D 32" is written between lines so that it obscures only the "3" in l. 2, and "Bitter
farewells . . . bring.'" is written after the pencil notes at the bottom of the page.
Emerson used the paragraph cited in Journal D, p. [152], later in "Religion," *Lectures*, III, 280 and 284, and partly in "The Over-Soul," *W*, II, 269.
[223] P. [81] is in pencil.

Strong man does the same as now [224] [D 100]

[82]   *Swedenborg*
His interlocutors ⟨speak⟩ Swedborg⟨e⟩ise [K 70]
Shakspeare & S. / K 83, D 95
Talk with S Reed   J 108
Modern Xy is trade in mummy   K 116
We conceive of Milton & Goethe as *great*   E 331½
All religions an excess of the organ of language   N
Nature at first & at second hand
Flowers are *our* poetry, not shittim wood   K 94

You shall not accept any man's person   J 82   K 6, E 293
Swedenborgianess   J 81

Marriage   H.33, 34, 84   J 111, E 331½, 340 [225]

[83]   ⟨Progress⟩
⟨The ⁿ simple Great   D 172   179   235⟩ [226]

[84] [227]   *Oct 1839*
Is it necessary as you suppose to govern so much[?]
Is it necessary that Men should have your precious example at
Church[,] at Elections & so forth?

[224] "All tragedy . . . the same" is expanded in "Tragedy," *Lectures*, III, 111.
The passages cited in Journal D, p. [21], C, p. [281], D, p. [48], C, pp. [280] and
[294], and D, p. [174], are used in "Tragedy," *Lectures*, III, 106–108; with the
passage in D, p. [100], cf. *ibid.*, p. 108, and with "Terror . . . Dislocation", cf.
ibid., pp. 108–109 and 110; "Want — More . . . now" outlines a section on pp.
107–108.
[225] The passages cited in Journal K, pp. [70] and [83], are used in the lecture
"Recent Literary and Spiritual Influences." Part of the paragraph in J, p. [108], is
used in "New England Reformers," *W*, III, 278. The passages in K, pp. [70], [83],
and [94], and J, p. [108], were later used in "Swedenborg," *W*, IV, 133–134, 94,
135–136, and 138. "You shall . . . 340", near the bottom of the page, may have
been added at another time; the passages cited in K, pp. [6]–[7], E, p. [293], and
H, p. [33], were used in "Nominalist and Realist," and E, p. [340], in "Experience,"
W, III, 227, 241, and 77.
[226] "Progress . . . 235" is heavily canceled.
[227] P. [84], in pencil, is indexed "New Subjects" on the front cover verso above.

Consider that this Establishment which you deem so needful to their sensuous pupilage will always form itself around such novices in nature. Therefore, you need not vamp it up.

Then Consider that you cannot with impunity contribute your example & vote to these paper hangings you call Church & State. Every tie pulls you down & now you are not a man but a church-warden[.]

[85]   Poet [228]

Altered Form

Nature's care for securing the agaric & the poem

Poet representative
Not Homer nor Hafiz but Man. It has the breadth of a universal problem

What first appears is that the poet is fanciful,   then imaginative; or, has a talent of using symbolical language

Wonderful effects of symbols
Singular liberating power of symbols: a wand to make skip & run about happy.
I think nothing valuable except the liberating.
Poets are free   & freemaking [229]
Effects of images
Examples of tropes

[228] Pp. [85]–[99] are apparently notes for "The Poet," *W*, III, 1–42, on which Emerson was working in November, 1843 (see Journal U, p. [90]), though notes on p. [97] may have been added later. Journal passages cited on p. [95] are later than the lecture "The Poet" (*Lectures*, III, 347–365), though outlines and some passages are evidently drawn from the lecture. Some passages went into "Poetry and Imagination," *W*, VIII, 1–75, possibly by way of other lectures.

[229] "Nature's care . . . poem" (Journal D, p. [123], and "Genius," *Lectures*, III, 74–75) and "Singular liberating . . . freemaking" are used in "The Poet," *W*, III, 22–24, 30, and 32. "Altered Form" and "Poet representative . . . symbols" are developed in sections of both lecture and essay; cf. "The Poet," *Lectures*, III, 354–357 and 352, and "The Poet," *W*, III, 3–6 and 13.

Language is fossil tropes
Poet is a Namer or language Maker [230] ↑printed↓

But this is done *fatally* not autocratically
i.e. The opaque is ⟨c⟩transparent to him & he makes [86] it
transparent to us; then we see things in true series & pro-
cession
Imagination is Sight
Rareness of Imagination
Power in the world of the Imagination

As a man's life is true, his mind comes into paralellism [n] with natural
laws, & he symbolizes

> How this stands in nature,
>   Body from soul,
>   Form from character,
>   Beauty from virtue,
>   Condition from quality,
>   Harmony from health,
>   [Spenser]

Swedenborg [231]

―――

All my /works/acts/ which I understand not are symbolic.

―――

Your employment is the fable of You.

―――

Ah what a Rhetoric is that of Things!

―――

Poet speaks by means of trifles a grave sense
(as Wordsworth's skating piece)

[230] With "Effects . . . of tropes", cf. "The Poet," *Lectures*, III, 352–353, and
"The Poet," *W*, III, 30–31. "Language is . . . tropes" is struck through in ink with
six diagonal use marks, "Poet is . . . Maker" with three, and both lines with another;
both are used in "The Poet," *W*, III, 22, 7, and 21.

[231] With "The opaque . . . procession", cf. "The Poet," *W*, III, 20. "Imagina-
tion is . . . health," is developed, and the lines from Spenser used, *ibid.*, pp. 26–28,
13, and 14. Swedenborg is discussed in both lecture and essay; cf. "The Poet," *Lec-
tures*, III, 361 and 513(notes), and "The Poet," *W*, III, 32 and 35–36.

A few symbols suffice, since each can be used with more simplicity
[E 170]

⟨Even the ⟨low &⟩ base, as, *Circumcision*.⟩ [232] [E 76]

[87] ————

The Charm of Nature for all men, elegant & coarse, lords & hunters & fishers, must be of this kind

————

Ineffable

————

animals
physics; nat. phil;

————

Inexhaustible

————

Every word millionfaced

This power in Nature because this Fate is in Nature. It so affects because it so is. All that is wondrous in Swedenborg[n] is that he was necessitated so to see. The world realizes the Mind. Better than images is seen through them[.]

————

Science an index of selfknowledge [233] [F 2, 163]
Ocean is still a god; fire, earth, sky,

————

Poet writes fable. I read truth

————

Poet must not only symbolize but have somewhat to convey by symbol.

————

Experience with thought, not androgynous. [E 7]

[232] "Your employment . . . You." is used in "Poetry and Imagination," *W*, VIII, 23. "A few symbols . . . *Circumcision*." is used in "The Poet," *W*, III, 17–18.
[233] "The Charm . . . nat. phil;" is developed in "The Poet," *W*, III, 15–16 and 21. "Inexhaustible . . . millionfaced" is used in an addition to "The Poet," *Lectures*, III, 513–514(notes). "This power . . . through them" is used in "Poetry and Imagination," *W*, VIII, 20, but cf. "The Poet," *W*, III, 13, where the thought is developed. "Science an . . . selfknowledge" is used in "The Poet," *W*, III, 15, and "Poetry and Imagination," *W*, VIII, 41.

[88]   Poet

Prolegomena   Poems
                        Popular notions
                   Poet representative
                        The Expressor
              Symbolist
                   Wonderful power of symbols liberating
                        This *secondary* yet eminent
                        Their *primary* power as signs

                        Origin of their power to symbolize, in the fact that
                        Nature is a symbol, or a secondary of the soul.[234]

[89]   Poet
Miscellanea   ⟨P⟩Goethe & every fine genius mocks his judge
——————

        The selection of the Image is no more ⟨one⟩ arbitrary than
the /significance/power/ of the image. The selection ⟨w⟩must follow
Fate.
————

        Cheerfulness of the Poet. All his pains are edged with pleasure
                                                            D 367 [235]

————

                        "Fletcher's wit
              Was not an accident to the soul but it
              Only diffused; thus we the same sun call
              Moving in the sphere & shining on a wall."
                                        E. Powell [D 275]

        Biography of the poet is the catalogue of his works   D 366

————

        [234] "Prolegomena . . . signs" is an outline of "The Poet," *W*, III, 4–34; cf. also
sections on "Poems" and "The Expressor" in "The Poet," beginning in *Lectures*, III,
348. With "Origin of . . . soul.", cf. "The Poet," *W*, III, 13, and "Poetry and
Imagination," *W*, VIII, 15.
        [235] "The selection . . . Fate." and "All his . . . pleasure" are used in "Poetry
and Imagination," *W*, VIII, 20 and 37. With "Cheerfulness of the Poet.", cf. also
"The Poet," *W*, III, 29.

"Artist natures do not weep" Poet draws his revenues from sin & from suffering also. Cheerful & glad   He is the glad man. The Exempt. he knows   that every set sun rises.   & he reads the death of his friend into verse.[236]

[90] The Carpenter's cord if you hold your ear close enough is musical in the breeze. [K 114]

It is well ⟨&⟩said by Taylor in note to Proclus that the infirmities ascribed to the gods, as lameness to Vulcan   blindness to Love   &c express transcendences   [See Proclus in Tim. Vol I, p. 120 [237]

   Nature   in Ж p 33
____

Poetry is "wanton heed & giddy cunning." [K 118]
____

Real words good as real actions   E 226
____

all poems unfinished   H 112
____

Music first before thought   F.55
____

Every word a trope   G 43, 57, 60.[238]
____

Power to affect me in natural objects impersonal & unrepenting. H 45
____

   Every promise many fulfilments   F 112

Perpetual miracle   wonder & rapture   See Lecture [239]

[236] Cf. "The Poet," *Lectures*, III, 357–358.
[237] *The Commentaries of Proclus on the Timaeus of Plato*, trans. Thomas Taylor, 2 vols. (London, 1820); this and the preceding entry, struck through in ink with single vertical use marks, are used in "The Poet," *W*, III, 13 and 18.
[238] Passages in Journal G, pp. [43]–[44] and [57], are used in "The Poet," *Lectures*, III, 352–353, and "The Poet," *W*, III, 18 and 17.
[239] "The Poet," *Lectures*, III, 360.

[91]   Prolegomena

                              Poet representative
                                Expressor
                                Symbolizer
                                        Power of ⟨t⟩symbols to liberate
                                        Power of symbols to symbolize
                                Rejoicer
                              Sanative power of verse antagonistic to
the sepulchral tendencies of Ch. My woods & Flora & not that of
Moses. No fagots. (Salvage p. 20)
        Gold skies I must have. ——

Hilarity of Beauty
Hilarity of metamorphosis
Hilarity of emancipation
        Imagination sees metamorphosis [240]

[92] We sidle towards the problem. If we could speak the direct
solving word, it would solve us too; we should die, or be liberated, as
the gas in the great gas

This hovering unlaid ghost which haunts nature & every piece of
nature, this omnipresent residuum is the magnetic stream which shows
the tendency of things; ↑shows↓ which is *from* & which is *toward*;
shows that soul made body, & not body soul.

        ⟨Pope translated the⟩ Odyssey   Greenough

To Science the world is homogeneous & therefore transparent, ⟨kno⟩
Itself sharing the same ⟨r⟩ path or circuit which things share[,] it finds
its way through them & makes them translucid to others.[241]

Is the cheerfulness of the poet due to his power to emancipate? He is

---

[240] "Poet representative . . . to symbolize" and "Hilarity of Beauty . . . sees
metamorphosis" are developed in "The Poet," *W*, III, 5–37; cf. also "The Poet,"
Lectures, III, 348 and 354.
        [241] "We sidle . . . gas" is struck through in ink with two vertical use marks,
or possibly offset from something laid on the page. With "soul made . . . soul.",
cf. "The Poet," *W*, III, 14. "Itself sharing . . . others." is used, *ibid.*, p. 26.

free[;] [242] he will not come under the power of any; loves Be⟨u⟩auty only, not commodity,[n] [93] not even safety, or any finite well being which Conscience so rapidly lapses to respect.

Homer Chaucer & Shakspeare⎫
Ariosto & Scott↑, Hafiz,↓   ⎭   are not sad.

This is the wine, this freedom, we are slugs & snails half-entombed already, pawing to get free; all partialists, one a brandy-sot, & one an order-sot, or precisian; & one a fact-sot or practical man; date hunter; every one mad with some madness, sot of ⟨one⟩some bottle.[n] This goes to free, to universalize us, it even attacks the excess of the Conscience, & therefore the Church Fathers well & naturally called poetry ⟨W⟩-Vinum daemonum[,] devils' wine, and some ↑abused↓ poetry is; but Poetry is God's Wine.

Cheerfulness of the Poet is the Cheerfulness of Nature ⟨He is tipsy with WATER.⟩

His power is—that he is victim ⟨as well as⟩ ↑that he may be↓ victor, sails with the current, not an offish observer like your scientific spy.[243]

[94] Poet   Poet
        Representative
            Whole man
            Expressor
            Symbolizer
            Emancipator
    The world projects a hand & writes the poem
Symbols.   Hermaphrodite
                Working King
                Magnetic needle ↑which only draws the true metal
                            out of dust & gravel↓
        a Diamond Merchant

[242] Cf. "The Poet," *W*, III, 30–32.
[243] With "devils' wine . . . WATER." and "sails with . . . spy.", cf. "The Poet," *W*, III, 29 and 26.

Poet a seer
     a namer
     an affirmer
     a creator when inebriated by the vinum deorum and then not an-
alysable, creator of the expression. It is his *child*.[244]

[95] I have ‖ ... ‖ written in the newspapers that I am called a
holy man   I ‖ ... ‖ plainest disclaimer to any such life & I am not
holy ‖ ... ‖
The simplicity of which ‖ ... ‖ speak [245]

Poet
     Mysticism   N 123
     Naming   Z 126   N 33
     Earth spirit   Z 109
     Courage of treatment   R 62
     Intoxication   R 64
     Liberation   Z 95
     Midsummer's Night's dream is an affirming   J 17
     Tipsy with water, [R 125$_2$] again   K 16
     Words as good as things   N 10, 128   Sayers.

H.D.T.'s poetry; poetry pre-written; mass a compensation for
                                          quality   N 24
     Literature of Epic & Drama empirical   N 80
     Superiority of Drama   N 80
     Tennyson, &c   E 346 [246]

[244] "Poet", at the left, and "Representative . . . Emancipator", in light pencil,
are developed in "The Poet," *W*, III, 5–30. The centered heading, "Poet", "The
world . . . the poem", and "Poet a seer . . . *child*." are in darker pencil, as is
"Poet . . . E 346" on p. [95] below. "The world . . . poem", "a Diamond Merchant", and "Poet a seer" are used in "Poetry and Imagination," *W*, VIII, 71 and
26. With "Poet a seer", "a namer", and "a creator . . . deorum", cf. "The Poet,"
W, III, 20 and 26, 7 and 21, and 27–29. With "It is his *child*.", cf. "The Poet,"
Lectures, III, 359.

[245] "I have . . . speak", five lines in erased pencil, only partially recovered,
is overwritten by "Tipsy with . . . empirical" below.

[246] Passages cited in Journal N, p. [123], R, pp. [64] and [125$_2$], K, pp.
[16]–[17], N, pp. [10], [128], [24]–[25], and E, p. [346], are used in "The
Poet," *W*, III, 34–35, 26–28, 29, 8, 7, 8, and 8–9.

[96] A bird's nest is a pretty rhyme enough; the love of the birds an idyl; a tempest is rough Tyrtaean ode; a summer with its harvest sown, reaped, & stored, a well proportioned Epic song; involving how many admirably executed parts, subordinating all; why should not the wonderful symmetry that modulates these, glide into our spirits when we do not pedantically close our doors, but humbly & joyfully live with nature. Organic poems, pre-written poetry, which we over-hear as the Destinies chaunt it, & dilute or deprave as little as possible in transcribing; that is what we want.[247]

The poet should read the symbol of nature but for its own beauty or ⟨for⟩ in other words for joy. Then his moral is pure & winged as is the moral of nature. But Swedenborg, though he reads the symbol, yet he reads it for good[,] not for beauty; & the impression corresponds; — it is sad & is preaching. Shakspeare is pure Poet.

[97] [248] Poet uses things as symbols or exponents
This power is called ⟨th⟩Imagination
It is primary & central
> The nature of things is flowing or a Metamorphosis
> The free spirit sympathizes not only with the actual form, but with the power or possible forms; but for obvious municipal or parietal uses, the God has given us a bias to fixed or today's forms.
> Hence the ⟨power⟩ shudder of joy with which we recognize the metamorphosis, because it is always a conquest, a surprise from the heart of things,[249]
> Once apprised of that power we must have it honestly or otherwise[.]

[98] Breadth of the problem   Poet representative of man
He is one of T⟨r⟩hree,   the Sayer
Primary

---

[247] With "A birds nest . . . want.", cf. "The Poet," *W*, III, 25–26, where "the love . . . nature." is used.

[248] Pp. [97]–[99] are in pencil.

[249] Irregular marginal markings to the left of "Poet uses . . . It is" may have been intended as a brace. "Poet uses . . . exponents" is used in "The Poet," *W*, III, 13, and cf. "Poetry and Imagination," *W*, VIII, 13 and 15. "The nature . . . Metamorphosis" is used in "The Poet," *W*, III, 20. "The nature . . . of things," is used in "Poetry and Imagination," *W*, VIII, 71.

     Organic & Universal Affirmer, no Tennyson
     By Symbols
     Universe the externization of the soul
     Hence the attractiveness of Nature
      Symbol in whole & symbol in parts
   Poet is the Approacher, & Seer of the Metamorphosis [250]

[99] His expression is organic. Like the metamorphosis of things into higher forms, is their metamorphosis into melodies. The sea, the mountain ridge, Niagara, and every flowerbed preexist in prewritten poems & ⟨the poet⟩ ⟨into the poet's ⟨ear⟩⟩ they sail like odours in the air & when an adapted ear goes by, that is, a poet's, he hears them better or worse [251]

[100]   *Marriage*
Impossibility of Marriage in Spiritual World *E* 340 [252]
Defence of Marriage in Constitution *E* 331½
Marriage should be by gravitation *J* 111
Marriage *H* 34, 84,
Marriage of minds *H*.33
Menu, *D* 85
Woman inspires *J* 9   has crises. *K* 23
Marriage not ideal but empirical *G* 74, 90
Marry today, *G* 90,
Mr Vise & Miss Vane *G* 114

[101] [253]
[102] [254] Influences on American Literature

---

[250] "Breadth of . . . Metamorphosis" is an outline for "The Poet," *W*, III, 6–21.
[251] This unfinished paragraph is used in "The Poet," *W*, III, 24 and 25.
[252] "Marriage" is listed in Notebook Ж, p. [169] below, among possible topics for the series on "The Times" in 1841–1842. The paragraphs in Journal E, p. [340], are used in "Experience," *W*, III, 77.
[253] A horse and rider are sketched on the lower half of p. [100], and p. [101], indexed "Edward's sketching," is filled with sketches of a train, a bow, quiver and arrows, and a horse-drawn sleigh flying a flag on which is written *"EDWARD EDWARD EMERSON"*.
[254] Emerson has written over pencil sketches of a coach on p. [102] and a horse on p. [103], both by his son Edward.

Carlyle, King Saib. G 17 ⟨E⟩D 15, 346 E 184, 173
  isolation 122 ↑J↓ [255]
Dickens D 361
Goethe J 90, D 319

Scott K 14, N 72
Shelley G 133, J 96
Tennyson

Swedenborg, J 81, 71, J 108, K 64, 83, D 25, 48, D 167 E 316, 90,

Shakspeare K 83,[256] E 331½   .

Wordsworth K 121 N 73
Manzoni Silvio Pellico
Edinb. Review —

  [103] Travelling N 74 E 330½ J 136

England N 75

Calvinism N 72 J 102, 85, 29, E 307

Transcendentalism Osric K 19 J 25

Cambridge H.85, J 34,

Socialism K 85 K 60, 49, 50, H 30, J 84, K 46, 90

Novels E 192 E 147, 230, 258,
Poetry K 90 J 86
Lectures E 118

---

[255] "J" is added in pencil.
[256] With "Carlyle", cf. Notebook F No. 1, pp. [149] and [154]–[159] above. The passages cited in Journal G, p. [17], E, p. [184], K, pp. [64] and [83], and E, p. [90], are used in the lecture "Recent Literary and Spiritual Influences." The paragraph in J, p. [90], is used in "Europe and European Books," *The Dial*, III (April 1843), 520–521.

353

Mesmerism
Phrenology [257]

Copyright K 130

[104]   / American Genius   D 296 [297]
Everett

Webster [258]

Allston

Channing
Greenough
Franklin
Alcott
Lowell
Holmes
Thoreau
C K Newcomb
P.P.Randolph
Sampson Reed

[105] Few Cosmogonies   E 141
When the great Yankee shall come   N 73
Dickens outAmericaed us   N 72
New England most religious & ideal   N 16 [259]

[257] The sentence cited in Journal N, p. [75], is used in the lecture "Genius of the Anglo-Saxon Race." The paragraph in J, p. [34], is used in the lecture "Trade." Part of the paragraph cited in E, pp. [118]–[119], is used, and "Mesmerism" and "Phrenology" discussed, in the lecture "Manners and Customs in New England." The passages cited in K, p. [50], and E, p. [230], are used in "New England Reformers," W, III, 264–265 and 285. The passages in J, pp. [136] and [86], and E, p. [258], are used in "Europe and European Books," *The Dial*, III (April 1843), 512, 518, and 520.

[258] Emerson discusses Everett and Webster in the lecture "Manners and Customs of New England."

[259] The passage cited in Journal N, p. [73], is used in the lecture "Recent Literary and Spiritual Influences." The paragraph in N, p. [16], is used in the lecture "Genius of the Anglo-Saxon Race."

[106] [blank]

[107]   Divine Persons

Divine persons chuckle   K 52

I wonder they are not million   K 23, 53, 54, E 330

Divine souls. Parmenides   K 53,   23

Osman   & Osric & Schill

Sanity very rare.   *& Salvage 29*

Children of the gods   J 96

Osman's apology   K 115 [260]

[108]   Men

Is not each Character entitled to large interpreta[tion] H 33

Criticism   E 243

You shall not accept any man's person   J.82   K 6

Presence of a genius is a star behind   J 89

Every man baulks expectation

Men suggest what they shall be   G 151

Hints & scintillations   G 166

We embellish all persons   G 88   E 51 [50]

⟨We hear from each his best & think it habitude   K 46⟩

A sane & an insane in every man   J 124

⟨What is best in each kind, the average of that   K 123⟩

We want the great man for riches not for bread   K 125

———

I wonder not at one bible or one divine man but that there should not
be million   K 23, 53, 54   E 330

———

We have never seen a man   K 99

All model heroes fail in one point   K 7   E 51, 293

We identify each with the Soul   E 51

Divine persons

We hear from each his best thought & think it habitude   K,46

What is best in each kind we count average of that   K 123 [261]

[260] "Sanity very . . . K 115" is in pencil. The quotation in Journal J, p. [96],
is used in a section on "Divine persons" in "Character," *W,* III, 109.

[261] The page to this point is in pencil; "Men" is overwritten by the same in ink.
The passages cited in Journal H, p. [33], E, p. [243], G, p. [88], and E, pp. [50]

Keep yourself pure of the Race. J 120
Wise man leaves the few as well as the many   K 122
Institution must be in Institutor   K 85
Men delicate ware to fetch over   N 121
Fool to rail at men; their nonsense is educative   N 83
We require all of each   G 101
Immense force of men whose part is taken   Z 163 [262]
[109] Intellectual man has a philanthropy which costs nothing   E 352
Styles of men, N 61, 113, E 353,[263]

[110]   *October 1842*
              Miscellanies [264]

———

A man can neither be praised nor insulted   H.17

———

Luther Lawrence of Women. H 16

———

None should be rich but those who understand it. 23

———

    Spend 5 months of every year in reading newsp. 2⟨4⟩3

———

Inaptitude
Men inapt for their appointed works   H 28

———

We have a hold on selfish man; his value of reputation &c. 29

———

and [293], are used in "Nominalist and Realist," *W*, III, 241–242 and 226–227. In K, pp. [7] and [125] are torn out, but are probably used, *ibid.*, pp. 227 and 240. The passage cited in K, p. [99], is used in "Character," *W*, III, 113–114.

[262] The passages cited in Journal K, pp. [122] and [85], and N, p. [121], are used in "Character," *W*, III, 100, 101–102, and 107. The passage in N, p. [83], is used in "Experience," and Z[A], p. [163], in "New England Reformers," *W*, III, 57–58 and 280.

[263] With the three passages cited in this line, cf. "Nominalist and Realist," *W*, III, 239.

[264] Emerson probably began the 18-page survey of his journals which follows for the 1843 lecture series on "New England," but the pattern of use marks indicates that he used it again in writing essays and revising lectures for *Essays, Second Series*; he may also have scanned it in preparing later lectures, such as "Discourse at Nantucket" in 1847 and lectures in the 1851 "Conduct of Life" series.

"The *Community*," advantage of seeing friends,   H 30   J 84

————

S.A.R.   H.32

————

Marriage of minds   33
↑————↓
   Is not munificence the only insight   } ↑H 33↓
   Is not each character entitled to largest interpretation
⟨————⟩
   ↑See also what is said of Criticism   E.243↓
↑————↓
Marriage   H 34 (temporary); 84,

————

Continuous effect not produced by discon. thought. ⟨E⟩H 36

————

Wis wis [H 45–46]

————

Life—eagerness to get the grip & grit of ↑the↓ fact⟨s⟩ H.48
      [See also what is said of Grief   J.62]
   Most of life mere advertisement of faculty   H 49 [265]
   The two directions   49
      Patience & Preparation   H 50, 51, 52

————

   Our Greek men & women   H 62

————

[111] Music   H 6⟨6⟩7

   Impossibility of intercourse   H 71

The Rowdies & Paddies make the law. Is it not their right   H.75
   See also N 42

[265] "A man . . . H.17" is struck through in ink with a vertical use mark, and
"*Life*—eagerness . . . J.62]" with a diagonal one. The passage cited in Journal
H, p. [17], is used in "Character," *W*, III, 106–107. "None should . . . understand
it." is used in "The Young American," *The Dial*, IV (April 1844), 500, and "Discourse at Nantucket." The passages cited in H, pp. [33]–[34], and E, p. [243], are
used in "Nominalist and Realist," H, p. [48], in "New England Reformers," and H,
p. [49], in "Experience," *W*, III, 241–242, 274, and 73.

What there is anywhere there is everywhere   H.75, N 96
Loss of vents. H 78

Rhine of the Divinity School   H 85

Leaders of great causes are vulgar & cunning   89

Parties. Every member of party wishes every other committed   97

Contemporaries; one set.   97

Books — are either for antagonism or Confirmation   118

↑I read Proclus for nature & fate   J 121↓
We have not quite yet served up to our thought. [H] 120

Few as I have seen I could do with fewer   H 128

False valuations   135

Why Cupid did not assault the Muses. Rabelais 3 Vol p 25 [H 142]

Queenie's Dream of the statue. H 142

Keats. Keats.

It is not worth while to worry people with your contrition   J 7

Dead writing   J 4   It will soon subside   J 135 [266]

Woman inspires   J 9

We ask to be selfsustained [J 9]

[266] "I read . . . thought. 120" is struck through in ink with two vertical use marks, one of them discontinuous. The passage cited in Journal J, p. [121], is used in "Nominalist and Realist," H, pp. [120] and [135], in "Character," and J, p. [135], in "New England Reformers," W, III, 233, 102 and 101, and 284.

[112]   *Oct 1842*   Miscellanies

We ask all things of society. J 10

———

⟨Gifts   J 9, 11,⟩

———

⟨All books & journals written by the successful class⟩ J 14
⟨The taking my cloak⟩ is beautiful, if original in you. J 15, 18,

———

Whigs love, Protestants hate   J 16
Transcendentalism   J 25

———

Pis aller of Romanism   J 26, 104

———

Masses   J 28, 70, 72
⟨Religion indemnity for inferiority   J 29⟩

———

Infirmities of & inaptitudes of genius   J 31
Inaptitude   H.28

———

⟨Credit eternal   J 33   Credit will be more & more⟩ [J 33].

———

        The two liberties   J 33

———

Harvard has much & therefore should have more   J 34

———

⎧Departure from routine a great fact   J 36
⎩Nonconformity   N 112, 136   J 7
⟨Don't be so grand with your⟩ one objection   J 39, 118   139
⟨You are⟩ not good enough to be such a reformer
Grief. J.62

Use of Bores   J 77
My life optical not practical   J 78 [267]

———————

        [267] "The taking . . . J 15, 18," is also struck through in ink with two diagonal

NOTEBOOKS OF RALPH WALDO EMERSON   Φ

The Swedenborgianess   J.81

[113] ——

You shall not accept any man's person   J 82, K 6 ↑E 293↓

Every man baulks expectation. J 82   ↑Sane & insane   J 124↓
⟨——⟩   ↑(See Inaptitude ⎤   ↑G 166, 151   E 293↓
    Whitewashing   G 88, K 46,↓⎦²⁶⁸

⟨Grand is a good understanding betwixt two   J 84⟩

You may come ever so near men if there be bounds   J 84

⟨Ghostlike we glide through life nor know the place⟩ J 85, 130

⟨Calvinist's constitutional⟩ ⟨8⟩J.85

Our poetry like catbird's   86

Few opinions. J 86   Salvage   55

⟨A poet an affirmer⟩ [J 87]
⟨E⟩Unaffirming geologists &c   J 87

Talent makes comfort, The Atheneum   J 88

    Intellect & Conscience is a Man-Woman   89

---

use marks. The passages cited in Journal J, pp. [10], [9], and [11]–[12], are used in "Gifts," W, III, 162–163. The passages cited in J, pp. [15], [39], [118], and [139], are used in "New England Reformers," W, III, 254, 262–263, and 283; with "You are . . . reformer", cf. ibid., pp. 261–263. The passages cited in J, pp. [28] and [34], are used in the lecture "Trade." The passage cited in J, p. [36], is used in "The Poet," N, p. [112], and J, p. [7], in "Character," and J, p. [78], in "Experience," W, III, 32, 99–100, 105–106, and 74–75.

²⁶⁸ "Sane . . . J 124", "Whitewashing . . . K 46," in a smaller hand, and the brace, were probably added later, when the short rule was canceled. "G 166 . . . E 293" was probably added after "Sane & insane J 124". Journal K, p. [7], is torn out, but the passage in K, pp. [6]–[7], is probably used in "Nominalist and Realist," W, III, 227; the passages cited in E, p. [293], and G, p. [88], are used, ibid., pp. 226–227.

Presence of a genius is a star behind   J 89

Wilhelm Meister   J 90

Dr Bradford concerning Children   J 94

Literary Criticism   94, 97
Intellect grows by obedience   95
Gods are to each other not unknown [J 95]
Depth of Fire   J 96
Character *must be* trusted   J 96 [269]
Shelley   J 96
New genius always flies to old   97

[114]   Oct 1842   Miscellanies

Language should describe not suggest. J 100

A man is not holden by his profession but by his belief. J 101, K 22,

The Scholar   J 101
Sunday   J 102
Increasing value of the present moment [J 102]
Romanism   J 104   A A.

⟨S⟩Talk with S. Reed. J 108   Here or nowhere the whole fact
    ⟨n⟩No devils; All my concern, with subjective truth. J 108

Every consciousness a sliding scale   J 110

---

[269] "Ghostlike . . . 130" and "Wilhelm Meister J 90" are struck through in pencil with single vertical use marks; "Gods are . . . unknown" is struck through in ink with a vertical use mark. Both passages cited in J, p. [85], J, p. [130], and the paragraph in Notebook S (Salvage), p. [55], are used in "Experience," W, III, 45–47 and 51. "Ghostlike . . . place" is also used in "New England Reformers," W, III, 273. "Intellect grows by obedience" is used in "Discourse at Nantucket." The quotations in J, pp. [95] and [96], are used in "Character," W, III, 112 and 109.

Marriage should be by gravitation J 111

Debate not wholly useless   J 111   Bartlett 110.

⌈ Good men must not obey the laws   J 112, E 42

⌊   I like best the unconscious Conservative   J 115

    Animal Magnetism   J 118

    Keep thy self pure from the Race   J 120 K 122

Genius has a necessity of isolation, & Carlyle must not read Lane
                                        J 122   B 288   Naphtha

Carlyle   J 123

Sane & insane in every man   J 124

Understanding, lame & laughable   J 124

    There is a necessity to be beautiful in the landscape   J 125

Chaucer Saadi   J 126
        Intellect must be cheerful & limitary   126
        Lay a ray of light under every fact   127 [128]
        Goodwill makes insight   J 129
        Pope's Odyssey   J 129 [270]

---

[270] "Increasing value . . . scale J 110" is written in a progressively smaller
hand; part or all of it may have been added. The first word in "I like . . . J 115"
is written over an earlier short rule; the line may have been added. The "No devils"
passage in Journal J, p. [108], and the quotation in J, p. [112], are used in "New
England Reformers," *W*, III, 278 and 280; the passage cited in J, p. [118], is used
in the lecture "Manners and Customs of New England," and J, p. [129]("Goodwill
. . . "), in the lecture "Recent Literary and Spiritual Influences." With "Bartlett
110.", cf. "Experience," *W*, III, 47. "Good men . . . laws" is used in "Politics,"
the sentence in K, p. [122], in "Character," the sentence in J, p. [125], in "Nature,"
and the paragraph in J, p. [129]("Popes Odyssey") in "Nominalist and Realist,"
W, III, 208, 100, 176, and 232–233.

[115] All our days are so poor whilst they pass that 'tis strange where we got any thing ever. J.130   J 85

The greatest genius only detaches something, not adds. & should make us feel our wealth   J.131

Fate & the music box   J 131   N 9
Zanoni [J] 132, 140, Novels 132, Sig Blitz.   D 126 order of wonder
Vivian [J] 134
Dr A & Prof. B will set the town right concerning themselves   135
Theory of Travelling; Doors: J 136
Love of anecdotes about trifles shows each should make his New 138
See that you work; paid or unpaid   J 1⟨1⟩38   G 43
A ship; the curse settles on our own. [J] 139   N 121
        Gold represents labor   Labor is higher   J 140
Compound interest on Temperance   141
Nature interrogates   143
I was always indolent   J 143
        Character.   abide by truth   K 1
Middle region of our being is the zone of life & thought. K 4, ↑131,
                                            N 90, D 126↓

An Opium is instilled into all pain   K 4   Grief J 62

———

        All model heroes fail in some one point   K 7, J 82
S. Robbins & the egg   K 7

———

The Dial   K 13

———

Life goes headlong; but the moment is all in all noble relations   K 14,
                                            K 19, G 106,²⁷¹ J 102,

²⁷¹ "All our . . . J 85", "Fate & . . . N 9", "Dr A . . . 135", "See that . . . G 43", and "Life goes . . . J 102," are struck through in ink with single diagonal use marks, and "Middle region . . . tho't." with two. The passages cited in Journal J, pp. [130], [85], [131]("The greatest . . . "), [139], N, p. [121], K, p. [131], N, p. [90], K, p. [4], and G, p. [106], are used in "Experience," W, III, 46, 45, 80, 46, 63–64, 62–63, 62, 48 and 49, and 50; J, p. [62] is torn out, but cf. ibid., pp. 48–49. The passages cited in J, pp. [85], [135], and [138]("See that . . . "), are used in "New England Reformers," W, III, 273, 284, and 283. The passages cited

[116]   *1842   October   Miscellanies*

. In cities all is surface   K 15

In reading "Lord of the Isles," I felt   K 14

The least differences in intellect are immeasurable [K 16]

A man at peace would command nature by his eye   K 16

The spirit of the landscape will not come out to coffee   17

The Scholar & the Banker ↑K↓ 19

Osric was great in the present time   K 19

⟨In⟩You are responsible for the civil law. You eat it in your bread & wear it in your shoes   K 22, J 101,

Wit knows itself; and we if we have seen wit we know it. K 23

Woman has crises. K 23

Clare's poor man   K 24

A.B.A.   K 30   E 338

We have no terror but in dreams. K 44

We hear from each his best thought & think it habitude   K 46

in J, pp. [140]("Zanoni"), [134], and [136], are used in "Europe and European Books," *The Dial*, III (April 1843), 519, 521, and 512. Passages cited in K, pp. [1] and [19], are used in "Worship," *W*, VI, 230 and 234. The passage cited in K, p. [7]("All model . . . "), though torn out, is used in "Nominalist and Realist," and K, p. [14] and G, p. [106], in "Character," *W*, III, 227, and 113 and 96.

I may be surprized by contentment, what room for Fourier phalanx
K 46, 90

———

E. Palmer   K 46

———

G R's project   Difficulty of meeting an expectation. *K* 49

———

When a man unites with phalanx, he is less than one   K 50

———

Divine persons presently chuckle   K 52
Yet we believe in ecstasy   *K* 53
     Genius, Virtue have a first right in every piece of bread / K 53 [272]
"Divine souls" — Parmenides   53, 23
     I would not surprize a truth as a lion surprizes prey   K 54
     As a man's life comes into union with nature [117] his thoughts
     run parallel with the creative laws   K 55
Platonists, nobly pious   K 56
Population of the world conditional   K 57
     Objections to Phalanxes   *K* 60, 50,
Tremendous energies flow in safety through us & through the feeblest
babe. K 64
Swedenborg
     His interlocutors ⟨speak⟩ Swedenborgise [K 70]

You should never ask what I can do. K 70
     It is never a question whether to do wrong   71
History of Christ a document of Character   76
Idolatry retrospective, Health prospective   80
     Poet should have an adequate errand. *K* 81
     Shakspeare & Swedenborg   K 83, D 95

———

[272] "The spirit . . . coffee 17" and "A.B.A.   K 30," are struck through in ink
with single vertical use marks. The paragraph cited in Journal K, p. [17], is used
in "The Poet," *W*, III, 29. The paragraph in K, p. [50], is used in "New England
Reformers," *W*, III, 264–265, and the paragraph in K, p. [90], in "The Young
American," *The Dial*, IV (April 1844), 498. The paragraph in K, p. [53]("Genius,
Virtue . . . "), is used in "Discourse at Middlebury College." The paragraph in K,
p. [19]("Osric . . . "), and the sentence in K, p. [53](" . . . ecstasy"), were used
later in "Worship," *W*, VI, 234 and 213.

The Institution must be in the Institutor   K 85

Preacher is cunning   K 87
We skip the recording of what we best know   K 89
From the mountain see the mountain   K 89
  Dewey's Report on Botany   K 90
    The flowers jilt us   K 93
    Flowers are our poetry not shittim wood   K 94
    Gates of thought slow to show   K 96
Babe not disconcerted   K 96½
I like a meeting of gentlemen   96½
  Mrs Black   97½
  We have never seen a man   K 99 ²⁷³

[118]   Oct 1842   Miscellanies
Effects of reading Proclus   K 104
The way of Thought   I do not make it
                    It affirms continuance   K 105
Life is a series, one stair of a scale   K 106

Beauty deserts an object in possession   K 144 [114]

⟨Y⟩We do not know whether today we are busy or idle: 114

The Carpenter's cord: 114 ²⁷⁴

²⁷³ "History of . . . 76" is struck through in ink with two diagonal use marks,
and "The Institution . . . K 85", "From . . . mountain K 89", "The flowers . . .
K 93", and "We have . . . K 99" are each struck through with one. The paragraph
in Journal K, p. [50], is used in "New England Reformers," W, III, 264–265. The
passages cited in K, pp. [70]("His . . . "), [83], and [89]("We skip . . . "), are
used in the lecture "Recent Literary and Spiritual Influences." The passages cited
in K, pp. [76], [85], and [99], are used in "Character," and K, pp. [90] and
[93], in "Nature," W, III, 114, 101–102, 113–114, 172, and 182.
²⁷⁴ "I do . . . K 105" and "Life is . . . K 106" are struck through in ink with
single diagonal use marks. "⟨Y⟩We do . . . idle: 114" and "The Carpenters cord:
114" are struck through in ink with single diagonal use marks, and both lines with
another. The passages cited in Journal K, pp. [104], [105], [106], and the first two
in [114], are used in "Experience," W, III, 71–72, 45, and 46. "The Carpenters
cord" is used in "The Poet," W, III, 13.

Inhospitality of disputing. [K 114]
⟨Osman never made an apology to the person aggrieved⟩ 115

Modern Xy. is the trade in mummy. K 116

———

We ^{n} demand both continence & abandonment   118

———

To wish for war is atheism   K 118

———

I am not ashamed that I am ashamed.

———

I cannot say Kitty Kitty any longer   119

———

'Tis said we still learn the language when we disuse it   1⟨2⟩19

———

Wordsworth's "difficult of tasks" elegy of the times   K.121

———

"Men should live by their strength not weakness"   K 122

———

Wise man leaves the few as well as the many   122

———

Boldness, yes; but whence boldness?   K 122

———

What is best in each kind the average of that   123

———

Do the gods bless by halves? K 123 ↑E 354↓
Imbecility   124
Clay & Clay differs   124
We want the great man only for riches, not for daily bread   125 [275]

———

[275] "Osman never . . . 115" is struck through in ink with two diagonal use
marks. "Wise man . . . many 122" is struck through in ink with a vertical use mark
and "We want . . . bread 125" with a diagonal use mark. "E 354" is added in
pencil. In Journal K, pp. [115]–[116] are torn out, but with "Osman never . . .
aggrieved", cf. "Character," W, III, 102–103, and "Worship," W, VI, 236; with
"Modern Xy. . . . mummy.", cf. "Worship," W, VI, 209. The first passage cited
in K, p. [122]("'Men should . . . "), is used in "Discourse at Middlebury College"
and the second ("Wise man . . . ") in "Character," W, III, 100. K, p. [125], is torn
out, but with "We want . . . bread," cf. "Nominalist and "Realist," W, III, 240.

Habit of contradicting spoils society   K 125
We are bound to gentilize society   K 126
Reform is dangerous because partial   Better remain [119] in the
Establishment better than it. 130

Copyright   130

People's superlatives & Dr J. Jackson   130
Life in the middle zone; /musquash/woodchuck/ is also superficial
K 131; 4
E. H's Morning & Evening   K 132;   and afternoon   113
Fate   K 78
Fate & Character   K 78
Defeated all the time yet to victory born   K 79
I wonder not at one Bible or one divine man, but that all are not divine
K 23, 53, 54   E 330

⟨Lucky to get off from those you have served without a slap⟩ E 330

Death the only poetic fact in the life of most   E 331

Lord Ashburton at ΦBK. Truth due from diplomatists   E 331

Classic & Romantic. E 3⟨4⟩31

Equality of an apprehender to a great poet ⟨3⟩E 331

S. Travelling in Italy   E. 330½

Omens   E.330½

Men not pious but lovers of pious   E 330½

⟨We owe men behaviour & we offer money   E 331½⟩

Understanding is a Malthusian   E 331½ [276]

[276] "Reform is . . . it. 130" is struck through in ink with three diagonal use

We conceive of Milton, Goethe, &c as *Great*   331½

Defence of Marr↑i↓age in constitution ⟨3⟩E 331½

Sunset wanted men. E 332

Lunatics swear   E 333
    Olympian Criticism let it be   E 334
Scholar has no family   E 335   ↑Scholar   G 52   G 132   J 101↓
Scholar's feet cold & head hot
You have come here to spy

    Betrayed me to a book & wrapped me in a gown [277] [N i]

[120] Poetry has been written here in your house   E 335

    We may well be slow of belief before Genius [E 335]

I could not stand with my penurious forces a flowing friendship E 335

    A few noble victims. Every deed deepens literature   E 336

Nature & Literature subjective phenomena   E 337
Temperament, in the moment seems Impulse. E 337
'Fiddle-faddle,' a fine answer [E 337]
My company   E 338
Mr Cushing & his Boston house   E 339

---

marks on p. [118], and four on p. [119]. "Life in . . . superficial" is struck through
in ink with four diagonal use marks; "woodchuck" is added in pencil. "Defeated
all . . . K 79" is struck through in ink with a diagonal use mark. The passages cited
in Journal K, pp. [130] ("Reform is . . . ") and [79], and E, p. [331] ("Death
. . . " and "Equality of . . . "), are used in "New England Reformers," *W*, III,
261, 283, and 281; with "We owe . . . money" in E, p. [331½], cf. *ibid.*, p. 256.
The sentence in K, p. [79], is also used in the lecture "Manners and Customs of New
England." The paragraphs cited in K, pp. [131] and [4], are used in "Experience,"
W, III, 63–64 and 62. The paragraph in E, p. [330] ("Lucky to . . . "), is used
in "Gifts," *W*, III, 163. The passage cited in E, p. [331½] ("Understanding . . . "),
is used in "The Young American," *The Dial*, IV (April 1844), 493–494.
   [277] "Sunset wanted men." is used in "Nature," *W*, III, 178. "Betrayed me . . .
gown", struck through in ink with five diagonal use marks, and "Scholar's feet . . .
hot" are used in "Montaigne," *W*, IV, 155.

[278] "Poetry has . . . E 335" is struck through in ink with a diagonal use mark; the passages cited in Journal E, pp. [335]("Poetry has . . . ") and [343], are used in "The Poet," W, III, 10–11 and 8. The paragraphs cited in E, pp. [337]("Nature & . . . Impulse."), and [340]("Impossibility . . . "), are used in "Experience," W, III, 50, 52, and 77.
[279] "E 330½" is added in pencil.

Shortness of Memory   Z 3

After all our accumulation of facts we are just as poor in thought. Z 3

Cultivated life. Li. 166,

Persians & Dorians, Li. 166.
Oliver Cromwell   D ⟨1⟩362
Kitty & her tail   N 30
Magic Palmistry ghostcraft, all real. N 31 [280]
    Naming of the Disease   N 33
    Literature names   N 32

[122₁] [281]   *Oct 1842*   *Miscellanies*
Each science will have its culmination   N 32
Love is blind but Self is Blind↑er↓ [282] N. 36
Masses   N 37   J 70   D 281
⟨A man should give me sense of resistance⟩ N 37
    We want More. The gods can't help us. N 38

⟨Gifts. The only gift a piece of Thee   N 39⟩

Problem; *Given* a bandit & opportunity, to save wit by wit. N 40
                      D 214   D 343
Sculpture, good for calm manners   N 41, 48

Rich & poor   N 42, ↑K 24, D 356↓   Cheaters & Cheated. N 42

---

[280] "Napoleon . . . battalion", struck through in ink with a diagonal use mark, is used in the lecture "Trade." The passages cited in Journal G, p. [61], and N, p. [31], are used in "Character," and G, p. [113], in "Nominalist and Realist," *W*, III, 112, 110, and 235. The passage on the "Wineglass—system" is used in "Discourse at Middlebury College." "Kitty & her tail" is struck through in ink with two diagonal use marks; "Believe in . . . exception" and N, p. [30], are used in "Experience," *W*, III, 74 and 80.

[281] The page numbers of this and the following page are repeated.

[282] "er" has been added in pencil.

Highest Criticism should be written in poetry   N 43

_____

Praise of Cities N 44   ↑Harvard   J 34↓ [283]
Persons are puzzle until we get the key   N 45
⟨Men follow⟩ success not skill as P.J.   N 45
Plants are the young of the world   N 45

_____

Poet disposes of facts very fast   Great is Being   N 46, 75. Z 3,
Shakspeare & his apprehender   E 331

_____

Some men ⟨achieve not⟩ work on false tendency & yet are great
otherwise   N 47

_____

A song no song without good cause   N 49

_____

White lies. 50
Poet cannot walk until he is alone   50
Everett   N 52
Walk to Shakers   N 62
Country unpeopled of good brains   N 63
Shakers' model-farms   N 69
Shaker faith   N 71 [284]
I hate family painting. N 70   Mr Pickens
Two Abandonments   D 343
[123₁] Dickens outAmericaed America   N 72
When the great Yankee shall come, English writers will write to
    America   N 73

_____

[283] "Harvard J 34" is added in pencil.
[284] "Plants are . . . world" and "Poet disposes . . . Being" are struck through
in ink with single diagonal use marks, and "Plants are . . . Being" with two more.
"A song . . . cause N 49" is struck through in ink with eleven short diagonal use
marks or cancellations. The passages cited in Journal N, pp. [44] and [63], and J,
p. [34], are used in the lecture "Trade." The passages cited in N, pp. [45]("Men
follow . . . ") and [52], are used in the lecture "Manners and Customs of New
England." The passage in E, p. [331], is partly used in "New England Reformers,"
W, III, 281. The passage cited in N, p. [37], is used in "Character," N, p. [39], in
"Gifts," N, p. [45]("Plants are . . ."), in "Nature," and N, pp. [46] and [75],
in "The Poet," W, III, 99, 159–161, 181, and 18–19. The paragraph in N, p.
[71], is used in "Discourse at Nantucket," and "Worship," W, VI, 237.

Wordsworth N 73
Scott N 72
As we grow old we count Niagaras unseen N 73
Calvinism leans on Calvinism ⎱ N 72
Connecticutt   ⎰
England held up by all dollars N 75
We are not satisfied with a boy's wonder at the city   N 75
The Farm, pig farm, horse farm, N 77
A good exception as good as rule N 78
Merchants N 45↑, 104, 114↓
One needs not eyes in order to see
To fill the hour is happiness N 33
    Why need we answer catechism in words, whilst the fact to be
    translated never disappears. N 34 E 26

———

Mrs Wells' verses on the Boy. E.201

———

Montaigne. D 95
⟨I⟩Every man led by the nose by some verb D 219
All religions, excess of organ of language N [94–95]

———

"The deaf man's hearing & the blind man's sight" is memory
[T 63]

———

Value of Reading: Books D 282

———

Artificial Memory: Value of a Catalogue: Knot of Now & Then   D 282

———

Rhyme D 326, 7,
We suppose defects to be organic D 345 [285]

[285] "We are . . . city N 75" and "To fill . . . N 33" are struck through in
ink with single diagonal use marks. ", 104, 114" is in pencil. With "When the . . .
America", cf. the lecture "Recent Literary and Spiritual Influences." The sentence
cited in Journal N, p. [75]("England . . ."), is used in the lecture "Genius of the
Anglo-Saxon Race." The paragraph in N, p. [75]("We are . . ."), is used in
"The Poet," W, III, 19. The passages cited in N, pp. [77] and [114], are used in
the lecture "Trade." The passage cited in N, p. [45], is used in the lecture "Manners
and Customs of New England." The passage cited in N, p. [33], is used in "Ex-

[1222] ⟨p⟩Prophecy not more sacred than knowledge of the present. Do not throw up your thought because you cannot answer objections   E 26   N 34

Gods & demigods must seat themselves without seneschal   E ⟨2⟩31
Only known to Plato that we can do without Plato [E 37]
Death   E 68
We are prisoners of our way of thinking   E 69, N 10
Economy of the Scholar; his place in the state. E ⟨128⟩ 75 —
The country is governed in barrooms. E 78
Few Cosmogonies   E 141
Circus; order of wonder. E 147
The life of love   E.162
Strong speech of the Mob   E 173
Excessive craving of sympathy   E 171
The life of man is the true romance   E 230
World is plastic to wit. E 236,

Scholars, persons, & virtues need perspective, E.260

Concert, as individuals   E 292 [293]

What man is. What Heart is. E 317

Man an exaggerator   E 321

He makes *Virtu* of all his things; of Persons also   E 321

Man of practick sense requires such a preacher as he, were his heart in the pulpit. Character is logical   E 329 [286]

perience," *W*, III, 59. The paragraph in N, p. [34], is used in "New England Reformers," *W*, III, 282; with D, p. [345], cf. *ibid*., pp. 268 and 270.

[286] "Gods & . . . seneschal" is struck through in ink with a vertical use mark, and "The life of man . . . E 230" with a diagonal one. The passages cited in Journal N, p. [34], and E, pp. [230] and [293], are used in "New England Reformers," *W*, III, 282, 285, and 265–266. "The Country . . . barrooms" is used in the lecture "Trade." The paragraph in E, p. [329], is used in "Discourse at Middlebury College."

Skeptical Scholars speak the sheriff fair. E 237
The recent mourner not yet a mourner, nor the new reformer reformed
N 88

Corporal Spohn true. N 90
There is no peau d'ane. N 90
[123₂] G.B a historical democrat   N 4
Four walls a good institution   N 4
⟨Theory of Union   Union must be Ideal   N 6⟩
If there were constancy great men would dwindle   N 8, N 88,
A man cannot jump out of his skin   N 10, E 69
⟨Words & deeds indifferent modes⟩ N 10
Several steps—   Architecture, progress   N 11, 134, E 98
We have our own method of answering objections   N 12
Every man would be a Benefactor: N 12
Discussion has its dangers   N 15
Associate on what ground you please, but do not preach it   N 16
New England population ideal   N 16
You take great liberty to lend me a book   N 17
A book only adds one word   N 17
Do not gloze, but call spade spade   N 18
Wit selects in labor & so destroys drudgery   N 20
Not too sqeamish about your acts & lectures   N 21
In N.E. mechanics keep School   N 22
⟨Riemer's biography of Goethe   N 79⟩
Merit of a poem or tragedy a thing of experience   80
No magic in making money   N 82
Divinity behind prayer & pottage saint & city   83
Prosperity of Boston   N 83
Try Olympian experiments   85
⟨Only by following your genius can you go out of prison⟩ N 86 [287]
Temperance is Rus Ruris [N 87]

[287] The passages cited in Journal N, pp. [6], [12]("Every man . . ."), and [86], are used in "New England Reformers," W, III, 266–267, 277–278, and 284–285. The passages cited in N, pp. [20], [82], and [83]("Prosperity . . ."), are used in the lecture "Trade." The sentence cited in N, p. [22], is used in the lecture "Genius of the Anglo-Saxon Race." The passage cited in N, p. [10]("Words . . ."), is used in "The Poet," N, p. [79], in "Character," and N, p. [83]("Divinity . . ."), in "Experience," W, III, 8, 103–104, and 57–58.

Dr Channing   N 87   92

[124] Every thing good on the highway   N 90, D 126   K 4, 131

⟨Description of Ulysses in Homer⟩

Do not refuse the employment the hour brings   N 91

Be sure you don't get imposed upon   N 93

Language flagellates the attention; Scald & Indian tell their the-ogony in good faith, being led by the nose by a verb   N 94, 139,

Every man holds every one responsible *but* himself: Otherism;
N 95

What is in any other is in every other   N 96, 23,

⟨Two or three words will make any man sad⟩ N 97

No man is fit for society who has fine traits   98

Glee of the Babe   N 100

T. asked always for the salvation of Soul. N 101

Every one make the dareGod & daredevil experim. N 102

Rabelais   102

Men culminate too fast   N 106, Φ 171,

Eustis   G 96

Tennyson   E 346

Every one has his trick of thought which you soon learn   E 353   N 113

Wineglass system   E 354↑, K 123,↓

Romeo [E 359]

Beauty of Casualty   E 279   Z[[A] 150]

No great man has a son   E 280

Private economy better than public: Z 133   Malthusian

⟨Net amount of man & man much the same⟩ Z 106

Value of demonology; omens. E 330½ [288]

---

[288] "Every thing . . . highway" is struck through in ink with a diagonal use mark. "Description of . . . Homer" is struck through in ink with five use or cancellation marks, and "Two or . . . sad" with seven; both passages are used in "Eloquence," *W*, VII, 72 and 63–64. ", K 123," is added in pencil. "Beauty of Casualty" is struck through in ink with two vertical use marks. "Net amount . . . same" and "omens." are struck through in ink with single vertical use marks. The passages cited in Journal N, p. [90], K, p. [4], N, p. [95], and the passages on "Beauty of Casualty", actually in E, pp. [280]–[281], and Z[A], p. [150], are used in "Experience," *W*, III, 62–63, 47, and 68. The passage in N, p. [98], is used in "Nominalist and Realist," E, p. [346], in "The Poet," and Z[A], p. [106], in "New England Reformers," *W*, III, 227–228, 8–9, and 281. The passages cited in

Swedenborg's selfequality   J 71

[125] Ah if the rich could be rich as the poor fancy riches! J 92 [289]

Sect of Impossiblists   K 86

[128] [290]   Oct 18⟨3⟩42   Scholar

Nature & Scholar. Nature never ⟨f⟩cares that scholar cannot express
    her   G 151

All books & journals written by the Successful   J 14

                    written by the unmagnetic   E.148

    When I shall be deserted, said the scholar   J 101

We all know enough to be endless writers   G 52

    Classic & Romantic   E 331

Immunity of the Scholar   D 86

Real History   E 256

    Economy of the Scholar: his place in the state   E 75

    Pope's Odyssey   J 129

    Literary Criticism   J 94, 97

Intellect grows by obedience   J 95   ↑*faith*↓

Scholars need perspective   E 260, C 231, G 132

    Language should describe   J 100

    Mysticism   N 123

Scholar must be isolated as some substances must be kept under naptha
                                   ↑B 288   J 122↓

Often so little affinity betwixt the man & his works, that the wind must
    have written them   J 130

Copyright   K 131 [130]   N 43

The good Aunt   D 115

A man's subject lies in his recent thought   E 42

Skeptical Scholars speak the sheriff fair   E 237

Too old to read   N 124

E. pp. [354] and [359], are used in "Discourse at Middlebury College." With E,
p. [330½], cf. the lecture "Manners and Customs of New England."

  [289] "Ah if . . . riches!", struck through in ink with two diagonal use marks,
is used with a paragraph in Journal J, pp. [91]–[93], in "Nature," *W*, III, 174–175.

  [290] After repeating two page numbers, Emerson skipped 126 and 127, correcting
the pagination.

Scribaciousness of ⟨A⟩Burton, Agrippa, &c   N 126,[291]
Pusillanimity of scholars   E 286, 289,
[129] Scholar has no family   E 335   E 259
Scholar's feet cold & head hot

————

"Betrayed me to a book & wrapped me in a gown" [N i]

————

You have come here to spy.
"How dare I go to be a psychological fact"   G 132,
Infirmities & inaptitudes of Genius   J 31, H 28
I would not surprize a truth as a lion his prey   K 54
Scholar also an Achilles   E 284   ↑*faith*↓
My life optical not practical   J 78
Paracelsus   N 129, 130, 133, H.48   E 347,
Rabelais   N 18, 102, 104, 109,
Theophrastus, of Books & Men. N 113   ↑*faith*↓
Confusion of the point of Conscience & Intellect   N 122
Value of a reader of Greek to America   N 108
Short Memory: after all accretion poor   Z 3
Writing a knack   J 43   E 353, N 113   ↑Intellect↓
          ⟨No crime to Intellect   N.41,⟩ 49
          Intellect grows by obedience   J 95
          Intellect makes interval
          Least differences immeasurable   K 14
          Way of thought; 1. I do not make it
                              2. It affirms continuance K 105
"Commencement" G 76,[292] 92   B 227   N 106

[291] "All books . . . Successful" is struck through in ink with seven diagonal use or cancellation marks; this sentence and the passage in Journal N, p. [126], cited below, were later used in "Books," W, VII, 195 and 211–212. The paragraph cited in J, p. [129], is used in "Nominalist and Realist," and the paragraph in N, p. [123], in "The Poet," W, III, 232–233 and 34–35. The paragraph in J, p. [95], is used in "Discourse at Nantucket."

[292] "Way of . . . K 105" is struck through in ink with three diagonal use marks; the passages cited in Journal N, pp. [122], [41], and [49], and K, p. [105], are used in "Experience," W, III, 79 and 71–72. The passage cited in H, p. [48], is used in "New England Reformers," E, p. [353], in "Nominalist and Realist," K, p. [14], in "Character," and G, p. [76], in "Manners," W, III, 274, 239, 113, and 130. The passage cited in E, p. [284], is used in "Discourse at Middlebury College." The sentence in J, p. [95], is used in "Discourse at Nantucket."

God hates inqu⟨s⟩isitive people, said Euclides. [K 122]
Education (Pericles) K 69

No one of the gods   says Diotima   philosophizes   *Proclus*   [Z 100]

⟨Every one, his trick of thought, which we soon learn⟩ E 353, N 113
We are prisoners of our way of thinking   E 69, N 10
    [130] The hawk — See Lect. on *Pres Age XI*
Yankee pedlar   Z 137   N 22   ABA & ⟨N⟩F
⟨Economy of private management better than public   Z 133⟩
Styles of men   N 61   113   E 353
    Thunder at a distance cheep small in a chamber   G 132
    Originality   R 69

things facts   ⎧ Dreams
             ⎪ Memory
             ⎨ Screens
             ⎪ Ambiguity of consciousness
             ⎩ Prophecies, omens, fables, all anthropomorphic
               Like sunshadows
softness of darkness [C 224]
fortunate men L.B.   boundless selftrust: the heroic: Epaminondas
Answer[n] (O Neptune &c) [Enc. 167]   So *Guesses*
Shakspeare's Octavius & A⟨m⟩ntony
Scott's Something that neither stood nor fell
abdication of will
amulets, sorceries, magicians;
ghosts
Animal Magnetism
power of awaking at a certain time
coincidence; sortes;   Dreams
Animals   Anim Mag
Trees   Ambig Consc
                                     Genius
                                     Ghost
                                     Amulet [293]

---

[293] "things . . . Amulet", in pencil, was inscribed first on p. [130] and is
overwritten in ink as far as "Prophecies," by "Yankee . . . R 69", printed above.

[131]   Dreams
        Omens   Complement
        prophecy
Dreams Van
    separate
    landscape   Bacon's rule
    dream house   Omens of Homer & Lucan
    animal   Guesses of Plutarch
    Agree to general law sub & ob.   Prayer to Neptune
    are within nature   Swans of Plutarch
    are prophetic   Masollam the Jew [294]
        stabbing [295]

    Animal mag directed

Omens
  Signs
fables
Anthropomorphic
    G
⟨An⟩ Genius
    Anct opinion, Shakspeare
    Goethe
    fortunate men   lucky hand
    Scott

This and pp. [131] and [132], also in pencil, are notes and outlines for "Demonology," *Lectures*, III, 151–171; much of the lecture was later used in "Demonology," *W*, X, 1–28. "Dreams . . . sunshadows" is developed in "Demonology," *Lectures*, III, 152–158, only partly in this order; "fortunate . . . nor fell", struck through in pencil with a diagonal use mark, is developed, *ibid.*, pp. 161 and 166 (with a quotation from "Lord Bacon"), 159, and 162–163; with "abdication . . . ghosts", cf. p. 162; "Animal . . . time" is developed on p. 167, "coincidence; sortes;" on p. 157, and "Animals" on p. 154. The column, "Dreams . . . Amulet", may have been added when p. [131] was written; cf. "Demonology," *Lectures*, III, 152–157, 167, 154, 160–161, and 162.

    [294] "Bacons . . . Plutarch" is struck through in pencil with a diagonal use mark; "Bacons . . . Jew" is used in "Demonology," *Lectures*, III, 166 and 159–160.

    [295] "Dreams . . . prophecy", treated separately in "Demonology," *Lectures*, III, 152–157, 156, and 155, is also used in one paragraph, *ibid.*, p. 157. "Dreams Van . . . stabbing" is an outline in nearly final order of pp. 152–156 of the lecture.

Young men's
Ghosts, amulets,[296]
All this is exaggeration of the Individual which nature steadily postpones. The man is made great by union[,] by publicity. You cannot
speak little enough of y[ou]r family[,] of y[ou]r sickness[.] [297]

[132]
It seems to me here are the questions { of science
of structure
of commodity

Demonology is the shadow of theology[,] the perverted image of
truth. The whole world is an omen & a sign. Why look so wistfully
in a corner? Man is sacred. Why run after a ↑ghost↓ raven or thunder
or Fridays or coincidences? The voice of divination resounds everywhere & runs to waste as the mountains echo with the bleating of
cattle[.] [298]

[133]   ⟨First word of lit. *Fall*⟩
⟨Confession around us. Trace it home⟩
⟨Man in the actual lapsing⟩
⟨Each individual is born pure⟩
⟨the world owes him life: heroic:⟩
          ⟨He protests⟩ against property
                    Choice of pursuit
                    traditions
                    Charities
                    Society
                    institutions
See this great protest as it lies against every abomination. The
pure God speaketh out of some one heart against every crime & every
folly[.]

---

[296] With "Animal mag directed", cf. the passage on "Animal Magnetism" in
"Demonology," *Lectures*, III, 167. "Omens . . . Anthropomorphic" is developed
ibid., pp. 156–158, and "Genius . . . amulets," on pp. 160–162.
[297] "All this exaggeration . . . postpones" (cf. Journal D, p. [248]) is used
in "Demonology," *Lectures*, III, 165. With "You cannot . . . sickness", cf. C, pp.
[139] and [221].
[298] "It seems . . . commodity" is developed, and "Demonology . . . cattle"
used, in "Demonology," *Lectures*, III, 167–168 and 170.

Trees look like imperfect men. It is the same soul that makes me which by a feebler effort arrives at these graceful portraits of life. I think we all feel so. I think we all feel a certain pity in beholding a tree[;] rooted there the would be Man is beautiful but patient & helpless. His boughs & long leaves droop & weep his strait imprisonment[.] [299] [D 58]

[134] [300] *Protest*
    The Fall of Man
↑⟨C⟩ D 15, 25, 17,
Stranger   D 104, 107, 110↓
    Ideal & actual   C 31⟨1⟩3 [301]

    The Redemption of man by ⟨C⟩Resistance
    Genius Protests
        against society   hates soirees
        against cities   loves nature
        against institutions   reforms

Counter action of society to soul
    ↑Few sanities 61↓
    Society loves the past   C 287   desponds; serves; sits;

---

[299] P. [133] is in pencil. "First word . . . institutions", and probably "See this folly" also, were inscribed on p. [133] first; then "Trees . . . imprisonment" was written around "First word . . . protests", which Emerson canceled. "First word . . . institutions" is an outline of "The Protest," *Lectures*, III, 86–95, and of summary paragraphs, *ibid.*, pp. 91 and 92; it was probably written after the collections for "The Protest" that follow on pp. [134] and [135]. "See this . . . folly" is expanded, *ibid.*, p. 89. "Trees . . . imprisonment" is used in "Nature," *W*, III, 181, but see p. [130] above, where Emerson lists "Trees" in notes for "Demonology."

[300] Pp. [134]–[135], in pencil, are notes for "The Protest," *Lectures*, III, 85–102. See also pp. [140] and [142] below, which have notes used in both "The Protest" and "Genius."

[301] "The Fall of Man" and "Ideal & actual" are discussed in "The Protest," *Lectures*, III, 86–87 and 89, and 94, though the passage in C, p. [313], is not used. "⟨C⟩ D 15 . . . 110", in heavier pencil, was probably added; an erased or incomplete word, of which only "Th" can be read, is under "Stranger", aligned with the first entry. Passages in Journal D, pp. [15] and [25], are used in "The Protest," *Lectures*, III, 100, 96, and 90.

History should awaken
Our sympathy too strong   D 61
People live from memory   D 118
French noblesse   D 46
Least woodthought better   D 141
Position of perpetual inquiry   D 42
Love of solitude   D 206
Pseudo reform — Temperance   D 51
Set y[ou]r own rate [D 245] [302]
Trades & callings an opiate

[135] Every young man & young woman must meet that question
Wilt thou be like one of us?
Every reformer partial   D 163, 231

Every reformer said No & then Yes
Michel Angelo
Columbus

Nature affirms
Art affirms

Society
In proportion to nobleness, alone   186
Holy hurra
put me not in society where
society dispirits   B 24
night chair [D] 153
if people were true infinitely deep   D 192 [303]

Despondency   D 103

[302] "The Redemption . . . reforms" is developed in "The Protest," *Lectures*, III, 90, 421 (notes), 95–96, 97–98, and 91. Each line of "Society loves . . . D 46" is struck through in pencil with a single vertical use mark; phrases in "Counter action . . . D 46" are developed and the cited passages used in "The Protest," *Lectures*, III, 86, 85, 97, 89, 98, 96, 95, and 89. Passages cited in Journal D, pp. [42] and [245], are used in "The Protest," *Lectures*, III, 99, 100, and 101–102.
[303] "Every young . . . Columbus" is developed and passages cited in Journal D, pp. [163]–[164] and [231], used in "The Protest," *Lectures*, III, 90, 91–92, 91, and 100–101. Passages in D, pp. [186] and [192], and "society dispirits" are used, *ibid.*, pp. 96 and 95.

[136] [blank]
[137] [304] What is Genius

The spontaneous perception & exhibition of truth
    Of truth
    Truth the object
    Soul speaks because it hath what to say; its word implies sight;
    & it pauses never but advances unceasingly
    It is articulate   precise
    It utters things for their own worthiness
    And takes place of all else
    But here is the reason why Genius is sneered at as playing with
moonshine & building air-castles, viz because its sight is piercing,
& it pauses not like other men at the surface of the fact but looks
through it for the Causal thought. It sees the all in each[.]

    And we learn that ↑⟨th⟩↓ there the fact & every fact can be
undermined & that ⟨we can⟩ facts are not ultimates[,] that a state
of mind is the ancestor of every thing.
    ↑Ideal truth the object
        Sculpture   Painting↓
    And here let me

[138] [305]   Love
All other pleasures are not worth ⟨his⟩its pains [306] [Enc. 105]
Oft in the stilly n↑i↓ght
C 189   attractiveness of every love tale   C 340 [307]
C 216   The cedar birds
Love men & do what you will with them

---

[304] P. [137], in pencil, is an outline of "Genius," *Lectures*, III, 68–74. See also
notes for "Genius" on pp. [140]–[143] below.

[305] Pp. [138] and [139], in pencil, are probably notes for the lecture "Love,"
most of which was used in the essay "Love," *W*, II, 167–188. See also p. [33] above.

[306] This quotation, struck through in pencil with a vertical use mark, is used in
"Love," *Lectures*, III, 57.

[307] This entry is struck through in pencil with a vertical use mark. Passages from
Journal C, pp. [189] and [340], are used in "Love," *Lectures*, III, 55.

C 326   Load yourself with love.   D ⟨1⟩49 remedy for More & Less.
C 340   How we glow over these novels!
C 38   Libertine a dupe   B 16   B 21
D 120   Casella [308]
Friendship   D 260 J.S.
D 1⟨66⟩55–6   Universal charity. Edw. Palmer.
Aphrodite
    Fancies   D 51
Boys & girls   D 236
Supererogatory household nicety of woman   C 159
    Grief of women   C 196
    Woman must keep her Countenance   C 298
    Women must take possession of society   A 57
    Base views of women; Cellar views   A 115 [309]
    Recollections of E[llen].   C.272, B 6 [310]
Music

[139]   The great Enchantment
visible in nature the melody of woods
    the marriage of plants↑,   2↓   , motions of animals [311]
rises in man, quickens all things   the bird articulate
the waving bough seems sympathetic   cloud & waters
one would scarce trust with the secret they invite it so [312]
    Let us not be immersed in the facts
let if we are every life hath a slime   If we are not every life the
coarsest lies pillowed on fairest Ideas [313]

[308] Passages in Journal C, p. [326], and D, p. [49], are used in "Tragedy," *Lectures*, III, 119 and 107; D, p. [49], is also used in "Compensation," *W*, II, 123–124. Passages cited in C, pp. [340] and [38], and D, p. [120], are used in "Love," *Lectures*, III, 55, 62, and 63–66. C, p. [38], is omitted in the essay "Love."

[309] Passages cited in Journal D, p. [236], C, pp. [159], [196], and [298], and A, pp. [57] and [115], are used in "Love," *Lectures*, III, 55–56, 63, and 62. Those in C, pp. [159], [196], and [298], and A, p. [57], are omitted in the essay "Love."

[310] The passage cited in Journal C, p. [272], is used in "Love," *W*, II, 171; that in B, p. [6], is used in "Love," *Lectures*, III, 56–57.

[311] With "The great . . . animals", cf. "Love," *Lectures*, III, 52. Only "The great Enchantment" is in "Love," *W*, II, 169.

[312] With "rises . . . invite it so", cf. "Love," *Lectures*, III, 58.

[313] With "Let us . . . Ideas", cf. "Love," *Lectures*, III, 54 and 55. With "Let us . . . slime", cf. "Love," *W*, II, 171, and Journal D, p. [11].

Attractiveness of love tales
Boys & girls

Love	Woman
Music. Richter	oracular
Purple / roselight	tender
Poetry : Art	must keep
Fancies	
Casella	

Progress of the change
Love in mature life
Rubs
    Gr↑i↓ef
    nicety
    Woman must
          I
          2
       oracular nature
       violet [314]

[140] [315]   *Genius*
Spontaneity
   This is the link between Genius or natural bias
              & Genius the perception of truth
↑Great by genius, by casualty
God hates inquisitiveness, said Euclides↓
    Genius the child

[314] Entries from "Attractiveness" to the bottom of the page are notes for the lecture "Love"; see p. [138] above for Journal passages. "Woman . . . keep" and "Grief . . . violet", in a smaller hand, may have been added. For "Attractiveness . . . Casella" see *Lectures*, III, 55–60, 63, 60, and 63–66; "Woman . . . keep" and "Grief . . . nature" are developed, *ibid.*, pp. 62–63; see also p. 55 for "Grief". With "Progress of . . . Rubs" and "violet", cf. *ibid.*, pp. 54–55, 61, 63–67, and 58.

[315] P. [140] is in pencil, except for "Great by . . . Euclides", added in ink, the second line written over "Genius the Protestant". "Spontaneity . . . truth" and "Genius the child" are developed in "Genius," *Lectures*, III, 70–71 and 74. With "Spontaneity" and "Great by . . . casuality", cf. passages in Journal Z[A], pp. [97] and [150], and E, pp. [280]–[281], used in "Experience," *W*, III, 67–68; Emerson may have used pp. [140]–[141] in preparing this essay.

Genius the Protestant
  The Fall of Man
  The lapsing tendency
    A man's deed is his enemy
    The prayer of Jesus hinders the praying of Xdom
    In Anna's wars
    The inventor.   30 years men
  World always sensual slumberous & so malignant
    Genius protests
    ↑All Genius protestant   Luther   Bacon   *Shakspear*↓ ⁿ
    loves nature
    hates society
    Yet to young Genius, society is somewhat great
    And so it is unhappy morose unlovely saying no.
    Reforms

    When Genius has got through saying No it
Genius Affirms ³¹⁶

[141] ³¹⁷ All men of genius impersonal. Napoleon   C 349

                        Drawing
                        ———

        C 220   Graeter must know then he can draw
        C 251   We know a priori the form
        D 211   Drawing of dreams ³¹⁸
  B 12   Man of genius cannot finish his work
B 255, 228,   Artist appeals to eternity

Genius never smells of fagots   C 295   Φ 157   ↑A 39↓
⟨Inspiration B 113, 109,⟩   ↑works in sport↓ ³¹⁹ [B 259]

---

³¹⁶ Though "Genius the Protestant . . . Genius Affirms" was apparently outlined as part of "Genius" at this stage, Emerson developed it in the following
lecture, "The Protest," *Lectures*, III, 421(notes) and 85–102, in roughly the order
above. With "The Fall of Man", cf. "Experience," *W*, III, 75.
³¹⁷ Pp. [141]–[143] are in pencil.
³¹⁸ The anecdote in Journal C, p. [220], is used in "History," *W*, II, 16–17,
with passages taken from the lecture "Genius." The passages cited in C, p. [251],
and D, p. [211], are used in "Genius," *Lectures*, III, 74, and "Intellect," *W*, II, 337.
³¹⁹ "B 12 . . . eternity" is struck through in pencil with one diagonal use

Genius surprises   B 286   ⟨C 129⟩ D 18
⟨Genius works ever in sport⟩ [B 259]
⟨Genius   D 56⟩
T⟨r⟩he ray alighting
C. Wren   B 255
Galvanized Webster   B 113
⟨Genius when it comes is complete in every word   D 56⟩
Genius is selfrelying   C 269
          disinterested
          sportful
          unpredictable [320]

[142]   Protest
Love of Nature   D 87
⟨S⟩Love of Solitude   D 206
Projects of Reform
Protestant   D 212, 86, 25   16⟨4⟩3   15, 231 [321]
Reformers   D 157
W.H.C[hanning].   D 116
Youth can speak to its cotemporary   D 114
Despondency of our society   D 103
Pseudo reform   D 51
Position of perpetual inquiry   D 42
French noblesse   D 46

---

mark, and "Genius . . . fagots" with another; "Artist . . . eternity" and the quotation in Journal B, p. [255], passages in C, p. [295], Φ, p. [157] below, A, p. [39],
and B, p. [259], are used in "Genius," *Lectures*, III, 76–77 and 80–81.

[320] The paragraph cited in Journal B, p. [113], is used in "The School,"
Lectures, III, 36; with the sentence in B, p. [109], cf. both "The School," and
"Genius," *Lectures*, III, 36 and 76. Passages in C, p. [129], and D, pp. [18]–[19],
are used in "Genius," *Lectures*, III, 79 and 80; cf. also "Experience," *W*, III, 68.
The paragraph in D, p. [56], is used partly in "The School," and partly in "Genius,"
Lectures, III, 45 and 78–79. The last four lines on p. [141] outline the four numbered
sections in "Genius," *Lectures*, III, 77–81, though not in Emerson's final order.

[321] "Love of Nature" is developed in "The Protest," *Lectures*, III, 97–98,
though the passage cited is not used. Passages in Journal D, pp. [212], [86]–[87],
[25], [163]–[164], and [231], are used, *ibid.*, pp. 94, 101 and 102, 96 and 90, 89
and 91–92, and 91.

Solitude of Genius
Genius
Our sympathy too strong   D 61
    Few sanities   D.61
People live from memory   D 118
Least wood thought better   D 141 [322]

    The origin of Genius is very high
        Kindred of works of nature & art
        Analogy between virtue & genius
        Man of genius cannot finish   B 12
        Genius appeals to Eternity   B 255   228, Φ 143, [323]

[143] And the reason why the work of genius fits the wants of all ages is because that which is spontaneous is not local or individual but flows from that internal soul which is also the soul of every man.

What is this difficulty of doing what we think? of realizing the ideal (as in B 109)? I think it is disobedience

    Genius is selfrelying
        To believe y[ou]r own thought is genius
        Wordsworth &c   C 269
        Trust yourself &c   B 102
        The reason of this trust is indeed very deep
        Infinitely rich   D 56   Dissipates earth to ether.

(2)   Genius sportful   humane
        smells no fagot   C 295
        heart in place   Φ 1⟨9⟩57
        Best persons freest speakers   A 39
        no fanatic

[322] Passages in Journal D, pp. [42]–[43], [46], [61], and [118], are used in "The Protest," *Lectures*, III, 99 and 100, 89, 96 and 85, and 95. The passage cited in D, p. [157], is used and "D 141" is listed for use in "The School," *Lectures*, III, 42 and 402 (notes).

[323] "The origin . . . high" is canceled, and "Kindred of . . . virtue & genius" used, in "Genius," *Lectures*, III, 415 (notes) and 76. Passages cited in Journal B, p. [255], and Φ, p. [143] below, are used, *ibid.*, p. 77.

⟨1⟨   Genius unpredictable
      Surprises   B 286   D 18   C 129

   Genius representative
      Collins Burns &c   B 16
      Man of Genius apprises of the Commonwealth
      The world always is at last on its side ↑Shelley↓
      Inspires us with a boundless confidence
      B 334 [324]

[144] [325] ⟨T⟩Sentiments
Instinct of truth   of society   of hope or trust
    Superiority of any wood-thought
       Selection
B 12⟨4⟩5   A man is a method &c
⟨⟨C⟩D 68   A scholar⟩ is a selector
⟨D 234   Respect all your impressions⟩
D 178   Emphasis of facts & persons nothing to Time
D 207   Nothingness of Magnitude of time or space
D 141   Superiority of any wood thought to Books
Φ 160   My will never gave things the rank they have to me
B 113, ↑109↓ Intuition
Φ 162   God makes prophet   unmakes not man
C 249   Expressiveness of ⟨facts⟩ certain facts to me [326]
C 175

---

[324] "And the reason . . . man." is used in "Genius," *Lectures*, III, 77. "Genius is selfrelying . . . ether." outlines the first of four numbered sections in "Genius," *Lectures*, III, 77–79. "(2) Genius sportful . . . no fanatic" outlines section 3, "⟨1⟨ Genius . . . C 129" section 2, and "Genius representative . . . B 334" section 4, *ibid.*, pp. 80–81, 79–80, and 81–84.

[225] Pp. [144] and [145], in pencil, are mostly notes for "The School." See also pp. [146₁], [147₁], and [148₁] below.

[326] "⟨T⟩Sentiments . . . trust" outlines a paragraph in "The School," *Lectures*, III, 39. "Selection" and the passages cited in Journal B, p. [125], and D, pp. [68], [234], [178], and [207], Φ, p. [160] below, B, pp. [113] and [109], and C, p. [249], are used, *ibid.*, pp. 36–38. "D 141" is listed in the lecture for addition; see *Lectures*, III, 402 (notes).

Condition
Climate
Laws of the world
Polarity or Dualism
Death
Sun & Moon
Sleep
Time & the Soul   D 171
"By the permanence of nature &c [B 183]
Independence of condition   D 100   Were it the will of Heaven
an osier bough [327]

[145]   (Tragedy of life consists in temperament not in events) [328]
          ↑*Teaching*↓   [D 244]
1   Instincts — from the soul sentiments from Organization instincts
2   Condition
3   Persons   love hatred competition conversation admiration
4   Books
5   Facts
    ↑significance of Nature   D 142↓

_____

          Obstruction

_____

1   Diversion from the soul to severalty in the organs
2   Vocabulary   ↑Worship of Effect   C 112↓
        or
    Classification
3   Temperament

    Persons
Society   men that answer to the sentiments

[327] "Condition . . . Sleep" outlines a paragraph in "The School," *Lectures*, III, 40; a curved pencil line links "Condition" with "nothing to Time" above. The passage cited in Journal D, p. [171], the sentence in B, p. [183], and "Were it . . . bough" (see Notebook Δ, p. [125] above) are used in "The School," *Lectures*, III, 38–39, and 41.
[328] "Tragedy . . . events" is used in "Tragedy," *Lectures*, III, 110, and may have been inscribed on the page before the notes for "The School" which follow.

who have power to wake all the emotion we call passion
Every man has something of me in keeping
How they lash us with those tongues   how quick they make the tear
start — & make us blush & whiten the cheek   soothe us to dreams
of hope & castles in air [329]

[146₁] [330]   The School
Nature
Health
Hand
Wants & faculties
Trade & profession
Aimless activity
Classification   D 35   120   207
Mighty Nature works through & cares not for costly apparatus   C 242
                                                                    T 19

    Makes apparatus of Society nature, books, ch[urc]hs, persons
    ⟨learn from all, sane & insane   D 166⟩
⟨A selector or choice⟩ B 125, ⟨98⟩   C ⟨187⟩   D 68, 234,
    Our joy in genius   B 16
    Books (few   C.229   their final value   B 311
    Nature becoming thought
    Facts   D 101   not the fact but the use. apercu
Scholar
    ⟨Mistakes of Education   C 112⟩
    Vocabulary
We are screened from premature ideas   B 255   D 195
    Outlive doubts   D 140
    Real Education   C 268

[329] "*Teaching* . . . Facts" is an outline of "The School," *Lectures*, III, 34–50,
and is used also in a summary sentence on the first page of the lecture. The passage
cited in Journal D, p. [142], is used, and "Persons . . . air" expanded, *ibid.*, pp.
41–42. The topics listed under "Obstruction" are treated briefly in Section II of the
lecture; Emerson may have intended to expand on them in an omitted lecture (see
Lectures, III, 170).
[330] Pp. [146₁]–[148₁], in pencil, are notes for the lecture "The School." Notes
for the 1846 lecture "Eloquence," written over and around these 1838 notes (see
Plate II), are printed as pp. [146₂]–[148₂] following p. [153₁] below.

True scholar ⟨E⟩formidable   D 68, 118 [331]
Sense of want & ignorance   inuendo
When you are deeply pleased without misgiving you are nourished

[147₁]   Books
An unestimable influence   Past Genius
    Effect of books   D 238
    Shakspear
    A few will serve: C 229   One even   D 101
        Not by books great poet made   D 209
        Entire literature unfair   D 101
        And all arrests of thought evil

Every man should write his own   B 98   Not by books great poet
                                                            made D 209
                                    great books   D 238
                                    One book good as all   D 101
                                    Lit unfair   D 101 [332]

            Facts
    D 101   Apercue
    D 142   I shall learn the meaning of the appletree
        144   Overvalue of facts — political
        50   Napoleon's fact
        42   Facts are tests
    1⟨90⟩14 ⎤ Fact placed & unplaced
        146 ⎦
        36   Day after day. Apercue [333]

[331] "Wants & faculties" and passages cited in Journal D, p. [207], C, p. [242], D, p. [166], B, pp. [125] and [98], and D, pp. [68], [234], and [101], are used in "The School," *Lectures*, III, 39, 38, 35, 42, 36–37, 38, and 49. "D 118" is listed in the manuscript, perhaps for addition to the lecture; see *Lectures*, III, 404(notes). "Scholar . . . Vocabulary" is overwritten in ink by "Eloquent man . . . Gratitude" (see p. [146₂] below).

[332] "Books . . . influence" is partially overwritten in ink by "Mosaic account . . . Keep your", and "great books . . . book good" by "day by day" (see p. [147₂] below). "Books . . . Lit unfair D 101" are notes for Section IV of "The School," *Lectures*, III, 43–47, and 405(notes).

[333] The "Apercue" paragraph in Journal D, p. [101], and the passages cited in D, pp. [114] and [36], are used in Section V [Facts.] of "The School," *Lectures*,

[148₁]   Facts abound
rich
they come asking questions of us
This was what the fable of the Sphinx meant
And men are men of facts or men of principle

Facts ⟨fall on⟩ encumber men tyrannize & make the men
of routine[,] the men of understanding[,] the men of
sense[,] but if the man is true to his allegiance & insists
on commanding[,] dwells with the soul & sees the principle[,] then the facts fall aptly into place[,] they know
their master & the meanest of them glorifies him[.]

The law being known[,] the fact obeys & takes its true
place & then first is beautiful[.]

The least fact in the eye of Soul is ⟨si⟩meaning [334]

[149] [...] [335]
[150₁] [336]   Home
⟨The child⟩ D 58, 59, 42, 24, 46, 219, ⟨B 289, 290   319ⁿ 15⟩ C ⟨22,
30,⟩ ⟨66⟩, ⟨70⟩, ⟨94⟩ ⟨134⟩ ⟨145⟩ ⟨168⟩ 178 ⟨184⟩ 211 ⟨269⟩ [337]
⟨The child & snow B 292⟩
Housekeeping D 19, 108 C 159
Man know ‖to‖ fish ‖&‖ hunt D 137
garden D 6, 21, 35, 55   108, 137, C ⟨94⟩, 101, 113, 136, 305

III, 49 and 47–48. The paragraph cited in D, p. [142], is used in Section II [Con-
dition.], *ibid.*, p. 41.

[334] "rich . . . ⟨si⟩meaning" is overwritten in ink by "no permanent . . . quick
enough" (see p. [148₂] below). The page is expanded in three paragraphs of Section
V of "The School," *Lectures*, III, 48–49.

[335] P. [149], left blank until 1846 when it was used for notes for the lecture
"Eloquence," is printed following p. [148₂] below.

[336] Pp. [150₁]–[153₁], in pencil, are working notes for the lecture "Home."
All four pages are overwritten in ink with notes for the lecture "Eloquence," printed
as pp. [150₂]–[153₂] below.

[337] Emerson wrote this entry across two pages; "66, . . . 269" is on p. [151₁].
Part of the paragraph in Journal B, p. [289], is used in "Home," *Lectures*, III, 32.
Passages in D, p. [24], B, pp. [289] and [15], and C, pp. [22], [94], and [145],
are used in "Domestic Life," *W*, VII, 103–105. The manuscript of "Home" is in-
complete; some of the missing pages may have been used in "Domestic Life" (see
Lectures, III, 23 and 24, n. 1).

Travelling   D ⟨160⟩, 163, 170, 178, ⟨229⟩ [338]

Gournou   Irishman   D 147 [A 116, B 280]

Tragedy of common life   B 16   C 166, D 48, 79, 95, 152, 174, Θ 101   D 225   ↑See Life in C↓

Tender ruffians   D 136

Natural affection is opportunity   D 102, B 289,

Man   Wife & son   D 85   102   105, ⟨M 116⟩

Feeble influence of thought in life

Nomads   D 67   111   112   127,

A man a stranger in his own body [D 111]

Man a selector & choice

Sleep   B 131, 298, C 10, 244, 320,

Aunts   D 2, 115

Woman   D 7, 59   65   69   78   85   91   105   194   236   B 5, 16, 21, C 38   43, 159, 162   169   190   195   284   285   296 [339]

Love of spoons [D 48]

    Shadows [C 145]

Boy D ⟨70, 93   114   21⟨8⟩9⟩ realizes) ⟨formidable observer D 93⟩:

                  to his cotempora. [D] 114

⟨Humble⟩ⁿ Eliot

    stranger   D 104, 107, 50ⁿ

Domestics   C 305 ⟨265⟩

---

[338] The paragraph on "Housekeeping" in Journal D, p. [108], is used in "Home," *Lectures*, III, 24–25. The paragraph on "Travelling" in D, p. [160], and part of the passage cited in D, p. [163], are used, *ibid.*, pp. 30 and 31; missing pages at this point in the lecture may have been used in "Self-Reliance," *W*, II, 80–81, where the passage in D, p. [163], is used; with the passages cited in D, pp. [170] and [178], cf. "Self-Reliance," *W*, II, 81–82.

[339] "See Life in C" refers to Emerson's index in Journal C, where "Life" is an index topic; see *JMN*, V, 522. Emerson may have used his journal indexes in collecting other entries on this page. The paragraph in Journal D, p. [102], is used in "Home," *Lectures*, III, 32–33; for "B 289", see above. Passages cited in Notebook Man, pp. [116]–[117] ("M 116"), and D, p. [111], are used in "Home," *Lectures*, III, 32, and 399(notes). The entry on "Woman" is written across two pages; "43 . . . 296" is on p. [151₁]; none of the passages cited have been located in "Home"; those in D, p. [236], and C, pp. [38] and [159], are used in "Love," *Lectures*, III, 55–56, 62, and 63.

Family   C ⟨242⟩ [340] 298 || ... ||
Any where but here

[151₁]   Edward Pyot   T 65

[152₁]   Home
    The same care which covers the seed warm under husks provides
for man the Mother's breast & the father's house, warm, careless,
cheerful, with good appetite, he runs in & out with boys & girls
    Welcome to the parents the little struggler comes with his comic
lamentations which soften all to pity & good humor[.]
        Domestic education   Shadows. [C 145]
        Natural affection opp[ortunit]y. [D 102]
        Boy, child & snow
        Poverty
        Domestics
        Housekeeping
              Mystics originals do not travel
              Stay at home like an axis
              Yet let your eyes see
              Travelling is objectiveness
              Homekeeping is subjectiveness
              Travelling for young it leans depends begs
              Home for the strong it lives radiates commands

Let him learn the tragicomedy of his house; of woman; of labor; of
near relations; [341]

[340] The paragraph cited in ·Journal C, p. [242], is used on a leaf now filed with
the manuscript of "Home" (see *Lectures*, III, 399–400[notes]) and is used in the
lecture "Genius of the Anglo-Saxon Race," and in "Domestic Life," *W*, VII, 119–
121.
      [341] "The same . . . appetite," "Welcome to . . . humor", and the passage in
Journal C, p. [145], are used in "Domestic Life," *W*, VII, 103–105. The paragraph
in D, p. [102], is used in "Home," *Lectures*, III, 32–33. See p. [150₁] above for
"Natural affection . . . snow", "Domestics", and "Housekeeping". With "Poverty",
cf. "Home," *Lectures*, III, 33, and "Domestic Life," *W*, VII, 119. "Let him . . .
relations;" is expanded in "Home," *Lectures*, III, 33, and "Education," *W*, X, 128.

[1531]   Philosophy of Home
      sub-object In Out
progressive transference   to Law to God
 Easy domestication a trait of great men   D 111
  All growth the endeavor to realize thought
  Philosophy is Homesickness
  Belzoni science would make Then Now [D 160]
Effect of univ. domestication to make partic. estrangm[en]t.
And so man comes to live a stranger and guest at home
  Advantages of home to the disengaged observer
  Not a duty less
   Home a school of human life
    a school human power
    a playground [342]

[1462]   Eloquence [343]
Brasidas
    Posthumous effect K 2
    Ashburton dinner E 331
    Boy playing ball is Jove E 159
      Pericles. Cousin's⎫ VI. 108 [344]
        Plato ⎭
     Test objects O 306 294 Y.39
      Webster's superfluous force U 161

Eloquent man must not speak too much
 St Cecilia V.7
  Gratitude O 80

Realism of New Eng[lan]d Orator O 349 [345]

---

[342] "Philosophy of Home . . . growth the" is overwritten in ink by "but a course . . . the right", printed on p. [1532] below. The pencil layer is an outline of "Home," *Lectures*, III, 25–33 and 24–25.

[343] Notes on pp. [1462]–[1532] are probably for the lecture "Eloquence," February 10, 1847; some are used in the lecture manuscript, which is fragmentary, and more are used in "Eloquence," *W*, VII, 59–100, derived from the lecture. See also Index Minor, p. [86] below, Journal O, p. [88], and JK, pp. [123]–[149].

[344] *Oeuvres de Platon*, trans. Victor Cousin, 13 vols. (Paris, 1822–1840), in Emerson's library.

[345] Except for "Eloquent man . . . O 80", which is written over "Scholar . . .

[147₂] Reality. Mosaic account. Plain tale that puts all down. Keep your feet on a fact [346]

Thee may sovran Destiny
Lead to victory day by day.

Crown with triumph day by day [347]

[148₂]   1846
Eloquence

There is no permanent orator.
The basis of the orator is a great personality, which, if it can have the singular advantage of adequate expression, produces beyond its usual ⟨force⟩ effect a beautiful effect. But the presence works, eloquent or not[.]
The measure of native force is parallelism or coincidence with things. It may be on high or on low planes that the ⟨genius⟩man stands. The audience know quick enough whether he is the tongue of things or only seems to be the tongue of things. Demades, ↑Luther,↓ Danton, have been formidable because stonewalls spoke by them and we are every day the victims of this eloquence if we go into the market [149]

Vocabulary" (see p. [146₁] above), the notes on p. [146₂] are fitted into blank lines and spaces around earlier pencil notes for "The School." "Brasidas" is listed in working notes for "Eloquence" now with the lecture manuscript; cf. "Eloquence," *W*, VII, 79. For "Boy playing . . . E 179", see Index Minor, p. [4] below. With the passage in Journal V, p. [7], cf. p. [151₂] below, and "Eloquence," *W*, VII, 99. The passage on "Gratitude" is rewritten on p. [153₂] below. "Realism of . . . O 349", written on a blank line at the bottom of the page, is developed in the lecture.

[346] "Reality . . . fact" is written over "Books . . . influence" (see p. [147₁] above). With "Reality.", cf. "Eloquence," *W*, VII, 88 and 99, and the lecture, where it is used with the paragraph on pp. [148₂]–[149] below and is followed by "Keep your . . . fact" (Journal V, p. [82]), which is used in both lecture and essay; see *W*, VII, 93. With "Mosaic account." (Journal O, p. [9]) and "Plain tale . . . down.", cf. *ibid.*, p. 93.

[347] "day by day" is written over "Great books . . . good" (see p. [147₁] above). "Crown . . . day" may have been added later.

or the wharf where anything is to be lifted, or burned, or mixed, or floated.[348]

Earnestness. The oration must be somewhat to the orator. He is not to say twice the same thing. A kick to this gun
He is compromised

There are many degrees on this scale
1   animal eloquence   .   . stove
2   ⟨oil or⟩ fascination   .   .   . ⟨oil⟩ sugar
3   village lawyer; rattle .   .   .   . gift of gab
4   personal ascendancy   .   .   . grit
    Balance of orator & audience
    Personal weight without eloquence is like beauty of form without beauty of face
    Add this power & 'tis best example of human power
5   personality determined to an aim ⎤
         or   ⎬ anthracite coal
    Earnestness   ⎦
    Envelopment
    Genius has always objects always a coincidence with things and Eloquence reaches great power only when ⟨mean⟩ ↑power↓ & aim coincide [349]

[150₂] Personality fashions this organ
and eloquence the focus
If the ⟨powers⟩ talents meet but not the personality there are good speakers receptive of the will of the audience its exponents and the audience is flattered by hearing its nonsense adorned. But if Personality then there is new power & audience must come down

[348] The notes for "Eloquence" on p. [148₂] are written over earlier pencil notes for "The School"; p. [149] was left blank earlier. With "There is . . . orator.", cf. Journal O, pp. [276]–[277], used in the lecture. "The basis . . . or not" is developed at length in "Eloquence," *W*, VII, 76–85. "The measure . . . floated." is used in the lecture, with notes on p. [147₂] above.
[349] "Earnestness." is developed in "Eloquence," both lecture and essay; cf. *W*, VII, 93. "There are many . . . Earnestness" is an outline of "Eloquence," *W*, VII, 65–93. Passages cited in "2" and "5" also survive in the lecture manuscript. "Genius has . . . coincide" is used in the lecture.

Columbus is come to Madrid not to show how ⟨France⟩ Spain can ⟨get⟩ gain a point with Rome or Flanders but how all Europe may be flung out & ⟨R⟩ Spain itself may transplant its dominion to a new world

---

Inconceivable levity of men [350] [O 133]
Everybody overrates their character. They have no meaning. They have heels, & it is the charm of noise *versus* the charm of eloquence.
[O 133]
If I could be surprised at anything, if the one lesson of life was — *not to be surprised*, I should admire the consternation & seriousness with which old ones take up this matter [1512] when they see that the very angels are often boys & divine persons chuckle & that the widest extremes are often reconciled in characters.[351]

Reality however has a sliding floor.
The height of Eloquence only reached when ⟨the⟩ all limits are taken away; which only can happen in the case of morality.

I think morals the only ground
↑Orator of masses must be moral↓
Truth snatches a clod & fashions it
The gods are come in the likeness of men.

All ⟨me⟩powers degraded into means as St Cecilia meekly would
Perish Egotism & show
⟨⟨The⟩One thought runs through Demosthenes⟩
Shame shame if you cannot convince us,
Is there opposition? it is opportunity.

Webster a paddy of the children of Reason
In this dominion of chance to find some principle of permanence to hold the object steady for scrutiny[,] to make the great great, & the small small [352]

---

[350] Notes for "Eloquence" are written over earlier pencil notes for "Home" on pp. [150]–[153]. "Columbus . . . world" is struck through in ink with a vertical use mark. "Personality fashions . . . come down" is rewritten, and "Columbus . . . world" and "Inconceivable . . . men" used, in "Eloquence," *W*, VII, 81, 82, and 91.

[351] Part or all of this paragraph may have been added; "I should admire . . . characters." is written in a progressively smaller hand.

[352] "Reality . . . floor." is used in the lecture "Eloquence." With "The height

[1522]   Eloquence

I hope you will see that it is an universal power and that its great masters whilst they valued & cultivated every means which they could attain & thought no pains too great to this end[,] like Kurouglou ⟨use⟩ⁿ had 17 weapons under his belt & used them all occasionally yet undervalued all means[,] never permitted the finest talent, voice, rhythm, poetic power, sarcasm, to appear for show but were grave men who preferred that integrity they cherished whether of their Country or of law or of reformation or of letters or of morals to the *whole world & to themselves*ⁿ also

There is so much to say which only requires high health[,] strength to the degree of frolic spirits & not special intellectual or moral gifts.

One ingredient then is Health ³⁵³

[1532] The people know very well whether you drive or whether your horses are running away with you.

⟨Ac⟩ Foster has not taken a course of lectures but a course of mobs

What gratitude does every human being feel to him who speaks well for the right

I am not only ⟨apprised⟩ reminded of my faith & my destiny but I am seized with gratitude to the speaker & could wash the feet of him who ⟨has⟩ⁿ seems to ha⟨s⟩ve put all mankind and the fraternity of rational beings under obligation[.] ³⁵⁴

Invigorating power of other men's vigor

. . . moral", cf. "Eloquence," *W*, VII, 97 and 98; with "All ⟨me⟩powers . . . would", cf. Journal V, p. [7], and "Eloquence," *W*, VII, 99; "Perish Egotism . . . opportunity." is developed, *ibid.*, pp. 99–100 and 97; "In this dominion . . . small", struck through in ink with a diagonal use mark, is used, *ibid.*, p. 98.

³⁵³ "Eloquence . . . also", struck through in ink with two vertical use marks, is used in "Eloquence," *W*, VII, 99–100; "Kurouglou . . . occasionally" (see Journal O, pp. [6] and [9]) also appears in notes in the lecture manuscript. "There is . . . Health" is developed in the lecture and in "Eloquence," *W*, VII, 67 and 69.

³⁵⁴ "The people . . . with you.", struck through in ink with a vertical use mark, is used in "Eloquence," *W*, VII, 91. With "Foster . . . mobs", cf. "Eloquence," *W*, VII, 96–97. With "I am . . . obligation", struck through in ink with two diagonal use marks, cf. Journal O, pp. [80] and [214].

[154]   "My own delighted laughing boy

            He sings aloud in medley mass
            Of nursery rhyme & infant lore
            No matter what the glorious theme
            He sings it o'er & o'er

            He cares not he for such as may
            ↑Those clamorous sounds annoy↓
            Unmindful of the sleepers near
            Who half awakened hear the strain
            And murmuring turn to rest again"
                                        Mrs Wells [355] [E 201]

Reality

Why answer ⟨a⟩catechism in words whilst the Fact abides   N 34
————
Shaker faith   N 71
————
⟨False valuations   H⟩ 135
————
We have not served up to our thought, H 120
————
Continuous effect not produced by discontinuous thought   H 36
        And Lit. Gazettes just
————
Character must be trusted   J 96
————
Work ↑away↓! paid or unpaid   J 138   G 43
————
⟨Institution in Institutor   K 85⟩
————
A man not holden by his profession but belief   J 101
————
⟨A & B will set the town right concern[in]g. themselves. J 135⟩
————
⟨Kitty & her tail   N 30⟩

[355] " 'My own . . . Wells" is in pencil, overwritten in ink by "*Reality* . . .
themselves. J 135", printed below.

Napoleon's fault was the defeat at Waterloo   D 50
Until History is interesting there is yet no history   D 61

Real History vs Bancroft   E 256

Chief is chief all the world over & not his plume   E 324

Man of practick sense requires such a preacher as he should be in
pulpit. Character is logical. E 329, H 36,
You should never ask what I can do.   K 70
Gods & ⟨demigods⟩ heroes must seat themselves without seneschal
E 31
Dead writing will soon subside   J 135

"⟨Re⟨s⟩ward of a thing well done is to have done it⟩" Seneca [C 9]

What there is anywhere, there is everywhere   H.75   N 96
⟨The only gift a piece of thee⟩ N 39   J 9, 11,[356]
[155] Shallow to rail at men: their nonsense educative   N 83
     On the art of speaking what you mean & are. N 75
     Body of rogue is yet sound   D 340
     All for thee; therefore all against thee   G 30
     Be calm. Are you there? then all   G 39,
     Quarrels would not exist if they could be reconciled   G 59, 86,
     No history true but what is always true   G 91
     The world gets on meantime   H 17
     Ask counsel of things. K 71
     The best of hospitality is fate also   N 127

[356] "We have . . . H 120" is struck through in ink with a vertical use mark,
later extended down through "Continuous effect". "Work . . . J 138" is struck
through in ink with a diagonal use mark. The passages cited in Journal N, p. [34],
and J, pp. [138] and [135], are used in "New England Reformers," W, III, 282,
283, and 284. The passages cited in H, pp. [135] and [120], J. p. [96], and K, p.
[85], are used in "Character," W, III, 101, 102, 109, and 101–102. The paragraph
in N, p. [30], is used in "Experience," and the passages cited in N, p. [39], and J,
pp. [9] and [11], in "Gifts," W, III, 80, and 159–161, 162, and 162–163. The
sentence cited in E, p. [324], is used in "The Young American," W, I, 386–387.
The paragraph cited in E, p. [329], is used in "Discourse at Middlebury College,"
and the paragraph on "Shaker faith" in N, p. [71], in "Discourse at Nantucket."

Every *thing* ⁿ is my cousin. IS[(Salvage)] 17 [C 120]
Truth is mine though I never spoke it   K 77
⟨Don't grieve you were not *there*:ⁿ Our force ubiquitous   J 79⟩ [357]

[156]   Affirmative

I take pleasure in coming near   G 28
Grand is a good understanding   J 84

Character is told overhead   G 13
Do not ask what I can do [K 70]

Good must not obey the laws too well   J 112

Force of men whose part is taken   Z 163 [358]

Daregod & daredevil experiment   N 102

[157] "Never was a man a poet or a lover of the works of poets who had
not his heart in the right place."   Scaliger [T 59]

> "For deathless powers to verse belong
> And they like demigods are strong
> On whom the Muses smile."
> W[ordsworth, "Sept., 1819 (Departing Summer)," ll. 25–27]

———

Whatever you do originally is good   J 15, 18

We have never seen a man [K 99]
Sanity very rare   S [(Salvage)] 29
        Character overhead   G 13
        Power behind & over us
        Immediate communications
        Truth mine though I never spoke it   K 77

[357] The passages cited in Journal N, p. [83] and J, p. [79], are used in
"Experience," N, p. [127], in "Gifts," and K, p. [77], in "New England Reformers," *W*, III, 57–58 and 74–75, 165, and 282. The paragraph in C, p. [120],
is used in "Eloquence," *W*, VII, 94.
        [358] P. [156] is in pencil. The quotation in Journal J, p. [112], and the sentence
cited in Z[A], p. [163], are both used in "New England Reformers," *W*, III, 280.

Genius casting behind   S ⟨8⟩21
Fact abides if I can't explain   N 34
Religion indemnity   J 29 [359]

[158] "And Virtue's whole sum is but know & dare." [T 183, C 90]

"M↑i↓nds that are great & free
Do not on fortune pause
'Tis crown enough to Virtue still her own applause."
Θ 29 [Enc. 264]
"Were it the will of Heaven an osier bough
Were vessel safe enough the seas to plough" [360] [A 167, T 185]
"There can be no true valor in a bad cause." *Ancient Gleeman* [Q 30, T 5]

[159]   Lect. V.
Tendencies [361]
        Great activity of thought & of experimenting.
        ⟨A⟩The Church or religious party falling from the Church
↑Visible↓ & appearing in Abolition & ⟨T⟩Non Resistance societies. Temperance, Farming, Palmer. Bible Convention,
        A keener scrutiny & criticism of institutions & domestic life than ever & much protesting. & changes of Employment. Some vaporing & backsliding
        In every movement a good result, a tendency to simpler methods & to an assertion of the sufficiency of the private man. An individual excommunicating a Church (good whilst original). Further in the gradual withdrawal of the best from organization
        Concert & Character
        They are the two who must play out the play

[359] " 'Never was . . . Scaliger" is struck through in pencil with a vertical use mark. "Whatever you . . . J 29" is in pencil. The sentence in Journal J, p. [15], "Power behind . . . communications", and the passages cited in K, p. [77], Notebook S (Salvage), p. [21], and N, p. [34], are used in "New England Reformers," *W*, III, 254, 281–282, 271–272, and 282.

[360] " 'Minds that . . . plough" is struck through in pencil with a vertical use mark; the first entry, misquoted from Ben Jonson, is used in "Duty," and the second, by Pindar, is used in "The School," *Lectures*, III, 149 and 41. For "Θ", see p. [14] above.

[361] P. [159] may be working notes for the fifth lecture in the "New England" series. See Index Minor, pp. [93]–[94] below, for a later outline of "New England Reformers."

A philosophy is getting up for Concert   Le Roux, Comte,
    Concert. Every member of party wishes
            Education
            Politics
            Social Reform

Though I have never spoken the truth it is here for me   K 77
Too slight & fickle: lose spring at 30:
Stimulating power of all genius   *Education* 46
Lect on *Character* Washington, H. Tooke, [D 144] *Valuation*[362]

[160] [a]/ In the garden, the eye watches the flying cloud & Walden woods, but turns from the Village. Poor society[!] what hast thou done to be the aversion of us all? [D 42] See also *The Hens*. C 298, & *Nature*[n] D 185

[b]/ I do not wish to know that my shell is a strombus or my moth a Vanessa but I wish to unite the shell & the moth to my being.[363]
[D 99, 160]

[c]/ Is not life a puny unprofitable discipline whose ⟨direct⟩ ↑amount of↓ advantage may be fairly represented by the ⟨direct⟩ ↑amount of↓ education that is got at College? C 26

[d]/ In Life all finding is not that thing we sought but somewhat else.
[e]/   The preponderance of nature over Will in every life is great.

---

[362] "Concert. Every . . . wishes", "Though I . . . K 77", and "Stimulating . . . *Valuation*" are in pencil. "Too slight & fickle:" is struck through in ink with a diagonal use mark. "Great activity . . . organization" is used in "New England Reformers," *W*, III, 251 and 253–255. With "Concert & Character", cf. *ibid.*, p. 263. Sections on "Concert . . . Social Reform" begin, *ibid.*, pp. 263, 267, 255, and 256. The passage cited in Journal K, p. [77], is used, *ibid.*, p. 282. "Too slight . . . 30:" is expanded in the lecture "Manners and Customs of New England." With "Stimulating . . . genius", cf. "Education," *Lectures*, III, 297–300, partly used in "New England Reformers," *W*, III, 270–271. The manuscript of the lecture "Character" does not survive, but cf. "Character," *W*, III, 89 and 101.

[363] "In the garden . . . Village.", struck through in pencil with a vertical use mark, is used with the passages cited in Journal C, p. [298], and D, p. [185], in "The Protest," *Lectures*, III, 98. "I do . . . being.", struck through in pencil with a vertical use mark, is used in "Home," *Lectures*, III, 30.

There is less intention in history than we ascribe to it. We impute deep laid far sighted plans to Caesar & Napoleon. The cement or the spine which gave unity to their manifold action was not their logic or long sight but the concatenation of events. My son cannot replace me. I could not replace myself said Napoleon. I am the child of Circumstances said Napoleon. [B 276]

He also said Nothing was more simple than his history [364]

[161] The characteristics of the New Age   D 46 [365]

My will never gave the images in my mind the rank they now take there. The four college years & the three years of divinity have not yielded me so many grand facts as some idle books under the bench at Latin School. We form no guess, at the time of receiving a thought, of its comparative value. [B 104, 276]   See g^n below [366]

f Newton called sculpture stone things & Terence a play book. [B 97] Ill success of almost all orations, &c [B 101]   The finest wits have their sediment. [B 53]

g. We do what we can & then make a theory to prove our practice the best.[367] [A 77] Every man idealizes his own life.

h. We should cleave to the usage until we are sure it is wrong.

i "The highest price we can pay for a thing is to ask for it." Landor.
[Enc. 186]

k Wrath is not worth carrying home though a man should ride. Landor
[B 21]

l By the permanence of Nature minds are trained alike & made intelligible to each other

[364] "The preponderance . . . his history" is struck through in ink with a vertical use mark; "He also . . . his history" is also struck through in ink with two short diagonal cancellation or use marks. "The preponderance . . . & Napoleon." is used in "The School," *Lectures*, III, 37, and "Spiritual Laws," *W*, II, 134.

[365] "The characteristics . . . D 46" is in pencil, overwritten in ink by "rank they . . . there. The", printed below; cf. "The Protest," *Lectures*, III, 89.

[366] "My will . . . value.", struck through in ink with a vertical use mark, is used in "The School," *Lectures*, III, 37.

[367] With "We do . . . best.", copied in Notebook Man, p. [48] above, cf. "Doctrine of the Soul," *Lectures*, III, 13.

^m A man should behave himself as a guest in nature not as a drone.

ⁿ I count no man much because he cows or silences me[;] any fool can do that but if his conversation enriches or rejoices ⟨y⟩me, I must reckon him wise. [A 21] [368]

^o Every man projects his own character before him[,] praises it, worships it.

[162] ↑a↓ "God, when he makes the prophet, does not unmake the man."
Locke. [BB I, 44, Y 220]

Montaigne   Chap 19   lib 1   On Death

[163]   *Oct 1832* [1842]   Manners [369]
Bad manners of the young men   G 36
Composure   G 39
Mr Cushing & his Boston house   E 339
We are bound to gentilize society   K 126
Wilhelm Meister   J 90
Cultivated life   Li 166,
Manners in the planting states   D 205
Conscience of Manners   D 226
Good sense the foundation   E 323

[164]   Religion [370]

Men not pious but lovers of the pious   E 330½   N 72
Religion indemnity for inferiority   J 29
You are not good enough to be Reformer   J 139, 39, 118
Grief   J 62

[368] "By the permanence . . . other", struck through in pencil with a diagonal use mark, is used in "The School," *Lectures*, III, 41. Emerson extended the use mark through "A man . . . drone." (Journal C, p. [109]); cf. "Home," and "Tragedy," *Lectures*, III, 32 and 113. For the passage in A, p. [21], see Notebook Δ, p. [7] above.

[369] See p. [1] above, where "Manners" is listed among what are probably topics for the lecture series on "New England."

[370] See p. [1] above, where "Religion" is listed among what are probably topics for the lecture series on "New England."

Calvinism constitutional   J 85   N 72
Intellect grows by moral obedience   J 95
  Sunday   J 102
    No devils   J 108
Good men must not obey the laws   J 112, K 22, E 42
Keep pure of the Race   J 120
Keep pure of the few as of the many   K 122
You are responsible for the civil law   K 22
Divine persons   K 52, 53, 23,   E 330
Platonists nobly pious   K 56
Never a question whether to do wrong   K 71
History of Christ a document of character   K 76
Preacher cunning   K 87
Mrs Black   K 97½   Z
Modern Xy trade in mummy   K 116
Boldness yes   but whence is boldness   K 122
Do the gods bless by halves   K 123
Church aerates   G 22
Unitarian   G 27
We cannot meet   G 34   C 287
Shaker Faith   N 71
Why need we answer catechism when the Fact abides   N 34 [371]
Ecstasy   E. 254 ↑257↓   Blessed are they who have no powers.
[165] ——
They call it Xy   I call it Consciousness

———

Swedenborgians must be humored   D 39
Beautiful is the veneration of men   D 46
Swedenborgianism & Manicheeism   D 148
Teaching that shows the omnipotence of the Will, Spiritual   D 271

---

[371] "History of . . . K 76" is struck through in ink with a vertical use mark; the passages cited in Journal K, pp. [122] and [76], are used in "Character," *W*, III, 100 and 114. The passages cited in J, pp. [39], [118], [108], and [112], and N, p. [34], are used in "New England Reformers," *W*, III, 261 and 262–263, 262, 278, 280, and 282. The passage in J, p. [85], is used in "Experience," and "Good men . . . laws" in "Politics," *W*, III, 51 and 208. The passages cited in J, p. [95], and N, p. [71], are used in "Discourse at Nantucket," and E, p. [42], and K, p. [116], in "Worship," *W*, VI, 237–238 and cf. 209.

The Capital Crime with which the Church stands charged is Poverty.
E 113

Excessive exaggeration of Persons   E 321
J. Bunyan's Life.
Complaint of Unit[arianis]m contra Calv[inis]m accuses Unitm
D 346 [372]

Always suppose God   C 112
⟨S⟩⟨X⟩Christ preaches the greatness of man but we the greatness of Xt
C 278

Humility of San Felippo
To him who said it before
Thanksgiving Sermon   O

> Trade in mummy   K 116
> Unitarian   G 27
> Poverty of Ch   E 113 [373]

[166]   *Human Life*

> Man
> Laws of the world, Dualism, Limitation,
> Moral laws
> Home, childhood, marriage
> Labor
> Friends, One Mind,
> Politics
> Letters   Books
> Mistakes
> Beatitude
> The Present Age
>
> Taste   Beauty   Art
> Faith

---

[372] The sentence cited in Journal E, p. [113], is used in the manuscript of the lecture "Recent Literary and Spiritual Influences." Emerson quotes a passage from Bunyan in the lecture "Genius of the Anglo-Saxon Race." With the paragraph cited in D, p. [346], cf. "New England Reformers," *W*, III, 279.

[373] "Trade in . . . E 113" is in pencil; all three entries are repeated from pp. [164]–[165] above.

Idols
Realism or the ⟨a⟩basis of every triviality in an Idea [374]

Religion   N. Eng. ⟨dissent⟩Puritanism [n]
In   Idealism
N.E.   Calvinism
        ↑J Bunyan
        Connecticutt N 72↓
        Refinement
        Sunday D 366, J 102
        Unitarianism
        Boston
        Channing
        Divinity School   Lect *PA* 39,[375] H 85,
        Rattles in the pod N 38   *wis wis* [H 45–46]
        Lyceum
                    German University D 294
        H. University.[376]
Φ 120—   Aeration G 22
        ⟨J⟩Swedenborgianism
        Shakers
        Commencement G 76, 92 B 227 N 106
        Cambridge H 85 J 34,
        Americans apologize for Scholarship D 99
        Books sell better for religion in N.E.[377]

---

[374] "*Human Life* . . . Idea", in pencil, is probably a list of trial topics jotted down during early planning for the "Human Life" lecture series in the fall of 1838. The topics are continued on pp. [167] and [169] below. "*Human Life* . . . Present Age" is partially overwritten in ink by "Idealism . . . Americans", printed below.
[375] *Lectures*, III, 457 (notes).
[376] "H. University." is connected with "Commencement" and "Cambridge" below by an ink line in the left margin.
[377] Notes in the ink layer of p. [166] are used in the first three lectures in the "New England" series. "Religion In . . . Refinement" and "Books sell . . . N.E." are developed in "Genius of the Anglo-Saxon Race." "Boston", "Shakers", and the paragraph cited in Journal J, p. [34], are used in "Trade," and the passage cited in D, p. [103], in "Manners and Customs of New England."

Englishman
Melancholy of Saxon Mind [378]
B 117   D 11, 103, 95,
Engd held up by all dollars   N 75

Trade in mummy   K 116 ↑N 38↓
Unitarianism   G 27
Poverty of Ch [379] [E 113]

[167] Demonology
  Comic
  Emphasis of parts of life, history, & literature
  Renunciation, non interference,
  The life & society of Truth
  Travelling
  Men of letters

1.	Introduction				
2	Child	Youth	Health		
3	Apprentice	⟨Protest⟩ Mistakes, Travelling,			
4	Love				
5	Duty	Protest			
6	Beauty	letters	Nature	Art	
7	Society. Politics				
8	Condition	Poverty & Riches		Love	
9	Church			Genius	
10	New Life			Duty	
				Society	

History: realism: Church
Reform   Domestic Service. Money. Animal food.

      Society
      Duty

[378] See "Permanent Traits of the English National Genius," *Lectures*, I, 233–252, much of which is used in the manuscript of the lecture "Genius of the Anglo-Saxon Race."

[379] "Engd held . . . of Ch" is in pencil. The sentence cited in Journal N, p. [75], is used in the lecture "Genius of the Anglo-Saxon Race." See pp. [164]–[165] above for "Trade in . . . of Ch".

Church
Sorrow [380]

Agriculture & Trade
Country
Farmers
Farms   pig N 77
Education: Valued
Pedlars
Schoolmasters, Preachers   Book agents
Country unpeopled of good brain [N 63]
Village traits   N 35, 22,
Wagon [C 27]
Bar rooms [E 78]
Teamsters' Mottoes [D 355]
Cornwallis [E 9–10]

Merchants
Cities
Boston   N 83

In cities, great contrasts seen: [B 294] Sacs & Fox. [C 209]
Praise of cities N 44   /   Harvard   J 34

Hands
Labor
Selection in labor   N 20
No magic in making money   N 82 [381]

---

[380] "Demonology . . . Sorrow", in pencil, is a continuation of the trial topics and titles for the "Human Life" series listed on p. [166] above. "Demonology" may have been added. "Comic . . . Beauty letters" is overwritten in ink by "Agriculture & Trade . . . Boston N 83" and "Church . . . Reform" by "In cities . . . Labor", printed below. "Introduction", "Child", and "Love" are struck through in pencil with single diagonal use marks.

[381] "Agriculture & Trade . . . N 82" is probably working notes for the lecture "Trade." "Pedlars", "Schoolmasters," "Country", "Bar rooms", "Teamsters Mottos", "Cornwallis", "Merchants", "Cities", "Boston", and "In cities . . . J 34" are struck through in pencil with single diagonal use marks. "Hands" may refer to the lecture

[168]   A new age   the old subjective   the new subjective
The age of the Soul   Justice has not been done to Man.
The irresistible inward advance of it   Much is dark & cannot be solved
but much can   We will be true to that
And its first revolution is the great soul   Let us not be too anxious
to weld the new to the old but accept the great gift of God & open it
as fast as we can.
↑Great is the Soul↓
     Magazine man; Ney; no boxes; extravagant souls;
pledges   Di|| ... || parle bien de dieu
We say the soul is great & the world must take its law
History has been irreligious, courtly, obtuse, external. Art poor &
low; Poetry feeble; Youth hopeless; Society degrading
The love of Nature a sign of revolution; in Wordsworth, &c
History of the Quakers; & Clarendon's Falkland
Great is the soul & we thereby wiser than we know.
We must obey it
                         Conclusion
Society true & false   Sanity rare   D 61
                        Simplicity   D 172
                        Sincerity   D 179
                        If I could utter D 183
                        There is always a higher   D 188
                        Obey the Upper power   D   196 [382]

"Doctrine of the Hands" and "Labor" to the lecture "Trades and Professions";
passages from both earlier lectures are used in "Trades."
    [382] "A new age . . . 196", in pencil, is overwritten in ink by "Climate, . . .
D 170", printed below. "A new age . . . true & false" is probably an early summary
or notes for "Doctrine of the Soul"; see also Notebook F No. 1, p. [102], and Δ,
p. [47], above. "A new age . . . to Man.", "And its first . . . great soul", and
"Magazine man . . . souls;" are developed in "Doctrine of the Soul," *Lectures*, III,
5–6, 9, and 11–14; for "pledges", see notes to p. 15 in *Lectures*, III, 392; "in
Wordsworth . . . Falkland", "Great . . . obey it", and "Society . . . false" are
developed in "Doctrine of the Soul," *Lectures*, III, 7–9, 15–20, and 16–17. "Conclusion . . . D   196" may have been added later. With the paragraph in Journal
D, p. [61], cf. "The Protest," *Lectures*, III, 85; passages in D, pp. [172], [179],
and [196], are in both "Religion," *Lectures*, III, 285 and 281, and "The Over-
Soul," *W*, II, 291–293.

Climate, Frost, Economy.   Uses of snow & Hurts
Manners & Genius
Hunger   N 76   H.48
Rashness. too much canvass
Want of steadfastness   Z.128
Love of intoxication [E 164]
Great elbowroom
Column of Am. population [E 283]
Internal Improvements
Great Travellers   N 74, J 136, E 330½

Love of Eloquence
    Faneuil Hall ↑C 227, 306,↓ [383]

Man of strong will more valued at south
Northerner & Southerner   E 352

Recent Intellectual influences
    Webster   Edin. Review
    Everett   Scott
    Allston   Byron
    Channing
    Wordsworth
    Carlyle
    Germany
    Phrenology
    Mesmerism ↑J 119↓
    Lectures, Lyceum & other   E 118
    Communities
    Reform
    Use of the Abolitionist   B 33   D 170

[169] Lecture I   Doctrine of the Soul
          II   Home
          III   The School
          IV   Love

[383] "C 227, 306," is added in pencil.

4 1 5

V.   Genius
VI.   The Protest
VII   Tragedy.
VIII. Comedy
IX.   Duty
X   Demonology.[384]

Politics   N 97
    Barrooms   E 78
    Rowdies & Paddies   H 75   N 42
    Parties   H 97
    Position of Woman

                    N 21 Do not be afraid to fail
                    Demosthenes in Burke
                    J Q A
                    Horsemanship — [Z[A] 127]

                    Climate &c
                    Indian Summer   C 136   N 108
                    Winter
                    Flowers   K.94

    Chevalier
    De Tocqueville
    Hudibras [385]

[170] Men should be placed; domesticated[,] centred; not as now out of place, slight, vagabond, disconcertable.

———

The life of man the true romance [E 230]

———

[384] "Lecture I . . . Demonology.", in pencil, is a list of the final titles for the "Human Life" lecture series. "Lecture I   Doctrine" is overwritten in ink by "Parties . . . Woman", printed below. See *JMN*, VII, 124, n. 362.
    [385] "Climate, Frost . . . D 170" on p. [168] and "Politics N 97 . . . Hudibras" on p. [169] are probably early notes for the entire lecture series on "New England"; entries are used or developed in all five lectures.

Men wish to hold others responsible, & to lay no finger to the load; but no disclaimer or protest will exonerate them.

———

You are not good enough to be a reformer
↑We marry no worse than we eat or speak. [J 118]
pedantry to give importance to property↓ [G 114]

———

After all our accretion of facts we are poor

———

Yet every man would be a Benefactor [N 12–13]

———

We have never seen a man. [K 99]
We have not quite served up to our thought [H 120]
Constancy   N 88

Obedience to genius the only liberation
Expect nothing from concert. Concert when concertors.
Cheerfulness.[386] Literature is disconsolate according to St Simon

[171] Men culminate too fast. [N 106] We must find a new & more powerful Spring. Education must. ↑It↓ Needs not to look out for doomsdays, overturns, & Millenniums, they are already here, death & death everywhere. Too easily pleased, American & European. Educated men, as easily; fatal facility. The college joke lasts forty years! A marriage, a removal, a setting up in trade, a fire, lasts as long, and is the date in a man's biography[.]

Eternity.   Identity   Past
Kitty & her tail [N 30]

Every thing is in Man. The idea of God is one of his possessions
He is coming to know his right estate

[386] The passages cited in Journal E, p. [230], J, p. [118], G, p. [114], N, pp. [12]–[13], and "Obedience . . . Cheerfulness." are used in "New England Reformers," W, III, 285, 262, 277–278, 284–285, and 265–266. The passages in K, p. [99], and H, p. [120], are used in "Character," W, III, 113–114 and 102.

he must be constant
cheerful
obedient to his genius
Nothing is so strong in place nor so slight when displaced [387]

[172] [388]   Vulgar reformers   D 53   154   173
Antimoney   D 154
Martyrs chiefly pseudo   C 343   347   D 97, 98, 99,
D 206, B 101

The great questions   C 245, D 11
The new Age   D 46 [389]

Politics
They are expressions of the Inevitable
power cannot part from *man*

or

things
men, it was claimed, should make the law for men
property   for property
But now & ever man has some right to things [390]

Art
p 100

[inside back cover]   Protest   134

Poet
symbolizes
& so emancipates

[387] "Men culminate . . . biography" may be notes for the lecture "Manners and
Customs of New England"; the passage in Journal N, pp. [106]–[107], was later
used in "Domestic Life," *W*, VII, 123–125. "Every thing . . . displaced" is in
pencil.
[388] Notes on p. [172] and the inside back cover are in pencil.
[389] The passages cited in Journal C, pp. [347] and [245], are used in "Reforms," and D, p. [98], in "Tendencies," *Lectures*, III, 268 and 256–257, and 310.
[390] Cf. "Politics," *W*, III, 201–205.

Symbols

Things are more beautiful as symbols than as ultimates
of a fair mother the fairer daughter [391]

μερος [392]

---

[391] Cf. "The Poet," *W*, III, 13 and 32.
[392] "Lot" or "portion" (Ed.).

Ж

1839–1842, 1851

Though there is only one date in Notebook Ж, Emerson evidently began it in October or early November, 1839, with a survey of his journals for his lecture series on "The Present Age," a list of possible topics or titles, several trial collections, and working notes for the composition of the lectures, given December 4, 1839, to February 12, 1840. He used it again, probably in 1840, to outline a paragraph in "Self-Reliance," and for notes for "Friendship" and the essay "Love" for *Essays* [*First Series*], and for notes for the lecture "Man the Reformer," given January 25, 1841. In the fall of 1841 he used it again for a survey of the journals, a list of titles and possible topics, and working notes probably for the lectures on "The Times," given December 2, 1841, to January 20, 1842. Notes dated 1851 are probably for lectures on "The Conduct of Life" given in 1851; Emerson probably scanned earlier notes in Notebook Ж for this series also.

Notebook Ж is a copybook with stiff coverboards measuring 16.2 x 21.2 cm and covered with blue and black marbled buff paper, and a spine of worn black leather crossed with 2 pairs of gold bars at the top and 2 at the bottom. The front cover is inscribed "Ж" in ink and has two ink blots. The leaves, faintly ruled, measure 16 x 20.5 cm. Including 2 front and 2 back flyleaves, there are 174 pages. After page 115, Emerson skipped two blank pages in numbering; the editor has renumbered the 4 pages following 115: 116$_1$, 117$_1$, 116$_2$, and 117$_2$. Pages numbered in ink are 1–23, 25, 27, 29–35, 40, 44–48, 50, 52–55, 57, 60, 62–63, 70–71, 74–75, 78–80, 82–84, 88–90, 98–102, 104–105, 107–113, 116$_2$, 120–123, 128, 130–132, 134, 136, 138–140, 142, 144, 146, 148, 150, 152, and 158. Numbered in pencil are pages 26, 36–39, 64, 66–67, 72–73, 92–97, and 124. Page 24 is numbered in ink over the same in pencil. The rest are unnumbered. Pages iii–iv, 21–22, 25–26, 28–29, 38, 40–46, 68–70, 72–73, 76–78, 80–82, 86–87, 96, 101–103, 105, 116$_1$–117$_1$, 118–119, 123, 131, 134–137, 140–141, 143–155, 157, and 167 are blank.

[front cover]   Ж

[i]   R.W. Emerson

[1] Although Emerson began Notebook Ж in 1839, he apparently did not index it
until 1841 or later. The first column below, in pencil partially erased, is a preliminary index. "Our Boston 104", in a smaller hand, may have been added.
"Lectures 128", at the top of the page, is also in pencil. The alphabetized second
column is in ink; "Fashion 126", in a smaller hand, may also have been added.

[ii] Metres

> In the desart a fountain is springing
> In the wild waste there still is a tree
> And a bird in the solitud[e] singing
> That speaks to my spirit of thee
> > [Byron, "Stanzas to Augusta," ll. 45–48]

——

> Come to Licoo the sun is riding [2]
> > [Anon., "Song of the Tonga-Islanders," l. 1]

——

> Not a drum was heard nor a funeral note
> > [Charles Wolfe, "The Burial of Sir John
> > Moore at Corunna," l. 1]

——

> I got me flowers to strew my way [3]
> > [George Herbert, "Easter Song," l. 1]

——

> The unearthly voices ceased
> —— [Scott, *The Lay of the Last Minstrel*, I, xviii, l.1]

[iii]–[iv] [blank]

[1]　　　　　　　　　　Miscellaneous Topics [4]

Communion service a document of Genius　　D 244
Only the Soul avails in dealing with a child　　D 245

[2] See *JMN*, I, 385, and Emerson's *Parnassus* (Boston, 1875), p. 380.

[3] This line is struck through in pencil with a diagonal use mark. These "Metres" may have been collected for a section on metre in "The Poet," *Lectures*, III, 358–359; Emerson lists "Herbert's . . . Easter" among examples of metre in "Poetry and Imagination," *W*, VIII, 55, an essay partly derived from this lecture.

[4] Pp. [1]–[10] are probably a preliminary survey of Emerson's journals for his 1839–1840 lecture series on "The Present Age." Only three of the lecture manuscripts in this series are complete; others have small gaps, and three are fragmentary or missing: "Politics" lacks fourteen leaves, only three brief fragments remain that can be assigned with any certainty to "Private Life," and "Ethics" is entirely missing. Some passages in the four essays Emerson had probably already written, "History," "Self-Reliance," "Compensation," and "Spiritual Laws," may have been used in these lectures, and some parts of "Private Life" may survive in "Friendship" and "Domestic Life." On p. [1], ll. 3, 7, 12, 13, and 23–25 have short vertical or diagonal marks in ink in the left margin, which may indicate use or transfer to another page; such markings are used only on pp. [2]–[10], [17]–[18], and [47] below. Similar but doubled marks are used in Notebook Φ, pp. [54]–[57], [61], [63] and [64], and Index Minor, pp. [6]–[7], all probably of later date.

Pleasures of sickness   D 246
If you can draw all lines why draw any?   D 246
Find a man's limitations & the game is up   D 246
Public speaking does not utter the character   D 247
A child's toys affecting   D 247
Easy as Falling. Falling   D 247 [5]
Insanity inconvertible   D 247
In morning the man walks, in eve[nin]g the feet. D 249
Epaminondas's silence   D 249
E.L.T.   D 249
Pathos his in small matters   D 252
Ask the tax gatherer if he be just
Memory *that & this*   D 255,
Music floats the discords   D 255
Belinda & Montreville   D 256
Child coughs to be somewhat   D 256
No age in talk   D 256
Village love puts distance between boy & girl   D 256
Brant's head   D 257
The Actual an optical illusion as in Brant's war   D 257
Extravagant compliment this reading   D 259
Church does not respect the Soul   D 259 [6]

[5] "Only the . . . D 245" is struck through in ink with a vertical use mark; the paragraph is used in "Religion," *Lectures*, III, 282, and "The Over-Soul," *W*, II, 279. A vertical use mark in ink through "If you . . . any?" has been finger-wiped. "Find a man's . . . character D 247" is struck through in ink with a vertical use mark; Emerson canceled the paragraph cited in Journal D, p. [246] ("Find . . ."), in "Education," *Lectures*, III, 497(notes), and used it in "Circles," *W*, II, 308; the paragraph in D, p. [247]("Public . . ."), is used in "Spiritual Laws," *W*, II, 152, and "Politics," *Lectures*, III, 244. "Easy as Falling." is struck through in pencil with a vertical use mark; the paragraph is used in "Spiritual Laws," *W*, II, 137.

[6] The passage about Ellen Tucker Emerson in Journal D, p. [249], is used in "Love," *W*, II, 178. "Music floats . . . D 255" is struck through in ink with a vertical use mark; cf. D, p. [262], which incorporates this phrase and is used in "Education," *Lectures*, III, 298–299. Emerson extended this use mark in pencil through "Belinda & Montreville 256", used in "Spiritual Laws," *W*, II, 149–150. "Village love . . . D 256" is struck through in pencil with a vertical use mark; the paragraph is used in "Love," *W*, II, 172–173. Emerson first struck through "Brants head" with a vertical use mark in ink, then extended it through "Church does . . . D 259"; the first passage cited in D, p. [257], is used in "History," *W*,

Need of the Ch[urch]. Visible only temporary   D 260
"Don't dishonor the Church"   D 260
[2] Isolation must precede society   D 260; 280
Stay at home in your *duties*   D 261
Not by running after Napoleon you Napoleonize   D 261
Conversation gives me self possession   D 262
Institutions illusions   D 263
Painting educates the eye   D 263
Popularity is for dolls. D 264
Men who are where we left them   D 264
Literature peeping   D 264 [7]
Work of art excludes all else   D 265
Conformist abdicates all. D 265
I do not wish to be Epaminondas   D 266.
"To him who said it before"   D 267, 288,
Identity a mercury. D 268
Always scorn appearances & you may   D 269
Cousindom   D 269, 371
Augustine's Aeneas & Dido, D 269 [8]

II, 16, the second in "Politics," *Lectures*, III, 240, and *W*, III, 199; the first paragraph cited in D, p. [259], is used in "Spiritual Laws," and the second in "Self-Reliance," *W*, II, 164–165 and 71; both are used in "Literature" [second lecture], *Lectures*, III, 231 and 228–229.

[7] Lines 1 and 2 on p. [2] are struck through in ink with a vertical use mark; all three passages cited are used in "Self-Reliance," *W*, II, 71–72 and 81; Emerson used "Stay at home" repeatedly; see "History," *W*, II, 8, and cf. "Literature" [second lecture], and "Politics," *Lectures*, III, 230 and 242. "Conversation gives . . . illusions D 263" is struck through in ink with a vertical use mark; the paragraph in D, p. [262], is used in "Education," *Lectures*, III, 298–299. Parts of the first passage cited in D, p. [263], are used in "Self-Reliance," and "Spiritual Laws," *W*, II, 63 and 71, and 155. "Painting . . . D 263" is marked in ink in the left margin; the paragraph is used in "Art," *W*, II, 356–357. "Men who . . . peeping D 264" is struck through in ink with a vertical use mark, and both lines are marked in ink in the left margin; the second passage is used in "Literature" [second lecture], *Lectures*, III, 230, and cf. "Spiritual Laws," *W*, II, 164.

[8] "Work of art . . . else D 265" is struck through in pencil with a vertical use mark; the passage is used in "Art," *W*, II, 355 and 356, and cf. "Religion," *Lectures*, III, 284. "Conformist . . . D 266." is struck through in ink with a vertical use mark; the first passage cited is used in "Self-Reliance," *W*, II, 54–55, and "Tendencies," *Lectures*, III, 309, the second in "Spiritual Laws," *W*, II, 162–163, and "Reforms," *Lectures*, III, 267. Lines 13 and 14 are marked in ink in the left

Xy as now preached caricatures Compensation   D 270
St Augustine concerning the Philosophers   D 271
Conventional character of English drawing   D 272
All foreign wonders once domestic   D 272
Good housekeeping impossible?   D 272
Best part of each writer nothing private   D 273
Eternity & omnipresence are proper   D 274
Realism of the poets; Fletcher Cartwright   D 275
Beaumont & Fletcher   D 276-7-8
The poet must be proper Caesar or cannot sing Caesar. D 278 [9]
[3] There must be epic as well as lyric   D 281
To each his own the liberal God supplies: My books my gallery ↑D↓ 282
Artificial memory: value of a Catalogue   D 282.
To know one you must know all. D 284   E 28.
Self trust & vanity   D 284
Authors don't like to see their readers   D 285
We would live with those we are used to. D 285
How great to do a little   D 286
Truth of character. Don't apologize for not visiting   D 286
Landor's Pericles. ↑287, 294,↓ Goodwill elegant. ↑287, 386↓ Honor the
philanthropies of the day   D 287
Strike sail to none. Nature has made wives for scholars   D 287
Beasts belong to the Hour   D 288
Pereant qui ante nos nostra dixerunt   D 288, C 156
The progressors Janus faced   D 288

---

margin; part of D, p. [268], is used in "Intellect," *W*, II, 340–341. "Always
scorn . . . may   D 269" is struck through in ink with a vertical use mark; the
paragraph is used in "Self-Reliance," *W*, II, 59, and "Tendencies," *Lectures*, III,
311. "Augustine's . . . D 269" is struck through with a vertical use mark and marked
in the left margin in ink; the quotation is used in "Literature" [second lecture],
Lectures, III, 231.

[9] "Conventional . . . drawing   D 272" and the last five lines on p. [2] have
marginal markings in ink. "Good . . . D 272" is struck through in ink with a
vertical use mark; the passage cited is used in "Domestic Life," *W*, VII, 112. The
paragraphs cited in Journal D, pp. [270] and [273], are used in "Compensation,"
W, II, 94–95 and 108. Part of the cited passage on "Beaumont & Fletcher" is used in
"Self-Reliance," *W*, II, 78. "The poet . . . Caesar. D 278" is struck through in ink
with a vertical use mark; parts of the paragraph cited are used in "Spiritual Laws,"
W, II, 165–166, and "Literature" [second lecture], *Lectures*, III, 231–232.

You know is it Truth or Tradition by the tone of the speech   289 [10]
Make daylight shine through your writing   289
All men's life superficial   D 289
↑D 207, 210,↓ God despiseth Size   D 289   Life in Moments. C 299 [11]
Propriety of great writers   D 290
One picture better than many   D 290   So one *man.*[n]
O unauthorized preacher pain & care are *things* [n]   D 291
Concealment impossible   D 292
Untune nobody   D 292
Fear goes before Rottenness   293 [12]
Germany & Bettina   D 294, 178,
A right college   D 294
[4] ⟨If I love you what is that to you⟩ D 295
Allston's genius & defect   D 296, 314, ↑332,↓
If the Absolute theory of life is wrong vae vobis   D 297
⟨The poor mind must *have* [n] somewhat⟩ D 298
⟨The Compensations of Calamity⟩ D 298
Self-help must be preached. Yankee boy   D 299 [13]

[10] Lines 1, 2, 6, and 7 on p. [3] have marginal markings in ink. "Truth of character." is struck through in ink with a vertical use mark; this passage in Journal D, p. [286], is used in "Spiritual Laws," *W*, II, 160–161. The paragraph on "philanthropies of the day" cited in D, p. [287], is used in "Reforms," *Lectures*, III, 260. "Strike sail . . . D 287", marked in ink in the margin, is used in "Spiritual Laws," *W*, II, 151. "You know . . . speech 289" and the two preceding lines are set off by marginal markings in ink.

[11] "Make daylight . . . writing" is also part of the paragraph "God despiseth Size" cited below, used in "Spiritual Laws," *W*, II, 161–162. *"All mens . . .* D 289", struck through in ink with a vertical use mark and marked in ink in the margin, and part of the paragraph "God despiseth Size" are used in "Reforms," *Lectures*, III, 259 and 266–267; cf. also "Domestic Life," *W*, VII, 109 and 110. The quotation in Journal C, p. [299], is used in "Politics," *Lectures*, III, 239.

[12] "Propriety of . . . writers   D 290" is marked in the margin; cf. "Literature" [first lecture], *Lectures*, III, 218. "Concealment . . . D 292 and the following line are both marked in the margin. "Fear goes . . . 293" is struck through in ink with a diagonal use mark; this paragraph and part of the first passage cited in Journal D, p. [292], are used in "Compensation," *W*, II, 111–112, and 116. "Untune nobody" is used in the "Discourse at Middlebury College" (July 22, 1845).

[13] All but ll. 3, 5, 8, 12, 25, and 26 on p. [4] have short vertical or diagonal marks in ink in the left margin (see Plate III). "The poor . . . boy   D 299" is struck through in ink with a vertical use mark; the first passage cited is used in "Spiritual Laws," the second in "Compensation," and the third in "Self-Reliance,"

The garden discovery   D 300
No History, Only biography. D 300, 322,
We disbelieve in the puissance of Today   D 301–2
Nature says, So hot Sir! D 303
A man amenable for his vocation   D 303
A man's Self travels ghost like with him   D 303
↑D 313, 304, 328,↓ Manual labor. Heroism of 1839, D 304 [14]
Why give the children all the romance of life   D 305
Lotus eaters. Damper of reform   D 306
We fear for the Not-Natural   D 307
Compression of style & ellipsis. D 307, 350, 354
Language, spolia opima   D 307
Our Scholars not learned & cannot be   D 308
The consecration of Sabbath owns the desecration of ↑the rest↓ D 308
List of reforms   D 309
Foreigners write as well as natives   D 309
My life a may game   D 309
Love thaumaturgic   D 309
Great man among small matters shows the divine in them   310
The riches of Nature in Dartmouth sheriff   D 310 [15]

W, II, 163, 126–127, and 75–76; the first and third are used in "Reforms," *Lectures*, III, 267–268, and 264–265. "332," is added in pencil.

[14] "We disbelieve . . . D 301–2", struck through in ink with a vertical use mark, is used in "Compensation," *W*, II, 124–126. "Nature says . . . Sir! D 303", struck through in ink with a vertical use mark, is used in "Spiritual Laws," *W*, II, 135, and "Education," *Lectures*, III, 299. "Manual labor." is struck through in ink with a vertical use mark, and "A man . . . labor." with four scribbled pencil marks, possibly to connect the ink use marks above and below; the second paragraph cited in Journal D, p. [303], is used in "Spiritual Laws," *W*, II, 140, and the third in "Self-Reliance," *W*, II, 81–82, and partly in "Tendencies," *Lectures*, III, 314. The paragraph on "Manual labor." in D, p. [328], is used in "Reforms," *Lectures*, III, 263–264; one sentence is used with the passage in D, p. [304], in a section on manual labor in pages probably substituted for a later reading of "Reforms," *Lectures*, III, 487–488(notes); both passages are also in a fragmentary lecture on labor and reform (ms. Houghton Library).

[15] The first passage cited in Journal D, p. [308], is used in The Present Age: "Introductory," *Lectures*, III, 194; cf. also "Thoughts on Modern Literature," *The Dial*, I (Oct. 1840), 154 (*W*, XII, 327). "The consecration . . . rest" is used in "Domestic Life," *W*, VII, 132. With the "List of reforms" in D, p. [309], cf. "Introductory," and "Reforms," *Lectures*, III, 196 and 257. "My life . . . thaumaturgic D 309" is struck through in ink with a vertical use mark; the first para-

Doctrine of the soul ↑D↓ 311
[5] Analysis legitimate & poetic   D 312
Two absolutions   D 312
Iteration   313
Manual labor consoles   D 313
All history subjective   D 314
⟨True prayers of farmer   D 314⟩
⟨The friends whom God sends me ↑D↓ 315–6⟩, E 92
Goethe teaches freedom of treating topics   D 319
The naturalist & artist must work by insight   D 319
⟨⟨N⟩Be sacred. None comes near but by my act   D 320⟩
⟨I would have friends, yet would seldom use them⟩ D 321
⟨Degrees of idealism   D 322⟩
Beauty a shield   D 324
A Defence of the Art of Composition   D 324
⟨What we are we must teach⟩ D 325, 356,[16]
⟨Rhyme & music may speak truth⟩ D 326–7
Chance pictures   D 326
Old Eng. poetry like old painting   D 327
Rembrandt paints reflections not substances   327
Reform must not be partial   D 328
Faith in suspenders   D 330
A friend is child & father of time   D 331
⟨Roses do not look back⟩ D 331, 338,

---

graph cited is used in "Reforms," the second in "Religion," *Lectures*, III, 268 and 279. "The riches . . . sheriff   D 310" is struck through in ink with a diagonal use mark; the passage cited is used in "Prospects," *Lectures*, III, 371.

[16] All but ll. 3, 5, 6, 9, and 27 on p. [5] have short vertical or diagonal marks in ink in the left margin. The paragraph on "Analysis" in Journal D, p. [312], is used in The Present Age: "Introductory," *Lectures*, III, 195. The second paragraph in D, p. [312], is used in "Self-Reliance," *W*, II, 74. Passages in D, p. [315], E, p. [92], and D, p. [321], are used in "Friendship," *W*, II, 194–195, and 214–216. One sentence on Goethe in D, p. [319], is used in "Literature" [first lecture], *Lectures*, III, 222. Part of the paragraph cited in D, p. [320], is used in "Self-Reliance," *W*, II, 72, and cf. "Literature" [second lecture], and "Reforms," *Lectures*, III, 234 and 260. The first paragraph cited in D, p. [324], is used in "Prospects," *Lectures*, III, 369, and part of the second in "Self-Reliance," *W*, II, 59, and "Tendencies," *Lectures*, III, 311. "What we . . . 356," is struck through in ink with a vertical use mark; both passages are used in "Religion," *Lectures*, III, 282, and "The Over-Soul," *W*, II, 286.

Transcendentalism   D 331   C 309
Secret of great pictures   D 33⟨5⟩3
⟨Doctrine of hatred   D⟩ 335 [17]
A Lecture   D 336
[6] ⟨Objection to conforming   D 337⟩
Obligation to the Reformers   337
Party makes men drunk, D 338
Hospitality   D 338
The miracle always spiritual. D 339
Extempore speech good & so is writing   D 339
⟨Past baked my loaf I break the oven⟩ D 339
⟨Common sense astonishes   D 339⟩
The body of the rogue is yet sound   D 340
Pity so near a painter & not paint   D 341
Bambino   D 341
Reform in Housekeeping   D 342 [18]
Two sorts of "Abandon"   D 343
Manners demonological   D 343
⟨Perception *fatal*   343⟩
Beside the great, solid men evanesce   D 343
We owe somewhat to poor pictures [D 343]
Summer Night Light   D 344
⟨A poet a Namer   D⟩ 344

[17] "Reform must . . . D 328" is struck through in ink with a vertical use mark; the paragraph is used in "Reforms," *Lectures*, III, 263–264. The first passage cited in Journal D, p. [331]("A friend . . . time"), is used in "Friendship," *W*, II, 214. "Roses do . . . 338," is struck through in ink with a vertical use mark; the passages are combined in "Self-Reliance," *W*, II, 67, and "Religion," *Lectures*, III, 283–284. The paragraph on "Transcendentalism" in D, p. [331], is used in "Tendencies," *Lectures*, III, 306–307. The paragraph cited in D, p. [335], is used in "Self-Reliance," *W*, II, 51–52.

[18] All but ll. 4, 7–11, 15, and 25 on p. [6] have short diagonal or vertical marks in ink in the left margin. Lines 1 and 2 are struck through in ink with one vertical use mark and ll. 2 and 3 with another. The first paragraph cited is used in "Self-Reliance," *W*, II, 54, and "Tendencies," *Lectures*, III, 309; the second is in "Reforms," *Lectures*, III, 259; the third was probably in "Politics" (see *Lectures*, III, 477 [notes], a torn leaf which can be reconstructed in part from "The Fortune of the Republic," *W*, XI, 519). "The miracle . . . spiritual. D 339" is struck through in ink with a vertical use mark; the paragraph is used in "Religion," *Lectures*, III, 279. "Reform in . . . D 342" is struck through in ink with a vertical use mark; cf. "Domestic Life," *W*, VII, 117–118.

⟨Friends are self elected   D 345⟩
⟨A thought imprisons   D 345⟩
We viciously esteem defects organic   D 345
Popular doctrine of Immortality false   D 345
⟨Conversation an evanescent relation⟩ D 346 [19]
Unitarian complaint of Calvinism accuses Unitarian[is]m   346
Burke a rhetoric   D 348,
Manners must be lazy   348
[7] Tedious self recollection of travellers   D 348
Man or Miracle?— Which? D 349
Appropriate the sentiments we read. 349
How to spend a day nobly   D 350   E 24
H. Mann's Address on Education   D 350
The Aurora Borealis no eye of faith behold, [D 351–352]
I hate preaching   It is a pledge   D 352   372
Chastity selfsufficing   D 353
The mob always interesting   D 353
A young man educated ten years comes out rotten   D 353 [20]
Let the age of words be followed by silence   353
It is base to remember   D 354
How many men can measure with a ton of coals   354
We hate Taxes 'Tis a satire on Govt   354
Wordiness incident to Man   D 354

[19] The paragraph on "Perception *fatal*" in Journal D, p. [343], is used in "Self-Reliance," *W*, II, 65. "Friends are self elected" is used in "Friendship," *W*, II, 209. "We viciously . . . organic D 345" is struck through in ink with a discontinuous vertical use mark; the paragraph is used in "Politics," and the first sentence in "Education," *Lectures*, III, 245–246 and 297. "Popular doctrine . . . D 346" is struck through in ink with a vertical use mark; with "Popular doctrine . . . false", cf. "Religion," *Lectures*, III, 277; the paragraph cited in D, p. [346], is used in "Friendship," *W*, II, 208.

[20] All but ll. 1–3, 5, 7–10, 12, 17, 18, and 21 on p. [7] have short diagonal or vertical ink marks in the left margin. "Man or . . . Which? D 349" is struck through in ink with a vertical use mark; the paragraph is used in "Religion," *Lectures*, III, 278–279. Part of the paragraph on "Education" in Journal D, pp. [350]–[351], is used in "Education," *Lectures*, III, 288 and 289, and "New England Reformers," *W*, III, 257. "The Aurora . . . behold," is struck through in ink with a vertical use mark; the paragraph cited is used in The Present Age: "Introductory," *Lectures*, III, 194; the paragraph on "The mob . . ." in D, p. [353], is canceled, *ibid.*, p. 458(notes). "A young . . . D 353" is struck through in ink with a vertical use mark; the paragraph is used in "Education," *Lectures*, III, 288.

Teamsters' mottos. D 355
J. Tuckerman's music   D 355
Literary debates   355
Rich will be ashamed of riches. D 355, E 56,
Dialogue not easy to write   D 356, 281
Water agreeable to the imagination[n]   356
Extempore speech of little moment, & written of little. 356
By doing without Shaksp. you can do sans his book [D 357]
Great man likes to be convicted. 357
Temperance that knows itself, not Temperance   357
To put off the foreign the only condition of insight   358 [21]
⟨These men   358⟩
[8] Oliver Twist   D 361
I must wait to know a friend   D 360
I will have the luxury of plain dealing   D 362
Oliver Cromwell   D 362
I prefer Artists to Generals. 363
Histories fawn on Princes [D 364]
In common hours thoughts do not sit for portraits   364
Milton's saying of wit & imagination   D 364
Sonnet to the woods. 365
Petrarch & his books   365
Life of a poet a catalogue   D 366
I love Sunday   D 366
Promise of great men   366
Seed vessels   367
Mankind right in their ⟨j⟩fames [D 367]
I ignore wo   367
Old Age   368, 370, C 261

[21] "How many . . . Govt   354" is struck through in ink with a vertical use mark; the first paragraph cited is used in "Education," *Lectures*, III, 289, and the second in "Politics," *W*, III, 215. The passage, "Rich will . . . riches.", actually in Journal D, p. [356], is used in "Self-Reliance," *W*, II, 88, and the passage in E, pp. [56]–[57], in "Domestic Life," *W*, VII, 114–115 and 118. "By doing . . . Temperance   357" is struck through in ink with a vertical use mark; the first passage cited is used in a leaf probably added to "Tendencies" for a later reading, *Lectures*, III, 507(notes); the last two are used in "Reforms," *Lectures*, III, 259–260 and 262. "To put off . . . insight" is used in both "Religion," and "Tendencies," *Lectures*, III, 284 and 313.

[22] All but ll. 1, 12, 13, 17, 20, 21, and 25–27 on p. [8] have short vertical or diagonal marks in ink in the left margin. The passage cited in Journal D, p. [360], is used in "Friendship," W, II, 201–202. "I will . . . dealing D 362" and "I prefer . . . 363" are struck through in ink with single vertical use marks; the passage cited in D, p. [363], is used in "Literature" [second lecture], Lectures, III, 225. "In common . . . portraits   364" is struck through in ink with a vertical use mark; the sentence is used in "Intellect," W, II, 336. "Mankind right . . . fames" is struck through in ink with a vertical use mark; the paragraph is used in "Literature" [second lecture], Lectures, III, 229–230. "In Soul . . . one 370" is struck through in ink with a vertical use mark; the sentence is used in "Religion," Lectures, III, 284, and "The Over-Soul," W, II, 269. "Faces on . . . sphere 371" is struck through in ink with a vertical use mark; the sentence is used in "Domestic Life," W, VII, 127, and a manuscript fragment which is probably part of the lecture "Private Life" (ms. Houghton Library).

Varieties of mood D 6.　　Varieties of want　D 2

Not safe to dispute　D 29, C 289, 343,

A few facts suffice　D 31, 101, C 310

Tragedy of women　D 66, 79,

The work not due we like best　D 68

Eloquence　D 72, 6⟨6⟩7,

Eyes　D 73

Society untunes　D 77

Easier to affront the cultivated than the uncul. D 97

Expression　D 104　C 174

A Stranger　D 107 [23]

Let us have a Scale　D 116

[10]　The youth can speak to his contemporaries　D 114

Sickness　D 126 ↑E 20↓

Distinctions of men immoveable　D 143

Facts　D 144

Each dog his day　D 119, 115

Many kinds of insight

Our faculties warrant inceptions only— D. 191

Memory　D 218

⟨*Ab extra* and *ab intra*　D⟩ 233

Wealth of New England　C 27

'Tis easier for philosophers to be poor. C 81

We paint on Time & say *Adam* n *was.* C 135

The crack in Phrenology. C 145

Coat　C 166

⟨*One* ⟨truth⟩ ↑*idea*↓ as bad as a draft of air⟩. C 255

---

[23] Lines 1, 3, 8–10, 12, 14, 15, and 18 on p. [9] have short vertical or diagonal marks in ink in the left margin. "I must . . . myself　D 374" is struck through in ink with a vertical use mark; the sentence is used in "Domestic Life," *W*, VII, 114, and incorporated in a paragraph in Journal E, p. [105], which is used in "Politics," *Lectures*, III, 243–244. "We never . . . uncultivated　D 376" is struck through in ink with a vertical use mark; both paragraphs are used in "Education," *Lectures*, III, 291 and 292–293. The paragraph cited in D, p. [384], is used in "Religion," *Lectures*, III, 277, and "The Over-Soul," *W*, II, 283–285. The paragraph in D, p. [68], is expanded in "Reforms," *Lectures*, III, 258, and used in "Works and Days," *W*, VII, 177. The paragraph in D, p. [97], is used in "Self-Reliance," *W*, II, 56, and "Tendencies," *Lectures*, III, 310. The paragraph in D, p. [107], is used in "Friendship," *W*, II, 192–193.

Growth of a great man *per saltu⟨s⟩m*.ⁿ C 296 [24]

Strong Will. C 313, D 214

Cultivated classes not so good as St Antoine   C 314, 254,

Two Emphases   1. Human Life;   2. Thought   C 339

Great men not alike   E 62,

System   E 60

Awkward Scholar   E 58

Philosophy of Comparison

Magic of learning languages   A 64

Half more than the whole   B 125

Mountains Z   Bad roads   C 17

Courage of 2 o'clock AM   C 299 [25]

Scholar like a cannon, not good near   C 231

Philanthropic Meetings   C 306

[11] [26] ⟨Most natures insolvent⟩

Is nature also dilettante? G 1

Tea & wine are frauds on time   G 1

[24] Lines 3, 10, 17, and 18 on p. [10] have short vertical marks in ink in the left margin. "The youth . . . D 114" is struck through in ink with a vertical use mark; the paragraph is used in "Self-Reliance," *W*, II, 48, and "Education," *Lectures*, III, 295. "Distinctions of . . . D 143" is struck through in ink with a vertical use mark; the passage is used in "Tendencies," *Lectures*, III, 305, and "Aristocracy," *W*, X, 35. The passage cited in Journal C, p. [296], is used in "Tendencies," *Lectures*, III, 312, and "The Over-Soul," *W*, II, 274–275.

[25] "Cultivated classes . . . 254," is struck through in ink with a vertical use mark; the quotation in Journal C, p. [314], is used in The Present Age: "Introductory," *Lectures*, III, 195, after a gap of two leaves; it is used with a passage in C, p. [254], in the lecture "The Spirit of the Times." "Great men . . . E 62," is struck through in ink with a vertical use mark; the first sentence is used in "Education," *Lectures*, III, 295, the entire paragraph in "Character," *W*, III, 108. "Courage of . . . C 299" is struck through in ink with a vertical use mark.

[26] Pp. [11]–[16] are probably a preliminary survey of Journals G, F No. 2, and E for the lecture series on "The Times," begun no earlier than October 30, 1841. Pp. [164]–[165] below may be a continuation of this survey. Of the manuscripts for these eight lectures, first delivered December 2, 1841–January 20, 1842, only "The Poet," "Prospects," and fragments probably from "Character" survive; see *Lectures*, III, 347–382, 482–483 and 524–525 (notes), and *JMN*, VII, 261–262. The introductory "Lecture on the Times," "The Conservative," and "The Transcendentalist" are printed in *W*, I, 257–359. Much of the other three probably survives in the essays, "Character," "Manners," and "Nature," *W*, III, 87–196.

Osman & Schill G 1, 48, ↑110↓ [27] F 37
⟨I love too well to pay attentions.⟩ G 5
You need your many coats: Godfrey has one G 9
I love not builders of dungeons in the air G 10 37
Power of circumstance in, Which tree shall I manure? G 11
"Days are dam long" G 13
Danger of piety in household service 13
⟨I skulk most of the time⟩ G 14
Double consciousness in our biography 15
Progress of Faith 15
Wo to the successful 16
Asiatic Sentences resemble Life G 16
We never forgive difference of opinion 17
If you are beautiful you shall not love beauty too much 20
⟨Better be solitary than keep bad comp⟩ [G 21]

———

When nature is forsaken by her lord be she ever so good she does not
survive [G 21]

———

⟨Too feeble fall the impressions of sense⟩ ⟨19⟩ 21 [28]

———

Bare feet in Athens G 21

———

Abstain modestly do enthusiastically G 25

———

⟨Cities are shells⟩ [G 25]

———

Vulgar man licentious when he travels G 26

———

Do not squander yourself in rejection 27
[12] ———
  ⟨I have pleasure only in coming near.⟩ G 28

[27] "110" is added in pencil.
[28] The paragraphs cited in Journal G, pp. [10] and [37], are used in "Prospects,"
Lectures, III, 368. Passages in G, pp. [14], [15], [21]("Better . . ."), and [25],
are used in "The Transcendentalist," *W*, I, 353–354, 347, and 359. The third
paragraph cited in G, p. [21], is used in "The Poet," *Lectures*, III, 355, and "The
Poet," *W*, III, 6.

Travel consists in sounding all the stops   G 2⟨8⟩9

All for thee therefore all against thee   G 30

No persons could live together on their merits   G 34

A[s]cending souls sing a paean ⟨D⟩G 37, 10, 97

Impudence which assumes you mean nothing   G 36

⟨Joy of the noble in loving   G 36⟩

Be calm. Are you not there? Then, all. G 39

He is very green who needs great people   G 41

Optimates   G 42, 43, 62, 51,
Expect the world to drop like a peach in their lap   43
Optimate Idleness   G 43
Every word a Trope   G 43, 57, 60
Great success to begin as fool & slip up   G 48
⟨Blue sky for background   G⟩ 49
Architecture bad because Arch. throws up his reason   49
⟨Better things to be said for Conservative⟩   G 50, 83
Optimates break off their flowers G. 51
Writing comes not of knowing   G 52   98
Great wit, great space   G 53
I expect more from Amos Kendall than Webster   G 54

⟨Measure⟩ G 54

⟨Of the principle one application suffices⟩ G 56

Yet there is choice in examples   57

436

⟨Meanest type most portable⟩ 57 [29]

⟨Screens   G 58⟩

Humoring people   58
Quarrels would not exist if they could be reconciled   59, 86
[13] ⟨Flaws⟩ 61
⟨Persistent character⟩ G 62
Hedge's Oration   G 64
Piety perhaps is not a philosopher   G 66

I have every inch of my merit allowed — no more   G 70

Robin's grace at dinner   G 72

Marriage not ideal but empirical   G 74, 90

    Be⟨e⟩acon st is also moral   G 75

⟨Yet the distinctions fast⟩ G 75
    Preaching   G 77↑, 106↓
Public born persons   G 79,
    Peculiar griefs of this Age   G 79
⟨World is of approximations⟩ 86
Black & white Art   87
    The best apology is none   G 88,
    Whitewashing of persons inevitable   G 88
    Marry today ⟨9⟩G 90
    ⟨Prayer performs perhaps: Caius Gracchus   G⟩ 90
    Dr Ripley & 19 April-men   G 91, 126,
    No history true but what is always true. 91

---

[29] "Acending souls . . . paean" is struck through in ink with a vertical use mark; paragraphs in Journal G, pp. [37] and [10], are used in "Prospects," and passages cited in G, pp. [97], [43], and [57], in "The Poet," *Lectures*, III, 368, 354, and 352–353. Passages in G, pp. [36] and [56], are used in "The Transcendentalist," *W*, I, 343 and 350. The passage in G, p. [49]("Blue . . ."), is used in "Nature," and G, p. [54], in "Manners," *W*, III, 174 and 139; with G, p. [48], cf. "Character," *W*, III, 105.

⟨Thoughts whereof Universe is celebration⟩ G 92
Class of 1821   G 92
Head is finished; trunk is blocked   96
Vary the dress with the mood like Walden weather [G 96]
⟨Holiday must be in the eye⟩ G 97
⟨Great man conquers by Presence⟩   G 97
⟨Tropes may be facts⟩   97 [30]
Reading & writing   98
[14] ⟨Screens, if guests can't entertain each other⟩ ↑G↓ 99
Pedantry, G 100
We require all of each   G 101
Plato dull if out of time   101
⟨Character often greater than acts⟩ G 102, 104
⟨Geniuses in trade   G 103⟩
⟨I taste the gas of the hour G⟩ 105
The least eccentricity remarkable   105
The moment is all, give us our swing   G 106
⟨We see no more than we animate   106⟩
In history the soul enormous   107
Great men are uncanonical   107
Availableness   107
One thought in all Demosthenes   107
Stubbed fellows wonder at the dandies of mor. sent. ↑G↓ 107   139
Genius takes three steps or four   G 109
People *live*[n] in circles   G 110
Osman & his berries   110
⟨Disgraceful amount of labor ↑G↓ 111⟩
Let not the profane speak of the sacred   112

---

[30] ", 106" in l. 10 on p. [13] is added in pencil. "Peculiar griefs . . . G 79"
is struck through in ink with a vertical use mark, which extends partly through the
line below it. The passage cited in Journal G, p. [61], is used in "The Transcendentalist," and G, p. [79]("Peculiar . . . "), in "Lecture on the Times," *W*, I, 344,
345, and 281–282. Passages cited in G, pp. [75] and [97]("Holiday . . . "), are
used in "Manners," G, p. [86], in "Nature," G, p. [88]("Whitewashing . . . "),
in "Nominalist and Realist," and G, p. [97]("Great . . . "), in "Character," *W*,
III, 129–130, 149, 190, 226–227, and 90. Passages cited in G, pp. [79]("Public
. . . ") and [92]("Class . . . "), are used in "Prospects," and G, pp. [90]
("Prayer . . . ") and [97]("Tropes . . . "), in "The Poet," *Lectures*, III, 371,
378, and 354.

⟨The Optimates are god like idle; G.⟩ 112   113
Pedantic to give so much importance to property   114
Mr Vise & Miss Vane   G 114
G. Ripley's community   G 116
⟨Transcendentalists' error   G 116⟩
⟨Manners make little Man great⟩   G 127 [31]
Every man once eloquent   G 128
Men boil at different temperatures   128
[15] ⟨Degrees in love   G⟩ 131
⟨Fine day   30 Oct G⟩ 130
Acquiescence   F 30

———

⟨Our quarrel with men is not with kind but amount⟩ F 31, E 202

———

Today always appears trivial   ⟨ E 192

———

Fine people & their Claude Lorraine glasses   F 106

———

When I was praised I lost my time   F 125

———

⟨The Stem is the Past   leaf the Present   F⟩ 127

———

Music   F 150
⟨Transcendentalism   F 160⟩
Less than a saint, love is but a goody   F 37
⟨If I quake what matters what I quake at⟩ E 212
Reality in affecting goodness to children   E 278
Genius by the oblique stroke   E 280
Concert   E 293 [32]

[31] Passages cited in Journal G, pp. [102], [104], [103], and [106]("We
see . . . "), are used in "Character," G, p. [106]("We see . . . "), in "Experience,"
G, p. [113], in "Nominalist and Realist," G, p. [114]("Pedantic . . . "), in "New
England Reformers," and G, p. [127], in "Manners," W, III, 89–90 and 92, 96, 50,
235, 262, and 149. The sentence cited in G, p. [107]("Great men . . . "), is used
in "Prospects," *Lectures*, III, 372. Paragraphs in G, pp. [111] and [112], are used
in "The Transcendentalist," W, I, 351 and 354.

[32] "Today . . . trivial" is struck through in ink with a vertical use mark; cf.
"Lecture on the Times," W, I, 267, Journal R, p. [102], and "Experience," W, III,
46. "Genius by . . . E 293" is struck through in ink with a diagonal use mark.

Tact or magnetism, Character, and Talent.
Dainty moods or Parian marble   E 1⟨4⟩3
Always & never the world is wise   Every book streams to wise   E 17
Homage paid to character demanded by others   E 22
We ought not to lose youth   E 29
Timidity of hosp↑i↓tality   E 53
Plutarch's memory   E 61
Death   E 68
We hardly conceive any other historic ideas than ours   E 69
Women see better than men   E 72
Plato   E 111
Pedantry to estimate nations by census   E 112
[16] Of books: written by unmagnetic   E 148
Old Age   E 151
Toys   E 159
Indian rule shames Graham rule   E 165
Of a man we should ask has he invented a day? E 167
People crave sympathy. E 171
Strong language   E 173
⟨What right has Genius to retreat from work⟩ E 188
⟨The good stands betwixt us & sun⟩ E 37
Inaccessibleness of every thought except that one you are in F.111 [33]

[17]   Literature [34]
Men to be seen as dramatic figures   D 377
Dante ↑E 16, 40,↓

Passages cited in G, p. [131], and F No. 2, p. [31], are used in "The Transcendentalist," and F No. 2, p. [127], in "The Conservative," W, I, 343, 344, and 300; G, p. [130], is used in "Nature," F No. 2, p. [160], in "The Poet," E, p. [212], in "Character," E, p. [280], in "Experience," and E, p. [293], in "New England Reformers," W, III, 169, 32, 98, 68, and 265–266.

[33] The paragraph cited in Journal E, p. [188], is used in "The Transcendentalist," W, I, 348. The sentence in E, p. [37], is used in "Character," W, III, 96. "Inaccessibleness . . . F.111" is struck through in ink with a curved diagonal use mark; the paragraph is used in "The Poet," W, III, 33.

[34] Pp. [17] and [18] are probably early collections for the two lectures on "Literature" in the "Present Age" series; in the earliest stage Emerson evidently planned only one lecture on the topic (see p. [163] below). For other notes for "Literature," see pp. [160]–[162] below.

Petrarch   D 365
Plutarch & books   D 365
Montaigne
Landor ⟨2⟩D 287, 294,
I prefer artists to generals   D 363
Extempore speech & Writing   D 339
Burke   D 348
Compression of style & ellipsis   D 307, 350, 354,   C.111, 126,
Language Spolia opima   D 307
⟨Our⟩ We have no Scholars   D 308
Foreigners write as well as natives   D 309
Old Eng. poetry old ⟨E⟩painting   D 327
Pereant qui ante nos nostra   D 288, 267, 285
Augustine   D 269, 271,
Beaumont & Fletcher   D 275-6-8,
    Authors would not see their readers   D 285
    Best part of each writer not private   D 273
Literature peeping   D 264
Propriety of great writers   D 290
Dialogue not easy to write   D 281   356,
A thought imprisons   D 345   an alibi
Histories fawn on princes   D 363 [364]
My books my gallery   D 282
A defence of Composition   D 324   C 83
Goethe teaches freedom of treatment   D 319 [35]
By doing without Shakspeare you may do without his book   D 356 [36]
[18] Defence of Carlyle's Mirabeau   D 15
The art of writing   D 26
Scholar formidable   D 68, 86,

---

[35] Both passages on "Dante" in Journal E, pp. [14]–[16] and [40], are used in "Literature" [second lecture], *Lectures*, III, 232–234 and 229. The anecdote in D, p. [365], is about Petrarch, not Plutarch. "I prefer . . . generals" and the passage cited in D, p. [363], are combined in "Literature" [second lecture], *Lectures*, III, 225. "Foreigners write . . . D 309" is marked with an "x" in ink in the left margin. The quotation from St. Augustine in D, p. [269], and passages in D, pp. [278] and [264], are used, *ibid.*, pp. 231, 231–232, and 230. A sentence on Goethe in D, p. [319], is used in "Literature" [first lecture], *Lectures*, III, 222.

[36] This line is in darker ink, as is p. [18] below; the passage is used in pages for a later reading of "Tendencies," *Lectures*, III, 507(notes).

Many books not so good as a few   D 92
Great to say things in order of cause & effect   D 124
History   D 129
Definitions of Literature   D 173, 264
⟨How a genius is understood; by diffusion of himself   D 175⟩
⟨Our faculties warra⟩Cowley & Donne. C 92
A good style   C 126
⟨The Bible original   E 70, 26⟩
Truth & originality go abreast always. [E 70–71]
⟨Shelley & modern poets E 82⟩   Byron   87
⟨Horace Walpole   E 1⟩
Criticism transcendental   E 2
No age to good writing   E 5   Plutarch
We would write without facts   E 7
Power of books today as ever   E 16,
A good sentence or verse rare   E 54
Burton's Anatomy of Melancholy ⟨F⟩E p 78, 67
⟨Subjectiveness   E 86,⟩
Not analysis but sleep the danger of Americans   E 63
Oliver Twist   D 361
⟨Mankind right in their fames⟩ D 367,
⟨Compare our proprieties with Bacon's nonsense⟩
————————————————————————————B 105, E 67,[37]
Scholar should be audacious as ⟨Attila⟩ ↑Danton↓ E 284

[19]   Love
Why give the children all the romance   D 305, 51,
I would have friends but seldom use them   D 321
The friends whom God sends   D 315–6
A friend is child & father of Time   D 331

[37] Lines 5–8, 11, 13–15, 18, 20, 21, and 25 on p. [18] have short diagonal marks in ink in the left margin. Passages cited in Journal D, pp. [124] and [175], and E, pp. [70], [82], [87], [1], [2], [7], [16], [54], [67], and [86], are used in "Literature" [first lecture], *Lectures*, III, 203, 211, 204–205, 217 and 218–219, 215–216, 213, 203–204, 203, 209, 209–210, 212–213, and 214 and 215–216. Passages cited in D, pp. [129], [173], and [264], E, pp. [2] and [16], and D, p. [367], are used in "Literature" [second lecture], *Lectures*, III, 227–228, 230, 226, 234, and 229–230.

Love thaumaturgic   D 309.
Friends are selfelected   D 345
I must wait to know a friend   D 360,
I will have the luxury of plain dealing   D 362
If I love you what is that to you   D 295, E 95
E L T.   D 249
We would live with those we are used to   D 285
⟨S⟩Be loved by predestined mates   D 287
The best effect of ↑a↓ fine person is found in absence   D 377 [38]
It does not hurt the eyes to look at eyes   D 31
Love is silent. D 69
Love sees no resemblances to persons. D 187
"Not on the store of sprightly wine." C 131
Love me for that I am. C 264
Love cannot be unrequited   E 95
Unfruitful joys of the affections   E 94
          Property in a friend's virtues   E 99
Love, only the reflection of the lover's worthiness   E 102
          The ancients exchanged names with their friends   D 162
          ⟨Village love interposes distance   D 256⟩
          ⟨Belinda & Montreville   D 256⟩
          Truelove & Faintlove   B 92
          Some we cannot divest of beauty   E 121 [39]

[38] The first fourteen lines of p. [19], "Love . . . absence   D 377", may have been collected for the lecture "Private Life," the manuscript of which is fragmentary, but which probably contained a section on friendship. "Friends are . . . D 345" and "I will . . . E 95" are struck through in ink with single diagonal use marks. The passages cited in Journal D, pp. [321]–[322], [315], [331], [345], and [360], and E, p. [95], are used in "Friendship," W, II, 214–216, 194–195, 214, 209, 201–202, and 216–217. The paragraphs in D, pp. [295] and [249], are used in "Love," W, II, 180–181 and 178. Emerson may have used and added to p. [19] in revising the lecture "Love" for the essay.

[39] The last fourteen lines of p. [19], "It does not . . . E 121", and p. [20] are in darker ink and were probably added late in 1840. The sentence in Journal D, p. [31], used in "Love," Lectures, III, 59, is omitted from the essay at the point where the paragraph in D, p. [249], listed above, and the passages in D, p. [187], and E, p. [121], are added, "Love," W, II, 178–179. The paragraph in D, p. [256], is used, ibid., pp. 172–173; see also Lectures, III, 55, n. 5, Emerson's note to add it to the lecture. The lines from Menander quoted in C, p. [131], are used in "Private Life," Lectures, III, 253, and "Domestic Life," W, VII, 128. "The ancients . . . D 162" is struck through in ink with a diagonal use mark; the passages cited in E,

[20] You cannot surprise me with your love. E 209
Diff of love of man & of woman   E 217
"May I gaze on thee" &c   E 21
Love gets official   E 162
How you raise me by rejecting my love   E 167 [40]
Love makes us little children   E 202
You would have me love you: What shall I love? E 222 [220]
A constitutional spousal love in Woman   E 234
A man's love no better nor worse than he   [E 264]
[Cupid did not assault the Muses   Rabelais Vol III. p 25] [H 142]
The good stands betwixt us & the sun   E 37

Less than a saint Love is a goody   F 37
Transcendant doctrine of Love   F 136,

[21]–[22] [blank]
[23]   The True Life
I must angle only with myself   D 374 [41]
I ignore wo   D 367
Men to be seen as dramatic figures   D 377
I would not be good by the whip   D 376
Great man would be convicted   D 357
By doing without Shaksp. you can forego his book   D 356.
We viciously esteem defects organic   D 345
Conversation an evanescent relation   D 346, ↑C 231,↓
Popular doctrine of Immortality false   D 345,
My life a May game   D 309
The poor mind must *have* [n] somewhat   D 298 [42]

---

pp. [95], [94], [99], and [102], and D, p. [162], are used in "Friendship," W, II, 216–217, 195, and 212. The paragraph in D, p. [256], is used in "Spiritual Laws," W, II, 149–150.

[40] Part of the paragraph cited in Journal E, p. [167], is used in "Friendship," W, II, 210.

[41] "I must . . . D 374" is struck through in ink with a vertical use mark; "I must . . . myself", actually on D, p. [375], is used in "Domestic Life," W, VII, 114, and incorporated in a paragraph in E, p. [105], used in "Politics," Lectures, III, 243; parts of the paragraph in D, p. [374], are used in "Religion," and "Education," Lectures, III, 281, 283, and 299, and "The Over-Soul," W, II, 295 and 296.

[42] Lines 5–6("I wd. not . . . D 357") on p. [23] are struck through in ink

Eternity & omnipresence are proper. D 274,
All men's life superficial   D 289
God despiseth size.   D 289, 286,
Untune nobody   D 292
Concealment impossible   D 292 [43]
Beside the great, solid men evanesce. D 343
Degrees of idealism   D 322
A man amenable for his Vocation   D 303
The actual an optical illusion as in Brant's War   D 257
Only the soul avails in dealing with the child   D 245
If you can draw all lines why draw any   D 246
Strike sail to none   D 287
Painting educates the eye   D 263
Be sacred none comes near b⟨y⟩ut by my act   D 320 [44]
The Transcendant is economy also. [D 379]
The great soul is plain   D 37, 172, 179 [45]

---

with a vertical use mark, which Emerson extended first through l. 9, then through l. 12. The paragraph cited in Journal D, p. [376], is used in "Education," and the passages cited in D, pp. [357], [309], and [298], in "Reforms," *Lectures*, III, 292–293, 259–260, 268, and 267–268; "We viciously . . . organic" (D, p. [345]) is used in both "Politics," and "Education," *Lectures*, III, 245–246 and 297. "By doing . . . his book", actually on D, p. [357], is used in a revised section of "Tendencies," *Lectures*, III, 507(notes), perhaps a later addition. The paragraph cited in D, p. [346], is used in "Friendship," *W*, II, 208; the passage cited in C, p. [231], is probably the paragraph used in "Prospects," *Lectures*, III, 370–371.

[43] "All men's . . . D 289" is struck through in ink with a vertical use mark which Emerson extended through "God . . . 286,"; both passages in Journal D, p. [289], are used in "Reforms," *Lectures*, III, 259 and 266–267. In the margin to the right of "Untune nobody . . . impossible D 292" are some random pen scrawlings and two practice A's.

[44] "Degrees of . . . D 303", "The actual . . . D 245", and "If you . . . D 320" are struck through in ink with single, connected, vertical use marks. "D 246" and "D 263" are connected by a diagonal line in ink. The paragraph in Journal D, p. [322], is used in "Circles," and the paragraphs in D, pp. [303] and [287], in "Spiritual Laws," *W*, II, 309, 140, and 151. The passage cited in D, p. [257], is used in "Politics," *Lectures*, III, 240, and *W*, III, 199, and cf. "Religion," *Lectures*, III, 273. The paragraph in D, p. [245], is used, *ibid.*, pp. 282 and 494(notes), and "The Over-Soul," *W*, II, 279. The sentence cited in D, p. [246], is incorporated in the paragraph in D, p. [263], which is used in "Art," *W*, II, 356–357. With "Be sacred", cf. "Literature" [second lecture], and "Reforms," *Lectures*, III, 234 and 266; the rest of the paragraph in D, p. [320], is used in "Self-Reliance," *W*, II, 72.

[45] This line is struck through in ink with a vertical use mark; all three passages

[24] Quietism　D 59
　　Utter things in order of cause & effect　D 124
　　Come to the platform above fear　D 192
　　Repose　D 195
　　Trust　D 196
　　I learn evermore. C. 34 [46]
　　True greatness content　C 261
　　Love me for that I am. C 264
　　Roses do not look back　D 331, 338
　　Do ↑not↓ respect thy writing or thine act　D 360 [47]
　　Speech indicates difference　D 69, 72, 79, 152, [48]

　　Buddhist hospitality　　E 155
　　Persons are ignes fatui at last　E 155
　　Of a man we ask Has he invented a Day　E 167
　　Never so fit for friendship as when we take ourselves to friend.
　　　　　　　　　　　　　　　　　　　　　　　　E 169

　　Little as good as much in knowledge & life　E 170
　　I cannot well go to see my relations　E 192
　　When shall we be not Patriot but Universalist　E 194
　　A man should never let me go　E 255
　　Extasy selfrelying　E 257
　　The mean Present will be great　E 258
　　Make secretly beautiful　E 300
　　Hospitality an outside fact　E 317 [49]

---

are used in "Religion," *Lectures*, III, 284–285, and "The Over-Soul," *W*, II, 290–292.

[46] "Quietism　D 59" is struck through in ink with a vertical use mark; this paragraph and the paragraph cited in Journal D, p. [196], are used in "Religion," *Lectures*, III, 281, and "The Over-Soul," *W*, II, 293. "I learn . . . C. 34" is struck through in ink with a vertical use mark; the paragraph is used in "Education," *Lectures*, III, 291.

[47] This and the preceding line are struck through in ink with a vertical use mark. The paragraphs cited in Journal D, pp. [331] and [338], are used in "Religion," *Lectures*, III, 282 and 283–284, and "Self-Reliance," *W*, II, 67.

[48] This line may have been added later, like those below the rule. The paragraph cited in Journal D, p. [69], is used in "Tendencies," *Lectures*, III, 314–315, and "Circles," *W*, II, 311. Part of the paragraph in D, p. [152], is used in "Religion," *Lectures*, III, 280 and 284, and "The Over-Soul," *W*, II, 269.

[49] Entries below the rule were added no earlier than May, 1841, probably as

[25]–[26] [blank]
[27]   Art
Conditions of criticism of pictures. D 2, 63,
We owe somewhat to poor pictures   D 343
Painting in Rome 1785   C 29
The American forester should make a different statue of a wood god
from an Italian work. C 137
Secret of great pictures   D 333,
Rembrandt paints reflections not substances   D 327
Chance pictures   D 326
Allston's genius & defect   D 296, 314, 332,[50]
Conventional character of Eng. drawing   D 272,
Pity so near a painter & not paint   D 341,

[28]–[29] [blank]
[30][51] Jar in life
        ⟨The woods make us feel the meanness of houses
        Cities make us mean
        Rail roads compromise us
        Wood looks as if man were royal
        The wood revives my faith in my Economy
        microscope & thermometer cannot praise us⟩ [52]

---

part of a survey for the series on "The Times." "Buddhist hospitality   E 155" and
"Never so . . . E 169" are struck through in pencil with single diagonal use marks;
the sentences cited in Journal E, pp. [155] and [169], and the paragraph in E,
p. [255], are used in "The Transcendentalist," W, I, 337, 347, and 346. "Persons
are . . . E 155" is struck through in ink with a diagonal use mark; the paragraph
is used in "Prospects," Lectures, III, 380–381, and "Nominalist and Realist," W,
III, 229. Parts of the passage cited in E, p. [170], are used in "The Poet," W, III,
18, and "Poetry and Imagination," W, VIII, 36–37. With the sentence cited in E,
p. [258], cf. "Lecture on the Times," W, I, 267.

[50] The passages cited in Journal D, pp. [333] and [296], are used in "Art,"
W, II, 360–362, and 355 and 356. P. [27] may be a collection for this essay.

[51] P. [30], in pencil, and pp. [31]–[34] below, may be notes for the lecture
"Relation of Man to Nature" (January 13, 1842); the lecture manuscript is missing,
but a considerable part of it may have been used in "Tantalus," The Dial, IV (Jan.
1844), 357–363, and "Nature," W, III, 167–196. See also Notebook Φ, pp. [69]–
[70] above, and Index Minor, pp. [40] and [96]–[99] below.

[52] With "Jar in life", cf. Journal D, p. [231], and "The Protest," Lectures,
III, 91. "The woods . . . praise us" is canceled with five angled pencil lines; cf.
"Nature," W, III, 171 and 173. With "microscope & . . . praise us", cf. D, p.

Nature an asylum Cities still serve me
⟨Cities will still serve⟩, Yet they demean
Rail roads compromise us
Woods accuse our Church & state
Microscope & thermometer   accuse
The very reason why we do like nature is because we do not
like man
Nature succours my faith
     I am not at home but a tangent
     We do not s⟨ee⟩ay Behold my peace
     Beauty of nature falls off from us
     Yet Flowers are flattery [53]

[31]   Nature
In nature all growth cotemporary   D 6
Summer heats   D 8   Summer night   D 8, C 329,
A few facts suffice   D 31
Moonlight   D 51
We do not transfigure the same object twice   D 58
The Doctor's Hill   D 104
The Mushroom   D 113
⟨Naturlangsamkeit   D⟩ 114   Secret of the World untold   H 93
Nature a Deist   D 117
Teeth limitary D 116   moral   D 168
Apples & Men   D 127
Lover of Nature not annoyed by being doubted   D 197
Throughout *things*," an effort at beauty   D 205
The streets & the fields   D 235
Flowers   C 40
⟨Nature says, "So hot!" D 303⟩

————

Seed vessels   D 367

————

————

[117], "Education," *Lectures*, III, 287, and the lecture "Recent Literary and Spiritual Influences."

[53] With "The very . . . man", and "I am not . . . flattery", cf. "Nature," *W*, III, 178, 190–193, and 182.

Nature leaves all doors ajar   H.C. Lect 2.

⟨Nature is the Circumstance that conquers all circumstance.
⟨U⟩see E. 312⟩

Dew   E 314

Sallad   E 312
⟨Magnificence   E 324⟩
⟨The ounce of overweight⟩ [54]
Need of excitement   H 78
Jew on the hip   H 29
[32]   ⟨Inappeasable hunger   G 86⟩
      Antagonism   H 118
Reality   H.135
Daguerrotype
⟨Identity   H 75⟩
⟨Sallads ↑E 312↓⟩
I taste the gas of the hour   G 105
⟨Fine Day   G 130⟩
Is nature also dilettante   G 1

"When nature is forsaken by her lord be she ever so good she does not survive." [G 21]

Mountains   Z
Power of Circumstance   G 11
⟨Blue sky for background⟩   ↑G 49↓
      Public born persons   G 79
      Every abuse stereotyped in generation. [H 24] Dartmouth   D 310
      Whitewashing of persons inevitable   G 88

---

[54] "Naturlangsamkeit   D 114" is canceled. The passage cited in Journal H, p. [93], is used in "Nature," *W*, III, 193–194. "D 303" is struck through in ink with a vertical use mark also; the paragraph cited is used in "Education," *Lectures*, III, 299, and "Spiritual Laws," *W*, II, 135. For "Nature leaves . . . Lect 2.", see "Doctrine of the Hands," *Lectures*, II, 235, from Journal B, p. [315]. "Nature is . . . circumstance." and passages in E, pp. [312] and [324], are used in "Nature," *W*, III, 169–170, 195, and 172–173. With "The ounce of overweight", cf. H, pp. [19]–[20], used in "Nature," *W*, III, 184–185, and probably in the lecture "Relation of Man to Nature"; see *Lectures*, III, 518(notes).

Thoughts whereof Universe is celebration   G 92
    Head finished trunk blocked   G 96
    Men boil at diff temp   G 128
    Ear not to be cheated   H 36
    ⟨Bit of Quartz predicts man⟩   E 218
    No time, No space, intercalated   E 263, H 61
    ⟨Nature's laws written on thumbnail   E 275⟩
Animals through probity make masters servants   E.277
Acorn   E 297
    ⟨Importance of scenery exaggerated   H 40⟩ [55]
[33] ⟨Day not profane in which I see nature   H 44⟩
The permitted as much characterizes God as the beloved   H 61
Nature invites to repose   E 181
⟨Today you come to a new thought & all nature typifies that   F 1⟩
Every promise of the soul many fulfilments   F 112
⟨Nature's method of advance transformation   F 116⟩

    Secret untold   H 93
    The beauty of the fable proves the importance of its sense
    Thoughts whereof the Univ is celebrat[io]n [G 92]
    The tropes have not one sense but many   F 1
    Otherwise no story would be intelligible
    Every promise of the soul many fulfilments   F 112

Thus ⟨c⟩N. converts herself into a vast promise. She will not be rashly
explained. Her secret untold. her curve not yet returned.[56]

---

[55] "E 312", "G 49", and "Public born . . . H 40" are in pencil. The passages
cited in Journal G,. p. [86], E, p. [312], and G, pp. [130] and [49], are used
in "Nature," *W*, III, 190, 195, 169, and 174. With "Identity H 75", cf. *ibid.*, pp.
182–183. The passages cited in G, p. [79], H, p. [24], and D, p. [310], are used in
"Prospects," *Lectures*, III, 370–371. Part of the paragraph in G, p. [88], is used
in "Nominalist and Realist," *W*, III, 226–227. The passages in E, pp. [218] and
[275], and H, p. [40], are used in "Nature," *W*, III, 182, 180–181, and 176.

[56] "Day not . . . E 181" is in pencil; part of the paragraph cited in Journal
H, p. [44], is used in "Nature," *W*, III, 172. With "Today you . . . that" in F
No. 2, p. [1], cf. *Lectures*, III, 514 (notes, possibly a draft for the essay "The Poet").
"Secret untold . . . returned." is in pencil. The passage in H, p. [93], and "Thus
. . . returned.", which includes it, are used in "Nature," *W*, III, 193–194. "The
beauty . . . sense" is used in "The Poet," *W*, III, 15; with "The tropes . . . in-

[34] [57] Ch[ristianit]y caricatures Ethics [D 270]
E|| . . . ||

An outrage to represent the life of Xt tantamount to Man   D 374
    Praise || . . . ||
The doctrine of compensation denies inspiration
                miracle[?] || . . . || miracles
                soul || . . . ||
                Christ || . . . || Christ's preach[in]g

Ch[ristianit]y old as the tradition   ↑E 17↓
    To him who said it before

    Do || . . . ||
        Doctrine of the soul   D 311, ⟨370⟩
            Do not vamp principles [E 25]
            Roses [D 331, 338]
            Never counts company   D 195
            Eternity & omnipresence proper   C 62, D 274
            God the whole   we parts   D 152   E 84
            A man's limitations,   D 246
            Acts of the soul   D 370
            God revealed in facts of old age &c   D 370
            ⟨God⟩ Pick no locks. Answer questions by life   D 384 [58]

Masses J   H 135

Ounce of overweight [H 19–20]

---

telligible", cf. *Lectures*, III, 513–514(notes). At least part of p. [33] was probably written early in 1844 when Emerson was working on *Essays, Second Series*.

[57] "Chy caricatures . . . life D 384", in partly erased pencil, and pp. [35]–[37] below, are notes for "Religion," *Lectures*, III, 271–285. "E|| . . . || . . . Doctrine" is partly overwritten in pencil by "Ounce of . . . quartz", printed below. "E 17" is added in ink.

[58] The paragraph in Journal D, p. [270], is used in "Compensation," *W*, II, 94–95. "An outrage . . . tradition" is developed in "Religion," *Lectures*, III, 281–283, 276–280, and 273–274. Passages in E, p. [25], D, pp. [331] and [338], [195], and [152], E, p. [84], and D, pp. [370]("Acts . . . ") and [384], are used in "Religion," *Lectures*, III, 278, 283–284, 282, 284, and 277.

hides ⟨the⟩ her necessity of progeny in the lover's private joy
                        partial speech   H 93
                        inappeasable hunger [G 86]
Compensation
        Sallad [E 312]
        Jew on hip [H 29]
        Ear not to be cheated [H 36]

        Power of circumstance

        Identity [H 75]
                quartz [59] [E 218]

[35]   ⟨P⟩Religion
Society will not allow of an irresponsible reporter   D 100
Popular religion   D 152, 201, C 22
Quoting Scripture   D 157
⟨Never counts company   D⟩ 195
The genius of the Divine Providence   C 22, 183, 192
Connecticutt Sunday   A 76
⟨Doctrine of Immortality   C 40⟩ 206, D 345,   E.↑78↓
Church does not respect the soul   D 259
"Don't dishonor the Church"   D 260
Christianity as now preached caricatures Ethics   D 270
Eternity & omnipresence proper   C 62, D 274
O unauthorized preacher pain is a thing   D 291
You know truth or tradition by tone of voice   D 289
Consecration of Sunday desecration   D 308
Doctrine of the Soul   D 311
⟨Miracle always spiritual   D⟩ 339
Unitarian complaint of Calv[ini]st accuses Unit[aria]n   D 346
Man or Miracle? D 349
I hate preaching   D 352, 372,
I love Sunday   D 366

---

[59] "Masses J . . . quartz" is in pencil. With "Ounce of . . . Sallad" and
"Power of . . . quartz", cf. "Nature," W, III, 184–185, 187, 193–194, 190, 195,
170, and 182–183.

Xy injurious   D 373 [60]
Not wholesome to say I love not Xt   D 374, 47,
We verify the facts of X's life   D 374
Content of man with wooden institutions   E 23
Need of Church visible only temporary   D 260
St Augustine de philosophis   D 271
[36] The compensations of calamity   D 298
    Roses do not look back   D 331, 338,
    The friends whom God sends me   D 315   E 92
    Ab extra & ab intra   D 233
    Christianity as old as the world   E 17   ↑[C 130]↓
    No lives that content us   E 50
    Not Plato or Kant may write of God   E 52
    Death & Suicide   E 68
    The Clerisy   E 75
    Power of the Jewish Idea   E.88
    Miracle not agreeable to this age   E 93 [61]
    The natural Theocracy   E 110
    The flower shows us our importance   C 40
    Our position in the Universe   C 41
    Always suppose God   C 112,
    Cause & Effect   C 112,
    Xt preaches the greatness of man but we the greatness of Christ
                                         C 278

    Accepted Xy caricature of real   C 304

[60] "Never counts . . . D 195" is struck through in pencil with a diagonal use mark. "Doctrine of . . . C 40" is struck through in ink with a diagonal use mark, and "78" is in pencil. "Miracle always . . . D 339" and the preceding line are struck through in pencil with single, connected, diagonal use marks. "Man or . . . D 349" is struck through in pencil with a diagonal use mark. Passages in Journal D, pp. [152] and [195], C, p. [40], and D, pp. [339], [349], and [373], are used in "Religion," *Lectures*, III, 280 and 284, 282, 277, 279, 278–279, and 283 and 277.

[61] "Roses do . . . 338," is struck through in pencil with a diagonal use mark; both paragraphs are used in "Religion," *Lectures*, III, 283–284, and "Self-Reliance," *W*, II, 67. "No lives . . . E 50" and the preceding line are struck through in ink with single, vertical, connected use marks; "[C 130]" is added in pencil. The paragraph in Journal E, p. [50], is used in "Religion," *Lectures*, III, 283, and "The Over-Soul," *W*, II, 295–296. "Miracle not . . . E 93" is struck through in pencil with a diagonal use mark, and this and the preceding line with a vertical use mark in ink; both passages are used in "Religion," *Lectures*, III, 274 and 278.

Can there be social worship   C 287
Miracle   C 303   D 105
God in nature   C 341
Fear to shock men is impotency of percep[tio]n   D 56
Do not speak of God much   D 17
Do not compare Gods   D 55, 29,
God the whole; we parts.   D 152   Man inflamed part [62]
Test of a religion the no. of things it explains.   D 241
[37] Acts of the soul   D 370
   Do not vamp principles   E.25
   Humility of San Felippo
   To him who said it before.
   I call it Consciousness
      ⟨No great lives   E 50⟩
   My relation to my friend & to his death   C 206
   ⟨Only the Soul avails in dealing with child   D⟩ 245 [63]

New England Religion   E 310, 309
Base poverty of Unitarianism   E 311
Pantheism   E 316 [64]

   Miracle to make stare ⟨D⟩   C 303
     The Capuchins   D 105
     Miracle not agreeable   E 93
     Always spiritual   D 339

[62] "The natural . . . E 110" is in pencil; cf. "Religion," *Lectures*, III, 276, and a sheet filed with "Politics," *ibid.*, p. 479(notes). "Miracle C 303. D 105" is struck through in pencil with a diagonal use mark and in ink with a vertical use mark; both passages are used in "Religion," *Lectures*, III, the first on pp. 278 and 279–280, the second on p. 278. "God the . . . inflamed part" is struck through in pencil with a diagonal use mark; much of the paragraph cited is used in "Religion," *Lectures*, III, 280 and 284; part is used in "The Over-Soul," *W*, II, 269.

[63] "Acts of . . . E.25" is struck through in pencil with a diagonal use mark. Lines 5, 7, and 8 are in pencil; ll. 6 and 8 are struck through in ink with single diagonal use marks. The passages cited in Journal D, p. [370], E, pp. [25] and [50], and D, p. [245], are used in "Religion," *Lectures*, III, 284, 278, 283, 282, and 494(notes); all but E, p. [25], are also used in "The Over-Soul," *W*, II, 269, 295–296, and 279.

[64] The rule and "New England . . . E 316" were added to p. [37] later in heavy ink; part of the paragraph in Journal E, pp. [309]–[310], is used in the lecture "Genius of the Anglo-Saxon Race."

Man or miracle   D 349
Love thaumaturgic   D 309
Eternity associates with truth love &c   C 40
The popular doctrine is duration & irreconcileable   D 345
In Literature   E 78
Eternity & omnipresence proper   D 274
The popular doctrine is duration[;] this the soul never teaches & Jesus therefore never teaches. In regard to all questions of this nature they are below in sense & the soul will not hear nor answer them. But it has its own way of treating them. Eternity associates with these. ↑C 40↓ Even with books   E 78   Higher still these things are proper to the soul[.] [65]

[38] [blank]
[39]   Manners
Do not quote texts nor gag your company with ⊖.   C 112, D 157,
Manners demonological. D 343
Two sorts of "Abandon"   D 343
Lethe adds to beauty   D 369   Lazy Manners   D 348
Faces on pivot & on sphere   D 371 [66]
Ecclesiastical manners   B 234

[40]–[46] [blank]
[47]   The Age [67]
Ill health. Nearsight   D 325,
Faith in straps & suspenders   D 330
No art because of unbelief   D 338
We talk about the Age & Virtue & self   D 353   D 354   E 27 [68]

[65] "Miracle to . . . D 309", struck through in pencil with a vertical use mark, and the rest of p. [37] are in pencil. The six use marked passages are used in "Religion," *Lectures*, III, 277–279. "Eternity associates . . . E 78" is set off in the left margin by a partial bracket in pencil; cf. *ibid.*, p. 277.

[66] This line is struck through in ink with a vertical use mark; the sentence cited is used in "Domestic Life," *W*, VII, 127, and a manuscript fragment which is probably part of the lecture "Private Life" (ms. Houghton Library).

[67] P. [47] and part of p. [48] are probably early collections for The Present Age: "Introductory." Several passages listed are used in other lectures in the same series; some that are use marked or apparently canceled may have been in pages now missing from the lecture manuscript. See also Notebook Δ, pp. [10]–[12], [17], and [27]–[32] above.

[68] "Faith . . . D 330", struck through in ink with a diagonal use mark, is

It is base to remember as we do ↑D↓ 354
The scholar comes out of college rotten ripe   D 353 [69]
This age ought to last some time yet   E 28
The Aurora Borealis   D 350
  We have no scholars   D 308, 9⟨9⟩6, 190, 99,[70]
  Each dog his day   D 91
  Our Martyrs   D 98, C 343, 347, B 101   D 97, 98, 99, 206,[71]
  Despondent   *D* 103   C 96
  *Against*ⁿ Reflectiveness   D 110, 166,
  Compare our proprieties with Bacon's nonsense   B 105, E 67 [72]
  Pius VII   B 280
  Contrasted with the religion of 60 years since. C 65, E 67 [73]
  Ocular; Advertising; ↑C 205, D 49,↓ sick, travelling,
  Want of faith in medicine as well as in theology. C 191
  Our philanthropies   C 306 [74]

---

used in "Montaigne," *W*, IV, 153. "No art . . . D 338", struck through in ink with a vertical use mark and marked with a marginal slash, is used in The Present Age: "Introductory," *Lectures*, III, 194. "We talk . . . self" is struck through in ink with a vertical use mark.

[69] This line is struck through in ink with a vertical use mark; the sentence is used in "Education," *Lectures*, III, 288.

[70] "The Aurora . . . D 350" is marked with both a marginal slash and a vertical use mark in ink; the passage, actually in Journal D, pp. [351]–[352], is used in The Present Age: "Introductory," *Lectures*, III, 194. The following line is also struck through in ink with a vertical use mark; passages in Journal D, pp. [308] and [99], are used, *ibid.*, pp. 194 and 195, and that in D, p. [96], is canceled in the lecture manuscript, *Lectures*, III, 456–457(notes). The passage in D, p. [190], is used in "Literature" [first lecture], *Lectures*, III, 221–222.

[71] Passages in Journal D, pp. [97] and [98], are used in "Tendencies," *Lectures*, III, 310, and *W*, II, 56; one in C, p. [347], and another in D, p. [97], are used in "Reforms," *Lectures*, III, 268.

[72] This line is struck through in ink with a vertical use mark; both passages cited are used in "Literature" [first lecture], *Lectures*, III, 211–213, and "Thoughts on Modern Literature," *The Dial*, I (Oct. 1840), 143–144. "*Against* Reflectiveness D 110," above, is canceled in the manuscript of The Present Age: "Introductory"; see *Lectures*, III, 457–458(notes).

[73] This line is struck through in ink with a vertical use mark; both passages cited are used in The Present Age: "Introductory," *Lectures*, III, 192–194.

[74] This and the preceding line are struck through in ink with a vertical use mark; the passage in Journal C, p. [191], is canceled in the manuscript of The Present Age: "Introductory"; see *Lectures*, III, 457(notes). With "Ocular . . . travelling," above, cf. "Men are sick, ocular, vain, and vagabond." in the lecture "The Spirit of the Times."

Teamster's mottoes   D 355
The greatness of this time not vitiated by my littleness   E 3
Dangers of Commerce   E 4
Objection to writing on subject too near   E 11
The greatness of this Time   E 12, 14, 19, 39, 56 [75]
    Defence of its alleged Brag   E 1⟨4⟩5, 50,
    Sacredness of the time   E 26
[48]   What is the Age   E 29
It revises reputations   E 40
The best information is acceptance, E 55 [76]
The woes of the time   D 379
Cant   C 82, 92, 293, 306, D 41
Sincerity Surprises & Commonsense   C 307   D 339
The great questions   C 245   D ⟨11⟩   154, 2, 65,
    Phrenology   C 145
    ⟨Adva⟩Americans apologize for learning   D 99,
    Analysis   D 312   E 62, 13, 19, 13 [77]
    Its culture does not recognize the Vast   D 105
    We timid crippled Uncles & Aunts   D 294,
    Commercial   E 4, 38, 65,
    ⟨P⟩Evils of Association   E 14,
    ⟨It cannot be overvalued E⟩ 56,
    Critical   E 62, 63,
    Age of Bronze ⟨or *Debris*⟩ E 64,
    Who desponds? [E 63]
    The measure of the ton of coals   D 354,
    Cultivated classes not so good as St Antoine   C 314, 254,

---

[75] The paragraphs cited in Journal E, pp. [12], [39], and [56], are used in The Present Age: "Introductory," *Lectures*, III, 199–201. Those in E, pp. [12] and [56], are also in the lecture "The Spirit of the Times."

[76] Passages cited in Journal E, pp. [29] and [55], are used in The Present Age: "Introductory," *Lectures*, III, 186 and 201; the first is also in the lecture "The Spirit of the Times." The paragraph in E, p. [40], is used in "Literature" [second lecture], *Lectures*, III, 229.

[77] With "The great questions", cf. The Present Age: "Introductory," and "The Protest," *Lectures*, III, 196 and 256–257, and "Lecture on the Times," *W*, I, 269–270. Passages in Journal D, pp. [99] and [312], and E, p. [62], are used in The Present Age: "Introductory," *Lectures*, III, 195–196; a paragraph in E, p. [13], is used in the lecture "The Spirit of the Times."

It has the feeling of the Infinite   E 82 [78]

Egotism   E 125
We are optative but must leave some mark   E 156
Our countrymen love intoxication: Spoonhunt & Lambkill   E 164
Bancroft's History   E 256
Modern Novels   E 258
Column of American population   E 283 [79]
[49] English & French Debates   E 290
Idea of the Gentleman   E 313
Phrenology: C 145
Philanthropic Meetings   C 306
See Δ 128
Promise in the books they love, in the daring of their thought, in

---

Only the inventor may boast of the model   G 34

---

perplexity   G 79

⟨The men are all loaded dice⟩
⟨World of approximations. all tantalizing   G⟩ 86
How customary we are   G 105

[78] "It cannot . . . E" is canceled in pencil. "Cultivated classes . . . 254," and the preceding line are struck through in ink with single, vertical, connected use marks. Passages in Journal E, pp. [56], [62], and [64], C, p. [314], and "It has . . . Infinite" are used in The Present Age: "Introductory," Lectures, III, 200, 195–196, 187, 195, and 196; those in E, p. [64], and C, p. [314], are also in the lecture "The Spirit of the Times"; with "Commercial", cf. the paragraph on "the Dangers of Commerce" which follows a gap in the lecture manuscript, Lectures, III, 190, and 454(notes). Passages in Journal D, pp. [105] and [354], are used in "Education," that in E, p. [14], in "Reforms," and E, p. [82], in "Literature" [first lecture], Lectures, III, 287 and 289, 265–266, and 217–219.

[79] Notes from the rule to the bottom of p. [48] and on pp. [49]–[51] below were added later, probably for the introductory "Lecture on the Times" (W, I, 257–291) or for that series, in November, 1841. The last four lines on p. [48] are struck through with a faint vertical pencil line, possibly a use mark. The paragraph in Journal E, p. [156], is used in "The Transcendentalist," W, I, 342. The paragraph in E, p. [164], was used in the 1843 lecture "Manners and Customs of New England" and the quotation in E, p. [283], in the lecture "Trade." The paragraph in E, pp. [258]–[259], was used in "Europe and European Books," The Dial, III (April 1843), 520 (W, XII, 375 and 376).

Genius uncanonical   G 107
Availableness   G 107
Whist players   G 113
Demand of the Spiritualist   G 135
Triumph is always over one who was once a victor   G 143
All men m[a]gnetisable by the great [G 144]
Sir have you wondered   G 147
Do not blame those who make the Outcry   G 158
A man must do all in great spirit   160
Inevitableness of the new. H 2
Disbelief in the existence of Mme Fichte   H.16
How the world gets on diagonally   H 17
Trials of the Age new   H.18
⟨Exaggeration a law of nature. H 19, 21,⟩ 48
⟨Whiggery & ⟨sy⟩Hospital system   H 26⟩ [80]
Religion in Bliss & E. Webster   H.46
[50] T. H. Benton & Vienna Protocols   H 61
Webster in Washington St.   H 68
Past baked the loaf I break the oven   D 339
Today always trivial   E 192
Stem past, Leaf present.   F 127
Repose & flexibility   Whig & ⟨v⟩radical
Whiggery rest at last on thin idea   F 23
Our cotemporaries   H 97
Portrait   98 [81]

[80] The passage in Journal E, p. [290], and part of the first paragraph on "the Gentleman" in E, p. [313], are used in "The Method of Nature," W, I, 206–207, and 219; the last paragraph in E, p. [313], is used in "Lecture on the Times," W, I, 263. "Promise in . . . thought, in" is in pencil; cf. "Lecture on the Times," W, I, 275. "perplexity G 79", "Demand of . . . G 135", "All men . . . great", and "Trials of . . . H.18" are struck through in ink with single vertical use marks; the passages cited in G, pp. [79] and [135], are used in "Lecture on the Times," W, I, 281–282, and 286. Passages in G, pp. [86] and [160], and H, pp. [19], [21], and [48], are used in "Nature," W, III, 190, 189, 184–185, 193, and 185; the essay may have been prepared from the missing seventh lecture in the "Times" series (see W, III, 328). Passages in G, pp. [107]("Genius . . .") and [147], and H, p. [2], are used in "Prospects," Lectures, III, 372, 378, and 522(notes). The sentence cited in H, p. [26], is used in "The Conservative," W, I, 322.

[81] Lines 2–5 and 9 on p. [50] are struck through in ink with single vertical use marks, the first four connected; the passages cited in Journal H, pp. [68] and [98],

[51] [82] We are society H.100   We the Age   G 45, 139
        Persons the age   G 46

                    Hope is great
                    The Ideal is enforced
                    It appears that each man lies in it
                    Inevitableness of New   H 2
            Religion & philosophy   H 46, 2,
                    Head & tail   H.10
                    New dignity of reform   H.110, 114, G 9, 134
                                                    ↑sold[ier].↓

                    Transcend[entalis]m should be dear   H 115
                    Transcendm demands thorough Spirit[ualis]m   G 135 [83]
            We can't forgive NonTrans   H.126
            Head

[52] [84] Are all experiments made
        If Plato had not been you'd say   no Plato
Each newborn an incompatibility
The wildest poetry has yet to be prized [n]
You that sit there have all
Imitation must go out of vogue

---

are used in "Lecture on the Times," W, I, 284 and 264–265; a sentence in E, p. [192], used in "Experience," W, III, 46, is incorporated along with "Today always trivial" in a paragraph in E, p. [258], part of which is used in "Lecture on the Times," W, I, 267. The sentence cited in D, p. [339], and the paragraph in F No. 2, p. [127], are used in "The Conservative," W, I, 305 and 300. "Whiggery rest . . . F 23" is in pencil; the paragraph cited is used in "The Transcendentalist," W, I, 331–332.

[82] P. [51] is in pencil.

[83] The passages cited in Journal H, p. [100], and G, pp. [45] and [46], are used in "Lecture on the Times," W, I, 266–267, 262, and 261. "Hope is . . . in it" is struck through in pencil with a diagonal use mark or cancellation; Emerson used "Hope is great" in "Tendencies," Lectures, III, 313; with "It appears . . . in it", cf. "Religion," Lectures, III, 280. The paragraph in H, p. [2], is used in a later reading of "Prospects," Lectures, III, 522(notes). The passages cited in H, pp. [110], [114], and [115], and G, pp. [9] and [135], are used in "Lecture on the Times," W, I, 273 and 274–275, 271 and 266, 287, 275, and 286.

[84] P. [52], probably notes for the lecture "Tendencies," Lectures, III, 302–315, is in pencil. See also pp. [53]–[54] below.

Strong will come in   Stronger trust. World a wave
Ends, causes, Effects; [85]
Each dog
Creation does not stop. On what limited experience we pronounce so magisterially. Hope always good
Dante & Cromwell halfmen
I live & will live in the faith that life may be yet beautiful & we less related to apes & dragons[.]

[53]   Progressors
Degrees in proficiency   D 379
Progressors Janus faced   D 288   C 346,
The true Germany in New England   D 178
These men   D 358
Believe that always you may be *circumscribed*. E 28
Great man likes to be convicted   D 357
To put off the foreign the condition of insight   D 358 [86]
Rich will be ashamed of riches   D 35⟨5⟩6
Transcendentalism   C 309   D 331
Great men impersonal   C 349, 310,
Growth of great man per saltum   C 296, 231
Popularity for dolls   D 264
Strong will   C 313   D 214
Great to do a little   D 286
Untune nobody   D 292
Courage of 2 o'clock
Rhyme & music   D 326
Scorn appearance & you may   D 269

---

[85] "Are all . . . prized" and "Strong will . . . trust." are used in "Tendencies," *Lectures*, III, 313 and 312. With "You that . . . Effects;", cf. also "Self-Reliance," *W*, II, 71 and 81–89.

[86] With "The true . . . D 178", cf. "Self-Reliance," *W*, II, 80–81, and "Literature" [second lecture], *Lectures*, III, 228. The paragraph in Journal D, p. [358] ("These men"), is used in "The Editors to the Reader," *The Dial*, I (July 1840), 2. "Believe that . . . D 357" is struck through in ink with a vertical use mark; the sentence in E, p. [28], is used in "Literature" [second lecture], and the passage cited in D, p. [357], in "Reforms," *Lectures*, III, 235 and 259–260. "To put . . . insight" (cf. D, p. [358]) is used in "Tendencies," and cf. "Religion," *Lectures*, III, 313 and 284.

A man's self travels ghostlike   D 303
Conformist abdicates all   D 265, 337
Why give the children the romance   D 305
Conversation evanescent relation   D 346   C 231
Observe without ceasing   B 164
Feeble influence of thought on life   C 319
Live all the time. Organizations   D 376 [87]
Each dog his day   D 119   115
[54] We fear for the not natural   D 307
Secret of great pictures   D 333
Love is silent   D 69
In Nature all growth cotemporary   D 6
The Man of skill makes his jacket invisible   E 10
Only safe to do what you like   E 51
You teach the boy to walk he learns to run himself [E 78]
When the state is unquiet personal qualities decisive   E 90
Great man sets light by the world of forms   E 90
Good contended against first then Embraced   E 91
Progress   D 8
A cheerful face is culture   D 97
Never rely on memory alone   D 112
Two abandons   D 343
Conversation evanescent relation [D 346]
Distinctions immoveable [D 143] [88]
Philanthropic Meetings   C 306

[87] "D 35⟨5⟩6" is corrected, and the rest of the page written, in darker ink. With the paragraph in Journal D, p. [356], cf. "Self-Reliance," W, II, 88. "Strong will . . . D 214", "Scorn . . . D 269", and "Conformist . . . D 265, 337" are struck through in ink with single vertical use marks. Passages cited in D, p. [331], C, p. [296], and "Strong will" are used in "Tendencies," Lectures, III, 306–307 and 312. Passages in D, pp. [269], [303], [265], and [337], are used in both "Self-Reliance," W, II, 59, 81–82, and 54–55, and "Tendencies," Lectures, III, 311, 314, and 309. The paragraph in D, p. [346], is used in "Friendship," W, II, 208, and that in C, p. [231], in "Prospects," Lectures, III, 370–371. Two paragraphs in D, p. [376], are used in "Education," Lectures, III, 291 and 292–293.

[88] The paragraph in Journal D, p. [69], is used in "Tendencies," Lectures, III, 314–315, and "Circles," W, II, 311. The paragraph in D, p. [112], is used in "Self-Reliance," W, II, 57. "Two abandons . . . immoveable" is in pencil. "Distinctions immoveable", struck through in ink with a vertical use mark, is used in "Tendencies," Lectures, III, 305.

[55] [89]
Antimoney Principle holds & the practice of all good men approaches it

Manual labor] ⟨is⟩Labor consoles   D 313
         plant & fish   D 137

    The Highest
       Love is silent
       Confucius eloquence
       Speech indicates difference   D 69, 72, 79, 152,
       Great man sets light by world of forms [E 90]
       Degrees in proficiency [D 379]
       Eternity & omnip proper [90]

[56] [91] Manual labor   *Selfr* 63D
    Temperance
    Antimoney
    Nonresistance
       Objection to modes   E 14, 25,
       Temperance hateful
       I hate y[ou]r personalities
       Caution to martyrs
       One idea bad   C 255
       ↑Don't vamp principles↓ [E 25]
       Value of Inaction   Simp 78

       Nobleness of reform
       ⟨Honor the Philan⟩ [D 287]
       ⟨Obligation to reform   D 337⟩

[89] P. [55] is in pencil.
[90] "Antimoney Principle . . . D 137" may belong with notes on p. [56] below; cf. *Lectures*, III, 485–488(notes), substitute pages for a later reading of the lecture "Reforms"; see also p. [61] below for "manual labor . . . D 313". The paragraph in Journal D, p. [137], is used in "Education," *Lectures*, III, 289, and "New England Reformers," *W*, III, 257–258. "The Highest . . . proper" is probably an outline for "Tendencies," *Lectures*, III, 314–315.
[91] P. [56] (see Plate IV), probably notes for the lecture "Reforms," *Lectures*, III, 256–270, is in pencil; see also the collection for "Reforms" on pp. [57]–[59] and notes on p. [61] below.

Don't quarrel with a man for percep   E 90
⟨Great man likes to be convicted   D 357⟩
Reality   ton of coals   D 354
Nonconformity   *Selfr* ⟨19⟩ 23 [92]

[57]   ⟨Books⟩ [93] ↑Reform↓
Obligation to the Reformers   D 337
[Reform in housekeeping   D 342
The problem how to spend a day nobly   D 350   E 24
Manual labor   D 304, 313, 328, 137,
The garden discovery   D 300
Damper of reform   D 306
List of reforms   D 309
Reform must not be partial   D 328
Consecration of S⟨a⟩unday desecration of Monday   D 308
Objection to conforming   D 337
The Doctrine of Silence   D 353 ↑152,↓   Epaminondas   D 249,
Temperance conscious is not Temperance   D 357, E 22,
Doctrine of Hatred   D 33⟨5⟩6, E 22
Licence   D 96
Potatoes   D 154
⟨How many men will measure with a ton of coals   D 354⟩
[Advantage of the orators of a principle   B 33
Anti money   D 154
Health   E 34
Nothing gained by admitting omnipotence of limitations   *E*.41
I cannot vote for your measure though good   E 14
Content of men with wooden institutions   E 23
Trust thyself   E 51

[92] The manuscripts of the essays are missing, but "Manual labor *Selfr* 63D" may refer to a paragraph in Journal D, pp. [299]–[300], used in "Self-Reliance," *W*, II, 75–76, and "Reforms," *Lectures*, III, 264–265. For "Value of Inaction Simp 78", see "Spiritual Laws," *W*, II, 161–163, also used in "Reforms," *Lectures*, III, 266–268. "Nonconformity *Selfr* ⟨19⟩ 23" is probably the section in "Self-Reliance," *W*, II, 54–56, used also in "Tendencies," *Lectures*, III, 309–310. Other entries on the page are evidently drawn from pp. [57]–[59] below and, except for ll. 10, 15, and 17, developed in "Reforms."

[93] See p. [63] below, where a collection headed "Books" is written over notes for the lecture "Man the Reformer" (January 25, 1841).

Honor the philanthropies of the day   D 287,[94]
Progressors Janus faced   D 288
Fear goes before rottenness   D 293
[58] ⟨Self help must be preached. Yankee⟩ boy   D 299
⟨Past baked my loaf   D 339⟩
I hate preaching 'tis a pledge   D 352   372,
A young man Educated ten years rotten   D 353
How many men can measure with a ton of coals   D 354
Water agreeable to the imagination   D 356
Great man likes to be convicted   D 357
To put off the foreign the condition of insight [D 358]
Our objection to your modes of reform   E 14
Do not vamp principles   E 25
Non Resistance   E 26
Solution of objections   E 26
Temperance   E 34, 53, 70, 80, 84,
Calomel of emulation   E 47
Mercuries of Fashion   E 49
It is only safe to do what you like [E 51]
In hard times cultivate yourself. E.52
Genius & Reform   E 83
Don't quarrel with a man for perception   E 90
Great good first opposed then married   E 91
Vulgar reformers   D 53   154   173
Antimoney   D 154
Martyrs chiefly pseudo   C 343   347   D 97, 98, 99   D 206   B 101
                                                                    C 306

The great questions   C 245   D 11
The New Age   D 46

---

[94] Brackets and single vertical use marks through "Reform in . . . D 342" and "Advantage of . . . B 33" are in pencil. With Journal D, p. [342], cf. "Domestic Life," *W*, VII, 117–118. The paragraph in B, p. [33], is used in The Present Age: "Introductory," *Lectures*, III, 197. "I cannot . . . E 51" is in pencil, and "Trust thyself E 51" is marked with an "x" in pencil in the left margin. Passages in D, pp. [337]("Obligation . . . "), [304], [328], [309], and [357], E, pp. [22], [34], [41], and [14], and D, p. [287], are used in "Reforms," *Lectures*, III, 259, 487(notes), 263–264 and 487–488(notes), 257, 262, 269, 265–266, and 260. The passages cited in D, pp. [137] and [354], are used in "Education," and "Objection to conforming" in D, p. [337], in "Tendencies," *Lectures*, III, 289 and 309.

That work agreeable not now due   D 68 [95]
When you are deeply pleased without misgiving you are fed [C 188]
Two sorts of abandon   D 343
[59] Feeble influence of thought on life   C 319
Popularity for dolls   D 264
Conformist abdicates all   D 265
⟨All men's life superficial   D⟩ 289
My life a May game   D 309
Chastity selfsufficing   D 353   organized   376
One idea as bad as a draft of air   C 255 [96] D 39
Don't be solemn on Temperance   D 51
 New England a nation of servants   H.C. Lect. 2.
Dr Abernethy's Rule, E 165
Principles the tools of Reform   F 34
 Selfhelp always elegant [F 2, 43–44]
 To ride in the railroad not best
 One looks back at the country roads as we go to town
 Better to go without what we cannot make
 Asia was conquered by the Saracen on barley [97]

ABolition   E 204

[95] Lines 1–2 on p. [58] are struck through horizontally in pencil. Lines 1, 6, 7, and 10 are struck through in ink with single vertical use marks. To the right of ll. 12–15 are "E", "ENTER", and "Entertainment" in pencil in ornate print-writing. "Vulgar reformers . . . Age D 46" is in pencil. "D 206 B 101", in pencil, and "C 306", in ink, are run over onto p. [59]. Passages cited in Journal D, pp. [299] and [357], E, pp. [14], [34], [53], [70], [80] and [84], C, p. [347], D, p. [97], C, p. [245], and D, p. [68], are used in "Reforms," *Lectures*, III, 264–265, 259–260, 265–266, 262, 260–261, 268, 256–257, and 258. The sentence in D, p. [339], is used in "The Conservative," *W*, I, 305. Passages cited in D, pp. [353], [354], and E, p. [47], are used in "Education," and D, pp. [97] and [98], in "Tendencies," *Lectures*, III, 288 and 289–290, and 310.

[96] "All mens . . . D 289" is struck through horizontally in pencil and with a diagonal use mark in pencil; this and the paragraph in Journal D, p. [309], are used in "Reforms," *Lectures*, III, 259 and 268. Notes after "C 255" were probably added later.

[97] The passage cited in Journal F No. 2, p. [34], is used in "Man the Reformer," *W*, I, 250–251. "Selfhelp . . . barley", probably notes for the same lecture, is in pencil; with "Selfhelp . . . elegant" and "Better to . . . barley", cf. *ibid.*, pp. 246–247, 245, and 251. See also pp. [60]–[66] below for notes for "Man the Reformer," which draws on the lecture "Reforms."

Monastery & convent did not quite fail   E 207
Perhaps 'tis folly to hope to bring together the good   E 222
"Community" would be Astor House again   E 238
    The Whites have no rights. Respect the burden, Madam. [E 255]

Pirates do not live on nuts   E 283
Pusillanimity of Scholars   E 289, 286
Remember to be disposed to believe   G 58 [98]

[60] [99] Reform seems to require first of all a confidence in man,
that kind of sportive health which brushes away difficulties[.]
⟨A confidence⟩ It requires Faith. We are such conformists we hardly
know the meaning of this & our deafness to projects of Reform is not
very Creditable. But Love means something
⟨A lead pencil is better than a mine of plumbago]
    Only as much principle as there is is there Hope
We must be willing to be fools of ideas
Idealism creditable: & the extravagance of it only shows the extravagance of materialism
    A great impulse to reform; in all things;
    very bad state of things [100]

[61]   Nature offers her stores

———

Our modes of living not agreeable to the imag

———

[98] Notes below the rule on p. [59] were added no earlier than August 22, 1841,
for a still later use, perhaps in the series on "The Times." Emerson had used part
of the paragraph cited in Journal E, p. [286], in "The Method of Nature" (August
11, 1841), *W*, I, 207–208. The sentence cited in G, p. [58], is used in "Instinct and
Inspiration," *W*, XII, 80, and "Ethnical Scriptures," *The Dial*, IV (April 1844),
536.

[99] Pp. [60]–[62], "Do not . . . labor" on p. [63], and pp. [64]–[66], all in
pencil, are probably notes for the lecture "Man the Reformer" (*W*, I, 225–256).

[100] With "Reform seems . . . in man," and "It requires . . . something", cf.
"Man the Reformer," *W*, I, 248–249 and 252–254. With "A lead . . . plumbago",
cf. Journal F No. 2, p. [170]. Notes on the rest of p. [60] are developed in "Man the
Reformer," *W*, I, 250–251, 229, 248, and 230–234.

Religion tends to the Hearth but the Reform must be greatly not partially conceived. [D 328–329]

———

Puniness of literary men   Nature teaches by rapid impoverishment
[D 304]

———

Difficulties of young man in Actual Society

———

Let the philosopher work & be poor

———

War may show the need of labor [Ж 64]
Honorableness of labor
Labor gives animal spirits
Variety of tastes
Every man's art should make him happy
Every man in his own place able
Two anomalies
Raise the Aim [E 137]
Our housekeeping cripples us [101]

[62] Let Man be
            Now customs are Fourth of July
            Rich men are.   I ought not allow it [F 2, 104]
            What does a man want of a climate
            What does he want of means. Arabs [E 218]

———

[101] Notes on p. [61] are probably for the lecture "Man the Reformer," though they drew on "Reforms" and the notes for it on pp. [55]–[59] above, and on "Doctrine of the Hands" and the notes for it in Notebook Δ, pp. [143]–[150] above. With "Nature . . . stores", cf. Journal B, p. [315], a paragraph used in "Doctrine of the Hands," *Lectures*, II, 235. "Our modes . . . the imag" is used in "Reforms," *Lectures*, III, 258, "Man the Reformer," and "Lecture on the Times," *W*, I, 243 and 271. "Religion tends . . . poor" is developed in "Reforms," *Lectures*, III, 263, 265–266, and 487–488 (notes), and "Man the Reformer," *W*, I, 248, 242, 230–231, and 241–243. There are sections on "Honorableness of labor" in "Reforms," *Lectures*, III, 263–264 and 487–488 (notes), and "Man the Reformer," *W*, I, 234–242. With "Labor . . . spirits", cf. the paragraph in F No. 2, pp. [120]–[121], probably expanded from D, p. [313], and F No. 2, p. [18], and used in "Man the Reformer," *W*, I, 236–238. "Our housekeeping cripples us" is used, *ibid.*, p. 243.

My income is convenient but there are Chestnuts & potatos
Let me lose in talents to gain in Character [E 247]

Trust a principle   Power of an Aim

Need of reform   We are poor & timid
                Our housekeeping base
                Our food unhandsome
                Our expense for conformity [F 2, 29]
                Our trade fraudulent
                Our property vicious
Let us not be pedants & superstitious
                Indians in diet
                Laborers but not farmers [E 133–134]
                Romantic not irregular [102]

[63] Do not confound Romantic with Irregular

Power of love   Agaric [E 216]
                Laws & Prisons costly [F 2, 133]
                People do not love rogues [E 210]
                Opposition between helper & help [E 124–125]

Specialties   Make sixpence a day
                Work
                Go without
                Help yourself

                Value of labor [103]

[102] The passages cited in Journal F No. 2, p. [104], and E, pp. [218] and
[247], are used in "Man the Reformer," *W*, I, 249, 251, and 256. With "Trust a
. . . Aim", cf. F No. 2, pp. [34]–[35], used, *ibid.*, pp. 250–251. "Need of . . .
vicious" lists sections developed, *ibid.*, pp. 227–234, 243–245, 245–247, 244–245,
230–233, and 234. "Let us not . . . irregular" is developed, *ibid.*, pp. 247, 251,
240–241, and 255–256; "Romantic not irregular" probably refers to Emerson's
revision of the paragraph in E, p. [247].

[103] The four passages cited in "Power of . . . help" are used in "Man the Reformer," *W*, I, 254, 252, 253, and 252–253. "Specialties . . . Help yourself" is
probably an outline of the section, *ibid.*, pp. 245–247. Drafts for the section on
"Value of labor", *ibid.*, pp. 234 and 236–242, follow on pp. [64]–[66] below.

⟨Books⟩

⟨The poorest wood thought better   D 141⟩ [104]
Bancroft's History   E 256
Carlyle's Mirabeau   D 15
De Clifford [H 28–29]
Modern Novels   E 258
H. Martineau   E 192
Oliver Twist   D 361
Burton's Anat. Melancholy   E 67, 78, 318 [105]

[64] See the need of labor ⟨c⟩taught in the constitution. What is war but the superabundant strength & irritability of Man & that magazine of power for want of an outlet running into peccant humors

The young man finds the ways of lucre blocked up. A corruption has come into trade [106]

[65] Every thing is surrounded with its proper enemies   as iron with rust, ⟨w⟩ cloth with moths, provisions with mould or acid or putridity or ⟨thieve⟩ money with thieves, timber with rot, and whoever ⟨a⟩ takes any of these things into his ⟨patronage or as he calls it⟩ possession, takes upon him the charge of defending them from this company of enemies or of keeping them in repair.

a pl⟨ow⟩anted field must be fenced from cattle must be daily cleared of weeds
an orchard with canker worms & caterpillars
a bridge with freshet
cattle with hunger

A man who supplies his own want with one of these   as for instance with a boat to go a fishing finds it quite easy to caulk it or put in a pin

[104] "Books" and "The poorest . . . D 141" are canceled with curved diagonal pencil lines and may be the earliest inscription on page [63]. "The poorest . . . D 141" is struck through in ink with a vertical use mark; the sentence cited in Journal D, p. [141], is used in "Literature" [second lecture], Lectures, III, 235. "Books" is listed as a possible topic on p. [163] below.
[105] "Bancroft's History . . . 318", in heavier ink, is written over "Do not . . . help", part of the pencil notes for "Man the Reformer" printed above. The passage cited in Journal E, p. [258], is used in "Europe and European Books," The Dial, III (April 1843), 520 (W, XII, 375, 376).
[106] "The young . . . trade" is used in "Man the Reformer," W, I, 230.

or mend the rudder but a man whose father had successively surrounded himself with all these things & who has orchard, bridge,
cattle, hardware, wooden ware, a great house, carpets, cloths, provisions, books, money, to look after & made none of [66] them himself
has his hands full to look after these things or means[;] they will no
longer be the means but masters[;] ⟨they will⟩ their enemies will not
remit, rust, mould, vermin, rain, sun, freshet, fire, all are seizing on
their own filling him with vexation, wrinkles, & premature age & he
is converted from a man into a watch⟨dog⟩↑man↓ or watchdog to this
warehouse of old & new litter

⟨First man can well look after his⟩
Inventor can well look after his inventions
⟨Receiver⟩ ↑Heir↓ becomes a sentry
Therefore as these should be means & the End of life is always spiritual
it is better that ↑a↓ man should renounce this plenty & take a voluntary
poverty[,] should not put too many walls & curtains & stoves & down-
beds between him & the earth & sky[.] [107]

[67]   The Over–Soul

Mankind right in their Fames   D 367
In the soul seer & sight are one   D 370
Doctrine of the Soul   D 311
We disbelieve the puissance of today   D 301–2,
The perception of identity a mercury   D 268
You know is it truth or tradition by the tone of voice ⟨2⟩D 289
Answer in words no answer   D 384
What we are we must teach   D 325, 356,
Condescension of Salvani   D 369,
Concealment impossible   D 292
We fear for the not natural   D 307
Chance pictures   D 326,
How much is supposed in every discourse   D 46
The divine soul takes care for heroes   D 47

[107] Pp. [65]–[66] contain a draft for "Man the Reformer," W, I, 238–240;
with the first paragraph, cf. Notebook F No. 1, p. [48] above; with the last paragraph, cf. also Journal E, pp. [138]–[139], used in "Man the Reformer," W, I,
242–243.

What can genius avail against facts. D 50
Relation of teacher to hearer   D 183
I see in the lip of the speaker his culture   D 187
Oversoul can find your friend if it will   D 196 [108]
Throughout *things* [n] an effort to be beautiful   D 205
The good in poor pictures & books   D 343   C 325
Alcott's School   C 334.

[68]–[70] [blank]
[71]   Poetry [109]
In common hours thoughts do not sit for portraits   D 364
Herrick
Sonnet to the woods   D 365, 370, E 77.
    Milton's saying of wit & imagination   D 364
    Petrarch & his books   D 365
    Life of a poet a catalogue   D 366
    A wood walk a dream   370
    A poet a namer   D 344
    Epic must be as well as lyric   D 281
        Summer night light   D 344
    Rhyme & Music may speak truth   D 326–7,
    Beauty a shield
    The poet must be Caesar to chant Caesarics   D 278
        Realism of the poets   D 275
        Analysis legitimate & poetic   D 312,
↑B 110↓ Wordsworth   D 60   Essential gifts of a poet [n]
        The talent of the poet   D 154

[108] "Mankind right . . . D 301–2," "Answer in . . . 356," and "I see . . .
D 196" are struck through in ink with single diagonal use marks. The paragraph
cited in Journal D, p. [367], is used in "Literature" [second lecture], *Lectures*, III,
229–230. The paragraphs in D, pp. [301]–[302], are used in "Compensation," *W*,
II, 124–126. The passages cited in D, pp. [370], [384], [325], [356], and
[196], are used in "Religion," *Lectures*, III, 284, 277, 282, and 281, and "The
Over-Soul," *W*, II, 269, 283 and 284–285, 286, and 293. See also p. [163] below.
[109] P. [71] may be a trial collection for the "Present Age" series. Emerson had
been considering "Poetry" as the subject of a lecture since 1838; see Notebook Φ, p.
[46] above. See also pp. [162], [163], and [168] below, where it appears among
possible topics for the "Present Age" and "Times" series, and pp. [97]–[100]
below, notes for the lecture "The Poet," where many of these entries are repeated.

Fine offices of the poet   D 230
Intellectual courage   D 236
Epitaph. C 111
Poetry precedes prose. C 211
Humanity of the poets   C 221
Shakspeare's threnes   B 225,
If poetry is not free it is nothing   C 318 [110]

[72]–[73] [blank]
[74] Reason of Selftrust is deep
Trust implies ⟨the⟩ Trustee
Who is Self
Spontaneity
That is, Intuition
We share the life of the World & then see it [111]

[75]   Ethics

Not wholesome to *say* I love not Xt.   D 374
Not safe to dispute   D 29   C 289, 343,
        Untune nobody   D 292,
        Roses d [D 331, 338]
        Two absolutions   D 312 [112]

---

[110] Lines 7, 9, 10, 12, 14, 15, and 19 on p. [71] are struck through in ink with single vertical use marks; l. 2 is struck through with a diagonal use mark and l. 14 with a second vertical use mark, both in heavier ink. The last nine lines on the page are in heavier ink. The sentence cited in Journal D, p. [364], is used in "Intellect," *W*, II, 336. "A poet a namer" is used in "The Poet," *W*, III, 7 and 21. The passages in D, p. [326], and C, p. [211], are used in "The Poet," *Lectures*, III, 359 and 358. The passage in D, p. [278], is used in "Spiritual Laws," *W*, II, 165–166, and "Literature" [second lecture], *Lectures*, III, 231–232.

[111] P. [74], in pencil, outlines part of a paragraph in "Self-Reliance," *W*, II, 63–64.

[112] P. [75] may be a collection for the missing eighth lecture in the "Present Age" series. The passages cited in Journal D, p. [29], and C, pp. [289] and [343], are used in "Prudence," *W*, II, 238–239; those in D, pp. [331], [338], and [312], are used in "Self-Reliance," *W*, II, 67 and 74, and both paragraphs on "Roses" are used in "Religion," *Lectures*, III, 283–284. Following the notes is a sketch of a rose, "R", and "Roses" written twice, all in pencil.

473

[76]–[78] [blank]

[79] Laws of the World

Chapter on Time B 275

Passenger pigeon B 257.

Condition of genius ⁿ always the same Δ 133

[80]–[82] [blank]

[83] Politics [113]

We hate taxes, & so accuse Government D 354

"As if their kingdoms were for them & not they for their kingdoms." *Pym.*

The low can best win the low & all people like to be made much of.
[B 308]

If America were to be sold today it would fetch more than it did yesterday.

Base politics C 318 A 92 B 307, 294, D 142 144

True politics Σ 13

See Δ 63

Our politics C 153, 297

Politics easy to a philosopher B 308

Public speaking does not utter the Character D 247

The actual an optical illusion as in Brant's war D 257

Institutions illusions D 263

Popularity for dolls D 264

All men's life superficial D 289

Party makes men drunk D 338

We viciously esteem defects organic D 345

Rich will be ashamed of riches D 355 E 56

H Mann's Address on Education D 350

Oliver Cromwell D 362

Society to be treated as children D 377

I would not be happy or good with uncultivated D 376

Society untunes D 77

---

[113] Pp. [83]–[85] are a collection for "Politics," *Lectures*, III, 238–247; the lecture manuscript is fragmentary; it was partly used in the essay "Politics," *W*, III, 197–221, and "The Fortune of the Republic," *W*, XI, 509–544. The collection draws on earlier lecture Notebooks Δ and Φ and on the manuscripts of essays which Emerson had not yet published, as well as regular journals.

Easier to affront the Scholars than the mob   D 97
Youth can speak to his contemporaries   D 114
Distinctions of men immoveable   D 143 [114]
[84] Wealth of New England   C 27
Despondency does no good
Is there any limit to the influence of character?   Φ 7
The soul must legislate
Napoleon   C 348, 349, 314, 315, 296,
Which are the hard times   B 38
Treat all men as gods   B 140
Benevolence   T 33   C 63
The condition of influence by virtue is time   C 302
        Sacs & Foxes   C 209
Chinese & English   C 171
Eberhard of Wirtemberg   Σ 13

        ⟦Stern Jove has in some Angry Mood
        Bereft us of his solitude⟧ [C 131]

Apples & men   D 127   224
The times   C 84   294   305
Nomads
Courage ⟦of 2 o'clock C 299)   C 15   348   145   Φ 158   D 240
Love of law   D 141
Convertibleness of every man   B 86
The first men had no glory   C 317   D 213
A king symbolical   *Essay. History*
Politics compensatory   *Essay Comp.*
Owe the Government nothing   *Essay Reliance*
When the state is unquiet personal merits avail   E ⟨11⟩90
Politics not concordant with the landscape   E 45

[114] "Politics easy . . . B 308" is struck through in ink with four diagonal use marks. Lines 2, 4, 8 ("Base politics . . ."), 9, 11, 13–16, 18–20, 22, 23, and 28 are marked in the left margin with single vertical or diagonal pencil lines which may be use marks. "The low . . . low" and the passages cited in Journal B, p. [294], Notebook Σ, p. [13], and Journal D, pp. [247], [257], [338], and [345], are used in "Politics," *Lectures*, III, 244–245, 241, 246, 244, 240, 477(notes), and 245–246; phrases in B, p. [308], and D, p. [338], were later used in "The Fortune of the Republic," *W*, XI, 518–519, and passages in D, pp. [354] and [257], in "Politics," *W*, III, 215 and 199.

This country governed in Barrooms   E 78 [115]
[85] Do not meddle too much — Non Resistance   E 26
True statesman looks at the measure & not Opinion   E 66
State should be governed by Ideas   Votes follow Ideas   E 100
Treat the state poetically   E 10⟨2⟩1
Nobody would be statesman who could be a friend ↑E↓ 103
The wise man is the state   E 105
Strong Will   C 348, 313, D 214
Moral effect of a victory — Undue power of a Fact   D 144, 364
Our national Union of little value. E 64 [116]

[86]–[87] [blank]
[88] We are always greenhorns   D 376, *Simp* 17
Sense of want & sin an innuendo [D 20]
Influence of nature
The vast an element. D 246, 105   143   Eternity & Omnip proper
                                                Rhyme & Music

Power of recurring to the sublime
I would not be happy or good with clowns [117]

[89]   Education

[115] Lines 3, 4, 7–9, 12, 20, and 22–27 on p. [84] are marked in the left margin
with single vertical or diagonal pencil lines. Only three phrases in Journal B, p.
[140], Notebook Σ, p. [13], and Journal E, p. [78], are used in what remains of
"Politics," *Lectures*, III, 245, 246, and 244, but the thought of many of the passages
cited on p. [84] is developed in the lecture. Emerson used the passages cited in C,
pp. [27] and [209], and E, p. [78], later in the lecture "Trade."

[116] Each line on p. [85] is marked in the left margin with a short vertical or
diagonal pencil line. Passages cited in Journal E, pp. [66], [100], [101], and [105],
are used in "Politics," *Lectures*, III, 244, 245, 239–240, and 243–244. With the
paragraphs in D, p. [144], and E, p. [64], cf. *ibid.*, p. 477(notes), and "The
Fortune of the Republic," *W*, XI, 519–520.

[117] Notes on p. [88], in pencil, are probably for the lecture "Education," *Lectures*, III, 286–301, a collection for which follows on pp. [89]–[90] and part of
p. [91]. "Eternity & . . . Music" is aligned with "Secret of . . . " and "Rhyme
& Music" on p. [89] opposite, and set off from "sublime" by a pencil slash. Except
for "Sense of . . . innuendo", all the notes are repeated from p. [89]. The sentence
cited in Journal D, p. [20], is used in "The Over-Soul," *W*, II, 267, and canceled
in the manuscript of "Education," *Lectures*, III, 499(notes). "*Simp* 17" probably
refers to the manuscript of "Spiritual Laws," titled "Simplicity" in early stages (see
p. [56] above), but the paragraph in D, p. [376], is not in the essay.

We are always greenhorns   D 376
Influence of Nature   D 303, 104,
Our unmanly Education   D 350   C 112
Conversation gives selfpossession   D 262
                    evanescent relation   D 346
Secret of great pictures   D 333
Rhyme & Music   D 326
Tedious selfrecollection of travellers   D 348
I would not be happy or good with the uncultivated   D 376
Strong Will   C 313   D 214
One idea as bad as a draft of air   C 255
The youth can speak to contemporaries   D 114
The Vast an element   D 246, 105, 143
Memory that and this   D 255, [218]
Eternity & omnipresence proper   D 274
A man's self travels ghostlike with him   D 303
Objection to Conforming   D 337
Extempore speech good, & so is writing. D 339, 356,
Perception fatal   D 343
A young man Educated ten years issues rotten   D 353
How many men may measure with a ton of coals   354 [118]
Magic of learning languages. A 64,
St Augustine   D 271
Germany in New England   D 178
Life of true man a catalogue   D 366
Power of recurring to the sublime   C 318

[90] Private Life

    Ought to be arranged from principles
    The house ought to show the man
We are not classic but composite

[118] Lines 2, 3, 4-5, 10, 13, 14, 21, and 22 on p. [89] are struck through in pencil with single vertical use marks. The passages cited in Journal D, pp. [376], [303], [350], [262], [376], [114], [246], [105], [353], and [354], are used in "Education," *Lectures*, III, 291, 299, 288-289, 298-299, 292-293, 295, 497 (notes), 287, 288, and 289. Emerson used the paragraph in D, p. [326], later in "The Poet," *Lectures*, III, 359, and D, p. [274], in "History," *W*, II, 9 and 23.

A house should be
A house is   Oppresses woman
   A man's tr
   Conjugal relation
   Relation to the poor [119]

   Observe without ceasing   B 164
   Phrenology   C 145
   Real Education   C 268
   Scholar loves society like D. of Ormond. see also C 156, 283
   Which are the hard times   B 38
   Feeble influence of thought on life   C 319
   Unconscious Culture   C 34
   Bifronted is every master   C 346
   Culture needs no costly apparatus   C 242   T 19
   Man should know how to plant & fish   D 137
   Find a man's limitations & the game up   D 246
   Why give the children all the romance   D 305
   We fear for the not natural   D 307
   Two *Abandons*   D 343
   A poet a namer   D 344
   Live all the time. Organizations   D 376
   Our faculties warrant inceptions only   D 191
   Growth of a great man *per saltum*   C 296
   Great men not alike   E 62
   Each dog his^n day   D 119, 115,
When will Education open the Sanscrit of Nature   E 174
Aim of Education to Emancipate man from Circumstance   E 186
Painting & Sculpture are but gymnastics of the eye. E 172
Toys. E 159
The capital or stock of man our estimates overlook   E 155 [120]

[119] "Private Life . . . poor", in pencil, probably notes for the lecture "Private Life" (January 8, 1840), is overwritten in ink by "Observe without . . . limitations", part of the collection for the lecture "Education" (February 5, 1840), printed below. "Private Life" is enclosed in an ornate box, and "Mont" written beside it. The manuscript of "Private Life" is fragmentary, but cf. "Domestic Life," *W*, VII, 109–129, and notes on pp. [91]–[95] below.

[120] "Unconscious Culture" and "Man shd. . . . D 137" are struck through in

[91] [121] I am by the soul selfsufficing
Where then is less & more
Is not all the mission of genius to reveal this
of nature
of society

Facts of common life   E 18
What can society do for friendship   E 96
Forms & faces around us   E 34   D 371
We never become superior to circ.   D 376
Reaction of our trade & habit   E 72
Object of man to idealize his life   D 289

Fathers would be fathers of the mind
Great men not alike. [E 62]   We fear for not-nat. [D 307]
Growth per saltum [122] [C 296]

[92] Cousindom   D 269
Tea very late   D 19
Hospitality (to soul   D 338) (cynical   D 371) (timid   E 53)
Good housekeeping impossible   D 272   Bad board   E 69
Reformed housek.   D 342
No property in Art E.72   Half & Whole   B 125
My expenditure E 22   Fear   D 293

---

pencil with single diagonal use marks, and "Great men . . . E 62" with a vertical one. The passages cited in Journal C, pp. [268] and [34], D, pp. [137] and [246], and E, p. [62], are used in "Education," *Lectures*, III, 289, 291, 289, 497(notes), and 295. "When will . . . E 155" was added in a smaller hand, no earlier than July 13, 1840; the paragraph in E, p. [159], was used in the lecture "Eloquence" (see Index Minor, p. [4] below); the rest are unlocated.

[121] Pp. [91]–[95] are in pencil.

[122] "Facts of . . . D 289" is probably notes for the lecture "Private Life"; the passage cited in Journal D, p. [371], is used in a manuscript fragment which is probably part of "Private Life" (ms. Houghton Library); passages cited in E, pp. [18] and [34], and D, pp. [371] and [289], are used in "Domestic Life," *W*, VII, 107–108, 127, 109 and 110. The paragraph cited in D, p. [376], is used in "Education," *Lectures*, III, 291. "I am . . . society" and "Fathers wd. . . . saltum" are notes for "Education" and were probably added a month later. With "I am . . . society", cf. *ibid.*, pp. 297–299; "Fathers wd. . . . mind" and one sentence of the paragraph in E, p. [62], are used, *ibid.*, p. 295.

Riches E 56   Wealth *le beau* E 104   New Engd C 67
We would live with those we are used to   D 285
A stranger   D 107

Germany & Bettina   D 294, 178
Inceptions   D 191
Romantic relations
Life a May game   D 309
I will live out myself sacredly   D 320
True generosity & right relations   E 57 .
Think not too much of Action   *Simp* 78 [123]
Doctrine of Hatred [D 335]

[93]   *Domestic Life* [124]
⟨Hospitality   D 338, 371, E 53⟩
Stay at home in y[ou]r duties   D 261
⟨⟨c⟩Cousindom   D 269, 371⟩
⟨Good housekeeping impossible   D 272⟩
My books my gallery   D 282
⟨We would live with those we are used to. D 285⟩
Great to do a little ↑D↓ 286
Good will elegant   D 287   366
⟨Wives for scholars   D 287⟩   *Simp* 48
All men's life superficial   D 289
God scorns size   D 207, 210, 289, C 299
O preacher pain & care are things   D 291
⟨Concealment impossible   D 292⟩
Untune nobody   D 292

[123] Notes on p. [92] are probably for the lecture "Private Life"; the manuscript is fragmentary, but parts of it were probably used in the essays "Friendship" and "Domestic Life." Passages cited in Journal D, pp. [272] and [342], and E, pp. [22], [56], [104], and [57], are used in "Domestic Life," *W*, VII, 112, 117–118, 109, 114–115, 113–114, and 118. A pencil line in the left margin runs from between ll. 2 and 3 to "Good housekeeping . . .", probably indicating a change in order. Most of the paragraph cited in D, p. [107], is used in "Friendship," *W*, II, 192–193. "*Simp* 78" probably refers to "Spiritual Laws"; cf. *W*, II, 161–163.
[124] Emerson listed this lecture as "Domestic Life" on p. [163] below, but "Private Life" in the final list on p. [166]. An unidentified pencil sketch fills the left margin of the page from "Fear before . . . " down to "Life a . . . ".

⟨Fear before Rottenness D 293⟩
⟨Germany & Bettina D 294, 178⟩
⟨If I love you, What?⟩ D 295
⟨Life a May game Love thaumat. D 309⟩
Great man small matters D 310
Dartmouth sheriff D 310
⟨Two absolutions⟩ 312
Manual labor consoles 313
⟨Friends God sends D 315 316 E 92⟩
⟨Friends not to be used D 321⟩ [125]
Reform must not be partial D 328
Bambino D 341
Old Age E 19   Sickness D 126 E 20
[94] Manners demonological D 343
     ⟨Reform in housekeeping D 342⟩
     ⟨Friends selfelected D 345⟩
     Conversation evanescing relation D 346
     Manners lazy D 348, 369,
     Spend a day well D 350 E 24
     Let the age of words be followed by silence [D 353]
     Men & the ton of coals D 354
     Riches E 56,
     ⟨I must wait to know a friend D 360⟩
     Luxury of plain dealing D 362
     ⟨Faces on pivot &c   D 371⟩
     Gleaning & gathering D 376
     ⟨We never become superior to Circums. D 376⟩
I would not be happy with the uncult. 376
     ⟨A stranger D 107⟩
     Tragedy of women D 66, 79

[125] Emerson used parts of the passages cited in Journal D, pp. [272] and [289], in "Domestic Life," *W*, VII, 112, 109 and 110, and passages in D, p. [313], E, p. [92], and D, p. [321], in "Friendship," *W*, II, 194–195 and 214–216. The paragraph in D, p. [287], is used in "Spiritual Laws," *W*, II, 151. Of the other entries with horizontal use marks, the first passage cited in D, p. [292], and the paragraph in D, p. [293], are used in "Compensation," *W*, II, 116 and 111–112; D, p. [295], is used in "Love," *W*, II, 180–181; the two paragraphs cited in D, p. [309], are used respectively in "Reforms," and "Religion," *Lectures*, III, 268 and 279; the paragraph in D, p. [312], is used in "Self-Reliance," *W*, II, 74.

⟨Sickness D 126 E 20⟩
⟨Our faculties warrant inceptions D 191⟩
⟨Wealth of N England C 27⟩
Coat C 166
⟨Half more than whole B 125⟩
Society should be treated as children [D 377]
Reality under sham-fight E 10
⟨Facts of common life E 18⟩
⟨My Expenditure E 22⟩
⟨Forms & faces around us E 34, D 371⟩ [126]

[95] ——

Friendship — God sends D 315, 316,
They come when we are fit ˙ E.6, 9, 19,
⟨Leave it to grow Dare not interfere E⟩ 36
⟨No peace without selfpossession⟩ E.83
My friends E 92   Wait to know friend D 360
⟨A new person a great event⟩ E 94
⟨Friendship *on one side*⟩ E 95
⟨Property in my friend⟩ E 99
Treat your friend as a spectacle. Respect him E 107
Friends selfelected D 345   Not to be used D 321
Belinda & Montreville *Simp.* 46 [D 256]
What can society do for Friendship   E 96
Friendship is the nut. [E 96] [127]

Wolsey's Orange E 44

[126] The passages cited in Journal D, pp. [345], [346], [360], and [107], are used in "Friendship," *W*, II, 209, 208, 201–202, and 192–193. The passages cited in E, p. [56], D, p. [371], and E, pp. [18], [22] and [34], are used in "Domestic Life," *W*, VII, 114–115 and 118, 127, 107–108, 109, and 108. The passage in D, p. [371], is used in a manuscript fragment which is probably part of the lecture "Private Life" (ms. Houghton Library).

[127] "Treat your . . . E 107" and "Friends selfelected D 345" are struck through in pencil with single vertical use marks. Passages in Journal E, pp. [83], [95], and [96], are used in both "Private Life," *Lectures*, III, 253–254, and "Friendship," *W*, II, 211, 216–217, and 201. The passages cited in D, p. [315], E, pp. [6], [36], and [92], D, p. [360], E, pp. [94], [99], and [107], and D, pp. [345] and [321], are used in "Friendship," *W*, II, 194–195, 212, 211–212, 194–195, 201–202, 195, 208 and 209, 209, and 214–216. "Belinda & Montreville" refers to a paragraph used in "Spiritual Laws," *W*, II, 149–150.

Use the Mercuries of fashion   E 49
⟨True generosity & right relations   E.57⟩
⟨Bad board   E 69⟩
⟨No property in Art   E 72⟩
⟨Reaction of our trade & habit, E 72⟩
Society spoils the best persons   E 89
⟨Love of wealth grows from Le Beau   E 104⟩
⟨Sitting still of Epam   *Simp* 78⟩ [D 266]
Poor mind must *have* something   *Simp* 80 [D 298]
Nunnery   D 376
Tragedy of common life   B 16, C 166   D 48, 79, 95   152
D 174, 225, Θ 101 [128]

[96] [blank]
[97] [129]   Genius
Growth of genius, one tree, one maid,   D 31
Coles & Briggs can end their sermon   B 12
Our exhaustion of men of genius   B 286
Aladdin's window   B 81   Talent & genius
Genius representative   not his wealth but Commonwealth   B 285
Hawk wheeling to heaven   *A* 38
Tax of snow & silence   C 25
Discriminative minims accumulated   C 129
We do not love the man that gives us thoughts   ⟨1⟩C 156   D 285
                                                    288   267
A devout sentiment in society has the effect of genius   C 307
        Men of Genius impersonal, Napoleon   C 349
When Genius arrives it writes itself perfect in a line as in a whole, D 56
        Genius's words the emanation of that they tell of   D 234
        ⟨Shakspeare *understands himself*⟩ D 175
        ⟨Poet is Caesar   D ⟨246⟩⟩ 278

[128] The paragraphs cited in Journal E, pp. [57] and [104], are used in "Domestic Life," *W*, VII, 114–115, 118, 113 and 114. The passages cited in "*Simp* 78" and "*Simp* 80" are in "Spiritual Laws," *W*, II, 162 and 163, and "Reforms," *Lectures*, III, 267–268. For "Θ", see Notebook Φ, p. [14] above.
[129] P. [97], in pencil, may be a trial collection for the "Present Age" series, though little was used there. Emerson may have drawn on it for the lecture "The Poet," notes for which follow on pp. [98]–[100].

483

Milton's saying of the delicacy of Wit   D 364
Life of an artist a catalogue of works. [D 366]
Communion service a document of genius   D 244
[Of Construction] Pity so near a painter & not paint   D 341

A poet a namer   D 344
Language [130]

[98]   The Poet
Religious
No cymbal clashed no clarion rang at the advent of Ideas.
Music first before thought. F ⟨9⟩55
⟨The namer⟩ [D 344]
The teller of news   F 100
⟨Can spare⟩ no pain   E 197, H.99
⟨How fond are the people of symbols⟩ E.206
⟨The Poet's life⟩ E 266
⟨Sweeter rhythms to be found   H 38.⟩
Poetry should surprize & capture us   H.39
A new person flings wide the doors of existence   39
⟨Difference between poetry & stock poetry 38⟩
Powers of the landscape ↑H↓ ⟨3⟩40
All poems are unfinished   H 112
Life of a poet a catalogue   D 366
Epic must be as well as lyric   D 281
⟨Rhyme & music speak truth⟩ D 326–7
Realism of poets   D 275
Fine offices of the Poet   D 230
Power to fix the life of objects   E 271
Every word a trope   G 43, 57, 60
⟨Poet only can know poet   E⟩ 266

---

[130] The passages cited in Journal C, p. [25], and D, p. [175], are used in
"Literature" [first lecture], and D, p. [278], in "Literature" [second lecture],
Lectures, III, 221, 211, and 231–232. With "Growth of genius," cf. C, p. [296],
used in "Tendencies," *Lectures*, III, 312. "A poet . . . D 344", used in "The Poet,"
W, III, 7 and 21, and "Language", probably a section of "The Poet," *Lectures*,
III, 358, may have been added in 1841, with notes for the lecture which follow on
pp. [98]–[100].

Every man tries his hand at poetry somewhere but most men don't
    know wh[ich]. their poems are [E 277]
⟨Nature did not make them black haired   E 296⟩ [131]
The balance of Individualize & Generalize   E 297
[99] Power to affect me in natural objects: impersonal   H.45
⟨H⟩Be expressed   express your confusion   H 47
Magic of liberty when we are expressed   H.47
Man is only half — Expression other half   53
We worship Expressors &c   53
Old age is expression   Expression is success   H.57
⟨Fanny Elssler⟩ 64, 69
Expression, how rare! few orators! poets! H.69 [132]
[War & Alcohol express   79]

⟨Too feeble fall the impressions of sense   G 21⟩
Ascending souls &c   G 37
⟨The world is *tropical*   G 43⟩
⟨The meaner the type the more portable   G⟩ 57
⟨Tropes becoming practical! G 97⟩
⟨Jones Very's value of his poems   G 116⟩
A man is a house
The only objection to Hamlet is that it exists
⟨Every trope is legitimate which occurred [n] without seeking⟩
⟨Poets are guardians of admiration⟩
⟨Poet the soul through which the universe is poured⟩
Poet is representative
Miracle of poetry

---

[131] Lines 3 and 6 on p. [98] are connected by penciled brackets in both margins.
"Music first . . . F ⟨9⟩55" and "Every word . . . 60" are in pencil. The passages
cited in Journal E, pp. [197], [206], and [266], H, pp. [38]("Sweeter rhythms
. . . ") and [39] ("Poetry . . . "), D, pp. [326]-[327] and [230], G, pp. [43]
and [57], and E, p. [296], are used in "The Poet," *Lectures*, III, 357, 353, 357–358,
359, 361, 359, 356, 352–353, and 356–357. "The namer" and the passages in E, p.
[206], and G, p. [57], are also used in "The Poet," *W*, III, 7 and 21, and 16–17.
[132] The passages cited in Journal H, pp. [53]("Man is . . . "), [57], and
[64], are used in "The Poet," *Lectures*, III, 349 and 350–351. The second passage
cited in H, p. [47], and both in H, p. [53], are used in "The Poet," *W*, III, 32–33,
and 5.

Dial   F 90 [133]
Swedenborg   E 90
Travel consists in sounding all the stops   G 27
[100] ——

"Things more excellent than every image are expressed through images."
Iamblichus

———

Man is ass, puppy, bat, owl, toad   house,

———

Milton wrote to his own ear. H 21 [134]

[101]–[103] [blank]
[104]   Our Boston Age
One ought to command the reason why no musical composer here.
Egotism of spiritualists   E 125
Boston needs 200 years more & moral interest   E 200
Our young speculative men monotonous rejectors   E 279
Man's life is but 70 sallads   [E 312]
⟨Opinion of Mr A. concerning Brattle st preacher⟩ E 313 [H 82]
Unitarianism   E 311, 313
Availableness
General Harrison   E 314 [135]

Not to be praised nor insulted [H 17]
Has pleasure only in coming near [G 28]

[133] "Miracle of poetry" and "Dial   F 90" are in pencil. The passages cited in
Journal G, pp. [21], [57], [97], and [116], are used in "The Poet," *Lectures*, III,
355, 352–353, 354, and 360. The first is also used in "The Poet," *W*, III, 6. "A
man is a house" and "Every trope . . . poetry" are used in "The Poet," *Lectures*,
III, 352, 353, 356, and 360.
[134] " 'Things more . . . Iamblichus", struck through in ink with a diagonal
use mark, is used in "The Poet," *W*, III, 13. "Man is . . . house," is used in "The
Poet," *Lectures*, III, 352. The paragraph in Journal H, p. [21], is used in "Prospects," *Lectures*, III, 375.
[135] The page to this point may be an early survey for the series on "The Times."
"Opinion of . . . preacher", apparently canceled with a wavy pencil line, and
"Man's life . . . sallads", are struck through in ink with single diagonal use
marks. "Man's life . . . sallads" is used in "Nature," *W*, III, 195, and the anecdote
in Journal E, p. [313], in "Lecture on the Times," *W*, I, 263; with "Our young
. . . rejectors", cf. *ibid.*, p. 282.

It takes no oath
Wholly real

Cannot drill [136] [E 54]

[105] [blank]
[106] [137] ⟨A great man conquers by Presence⟩ G 97
    ⟨Xenos & Iole⟩ E 117
    ⟨Impression of Character⟩   Angels shine   H 92
        ⟨Homage E 308   no foul⟩ word
        ⟨Magnetism⟩ E 176, 187, 296
        ⟨Good 'twixt us ⟨& sun⟩ &⟩ the sun ↑E 37↓
        ⟨slave ship of Washingtons⟩
        brings greatness; is greatness;   H 39

Love built on it,
Privacy of elevation
Marriage empirical   G 74, 90
I love too well to ⟨p⟩court   G 5
Marriage from Character ⟨C⟩H 84 [34]

Transcendant
        ⟨Not to be measured by works⟩ J 35 [138]
        ⟨Abolition trivial⟩   H.85
        Rely on Character   H 88   cars
        Judges reformers   H.127
        Character a theocracy

---

[136] "Not to . . . drill" is in pencil. These lines and pp. [106]–[111] below are probably notes for the lecture "Character" (January 6, 1842); cf. "Character," *W*, III, 106–107, 111–112, 101, and 108. The lecture manuscript is missing, but probably served as the basis for "Character," *W*, III, 87–115. See Index Minor, pp. [35]–[37] below, for notes for the essay; see *Lectures*, III, 483 and 524–525(notes), and *JMN*, VII, 261–262, for possible fragments of the lecture.

[137] P. [106] is in pencil; "E 37" is added in ink. Lines 1–7, 15, and 16 are apparently canceled with wavy pencil lines, though some of the passages are used.

[138] The passages cited in Journal G, p. [97], E, pp. [117], [187], [296], and [37], and J, p. [35], are used in "Character," *W*, III, 90, 94, 96, and 103. "slave ship of Washingtons" is used, *ibid.*, pp. 94–95, and in *Lectures*, III, 477(notes); cf. G, p. [142]. With "Love built . . . elevation", cf. "Character," *W*, III, 111–112, p. [109] below, and *Lectures*, III, 524(notes).

[107] [139] Alternation of Character & intellect   G 3
Character inspirations not literary   H 94

> Young to denounce
> ashamed of our virtue
> Aims at the circumstance of slave

⟨The sin against the Holy Ghost   H 132⟩

> Vulgar man licentious abroad [G 26]
> ⟨Assurance H 30⟩   Dandies   G 107, 139
> ⟨Permanence   H 116 Ilchester   G 62   They who never stoop⟩
> ⟨Not great and small but always great⟩   G 52
> Should never let us go
> > Buckminster [BB] Y [48–49, H 106]
> > Lose time in trying to resemble   J 18

⟨Oath of Character   G [E] 271⟩
⟨Not to be praised nor insulted⟩ [H 17]
> Best apology none

> A career

⟨Character loves to hear its faults⟩ [H 60] [140]
Window in the breast [G 152]

> Patience   H 51

[108]   Character
⟨A great character wants room   H 132⟩
⟨The sin we hate is insult to Character   H.132⟩

---

[139] P. [107] is in pencil. Lines 6, 8, 14, and 15 are apparently canceled with wavy pencil lines, though some of the passages are used.

[140] The passages cited in Journal G, p. [3], H, p. [132], G, p. [52], and H, pp. [17] and [60], are used in "Character," *W*, III, 104–105, 114–115, 90, 106–107, and 97. "Young to . . . slave" is struck through in pencil with a diagonal use mark; cf. "Lecture on the Times," *W*, I, 277–280. For "G 62 . . . stoop", see *Lectures*, III, 395 (notes).

Skepticism is unbelief in man   H.131, G 135–6,
⟨We are all involved in one folly: our vice not so bad as⟩ our virtue
                                        H. 127.

⟨Permanence & Count of Ilchester   H.116⟩
The Game of Life   H.48, 49,
No man stands by himself
De Clifford no perception of character   H.28
⟨Assurance concerning my friends⟩ H 30
⟨I like to hear of my faults⟩ H.60   E 227
⟨How noble in secret the men that have not stooped⟩ a little. G 62
Not to be denied that the pious youth may be partial   G 66
Certain places are guages of character (G 76)
When we quarrel, O for character! G 86
⟨Greatness conquers by *Presence* ⟨9⟩G 97⟩
⟨Character greater than actions; Chatham, Sidney, &c   G 102⟩
      Dandies of character   G 107   139
⟨The love which belongs to it   G 131⟩
A month ago I met myself   F 27
We use friends as expedients   F 108
⟨Make me feel that what you say holds   F 110⟩
⟨Character is a theocracy⟩ E 110, H.136,
⟨Xenos & Iole   E 117⟩
Sensibility: rest in motion: Willow: E 116
Emptiness of the landscape   E 200
Powerful influence should never let us go   E 248   255   322 [141]
Blessed the man who has no powers   E 252
[109] ⟨Oath of Character   E 271⟩
Acquiescence   E 272
Homage paid to character demanded by others, E 22

[141] "A great . . . H 132" is in pencil, struck through in ink; "The sin . . . H.132" is struck through in pencil; both passages are used in "Character," *W*, III, 108 and 114–115. "We are . . . bad as" is struck through in pencil; the passage is used in "Lecture on the Times," *W*, I, 280. Each line of "Assurance concerning . . . G 62" is apparently canceled with a wavy pencil line; with "I like . . . faults", cf. "Character," *W*, III, 97. The paragraphs cited in Journal G, pp. [97] and [102], and E, p. [117], are used, *ibid.*, pp. 89–90. "The love . . . G 131" is apparently canceled with a wavy pencil line; this and the paragraph in E, p. [255], are used in "The Transcendentalist," *W*, I, 343 and 346. The paragraph cited in F No. 2, p. [27], is used in "Prospects," *Lectures*, III, 380.

Criticism on Raphael & M Angelo. E 43
It is only low merits that can be enumerated   E 51
Reaction that we want   E 52
⟨No great man will drill   E 54, 62,⟩
⟨Fashionist must be a primary⟩ E 55
In stormy times personal qualities decisive   E 90
⟨Life needlessly long   E 112⟩
No measure may be preferred to man. E 112
⟨Magnetism   E 176⟩
The best not magnetic   E 176
⟨Magnetism by which higher overpower low natures by sleep⟩ E 187
⟨Magnetism through eyes   E 296⟩ [142]

Tests   E 272   G 133
⟨Character which suffered no foul word in its presence⟩ E 308
⟨Homage to Character⟩ E 308
Privacy of elevation of sentiment   CS Journal
Every ↑right↓ step is a step into union
⟨Is there a man in the House? H.43⟩
Eccentricity   H.62, 57,
Chastity selfsufficing   D 353 [143]
Character shall not be turbid   H.62
[110] [144] ⟨Genius does a feat & appears at one time great at another small but Character always great.⟩ [G 52]

———

Character & intellect   G 3
⟨If I quake what imports what I quake at? E 212⟩

[142] The passages cited in Journal E, pp. [51], [54], and [62], are used in "Character," *W*, III, 103 and 108. "Life needlessly . . . man. E 112" is in pencil; the first is used in "The Transcendentalist," *W*, I, 350. Emerson marked "Magnetism E 176 . . . E 176" with a partial bracket in the left margin, then extended the bracket to include the next two lines; the passages cited in E, pp. [187] and [296], are used in "Character," *W*, III, 94.

[143] "Character which . . . presence" and the following line are struck through in pencil. For "Privacy of . . . sentiment", see *Lectures*, III, 524(notes), an unplaced leaf headed "Character"; "CS" may be Caroline Sturgis. The passage cited in Journal H, p. [43], is used in "Manners," *W*, III, 134. "Chastity . . . D 353" is in pencil.

[144] Under ll. 7–15 on p. [110] is a pencil sketch of a running figure brandishing a hatchet; the sketch continues on p. [111] facing, under ll. 6–22.

Osman & Schill   G 1, 48, 110   F 37
I love too well to pay attentions   G 5
You need all your coats; Godfrey has *one*   G 9
Dungeons in the air   G 10, 37
Wo to the successful   G 16
We never forgive difference of opinion   G 17
Vulgar man licentious when he travels   G 26
I have pleasure in coming near   G 28
None could live together on their merits. G 34
⟨Joy of the noble in loving⟩ G 36
Be calm: are you not there? then all   G 39
Quarrels would not exist, if reconcileable   G 59
Persistent Character   G 62   H 116
⟨Great man conquers by Presence⟩ G 97
Marriage Empirical   G 74   90
The best apology is none   G 88
⟨Great men are uncanonical⟩ G 107
Vise & Vane   G 114
When I was praised I lost my time   F 125
Dainty moods   E 13
⟨Good betwixt us & the sun⟩ E 37 [145]
Theory of gifts   J 9, 11, 15,
[111] We lose time in trying to be like others   J 18
Affirming   J 16
Reformers & Conservers   J 19
We ⟨can seldom strike a direct⟩ stroke   J 20
⟨I will not measure benevolence by its works⟩ J 35
Permanence   H.116   Ilchester
We bore with our indigence & Siberia   H.43
⟨I cannot be praised nor insulted⟩. [H 17]

---

[145] "If I quake . . . E 212" is struck through in both pencil and ink. The passages cited in Journal G, pp. [52] and [3], and E, p. [212], are used in "Character," *W*, III, 90, 104–105, and 98. "Joy of . . . G 36", struck through in pencil, and H, p. [116], are used in "The Transcendentalist," *W*, I, 343 and 358. "Great man . . . G 97", struck through both in ink and with a wavy pencil line, is used in "Character," *W*, III, 90. "Great men . . . G 107", struck through in pencil, is used in "Prospects," *Lectures*, III, 372. "Good betwixt . . . E 37", struck through in pencil, is used in "Character," *W*, III, 96, and *Lectures*, III, 483 (notes).

Our hold on the selfish man   H 29
The ear is not to be cheated   H 36
Love   H 55, 71, ↑G 73↓
Marriage from Character   H 84
⟨Abolition trivial⟩ H 85
We shall learn to rely on character ↑[Cars.]↓ H 88
Buckminster made his own pertinence [BB] Y [48–49, H 106]
⟨Vast spiritual influence   H 108⟩
We blunder into victory   H 129 [146]
And where did you pick up this frippery   H 128
⟨Character   Window in the breast⟩ G 152
⟨Slave ship of Washingtons⟩ G 142
I wish to be of stellar un[di]min[i]shed light   G 52
Humoring   G 58
⟨One of those men of love in the shade there   G 67⟩
Make thy life secretly beautiful   E 300
Inaptitude   H 28
San F⟨i⟩elippo [147]
A man behind the sentence   F 32

[112]   ↑Whiggism↓
                        Conservative [148]

[146] "We can . . . J 20" is struck through in ink with a vertical use mark; the paragraph is used in "Gifts," *W*, III, 164. "I will . . . J 35" and "I cannot . . . insulted" are each struck through horizontally in pencil and with single vertical use marks in ink; the passages cited are used in "Character," *W*, III, 103 and 106–107. "G 73" is in pencil. "Abolition trivial" is struck through in pencil; the paragraph cited is used in "Lecture on the Times," *W*, I, 280–281. "Vast spiritual . . . H 108" is struck through in pencil; passages in Journal H, pp. [108] and [129], are used in "Prospects," *Lectures*, III, 372 and 370.

[147] "Character . . . San F⟨i⟩elippo" is in pencil; the first two lines are struck through in ink. "Slave . . . Washingtons" and the passage cited in Journal G, p. [142], are used in "Character," *W*, III, 94–95, and *Lectures*, III, 477(notes). "One of . . . G 67" is struck through horizontally in pencil. For "San F⟨i⟩elippo", see *JMN*, VIII, 339, and "Worship," *W*, VI, 227–228.

[148] Notes on pp. [112]–[115] are probably for the lecture "The Conservative" (December 9, 1841), printed in *The Dial*, III (Oct. 1842), 181–197, and *W*, I, 293–326; Emerson used some of the thought also in the related lecture, "The Transcendentalist" (December 23, 1841), printed in *The Dial*, III (Jan. 1843), 297–313, and *W*, I, 327–359, notes for which follow on pp. [116₂]–[117₂] and [120]–[122] below.

Pedantry of Whiggism   F 77
Whig asks what facts not what principles confirm you
Virtues of the senses   E 261
For skepticism of men of the world consult MS MME [149]
⟨Bank presidents will speak for Sunday   E 26⟩

⟨"Here's the hole & in thou must"⟩ [E 44]

On the maintenance of the Clerisy   E 75

———

When people are going to die &c
This country a Cacocracy   E 78
Wise who knows a mask from a man   E 183
To plant our foot on one action & go back to that as husband & wives
do — E 224
Dial good in Whig manner. E 236
Cannibalism & its varioloid   E 264
      Young men must live. [E 277] "And all for Quarter Day!"
      St Simon paints Fenelon   E 278   Dr R to Dr. R's. [F 2, 98]
Unitarianism   E 311, 313
General Harrison   E 314
Availableness   G 107
Lozenges for the sick, your whig religion   E 321
Power of circumstance   E 328
⟨"And all for quarter day!"⟩
Force of Custom; heads without bodies. ⟨E⟩H ⟨140⟩138
Indeterminateness of men   G 134
Duty to cry Hist-a-boy   H.26 [150]
It would be good to give lessons in Idealism   H 2
[113] Society does not love its unmaskers   H 84
      Faith in suspenders   D 330
      Body of a rogue is yet sound   D 340

———

[149] "MME" (Mary Moody Emerson) is boxed in ink (ms. Houghton Library).
[150] With "Whig asks . . . you", cf. "The Conservative," W, I, 318. "Bank presidents . . . E 26" and " 'Here's the . . . must' " are each apparently canceled with wavy pencil lines; with the first, cf. "The Conservative," W, I, 321; the second is used in "The Conservative," The Dial, III (Oct. 1842), 194, omitted in W, I. "Availableness" and "Lozenges for the sick," are used in "The Conservative," W, I, 318 and 320. The passage cited in Journal H, p. [26], is used, ibid., p. 322.

Value of a church as a publisher ⟨E⟩G 24
Whig Government should be parental   G 26
Whig rests at last on Transcend[entalis]m   F 23
The defence of Whiggery in the Burke defence of British Constitution [151]

Doctrine of instructing representatives   H 49
⟨Whiggery the doctrine of allowing for friction and of sickness, Hospital system   H 20, 24⟩

Better things for Conservatives. G 50

Strength not with Whigs but Locos, Kendall &c   G 54
Alas that Labor may easily exceed   G 83
Vast skepticism   G 136
Barbarous scriptures   G 161
Sickness its heroes   G 138
Temperance whose root is intemperance   G 132
Whiggery sacrifices to despair [G 128]
Do not waste y[ou]rself in rejection   G 27
The demand of Time Time   G 140
Shell & stem   F 127 [152]
Undue power of a fact   D 144

[114] [153] Goes to produce Universal falsehood

Goodwill

It would not make a difference to the hero
Ab⟨ic⟩dicate the law

[151] "Faith in . . . D 340" and "Whig rests . . . Constitution" are in pencil. The paragraph in Journal F No. 2, p. [23], is used in "The Transcendentalist," *W*, I, 331–332. With "The defence . . . Constitution", cf. "The Conservative," *W*, I, 309–310.
[152] "Whiggery the . . . H 20, 24" is apparently canceled with a wavy pencil line; both of the passages cited are used in "The Conservative," *W*, I, 319. The passages cited in Journal G, pp. [161] and [128], and F No. 2, p. [127], are used, *ibid.*, pp. 304, 318, and 300.
[153] P. [114] is in pencil; cf. "The Conservative," *W*, I, 309, 324–325, 322–323, 313, and 310. "Goodwill" is in print-writing.

Good will flow to him
Good will flow from him
He defies the law
It is my business to make myself revered & not in the power
of your law to protect me

It is of greatest importance to have motion & not a Chinese stag-
nation, war makes motion[,] forces each man to depend on his virtues
& not depend cowardly on a law which conceals his unworthiness[.]

But the present Law is the great Necessity got so far on.

Credit

[115] Pluck sun & moon & North star if you could (poll tax) &
thought. commodity, ornament, pride. same cause which ⟨abused⟩
unchecked by love leads you to this usurpation leads me to claim
my Earth.
Love would ⟨⟨p⟩right all⟩ rectify all

But why not trust the thought?
Because the power of circumstance; [154]
    Experience
    What men to deal with
    Give us Time Time [G 140]

A Radical must be a Whig first

I exist amid humiliations like Kehama

I am preoccupied

Parties ⟨are⟩ parody these two interests

[154] P. [115] is in pencil. "I am preoccupied . . . heaven in the face" is written
over pencil sketches, which include an angel's head and wings and the left profile of
a frowning man. "Pluck sun . . . Earth." is developed in "The Conservative," *W*,
I, 309. With "But why . . . circumstance;", cf. "The Transcendentalist," *W*, I,
334–335.

I am defrauded of myself. I do not wish to scuttle along the ground ducking here[,] apologising there[,] getting ⟨through the world⟩ my most apparent necessities answered by shifts & crooks but to look heaven in the face & be a man all ⟨the⟩ day long[.]

Life is short & we make it shorter by our indirection. Nothing can I do straightly but everything I must go long ways about to compass. I cannot marry after my character but after my Condition[.]

[116₁]–[117₁] [blank]
[116₂]   Transcendentalism [155]
Transcendental in Books   F 160

If the absolute theory is false vae vobis   D 297

Transcendentalism   C 309   D 331

[In last years Lecture on Tendencies] People hold to you whilst you hold to Ideal as a pretty dream, &c   E 41

Michel Angelo's pictures necessitated   E 88

Quarrel not with him who makes little of y[ou]r forms   E 90

Great good always contended against   E 91

A Man knows what thought is revelation & which not   E 93

Is God conscious   E 126

        Our moods not reportable by words   E 129

We are halves — When will the Foresight be   E 133

[155] Some entries on pp. [116₂] and [117₂] are repeated in notes for "Discourse at Middlebury College" in Index Minor, p. [117] below, and may have been added in 1845.

A few Cosmogonies go   E 141

⟨Beauty the mean between dowdiness & heartlessness⟩ E 147

⟨Buddhist hospitality   E 155⟩
⟨What vast demands we make.⟩ E 202
'It has never been,' a reason why it should be   E 266
Cowardice of us before opposition   E 286
⟨Nature is the circumstance that sports with Circumst⟩ E 312
Our faculties warrant inceptions only   D 191
Transcendentalism lies unsuspected on the bookshelves of all rankest
Whigs in splendid binding. Cudworth, Plato, St John,

      To him who said it before

What is divine shares the selfexistence   F 154
Calculation carried out is Transcm   H.126
The Inevitableness of T.   H.2 [156]
[117₂] Transcendental Ethics   F 150, 154
Transcendentalism in State Street   H.60
Whiggery rests at last on T————   F 23
      Jacobi
      Thought is a disease
      We cannot get away from ourselves
      Faith is trans   Jesus, Quakers,
Transs are expecters of miracles
      Play with thoughts [157]
[118]–[119] [blank]

[156] "If yᵉ absolute . . . D 331" and "Our faculties . . . D 191" are in pencil.
The paragraph in Journal D, pp. [331]–[332], is used in "Tendencies," *Lectures*,
III, 306–307. The passage cited in E, p. [41], is printed in "Reforms," *Lectures*, III,
269. The passages cited in E, pp. [147₂] and [155], are used in "The Transcendentalist," *W*, I, 355 and 337. With E, p. [202], cf. *ibid.*, p. 344. The passage
in E, p. [312], is used in "Nature," *W*, III, 169–170 and 195. The paragraph cited
in H, p. [2], is printed in "Prospects," *Lectures*, III, 522(notes), probably for a
later reading.
[157] The paragraph in Journal F No. 2, p. [23], is used in "The Transcenden-

[120]   Optimates
        ⟨Spirit of the Dial lonely   E 208, E 97, 192, 223⟩
A vast advantage you give me by rejecting my love because it is easy
to go up to a given level.
O age he who has thee has all ages   E 91   ↑See also F 125↓
Portraits   E 106
⟨Dowdy good & heartless true   E⟩ ⟨151⟩   147
——————

We are Optative but must leave some mark   E 156
——————

Carlyle   E 184   D 15
——————

I cannot well go to see my relations   E 192
——————

⟨What right has Genius to retreat from work   E 188⟩
Love & religion sequester   E 223
        Beauty of casuality   E 281
⟨The two theories of life⟩ E 282, 318
Obey the genius when he leads to uninhabitable   E 282
We are astonished & diverted by opposition   E 286
⟨Beauty the only sure sign⟩ E 297
We must play sometimes   E 297
Caryatids   E 309
⟨He who goeth to walk alone accuseth all⟩ E 314
The pundits saying   E 315
        Thy Heart   E ⟨2⟩317
        ⟨I sacrifice to the lust of freer demonstration of my gifts E⟩ 318
What sort of man is he of whom I do never think   E 32⟨3⟩2
⟨Great men never let us go⟩   E 248, 255 [158]
        One song a year   E 328
[121] The trials of this age new   H.18
——————

talist," *W*, I, 331–332. "Jacobi . . . thoughts" is in pencil; with "Jacobi" and
"Trans⁵ . . . miracles", cf. "The Transcendentalist," *W*, I, 335–336.
        [158] All horizontal use marks on p. [120] are in pencil. With "Spirit of . . . E
208," cf. p. [122] below, and "The Transcendentalist," *W*, I, 342. The passages
cited in Journal E, pp. [147₂], [156], [188], [297]("Beauty the . . . sign"),
[314], and [255], are used, *ibid.*, pp. 355, 342, 348, 354, 342, and 346. The entire
paragraph in E, p. [297], is used in "Prospects," *Lectures*, III, 367 and 369.

⟨I will sit still & perish ere I will go uncalled   H 19⟩
⟨All that is due today is not to lie.⟩ H.43
Most of life is mere advertisement of faculty. H.49

———

⟨The best persons hold themselves aloof⟩ H.86, 87

———

Alas that we know the best persons, H.57, 91

———

  Ennui of young Americans   H 92
⟨Where are the old Idealists⟩ H.92
⟨We could not speak if we knew our partiality   H 93⟩
⟨Soul not written when you thought it written   H.94⟩
⟨Hyperions wish to be loved   H ⟨9⟩102, 105⟩
  ⟨but do not wish curiosity   H.105⟩
⟨The Optimates go for beauty   H.112⟩
⟨Men for superior Chro[no]meters   H.116⟩
⟨Who can be misled who trusts to a thought? 118⟩
⟨It is with us a thought, not a spirit. H.⟩ 120
Patience   H.1, 51, 86, 135, 143, 138
I would not be happy or good with the uncultivated   D 376
The best effect of fine person is in absence   D 377
All men's life superficial   D 289
Flaws   H 31   G 166
The ⟨G⟩illuminated hour   H.13, 47, 49
A good Orson as good as a Valentine   G 166
Inevitableness of the new spirit. H 2 [159]
What vast demands we make   E 202

[159] All the horizontal use marks on p. [121], except those through ll. 9 and 10, are in pencil. "I will . . . H.43" is also struck through in pencil with a vertical use mark; both passages are used in "The Transcendentalist," W, I, 350–351 and 354. "Most of . . . H.49" is struck through in ink with a vertical use mark. "Hyperions wish . . . H. 120" is struck through in pencil with a diagonal use mark. Passages cited in Journal H, pp. [86], [87], [92]("Where are . . . Idealists"), [102], [105], [112], [116], and [51], are used in "The Transcendentalist," W, I, 348, 349, 341, 345, 343, 344, 354–355, 358, and 351. Passages cited in H, pp. [91], [135], and [2], are used in "Prospects," Lectures, III, 374–375, 377, and 522(notes). H, p. [92]("Ennui . . . "), is used in "Lecture on the Times," W, I, 284. The paragraphs cited in H, pp. [93] and [94], are probably used in "Nature," W, III, 188–189. H, p. [120], is used in "Character," W, III, 102.

[122] They are lonely they shed influences [160]

[123] [blank]
[124]   Behavior [161]   ↑Fashion↓
Base to remember   D 354
⟨Fashionist   E 49⟩
⟨Fashionist too must be a primary   E 55⟩
Behavior of Scholar at hom[e]   E 58
⟨"First in Beauty shall be first in might" E⟩ 85
"Fashionable Parties" E 89
Manners   E 121
      Beauty in behavior   E 187, 189,
⟨Manners make little man great   G 127⟩
⟨The Gentleman of modern times⟩ E 204, 313,
Tests of character   E 272
Scholar at a party   E 272
War carried on in full bottomed wigs   E 282
⟨Nothing is settled in Manners   E 322⟩
In the courtesy & riches of the rich the best thing is nature as in L's
park   E 325
Manners lazy   D 348   369
⟨Use the Mercuries of Fashion   E 49⟩
⟨Recamier   T p 24⟩   Vol III D.A. [*Memoirs of the Duchess*
d'Abrantès] p 65

Manners demonological   D 343
Lethe adds to beauty   ⟨Creoles⟩   D 369   348
Society untunes   D 77
Awkward Scholar   E 58
Impudence which assumes that you mean nothing   G 36
⟨Distinctions of Beacon st fast   G 75⟩ [162]

---

[160] In pencil; cf. "The Transcendentalist," *W*, I, 342.

[161] Notes on pp. [124]–[129] are probably for the lecture "Manners" (December 30, 1841); the lecture manuscript is missing, but much of it may survive in the essay "Manners," *W*, III, 117–155. Emerson may also have scanned these notes for "Behavior," *W*, VI, 167–197.

[162] "Behavior", "Base to . . . D 354", and "Manners lazy . . . E 49" are in pencil; "Use the . . . E 49" and "Creoles" are apparently canceled with wavy pencil lines. With "Base to remember", cf. "Manners," *W*, III, 124. Passages cited

Public born persons   G 79

[125] Head is finished, trunk blocked   G 96

⟨Holiday must be in the eye   G 97⟩

Fine people & Claud L. glasses   F 106

Women see better than men   E 72

⟨Perhaps no gentleman no lady in All England   H 31⟩

⟨The two ways of entering Almacks   H 102⟩

⟨Etiquette geographical. Remove two miles   H 119⟩

Deoxygenation of the ball room   H 125

Fashion the amends for the emasculation of wealth   H.125

The usual; ⟨its⟩headless men   H 138

⟨The spirit not the wit makes success   H 143⟩

Exclusives   H 58

⟨The natural a⟨s⟩ristocracy ⟨v⟩on the edge of the actual; H.74⟩

Intemperance is vulgarity   H 27

⟨Measure   G 54, 105⟩

Beauty redeeming   F 112

Do not confound romantic with irregular   E ⟨279⟩ ↑293↓

Novel of De Clifford   H 28

⟨Scott's lords are men of buckram   H 29⟩

⟨There must be romance of character   H 32⟩

Casualty   E 281

    Beauty   E 85,[163] 106

[126]   Fashion   Society

⟨S⟩Fashion

Society knows very well how to use a few words to express its dis-
pleasure,   Puppyism

---

in Journal E, pp. [49], [55], [85], [187], [189], [204], [313], [322], and [49],
and G, pp. [127] and [75], are used, *ibid.*, pp. 133, 132, 147, 149, 120–121, 131–
132, 133, 149, and 129–130. With "Manners lazy" and "Creoles", cf. *ibid.*, p. 140.

  [163] The horizontal use marks through "The spirit . . . H 143", "Scotts lords
. . . H 29", and "There must . . . H 32" are in pencil. "293" is added in pencil.
Passages cited in Journal G, p. [97], H, pp. [31], [102], [119], [143], and [74],
G, p. [54], H, pp. [29] and [32], and E, p. [85], are used in "Manners," *W*, III,
149, 147–148, 143–144, 152–153, 141, 146, 139, 148, and 147. With the passages
cited in G, p. [97], and H, p. [125], cf. "Behavior," with F No. 2, p. [106], cf.
"Illusions," and with E, p. [106], cf. "Beauty," *W*, VI, 180, 184, 315, and 299.
The paragraph cited in F No. 2, p. [112], is used in "Prospects," *Lectures*, III, 369.

Manners a perpetual involuntary emanation of character

Fashion is the Virtue of last year for City is yesterday's Country

Beauty of behavior   E 187   189
Holiday in the eye [G 97]
Head finished trunk blocked [G 96]
Recamier [T 24]
Romance of character   H 32
No gentleman in England   31
Scott's lords of buckram   H 29
Beauty redeeming ⟨F 112⟩   E 85
Manners make little great [G 127]

Was a man in house   H 43
Screens   G 99
Gentleman dodges not
Woman's instinct   H 104 [164]

[127]   An angel would pass into the Circles
Fashion hates nothing so much as pretenders
Hobnail will pass better than the halfbred
Fashion is founded on Character yet Character is not yet admitted

---

Lazarus will rise but the unfashionable shall not be fashionable
    Wholesouled men sleepy sense that disarms criticism
Good manners a certain average, in the Spirit not in the intellect betraying a firm temper
    Therefore it loves Measure
It rests on reality on reliance; must be primary   E 55
          on measure

[164] "Manners a perpetual . . . instinct H 104" is in pencil, the last four lines in a smaller hand; "Was a man . . . dodges not" is struck through in pencil with one diagonal and three vertical use marks. With "Manners a perpetual . . . Country" and "Screens", cf. "Manners," W, III, 149, 128, and 135. Passages cited in Journal E, pp. [187] and [189], G, p. [97], H, pp. [32], [31], and [29], E, p. [85], G, p. [127], and H, pp. [43] and [104], are used in "Manners," W, III, 147–150 and 134.

on cheerfulness
on originality
on beauty of nature
on romance

True gentility & riches   G 37, 41, 146

holiday in eye [G 97]
nothing sett[l]ed ^{n} in manners [E 322]
Re[c]amier
Composure   J 37 [165]

[128]   Lectures
Eloquence that can agitate is with Philosophers   E 18
Portraits (Garrison   E 25) (Egotists   E 125)
Best of RWE in lectures   E 58
Lectures   E 118
Egotists   E 125 [166]

You cannot say anything too good or too bad of fashion. It reaches
like everything in human nature from h to h

Permanence of fash[iona]ble distinc[tio]n
Fashion & her flock
Morgue of Etiquette
Air of Parties deoxygenated [E 89]

A career, a figure,[167]

[129] [168] Average result of the spirit of the Energetic class in the
whole world

[165] P. [127] is in pencil. With "An angel . . . Measure", cf. "Manners," *W*,
III, 131, 144, 146, 140, 141, and 139. Passages cited in Journal E, p. [55], G, pp.
[37], [146], and [97], E, p. [322], and J, p. [37], are used in "Manners,"
W, III, 132, 153–154, 149, and 131–132.

[166] "Lectures" is listed on p. [163] below with possible topics for the series on
"The Present Age." "Lectures . . . Egotists E 125", in ink, was probably inscribed earlier than the rest of the page. The passages cited in Journal E, pp. [18]
and [118], are used in the 1843 lecture "Manners and Customs of New England."

[167] "You cannot . . . a figure," in pencil, is probably notes for "Manners"; cf.
W, III, 121 and 127–130. With "Fashion & her flock" and "Air of . . . a figure,"
cf. "Behavior," *W*, VI, 186, 184, and 189.

[168] P. [129], in pencil, is probably notes for "Manners"; cf. *W*, III, 121, 149,

beams in the eye & moves in gesture
a badge of reality of strong will of original purpose
    self reliance
    good sense & loves *measure* & natural gifts

Also higher than this is the circle of romantic behavior, Sidney Shakspear

This end of a select wellbred circle ⟨is⟩seemed an end so important as to justify the pains that we take to be rich

[130]   Nature   See p 31
⟨The ounce of overweight
The need of excitement   H 78
The Jew on the hip   H 29
Secret of the world untold   H.93
Inappeasable hunger   G 86
Antagonism   H 118
Reality   H 135
Daguerrotype
Identity   H 75
Sallads⟩ [169]

[131] [blank]
[132]   Riches [170]
Best riches of the rich, in nature   E 32⟨4⟩5
Pedantic to give such importance to property   G 114
All of us are Property men; only an Idea on the other side   G 164.
None should be rich but such as understand it   H 23
It is an operose machine to a small end   H.23
⟨A splendid house without a man   H.43⟩

131, 123, 132, and 146–148. With "self reliance", cf. also "Behavior," *W*, VI, 186 and 190.

[169] "Antagonism . . . Sallads" is in pencil. The page is canceled in ink. See pp. [31]–[34] above, probably notes for the lecture "Relation of Man to Nature," where all of these notes are repeated.

[170] Pp. [132]–[133] may be a trial collection for the series on "The Times." "Riches" is listed among possible topics on pp. [162] and [169] below.

People say Law but mean Wealth
Riches our anthropometer   H.58
    Aristocracy & Wealth an operose method again   H 70, 122
Opposition of the Rich & the Rowdies   H 75
    Wealth sought to remove friction   H.122
    Real Riches must be Helpfulness   G 37, 146
    Telescope a screen   G 58
    ⟨Fashion permanent⟩ G 7⟨4⟩5
    ⟨Great hospitality of O; G 146⟩
Merchants cramp themselves & negro is more human   H 22
    ⟨Valiant yea & Nay ⟨G⟩H 24   Napoleonic arithmetic⟩
⟨Screens if guests cannot entertain each other.⟩ G 99, 9,
Gifts   J 9, 11,
Robin Hood   J 1
We demand infinite wealth   J 10
Credit indestructible   J.33
    Reason why Legislature should give to H. University. J.34
Our wealth should be unimportant   F 91
Dependence is the only poverty
Cannibalism & Varioloid   E 264
Maintenance of the Clerisy   E 75
[133] Value of Church as publisher   G 24
Modern Novels   E 258
    ⟨Sallad   E 312⟩ [171]
    Hospitality   E 317
All for thee   therefore all against thee   G 30

[134]–[137] [blank]
[138]   Condition
                          Power of circumstance

[171] Passages cited in Journal E, p. [325], H, pp. [70] and [122], and E, p. [312], are used in "Nature," *W*, III, 173 and 174, 190–192, and 195. Passages cited in G, pp. [114] and [164], are used in "New England Reformers," *W*, III, 262. Passages in H, p. [43], G, pp. [37], [146], [58], [75], and [99], are used in "Manners," *W*, III, 134, 153–154, 135, 129–130, and 135. The passage in H, p. [22], is used in "Prospects," *Lectures*, III, 371, and H, p. [24], in "Character," *W*, III, 93; those in J, pp. [9], [10], and [11], are used in "Gifts," *W*, III, 162–163.

Sickness   G 138   Heroes of sickness [172]

[139] [173]   1851
          Beauty redeeming   F 112
          Beauty   E 85, 106
          Beauty in behavior   E 187   189
          Popularity is for dolls   D 264
          Society does not love its unmaskers   H 84
          Salvani   D 369
A devout sentiment in society has the effect of genius   C 307
     Milton's saying of wit & imagination   D 364
     Chance pictures   D 326
     One idea bad as draft of air. D 39
     Humility of San Filippo [174]

[140]–[141] [blank]
[142] [175] In America a strong European influence
N A Review, Allston,

power of riches
          the Merchant
          the Fashionist

[143]–[155] [blank]
[156] Let him be forearmed against all skepticisms
A piercer to the Reality
     How to make use of Society

[172] For "Power of circumstance", see also pp. [112] and [115] above. The anecdote in Journal G; p. [128], is used in "Old Age," *W*, VII, 322–323, probably from an earlier lecture.

[173] Notes on p. [139], in pencil, probably for the 1851 lectures on "The Conduct of Life," are taken from other collections in Notebook Ж and indicate that Emerson scanned this notebook for that series. The page is indexed "1851 Salvage" on the inside back cover.

[174] Lines 2–4, 8, 10, and 12 on p. [139] are struck through in pencil with single vertical use marks. One sentence in Journal E, p. [106], is used in "Beauty," "Popularity is for dolls" in "Culture," "Society does . . . unmaskers" in "Illusions," and the story of San Filippo (see *JMN*, VIII, 339, n. 93) in "Worship," *W*, VI, 299, 163, 313, and 227–228.

[175] P. [142] is in pencil. See p. [132] above.

Men & women measures
Skin for Skin
How you serve me by rejection
    a few moments of love   H 49

   ⟨As I am I see   G 128⟩

But society instructs in solitude
   As I am I see
   If I look out of the window   It is Now; if in faces changes

    I see that it takes all to make ↑a↓ man
       they are hints
       ignes fatui; catch the light
       There is none but God only [176]

[157] [blank]
[158] Originality   G 154, 148
M.M.E's velocity   G 152
Have you wondered   G 147
Time Time   defect of force   G 140
Classmate known to Classmate   G 93
Remember to be disposed to believe   G 58   I can't read a little
Herrick without feeling how much more we know than we can say
                                       [J 45]
Quarrels   G 59
   Serving a friend   G 51, J 20   Oblique stroke   J 21
   Heaviest battalion   G 50
O. begun life as fool   G 48
All done by the successful class [J 14]
   Church aerates   G 22
   Life & Math[emati]cs leave us where they found [J 43]
   Friends are stoves
Topic of no importance   H 47
History true for once true always: & Bone once bone always   H 75

[176] P. [156] is in pencil. "As I . . . see" is used in "Experience," *W*, III, 79. The rest of the page is an outline of "Prospects," *Lectures*, III, 377–381.

⟨Opposition E 28⟨4⟩6,ⁿ 286⟩

Out of the eyes of Reformer stares God J. [19]

Gifts J.[9–12] [177]

Look out of the window it is Now: look in faces & it changes momently. J [44]

Bernardo could never fit his knowledge to needs J.[31]

Masses J.[28]

Acorn

Marriage H 84

Society untunes D 77, ⟨D⟩292
[159] [178] ⟨Rhyme & Music D 326⟩
⟨Strong Will C 313 D⟩ 214
Popularity for dolls D 264
⟨Conformist abdicates all D⟩ 265, 337,
⟨Always scorn appearances & you may⟩ D 269
Eternity & omnipresence proper D 274
How great to do a little. D 286
⟨Untune nobody D 292 Society untunes D 77⟩
If the absolute theory is wrong— D 297
⟨A man's self travels ghost like⟩ D 303
Why give the children the romance D 305

[177] "Classmate known . . . G 48" and "Church aerates . . . H 47" are in pencil; ll. 3, 5, 14–15, and 19 are struck through in pencil with single vertical use marks. The page is probably a collection for the lecture "Prospects." The passages cited in Journal G, pp. [147] and [93], J, pp. [45] and [43], "Friends are stoves", and J, p. [19], are used in "Prospects," *Lectures*, III, 378, 372, 378, 379, and 376. The passages cited in G, p. [51], "Oblique stroke", and J, pp. [9]–[12], are used in "Gifts," *W*, III, 162–164.

[178] "Mosaic" is written in pencil in an ornate hand in the top right margin of p. [159].

⟨Doctrine of hatred⟩ [D 335]
⟨Past baked my loaf   D 339⟩
⟨Conversation evanescent relation⟩ D 346
⟨The Stranger⟩ D 107
⟨These men⟩ D 358
⟨In common hours thoughts do not sit⟩ D 364
Lethe adds to beauty   D 369
Salvani   369
Chaste woman & nunnery   D 376
⟨Distinctions immoveable⟩ D 143
Growth of great man per saltum   C 296 [179]
Courage of 2 o'clock
Mountains
Painting   E 5

[160] [180] Not writ in extacy   ⟨Jack⟩
          Jack Downing
          Speeches
          Verses
          Phrenology prosaic, Abolition poetic
Too Rich in old books
      It hath an overloaded memory; but what have I to do with them
      The Age also writes a few. Faust, Wordsw. ⟨Criticism⟩

[161]   Lit lawful
                          Good writing necessary   E 2
                          Mank[ind] right in fame   D 367

[179] With "Strong Will", cf. "Tendencies," *Lectures*, III, 312. The passages cited
in Journal D, pp. [265], [337], [269], [303], and [143], and C, p. [296], are
used, *ibid.*, pp. 309, 311, 314, 305, and 312; the page may be a collection for this
lecture. See also p. [53] above, where most of these entries are repeated. The passages
in D, pp. [265], [337], [269], [303], and [335], are used in "Self-Reliance,"
W, II, 54–55, 54, 59, 81–82, and 51–52. The sentence cited in D, p. [339], is
used in "The Conservative," *W*, I, 305. Passages in D, pp. [346] and [107], are
used in "Friendship," *W*, II, 208 and 192–193. The paragraph in D, p. [358],
was used in "The Editors to the Reader," *The Dial*, I (July 1840), 2. The sentence
cited in D, p. [364], is used in "Intellect," *W*, II, 336.
[180] Pp. [160] and [161], in pencil, may be early notes for the 1839 lectures on
"Literature." See also pp. [17]–[18] above.

Bible orig   E 70[181]
Writing done by the soul   D 273
Caesarics

[162] Literature of the age.
It quotes, or prints all Elizabeth & the Commonwealth
It reads French & German
It boasts Goethe, Wordsworth, Landor, Coleridge
Byron   Shelley   Keats   Hemans   De Stael

Subjectiveness Brag [E 86]	Poetry
⟨A good sentence rare⟩ E 54	Riches
⟨The Bible original⟩ [E 70–71]	Character
⟨How a genius is understood⟩ D 175	Philosophy [182]

⟨Hor. Walpole⟩ [E 1]
⟨Criticism transcendental⟩ [E 2]
Great to say things in order of Cause & Ef [D 124]
Best part of writer not private [D 273]
By ⟨doing without Shaks.⟩ you do without his book [D 357]
Men dramatic [D 377]
Cause

⟨Men dramatic⟩

Men dramatic [183]

[181] Part of the paragraph in Journal E, p. [2], and the paragraph cited in E, p. [70], are used in "Literature" [first lecture], and the rest of E, p. [2] and the sentence in D, p. [367], in "Literature" [second lecture], *Lectures*, III, 203–205 and 229–230.

[182] These four titles, probably added in 1841, are repeated on pp. [168]–[169] below, among topics Emerson was considering for his lecture series on "The Times."

[183] "Literature of . . . Brag" is struck through in ink with two diagonal use marks; cf. "Literature" [first lecture], *Lectures*, III, 210–220. "A good . . . Men dramatic" (the rest of the page) is in pencil; "A good . . . transcendental" and "doing without Shaks." are apparently canceled with wavy pencil lines. The passages cited in Journal E, pp. [54] and [70], D, p. [175], and E, pp. [1] and [2], are used in "Literature" [first lecture], *Lectures*, III, 209–210, 204–205, 211, 213, and 203–204; with D, pp. [124] and [273], cf. *ibid.*, pp. 203 and 215. With the sentence cited in D, p. [357], cf. "Tendencies," *Lectures*, III, 507(notes).

510

[163]   Loci
Lectures
Farm
Goethe
The Age
Christianity
Books

The Household	1	The Age
Immortality	2	⟨Education⟩ Literature
Poetry	3	Literature
Compensations	4	Politics
Selfreliance	5	Social modes, Home,
Reforms	6	Religion
The OverSoul.	7	Ethics
The Will	8	Reforms
Transcendentalism	9	Philosophy
Education	10	Progress
Politics [184]		Education

Age
Literature
↑Literature↓
Politics
Reforms
Religion
Ethics
Domestic Life [185]

[184] "Loci . . . Immortality", in light pencil, are probably trial topics for the "Present Age" series. "Farm", "Goethe", and "Christianity . . . Immortality" are struck through in pencil with single, diagonal, connected use marks or cancellations. "Poetry" is in heavier ink and may have been added. "Compensations" is struck through in ink with a vertical use mark, which was extended diagonally through "Selfreliance", then finger-wiped. "Reforms" and "The OverSoul." are struck through in pencil with single, vertical, connected use marks. "The Will" is in pencil. "Education" is struck through in pencil and "Politics" in ink with single, diagonal, connected use marks.

[185] "1 The Age . . . Education" and "Age . . . Domestic Life", in pencil, are preliminary titles for the "Present Age" series; for final titles, see p. [166] below.

[164]   Miscellaneous
All martyrdoms ⁿ looked mean when they happened   E 192
Strange fact ⁿ of Abolition   E 204
⟨This bit of quartz predicts man   E 218⟩

———

Husbands & wives recite Goose melodies   E 222

———

Real words as good as real actions: pedantry to prefer one thing which
is alive to another thing which is alive   E.226

———

You shall not compliment me o prophet I⟨ai⟩saiah   E 227
Criticize a fine genius: you shall find you untrue   E 243
"Blessed the man with no powers" E 252
⟨Carlyle's Mirabeau.⟩ D 15
Bancroft's History   E 256
The mean Present will be great,— E 258
Modern Novels   E 258
I can spout when I cannot speak   E 260
Our virtues need perspective   E 260
Our virtues virtues of the senses   E 261
Unsay all things concerning labor of scholar   E 261
There is no time: no space intercalated ⁿ E 263
Cannibalism & varioloid cannib. E 264
Emancipation of art   E 269   Palenque
Pythagoras & his melodies   E 268
⟨Oath & affirmation   E 271⟩
⟨Nature's laws written on thumbnail   E 275⟩ [186]
Animals through probity make their masters servants   E 277
Rewards of virtue   E 277
I wish we had cafés   E 278
How holy I am when I punish the boy! E 278

———

[186] "All martyrdoms . . . happened" and "Criticize a . . . untrue" are struck
through in ink with single vertical use marks. This and the following page are probably a continuation of the survey for the lectures on "The Times" on pp. [11]–[16]
above. The passages cited in Journal E, pp. [192] and [263], are used in "Experience," E, p. [243], in "Nominalist and Realist," D, p. [15], in "Character,"
and E, p. [275], in "Nature," W, III, 46, 241–242, 89, and 180–181. With the first
paragraph in E, p. [258], cf. "Lecture on the Times," W, I, 267.

[165] ——
Our young speculators reject, monotonous, E 279

———

America peddles   280
No great man has a son   E 280
Beauty of casualty   E 279
Do not confound romantic with irregular
Our cowardice before opposition   E 286   289
Foibles of the great   E 293
Concert   E 293
We must play sometimes   E 297
The Potential painter in me   E 299
Wild freedom of M M E's genius   E 303
⟨Sallad   E 312⟩
⟨T⟩Meaning of Hospitality   E 317
Pantheism   E 316
What is the Heart? E 317
Genius & Talent   E 318
⟨Your fine Institutions are lozenges for the sick   E 321⟩
What sort of man is that whereof I need not think   E 322
⟨Blessed is Law   in Nature! E 326⟩
Power of circumstance   E 328
Heads without bodies   H 138
Scholar like the cannon   G 132   C 231 [187]

[166]
1.   Introductory.
2.   Literature
3.   Literature
4.   Politics.

[187] The last two lines on page [165] are in heavier ink and may have been added later. Passages cited in Journal E, pp. [280]("America . . ."), [286], [289], [299], [303], [318] and [321], were used in "The Method of Nature" (August 11, 1841), W, I, 191, 207–208, 206–207, 206, 218, 222 and 216, and 208. The passage cited in E, p. [279], is used in "Experience," the first passage cited in E, p. [293], in "Nominalist and Realist," the second in "New England Reformers," and E, p. [312], in "Nature," W, III, 68, 227, 266, and 195. The passage in C, p. [231], is used in "Prospects," Lectures, III, 370–371.

5. Private Life.
6. Reforms.
7. Religion.
8. Ethics.
9. Education.
10. Tendencies.

RWE proposes to deliver at the Masonic Temple a Course of Eight Lectures on The Times. The course will consist of Eight lectures to be delivered ↑once a week↓ on Thursday Evenings beginning on the first Thursday of December at 7 o'clock p.m.

1 The Times
2 The Conservative
3 The Poet
4 The Transcendentalist
5 Manners
6 Character
7 Relation to Nature [188]

[167] [blank]
[168]

Times
Transcendentalism
Poetry
Character
Whig

Prospects

Poet
Philosophy
Apology for Hermits
Character
Fashion
Conservatism

Prospects

[188] Titles at the top of p. [166] are final titles for the "Present Age" series, probably written after completion of the course on February 12, 1840. "RWE proposes . . . 7 o clock p.m.", in pencil, is the draft of a newspaper announcement

[169]
1   The Times
2   The Conservative

Beauty
Fashion
⟨Expression⟩
⟨Poet⟩
Riches & Poverty
Screens
Character
Transcendentalism
Whiggism
Marriage
Love
Power of Circumstance
Apology for Hermits [189]

[170]
3   Dr C T Jackson
3   T. Haskins
2   Mary Russell
⟨3⟩1   W B Greene
5   A. Adams
2   Dr N L F[rothingham]
2   Mrs Sampson
3   Dea Greele
5   M. Fuller
2   P Ford
2   S Clarke
⟨2⟩4   J.S. Dwight
2   S G. Ward
1   C[aroline]. S[turgis]
2   G.S. Hillard

of the series on "The Times" which Emerson began December 2, 1841; the list of titles for the series following it is incomplete, lacking the final lecture, "Prospects."

[189] Pp. [168] and [169], in pencil, are probably trial topics for the lecture series on "The Times"; "Apology for Hermits" may refer to a section in "The Transcendentalist" (cf. *W*, I, 342–351), but cf. also "Discourse at Middlebury College" (July 22, 1845), a paragraph used later in "Goethe," *W*, IV, 266–268. On p. [169], "Fashion", "Riches & Poverty", and "Screens" are connected with one pencil bracket in the left margin, and "Expression" and "Poet" with another.

1   G.P. Bradford
1   Dr Bartlett
1   CS Wheeler
1   ⟨E⟩ER Hoar
2   E[lizabeth]. H[oar].
1   J R Lowell
1   C Briggs
2   G.B. Emerson
1   W. Burton —
1   O.A. Brownson
1   C.S. Wheeler
2   Mercy Whitcomb
2   Hepsy [190]

[inside back cover]

5 S Ripley	2 W Ware	Delivered to JM & Co		
			season t.	96
2 C Francis	1 J Very	d[itt]o	do	50
2 C Stetson	1 Soph. Brown	do	do	25
6+ ⟨5⟩9 AB Alcott	1 G Briggs	do	do single t.	100
1 J S Dwight	2 Mrs S Ripley	do to Little & Co		
			season —	100
3 S M Fuller	2 C Larkin	do	do	50
⟨1⟩2 S Clark	3 E R Hoar	do	do single	100
1 S G Ward	1 K T Haskins	Do to Martin season		25
2 M Child	1 C.W. Upham	Do to Martin season		
3 G P Bradford	1 J Angier	10 to Mrs Larkin s.t.		10
2 T W ⟨C⟩Haskins	1 W H Snelling			
3 E P Peabody	2 Mr Gore			

[190] This is probably a list of those to whom Emerson gave tickets to the lecture series on "The Times," which began December 2, 1841. In addition to those previously or easily identified, it includes William Batchelder Greene (1819–1878), an Army lieutenant who fought in the second Seminole War between 1839 and 1841, later a contributor to *The Dial*, a Unitarian minister, and author of numerous pamphlets and books; Charles Briggs, pastor of the First Church at Lexington; probably Sarah Freeman Clarke, sister of James Freeman Clarke and a close friend of Margaret Fuller; Mercy Whitcomb appears in Emerson's accounts and Hepsy in letters as working in the Emerson household in 1838.

3	C T Jackson	2	Miss Lebaron	
	E. Hoar		Mrs Smith [191]	
4	A. Adams			
2+4	E. Palmer		In ⟨1⟩one packet	96
2	C A. Bartol		In one	75
2	N.L. Frothingham		In one	109
2	G. Ripley			
2	S Robbins		1851 Salvage p. 139	
1	O.A. Brownson			
1	H G O Blake			
1	R. Bartlett			
2	H. Ware jr			
1	C S Wheeler			
2	Mrs Sampson		96	
2	B Dodge		50	
3	E. Washburn		25	
	C.F. Barnard		10	
	H. Crooker		181 [192]	
3	S. Greele			
2	E Pritchard			
2	G. B. Emerson			
	⟨C. Larkin⟩			
	D.G. Haskins			
2	W G Ladd			
	H. Ropes			
3	T Haskins			
2	S Searle			

[191] "5   S Ripley . . . 3 T Haskins" in the first column and "Mrs Smith" in the second column are in pencil; numbers on ll. 4, 8, 15–17, 25, 27, 28, and 36 of the first column are added in ink. A line drawn between numbers and names links "C Francis" and "C Stetson". The list is of those to whom Emerson gave tickets for a lecture series, probably the "Present Age" series, which began December 4, 1839, in Boston. In addition to those previously or easily identified, the list includes Edward Washburn and John Angier, Harvard classmates of Emerson; David Greene Haskins, Emerson's cousin; William Ware, editor of the *Christian Examiner*; and Sophia Brown, Emerson's niece. S. Robbins and Mrs. Smith were probably Concord neighbors.

[192] "In ⟨1⟩one . . . 109", in pencil, is partly overwritten by "Do to Martin . . . s.t. 10", the last two lines above. "1851 Salvage p. 139" is in pencil in a hand like that on p. [139] above. The sum is in pencil.

Index *Minor*

1 8 4 3 – 1 8 4 7 ?

The title page of Index Minor is dated *"Oct. 1843"*. Emerson began it with a survey of his journals while he was working on *Essays, Second Series*. What seem to be topical collections are probably trial topics for essays, particularly "Experience" and "Nominalist and Realist," where notes headed "Life" and "Representative" are used, and for the revision of lectures in the "Times" series into essays. While working on the essays, he used Index Minor for working notes for the lecture "The Young American," given February 7, 1844, for an outline of "New England Reformers," delivered March 3, 1844, probably a revision of the fifth lecture in the "New England" series, and for notes for the "Address at the Second Church," March 10, 1844; the following year he entered notes for "Discourse at Middlebury College," given July 22, 1845. He used this notebook extensively for collections and working notes for the lectures on "Representative Men," first given as a series from December 11, 1845, to January 22, 1846. Later he added notes probably for the lecture "Eloquence," first given February 10, 1847.

Index Minor is a copybook with stiff coverboards measuring 16.3 x 21 cm and covered with yellow paper marbled blue and red, and a spine of worn black leather with seven sets of double horizontal gold lines. The cover is inscribed "INDEX", below that "MINOR", probably added at a later time, and "1843", all in ink. The leaves, faintly ruled, measure 16.1 x 20.3 cm. Including 2 front and 2 back flyleaves, there are 152 pages. Pages numbered in ink are 2, 4, 6, 10, 20, 26, 36, 40, 44, 46, 48, 50, 60, 74, 84–87, 90, 93, 9⟨4⟩5, 98, 99, 102, 106–109, 111, 115, 117, 120–121, 125, 129, 131, 133, 137, 142, and 143. Numbered in pencil are pages 1, 3, 5, 7, 11, 13, 15, 17, 19, 21, 23, 25, 27–33, 37, 39, 41, 43, 49, 51, 53, 55, 57, 59, 61, 63, 65, 67, 69–70, 72–73, 75–77, 79–82, 92, 96, 103, 110, 112, 114, 122, 124, 126, 128, 130, 132, 134–136, and 138. Pages 8–9, 34–35, 45, 47, 78, 94, 97, and 139 are numbered in ink over the same in pencil. The rest are unnumbered. Pages ii–iv, 12–19, 22–23, 29, 31, 33–34, 44, 49, 52–53, 58–59, 62, 64, 66, 68–69, 72–74, 77, 80, 84–85, 89, 91, 9⟨4⟩5, 100–102, 104–105, 108, 110, 113–114, 118–119, 122–124, 126–128, 130, 136, 138, 140–141, 144–147, and the inside back cover are blank. Laid in between the front cover verso and flyleaf i (but photographed between the last page and the inside back cover in 1955) is Index Summary, six leaves torn from a bound note-book, measuring 10.7 x 17.6 cm and held together with worn loose threads; the pages are lettered in the upper corner of outside margins as for an index: "DA", "DE", "D⟨E⟩ i", "Do.", "Du", "Dy.", "E.a.", "E.e", "E.i", "Eo.", "E.u", and "Ey". In addition to four alphabetized references to classical literature, probably written earlier, it contains an incomplete list of Emerson's journals and notebooks written in ink not earlier than 1870 on pages DA and D⟨E⟩ i. Pages 87 and 98 have four or more revisions of accidentals.

[front cover]

INDEX
↑MINOR↓
1843

[front cover verso] [1]	Age	60		
Result 135	Aristocracy	70		
Society 129	Autobiography	139		
Friendship 131	Character	35		
Miscellanies 1	Community	109		
Skeptic 25	Criticism	90		
Gulistan 30	Divine men	63		
Love 31	↑Demonology 40↓			
Character 35	Essays	⟨133⟩		
Life 45	↑Eloquence	86↓		
Essays 133	Friendship	131		
Poet 55	Greatness	106		
⟨Nature [n] 65⟩	Gulistan	30		
Manners 70 Aristocracy	House	92		
Property 75	Individual	133		
Politics 82 Party	Idealism	115	Identity	137
Literature 87 Criticism 90	Intellect	65		
House 92	Life	45		

[1] In the first column, "Result   135 . . . Reform   28", a preliminary index incorporated in the alphabetized second column, is in partially erased pencil; "Miscellanies   1" and "Skeptic   25" are overwritten in darker pencil by "Middle-bury Notes, 50.", printed below; "Property   75 . . . House 92" is overwritten by "Great men 106", in lighter pencil, and "Philosopher . . . Writer ⟨50⟩39", in print-writing in darker pencil, printed below. The second column, in a smaller hand, is in varying shades of pencil; "Greatness   106", "Individual   133", "Philosopher 111", and "Writer   39" were probably inserted later. "Identity   137" at the right resembles "Middlebury Notes, 50.", written over the first column, and may have been added at the same time.

Nature   97

Woman   103

Community   109

Idealism   115

Transcendentalism   117

Realism   120

Autobiography   139

New England   125

Reform   28

Middlebury Notes, 50.

     Great men   106

     Philosopher   111

     Mystic   78

     Writer ⟨50⟩39

[i]

Literature   87

Love   131

↑Mystic... 78↓

Manners   70

Miscellanies   1

Napoleon   20

Nature   97

New England   125   V Lect 93

Philosopher   111

Party   82

Politics   82

Poet   55

Property   75

Realism   120

↑Representative   40↓

Result   135

Reform   28

Society   129

Skeptic   25

↑Sermon   93↓

Transcendentalism   117

Writer   39

Woman   103

Oct. 1843
Index.
———

Rotation of friends — O 149

Memory, O.89

Texas   V 137, 129   166

W 47

W 69

say   15   W.E.C.[2]

[2] "Rotation . . . W 69" is in pencil. The paragraph cited in Journal O, p. [149], is used in "Uses of Great Men," *W*, IV, 19, and the paragraph in O, p. [89], in "Natural History of Intellect," *W*, XII, 91. "say 15 W.E.C.", in pencil, is upside down at the bottom of the page.

[ii]–[iv] [blank]
[1]

———

Miscellanies [3]

———

Faith in ecstasy consists with total inexperience of it   K 50
Life must have continence *and* [n] abandonment   K 118
Do the gods love to bless by halves   K 123
Literature names things   N 33, Z 126
A M's honesty & F's & J.T.'s   N 35, U [45, 44]
How dearly fine traits are purchased   N 98
Olympian Criticism   E 334, 354
Earth Spirit   R [Z[A] 109]
⟨Immense benefit of party   U 66⟩
⟨Flowers jilt us   K 93⟩
Alcibiades & lords of the world   D 165
If there could be an interval   E 263
Genius surprises   B 286. C 129   D 18
Turns   C 68, 231   D 101   119   132   146   wineglass
Sky   E 357   R 98, 113
Few Cosmogonies   E 141
Dualism; obverse & reverse. S [(Salvage)] 61
⟨One man wrote all the books & did all the things⟩ R.14, U 65, R 108,
                                                              J 129.
⎰⟨Men representative, not accurately & thoroughly great   R 27, N 128⟩
⎱⟨None dead: all alive   R⟩ 112   U 117 [4]

---

[3] In October, 1843, Emerson began gathering material for a second book of essays (*L*, III, 214); Emerson probably began pp. [1]–[5] then as a survey for the essays and for scattered lectures given in 1844, adding entries at various times.

[4] Passages cited in Journal N, p. [98], U, p. [66], C, p. [68], D, pp. [119], [132], and [146], R, p. [14], U, p. [65], J, p. [129], R, pp. [27] and [112], and U, p. [117], are used in "Nominalist and Realist," *W*, III, 227–228, 239–240, 238, 238–239, 246–247, 239, 232–233, 226, 244, and 228. The passages in K, p. [93], and R, p. [98], are used in "Nature," *W*, III, 182 and 172. "Earth Spirit" is used in the lecture "The Spirit of the Times," and "Life and Letters in New England," *W*, X, 329, both compiled from earlier lectures. With "wineglass", cf. E, p. [354], used in "Discourse at Middlebury College" (July 22, 1845; see pp. [50]–[51] below). The passage cited in Notebook S (Salvage), p. [61], is used in "Montaigne," *W*, IV, 149. The paragraph in R, p. [112], is also used in "Address at the Second Church" (March 10, 1844; see pp. [9₁] and [11] below).

Copyright   N 43   E 75–6,

[2] Beautiful is reverence in men [D 46] Duty 17

    Virtue surprises in an engineer [C 63] Duty 4

    Aristocracy: The humblest feudal retainer sat at his lord's table

                              J 20

"I have 200.000 000 in my coffers & I would give them all for Ney."

                            [C 348, D 10]

Odious to have to humour people   D 39

⟨Time is the drying wind   D 49⟩

True reformer never addresses bodies of men   D 53

Extempore eloquence "thinks on his legs"   D 56

Genius — The price of the picture   D 56

Every word of genius selfsame with its masterpiece   D 56

M⟨an⟩ore receiver, more man. D 69, 70

Abby Warren's genius for music   D 72

Hurry: no intercalation   E 263

In perfect eloquence hearer loses dualism   D 72

Eyes   S [(Salvage) 35–40]

See what makers are our eyes   D 73

Concord meetinghouse   D 78

Mummies   D 80

Grand Egyptian Architecture   D 80, 81

And Heeren's important observation on the culture of the Egyptians

                              D 81

Man sold by the pound. Sir Godfrey Kneller [5] [Man 9–10]

[3] Doctrine of Benefit   D 84

Of Bachelors   D 85

πλεον ημισυ παντος [Enc. 29, U 88] D 92

The Silken persecution   D 99

---

[5] "Duty 17" and "Duty 4" are circled in ink; both pages are missing in the lecture manuscript. With the passages cited in Journal D, p. [39], and E, p. [263], cf. "Experience," W, III, 55 and 46. Passages on "Eyes" in Notebook S (Salvage), pp. [37] and [40], are used in "Manners," W, III, 135 and 149. " 'I have . . . Ney.' " is used in "Napoleon," and "Man sold . . . Kneller" in "Montaigne," W, IV, 244 and 152–153.

Our love of near relatives is *opportunity*. D 102
Apples & Men   D 127
True writing of history   D 129
Aperçues,   Goethe   See B 159
Heroes in all ages. Alcibiades, Essex &c   D 165.
New position of the slaveholder in civilization   D 182
Do the gods bless by halves? K 123
Only that good is mine which I can taste with open doors   D 184

Music at church; fine voice. D 255
Rhyme   D 326, 327, 341   Iteration   D [313]

Doctrine of Labor   D 329
How rich the world is. D 330
What possibilities! D 340
To organize victory   D 349
Common sense of mankind in the fame of Jesus   D 367
The Soul always believes in itself   D 374
Foundation of aristocracy   D 377
Facts that turn curled heads at church   E 23
Never was aught gained by admitting omnipo. of limitations   E 43
[4] Expenditure of the Clerisy   E 7⟨6⟩5
And right to sell their Works   E 75
The Age. He who embraces his own finds all in that   E 91
    Grandeur of Today. E 102, 219, 214, 258
        The Blue of the irrecoverable days   E 258
Measure nations also subjectively   E 112
The Spiritualists were all egotists   E 125
    Reference versus Necessity. R 58
Consciousness & unconsciousness of God. E 126
Christianity. E 132, 141, F 100,
Cosmogonies   E 141
Scholar has no family   E 335
Coleridge's Three silent revolutions. B 53
    ⟨Opinion of President Fontanes   B 280⟩ [B 300]
↑In↓ The Golden Age—   E 143
A personal influence an ignis fatuus, E 155

523

Boy playing ball is a Jupiter   E 159   ↑*Eloquence*↓

No leap in nature. Bit of quartz predicts man   E 218 [6]

The morning is grey in the East —   E 214
—lest God prove a little too divine   E 214

I sit with the Cause grim or glad   E 230
I think I may never do a deed again   E 230
[5] What you call my indolence nature does not accuse. E 231

Astronomy. Mizar & Alcor   E 276
I am of the Maker not of the Made   E 276
We assume to be holy when we deal with children   E 278
Value of the Past   U 158
Adduce yourself as the only reason. E.286

Of legislative & parliamentary debates. E 289
We too have superstí↑ti↓ons. R 137
A man must be himself. E 329
Practical man requires in preacher such as he should be if he
were preacher: forgives no conformity to him. E 329
Huzza for the Present! the cabbage a shade tree. R 138
What Hafiz will do. E ⟨331⟩ 329
⟨Homoeopathy & mesmerism & phrenology good criticism⟩
                                    U 99, 121   64
Ashburton dinner at Cambridge   E 331

Olympian criticism   E 334, 354
Dr Channing   E 346

---

[6] "Opinion of . . . B 280", struck through in ink with two vertical and two
diagonal use marks, is used in "Napoleon," *W*, IV, 228. The paragraph cited in
Journal E, p. [155], is used in "Nominalist and Realist," *W*, III, 229. "Eloquence"
was added later, probably in 1846; see Notebook Φ, p. [146₂] above. "No leap . . .
E 218" is struck through in ink with a vertical use mark; the sentence is used in
"Nature," *W*, III, 182.

Murderous Buddhism. E 353
C.L. at Mr Whiting's E 357,
Romeo   E 359
⟨Young people admire parts, old people the genius. U 64⟩
Royal right of Genius in all things. K 53 [7]
[6] Phrenology. A Body an hourly mercury of Soul. F 6
Fate. The Spirit never gossips K 78
Poor thin Unitarianism H.41, 46 U 148
Fourier U 4, 7, V 10 19 41 125 139 146 151
Courage my own & other people's W 43,
Marshal Lannes; & the Imperial Guard V 72
No man passes for that with another, as with himself V 136

A man has too many enemies than that he can afford to be his own.

[V 109, 137]

Whig party observers. V 129
Diff between Abolitionist & Democrat V 137
We do blunder into victories. V 142
My life optical not practical J 78 We live with the tips of our finger⟨r⟩s W
A man not holden by profession but belief J 101 K 22
Compound interest on temperance   J 141
Our faculties warrant inceptions only. D 191
Superlatives & low style W 82
Every one to his own work. W 134, U 122,
        See Proclus, also.
Man Endogenous V 12.
Hahnemann's skin theory. W 138
Antony's diet in Shakspeare
In the "Tempest" the Utopia. [U 53]
Novels, V 46

---

[7] The paragraphs cited in Journal E, pp. [329]("Practical man . . .") and [359], and K, p. [53], are used in "Discourse at Middlebury College." U, p. [99], is torn out, but "Homoeopathy . . . criticism" is used in "Nominalist and Realist," W, III, 234–235; the paragraph in U, p. [64]("Young people . . ."), is used, ibid., p. 228.

Orator makes people wise after that which *he* knows   V 58 [8]

[7] Attractive industry   Proclus; Theol. of Plato, Vol. 1 p 52.

"⟨For it⟩The gods lead & perfect all things by a silent path, ⟨&⟩by their very being, & fill them with good. That which is according to nature is not laborious to anything &c. &c." [9] [T 101]

> Domesticating power of moral sentiment.   Antiskeptic.
> Injury done to men by political arrangement   V 58
> Necessity of Deity rushing into distribution   V 59
> Literature a quotation & our body & our life   V 65
> ⟨The moral sentiments make poetry of me⟩ V 71
> Steadiness of "Imperial Guard." V 72

↑Perfect↓ Health needful for some topics   V 73

> Great happiness to escape relig. education   V 73
> Fascination of individuals, as *S G W*. V 73
> ⟨S⟩Bruisers should not fear paddies. V 76
> Add as much more ↑intellect↓ to Napoleon, for *morale*   V 80
> Time the assistant of criticism   V 82
> Orator groping till he feels the stones   V 82
> Ground of Hope in the infinity of World   V 83
> Literature always falling behind Nature   V 108
> Literature how incidental! V 113
> Desperate circumstances; eating man; whale's mouth; &c. V 123

"Human nature in its wildest forms most virtuous" V 132 [131]

> How many degrees of power! V 129 [10]

---

[8] "Marshal Lannes . . . V 72", "live with . . . fingers W", and "Compound interest . . . J 141" are marked in the left margin with short double vertical lines in pencil. "A man . . . his own." is struck through in ink with a diagonal use mark. From "Our faculties" to the bottom of the page is in heavier ink like that on the following page. Passages on Fourier in Journal U, p. [7], and V, p. [139], are used in "Life and Letters in New England," W, X, 348 and 356. The paragraph in W, p. [43], is used in "Discourse at Middlebury College." With V, p. [136], and J, p. [78], cf. "Experience," W, III, 78 and 74–75. "A man . . . own." is used in "Montaigne," "We do . . . victories." in "Napoleon," and the sentence cited in V, p. [12], in "Uses of Great Men," W, IV, 160, 232, and 6. The paragraph cited in V, p. [58], is used in "Eloquence," W, VII, 84.

[9] See p. [106] below. "which is . . . &c. &c." is struck through in ink with two vertical and two diagonal use marks; "Attractive industry" is used in "Life and Letters in New England," W, X, 350.

[10] With "Domesticating . . . sentiment.", cf. "Montaigne," W, IV, 183. The sentence in Journal V, p. [71], is used in "Swedenborg," W, IV, 93–94. "Fascination

[8₁] [epw] [11]

[9₁] [n]   While we wait, we beguile by fetch & carry [G 113]
    Beautiful veneration in men (Duty 17) D 46
    Humility   Filippo Neri
    Edw. Pyot   T 65
        Not too much of God.   U ult. pag. [U 166]
Unbelief   Society ‖ . . . ‖ Chh as [n] amusement, & Education & police
                                                    [U 108]

    Your criticism of reformers does not impose on   U 87

    Condition makes you; seed in manure   U 83
    Act for great masses you are moral & feminine   U 31
    We ought to thank the Nonconformist for all his good   U 40
    Preoccupation of mind the only reason against reform   U 109
    The Uncertain Sciences good criticism
    Telemachus   & the lamp [12]

[8₂] ——
Commonsense the wick of the candle [V 136]

——

Flake of snow brought the avalanche down [V 136]

——

⟨Progress of life. Once you saw phoenixes, &c   V 150⟩

——

We alternate an appetite for the exact & the mystical   V 151

. . . V 73" is marked in the left margin with two short vertical pencil lines. With
"How many degrees" (V, p. [129]), cf. "Uses of Great Men," *W*, IV, 20.
    [11] At least eleven lines in light pencil, mostly erased, underlie "Commonsense
. . . world W 49", printed on p. [8₂] below. The only recovered words are the
heading, "Sermon", and "That   We are lovers of truth more than of ourselves"
(l. 7), "Lovers of" (l. 8), "Lovers of a better life" (l. 9), "in divine persons"
(l. 11), "⟨C‖ . . . ‖ great life⟩" (l. 12), "of life" (l. 14), and "Oversoul" (l. 18).
See pp. [93]–[94] below; the page is probably notes for "New England Reformers."
    [12] "While we . . . lamp", in pencil and overwritten in ink by "All conversa-
tion . . . caricaturist." printed on p. [9₂] below, is probably a collection for the
"Address at the Second Church"; the manuscript is incomplete, but "While we . . .
carry", the Pyot quotation, and "Telemachus . . . lamp" are used in surviving
pages. The story of San Filippo Neri (see Z[A], p. [90]) is used in "Worship," *W*,
VI, 227–228, an essay in which other parts of this Address may have been used.

Alternation again in fortunes. V 152

Alternation again in power of individuals   V 153
Cold correctness of the Unitarian era   V 163
All wise in capacity few in energy & need but one wise man   V 164
Country people ask the Scholar to a Temperance Lecture   W 10
Genius & Talent   W 11, 18
    Sea-Shore[n] W 12   U 79 ↑Croisements.↓   Alternation.
Friction of the social machine absorbs all the power. W 17
Art requires a living soul. W 19
Every work repeats in small the workman. House; W 22
Practical Man [W 26]
Perjury of Bishops   W 45
Only religious can have succor of religion. W 44
You shall not know too much of the world   W 49
Only poetry inspires poetry   W 55
Want of insight the reason why we are so slow   W 75
We are educated to wish to be first   W 76
Society a great boardinghouse. W 82
Animal spirits perfectly blend   W 83
The head smokes as seen on white wall   W 86
A fluxional philosophy. W 86 [13]
    Farm once more   W 94
[92] All conversation & all literature is rhetoric. W 103
Eloquence of Father Taylor   W 108, 114 [115], Y 3
Born educable, born lawful, W 119. 127½
We do not absorb thoughts ↑or adequately receive them   W 120↓
Base life   W 120
M. Kickee goes for philanthropy   W 123

---

[13] The passages cited in Journal V, pp. [150] and [164] (a missing leaf), and W, p. [76], are used in "Uses of Great Men," *W*, IV, 34, 25, and 22. The passages cited in V, p. [153], and W, p. [86]("A fluxional philosophy"), are used in "Montaigne," *W*, IV, 156–157 and 160–161. The paragraph in W, p. [11], is used in "Discourse at Middlebury College," and "The Scholar," *W*, X, 285. With "Genius & Talent   W 11, 18", cf. "Plato," *W*, IV, 52 and 54. "Only religious . . . religion." is used in "Discourse at Nantucket." One sentence of the paragraph cited in W, p. [83], is used in "Swedenborg," *W*, IV, 121.

The two histories. W 124   U 135

    Stimulus, tonics, mesmerise ourselves   W 126

Last value of experience   W 127

⟨In⟩ all teaching a diagonal between teacher & pupil   W.126 [127½]

See how white souls are born   W 127½

Every director is also a bank.   W 127⅔

————

There are no common people   W 128

Games & toys follow the sciences   W 130

Not practical? We are not yet poetical.   W 131

The propriety, over all enumerable merits   W 131

Cruikshank no caricaturist.   W 134

Easy to a bundle of nerves to go   W 134

State is a great apparatus for small end   W 134

Court, jury, & lawyers, Webster   W 135

Hahnemann's skin doctrine   ⅞   W 138

All the trial in court is for two or three phrases   W 138

Ever the thing done avails, not the reputation   W 139

Character. Not to know oneself defeated   W 139

Eloquence   W 115, 108, 47

Every man has his Diminisher. Genius relative   U 99 [14]

[10] Nervous union of Shakers   U 110,

    ↑Idiodynamics↓   W 114, 134, 94

Every one to his own work   U 122, 135   Y 31, 84, W 44

The Two histories   U 135

Poet   *U* 144   122

Eternal resurrection of the Past   U 158

People's Superlatives. Dr J. Jackson   K 130

Truth due from diplomatists   E 331

Wineglass again   E 335   K 123

Superlatives, Dickens outamericaed America   N 72

Superlatives. E 321, Y 47, E 333

[14] The passages cited in Journal W, pp. [115], [135], [138]("All the trial . . ."), and [47], are used in "Eloquence," *W*, VII, 63, 85–88, and 93. One sentence in W, p. [124], is used in "Montaigne," *W*, IV, 151. "There are . . . people" is used in "Uses of Great Men," *W*, IV, 31; U, p. [99] is torn out, but cf. *ibid*., p. 32.

Temperance is *rus ruris* [N 87]
Fable a good hamper or basket
⟨Man by the pound. M 9⟩
Astronomy appeasing   C 287,
Virtue not to be taught. Pericles   K 69
Time inverse measure of spirit   G 140
Superlatives. Every writer nowadays is the best since Milton.
Corinthian brass. Y 119
Order of Wonder   W 80   Y 142
Bishops, W 45
Every being weaponed. Gossip   W 126
We Americans bide our time with our peddling too long   W 10, 58,
Oriental durations: the songs of the hahas
We speak the sheriff fair   E 237 [15]
Fate   K 78
[11] [16] He never hears it as he knows it. W 44
            I think nothing so beautiful as reverence
                    Humility
                    Edw. Pyot   T 65
            We believe in Ecstasy
                    Saadi   Σ [34]
Thomas Taylor *Elenctic* paradigm anagogic
            The spirit judges from the totality   U 105
            Therefore uncertain sciences are good criticism
                    and Swedenbo⟨g⟩rgism good criticism

It is the beautiful order of nature that whatever does not concern us is
concealed from us. As soon as a person is not related to our present
interests he is concealed or dies as we say.
and whatever belongs to us enlarges[,] brightens as if some god held
a lamp before it[.] [17]

[15] The quotation cited in Journal Y, p. [84], is used in "Plato," *W*, IV, 66.
The anecdote in Notebook Man, pp. [9]–[10] above, and the passage cited in W,
p. [80], are used in "Montaigne," *W*, IV, 152–153 and 170. With "Oriental . . .
hahas", cf. Journal Books S[I], p. [4], and Y, p. [260]; the story is used in the
lecture "Eloquence." "We speak . . . E 237" is in pencil.

[16] "He never . . . W 44" and "Thomas Taylor . . . anagogic" are in ink;
the rest of p. [11] is in pencil.

[17] Like p. [91] above, pencil notes on p. [11] are probably for the "Address at

[12]–[19] [blank]
[20]   Napoleon [18]
N. was France. a great man receptive & representative ⟨U⟩ V 92, 114
Citizen before he was Emperor, V 93, 114, C 299, cent mille hommes
                                                              [C 318]

His theory of war   V 94, 95, 119,
N. is the incarnate Democrat. V 98   C 298, 299, 314
N. the Cipherer   V.98, 125, 115,
His search for Men   V 99. Ney; Ormond;
His *abandon*   V 98
And his prudence   V.118, 124
N. the modern average man V 114, 124
Instinct of the liberals still applauds him   V 125, 76. C 340
                                              ↑U 84↓ [19]

Destitute of Worth   V 126
A real king, understood his business   V 76
N. had a ⟨religion⟩ free speculation on religion letters medicine
see V 88, 118,
        His love of music   V 80   his superstition   V 90
His troops   V 91, 124   C 314   315
His thoroughness   V 124
His originality   V 93
His proclamations   V 93, 97   C 318   Speeches   C 348
His self reliance   V 95   C 31⟨5⟩4
His good sense: Alps   V 96, 118
Realist   V 97
His regard to Faubourg St Germaine   C 296
Excellent speculation on himself   C 297
His bon-mots   C 297, 299, 340, 349 [20]
His good-nature   C 311

---

the Second Church"; "I think . . . Pyot" and "It is . . . before it" are developed
or used in the remaining manuscript; "uncertain sciences . . . as we say." is used in
"Nominalist and Realist," *W*, III, 234–235 and 243.

[18] Notes on pp. [20]–[21] are for the lecture first delivered in Concord on
April 2, 1845, as "Bonaparte," and later included in the "Representative Men" series
as "Napoleon, or the Man of the World" (*W*, IV, 221–258).

[19] "U 84" is added in pencil; see p. [21] below.

[20] Passages cited in Journal V, pp. [76]("A real king . . ."), [88], [90], [92]–

[21]   [Incidental topics]
              Want of a Legion of Honour   V 57
              Cagliostro power of face   U 30
              Genius owns the world   U 84
              The Nays have it [U 105]
              The tone of society   U 92, 105, 108, 129, 138
          ⌠ Able men only ask ability, not *their* ⁿ ability   U 161
          ⌡ Power fraternizes with power   R 56 [21]

Plebeian. C 298   314
He fought sixty battles [C 299]
Perfection of his Constitution ⟨V⟩C 349
A Working King ⟨U⟩V 76 [R 46]

Fourier's account of Napoleon   U [4]
Strong practical man   W 26 [22]
Black men built railroads for blue eyes to ride in   W 6⟨6⟩8

[22]–[23] [blank]
[24]   Montaigne [23]
Our farmers use 50 words.   Laborers &c. W 99   E 173
⟨There are several things⟩ in the world & unlike. W 46
⟨S⟩Not whether employer swears, but whether he pays   W 49
The lesser ⟨e⟩Experience; as small house   W 54

---

[96], [99], [114], [115], [118], [119], and [124]–[126], and C, pp. [297]–
[299], [314], [340], and [348]–[349], are used in "Napoleon," *W*, IV, 225–227,
229–233, 235–246, 248–251, and 253–254, though not in the order listed. V, p. [98],
is torn out, but cf. "Napoleon," *W*, IV, 224 and 239–240.

21 [Incidental . . . R 56" is in pencil and may have been inscribed earlier
than the collection for "Napoleon" continued below. Journal U, p. [84], is used in
"Discourse at Middlebury College" (July 22, 1845). The paragraph in U, p. [129],
is used in "Nominalist and Realist," *W*, III, 246. The paragraph cited in U, p. [161],
is used in "Goethe," *W*, IV, 268. But Emerson may have used the thought of some
entries in "Napoleon"; cf. especially *W*, IV, 223–224 and 256, 229, and 242–245.

22 Passages cited in Journal C, pp. [298], [314], [299], and [349], V, p.
[76], and W, p. [26], are used in "Napoleon," *W*, IV, 240, 245, 236, 231, 232–
233, and 247.

23 Pp. [24]–[27] are notes for the lecture on "Montaigne, or the Skeptic" in
the "Representative Men" series, much of which was probably used in the essay, *W*,
IV, 147–186.

Stygian anniversaries at Cambridge   W [83]
Intoxication for lockjaw   W 101

———

A sort of wanton observation; as Goethe's remark on the fondness
men have of hearing the Devil spoken of. [Y 32] Swedenborg's liberty
in looking at the back of the head
    Every man reserves to himself alone the right to be tedious   U 98
    Prudent Life: Sleep. health. U 114
    Superficialness & lateralness of nature   U 119
Montaigne   B 59, 94   C 205, 278, D 95
A man cannot jump out of his skin   N 10   E 69
Quarrels would not exist if they could be reconciled. G 59, 86,
Robust way of living, travel, &c, M   Le Grand
Montaigne pretends to most vices [24]

[25]   Skeptic
⟨Imm⟩Mortality not so satisfactory to our pride   F 6
⟨Whether sot ⟨of⟩or man of worth, not so material as they say U⟩ 116
Buddhism   E 353
Labor injurious to the form
Unequal marriages make the best children

"Who knows whether to live is not to die & to die is not to live?" Euripides
                                    ap. Plato in Gorgias

In America we are rowdy & therefore skeptical   V 18
⟨S[amuel].H[oar]. constructive & therefore valued rightly⟩ V 39
Alternation in fortunes   V. 152,   in lit. tastes   V 151
⟨Of what use that I should rattle when one neighbor⟩ will pin me
                                            V 153

Religion & rape & success in both   V 163
Surfaces are safe   W 20
My limitariness   W 31
⟨Nothing but wine & nuts⟩ W 42
Parade speeches, but, if we buy & sell, poets & grocers agree. W 42

---

[24] With the passages cited in Journal D, p. [95], and N, p. [10], cf. "Montaigne," *W*, IV, 167 and 168. With "Robust way . . . travel, &c," cf. *ibid.*, p. 166. "Montaigne pretends . . . vices" is used, *ibid.*, p. 165.

⟨No account made of masses of men⟩ W 42
⟨Our life, an ass with hay⟩ W 46
Bounds & limits   W 66, 58
Of what use to put whole thread in rotten web   W 74
⟨Skepticism dispirits⟩ W 80   profits, 80
Poltroonery   W 95
Base life, thievish manners. W 120,
We are of many sires. W.122, 118
See-Saw   W 122
The two histories   W 124 [25]
[26] ⟨We expose our skepticism out of probity⟩ W 127
     Honor among thieves. truth in skeptics   W 12⟨6⟩7½
     Hunger skeptical, Boston streets   W 32
Lord Bo⟨o⟩lingbroke's opinion   T 27

"Les nerfs, voila tout l'homme," Cabanis [T 118]

The Devil has come into favor ⟨W⟩Y 32, ⟨13⟩U 135, 138,
Skeptic   U 44   65   103   105   116   159   *109, 115,* 119
                                        129   *135*
     Irreconcileableness of theory & practice of life   U 11⟨6⟩5
     Indifferency of circumstances   U 116
     I wish the incompatible   U 159
     Greatness of centuries out of the paltriness of the days ⟨1⟩U 118
     A good exception ↑as↓ good as a rule   N 78
Panurge   N 104
Vulgar man licentious when he travels   G 26
Vast Skepticism   G 136
De⟨finition⟩↑scription↓ of Skeptic in Phaedo
There is always the rumour that the race of man is dwindling

"Hell is a circle about the unbelieving." *Mahomet* [Y 82]

Are we to make believe think & feel? W 42

---

[25] The paragraph cited in Journal U, pp. [115]–[116], "Labor . . . form", and passages in V, pp. [39] and [153], and W, pp. [46], [80], and [124], are used in "Montaigne," *W*, IV, 178–179, 158, 170–171, 156–157, 154, 170, and 151. The third paragraph cited in W, p. [42], is used in "Uses of Great Men," *W*, IV, 30–31.

Are any or all the institutions worth being lied for? W 126

[127½]

⟨"Whether you take a wife or not, you will repent it"⟩ *Soc.*[rates]
ap. Stobaeus

Society does not love its unmaskers   H 84
Perceivers of difference & perceivers of Identity   U 126
Timing   Y 130 [26]
Liars also are true   W 68
Belief & Hope greater   R 126
Truth is that whose existence we cannot disimagine. *Norris*. [B 60]

[27] [27]   Two Histories   Trilobite & god   W [U] 135   [W] 124
Identity & difference   U 126
Fenelon & Plotinus lean on one side
Animals & practicals on the other
Scoffer speaks their speach
Cabanis [T 118] Bolingbroke   T 27
Rabelais
Wine & nuts; [W 42] ass with hay; [W 46] man by the
pound [Man 9–10]

Skeptic plants his feet; will be beam of the balance
will not go beyond his card, world in hand worth two in bush,

points at the false extremes; wife or no wife bad; state & no state;
labor hurts the form; a Bank makes the population; unequal marriages

Society hates the unmaskers   H 84

[26] Emerson struck through l. 4 on p. [26] with a vertical use mark in pencil,
then extended it through l. 5; ll. 4–6 are struck through in ink with an additional
vertical use mark. The quotations in Journal T, pp. [27] and [118], are used in
"Montaigne," W, IV, 154 and 153. With the paragraph in U, p. [135], cf. "Goethe,"
W, IV, 277. Passages cited in U, pp. [44], [115]–[116], and [129], and the
quotation from Socrates are used in "Montaigne," W, IV, 154, 178–179, 154, and
157. "De⟨finition⟩ . . . Phaedo" is in pencil. "Perceivers . . . U 126" is struck
through in pencil with a vertical use mark; the paragraph is partly used in "Montaigne," W, IV, 150. "Timing   Y 130" is in pencil.

[27] P. [27] is in pencil.

Out of probity too. ↑127↓ Are they worth being lied for? W 126 [127½]
      Shall we make believe think & feel W 42
      See that poet & priest trade as the rest
      All accept the accom⟨d⟩odations V 48

Degrees of Skepticism Fluxional Philosophy W 86 Y 56
      ↑See Saw↓ [W 122]
      No convergence U 115
      Vast skept[icis]m G 136 Y [106] [28]

[28] [29]   Reform
Who shall ask Reformer what he compounds with U 41
_____

Reformer proves too much 'Tis a *reductio ad absurdum*
_____

The only ⟨good⟩ valid plea for not reforming is preoccupation of
mind, or your own genius U 109
_____

You must be born a reformer or be none for your system counts,
& not your particular actions
How did great man get his living R 12
Pudency of life must not be violated R 48
The golden age of reform R 132
Persistency N 88
Lovers of men safe as the sun R 161

[29] [blank]
[30] [30]   Gulistan
Alcott & the Egg K 7
Alcott & the potatoe row CS Journal

[28] The passages cited in Journal W, p. [124], U, p. [126], Notebook T, pp.
[118] and [27], W, p. [46], and Man, pp. [9]–[10], are used in "Montaigne,"
W, IV, 151, 150, 153, 154, and 152–153. With "Fenelon & . . . speach", cf. *ibid.*,
pp. 150–154. "Skeptic plants . . . bush," is used, *ibid.*, pp. 155 and 159. With
"points at . . . the form;" cf. *ibid.*, pp. 155–158. The passages cited in W, p. [86],
U, p. [115], and Y, p. [106], are used, *ibid.*, pp. 160–161, 178–179, and 155.
 [29] P. [28] is in pencil. See p. [133] below, where "Reform" is listed among
possible topics for "New Essays".
 [30] P. [30] is in pencil. With "Le peau d'ane", cf. "Uses of Great Men," W, IV,
21.

Day & diamond
Osman
Theanor & Amphitryon
Le peau d'ane   N 90
Dream of the statue   H 142

[31] [blank]
[32] [31]   (Gulistan)   Men & times
        Everett
Webster
Alcott
M F
E
W E C | E 343
C S
G P B
C.L.
Jones Very
C N
Jones Very D 168, 176, 183, 185, 230, 316, 322, E 9, 237, F 8, 110
        G 116, C 300   J 2, Y 144, DL 227, CO 38, MORALS 184,
        GULISTAN 135, FOR 86, LN 5, ZO 304,
E. Palmer   D 154, 336,
L.E. | D 162
S
S.A.R | D 174
⎯⎯⎯⎯
E.T.E | D 249

M M E.   E 303,

H D T | F 221

[33]–[34] [blank]

---

[31] "(Gulistan) . . . C N" is in pencil; "Jones Very" and "C N" are over-
written in ink by "Jones Very . . . C 300". "H D T | F 221" is in pencil.

[35]   Character [32]

The nobleman   R 120, 121
   Superficial Enthusiasm   R 129
In reading Lord of the Isles I felt &c   K 14
A ⟨man not praisable nor insultable nor victimizable⟩ N 12[1] H 17
Men of aim must rule the aimless   N 112, 136, 141,
   Osric great in the present   K 19
   ⟨Every man would be a Benefactor &c⟩ [N 12–14] N.E. Lect V
   Persistency   N 88
   Saadi   J 126
   Character is logical   H 36. E 329
   You should never ask what I can do   K 70
   Beautiful is veneration in men [D 46] Duty p 17
   ⟨A reputation for benevolence founded on expenditure⟩ J 34
   Society values inoffensive & tasteful persons   U 10, 17,

   Virtue expected in us, not in engineer [C 63] Duty 4 [33]
What an adulation of England is all our brag on our Revolution!
                                 U 40
   To organize victory   D 349
Never anything gained by ascribing omnipotence to limits   E 43 [41]
The great man   E 42
The nonconformist. E 90
   Scott should not have given his book to Ballantyne. E 146

   Pythagorean noviciate   E 268   Persistency
[36] Adduce yourself as your reason. E 286

---

[32] The heading is in ink written over the same in pencil. Pp. [35]–[37] are probably notes for the essay "Character," *W*, III, 87–115; see Notebook Ж, pp. [106]–[111] above, for notes for the lecture on which it was probably based. "N.E. Lect V", "Duty p 17", and "Duty 4", references to lectures, are circled in ink.

[33] The two paragraphs cited in Journal R, pp. [120] and [121], are used in "The Young American," *W*, I, 387. The passages cited in H, p. [17]("a man . . . insultable"), N, pp. [121]("nor victimizable") and [112], are used in "Character," *W*, III, 106–107 and 99–100; with "A reputation . . . J 34", cf. *ibid.*, p. 103. The passages cited in N, pp. [141] and [12]–[14], are used in "New England Reformers," *W*, III, 278–279 and 277–278. The pages Emerson cites in the lecture "Duty" are missing from the manuscript; see *Lectures*, III, 138.

Osman. F.37

It imports not how many propositions but what platforms. U.40

⟨Young people admire details   older people totalities⟩ [U 64]

Live by your strength not by your weakness. K 122

Though you cannot argue cleave to the truth, & to God against the
name of God. K 2

⟨I am always environed by myself.⟩ U 152 [34]

[37] [35] Definition   latent incomputable presence
elemental
direct

Substance

Privacy

Distinguished from intellect   —   Elemental
Distinguished from action   Elemental
Divine persons   Elemental

Ethics distinguished from crystallography
Advance of character
persistency

_____

Character identical with morals; thence its reality or the succour
of the Spirit to our spirit

_____

failure to honor character

[38]   GOETHE
A 59   B 274, ⟨148⟩   153   158   144. C 25, 38, 50, 208
D 7   15   18   128   C 31

Nothing indicates the Writer more than the bag of Acheson or the like
in which he collected things, & was afraid of falling into.

[34] The paragraph cited in Journal U, p. [64], is used in "Nominalist and Realist," W, III, 228. The passage in U, p. [152], is used in "Character," W, III, 98.
[35] P. [37], in pencil, is an outline for "Character," W, III, 89–115.

539

See C p 17   two quotations

Goethe lays a ray of light under every fact.[36] J 127 [128]

The day is immeasureably long to him who knows how to value & use it
[A 20]

[39]   Writer
Hugh & the writer   V 54
Aim of writers to tame the Holy Ghost &c   V 134
England full of clever Praeds &c [W 9]
     Rogers or Pillsbury. W 50
Literature has been before us wherever we go, like botany W 121

———

That none but writers should write.

———

Every one to his own. U 122
By acting rashly we buy the power of talking wisely   U 146
Intel. men attractive to women   U 145
Two affirmatives & again two   U 160
The great describer   U 12
Scholar   G 52, 132, J 101   E 335   feet cold, head hot, betrayed to
a book

Every discourse should resemble an animal *Phaedrus* T.P III p 352

Anxious, dragon-driven. Y 78
Scholar & Banker   R 19
Objection to Action [37]

---

[36] Pp. [38] and [39] are collections for the lecture "Goethe, or the Writer," in the "Representative Men" series. "A 59 . . . C 31" is copied from Notebook Φ, p. [10] above. Emerson had written on Goethe in "Literature" [first lecture], *Lectures*, III, 219–223, then used and added to that part of the lecture in "Thoughts on Modern Literature" in *The Dial*, I (Oct. 1840), 137–158. The passages cited in Journal B, pp. [148] and [158], and C, pp. [25], [38], and [31], had been used in both the lecture and the *Dial* essay. Part of the paragraph in D, p. [128], and "Goethe . . . fact." are used in "Goethe," *W*, IV, 287 and 284.

[37] The paragraphs cited in Journal V, p. [54], and "By acting . . . wisely" are used in "Goethe," *W*, IV, 262–264; with "Aim of . . . Ghost", cf. *ibid.*, p. 263; "Objection to Action" is developed, *ibid.*, pp. 266–268. "feet cold . . . book" (cf. N, p. [i]) is used in "Montaigne," *W*, IV, 155.

⟨Wh⟩Leaders of great causes are vulgar & cunning ↑H 89↓
Americans coaxed into Fed. Constit.
Religion of men leads from it. Y 211
Every member of party wishes every other committed.

H 97

[40]   ⟨Representative⟩ [38]
[epw]
Nature delights in contraventions of her own laws
She separates all things by space then takes an animal & adds a few
feathers to its side by which it may reduce the power of space & be as
easily present in a thousand places as a worm in its inch.[39]

———

Demonology

———

Insurance of life by our task   U 47
Loved by Nature   ⟨U⟩V 36↑, 42↓
See *Goethe*. Nachgelassene Werke, vol. 5. p. 146,ⁿ 296
          ↑Queenie's Sortes Biblicae   E↓ [40]
Rix-dollar Providence of Stilling. [W 28]
Neurology   U 121   Fools rush in where angels fear to tread.
Mesmerism
⟨Z⟩Chaldean Oracles   U 120
Lurking, latent, V [134]
Triviality of the stake unimportant   E 330½
          Omens   E 330½

---

[38] Following "Representative", written and canceled in ink, are at least seven
lines in partially erased pencil overwritten in ink by "Demonology . . . p. 314",
printed below. The only recovered words are "of all under" (l. 4), "The cards beat
all at last" (l. 6), and "The Genius of nature[?]
                    of literature
                    of nations[?]
                    of Society" (ll. 8–11).
Cf. "Nominalist and Realist," *W*, III, 241, 233 and 244, 232–233, 229–230 and
226–227. "Representative" may have been Emerson's first title for this essay; see pp.
[132]–[133] below.
[39] "Nature delights . . . inch." is in partially erased pencil; "her own laws" is
partly overwritten in ink by "Taylors P . . . 314", printed below. The paragraph,
rewritten from Journal B, p. [257], is used in "Nature," *W*, III, 181.
[40] ", 42" and "Queenie's . . . E" are added in pencil.

"Greatest goods come to us thro mania" Plato.

Taylor's P Vol 3 p 314 [41]

[41] [42] We exaggerate all persons identifying with soul [E 50]
    there's no Jesus

Each man is a partiality & a tyrant [U 150]

Yet is each individual entitled to honour

Benefit of party [U 66]

Each man also a universalist
    Nothing ⟨but⟩ we prize but we turn & rend [D 132]
    I am always insincere   U 116
    If we were not of all opinions S 170 [U 116]
    Every thing its flower   D 205 [43]

[42] Man is relative & represent[ati]v[e]
Each a hint [U 130]
You can't get their own quality from them [U 20]
Each expresses himself very imperfectly [U 121]

    The genius is all. Magnetism alone respectable [U 117]
    Young like talent old genius [U 64]

        genius of nature in musicians [U 102]
                in language [U 161]
                in municipal provisions [U 22-23]
                in national character
                in literature [U 65]
                in Exceptions as Homoeopathy &c

[41] *The Works of Plato* . . . , trans. Floyer Sydenham and Thomas Taylor, 5 vols. (London, 1804); in Emerson's library.

[42] Pp. [41]–[43], in partially erased pencil, are notes for "Nominalist and Realist," *W*, III, 223–248.

[43] The passages cited on p. [41] are used in "Nominalist and Realist," *W*, III, 227, 239–240, 245, 246, 247, and 236–237.

Eripitur persona   Cards beat all [U 161] [44]

[43]   Each man a partiality
        Great but not symmetrical [R 27]
        No such men as we say; no Jesus &c
        ⟨I⟩Fine traits unfits man for society
        Parts & turns & tricks
        Each man a tyrant in tendency [U 150]
        Benefit of party [U 66]
        Sanity of Society [U 80]
        Condiment

    But ⟨n⟩it is idle talking. Nature will vindicate herself[;] as much
as a man is a whole so is he also a part & it were partial not to see it[.]

        It is a rebellion of the parts against the whole
        Poet is dazzled by details
        Art consists in proportion
        God is no respecter of persons [45]

[44] [blank]
[45]   Life [46]
How dearly are fine traits purchased   N 98
Ecstasy   K 53, E 253, 257, D 322
Here or nowhere the whole fact   J 108
After all accumulation of facts we are as poor in thought   Z 3

----

[44] "Man is . . . Homoeopathy &c" is an outline for "Nominalist and Realist,"
W, III, 225–235. See Journal U, p. [161], where Emerson calls this his "piece on
the Genius of Life." "Cards beat all" is used in "Nominalist and Realist," *W*, III,
241.

[45] With "Each man a partiality . . . Condiment", cf. "Nominalist and Realist,"
W, III, 245, 226, 227, 236, 238–239, 237, and 240. "But ⟨n⟩it . . . see it" is used,
ibid., p. 236. With "It is . . . persons," cf. *ibid.*, pp. 236, 234, and 228–229.

[46] "Life" is written in ink over the same in pencil. See pp. [132]–[133] below,
where "Life" is listed among proposed titles for *Essays, Second Series*. Pp. [45]–
[48] may have been notes for "Experience," though many passages in the earlier
pages were used in "Nominalist and Realist"; see also the outline for "Experience"
in Journal R, p. [126], and notes in Notebook Φ, pp. [50], [140], and [171]
above.

Moment is all in all noble relations   K 14, 19, G 106, J 102
⟨Chief is chief   E 324⟩
We can only dispose of our own facts   N 24
We cannot spare the coarsest guard of virtue   N 101

———

Experience indispensable; but all musty again without Idea.

———

Roads of life   J 129,

———

We shed our contritions   F 97

———

Every promise of the soul has many fulfilments   F 112
Wine glass system   G 113   E 354   N 113
Buddhism   E 353
Men culminate too fast   N 106   Φ 171
In life all finding ^{n} is not that thing we sought, but somewhat else C 27
Earth Spirit [Z[A] 109]
>   Defeat door of victory
>   Our possibility; king's brood
>   While we wait we beguile by fetch & carry. [G 113]
>   ⟨Sanity a balance of insanities   U⟩ [80]
>   "Surprise." [47] You interest me as long as you have not been before
>   me &c

[46₁]   ↑LIFE↓
You shall not accept any man's person   J 82, K 6[–7], E 293,
                                         K 125, G 166, 151,

———

[47] "Moment is all" and "We can . . . facts N 24" are struck through in ink with single diagonal use marks; cf. "Experience," *W*, III, 60 and 81. "Moment is . . . N 24" is also struck through in ink with a vertical use mark; the passage in Journal K, p. [14], is used in "Character," and one sentence in G, p. [106], in both "Character," and "Experience," *W*, III, 113, 96, and 50. The passages cited in N, p. [98], G, p. [113], and U, p. [80], are used in "Nominalist and Realist," *W*, III, 227, 235, and 237. Passages cited in K, pp. [53] and [19], N, p. [101], and "Defeat . . . victory" are used in "Worship," *W*, VI, 213, 234, 222, and 234–235, and "While . . . carry." is also used in the "Address at the Second Church" (March 10, 1844). With "Our possibility;" cf. R, p. [126], and "Experience," *W*, III, 67–70, the section on "Surprise." The sentence cited in E, p. [324], is used in "The Young American," *W*, I, 386–387.

⟨We want the great man for riches   K 125,⟩
        Sane & insane   J 124
        Inaptitude   H 28
        Whitewashing   G 88   K 46
Life goes headlong but the moment All. K 14, 19, G 106 [48] J 102

[epw] [49]

[47₁]   Subjectiveness
———

    We have found out we exist & we suspect our instrum[en]ts
    ———

        Nat lit. events, persons; chagrins, idolatries, all subjective.
        ———

        So Marriage.
        ———

        ˙ Co-life impossible
        ———

        Great men the mind's deputies
        ———

        The world a kitten & her tail
        ———

        ———

        We cannot be lost, we think
        ———

        Nor we commit crimes so black as others
        ———

        For intellect has no crime
        ———

---

[48] With Journal K, pp. [6]–[7] and [125], both torn out, cf. "Nominalist and Realist," *W*, III, 227 and 240; the passages cited in E, p. [293], and G, p. [88], are used, *ibid.*, pp. 226–227. "Life goes . . . moment All." is struck through in ink with four vertical use marks; see p. [45] above.

[49] Traces of an earlier layer of erased pencil writing are visible under most of the ink layer printed on p. [46₂] below, the only recovered words being "Orestes & Apollo & preoccupied attention" (l. 20), and "It is worse than a crime it is a blunder said Napoleon speaking the language of the intellect" (ll. 24–26); both are used in "Experience," *W*, III, 82 and 79.

Yet is this good in subjectiveness, that it does not waste its efforts; or adopt other people's facts

———

America an easy-fool

———

Orestes & Apollo [R 88] & preoccupied attention [50] [R 109]

———

[46₂] We do blunder into victories   V ⟨32⟩142
Power of truth   V 65, W 34, 40,
As a man's life comes into union with nature his thought runs parallel with creative laws. K 55
Fortune & character   V 36
    The Long Life, or great Year   V 42
Guest in house, & in thought, Who is he? — V 52
Life so affirmative that vigour is contagious   V 56
Wisdom the power (mathemat.) of the present hour   V 56
No man passes with another for that he passes for with self V 136 [51]
Degrees; no huddle. W 32 ↑Woman would not be her lover, &c↓
    We transcend the circumstance continually   W 56
Life a game between God & man   W 57
Life a long protean march   W 57
Virtue runs in a rill; no freshet. W 58
How hard to find a man   W 58

———

The farmers must have compounded some day and sold themselves to the devil for cheese mites   W 60

———

We allow a man any length of line who has not given up the holy ghost. W 102
    The rich take up more world into life   W 107

[47₂]   ↑LIFE↓
Subjectiveness. We never see nature in undress, because nature is *our eye*.

---

[50] "Subjectiveness . . . attention", in pencil and struck through in pencil with a diagonal use mark, outlines a section of "Experience," *W*, III, 75–82. "Subjectiveness" is overwritten in ink by "saints also are born", printed below, p. [47₂].

[51] With "Wisdom . . . V 136", cf. "Experience," *W*, III, 60 and 78.

Last value of experience   W 127 [52]

  See how saints also are born ↑W↓ 127½

Travel & going abroad needful. M

[48]   ↑LIFE↓

⟨We forgive nobody's sin but⟩ our own   Duty 10

A sentiment lifts man out of the mire   D 51

After 30 a man feels the limitations   D 99

A new day   E 9

Older, older; we wish these signs   E 37

Death?   E 68, 313, Σ   Saadi

How stout look the Sforzas, Dorias, Merovingians! E 313

No hope so bright but is beginning of its fulfilment   E 91

Our moods never trans⟨ferab⟩lateable by words. Selfreliance. E 129

Hurry, hurry: no intercalation. E 263

————

  Enlarge not th⟨e⟩y destiny. Μη συ ανξανε την ειμαζμεν⟨ε⟩ην

                              [E 327, RS 9]

————

"Let the immortal depth of your soul lead you!" *Zoroaster*. [E 327]

Let us think the ⟨tragedy⟩ ↑grief↓ of others as slight & medicable as our own, F 122

Life is the true romance [E 230] N.E. ⟨3⟩V.

Progress of life. U 105

⟨The true romance   U 86⟩

⟨The individual always mistaken⟩ U 104

⟨We cannot spare the fools & sots⟩. R 159

⟨Succession⟩ U 122↑, 76↓

If one had any security against moods   U 76 [53]

[52] With "Subjectiveness. We . . . *eye*.", cf. "Experience," *W*, III, 75–76, and p. [47₁] above. With the paragraph cited in Journal W, p. [127], cf. *ibid.*, p. 85.

[53] "Duty 10" and "N.E." are circled in ink; with "We forgive . . . own", cf. "Experience," *W*, III, 78. With "Life is . . . romance", used in "New England Reformers," *W*, III, 285, cf. "The true romance . . . power." in Journal U, p. [86], used in "Experience," *W*, III, 86. Passages in U, p. [104], and R, p. [159], are used, *ibid.*, pp. 69–70 and 62. ", 76" is added in pencil; "If one . . . U 76" is in partly erased pencil; the paragraph in U, p. [76], is used in "Nominalist and Realist," *W*, III, 247, but cf. the section on Succession in "Experience," *W*, III, 55–58.

Form always stands in dread of power   R 48
Every one would make the dare God dare devil experiment   N 102

[49] [blank]
[50]   Middlebury Notes [54]
                    Literature
        No law but comes prisoner to the bar in its turn   U 138
        The highest should alternate contemplation & energy   U 122
Literature is consolation not decalogue. V 132 [131]
        Audacity of scholars like Danton's   E 284   V 29
        King René period. R 47
        Dr Kraitsir.
        ⟨O⟩Right Education. Gold & silver grow in the earth from the
        celestial gods, an effluxion from them. *See Procl. on Tim.* Vol. 1,
        p 36. [W 75]
Fitchburg stock is not private property   W 7⟨4⟩5

A peal in the breast attends the perception of truth   W 34

        All the arguments are against literature, yet one verse disposes of
them into dancing rhymes

Only the religious can expect the succour of religion. W 42   44
Many courages   W 43
Scholar shall not propose to himself model or comparison   V 29
End of the oration to change for many men the course of life in half
an hour.
        Persons, W 60, 66,
Whatever can be thought can be spoken   V 54
Intellect is the King
The Philistines also share the ⟨lif⟩ ideas of the time   V 37 [55]

---

[54] Pp. [50]–[51] and the later layer of p. [54] are notes for "Discourse at
Middlebury College" (July 22, 1845). Emerson used parts of the lecture in
"Goethe," *W*, IV, 261–268, "Montaigne," *W*, IV, 181–186, and "The Scholar," *W*,
X, 261–289. See also lecture notes in Journal W, pp. [62], [90], [97], [105], and
[144]–[145].
        [55] "The highest . . . U 122" is in pencil. The passages cited in Journal U, p.
[122], V, p. [131], W, pp. [75], [34], [43], and [60], "Whatever can . . .

[51] Saadi   U 58
Hear an orator to know how presentable truth is. V 31

Guest in his house, guest in his thought, V 52
Life affirmative & to hear of vigor invigorating   V 56
The Pharos class. V 57
For the fine things, I make poetry of them, but the sentiments make poetry of me [V 71]
In the antislavery–conventions, the clock: but give me a thought or a law — V 135

Needs only one wise man to a company. V 164
affected worldliness of the Poet also. W 50
Plenty of wild wrath, but great want of talent   W 60.
Character-destroying civilization   V 36
Spirit of the age   V 37, 44, 48, 150, 152, 162.
Able men love ability, not *their* ability only.
Only live; Suicide is the rule, life the exception   W 102
Nature makes secondaries, so that there is nothing that is not related to man, & that is not ratified [56]
⟨a⟩Animals through probity make their masters servants. E 277
We owe to every book certain words   W 107

[52]–[53] [blank]
[54] [57]   ↑Poet↓

---

spoken", and V, p. [37], are used in "Discourse at Middlebury College." With "All the . . . rhymes", cf. W, pp. [50]–[52], and with "End . . . hour.", cf. W, p. [62], both used in "Discourse at Middlebury College."

[56] "For the fine . . . of me" is struck through in ink with three diagonal use marks. "Needs only . . . V 164" is struck through in ink with one diagonal use mark. "Nature makes . . . ratified" is in pencil. The passages cited in Journal V, p. [31], W, pp. [50] and [60], V, pp. [36] and [37], and "Able men . . . only." are used in "Discourse at Middlebury College." "For the fine . . . of me" is used in "Swedenborg," W, IV, 93–94, but cf. W, p. [90], probably notes for "Discourse at Middlebury College." The paragraphs in V, pp. [135] and [150], and "Needs only . . . company." are used in "Uses of Great Men," W, IV, 21–22, 34, and 25.

[57] "Poet" has been added in heavy ink, probably at the same time as "so little . . . J 130" below. "Symbolizer . . . this Metamorphosis", in faint, partially erased pencil, was probably incribed first; the first ten lines are overwritten by "Scholar is . . . without", in pencil, and "so little . . . J 130", in heavy ink.

Symbolizer
P   Employs natural objects as symbols
Everything in nature has expression
Soul makes body
‖ ... ‖ holy place
Universe ‖ ... ‖ the Soul. Heavens retinue of us
‖ ..... ‖

———

A few symbols suffice   use each more simply

———

We use defects & deformities to sacred end

———

Poet reattaches things to Nature & disposes of all
World being thus put under mind Poet is Spokesman, Namer,
He comes a step nearer to things & sees the Metamorphosis
All the animal facts express this Metamorphosis [58]

Scholar is sane-man, connector, generalizer, spiritualist

He is to have talents
     They are good
Or he is to have no talents but
He is to be somewhat
Thence courage
Thence connection or generalizing
Thence ability to do without [59]
so little affinity twixt writer & works; the wind must have writ them
                                                        J 130 [60]

[55]   Poet
Inspiration   U 72
All things must be treated poetically   E 101

---

[58] Between "Universe . . . of us" and "A few . . . simply" are four lines in
pencil, unrecovered except for "with self exis‖tenc‖e" at the end of l. 9, "who
must be" at the end of l. 10, and "& more" at the end of l. 12. "Symbolizer . . .
this Metamorphosis" is an outline of "The Poet," W, III, 13–21.
[59] "Scholar is . . . without" is an outline of "Discourse at Middlebury College."
[60] "so little . . . J 130" is struck through in ink with a diagonal use mark.

⟨S⟩Mania or inspiration, in Phaedrus. Taylor Vol III p 319 [61]
    What Hafiz will do E 3⟨31⟩29
    Veeshnoo Sarma's Man of feeling, T 97
    Saadi's ecstasy Σ^n 34
    Charms of poetry according to Epicurus T 59
    Poet, in Zoroaster, U p 144
    Poet's Charter R 116
    Mythology see Taylor's note Procl. in Tim. vol 1 p 120 [62]
    We must have our own poetry & not some foreigner's K 93

———

Shakspeare preferred a divided fame to a small originality

———

Malone's computation that in the historical series of 6043 lines, 1771
    were written by some author preceding Shaksp. 2373 by him on
    the foundation la↑i↓d by his predecessors & 1849 were entirely
    his own.

———

Luckily the playhouse & plays were despised W 141 [63]
Novels, V 46
Poet so rare because of his incompatible qualities V 165
All men of genius are melancholy. *Aristotle*
Only poetry inspires poetry W 55

[56]   Conclusion

We dare not sing our own circumstance
But if we would write of poet must not read the poets
Yet our America is a poem in our eyes & will not long wait to be such
    in the intellect

[61] *The Works of Plato* . . . , 1804.
[62] *The Commentaries of Proclus on the Timaeus of Plato* . . . , trans. Thomas
Taylor, 2 vols. (London, 1820); in Emerson's library.
[63] "Poet . . . E 101" and "Mythology . . . K 93" are in pencil, "We must
. . . K 93" probably written at a different time. "Shakspeare preferred . . . W
141" is struck through in ink with a vertical use mark. One quotation in Journal U,
p. [144], is used in "Poetry and Imagination," *W*, VIII, 19. The paragraph beginning on R, p. [116], is used in "The Poet," *W*, III, 41–42. The passage cited in K,
p. [93], is used in "Swedenborg," *W*, IV, 135–136, but cf. "The Poet," *W*, III, 37–
38. With "Shakspeare preferred . . . W 141", cf. "Shakspeare," *W*, IV, 193–197.

But I will not poorly limit to persons but say a little boldly what the Muse says of Expression

↑SHAKSPEAR

⟨2⟩D 207, 211, 212, 217, 102
Threnes B 225↓[64]

Eloquence of Father Taylor. W 108   114 [115] Y 3
Eloquence   W 47

Propriety over all enumerable merits   W 131
⟨W⟩Order of Wonder   W 80   Y 142
Poetry sometimes good for mass   N 26
Merit of poem a thing of experience   N 80

Shakspeare's   Expression
                        Hilarity

Cheerfulness of the poet all his pains are edged with pleasure D 367

"Artist natures do not weep." Bettina.

Sanative power of verse antagonistic to the ⟨sad &⟩ sepulchral tendencies of Ch[urch]
My woods & Flora not Moses's. No fagots. Salvage 20 [65]
[57] cheerly & sovereignly [66] [J 126]

[58]–[59] [blank]
[60]   The Age
Realism of Abolitionists & of Fourier. V 82
Unitarianism & trifles. V 28,

[64] "Conclusion . . . Expression", in pencil, is an outline of "The Poet," W, III, 37–38. The "C" in "Conclusion" is partly overwritten by "SHAKSPEAR . . . B 225", added above it; see Notebook Φ, p. [10].

[65] The passages cited in Journal W, pp. [115] and [47], are used in "Eloquence," W, VII, 63 and 93. See "Shakspeare," W, IV, 213–216, for sections on "Expression" and "Hilarity". The sentence cited in D, p. [367], is used in "Poetry and Imagination," W, VIII, 37. The notes cited in Notebook S (Salvage), p. [20], are used in "Genius," Lectures, III, 80–81.

[66] This phrase is used in "Discourse at Middlebury College," and "Shakspeare," W, IV, 216.

Millerism. R.89
Cheap press   Z
Rail Roads   Z   V 53,

Civilization   V 36
The nays have it [U 105]

Better that our poets should be pets of society than dandies   V 44

Small difference between good & bad: all have accepted the accommodations of the Hotel   V 48, 87,

---

D Shat & all philistines share the idea of the age. V.37, 30,

---

⟨Once you saw Phoenixes, but now Representatives. V.150⟩

No sterile ages. V.162

Was it fit after so many sacrifices, France should reassume the old civilisation? ⟨U⟩V 152.

Texas & the world spirit. V 165,

When it is felt, "Those men occupy my place," the revolution is near.

See how large not how small is the effect of a thought   V, ⟨30⟩, 30,

---

Aperiency. V 36
No nobility   V 57
Buonaparte great by intellect, V.80, 45,   U 161
⟨There was nothing new in war, said they, when Napoleon came⟩
V.138
⟨Goethe & Napoleon. V⟩ 101 [67]

[67] The passage cited in Journal V, p. [150], is used in "Uses of Great Men," W, IV, 34. The paragraph in V, p. [165], is used in "Montaigne," W, IV, 185. Passages cited in V, p. [45], U, p. [161], and V, p. [101], are used in "Goethe," W, IV, 268 and 289. The paragraph in V, p. [138], is used in "Napoleon," W, IV, 247.

Value of a man of truth   V 101
No black blood   U 148
[61] We must be sick with its sickness to see the age from the inside.
V 132

Sympathetic   V.142, 132, 165,
Convict.
Alypius   The Modern Alypius   V 135, ⟨1⟩87, 48,

Majorities, the asylum of weakness, the reason of fools. Y [183]
Fourier   V 10, 19, 41, 125, 139, 146, 151   U 4, 7,
Hahnemann's skin diseases   W 138
Men now alternate a faith in love & ⟨righ⟩Truth   W 92
Travelling seems a modern invention   W 127½
Beckford Byron Warburton Humboldt.
Every past man is quotable & available. Y 109
True office of America to emancipate Man
We Americans peddle a little too long   W 10, 58,

[62] [blank]
[63]   Divine Men
        Divine men   Plotinus p 285 [68]

[64] [blank]
[65]   ⟨Nature⟩Intellect
⟨Trees imperfect Men   D 58⟩
⟨The flowers jilt us   K 93⟩
⟨Zoroaster de Natura. E 195⟩
        Law of Adrastia [R 68]
        Charm of poetry. T.59
⟨Bit of quartz predicts man E 218.   *no saltus.*⟩
Cheerly & Sovereignly
Plotinus makes no apologies   v[ide]. Plot. 86
Shakspeare & Swedenborg [K 81, 83–84]
Identity;   *Diogenes of Apollonia*, see T.111

[68] *Select Works of Plotinus*, trans. Thomas Taylor (London, 1817); in Emerson's library. See Journal U, p. [92], and p. [65] below.

554

⟨The drop too much, or excess of direction in man. F 113⟩ [H 19]
Divine men. *Plotinus* p. 285

⟨"Natura sibi semper est similis." *Linnaeus*⟩

⟨What a little gets spoken & how accidentally, of all we know. U⟩ 125 [69]
Memory is stability of knowledge.   *see* Plotinus p. 379
Gates of thought slow to s⟨l⟩how   K 96
Platonists nobly pious   K 56

[66] [blank]
     [67] *Genius* [n] & Talent

Genius ⟨I⟩an emanation of that it tells of.   *Duty* p 5 [70] [D 234]
Genius   D 56, 31, B 286, 12,
Fancy & imagination   D 93
Genius surprises   B 286   C 129   D 18
Genius takes ⟨3⟩three steps or four   G 109
Genius uncanonical   G 107
Genius, two affirmatives, & again two, & so on. U 160

Talent makes comfort; Atheneum; J 88

[68]–[69] [blank]
[70]   Manners
Qu'est ce qu'un noble? R 27
How necessary to live with good taste — more than with truth   R 36

[69] "Nature" was inscribed in pencil, erased, and overwritten with "Intellect" in pencil. "Law of Adrastia" is in pencil. Lines 3 and 12 are struck through horizontally in both ink and pencil, and ll. 4, 7, and 14 in pencil. "Cheerly & . . . Swedenborg" is in darker pencil. The passages cited in Journal D, p. [58], K, p. [93], E, p. [218], and "The drop . . . in man." are used in "Nature," *W*, III, 181, 182, and 184–185. "Law of Adrastia" is used in "Experience," *W*, III, 84. "Shakspeare & Swedenborg" and " 'Natura sibi . . . Linnaeus" are used in "Swedenborg," *W*, IV, 94, 104–105, and 107. The passage cited in U, p. [125], is used in "The Poet," *W*, III, 39–40.

[70] "*Duty*" is circled in ink. See *Lectures*, III, 138. The sentence is used in "Discourse at Middlebury College." Emerson dealt with Genius and Talent repeatedly in this period; see "The Poet," and "Nominalist and Realist," *W*, III, 11 and 228, "Discourse at Middlebury College," and "Montaigne," *W*, IV, 150 and 170. Emerson may have drawn part of these notes from earlier collections; see Notebook Ж, p. [97] above, and Φ, pp. [43]–[45] above.

Humblest feudal retainer sat at lord's table   J 20
Manners of the southerner hold me at arm's length   E 121
Foundation of aristocracy   D 377
Alcibiades & lords of the world   D 165
Aristocracy in Montaigne's time   U 42
A shade ⟨on⟩falling on English arist. U 46
⟨A man must always carry his associates with him⟩ U 111
Lawful heir humbles himself to the bastard   U 92
Hero does nothing apart & odd   Z 106
American nobles   Z 106
Pride & vanity   R [17]
Fruitland nobles   R 160
Ten acre farms not agreeable like parks   R 120
Animal Spirits. U 17, 24, 26,
The men all stood round me like castles.
Manners need time   V 136,
Poo⟨or⟩rer class encrusts itself with vulgarity as defence   V 8
Deference in acres   V 8;   in house in the woods, V 20
Please himself & he will please me. V 51
Our relations to fine people whipped cream   V 70
Deference in conversation. Don't talk of sickness   W 78 [71]
Caesar's ointment on the asparagus, in Plutarch. Life of Caesar

[71] [72] fas

Gentilesse loves measure & proportion
                reality
                Sociality

[71] "Manners" and "The man . . . castles." are in pencil; a small, unidentified pencil sketch underlies "time V 136 . . . V 8;". This and the following page are probably notes for the revision of the lecture "Manners" for the essay; see Notebook Ж, pp. [124]–[129] above, for lecture notes. The passages cited in Journal R, p. [36], and U, pp. [42] and [111], are used in "Manners," W, III, 138, 136, and 132–133; with U, p. [17], cf. ibid., p. 124. With the entries on "Deference", cf. ibid., pp. 136–138.

[72] P. [71], in faint pencil, is an outline of the thought in "Manners," though not in final order; cf. W, III, 122, 139, 133, 139–141, and 136–138; fashion is discussed throughout. In the bottom left-hand corner of the page is a pencil sketch of the bust of a man in left profile.

Gentilesse is deferential

[72]–[74] [blank]

[75]   Property   Property   Rich & Poor

Pecunia est alter sanguis [N 87]

    No magic in making money   N 82   or in learning a language
    Credit eternal   J 33   will be more & more
    Power of dead labour   R 125

⟨None should be rich but they who understand⟩ it, H.23

Few understand it. R

Feudal retainer sat with his lord   J 20

Credit   J 33

    The Farmer's dollar heavy. U 63

⟨Ah if the rich could be rich as poor fancy⟩ rich! J 92

Rich & poor   N 42   K 24   D 356

Clare's poor man [K 24]

M M E's

The one thing I wish to know of the great man how he ⟨managed⟩ got his living. R 12

Theanor   Z 161

Gold & Labor. J 140

Pedantry to give such importance to property   G 114

All on the property side   G 164,

How the Farmer enriches me, U 13

Repudiation. Story of Glaucus   Duty p 53

⟨You can never repudiate but once.⟩

Poverty makes pirates   D 59

The rich will yet be ashamed of his riches   D 356

Understanding perpetual skeptic on sumptuary laws, &c. E 331½ [73]

---

[73] "Property", centered, is in pencil. With "None should . . . Few understand it.", cf. "Discourse at Nantucket" (May 8, 1847); both lines are used in "The Young American," *The Dial*, IV (April 1844), 500. "Ah if . . . rich!" is used, with the paragraph in Journal J, pp. [91]–[93], in "Nature," *W*, III, 174–175. The passages cited in G, pp. [114] and [164], are used in "New England Reformers," *W*, III, 262. "Duty p 53" is circled in ink; see "Duty," *Lectures*, III, 147–148. "You can . . . once." is used in a section on repudiation in "The Young American," *W*, I, 389; the passage cited in E, p. [331½], is used, *ibid.*, p. 374. Passages in N, pp. [87] and [82], U, p. [63], and R, p. [12], were later used in "Wealth," *W*, VI, 125, 100, 101–102, and 85.

[76] ⟨Ah if the rich could be rich as the poor fancy riches   J 92⟩
    True riches & poverty   R 132 [74]
    Vulgarity a defence of the poor   V 8

[77] [blank]
[78]   Mystic [75]
    Jesus never preaches personal immortali↑t↓y   V 22
    J. Behmen   V 23, 24,
    Religion a crab fruit   V 25, 132,
    We alternate an appetite for mysticism & French ↑Science↓ V 151
    If we could sequester ourselves   V 163, W 10, 18
    Rix thaler Providence   W 28

    _____

    Only religious can expect succor from Religion   W 44

    _____

    Worship   W 106

    _____

    Any length allowed to him who has not given up the Holy Ghost
                                    W 102
    Thick starred Orion his companion   U 159
    The moral sentiments make poetry of me, V 71
Ecstasy = absence, αποχωρωσις εκ του σωματος εις εννοειν getting out
of their bodies to think.
    Socrates in "the Banquet"

            The realms of being to no other bow
            Not only all are thine but all are thou. *Persian*

After this generation, one would say, Myst[icis]m would go out
                                    ⟨U⟩V 150

We are educated to wish to be first. W 76
Swedenborg's self equality   J 71
Spirit never gossips   K 78

---

[74] "Ah if . . . J 92" is canceled; see p. [75] above. The sentence cited in
Journal R, p. [132], is used in "Discourse at Middlebury College," and
"Wealth," W, VI, 97.

[75] Pp. [78], [79], and [81] are notes for the lecture "Swedenborg, or the
Mystic" (December 25, 1845).

Here or nowhere the whole fact   J 108,[76] H 75, N 96, G 91,
Every man a private play of his own enacting

[79] Negative Conscience [77]
Swedenborg a wonderful ⟨example⟩ ↑specimen↓ of ore
We wish to get oxygen we collect it from many things but best from
conferva rivularis [RS 164]

"Hell is a circle about the unbelieving" Mahomet [Y 82]

Swedenborgism Manicheeism   D 148
Swedenborgians must be humoured   D 39
Teaching that shows the omnipotence of the will spiritual   D 271
Crime of the Church is Poverty   E 113
Xt preached the greatness of man, we the greatness of Xt   C 278
Trade in mummy. K 116
Boldness, but whence boldness? K 122
Do the gods bless by halves? K 123
Keep pure of the race, pure too of the few. K 122
⎡Great happiness to escape a religious education   V 73
⎨Human nature in its wildest forms most virtuous   V 132
⎣See how white souls are born   W 127½ [78]

[80] [blank]
[81]   SWEDEN⟨b⟩BORG
     B 127, 130   D 25, 35, 41, 48, 148 [79]

Swedenborg had the grammar, knew all the rudiments of the Ur-
sprache; how ⟨can he⟩could he not read off one strain into music? [n]

[76] Behmen is discussed in "Swedenborg," *W*, IV, 117 and 142–143. "Ecstasy
. . . Socrates" is marked with a curved ink line in the left margin, and "The
realms . . . *Persian*" with a single square bracket; "Swedenborgs . . . J 71"
is in pencil. The passages cited in Journal V, p. [71], "Ecstasy . . . thou.", and
J, pp. [71] and [108], are used in "Swedenborg," *W*, IV, 93–94, 97, 95, 102–
103, and 138.
[77] Cf. "Swedenborg," *W*, IV, 139–140.
[78] Emerson drew the brace first around "Great happiness . . . Human nature", then extended it to include the following line.
[79] "SWEDEN⟨b⟩BORG . . . 148", in heavy print-writing, may have been
added later; see Notebook Φ, p. [10] above. With Journal B, p. [127], and D,
pp. [25] and [48], cf. "Swedenborg," *W*, IV, 125, 126, 134, and 123.

Was he like Saadi, who forgot in the intoxication to bring the flowers away? Or, is it ⟨not⟩ a breach of the manners of that society? Or was it that he saw it intellectually, & hence that chiding of the intellectual that pervades his book. I hold him accountable for every yawn of mine.[80] [Books S [I] 22–23]

[82]   Politics

Both parties Whigs   N 97
G B historical democrat   N 4
⟨Immense benefit of party. U 66⟩
Whoever wants power must pay for it   M M E
Whigs die, democrats are born.
Salary & stealings
All scholars are democrats but in the want of a just representative of democ[rac]y vote with Whigs
Great voting   E 100
measure nations subjectively   E 112
Condition of participation   U 80
Leaders of great causes are vulgar & cunning   H 89
          Any form in which the rulers were gentlemen   U 23

———
Polity. *Proclus on T⟨u⟩imaeus*   Vol. 1, p. 26 [81]
Indifferency of events to the world spirit   V 165

"Put men to death by the principles which have for their object the preservation of life, & they will not grumble." Hea Mung) R 123

          Our neighbors are the State. ⟨U⟩V 136
          Perjury of Bishops. Brougham)   W 45
          State absorbs all the power in friction. W 17, 134,[82]

[80] This paragraph, struck through in ink with a vertical use mark, is used in "Swedenborg," *W*, IV, 143–144.
[81] *The Commentaries of Proclus on the Timaeus of Plato* . . . , 1820.
[82] "Politics . . . N 4", "Leaders of . . . U 23", and "State absorbs . . . W 17, 134," are in pencil. The passage cited in Journal U, p. [66], is used in "Nominalist and Realist," *W*, III, 239–240. The paragraph cited in V, p. [165], is used in "Montaigne," *W*, IV, 185.

[83]   Party

Entrenched in another man's mind   D 41

Partisan wants you also committed. H 97, U 80,[83]

[84]–[85] [blank]

[86]   Eloquence   [S 31

⟨a⟩Animal eloquence   U 26

Realism   U 12

Audiences   U 98

Teachings of an assembly   U 123

tediousness   U 98

Father Taylor   W 108, 114 [115],[84] Y 3

Pericles, in Phaedrus, Cousin Vol VI 108

          Realism. Speak & leave the antagonist out   J 79 [78]

Words are organic

[87]   *Literature*   ↑| *Scholar*↓

     ⟨One man wrote all books   U[65]   R 108⟩

     The true romance or novel   U 86   Novels   U 48

     Milton the most literary man in literature

     Our King Rene period   R 47

     Copyright   N 43

     Difference between educated men — faith in ideal standard   D 78

     Beautiful immunity of the Scholar   D 86, 100,

     How few writers! D 90

     Short accounts of literature   D 173

     Religion of Chaucer & the old poets   D 194

     Use of mass in writing; as in Drama   D 281

     Propriety of the great writers   D 290

---

[83] "Party . . . U 80," is near the middle of the page, opposite "want of . . . E 112" on p. [82] facing. One sentence in Journal U, p. [80], is used in "Nominalist and Realist," *W*, III, 237.

[84]"[S 31", in pencil, refers to Notebook S (Salvage), p. [31], headed "*Eloquence*." The passages cited in Journal U, pp. [26], [12], and [98], and W, p. [115], are used in "Eloquence," *W*, VII, 69, 94, 66, and 63; the first is also in the lecture "Eloquence." See Notebook Φ, pp. [146₂]–[153₂] above, and Journal O, p. [88], for notes for the lecture.

↑The↓ Lecture   D 336   R 17
   Death in novels & plays   E 122
   Books are written by the unmagnetic. E 148
   Literary man unfit for labour. E 261
   Robust courageous Scholar   E 284
   Scholar has no family   E 335
   Literature & the snow. E 253
   Ever new values of the Past   U 158
   Literature the volatile sphere of the spiritual solid. U 103
   Quotation   U 145
   Saadi, U 138, 58, 61,
   Literature   U 65, 88, 101, 103, 107,
   Naming   Z 126   Reporting ⟨U⟩V 54 [85]
[88] The orator ⟨U⟩V 58
Law of writing ⟨U⟩V 73
Scholar like the cannon   C 231, G 132,
The low style & superlative   W 82
Not to fight often with the same enemy   W 140
   Pseudo Homer, Pseudo Plato, pseudo Shakspeare   140
The arts of literature rapidly learned   140
There never was wanting a translation of Plutarch   142 [86]
Scholar like Russian bather   W 61
Abuse of Superlative   B 46, 98, 328   D 116, 171

[89] [blank]
[90]   Criticism
A scholar is a diamond merchant [R 46]
Ruin of unseasonable criticism   R 90
No character in the novel should act absurdly   R 112

[85] The passages cited in Journal U, p. [65], and R, p. [108], are used in "Nominalist and Realist," W, III, 232 and 233. The sentence cited in U, p. [86], is used in "Experience," W, III, 86. Passages cited in D, p. [281], E, p. [284], and U, p. [88], are used in "Discourse at Middlebury College." Passages in U, pp. [138] and [58], are used in "Shakspeare," and U, p. [101], and V, p. [54], in "Goethe," W, IV, 197, 216, 277, and 262–264.

[86] The paragraph cited in Journal V, p. [58], is used in "Eloquence," W, VII, 84; with the sentence in V, p. [73], cf. *ibid.*, p. 67. The first paragraph cited in W, p. [140]("Not to . . . enemy"), is used in "Uses of Great Men," and the passage cited in W, p. [142], in "Shakspeare," W, IV, 13 and 200–201.

Ease of ⟨cr⟩literary & biographic criticism; as Goethe's   D 119   128
True History   D 129
True conciseness   D 350
Plutarch   E 61   Burton   E 78   Agrippa   Plato   E 111
The Divine Critic   E 91
Transcendental Criticism   E 140, 145, 146
Montaigne. E.173
Criticize a fine genius, 'tis odds you are wrong. E 243
Bancroft's History. E 256
Classic & Romantic Schools, E 331
Olympian Criticism   E 334, 354,
Merit of a poem or tragedy a thing of experience   N 80
Scholars either play with thoughts or trade with thoughts
Phrenology, homoeopathy, &c. good Criticism. U 99, 121,
Value of first thoughts   W 36
        Scholar like a cannon. *C* 231 [87]

[91] [blank]
[92]   House
     Its situation like genius
Internal convenience — water — cover., baths.
   varnished not painted rafters
   never need go out
   furniture; selected; not a warehouse yet not a museum
   pictures
Sculpture   —   Sterling   N 41, 48
   In taste half is much more than the whole
   I dream of white marble houses
   a study in a turret or a cave [U 57]

---

[87] "Scholars either . . . thoughts" and "Scholar like . . . *C* 231" are in pencil. "A scholar . . . merchant" is used in "Discourse at Middlebury College." The passage cited in Journal D, p. [128], is used in "Goethe," E, p. [111], in "Plato," and E, p. [173], in "Montaigne," *W*, IV, 287, 61, and 168. The passages cited in E, p. [243], and U, p. [121], are used in "Nominalist and Realist," *W*, III, 241–242 and 240; U, p. [99] is torn out, but cf. *ibid.*, p. 234. Emerson had used the paragraph in C, p. [231], in "Prospects," *Lectures*, III, 370.

gardens: never need travel

___

Lord Bacon's ponds at Gorhambury

___

{ whole subject, as soon as the tenant is considered becomes like
{ the recipe for cucumbers—   out of the window

___

It has the apology that it treats man respectfully

___

Concord a park, & sky a ceiling

___

In his own house let him be guest. [R 96] Athenaeum   Salve [88]

In a hot house should be.   see D 77
Fit for man to build   D 83
Household tasks subjects of Greek gems   D 356. E 299

[93] [89] *Sermon.*   V Lecture on N. England
Synopsis. Great activity of Speculation in young N.E
         Dissent in diet; use of animals; commerce;
           some serious protests & reforms.
         in politics, ⟨p⟩non-jurors, non-payers,
       Episode on Concert.
         in Education   want of things
                rejection of Lat & Greek
In all this dissent a casting off of means & new Selfreliance
    Fault of the reformers *partiality*
    Second fault, *want of faith* as exhibited in Concert
True office of N.E. to Emancipate Man

    Particulars of the Faith in Man

___

[88] "House . . . Salve" is in pencil; "Salve" is circumscribed in pencil. P.
[92] is notes for a section of "The Young American" (February 7, 1844), *The
Dial*, IV (April 1844), 488–490, partly printed in *W*, I, 367–368; cf. Journal
U, pp. [27]–[29] and [56]–[57]. With "not a museum", cf. "Domestic Life,"
W, VII, 130.
[89] Notes on pp. [93]–[94] are an outline of "New England Reformers,"
W, III, 251–285. "Episode on Concert." is in pencil.

[Cardinal vice of the age is its want of Faith
    Education a system of despair
Counterstatement]

              Men are all geniuses
                    radicals
                    devotees
      (the very Caesars & Adamses are such)
                    want superiors not gossips
                    and to be benefactors
                    are lovers of truth & fidelity
        A man equal to the Church
              to the State
              to every other man

[94] *Sermon continued*
              our connexion with the Spirit
              the Future man
              The Law
                    Work paid or unpaid
                    The pretender sets the people right
                    Obedience to our genius is all
                    The life of man is the Romance,
                    of romances.

[9⟨4⟩5] [blank]
    [96] In writing of nature, I do not wish to fall into euphuism. I prefer facts. Nature does not lisp or ⟨dawdle⟩ ↑drawl↓. I should like to read a wood cutter's gazetteer, or such facts as would really interest a wood chopper, would be those most engaging to such as never saw the forest.

The facts of th↑e↓ bookmaker are few among m

books are meagre & indigent of facts. how few go to the making of the best book of travels. It must go like a beau & have in mind all that went before. I should like to read a wood cutter's gazetteer. The

secrets of the forest which a wood chopper would care to know would
be those most engaging to such as never saw the forest [90]

[97]   Nature
⟨Natura sibi semper est similis. *Linnaeus*⟩ [91]
Nature & Montaigne   Z[[A] 126–125]
Nature so respective of the future that pregnancy insures life
Space   R 119
Walks   R 119, 135,
Water
Sky   E 357,
Fire   D 218
Earth
Air
Stars   R 122
The Mountains   R 140
     Tuckis⟨*i*⟩*ch* ⟨If you baulk water you shall be drowned next time.⟩
          Notch & Profile mountains   D 347
⟨Plants are the young of⟩ the world   N 45
A certain temperature good for prediction. *Plutarch* | E 7
Olympian Criticism. E 334
⟨Ah if the rich were rich as⟩ the poor fancy riches [Φ 125] J 92
Hurry, hurry: there is no intercalation. E 263
     Flowers jilt us   K 93
Trees imperfect men   D 58
Zoroaster *de Natura*   E 195
The drop too much   F 113
Bit of quartz   E 118 [218]   no leap [B 284]
Nature does not Entrance   U 119
"Nature tells everything once."   *Goethe*.[92] [A 20, 21]

----

[90] P. [96], a rough draft for "Nature," *W*, III, 177, is in pencil; "I should
. . . among m" is struck through in pencil with two vertical use or cancellation
marks. See also p. [40] above and pp. [97]–[99] below for notes for this essay,
and Notebook Ж, pp. [30]–[34], for notes for the lecture "Relation of Man to
Nature," on which it was probably based.
     [91] See "Swedenborg," *W*, IV, 104–105, where Emerson translates this, "Na-
ture is always like herself".
     [92] The heading "Nature", "Nature & . . . life", and "Flowers . . . K 93"
are in pencil; with "Nature so . . . life", cf. "Nature," *W*, III, 186–187. The

Nature no exaggeration   E 333

[98]   ↑NATure↓
   Is Nature also dilettante   G 1
   Surprise & casualty the apples of her eyes   [JK 64]
There's a necessity to be beautiful in the landscape   J 125
As ⟨A⟩the life comes into a man with nature, his thoughts parallel &c
                                                               K 55

"The greatest goods produced through mania." T.'s Plato Vol 3 p 314

Nature = Natura; is not, but becomes. See *Philosophy* [93]

[99] [94]   No leap in nature
            ever on, but ever with the first elements,
            runs to ruin, ⟨but⟩ if left without one of the threads
            plants are the young of the world
            trees imperfect men
            but as we grow old the flowers jilt us

   For ⟨such is the⟩ ⟨whether we are too clumsy for so subtle a topic⟩ ⟨it is certain that whilst⟩ all men are naturally hunters & inquisitive of wood craft & would rather have such a gazetteer as woodcutters & Indians would ⟨make⟩ ↑furnish↓ than all the "Chaplets" & "Wreaths" of the bookshops, yet ordinarily because we are too clumsy for so subtle a topic as soon as men ⟨set out⟩ begin to write on nature they fall into euphuism[.] [95]

---

passages cited in Journal D, p. [347], N, p. [45], Notebook Φ, p. [125], and J, p. [92], K, p. [93], E, p. [218]("Bit of quartz"), and "no leap" are used in "Nature," *W*, III, 175, 181, 174–175, 182, and 179. With "no leap" and the quotation from Goethe, cf. "Humanity of Science," *Lectures*, II, 31 and 26.
   [93] The sentence cited in Journal J, p. [125], and "Nature=Natura; . . . becomes." are used in "Nature," *W*, III, 176 and 179. "See *Philosophy*" may have been added; see pp. [111]–[112] below, headed "Philosopher"; "Nature=Natura" is expanded on p. [112]. Below the written matter, the head of a child is sketched in pencil.
   [94] P. [99] is in pencil.
   [95] "No leap . . . jilt us" outlines a section of "Nature," *W*, III, 181–182. "men are . . . euphuism" is used, *ibid.*, p. 177.

[100]–[102] [blank]
[103]   Woman

A constitutional nuptial affection. E 234
⟨Tragedy of⟩ life of women pathetic   D 66, 79
Woman has crises   K 23

We need all the conventions for marriage against our evil. E 331½
    Marriage impossible in spiritual world. E 340   F 136
    Medical Skepticism, amplification of a system
    Slavery Skepticism selling woman by the pound
    Poetic   Skepticism knows woman only in the plural
    Woman acquires easily all her husband's results   S 211 [96]

[104]–[105] [blank]
[106]   Great Men
    The gods lead & perfect all things by a silent path, by their very
being & fill them with good

That which is according to Nature is not laborious to anything &c &c
        Proclus. Theol. Plato   Vol 1 p 52 [T 101]

Attractive Industry [K 26]   } W 134

———

Necessity of Deity rushing into distribution. V 59

———

Our faculties warrant inceptions only   D 191
Inference that life is a great inception; considered with transmigration.

———

Human nature in its wildest forms most virtuous, V 132 [131]

———

How many degrees of power! V 129

———

⟨We need but one wise man⟩. V 164

———

[96] "Woman" is in pencil. With "Woman has crises", cf. Journal N, p. [106],
used in "Domestic Life," W, VII, 123–125. The paragraph in E, p. [340], is
used in "Experience," W, III, 77, and the paragraph in F No. 2, p. [136], in
"Swedenborg," W, IV, 128–129. With "Woman acquires . . . results" (Notebook S (Salvage), p. [211]), cf. "Woman," W, XI, 406–407.

No common people   W 128 [97]

Idiodynamics ⟨U 122, 135, W 94, 114, 134, Y 81, 84⟩
Men born with peculiarities of power, for music, animals, &c   W 94
 Each has a drama to his private box   W 114
 We misapply men ↑& so neutralize↓, but to a fagot of nerves it is
  easy to go   W 134   U 122
 ⟨What is acc. to Nature is not laborious⟩   T 101,
 Misassociation an extempore Auburn or Sing⟨s⟩Sing   W 129
 ⟨Men have their metal ⟨l⟩as of gold or silver   ⟨W⟩Y 81
 Every class rejoiceth in his own
 Ali created near by intellect   Y 62
 ⟨Men who knew the particular deity from whom they descend⟩
               U 13⟨4⟩5

Bring me a law & I count not the clock   V 135 [98] W 70
[107] * Immense force of men whose part is taken [99] Z 16⟨9⟩3
In reading the old mythology, how easily we detect the men &
women we know, clothed there in colossal masks, & stilted on high
buskins, to go for gods & goddesses. [W 140]

The gods of fable are of course the shining moments of great
men.   "But they remain seated around the gold tables," &c: The
aristocracy of Nature grinds & torments,—

* Robert Owen ↑seen↓, *in society*, is an example of that.

[97] With the quotation from Proclus and "Attractive Industry", cf. "Life and
Letters in New England," *W*, X, 349–350. The quotation in Journal V, p. [131]
is used in "Worship," *W*, VI, 214. With the quotation from Proclus and the
paragraph cited in V, p. [129], cf. "Uses of Great Men," *W*, IV, 7 and 20. V,
p. [164], is torn out, but the passage is used, *ibid.*, p. 25. The sentence cited in
W, p. [128], is used, *ibid.*, p. 31.
[98] The horizontal use mark through "U 122, 135, . . . 84" is extended down
to "U 13⟨4⟩5" in the right-hand margin to enclose the nine entries on "Idiodynamics"; cf. "Uses of Great Men," *W*, IV, 6–7. The passages cited in Journal
Y, pp. [81] and [84], are used in "Plato," *W*, IV, 66 and 52. The passage cited
in W, p. [129], is used in "Society and Solitude," *W*, VII, 14. With "Every
class . . . own", cf. "Uses of Great Men," *W*, IV, 24. The paragraph in V,
p. [135], is used, *ibid.*, pp. 21–22.
[99] Cf. the discussion of Robert Owen in "Life and Letters in New England,"
W, X, 346–347.

The sympathetic force of energy & toil
Life is fictitious & we would have it real, &c. Y 53 [100]

[108] [blank]
[109]   Community
↑N ⟨140⟩   K ⟨49⟩, 90, 46   ⟨E 258⟩⟨Z 133⟩   G 116↓

Communities will never have men, but halves, &c   N 127

Of "Attractive Industry" see Proclus. *Theol* of *Plato*   Vol 1. p 52

G. & S. Ripley's visit. Oct 1840,   E 238

In Orpheus the Demiurgus interrogates Night

"Tell me how all things may as one subsist
Yet each its Nature separate preserve." [E 353]

Advantage of seeing friends   H.30, J 84
Objections to Phalanxes   K 50   60
Institution in the Institutor   K 85
Permanence of the Shakers N 62[–69]
Brook Farm   U ⟨10⟩, ⟨16⟩, ⟨13⟩, ⟨85⟩, ⟨88⟩, ⟨91⟩   R 63, 84, 94, 96,
                                                                        152, 101
C L's remark that our communities had better women than English
                                                                        N 140
Danger of Charlatanism to the founders   K 49
Harvest better preserved by individuals   Z 133
Founders of B.F. have made the most agreeable residence   U 16
Unwillingness to work   U 10
Fourier's noble thought   U 13
⟨Equal pay of talent & labor   U 85⟩
Married women decided against them   U 88

[100] The sentence in Journal Z[A], p. [163], is used in "New England Reformers," *W*, III, 280. "The gods . . . great men.', struck through in ink with
a diagonal use mark, is used in "Uses of Great Men," *W*, IV, 4. Y, p. [53], is
torn out, but cf. *ibid.*, p. 20.

Stock Companies   U 91 [101]
Society a boardinghouse. W 82

[110] [blank]
[111]   Philosopher
Man feels that he has been what he is from all eternity   Schelling
                                                              see V 13
Man endogenous   V 12
All are born with the secular idea   V 37
Form the visibility of spirit   V 44
⟨Bring me a law & I count not the clock   V 135   W 70⟩
Let us have the theory of America   W 1⟨5⟩3
Integrating power of ideas ascribed to multitudes   W 46
Life Identity in variety & a protean march   W 57
Bounds & limits   W 66
Tendency; Star in Hercules
Tendency; hence mystic
Tendency; world thinks for us. W   Fame W 67
A fluxional philosophy must be. W 86
Philosophic Abgrund   W 86
⟨Others may build cities, he should understand⟩ & keep them in awe
                                                              W 93
Literature has been before us into secretest experience   W 121
Arithmetic science of surfaces; probity, of essences. W 125
Obedience to one's genius the particular of faith: By & by shall come
the universal of faith   U 109
Intellect always puts an interval   E 340
Nature & literature subjective   E 337
Order of wonder   E 147, W 80   Y 142

---

[101] "Institution . . . K 85" is struck through in ink with a vertical use mark; the paragraph is used in "Character," *W*, III, 101–102. Passages cited in Journal K, p. [90], N, pp. [63]–[64], U, pp. [16], [13], [85], [88], and [91], are used in "The Young American," *The Dial*, IV (April 1844), 498, 490–491, 486–487 and 493, and 498–499 (*W*, I, 382–383, 368–369, 454[notes] and 373, and 382–384). Passages cited in N, p. [127], and K, pp. [50] and [60], are used in "New England Reformers," *W*, III, 264–265 and 267. Passages cited in K, pp. [49] and [60], and U, pp. [10] and [16], are used in "Life and Letters in New England," *W*, X, 354, 368, 366, and 364; with "Of 'Attractive . . . p 52", and R, pp. [63], [84], and [94], cf. *ibid.*, pp. 350, 367, 365, and 368.

Want of insight the reason why we are so slow   W 75
⟨Dualism.   Obverse & reverse   S 61⟩
⟨Adaptiveness. W 86   Y 56⟩
Identity,   T ⟨‖ ... ‖⟩ 111,[102]

[112] Nature = natura, future participle   Nothing is, but all becomes. The universe is only in transit, or we behold it shooting the gulf from the Past to the Future —

[113]–[114] [blank]
[115]   Idealism
"Matter is privation," &c   *Plutarch*. See E 1

The soul is in this body as ↑in↓ a fiction. *Hermeas. Taylor's Plat.* Vol 3 p 334

[116] [103] Spinoza
Motion   & rest
Will   & understanding
        Identity , affirmation
        Difference   negation

    misfit

[117]   Transcendentalism [104]
↑J 25, F.160, C 309   D 331,↓
Transcendentalism for health, but not empirical. E 104
Why the Scholar tends to Idealism   E 151
Ecstasy   K 50, E 257, 253, Saadi Σ   K 53, D 322,
Buddhism   E 353

---

[102] The passages cited in Journal V, pp. [12] and [135], are used in "Uses of Great Men," *W*, IV, 6 and 21–22. Passages in W, pp. [86]("A fluxional . . . ") and [80], S (Salvage), p. [61], and Y, p. [56], are used in "Montaigne," *W*, IV, 160–161, 170, and 149. The sentence cited in W, p. [93], is used in "Swedenborg," *W*, IV, 93. With the quotation in Notebook T, p. [111], cf. the section on Unity in "Plato," *W*, IV, 47–52.

[103] P. [116] is in pencil. "Spinoza" is circled, and to the right of it is a rough sketch of a man's head. Cf. "Plato," *W*, IV, 51 and 62.

[104] Notes on p. [117] are probably for "Discourse at Middlebury College"; see also pp. [50]–[51] above and notes for "The Transcendentalist" in Notebook Ж, pp. [116₂]–[117₂] above.

Transcendentalist does not go beyond his experience   R 73

———

I think men of the world thoroughly entitled to know if this be anything, a substance. V 45, & U 161, V 31,

———

Transcendentalism in State Street. H 60

———

Men have an instinct — who threatens the stocks   U 160

———

Inevitableness of Transd—m; H 2
Calculation carried out is T.; H 126
Whiggery rests at last on T.   F.23
T—ists play with thoughts [105]
T—m is an attempt to jump out of one's skin.

[118]–[119] [blank]
[120]   Realism
Reference versus Necessity. R 58
Identity. T 111
The Divine Critic   E 91
Young people admire parts; the old, Genius. U 64↑, 105,↓
⟨A man behind the book   F⟩ 32,
Ecstasý selfrelying. E 257
        Measure nations subjectively   E 112
Poorness of our experience makes no difference: We must affirm the
        law. E 265
What had they to conceal? what had they to exhibit? R 160
        ⟨φυγη μονου προς μονον⟩ [106] [E 277]
The rich man steals his own dividends; U 81
All knowledge is assimilation to the object of Knowledge. [E 277]

[105] "J 25 . . . D 331," is added in pencil. "K 53" is written in ink over the
same in pencil. Passages cited in Journal V, p. [45], U, p. [161], V, p. [31], H,
p. [60], and "T — ists . . . thoughts" are used in "Discourse at Middlebury College." Passages in V, p. [45], and U, p. [161], are also used in "Goethe," W, IV,
268. The paragraph in F No. 2, p. [23], is used in "The Transcendentalist," W, I,
331–332.
[106] Emerson uses a translation of this quotation from Plotinus in "Swedenborg,"
W, IV, 97; cf. also Journal D, p. [374], used in "Religion," and "Education," Lectures, III, 283 and 299.

⟨"Is he anybody?"⟩ V 45,

I met myself. F 27

Qui s'excuse s'accuse.ⁿ [E 277]

Here or nowhere the whole fact— J 108, ↑H 75, N 96↓ No history
true but what is always true. G 91

Our assumption of holiness when we deal with children. *E* 278

Biography above biography *E* 287

I did not mind what B said about the ox I asked the ox. said E[liza-
beth] H[oar] [107]

We do not live by times but by qualities. R [136]

Inextinguishableness, U 159

Liars also true W 68

We transcend circumstance continually W 56

After all our accumulation of facts, we [121] are just as poor in thought
Z 3

Character is logical E 329

There is no *peau d'ane* N 90

They are not kings who have thrones, but they who know how to
govern.

What there is anywhere there is everywhere H 75 N 96

Speak & leave the foolish antagonist out. J 79

The Real Emperor. Chinese proverb. R 75

———

When it is felt 'Those men occupy my place,' the revolution is
near.

———

Life is fictitious & we would have it real. Y 53 [108]

The thing done avails, not the reputation W 139

---

[107] "105," and "I did . . . E H" are in pencil. "No history . . . G 91" continues onto p. [121] facing, connected by lines above and below to "whole fact".
The paragraph in Journal U, p. [64], is used in "Nominalist and Realist," *W*, III,
228; passages in U, pp. [64] and [105], are used in "Worship," *W*, VI, 227. The
paragraph cited in F No. 2, p. [32], is used in "Goethe," *W*, IV, 282; the sentence
cited in V, p. [45], is used, *ibid.*, p. 268, and in "Discourse at Middlebury College."

[108] The paragraph cited in Journal E, p. [329], is used in "Discourse at Middlebury College." With *"peau d'ane"*, cf. "Uses of Great Men," *W*, IV, 21; Y, p. [53],
is torn out, but cf. *ibid.*, p. 20.

[122]–[124] [blank]
[125] America: New England:

                      Is it not curious that the French have
no word for *to stand*? *E* 156,

    Lectures. U 12, R.17,

City of Washington, R 92
America out of doors & in doors, a market & a stove. R 93
America not pleasing to the imaginative R 104
Fill it with incident R 138
Bunker Hill & Webster R 148
Plymouth R 171
The West is the native American element. ⟨R⟩U 82 [109]
Yankee is like a goose in a deluge [U 64]

[126]–[128] [blank]
[129]   Society

Life makes us acquainted faster than thought. E 353

[130] [blank]
[131]   Friendship. Love

How fast life & real interests make us acquainted. *E* 353
We use friends for expedients as we do stoves. *F* 108
Lover loves nature in his mistress. *U* 70
Love is the road builder
The flattery of omens.
Lover transcends the person of the beloved. *V* 82
⟨L⟩To lover occurred magical communication. *V* 164
    Attributes of love. *W* 98
    Medicinal or educative power.

---

[109] The passages cited in Journal R, pp. [93], [104], and [138], and U, p. [82], are used in "The Young American," *The Dial*, IV (April 1844), 501–502, 505, 507, and 491 (*W*, I, 388, 392, 395, and 369–370).

Lovers of Men as safe as the sun. *R.*⟨1⟨3⟩61⟩ ↑161↓

[132]¹¹⁰   The Poet
          Life   32
          Character   16 pp
          Gifts
          Manners   25
          Nature
          Representative   18

Order
1   Poet
2   Nature
3   Experience
4   Character
5   Manners
6   Gifts
7   Representative

          Nat   20
          Poet   40
          L   32
          C   16
          M   25
          Nat   20
          Rep   18
          G   5
                  ───
                  176

[133]   New Essays
     The Poet
     Life
     Character
     Nature
     Gifts

¹¹⁰ P. [132], early titles for *Essays, Second Series*, is in pencil; "Order" is circled.

Representative U ⟨132⟩, ⟨9⟩ / ⟨20⟩, / ⟨117⟩ ⟨89[?],/ ⟨102⟩ /
⟨63⟩ / ⟨99⟩ / 130 R 27 N 128

⟨Tragedy⟩   Manners
Protest[?]
Reform ‖ ... ‖
D‖emo‖nology

Representative

Tax we must pay for foreign talent is its Encroachment. Swed

Mrs Hildreth
Mathews
Haggerty
Martineau
Cranch
Lowell
Miss Sales
Mary Adams [111]

Individual

A man has too many enemies than that he should be his own   *V* 137,

Everything wishes to remain itself even Abolitionists   *W* 33

And women   W 32

He never hears it as he knows it. W 44

What is the use of trying to be somewhat else. *W* 61

Universal triumph of the Genus over Individual. *W* 68

Colleges not gracious to geniuses. W 73

We Saxons all require to be *first*. *W* 76

Genius of the world spreads his ability over the whole. W 81

⟨Individuals protected from individuals⟩ W 91

Every man has a private play of his own enacting   *W* 114

[111] "New Essays . . . Mary Adams" is in pencil; "New Essays . . . D‖emo‖nol-ogy" is overwritten by "Individual . . . Individuals protected", printed below. The passages cited in Journal U, pp. [20], [117], [102], [63], and [130], and R, p. [27], are used in "Nominalist and Realist," *W*, III, 225, 228, 233, 236, and 225–226. Passages in U, p. [132], and N, p. [128], are used in "The Poet," *W*, III, 40–41 and 7. The names are of people to whom Emerson sent copies of *Essays, Second Series*, on October 15, 1844; see Journal V, pp. [69]–[70].

Limits of personality. *W* 66 [112]
Lotus of Individualism   *W* 114
    Seed of the tree of ignorance. *Y*.90

[134] [113]
[135]   Result
Population of the world Conditional   K 57
Ah if our genius were a little more of a genius
If one could have any security against moods! U 76
Sanity of society is a balance of a thousand insanities [U 80]
The true romance the transformation of genius into practical power
                                                         U 86,

Is there method in your consciousness? &c ⟨V⟩U 166
Liars also are true. *W* 68
Universal triumph of the Genus over Individual   *W* 68
⟨History of the Universe only symptomatic. *W* 127⟩
Last value of experience   *W* 127
Intellect sees by moral obedience. *U* 109 ↑J.↓ 95.
To the vigilant the history of the universe is only symptomatic, & life
mnemonical. *W* 127 [114]

[136] [blank]
[137]   Identity [115]
No hope so bright but is the beginning of its fulfilment   E 91

[112] The sentence cited in Journal V, p. [137], is used in "Montaigne," *W*, IV,
160. The passages cited in W, pp. [76] and [91], are used in "Uses of Great Men,"
W, IV, 22 and 28–29. The paragraph in W, p. [66], is used in "Eloquence," *W*,
VII, 80–81.

[113] P. [134] is filled with practice writing in pencil; "Concord" is written 43
times, "1843" twice, and "Estimate" once, in addition to other apparently meaning-
less lines.

[114] "Result" is in pencil. "Ah if . . . U 86" is struck through in ink with two
vertical use marks; the paragraph in U, p. [76], and the sentence in U, p. [80], are
used in "Nominalist and Realist," *W*, III, 247 and 237; the sentence in U, p. [86],
is used in "Experience," *W*, III, 86, but cf. also E, p. [230], used in "New England Reformers," *W*, III, 285. The paragraph cited in U, p. [166], is used in "Discourse at Middlebury College." "To the vigilant . . . mnemonical." in W, p.
[127], is used in "Uses of Great Men," *W*, IV, 32; with W, p. [127]("Last value
of experience"), cf. "Experience," *W*, III, 85. "Intellect sees . . . obedience." is
used in "Discourse at Nantucket."

[115] Cf. notes for "Plato" in Journal Y, p. [197]. "Every thought . . . tells of."

Every thought of genius an emanation of that it tells of. [D 234]
Life a game betwixt ⟨g⟩God & Man   W 57
Coarse & fine   W 62   Plato & Plesiosaurus
Only poetry inspires poetry   W 55
Only the religious can expect the succor of religion [W 42, 44]
⟨E⟩He only is righ↑t↓ly immortal to whom all things are immortal
Every director is also a bank   W 127⅔

[138] [blank]
[139]   Autobiography

In some hours I walked in a world of glass   E 99

Of writing Lectures, E 91

The spiritualists were all egotists, E 125

Too sympathetic, E 131

In these years I wanted to buy a master   E 152

"Essay on Love"   see E 162

Of the Reforms. E 165, 255,

A puny limitary creature I   E 259, 261, 335,
I could not stand the dissipation of a flowing friendship   E 335
In public assemblies I desired to be eloquent   U [123]
"secret of popularity"   U 136

Self defended   O 199
Individualism   E 368

[140]–[141] [blank]
[142] [116]   ⎡"From an original painting by Saml
                 ⎣Lawrence, London, Feby, 1845"

---

is used in "Discourse at Middlebury College," and "Only the religious . . . religion"
in "Discourse at Nantucket."

[116] Pp. [142] and [143] are in pencil. See *CEC*, pp. 374–375.

[143]

imprisoning
fettering
pinched
galling
taming
chai⟨r⟩ning
inextricable
impassable
fatal
stern

[144]–[147] [blank]
[148]¹¹⁷   1

2   Plato

3   Swedenborg

4   Montaigne

5   Shakspear   Saadi

6   Goethe

7   Napoleon

8   Fourier

[θεου θελοντος και επι ριπον αν πλεοις]¹¹⁸ [CD i]

[inside back cover] [blank]

---

[117] P. [148], in pencil, lists titles considered for the "Representative Men" series.

[118] This line, in pencil, is written vertically downward in the right margin; a verse translation is used in "The School," *Lectures*, III, 41.

$\mathcal{BO}$ $\mathcal{C}$onduct

1851

Emerson dated this notebook October, 1851, and used it to collect
material for lectures in the "Conduct of Life" series; most of these lectures
had been given earlier, some as single lectures, but the first known series to
include the lecture "Fate" was a private series given in Boston between
December 22, 1851, and January 26, 1852. There is a concentration of
material for "Fate." Although there are scattered entries used in all of the
lectures and essays later printed as *Conduct of Life*, concentrations of notes
for "Wealth," "Economy," "Culture," and "Worship" are probably for
revision of earlier lectures.

BO Conduct is a notebook with a moiréd blue cover of heavy paper about 20.2
x 24.6 cm, separated from the rear cover, which is evidently lost. There are various
rips and tears around the edges, and a big tear at the upper left corner, so that on the
inside front cover, at the top right, the remaining inscription is "R. W." Pasted
on the cover is a label in ink reading "BO / October 1851 / Conduct of Life", not
in Emerson's hand.

The pages are faded blue, approximately 20.4 x 24.5 cm. The discrepancy
between the width of the page and the width of the cover occurs because much of the
cover near what would have been the spine is lost. The pages are numbered in ink;
unnumbered pages are 42, 43, and 46–48. Pages 18–19, 42–43, and 45–46 are blank.
The notebook is composed of 48 pages, sewed through between pages 24 and 25, in
three sew holes.

Laid in between pages 46 and 47 are several sheets of the kind of paper used in
lectures, as follows:

1) One folded sheet of blue lined paper; the first page is numbered 73, the third
   75, both in pencil, and both inscribed. The sheet has several sets of sew holes,
   indicating that the contents were used in different lectures. Page [74] is
   inscribed, page [76] blank.

2) A single leaf of unlined blue paper, the first page numbered 81 in pencil.
   The leaf has been pulled away from a sheet and is inscribed on recto and
   verso. The papermaker's mark, in the upper left corner, is D. & J. Ames on
   a scroll within an octagonal double frame.

3) A leaf of the same kind of paper as in no. 2), with the same papermaker's
   mark. It has been pulled away from a sheet. It is numbered 66½ and inscribed
   on the recto only.

4) A cream-colored folded sheet of four pages numbered in ink 9, 10, and 12. It is inscribed on all four pages, but the top half of 12 is blank. The bottom halves of pages [11] and 12 have a continuous inscription in prose by Mary Moody Emerson which Emerson writes on page 12 that he copied in Notebook MME 3, page 141.

5) A folded sheet of unlined blue paper, numbered 65 in pencil, upside down and at the bottom of the last page. The recto of the first page is inscribed; the inscription in pencil on the page numbered 65 is

> "True tone
> High tone"

All pages in numbers 1–5 range between 19.6 and 18.9 cm wide x 24.9 and 24.4 cm long. They are probably stray leaves from lectures and are omitted here.

6) A single leaf of cream-colored paper, 11.5 x 18.1 cm, with chain links and part of the watermark visible. It is inscribed in ink.

7) A single leaf of bluish paper, 11.0 x 18.2 cm, with a round but scarcely discernible papermaker's mark in the top right corner. These two leaves, numbered 46ₐ and 46ᵦ by the editors, are printed following page 46.

[front cover]

BO
October 1851
Conduct of Life

[front cover verso]
Conduct of Life   p. 26   R.W.‖msm‖ [1]

Fate   1
Power   7
Wealth ⟨14⟩13.
Culture   20, 28, 36
Religion   30
Intellect   38
Prudence   16
Economy   15
Miscellanies   44 [2]

"Or if the Soul of proper ‖msm‖
Be so perfect as men ‖msm‖
That it wot what is to com‖msm‖,
And that he warneth all & some
Of every of their aventures,
By previsions, or figures;
But that our flesh hath not might
It to understand aright;
For it is warned too darkely;
But why the cause is, wot not I." [3]

Chaucer: [CO 158]

---

[1] The upper right-hand corner of the page is torn off.

[2] "13", "36", and "Prudence   16 . . . Miscellanies   44" are in darker ink and were probably added later.

[3] This quotation is used, except for the last line, in "Fate," *W*, VI, 46.

"Success shall be in thy Courser tall,
Success in thyself, which is best of all,
Success in thy hand, success in thy foot,
In struggle with man, in battle with brute,
The Holy God & Saint Drotten dear
Shall never shut eyes on thy career
Look out, ⟨look out⟩look out, Svend Vonved!"[4]

[1]   Oct 1851
Fate   ↑If a more powerful horse than ordinary ⟨TU 170⟩↓ ↑EO 67.↓
Instinctive action. BO 182
Event & Person meet, & Shakspeare must be English. ↑CO 106↓

For the ⟨high⟩ overpowering high riding well-willing Destiny, which is God, see *Religion*

———

House of Fame   CO 158

———

Fate. Families. In a family all the qualities of the progenitors appear to be potted in several jars, the best, the middling, and the inferior; and some times the unmixed temperament is drawn off in a separate jar. *CO* 251

———

A Facility comes by, at last. *CO* 260
Providence not to be whitewashed. CO 257

———

In some men, incapacity of. melioration. *BO* 23

———

Shall not a man have better insurance than chlorine? *BO* 98
      Population of the world conditional. K 57
Unity in human structures pervasive: hump appears in intellect, too.
                                                    BO, 137.
Man hooped in by necessity, which he touches on every point, until he learns its arc   AZ 36[5]

[4] These lines, used in "Success," *W*, VII, 287, are from a Danish ballad translated by George Borrow in *Romantic Ballads, translated from the Danish; and Miscellaneous Pieces* (London, 1826), p. 64, ll. 38–45; cf. Journal U, p. [18].
[5] "Fate   If . . . ordinary", "Fate. Families . . . *CO* 251", "Providence not . . . CO 257", and "Unity in . . . AZ 36" are struck through in ink with single

All above as below is organized   CO 208

[2] "Men are everywhere exactly what their mothers make them." *St John*
[AZ 94]

_____

"Fate is nothing but the deeds committed in a former state of existence."
[AZ 97]

_____

Fate or Nature has no nonsense, but establishes a despotism at a fire, in a seastorm, in the streets of a revolutionary Paris, &c. See AZ 247

_____

Greatness of fate, well; the nobility of the sentiments is in resisting or in accepting it   RS 202

_____

Event & person indissoluble. TU 248, 246.
                    CO 168   169, 186, 106
        ↑Events are subpersons. *RS* 273↓

_____

Fate = Passion   antagonist force is Science
Man & his things all of a piece   *CO* 163
Expense of ends to means is Fate [6] [CO 164]
Victory is born with victors   *CO* 165

_____

The fate fits like a glove. *CO* 57   Fate in the bill of the bird. Y 113

_____

Intellect conquers fate, & Insight is serene. They who talk of fate, invite it. *CO* 70

_____

vertical use marks. The passages cited in Journal TU, p. [170], and Notebook EO, p. [67], CO, pp. [158], [251], and [257], K, p. [57], and AZ, p. [36], are used in "Fate," *W*, VI, 35, 46, 9-10, 8, 16, and 19-20. With CO, p. [106], cf. *ibid.*, p. 39. BO, p. [137], is torn out but "Unity in . . . intellect, too." is used, *ibid.*, p. 45. The passage cited in BO, p. [23], is used in "Culture," and BO, p. [98], in "Worship," *W*, VI, 140 and 232. The passage cited in CO, p. [260], is used in "Powers and Laws of Thought," *W*, XII, 47. With K, p. [57], cf. U, p. [152].
    [6] " 'Men are . . . existence.' ", "Event & . . . 246.", and "Expense of . . . Fate" are struck through in ink with single vertical use marks. The two quotations are used in "Fate," *W*, VI, 10 and 12. The passages cited in Journal TU, pp. [248] and [246], and RS, p. [273], are used, *ibid.*, p. 41, and those in CO, pp. [168] and [169], *ibid.*, pp. 42 and 46. "Expense of . . . Fate" is used, *ibid.*, p. 8. For CO, p. [106], see p. [1] above.

We shall have what we wish. CO 71

Power & Circumstance. *CD* 141 [7]

Calvinism complexional. J 85   Differences of opinion organic. J 110

[3] We pass from thought to thought easily, but o how slowly from realization to realization! [CO 120] The wise hand does not all that ⟨her⟩the foolish tongue saith. [Q 19]

We must accept a good deal as fate. &c. RS 175
Quetelet's "Destiny" & "Circumstances." *RS* 220

As soon as the children are good, the mothers are scared, & think they are going to die. [LM 102]

"The liberation of the Will from the Daemon is the end & aim of this mundane state."

In feeble individuals, sex & digestion are all, i.e. they are children of fate. *CO* 30 [8]

Greek & Indian Fate. Y, 148.

Solution of the riddles. *CO* 36 [9]
Every atom displaces every other atom; & every soul unspheres every soul but itself   See *CO* 208

"Marchez sans le peuple, et vous marchez dans les tenebres." *CO* 223

Wo to him that suffers himself to be betrayed by Fate. AB 129

[7] "The fate . . . *CD* 141" is struck through in ink with a vertical use mark. The passages cited in Journal Y, p. [113], and CO, pp. [70] and [71], are used in "Fate," *W*, VI, 9, 23, and 47. With CD, p. [141], cf. *ibid.*, p. 14.
    [8] With " 'The liberation . . . state.' " and the passage cited in Journal CO, p. [30], cf. "Fate," *W*, VI, 36 and 11. "As soon . . . die." is used in "Considerations by the Way," *W*, VI, 259.
    [9] A sum is inscribed in pencil to the right of "*CO* 30 . . . *CO* 36".

⟨The⟩ Nature's Police. AB ⟨58⟩ 79

Fate in the proceeding of the fossil ages [CO 175]

Schelling's preexistence, V 13 [10] [TU 51]

Temperament the last form this most poetic Spirit took, the self-imposed limitation. See V 24

Daemonology, faith in nature. V 36
     K 78 [11]
     [4] Will you dare play at ball or props with Fate? ↑to↓ play Providence, & be the little Prometheus of your family Circle? When the heroes, in the Iliad, saw that the gods interfered in the fight, they prudently drew ⟨f⟩off. And so, when wary fathers & guardians see what potencies mingle in this game of love & marriage, they will hardly dare to advise, dare to dissuade, & incur the ⟨heavy⟩ life-long responsibilities of making or marring a marriage. Treat the gods with respect, even if you detect them among your own children.

Seven or eight of them under one skin. *BO* 170[–171]   *W* 122

Our circumstance fit mythic costume. K 88[–89]

None acts absurdly; every one constitutionally true: nonsense will not keep its nature, if, you come into the humorist's point of view. &c.
                                                                                    [R 112]

Whence does the light come from that shines on things? Plotinus,
                                                              p. 452 [U 92] *E* 17

[10] "Solution of . . . *CO* 36", "Wo to . . . AB 129", and "Schellings preexistence, *V* 13" are struck through in ink with single vertical use marks; the passages cited are used in "Fate," *W*, VI, 47, 29, and 13. The passage cited in Journal CO, p. [223], is used in "Power," and AB, p. [79], in "Worship," *W*, VI, 70 and 222–223. With "Fate in . . . ages", cf. "Fate," *W*, VI, 15, and with "Wo to . . . Fate.", cf. also "Persian Poetry," *W*, VIII, 245.
     [11] In pencil.

The circumstance of circumstance is timing & placing.[12] &c. *CO* 85

———

Oceanic working of nature, which accumulates a momentary individual, as she forms a momentary wave in a running sea.[13] [LM 29,
S (Salvage) 163]
[5] We read for Fate, J 121.   Fate takes in holidays. J 131,
Temperament. Black eyes build roads for blue to ride in. W 68
Quarrels would not exist, if they could be reconciled. G 59, 86,
Universal triumph of Genus over Individual. W 68
Freedom is frivolous beside the tyranny of our Genius. [R 98, JK 29]

———

Animalcule system, ferocious maggot & military grub who bite & tear,
yet make up the fibre & texture of nobler creatures. *BO* 11
Open a new chamber in the brain, & what then? *CO* 243, 146

———

Most men ⟨are⟩& women are merely one couple more. *CO* 31

———

Election by weight   *CO* 40

———

Some men have several tickets. CO 4

———

Heterogeneity, or the man that is *not* felt to the centre of Copernican
System   *CO* 72
The representative men of Boston, Lowell, Taunton, &c   CO 8⟨9⟩7

———

Which are realities? & who is wanted? CO 170

———

People made now cannot be made next millennium   CO 175

———

You can't detach Tom without injustice. *CO* 201

———

Michel de Bourges   *CO* 222[–223]

———

[12] "Seven or . . . skin." is used in "Fate," *W*, VI, 10, "nonsense will . . .
view." in "Powers and Laws of Thought," *W*, XII, 54, and "The circumstance . . .
placing." in "Social Aims," *W*, VIII, 83.
[13] "Oceanic . . . sea." is marked in the left margin with two vertical pencil
lines, perhaps use marks.

⟨In n⟩Nature hits the white as seldom as we. *TU* 180, *AZ* 43 [14]

Nature's severity in levelling. *AZ* 136, *TU* 170

Fate the Schoolmaster   *AZ* 177   ↑Sig. Quadro↓

Text of life & gloss of dreams   U 127
Parasites. *TU* 67   Important passage on Reform. *S* [(Salvage)] 64
                                                                [J 19] [15]
Inevitable civilization   LM 64

[6] *Fate*   Goitres follow strata. C 253
No luck; all the fortune earlier than action, in the race & the brain.
                                                    GH 92[–94]

"a flame tormented by the wind" [MFO 1]

Newton's theory of transparency [H 16, RS 162]   ↑??↓

Nerves pervade the Universe, & ⟨c⟩the world is a company where
every atom is guaranteed by all the stockholders. Not a particle, but
the sun must answer for; and the sun cannot lose a ray, ⟨without⟩ but
every worm will suffer. This new experiment of telegraphing by
means of snails ⟨is true or fa⟩ may be true or fabulous in its details, but
is founded in truth.[16]

[14] "The representative . . . CO 170" and "⟨In n⟩Nature . . . AZ 43" are
struck through in ink with single vertical use marks. With "Temperament . . . ride
in.", "The representative . . . Taunton, &c", and "People made . . . millenium",
cf. "Fate," *W*, VI, 9, 42, and 15. "Most men . . . more." and the passage cited in
Journal CO, p. [40], are used, *ibid.*, pp. 11 and 14. The passage cited in BO, p. [11],
is used in "Address to the Adelphic Union of Williamstown College," August 15,
1854. With "Heterogeneity . . . System", cf. "Beauty," *W*, VI, 283. For the French
quotation from Michel de Bourges, CO, pp. [222]–[223], see p. [3] above. TU,
p. [180], is torn out, but with "Nature hits . . . we.", cf. "Considerations by the
Way," *W*, VI, 250.
    [15] "Parasites. *TU* 67" is struck through in ink with a vertical use mark. "Im-
portant passage . . . *S* 64" is enclosed by a three-sided box to separate the entries. The
passages cited in Jounrnal TU, pp. [170] and [67], are used in "Fate," *W*, VI, 35
and 45.
    [16] "Newton's theory . . . in truth." is struck through in ink with two vertical,

All above as below is organized, & into the inmost being man may not enter. ⟨O⟩*CO* 208

Illusion, *CO* 247–8

Seven or eight rolled up in each skin. *BO* 170[–171]
As a tree is a congeries of living vegetables, so a man of living spirits.
B 26

Who dare say how far, how high, this organism may go. All above as below is organized [*CO* 208]
If he is, he is wanted. *BO* 170[17] ↑Every man wants a bit of Fate
as *abgrund*. *S* 163[–164]↓
The Locomotive, Destiny   *S* 158

[7] Power.   Equal to whatever may happen. [*BO* 193]
   ⟨Th⟩He stands well on the world. *BO* 197
↑*AZ* 20, 22,↓
      Where is the shop of power. *CO* 240

Instinct. Marchez sans le peuple, et vous marchez dans les tenêbres. La Providence n'est pas avec vous.
CO 222 [223]
   Election goes by avoirdupois weight. — *CO* 40

Farmers   *AZ* 2⟨1⟩5,

Working-talent. *AZ* 31   *BO* 112, 162,

---

discontinuous, curving use marks. The two question marks following "transparency" are in pencil. The passage cited in Journal GH, pp. [92]–[94], is used in "Aristocracy," *W*, X, 44–45.
   [17] "If he . . . *BO* 170" is in pencil. A three-sided box around "Every man . . . *S* 163" separates the entries. With "Illusion, *CO* 247–8" and "Seven or . . . skin.", cf. "Fate," *W*, VI, 40 and 10. "If he . . . wanted." is used in "Considerations by the Way," *W*, VI, 252.

Reaction. They who govern themselves govern others. [AZ 100]
↑[Fate in ideas   *GH* 108↓
Feats   TU [9–]10

Conversion of come & go of pendulum into steady push. *CO* 213

———

Boy's speech went forth clean, wholly disengaged. *CO* 73

———

Farmer's Power. A Moore   CD 94

———

Power & Circumstance. *CD* 141 [18]
The art of playing on men. CO 63
Fouché said of Napoleon, "ce n'est pas là un homme à arreter; e⟨t⟩ncore, ne suis je pas ⟨la⟩l'homme qui l'arrétera." [T 94]

———

I do not wonder at feeble men being advocates for slavery. No feeling of worthiness assures them of their own safety⟨. I⟩in a new state of things. &c   *V* 75
But strong men should be abolitionists   V 76

[8]   *Power*
Muscadins, *V* 44

"Will is the measure of Power." *Proclus* [R 29]

Power fraternizes with power; & wishes you not to be like "*him*," but your[s]elf. Echo *them*, & they will see fast enough that you have nothing for them. They came to you, for something new. A man loves a man.[19] [R 56]

———

[18] The passages cited in Journal BO, p. [193], and CO, p. [223], are used in "Power," *W*, VI, 56 and 70; with the first, cf. also "Worship," *W*, VI, 232. The passage in CO, p. [40], and "Power & Circumstance." are used in "Fate," *W*, VI, 14. The passage cited in BO, p. [112], is used in "Wealth," *W*, VI, 91–92, and those in TU, pp. [9]–[10], and CO, p. [213], in the lecture "Economy," March 27, 1851. The passages cited in BO, p. [197], and AZ, p. [22], are used in "Farming," *W*, VII, 153. With "Where is . . . power.", cf. "Inspiration," and with "They who . . . others.", cf. "Greatness," *W*, VIII, 269 and 320. The passage cited in CD, p. [94], is used in "Country Life," *W*, XII, 145.

[19] " 'Will is . . . loves a man.' is struck through in ink with a diagonal use mark. " 'Will is . . . Power.' " is used in "Result," *W*, V, 305, and "Powers and Laws of Thought," *W*, XII, 46. "Power fraternizes . . . new." is used, *ibid.*, p. 30.

"I have heard⟨,⟩ my master say," says Confucius, "that a man cannot fully exhaust the abilities of his nature" [20] [R 123₂]

Add to what was said of M. Angelo's ochres, [AZ 230] M. Angelo's skeleton sketches, and Page's modelling his figure in clay. [TU 186]

Incredibility of Animal spirits. U 24

Diners at the American House. *CO* 4

Adherence — *CO* 65

The steady push. *CO* 21⟨2⟩3.

The daguerrotypist sets his boy in freedom ⟨by⟩ & expression by a lively song. [CO 63]
The art of playing on men [CO 63]

Is power contagious?   The chief want of life is some one to make me do what I can. *BO* 109 [21]

[9] "My experience, that men of great talents are apt to do nothing, for want of vigor." [*Memoirs of Sir Thomas Fowell*] Buxton [(London, 1848),] p 166

"Vigor, ⟨energy,⟩ [22] resolution, firmness of purpose, these carry the day." [*Ibid.*, p. 166]

Hunter, surgeon. "Is there one who *will* conquer,—that kind of man never fails" [*ibid.*, p. 167]

"And all that cowards have is mine." [TU 88]

[20] This sentence, marked in the left margin with a vertical line in pencil, is used as the motto for "Social Aims," *W*, VIII, 78. See also p. [34] below.
[21] With "M. Angelo's . . . sketches," cf. "Power," *W*, VI, 72–73. "Page's modelling . . . clay." is used in "Powers and Laws of Thought," *W*, XII, 49. The passage cited in Journal U, p. [24], is used in "Society and Solitude," *W*, VII, 12. The passage cited in CO, p. [65], is used in "Fate," and "The chief . . . can." in "Considerations by the Way," *W*, VI, 24 and 272.
[22] Canceled in pencil.

Napoleon aggressive. AZ 249

———

"Troops act, as they are handled at first." *Eng. paper*

———

Why should we who believe in the Intellect ever speak to a public meeting, without yielding the company a spark of lightning, some word of transforming, upbuilding truth? [CO 63]

———

Heterogeneity   *CO* 72

———

Where is the shop of power? *CO* 240

———

Power, facility, *CO* 260

———

Manners of Power. *BO* 18,

———

Give me the leader, you may have the baggage. *BO* 138

———

Govern self, govern others. *BO* 117

———

Equal to whatever may happen [BO 193]

———

Does he stand well in the world? *BO* 197, *AZ* 20, 25, ↑22↓ *O* 152,

———

One, two, & three shocks. *BO* 160

———

We do not try our amulets & talismans. *BO* 15

Wild liberty develops iron conscience; centrip. centrif. Z[A] 115 [23]
[10] We live & grow by use: sit down to write with weak eyes, & awaken your imagination; your eyes will be strong enough. [24] [B 26]

---

[23] " 'Troops act . . . first.' " is used in "Behavior," and "Equal to . . . happen" and "Wild liberty . . . conscience;" in "Power," *W*, VI, 184, 56, and 64. The passage cited in Journal BO, p. [160], is used in "Poetry and Imagination," *W*, VIII, 72. For "Heterogeneity *CO* 72", see p. [5] above; for "Does he . . . 22", see p. [7] above. "22" is added in pencil, directly beneath "25,".

[24] This sentence is marked in the left margin with two vertical lines in pencil, possibly use marks.

If you wish to know what nobody knows, read what every body reads, just one year after it is published. [B 55] ↑printed in *"Books"*?↓ [25]

———

Gipseys more attractive than apostles. K 64
    Barbour's verse, *A* 25

———

Affirmative Action⟨,⟩ rare. *RS* 200   to follow the passage about *Imbecility* in Lecture

———

I like people who can do things.[26]

———

Inaction disgusts. We bow, but 'tis a farewell bow; it is never complimented with a summons   *RS* 30

———

[11] [27] ⟨R⟩ 2   E[lizabeth] Hoar
        2   Mrs Lowell   Ripley
        2   Dr Frothingham   Alger
        4   Dr Dewey   ⟨Bartol⟩
        2   Mrs Cobb
        2   Miss Peabody
        2   Sarah Clarke
        2   Theodore Parker
        2   J Nash
        4   C T Jackson

[25] "printed" is enclosed on the left-hand side by a three-sided boxed line. With "If you . . . published.", cf. "Books," *W*, VII, 196.

[26] "*RS* 200" is followed by a vertical use mark in ink. With "the passage about *Imbecility*", cf. "Power," *W*, VI, 54. "I like . . . things." is used in "Powers and Laws of Thought," and "The Celebration of Intellect," *W*, XII, 47 and 119.

[27] P. [11] is in pencil. This list may represent persons to whom Emerson intended to send lecture tickets. Of the names not previously mentioned or easily identified, "J Nash" may be Joshua Nash, husband of Paulina Tucker; "Dr Solger" is probably Reinhold Solger (1820–1866), scholar and author, who arrived in New York with Kossuth early in December, 1851, and who was for a time a teacher in Concord; "W Robinson" is probably William Stevens Robinson (1818–1876), Concord-born journalist with antislavery views; "Professor Brown" may be James Baker Brown, Concord schoolmaster; and "Alger" may be William Rounseville Alger (1822–1905), Unitarian clergyman in Roxbury, Mass. "Professor Brown" is circled in ink, and "Ripley . . . ⟨Bartol⟩" is partly enclosed on the left by a curved ink line.

2   Dr Solger
1   G[eorge] S Phillips
2   G B Emerson
2   S G Ward
2   P. B. Ripley
1   G. P. Bradford
2   A B Alcott
2   Dr Hedge
2   C A Bartol
1   W Robinson
     Professor Brown
3   A Adams

[12] *Fate*
Every creature has a tail. The brain has not yet availed to drop that respectable appendage. *O* 6

[13] Wealth
Wilkins bought the Bhagavat; Petrarch learned Greek; Elgin bought the Marbles: Wallraf the Medusa.

[14] Wealth

———

    Lord Mansfield's saying   *CO* 105

———

    Easier to invest the first million than the second. *CO* 105

———

    In England, Crystal Palace must pay for itself. *CO* 154

———

Credit eternal; & will be more & more. *J* 33 [JK 37]

———

Every sound man stands for the support of 14 or 15 sick. R 120

———

The farmer's dollar. *U* 63[–64]
Shingling. *65 U*

———

Puzzle of currency remains. *CO* 291, 292

———

High salaries for talent in the mills. *BO* 144

——

Value of farm compared with city values. *BO* 145

——

If a p⟨air⟩ear sells for a shilling, it cost a shilling to raise it. If the best securities offer 12 per cent for money, they have just 6 per cent of insecurity.

The worth of any thing,
Is so much money as 'twill bring. [AZ 141]

——

"Grave moral deterioration that follows our empty exchequer." [AZ 162]

——

We must have an intellectual property in property *BO* 37

——

Wealth of Boston & Massachusetts. *BO* 53

——

Value of cultivated labor; superintendant. *BO* 144

——

Inflated values. Boston, & Farm. *BO* 145 [28]
Eng. & American love money. who does not? *BO* 178

——

Attractive are house, orchard, hillside. *CD* 44

——

Man must be dressed in house, grove, statue. *AB* 62 [29]

——

J. Richardson U 63

[28] "If a p⟨air⟩ear . . . insecurity." and the passage cited in Journal U, pp. [63]–[64], are used in "Wealth," *W*, VI, 108 and 101–102. "High salaries . . . *BO* 144" and "If a . . . insecurity." are struck through in pencil with single vertical use marks, which Emerson then connected through "Value of . . . *BO* 145". "Wealth of . . . Farm. *BO* 145" is struck through in pencil with a vertical use mark. With the passages cited in BO, p. [145], cf. *ibid.*, p. 102. With the passage cited in R, p. [120], cf. "Considerations by the Way," *W*, VI, 250. "We must . . . property" is used in "Culture," *W*, VI, 158. With the passages cited in CO, pp. [154] and [291], cf. "Wealth," *W*, V, 156 and 168–169; " 'Grave moral . . . exchequer.' " is used, *ibid.*, p. 154. With the passage cited in J, p. [33], cf. "Social Aims," and with CO, p. [292], cf. "Poetry and Imagination," *W*, VIII, 84 and 37.
[29] With this passage, cf. "Society and Solitude," *W*, VII, 10.

[15] *Economy*
Sylvan's Garden. CD 80
You have worn out your shoes, but thatched your body: you have worn out oxen, but their strength is in the farm: you have worn out three horses; but the victory is yours. CO 131

———

Economy, *V* 9
Of B⟨y⟩uying woodland   V 20

———

Farmer's dollar heavy. U 63[–64]

———

Levi Bartlett's farm. [TU 149]

———

Nature's frugality. Neither can you waste a drop or a splinter in her house. She ↑re-↓distributes her elements, when you burn or throw away, as a compositor re-distributes his types from the form.

———

Crystal palace must pay. CO 154

———

A bag of coffee is good as money at interest [BO 53]

———

Ascending investment   BO 90;
The young minister's tulips. CO 46

Wealth
     The puzzle of currency remains for rich & poor. I never saw a rich man who thought he knew whence the hard times came.
But Free trade must be right, & the annexation of England to America. And as for tariff, that interests only a few gentlemen in Boston. Railroad capital exceeds Manufac.
But we shall not understand Polit. Econ. until Beranger & Burns write it in songs. [CO 291–292] [30]

    [30] "You have . . . yours.", "Farmer's dollar . . . U 63", "Nature's frugality . . . CO 154", and "Ascending investment . . . CO 46" are struck through in pencil with single vertical use marks. With "You have . . . yours.", "Nature's frugality . . . form.", and the passage cited in Journal BO, p. [90], cf. the lecture "Economy." With "Nature's frugality . . . form.", cf. also R, p. [77], and with BO, p. [90], cf. also "Wealth," *W*, VI, 125. For the passages cited in U, pp. [63]–[64], and CO, pp. [154] and [291]–[292], see p. [14] above.

[16]   *Prudence*   *Economy*

Timeliness. When the husbandman comes out of his door what a train of invisible works are behind him! He has done them all in their hour. The North wind blows at sea three days. The seaman has kept his ship in such trim that he has got every mile it would yield, from it; and he knows, that, at the end of it, there are fresh relays of the same wild horses all along the road, to his port.

Reticence—don't be leaky; or ridden, & forced to say what you do not wish to say.

———

Don't take the stiffening out of a man.

———

A libertine is a dupe. C 38   B 16, 21,

———

The reaction of the end on all the means. *CO* 248

———

Shoeleather's use   *CO* 131

———

Nature's low fare system. *CO* 147 [31]

———

The manifest economy of seeing that all jobs or feats which consume so much time (like fine carving with a penknife) shall be in the line of your genius or general plan. Webster may well spend a month on a petty lawsuit of ⟨a⟩ trifling amount, provided it involves history & principles that will be [17] treasures to him a little further on in his career. ⟨Nor⟩ That recommends the office of teaching to the young graduate of our colleges, that the act of teaching is the best ⟨review⟩ ↑rehearsal↓ & ⟨certifying⟩ ↑reprinting↓ of the elements of grammar & ↑of↓ figures in his memory.

   Newton   The ⟨arch⟩ miracles of Chemistry which make our material power were ↑never↓ got in grand theatres, but in ⟨mean places⟩ ↑much practice↓ with few & simple elements. ⟨But⟩ ↑And↓ the

———

[31] "Timeliness . . . port." and "Shoeleather's use . . . *CO* 147" are struck through in pencil with single vertical use marks. With the passages cited in Journal CO, pp. [131] and [147], cf. the lecture "Economy." The phrase "don't be leaky;" occurs in CO, p. [213]; cf. "Behavior," *W*, VI, 195–196. For "A libertine . . . 21," see p. [34] below.

best paid works *off a man's line*,[32] however well paid, must bankrupt him, & make him useless to the world.

———

Faraday's subjects were a teakettle, a chimney, fire, ashes, &c

———

[18]–[19] [blank]
[20] Culture

———

The art now lets him ⟨do⟩make in one year six pictures   *CO* 110

———

Drill[n] makes courage. *CO* *112*[–113] ↑& Marshal Lannes' opinion.
                                    [V 72] *Morals.* 51↓

———

Mechanical and spiritual of course become one meaning at last. God is geometer. See what I wrote of the mill: and this is to be the doctrine of the Nat. Hist of Intellect. See what is said of manufacturing[,] the genius of the people. *CO* 115
Politics poor tinkering. Anticipate by Education. *CO* 162

———

We have not learned the art to avail ourselves of the virtues & graces of others. *TU* 41

———

Melioration.   Today's people will not be organizable at a riper epoch.
                    CO 175   S [(Salvage)] 106[33] [V 61]
We all believe, too, in a good stock of kenned folk. *CO* 181
    One of these days, we shall do without this dismal multitude, & have the family instead of the mob. Leisures. *CO* 121, 77,
                              ↑A census conveniently small↓

———

Characteristics of the XIX Century   *CO* 49

———

"No happiness but in intellect & virtue." *CO* 56

———

   [32] The underlining has been added. With "And the . . . world.", cf. "Wealth," *W*, VI, 112, and the lecture "Economy."
   [33] "& Marshal . . . 51", "Politics . . . *CO* 162", and *"Melioration* . . . S 106" are struck through in ink with single vertical use marks. With the passages cited in Journal CO, pp. [112]–[113], [162], and [175], and Notebook Morals, p. [51], cf. "Culture," *W*, VI, 139, 140, 166, and 139.

Low tone. *CO* 58

Men of one idea.   Conceit   *RS* 65

Christianity was European Culture. *RS* 142

Trifles. RS 42   CO 280, ↑254,↓
    Reaction of things. *CO* 273, ↑28↓
Melioration. Wrenching of paltry means to grand results. *CO* 270 [34]

[21] ↑CULTURE↓

    'Keep the body open' *and the Mind*   CD 23
Rotation is the remedy for loaded individuals. [CD 36]

What have we to do with reading that ends in reading? *CD* 50 [49]

Melioration. The hope of Socrates. *CD* 60
        Owen & Fourier say, we shall make men yet of the right sort.
        S [(Salvage)] 106
        LM 64   Civility inevitable as we.

Learn the lesson which all our arts teach the mind   CD 122

Man a manufacturer.↑chiffonier.↓ makes sense out of nonsense   wealth
out of rags, time out of space, & day out of night [35]

---

[34] With "Low tone. *CO* 58", struck through in ink with two vertical use marks, and the passage cited in Journal CO, p. [254], cf. "Culture," *W*, VI, 150–151 and 153. "Christianity . . . Culture." is used in "Worship," *W*, VI, 206. " 'No happiness . . . virtue.' " is used in "Works and Days," *W*, VII, 179. CO, p. [270], is torn out, but with "Wrenching . . . results.", cf. *ibid.*, pp. 160 and 166; cf. also CO, p. [271], and BO, p. [17].
[35] With "Man a . . . night", struck through in ink with a vertical use mark and marked in the left margin in pencil with a large square bracket, cf. "Works and Days," *W*, VII, 161, Journal BO, p. [73], and AB, p. [94]. With the passage cited in CD, p. [23], cf. "Persian Poetry," *W*, VIII, 247. With "Rotation is . . . individuals.", cf. "Uses of Great Men," *W*, IV, 19.

It is a⟨n a⟩reason for *travelling*, that we use up ⟨f⟩ our scenery, our environment, after a time, & cease to be excited by it to rhyme or to writing. That is, our youth is gone. Then go to new country, to new men, to Englishmen, Frenchmen, to Polynesia, to Typee, & you have a new youth, a second, a third youth.   — Travelling   see R 76

Damascus steel. *CO* 210

Men are as their relatedness is. A fop carried a few miles out of town is as good as killed: but Archimedes, Newton, Goethe, are felt to the centre of the Copernican System.

Culture of Calamity. *CO* 221
Capital secret of Culture is, to know the few great points. *CO*   221, 48,[36]

[22] Culture
Infirm class. American scholars, fit only for sons in law. *U* 31
Totality   F 28
Friends too are stoves   F 108
End of Culture, Self-creation. *CO* 253

Culture can spare nothing; wants all the material. *CO* 261 [37]

The manners of the celestial mind. *TU* 230

Hazlitt   *AZ* 199

Culture will absorb the hells also. *CO* 287, 289

[36] "It is . . . R 76" is struck through in ink with two diagonal use marks. With the passage cited in Journal R, p. [76], cf. "Culture," *W*, VI, 145. With "Culture of . . . *CO* 221", struck through in ink with a vertical use mark, cf. *ibid.*, p. 161. With "Men are . . . System.", marked in pencil in both margins with single vertical lines, cf. "Beauty," *W*, VI, 283, and p. [5] above. With the passage cited in CO, p. [48], cf. "Illusions," *W*, VI, 325.
[37] With "End of . . . *CO* 253", marked in pencil with a single vertical line in the left margin and two vertical lines in the right margin, cf. "Education," *W*, X, 131. "Culture can . . . material.", struck through in ink with a vertical use mark, is used in "Culture," *W*, VI, 166.

And lower kinds will at last go out. *CO* 288 [38]

———

With culture selfdirection develops. *CO* 290

———

The selfacting siphon. *CO* 278

———

Culture from Calamity: Ben Jonson to his Muse   *LI* [40]
And Dr Johnson's "Primogeniture makes but one fool in a family"
⟨Fine society starves us⟩; people wish to be amused, but I do not wish
to be amused. [O 80]

———

Currency   *LM* 30   Merchant & Scholar   *AZ* 252
Hazardous Education   *AZ* 177   Sig Quadro

———

Mead! [n] Meliorate! 'tis the law of nature.

———

Manners   ⟨r⟩true refinement. CO 53 [39]

[23] A man in pursuit of greatness feels no little wants.
The greatest geniuses have died ignorant of their power & influence
on the arts & sciences. [MME 1, 121–122]

Very few men can be said to be disengaged from the lingering
quadruped organization. After an attack of rheumatism, if the weather
becomes damp & raw, we still feel the old cramp. And so, when our
fears & affections are addressed, we still feel the remains of fox &
snake & goat & tiger in our meliorated blood. We call these millions
men, but they are not yet men.

[38] "Culture will . . . *CO* 288" is struck through in ink with a vertical use
mark. "Culture will . . . 289" is marked in pencil with a vertical line in the left
margin; two vertical pencil lines are drawn between "also." and "*CO*". With the
passages cited in Journal CO, pp. [287], [289], and [288], cf. "Culture," *W*, VI,
166 and 165.
[39] "Culture from . . . *LI*", struck through in ink with two vertical use marks,
is used in "Culture," *W*, VI, 161–162. "Mead . . . CO 53" is marked in pencil
in the right margin with two vertical lines. "Mead . . . nature." is used, *ibid.*, p.
140; cf. also "The Sovereignty of Ethics," *W*, X, 188. "And Dr . . . family'",
struck through in ink with a diagonal use mark, is used in "Aristocracy," *W*, V,
196. "people wish to be amused . . . amused." is used in "Considerations by the
Way," *W*, VI, 247.

I stand here for humanity   TU 230
Popularity is for dolls   D 264 [40]

Highest Culture   *BO* 13, 14, 15.
And true Culture   AZ 270 [41]

[24] Half engaged in the soil, Man needs all the music that can be brought to disengage him. If Love, if War with his /drum/cannonade/, if ⟨Ch⟩ Want with his lash, if Trade with his money, if ⟨r⟩Christianity with its Charity, ↑Art with portfolio↓ can set his dull nerves in vibration, &, by tapping on the Chrysalis, can break its walls, & let the new creature emerge, erect & free[,] that is something; that is much; but not all. He is yet the subject of culture only to be the subject of culture again. He has yet clogs, & earth, & fate, to get rid of; he is to shed this poor belly which drags him down. Culture[,] Religion are to put wings on his feet; wings on his brain. The age of the Belly is to go out, & the Age of the Brain & of the Heart to come in. [42]

[25] You are to send him,—(the poor boy, the poor girl that is born,) — to effective schoolmasters, but the least ⟨ar⟩of these is ⟨F⟩Books. Books surely (o yes, give them all the geography, figures, copy slips, & language, you can,) but Love[,] red love[,] is to teach them tears; Want is to put them to starve & pine; Ambition is to set them on Vigils; Ice & snow, River, Sea, & Mountain chains, are the toys & barrows & tools they are to work with. The Animals, also the inferior races, the slaves, ↑the legal & the real,↓ and the army of people with

---

[40] "A man . . . wants.", struck through in ink with a diagonal use mark, is used in "Culture," *W*, VI, 154. With "Very few . . . men.", struck through in ink with a wavy, diagonal use mark, cf. *ibid.*, p. 165. "Popularity . . . D 264" is in pencil. The sentence is used, *ibid.*, p. 163. With the passage cited in Journal TU, p. [230], cf. "Behavior," *W*, VI, 197, and C, p. [58].
[41] "Highest Culture . . . AZ 270" is marked in pencil in the right margin with a vertical line. The passages cited in Journal BO, pp. [14] and [15], are used in "Works and Days," *W*, VII, 163.
[42] "Half engaged . . . all.", struck through in ink with a wavy, diagonal use mark, and "The age . . . come in.", struck through in ink with two diagonal use marks, are used in "Culture," *W*, VI, 165–166.

whom he deals[,] the customer, the enemy, the creditor, the patron, the client,   all these are tutors[.]

Then the Carnival[,] the Masquerade. Nobody drops his domino[;] the unities[,] the illusions of the piece, it would be an impertinence to break[.] [43]

[26]   Conduct of Life
     Let us yield gracefully to the young   TU 236

How bad we are! TU 242   *AZ* 250   The Guano Age   *CO* 28[–29]
Fribbles & whigs   *CO* 26, 42, 92,   *RS* 144

How to live with unfit companions. *CO* 11,
Timeliness   *CO* 18
Prudence   *CO* 2, 11, 13, 18, 48, 58, 105,
Doctrine of Leasts. *RS* 45 [44]

_____

But Books? Literature does not represent Nature. *CD* 50

_____

The savage rides on the rollers, the ⟨v⟩Canadian Voyageur on the rapids[;] ⟨the joy of⟩ this delicate guiding is great pleasure. Cannot we guide life, & "see what we foresaw"? [45] The game is his who has the most presence of mind & sees what he foresaw. The alphabet really contains all the posterior combinations, and life might be anticipated in the closet; as Leverrier said, "the planet is geometrically there, Look for it ⟨if⟩, who will." [46]

[27] How slowly we bethink ourselves, or arrive at ⟨the first⟩ even

[43] With "red love . . . Vigils;", struck through in ink with a diagonal use mark, cf. "Culture," *W*, VI, 165. "Then the Carnival . . . break" is used in "Illusions," *W*, VI, 312–313.
[44] The passage cited in Journal CO, pp. [28]–[29], is used in "Fate," CO, p. [92], in "Wealth," CO, p. [11], in "Considerations by the Way," and CO, p. [48], in "Illusions," *W*, VI, 16–17, 108, 270, and 325. With RS, p. [45], cf. "Uses of Great Men," *W*, IV, 6.
[45] Wordsworth, "Character of the Happy Warrior," l. 54.
[46] With "as Leverrier . . . will.'", cf. Journal TU, p. [10], and "Success," *W*, VII, 286.

the premises, or stipulations of the first necessity! My feet must not be in the air. I must have basis. I must have the courage, which only the knowledge that I have means of support, weapons of defence, weapons of aggression, can give.

What questions an autobiography would answer   AB 110

A personal influence towers up. *CO* 284

---

[28] *Culture*

"Gold teaspoons constrain us, if we are used to silver"
                                        ↑*Goethe*↓ [CO 254]

Knowledge of Greek letters mark of a gentleman

See *Eckermann*[47] II 46

Questions are always about to be asked: You[n] need not know them, until you have gone up to a certain plane. Then you must answer them, or lose caste.

Yesterday, X was asked the meaning of *Entelecheia*. It was no great shame ⟨that⟩ to such as him that he did not know: but if ↑S.↓ ⟨S⟩ ↑or N. or *A*.↓ had been in the company, he must know or lose rank. *Solidarity*. Question arises concerning Martial, Catullus, Tibullus, & Persius. It cannot be hid: — no silence will hide— how much or how little he knows.

Eckermann.

"The audacity & grandeur of Byron must certainly tend towards culture. Take care not to be always looking for it in the decidedly pure & moral. Everything that is great promotes cultivation, as soon as we are aware of it."

[29] Unpretendingness is a mark of culture; and so is retentiveness. Don't be leaky. "Have more than thou showest, speak less

[47] Goethe, *Conversations of Goethe with Eckermann and Soret*, trans. John Oxenford, 2 vols. (London, 1850). For *"Entelecheia."*, see Journal RS, p. [27].

than thou knowest." [48] It is important part of culture, that you shall be able to articulate what you are & know. But it is also good to hold your tongue.

He who has spoken a thing,— that thing seems less to be in him[.]

You are to have the ability so thoroughly that it needs no abutments of reputation
⟦The Illustrations in modern books mark the decline of art. 'Tis the dramdrinking of the eye, & candy for food.⟧
as whales & horses & elephants produced on the stage show decline of drama⟧

[*St Simon*]
"The golden age is not behind, but before us: it consists in the perfection of the social order. Our fathers have not seen it. Our children will realize it." [Z[A] 108] [49]

[30] Religion

———

Whiggery even is much his friend. CO 124

———

And out of paltriness is grandeur made. *CO* 270

———

We are born believing   *CO* 153

———

The reaction of a high aim. *CO* 248

———

Providence a rough rider, & does not admit of any whitewash, &c.
                                                            CO, 257

———

The overruling of paltriness to grand ends, as Acton farms make up the picture. *CO* 270.   *BO* 11[−12], 17, 57,   U 118,
        ↑Great effect by cheap means   RS 45↓   ↑199↓
The great Patience,   We lost the Election, & expected to lose, but we saw longevity in the cause. *CO* 54

[48] Shakespeare, *King Lear*, I, iv, 131–132. For "Don't be leaky.", see p. [16] above.
    [49] " 'The golden . . . us:" is used in "Resources," *W*, VIII, 142. "*St Simon*" is written vertically up in the left margin, from "seen it." to " 'The golden".

↑Patientia maxima   CO 167↓

Law-abiding,—yes, made to cohere. *BO* 17   *AZ* 251

The very love of life, so disproportioned to the particulars, points at immense reserves & possibilities. *BO* 34

Religion of W. L. F⟨.⟩↑isher↓   *BO* 41

———

Let a man's life be insured by his aim. *BO* 98, *Morals* 142, V 75, 76, 47
I am not afraid of accident as long as I am in my place. [AB 101] [50]

[31] Immortality. *BO* 147

Greatness   AZ 33
  Nor is life long enough for Friendship which is solemn & timeous
  affair. AZ 44

Reaction. They who govern themselves, govern others. [AZ 100] [51]
  ↑I am never beaten until I know I am beaten   CO 178
  How the Furies walk disguised. CD 76   AB 79
  What living creature slays or is slain [Y 167] AB 83↓

⟨Religion.⟩ Quality and Amount. Affection gives the first; intellect, the second. Fine disposition essential as talent. AZ 272 See also AZ 279

———

A good writer will allow full swing to his skepticism, will dip his pen

[50] The passages cited in Journal CO, p. [153], BO, p. [17], AZ, p. [251], BO, p. [98], Notebook Morals, p. [142], and AB, p. [101], are used in "Worship," *W*, VI, 203, 202–203, 232, 235, and 232. The passage cited in CO, p. [257], is used in "Fate," and BO, pp. [11]–[12], in "Considerations by the Way," *W*, VI, 8 and 256. With "Great effect . . . means" in BO, pp. [17] and [57], cf. "Works and Days," *W*, VII, 160, 166, and 178. For CO, p. [270], see p. [20] above. With the passages cited in RS, pp. [45] and [199], cf. "Uses of Great Men," *W*, IV, 6.

[51] The passage cited in Journal BO, p. [147], is used in "Immortality," *W*, VIII, 336, and AZ, p. [33], in "The Superlative," *W*, X, 174. "Nor is . . . affair." is used in "Considerations by the Way," *W*, VI, 273. For "Reaction . . . others.", see p. [7] above.

in the blackest of the pot, because he does not fear to fall in. ——
AZ 272   CO 257   ↑W 122↓

———

Providence appears to the ⟨man tr⟩husband in tradesman's bills, & to his dame, in coming & going of cook & chambermaid. *CO* 217

———

But what a day dawns, when we have taken to heart the doctrine of Faith! ⁿ to prefer as a better investment being to doing, being to seeming; logic to rhythm & to display; the year to the day, the life to the year, character to performance   and come to know that Justice will be done us, & if our genius is slow then the term will be long.[52]

[32] Every god is good, & every god is alive yet. *CO* 48

———

Let us sacrifice to the immortal gods. ⟨CO⟩RS 63

———

Faith   *RS* 112

———

our Teutonic Philosophers. *RS* 176

———

Richard of Devizes. *RS* 275   BO 81,   ↑*Index* [Major] 119↓

———

What is stronger than fire? Σ 43 [AB 99]

———

Scholar's courage should grow out of his conversation with spiritual nature, not out of brawn, &c. ⟨C⟩AB 101[–102]
Faith in Nature; Daemonology; V 36, 43,
Faith, totality, not medicines. F 28
Key to the riddle. *CO* 36[–37]
"Piety an essential condition of Science"   AZ 257

———

Grandeurs do not ultimate themselves in grandeurs, but in paltriness
BO 15, 16, 17.

---

[52] The passage cited in Journal CO, p. [178], "A good . . . fall in.", struck through in pencil with a vertical use mark, and "But what . . . long.", struck through in pencil and in ink with single, vertical use marks, are used in "Worship," *W*, VI, 234–235, 201, and 215–216. With the passages cited in AB, p. [79], and *W*, p. [122], cf. *ibid.*, pp. 222–223 and 202. "Fine disposition . . . talent." is used in "Considerations by the Way," *W*, VI, 264.

"Every seed will grow." [53]

Every thing has its judgment day. CD 76
The young not forsaken, but later, mirac. protection withdrawn   B 46

[33] Fear God, & where you go men shall think they walk ⟨in⟩ in hallowed Cathedrals. ↑Worship↓
"any absorbing passion has a noble effect to deliver from the little coils & cares of every day." Heat, heat enough to surmount the friction of first addresses in society & crossing thresholds.

Question   "Will not commerce serve for Xy" &c   M M E [1] p 142

Christianity was European Culture. RS 142
Religion latent but great. AZ 30

For miraculous legends the youth of today has no ears.

Every sensual pleasure private & mortal   G 22
Choices in the street   E 259   G 23?

with culture selfdirection develops. [54]

The true does not come with jangle & contradiction, but it is what all sects accept, & what recommends their tenets to rightminded men.

---

[53] "Richard of . . . BO 81," is struck through in ink with two diagonal use marks. The passages cited in Journal RS, p. [275], BO, p. [81], V, p. [43], BO, p. [17], and " 'Every seed . . . grow.' " are used in "Worship," W, VI, 206, 205, 235, 202–203, and 231. The passage cited in CO, pp. [36]–[37], is used in "Fate," W, VI, 47. With CO, p. [48], cf. "Illusions," W, VI, 325. "Scholars courage . . . &c." is used in "Greatness," and " 'Piety . . . science' " in "Progress of Culture," W, VIII, 311–312 and 228. "Grandeurs . . . 17." is struck through in ink with a vertical use mark.

[54] "Fear God . . . Cathedrals." and " 'any absorbing . . . thresholds.", each struck through in ink with three diagonal use marks, are used respectively in "Worship," and "Considerations by the Way," W, VI, 231 and 259. "Christianity . . . AZ 30" is struck through in ink with a diagonal use mark; "Christianity . . . Culture." is used in "Worship," W, VI, 206. With "with culture . . . develops.", cf. "Progress of Culture," W, VIII, 217.

[34]   A libertine a dupe. C 28 [38] B 16, 21,
    Why gipseys more attractive than bishops. K 64
I have heard my master say, says Confucius, &c [R 123₂]

————

Reaction of end on all the means   CO 248

————

Liars also are true. W 68
We don't care for you, but for him behind you. O 323

————

In the progress of character, an increasing faith in the moral sentiment,
& a decreasing faith in propositions. [U 105]

————

"Napoleon visited those sick of the plague, in order to prove that the man
who cd. vanquish fear, cd. vanquish the plague also. And he was right— It is
incredible what force the moral will has, in such cases It penetrates, as it
were, the body, & puts it into a state of ⟨healthful⟩ activity, which repels
all hurtful influences. Fear is a state of indolent weakness & susceptibility,
wh. makes it easy for every foe to take possession of us" [55]
                                        Eckerman. II. 167

[35] ——
    If you succour the flagging spirits with wine or opium, the poem [n]
you write will characterise itself as Hotel Poetry. If you set out to
build a cheap dear house it will appear to all eyes as a cheap dear
house[.] [56]

————

[36] *Culture again*

They wish to be amused by thoughts, they wish to be amused by love
of nature, & they summon a lecturer or a poet to ⟨entertain⟩ ↑read to↓
them for an hour. ↑And so they do with a priest.↓ But the thoughts,
could they once enter, would revolutionise them, & turn the good

---

[55] The passage cited in Journal O, p. [323], "In the progress . . . propositions.", and " 'Napoleon . . . us' " are used in "Worship," *W*, VI, 228–229, 227,
and 232–233.
    [56] "If you . . . house" is used in "Worship," *W*, VI, 223.

patrons out of doors. The love of nature * They think these elemental forces   like fire, & like brandy & ether, are ⟨good⟩ pretty servants, but bad masters.

⟨The love of natur⟩There is no logic, no continuity in our living, but this dilettantism.

———

A successful man on the two platforms — *RS* 20 [57]
(is an important note to the Essay.)

[37] But of topics of culture. People do not wish to be cultivated. ↑If↓ neither[n] you who hear, nor I who speak, wish really to have our ⟨bareness⟩ ↑emptiness↓ exposed, ⟨and⟩ ↑or↓, mean, when convicted, to reform, what's the use ⟨then⟩ of talking?

———

Thus it will be seen, that, one after the other, all the material badges are dropped, like so much tattoo & heraldry, & those powers only worn which subjugate nature.[58]

———

> *Trifles.*   Gold spoons [CO 254]
> What if a child cried [G 146, U 141]
> New Englander hears every coffeemill. GH 21
> trinkets

[38] *Intellect*

God has only to open the new cellule in the brain & the naked are clothed   *CO* 146

———

I wish a "Farmer's Almanack" of the mental moods. &c. *CO* 244

———

* The love of nature received & obeyed would break up this bandbox of a parlour, shatter that rosewood piano, end this card case, & amiable idiocy of fashionable calls.

[57] "They wish . . . masters." is used in "Address to the Adelphic Union of Williamstown College." With the passage cited in Journal RS, p. [20], cf. "Success," *W*, VII, 311.
[58] With "Thus it . . . nature.", cf. "Greatness," *W*, VIII, 312.

Ah if we could only plant instruments & take the angles of the true glory!—245

——

Strong thinking dissolves the material Universe   *CO* 257

——

New Metaphysics. *CO* 258
The somewhat better than Homer & Shakspeare, 258, BO 13

——

    Memory & Inspiration. *CO* 76, 118

——

Excellence of fa⟨ir⟩eries to be small. Little head carries command power of assimilation   Swedenborg. &c   *CO* 77, 123
    And in each town, one man understands the town. *CO* 87   *BO* 55 [59]

——

Inspiration   *CO* 89   All that is done is done so

The Value of the new generalizations that two talkers reach.
                               BO 13↑–16,↓   *CO* 258,
    Sculptor's feat   AZ 194   ↑Feats *TU* [9–]10,
Pook's ship, a formula in numbers.   a feat.↓ [TU 10]
    Columbus's course to Veragua; a feat. BO 162 [162_2–163_2]
    Ben Jonson can the paper stain.   a feat   AZ 183
Intellect & Morals. Luther's push. *BO*.100,—[101–]102,[60] AZ 257,

[39] We must have intellectual property in all property, or we have it not truly. *BO* 37

——

[59] "Strong thinking . . . Universe" is used in "Fate," *W*, VI, 28. With the passages cited in Journal CO, pp. [123] and [87], and BO, p. [55], cf. *ibid.*, pp. 42–43. With the passage cited in CO, p. [244], cf. "Powers and Laws of Thought," and with CO, p. [76], cf. "Memory," *W*, XII, 11 and 95. With the passages cited in CO, p. [258], cf. "Poetry and Imagination," *W*, VIII, 63, and with CO, p. [77], cf. "Works and Days," *W*, VII, 176.
[60] The passage cited in Journal AZ, p. [194], is used in "Beauty," and that in BO, pp. [101]–[102], in "Power," *W*, VI, 302 and 62–63. The passage cited in CO, p. [89], is used in "Inspiration," *W*, VIII, 271. "Columbus's . . . feat." is used in "Success," *W*, VII, 285. For TU, pp. [9]–[10], see p. [7] above. "Sculptor's feat   AZ 194" and "Columbus's . . . AZ 183" are in a smaller hand and may have been added.

Abandon   BO 182, AZ 182

The little air chamber, the camarilla, of Heat, of Imagination, in the brain. *BO* 188[–189]

Affirmative talent. AZ 94, 9,[61]

Memory, Imagination, Reason, the same power. AZ 182   ↑CO 166↓
     Interest of these topics. AZ 271,

Every great fact in science divined by the presentiment of somebody.
           AZ 282

It is really surprising how few heads carry on society.
All that all the English think & say is in the Times Newspaper. AZ 68
No Terminus in Metaphysics. AZ 166,

———

Short & long. AZ 167 [62]

———

Fate or Nature does much in Intellect. AZ 176, 177,

———

     Genius is natural method, or real principle of order. Angelo
     Napoleon   distribute chaos into beauty   AZ 273

[40] Intellect
     Copernicus Newton Laplace Humboldt Archimedes   are
     always in the world   AZ 282

———

Do not keep on the stretch. Collapse of the Intellect. *CO* 194

———

Perpetual seesaw of mind & matter, *CO* 123, 241.

———

The subject indifferent; the reading indifferent. AB 80.

———

[61] To the right of this entry are two sums in ink.
[62] "We must . . . truly." is used in "Culture," *W*, VI, 158. With the passages cited in Journal AZ, pp. [94] and [282], cf. "Fate," *W*, VI, 10 and 18. With "All that . . . Newspaper.", cf. "The Times," *W*, V, 268. With the passage cited in AZ, p. [167], cf. "Memory," *W*, XII, 109.

Intellect sees by moral obedience   U 109   J 95 [63]

A thought would destroy most persons   AZ 248

[41] But where is great design in modern poetry?
$\qquad$ Y 189   K 81   CO 16, 63, O 327, V 19 [64]
Whole use of literature is moral.   AB 48

[42]–[43] [blank]
[44]   Miscellanies

Boston   CO 91–2, [91–93]

The immigration to America is sifted. CO 102

Currency, or else impassivity. CO 104, BO 82,

Byron suggests, like Greenough, partnership in literature [AZ 105]

Life a ⟨c⟩ one cent farce. CO 192

Law abiding, loyal, &c   BO 17, AZ 251,

Opportunity. O 294, 306, [65]

[45]–[46] [blank]

[63] With the passages cited in Journal AZ, p. [282], and CO, pp. [123] and [241], cf. "Fate," W, VI, 18 and 43. "Intellect sees . . . obedience" is used in "Discourse at Nantucket."

[64] "But where . . . poetry?" is used in "Literature," W, V, 256. The passages cited in Journal K, p. [81], CO, p. [16], and O, p. [327], are used in "Poetry and Imagination," W, VIII, 65, 63, and 33.

[65] With the passages cited in Journal CO, pp. [91]–[93], cf. "Boston," W, XII, 208 and 185–186, and with CO, p. [92], cf. also "Wealth," W, VI, 108. The passages cited in BO, p. [17], and AZ, p. [251], are used in "Worship," W, VI, 202–203. The passages cited in O, pp. [294] and [306], are used in "Poetry and Imagination," W, VIII, 70.

[46ₐ] Vocabularies

    Burton
    Cornelius Agrippa
    Rabelais   N 102[–103]

    Behmen

[46♭] English Literature
———

Bacon

⟨Johnson⟩ C⟨a⟩larendon
Burke
——————

Edda & Turner [66]
———

[47] Whilst I suffered at being seen where I was, I consoled myself with the delicious thought of the inconceivable number of places where I was not.[67]

[48] [blank]

[66] Pp. [46ₐ] and [46♭] are two small leaves laid in between pp. [46] and [47]; see p. 581 above. With "Vocabularies . . . Behmen", on p. [46ₐ], cf. Journal N, pp. [17]–[18], and "Books," W, VII, 190. With "Rabelais N 102", cf. "Quotation and Originality," W, VIII, 181. With p. [46♭], cf. "Books," W, VII, 206–209.

[67] "Whilst I . . . not.", struck through in ink with three vertical use marks, is used in "Society and Solitude," W, VII, 4.

Appendixes
Textual Notes
Index

Designation	Harvard edition
R (1843)	VIII, 349–441
RO Mind (1835)	V, 269–276
RS (1848–1849)	XI, 3–86
Scotland and England (1833)	IV, 209–235
Sea 1833 (1833)	IV, 236–248
Sea-Notes (1847)	X, 200–207
Sermons and Journal (1828–1829)	III, 119–158
Sicily (1833)	IV, 102–133
T (1834–?)	VI, 317–399
Trees[A:I] (1843–1847)	VIII, 518–533
Trees[A:II] (1847)	VIII, 534–549
TU (1849)	XI, 87–182
U (1843–1844)	IX, 3–92
Universe 1–7, 7[A], 8 (1820–1822)	I, 358–394
V (1844–1845)	IX, 93–181
W (1845)	IX, 182–255
Walk to the Connecticut (1823)	II, 177–186
Warren Lot (1849)	X, 489–493
Wide World 1 (1820)	I, 3–32
Wide World 2 (1820–1821)	I, 33–58
Wide World 3 (1822)	I, 59–90
Wide World 4 (1822)	I, 91–113
Wide World 6 (1822)	I, 114–158
Wide World 7 (1822)	II, 3–39
Wide World 8 (1822)	II, 40–73
Wide World 9 (1822–1823)	II, 74–103
Wide World 10 (1823)	II, 104–143
Wide World 11 (1823)	II, 144–176
Wide World 12 (1823–1824)	II, 187–213
Wide World XIII (1824)	II, 214–271
Xenien (1848, 1852)	X, 458–467
Y (1845–1846)	IX, 256–354
Z (1831? 1837–1838, 1841?)	VI, 287–316
Z[A] (1842–1843)	VIII, 309–348

Appendix II

A loose leaf found in Journal A between pages [40] and [41] and numbered "40ₐ" in pencil, omitted in printing Journal A (see *JMN*, IV, 283–284, n. 103, for description), contains notes for the 1837 lecture "Literature" and is printed below.

[40ₐ] [recto]
Literature is the conversion of action into thought for the delight of the Intellect. It is the turning into thought of what was done wit⟨t⟩hout thought.
It aims at ideal truth. But it is only approximation. The word can never cover the thing. You don't expect to describe a sunrise

⟨Art idealizes action⟩
Art actualizes thought
Literature idealizes action
Mission of the intellect

What changes —— [1]

[verso]   Literature part of Art
             Delight of a thought written [B] p 243
                     Otherism   216
                                      p 315
             genius apprizes us of *ours*   p 285

Literature
        Underlies a necessity
        Shakspear's relation to stage [B 165]
        Fit word comes at fit time [B 271]

        Literary Genius   p
            extent   p 310
            humanity   p 225

[1] "What changes ——" is upside down. With the rest of the page, cf. "Literature," *Lectures*, II, 55–56 and 59.

recognizes rejected thoughts [B 102]
Landor's word p 25
Talent & genius/Aladdin/p 81
Consists in new Sight   p 38 [2]

[2] "Literature   Underlies . . . Sight" is in pencil. "Literature part . . . humanity" notes passages used in "Literature," *Lectures*, II, 55–63. The passage in Journal B, p. [102], is used in "Self-Reliance," *W*, II, 45–46. With "Landors . . . p 81", cf. "The Senses and the Soul," *The Dial*, II (Jan. 1842), 377 (printed as "General Views," *Lectures*, II, 361). The passage in Journal B, p. [38], is used in "Genius," *Lectures*, III, 71.

Textual Notes

L *Concord*

5 mem[2]bers | ass-[3]istants **9** element; **12** accompan **15** ad*vis*ing. **18** so, **22** [dot added to "e" to make "i"] | ⟨enabled⟩ **26** one **27** principles. | or [blotted] | m⟨e⟩American **28** agai **32** pride₂ & excess₁

L *Literature*

37 inexhaust⟨ˢ⟩↑ibleness↓. **39** prevailed. **40** here. **49** things. **54** a*mus*e

Man

59 said. | Nature, | province. **60** other. **63** base. **66** upon. **67** world, **71** arrived,

F *No. 1*

80 Circ.↑umstances↓ [expansion Emerson's?] **86** T*hey* **109** political. | ↑force.↓ **123** dollars. **127** he [blotted] | puts, **131** [If y] **136** each [blotted] **137** short [blotted] | ["n" dotted to make "i"] **142** none. **144** miracles. **152** free d⟨u⟩om **153** crime. **157** ["s" blotted] **159** ⟨⟨3⟩221⟩ ↑221↓ **163** ["n" dotted to make "i"] **164** up. **168** man. **171** ⟨⟨matchless⟩⟩ [parentheses and cancellation in pencil] | the | time. **172** style. **173** Indi⟨v⟩↑duals↓

Δ

183 ⟨⟨being⟩⟩ | yo*ur* **185** the **186** enemy. **187** ⟨⟨apply the s⟩⟩ ↑lo↓ | wages. **192** worship. **199** And **200** propitiated. **201** but⟨,⟩↑,↓ | choir. **204** (& th) **210** time. **216** ⟨⟨that⟩⟩ ⟨⟨exists⟩⟩ | ⟨⟨to him⟩⟩ | ⟨⟨ample⟩⟩ **218** anything. | men. **219** life. **226** friend. |Be-[100]cause **227** together. **228** ["Lao" blotted] **237** complainters **239** Mam's **256** Remote, | sensations.

Φ

283 ["d" blotted] **291** yo*ur* **302** corrcet **313** D*u*alism **318** you **322** [Σ reversed] **325** [Σ reversed] **327** Or*lean*s **335** ↑h↓hghly | [Σ reversed] | D [blotted, possibly canceled] **342** The [blotted] **344** par-[line end]ralellism **345** Swedenb⟨.⟩↑org↓ **349** commod[93]ity, | bottle, **367** We [blotted] **368** re--[119]main **379** Amswer **387** Sh*a*kspear **394** 319[?] **395** ⟨humble[?]⟩ | 50[?] **401** use | *the*mselves | has **404** t*hin*g | there: **406** N*at*ure **407** g[?] **411** ⟨dissent[?]⟩Puritanism

Ж

426 *m*an. | t*hin*gs | have **431** ⟨imagination⟩ [finger-wiped] ↑imagination↓ **433** *A*dam **434** *per* sa*ltu*⟨s⟩m **438** li*ve* **444** ha*ve* **448** thi*n*gs **456** Against **460** prosed[?] **472** t*hin*gs, | ⟨poet⟩ [finger-wiped] **474** ["us" blotted] **478**

623

["i" blotted]   **485** ["cur" blotted]   **503** ["tt" not crossed]   **508** 28⟨4⟩6, [blotted]
512 marytyrdoms | fact ["t" not crossed] | intercalated [second "t" not crossed]

Index Minor

519 ⟨Nature[?] 65⟩   **521** a*n*d   **527** ["p 9" in pencil, "9" in ink] | as[?]
528 S*ea*-S*ho*re   **532** th*ei*r   **541** 14b,[?]   **544** ["ing" blotted]   **551** [Σ reversed,
canceled, corrected]   **555** Geni*us*   **559** music.   **574** ["cu" blotted]

BO Conduct

598 Drill.   **601** M⟨‖ ... ‖⟩ead!   **604** you [at end of line] You   **607** Faith.
609 poems   **610** Neither

624

Index

This Index includes Emerson's own index material. His index topics, including long phrases, are listed under "Emerson, Ralph Waldo, INDEX HEADINGS AND TOPICS"; the reader should consult both the general Index and Emerson's.

References to materials included or to be included in *Lectures* and to missing lectures are grouped under "Emerson, Ralph Waldo, LECTURES." References to Emerson's letters, whether quoted in the text or cited in notes, are grouped under "Emerson, Ralph Waldo, LETTERS." Under "Emerson, Ralph Waldo, WORKS" are references to published versions of poems, to lectures and addresses included in *W* but not in *Lectures*, and to Emerson's essays and miscellaneous publications. Kinds of topics included under "Emerson, Ralph Waldo, DISCUSSIONS" in earlier volumes are now listed only in the general Index.

627

www.smpl.org